Treaty Series

Treaties and international agreements registered or filed and recorded with the Secretariat of the United Nations

VOLUME 3116

Recueil des Traités

Traités et accords internationaux enregistrés ou classés et inscrits au répertoire au Secrétariat de l'Organisation des Nations Unies

United Nations • Nations Unies
New York, 2025

Print ISBN: 978-92-1-003069-4
e-ISBN: 978-92-1-358843-7
ISSN: 0379-8267
e-ISSN: 2412-1495

TABLE OF CONTENTS

I

Treaties and international agreements registered in March 2016 Nos. 53560 to 53563

No. 53560. Finland and United States of America:

Agreement between the Government of the Republic of Finland and the Government of the United States of America to improve international tax compliance and to implement FATCA (with annexes and memorandum of understanding). Helsinki, 5 March 2014 3

No. 53561. Finland and Turkey:

Agreement between the Republic of Finland and the Republic of Turkey for the avoidance of double taxation with respect to taxes on income (with protocol). Istanbul, 6 October 2009 99

No. 53562. United Nations and Netherlands (in respect of Aruba):

Exchange of letters constituting an Agreement between the Government of the Kingdom of the Netherlands, on behalf of the Government of Aruba, and the United Nations regarding the hosting the Aruba Public-Private Partnerships Conference, to be held in Oranjestad, Aruba, from 22 to 24 March 2016. New York, 18 March 2016 201

No. 53563. Turkey and Bosnia and Herzegovina:

Agreement between the Government of the Republic of Turkey and the Council of Ministers of Bosnia and Herzegovina on cooperation in the field of health. Ankara, 11 May 2010 203

II

Treaties and international agreements filed and recorded in March 2016 No. 1378

No. 1378. United Nations and World Tourism Organization:

Agreement between the United Nations and the World Tourism Organization (with Protocol). Beijing, 24 October 2003, and New York, 23 December 2003 219

ANNEX A

Ratifications, accessions, subsequent agreements, etc.,
concerning treaties and international agreements
registered in March 2016 with the Secretariat of the United Nations

No. 2997. Multilateral:

Statute of The Hague Conference on Private International Law (revised text). The Hague, 9 October 1951 and 31 October 1951

Acceptance: Republic of Moldova 246

No. 9464. Multilateral:

International Convention on the Elimination of All Forms of Racial Discrimination. New York, 7 March 1966

Declaration under article 14 (1): El Salvador 247

No. 14668. Multilateral:

International Covenant on Civil and Political Rights. New York, 16 December 1966

Notification under article 4 (3): Peru 249

Notification under article 4 (3): Peru 257

Notification under article 4 (3): Peru 266

No. 15705. Multilateral:

Convention on Road Traffic. Vienna, 8 November 1968

Amendments to articles 8 and 39 of the Convention on Road Traffic. Geneva, 23 September 2015

Entry into force 274

No. 16908. Multilateral:

Convention for the protection of the Mediterranean Sea against pollution (with annex and Protocol for the prevention of pollution of the Mediterranean Sea by dumping from ships and aircraft and Protocol concerning co-operation in combating pollution of the Mediterranean Sea by oil and other harmful substances in cases of emergency). Barcelona, 16 February 1976

Amendments to the Convention for the protection of the Mediterranean Sea against pollution (with Final Act). Barcelona, 10 June 1995

Ratification: Lebanon 275

No. 20337. Federal Republic of Germany and France:

Agreement between the Government of the Federal Republic of Germany and the Government of the French Republic on exemption from certain prior educational requirements for admission to university courses in the humanities and natural sciences in the partner country. Bonn, 10 July 1980

Termination 276

No. 20378. Multilateral:

Convention on the Elimination of All Forms of Discrimination against Women. New York, 18 December 1979

Territorial application in respect of Anguilla and the Cayman Islands (with reservation): United Kingdom of Great Britain and Northern Ireland 277

No. 21934. Finland and Luxembourg:

Convention for the avoidance of double taxation with respect to taxes on income and on capital. Luxembourg, 1 March 1982

Protocol between Finland and Luxembourg for amending the agreement for the avoidance of double taxation with respect to taxes on income. Luxembourg, 1 July 2009

Entry into force 278

No. 22495. Multilateral:

Convention on Prohibitions or Restrictions on the Use of Certain Conventional Weapons which may be deemed to be Excessively Injurious or to have Indiscriminate Effects (with Protocols I, II and III). Geneva, 10 October 1980

Accession: Bahrain 287

Additional Protocol to the Convention on Prohibitions or Restrictions on the Use of Certain Conventional Weapons which may be deemed to be Excessively Injurious or to have Indiscriminate Effects (Protocol IV, entitled Protocol on Blinding Laser Weapons). Vienna, 13 October 1995

Consent to be bound: Bahrain 288

Protocol on Explosive Remnants of War to the Convention on Prohibitions or Restrictions on the Use of Certain Conventional Weapons which may be deemed to be Excessively Injurious or to have Indiscriminate Effects (Protocol V). Geneva, 28 November 2003

Consent to be bound: Bahrain 289

No. 22514. Multilateral:

Convention on the Civil Aspects of International Child Abduction. The Hague, 25 October 1980

Acceptance of accession of Kazakhstan: Switzerland 290

Acceptance of accession of Guinea: Ukraine 290

Acceptance of accession of Iraq: Ukraine 290

Acceptance of accession of Kazakhstan: Ukraine 291

Acceptance of accession of Lesotho: Ukraine 291

Acceptance of accession of the Republic of Korea: Ukraine 291

Acceptance of accession of Zambia: Ukraine 291

No. 24841. Multilateral:

Convention against Torture and Other Cruel, Inhuman or Degrading Treatment or Punishment. New York, 10 December 1984

Ratification (with reservation): Fiji 292

No. 27531. Multilateral:

Convention on the Rights of the Child. New York, 20 November 1989

Objection to the reservations made by Somalia upon ratification: Austria 294

Objection to the reservations made by Somalia upon ratification: Latvia 295

Objection to the reservations made by Somalia upon ratification: Netherlands ... 296

Optional Protocol to the Convention on the Rights of the Child on the sale of children, child prostitution and child pornography. New York, 25 May 2000

Accession (with reservation): United Arab Emirates 298

No. 30619. Multilateral:

Convention on Biological Diversity. Rio de Janeiro, 5 June 1992

Nagoya Protocol on Access to Genetic Resources and the Fair and Equitable Sharing of Benefits Arising from their Utilization to the Convention on Biological Diversity. Nagoya, 29 October 2010

Ratification: Senegal 299

No. 30795. Finland and Switzerland:

Agreement between the Swiss Confederation and the Republic of Finland for the avoidance of double taxation with respect to taxes on income and on capital. Helsinki, 16 December 1991

Protocol between the Republic of Finland and the Swiss Confederation amending the Agreement for the avoidance of double taxation with respect to taxes on income and on capital and the protocol, signed at Helsinki on December 16, 1991, as amended by the Protocols signed at Helsinki on April 19, 2006 and 22 September 2009. Helsinki, 18 September 2012

Entry into force.. 300

No. 32888. Multilateral:

Agreement for the Establishment of the Indian Ocean Tuna Commission. Rome, 25 November 1993

Withdrawal: Guinea... 309

No. 34028. Multilateral:

Convention on Environmental Impact Assessment in a Transboundary Context. Espoo, Finland, 25 February 1991

Protocol on Strategic Environmental Assessment to the Convention on Environmental Impact Assessment in a Transboundary Context. Kiev, 21 May 2003

Ratification: Latvia 310

Amendment to the Convention on Environmental Impact Assessment in a Transboundary Context. Sofia, 27 February 2001

Ratification: Latvia 311

Acceptance: Republic of Moldova 311

Ratification: Serbia 311

No. 34380. Netherlands and Chile:

Convention on social security (with Administrative Agreement of 4 December 1996). Santiago, 10 January 1996

Agreement on social insurance between the Kingdom of the Netherlands and the Republic of Chile, amending the Convention on social insurance between the Kingdom of the Netherlands and the Republic of Chile signed in Santiago on 10 January 1996. The Hague, 15 June 2005

Entry into force 312

No. 37794. Austria and Finland:

Agreement between the Republic of Austria and the Republic of Finland for the avoidance of double taxation and the prevention of fiscal evasion with respect to taxes on income and on capital. Vienna, 26 July 2000

Protocol and Supplementary Protocol amending the Agreement between the Republic of Austria and the Republic of Finland for the avoidance of double taxation and the prevention of fiscal evasion with respect to taxes on income and on capital signed at Vienna on 26 July 2000. Helsinki, 4 March 2011

Entry into force 325

No. 38544. Multilateral:

Rome Statute of the International Criminal Court. Rome, 17 July 1998

Accession (with declaration): El Salvador 342

Amendment to article 8 of the Rome Statute of the International Criminal Court. Kampala, 10 June 2010

Ratification: El Salvador 343

Ratification: The former Yugoslav Republic of Macedonia 343

Amendments on the crime of aggression to the Rome Statute of the International Criminal Court. Kampala, 11 June 2010

Ratification: El Salvador 344

Ratification: The former Yugoslav Republic of Macedonia 344

No. 39126. Netherlands and Philippines:

Agreement between the Kingdom of the Netherlands and the Republic of the Philippines on the export of social insurance benefits. Manila, 10 April 2001

Protocol amending the Agreement between the Kingdom of the Netherlands and the Republic of the Philippines on the export of social insurance benefits. Manila, 21 April 2015

Entry into force.. 345

No. 40214. Multilateral:

Stockholm Convention on Persistent Organic Pollutants. Stockholm, 22 May 2001

Accession: Iraq 348

No. 40879. Finland and Singapore:

Agreement between the Republic of Finland and the Republic of Singapore for the avoidance of double taxation and the prevention of fiscal evasion with respect to taxes on income. Singapore, 7 June 2002

Protocol amending the Agreement between the Republic of Finland and the Republic of Singapore for the avoidance of double taxation and the prevention of fiscal evasion with respect to taxes on income signed at Singapore on 7 June 2002. Singapore, 16 November 2009

Entry into force.. 349

No. 42632. Multilateral:

Agreement on the conservation of African-Eurasian migratory waterbirds. The Hague, 15 August 1996

Amendments to Annexes 2 and 3 and to Table 1 of the Agreement on the conservation of African-Eurasian migratory waterbirds (with annexes). Bonn, 14 November 2015

Reservation: Czech Republic 355

No. 42671. Multilateral:

Convention for the Safeguarding of the Intangible Cultural Heritage. Paris, 17 October 2003

Acceptance: Guinea-Bissau 356

No. 43345. Multilateral:

International Treaty on Plant Genetic Resources for Food and Agriculture. Rome, 3 November 2001

Ratification: Chile 357

Accession: Guyana 357

No. 43977. Multilateral:

Convention on the Protection and Promotion of the Diversity of Cultural Expressions. Paris, 20 October 2005

Accession: South Sudan 358

No. 44004. Multilateral:

International Convention for the Suppression of Acts of Nuclear Terrorism. New York, 13 April 2005

Ratification: New Zealand 359

Territorial exclusion: New Zealand 359

Ratification: Uruguay 360

No. 44910. Multilateral:

Convention on the Rights of Persons with Disabilities. New York, 13 December 2006

Optional Protocol to the Convention on the Rights of Persons with Disabilities. New York, 13 December 2006

Objection to the declaration made by Turkey upon ratification: Austria 361

Objection to the declaration made by Turkey upon ratification: Greece 362

No. 45694. Multilateral:

Convention on the protection of the underwater cultural heritage. Paris, 2 November 2001

Acceptance: Guinea-Bissau 364

No. 46241. Multilateral:

Convention on the international protection of adults. The Hague, 13 January 2000

Ratification: Monaco 365

No. 48455. Multilateral:

Protocol on Integrated Coastal Zone Management (ICZM) in the Mediterranean. Madrid, 21 January 2008

Ratification: Israel 366

No. 52481. Germany and Uzbekistan:

Convention between the Federal Republic of Germany and the Republic of Uzbekistan for the avoidance of double taxation with respect to taxes on income and capital. Berlin, 7 September 1999

Protocol amending and supplementing the Convention of 7 September 1999 between the Federal Republic of Germany and the Republic of Uzbekistan for the avoidance of double taxation with respect to taxes on income and capital. Berlin, 14 October 2014

Entry into force... 367

No. 53490. Multilateral:

Agreement on Establishing the Center of Excellence in Finance (CEF). Bled, 3 September 2013

Ratification: Montenegro 404

Ratification: Republic of Moldova 404

Ratification: Romania 404

No. 53511. Multilateral:

Agreement on the Eurasian Group on combating money laundering and financing of terrorism. Moscow, 16 June 2011

Ratification: China 405

Ratification: Kazakhstan 405

Ratification: Kyrgyzstan 406

Notification: Russian Federation 406

No. 53515. Austria and China:

Agreement between the Republic of Austria and the People's Republic of China on the promotion and reciprocal protection of investments. Beijing, 12 September 1985

Exchange of notes constituting a Protocol amending the Agreement between the Republic of Austria and the People's Republic of China on the promotion and reciprocal protection of investments. Peking, 4 September 2012 and 17 September 2012

Entry into force 407

No. 53553. Multilateral:

Agreement for the establishment of the African Legal Support Facility. Tunis, 19 June 2008

Accession: African Development Bank 418

Accession: African Union 418

Ratification: Burkina Faso 418

Approval: Chad 419

Accession: Comoros 419

Accession: Congo 419

Accession: Egypt 419

Accession: France 420

Ratification: Gambia 420

Accession: Islamic Development Bank 420

Accession: Mali 420

Accession: Mauritius 421

Accession: Morocco 421

Accession (with reservation): Netherlands 421

Accession: Niger 422

Accession: Organization for the Harmonization of Business Laws in Africa 423

Ratification: Rwanda 423

Accession: Sierra Leone 423

Ratification (with declaration): Tunisia 424

Accession (with reservation): United Kingdom 425

Accession: West African Development Bank 426

Governing Council Resolution ALSF/GC/2012/01 amending Article VIII and XXVI of the Agreement for the establishment of the African Legal Support Facility. Arusha, 29 May 2012

Entry into force 426

ANNEX C

Ratifications, accessions, etc.,
concerning League of Nations treaties and international agreements
registered in March 2016 with the Secretariat of the United Nations

No. 2623. Multilateral:

International Convention for the Suppression of Counterfeiting Currency. Geneva, 20 April 1929

Succession: Serbia 436

Protocol to the International Convention for the Suppression of Counterfeiting Currency. Geneva, 20 April 1929

Succession: Serbia 436

TABLE DES MATIÈRES

I

Traités et accords internationaux
enregistrés en mars 2016
Nos 53560 à 53563

N° 53560. Finlande et États-Unis d'Amérique :

Accord entre le Gouvernement de la République de Finlande et le Gouvernement des États-Unis d'Amérique relatif au renforcement du respect des obligations fiscales internationales et à la mise en œuvre de la loi FATCA (avec annexes et mémorandum d'entente). Helsinki, 5 mars 2014 3

N° 53561. Finlande et Turquie :

Accord entre la République de Finlande et la République turque tendant à éviter les doubles impositions en matière d'impôts sur le revenu (avec protocole). Istanbul, 6 octobre 2009 99

N° 53562. Organisation des Nations Unies et Pays-Bas (à l'égard d'Aruba) :

Échange de lettres constituant un Accord entre le Gouvernement du Royaume des Pays-Bas, à l'égard du Gouvernement d'Aruba, et l'Organisation des Nations Unies concernant l'organisation de la conférence sur les partenariats public-privé d'Aruba, qui se tiendra à Oranjestad, Aruba, du 22 au 24 mars 2016. New York, 18 mars 2016 201

N° 53563. Turquie et Bosnie-Herzégovine :

Accord entre le Gouvernement de la République turque et le Conseil des ministres de la Bosnie-Herzégovine relatif à la coopération dans le domaine de la santé. Ankara, 11 mai 2010 203

II

Traités et accords internationaux
classés et inscrits au répertoire en mars 2016
N° 1378

N° 1378. Organisation des Nations Unies et Organisation mondiale du tourisme :

Accord entre l'Organisation des Nations Unies et l'Organisation mondiale du tourisme (avec Protocole). Beijing, 24 octobre 2003, et New York, 23 décembre 2003 219

ANNEXE A

Ratifications, adhésions, accords ultérieurs, etc., concernant des traités et accords internationaux enregistrés en mars 2016 au Secrétariat de l'Organisation des Nations Unies

Nº 2997. Multilatéral :

Statut de la Conférence de La Haye de droit international privé (texte révisé). La Haye, 9 octobre 1951 et 31 octobre 1951

Acceptation : République de Moldova 246

Nº 9464. Multilatéral :

Convention internationale sur l'élimination de toutes les formes de discrimination raciale. New York, 7 mars 1966

Déclaration en vertu du paragraphe 1 de l'article 14 : El Salvador 247

Nº 14668. Multilatéral :

Pacte international relatif aux droits civils et politiques. New York, 16 décembre 1966

Notification en vertu du paragraphe 3 de l'article 4 : Pérou 249

Notification en vertu du paragraphe 3 de l'article 4 : Pérou 257

Notification en vertu du paragraphe 3 de l'article 4 : Pérou 266

Nº 15705. Multilatéral :

Convention sur la circulation routière. Vienne, 8 novembre 1968

Amendements aux articles 8 et 39 de la Convention sur la circulation routière. Genève, 23 septembre 2015

Entrée en vigueur 274

N° 16908. Multilatéral :

Convention pour la protection de la mer Méditerranée contre la pollution (avec annexe et Protocole relatif à la prévention de la pollution de la mer Méditerranée par les opérations d'immersion effectuées par les navires et aéronefs et Protocole relatif à la coopération en matière de lutte contre la pollution de la mer Méditerranée par les hydrocarbures et autres substances nuisibles en cas de situation critique). Barcelone, 16 février 1976

Amendements à la Convention pour la protection de la mer Méditerranée contre la pollution (avec acte final). Barcelone, 10 juin 1995

Ratification : Liban 275

N° 20337. République fédérale d'Allemagne et France :

Accord entre le Gouvernement de la République française et le Gouvernement de la République fédérale d'Allemagne sur les dispenses de scolarité, d'examens et de diplômes pour l'admission aux études universitaires dans le pays partenaire en sciences, lettres et sciences humaines. Bonn, 10 juillet 1980

Abrogation 276

N° 20378. Multilatéral :

Convention sur l'élimination de toutes les formes de discrimination à l'égard des femmes. New York, 18 décembre 1979

Application territoriale à l'égard d'Anguilla et des Îles Caïmanes (avec réserve) : Royaume-Uni de Grande-Bretagne et d'Irlande du Nord 277

N° 21934. Finlande et Luxembourg :

Convention tendant à éviter les doubles impositions en matière d'impôts sur le revenu et sur la fortune. Luxembourg, 1er mars 1982

Avenant en vue de modifier la Convention entre la Finlande et le Luxembourg tendant à éviter les doubles impositions en matière d'impôts sur le revenu et sur la fortune. Luxembourg, 1er juillet 2009

Entrée en vigueur 278

N° 22495. Multilatéral :

Convention sur l'interdiction ou la limitation de l'emploi de certaines armes classiques qui peuvent être considérées comme produisant des effets traumatiques excessifs ou comme frappant sans discrimination (avec Protocoles I, II et III). Genève, 10 octobre 1980

Adhésion : Bahreïn 287

Protocole additionnel à la Convention sur l'interdiction ou la limitation de l'emploi de certaines armes classiques qui peuvent être considérées comme produisant des effets traumatiques excessifs ou comme frappant sans discrimination (Protocole IV, intitulé Protocole relatif aux armes à laser aveuglantes). Vienne, 13 octobre 1995

Consentement à être lié : Bahreïn 288

Protocole relatif aux restes explosifs de guerre à la Convention sur l'interdiction ou la limitation de l'emploi de certaines armes classiques qui peuvent être considérées comme produisant des effets traumatiques excessifs ou comme frappant sans discrimination (Protocole V). Genève, 28 novembre 2003

Consentement à être lié : Bahreïn 289

N° 22514. Multilatéral :

Convention sur les aspects civils de l'enlèvement international d'enfants. La Haye, 25 octobre 1980

Acceptation d'adhésion du Kazakhstan : Suisse 290

Acceptation d'adhésion de la Guinée : Ukraine 290

Acceptation d'adhésion de l'Irak : Ukraine 290

Acceptation d'adhésion du Kazakhstan : Ukraine 291

Acceptation d'adhésion du Lesotho : Ukraine 291

Acceptation d'adhésion de la République de Corée : Ukraine 291

Acceptation d'adhésion de la Zambie : Ukraine 291

Nº 24841. Multilatéral :

Convention contre la torture et autres peines ou traitements cruels, inhumains ou dégradants. New York, 10 décembre 1984

Ratification (avec réserve) : Fidji 292

Nº 27531. Multilatéral :

Convention relative aux droits de l'enfant. New York, 20 novembre 1989

Objection aux réserves formulées par la Somalie lors de la ratification : Autriche 294

Objection aux réserves formulées par la Somalie lors de la ratification : Lettonie 295

Objection aux réserves formulées par la Somalie lors de la ratification : Pays-Bas 296

Protocole facultatif à la Convention relative aux droits de l'enfant, concernant la vente d'enfants, la prostitution des enfants et la pornographie mettant en scène des enfants. New York, 25 mai 2000

Adhésion (avec réserve) : Émirats arabes unis 298

Nº 30619. Multilatéral :

Convention sur la diversité biologique. Rio de Janeiro, 5 juin 1992

Protocole de Nagoya sur l'accès aux ressources génétiques et le partage juste et équitable des avantages découlant de leur utilisation relatif à la Convention sur la diversité biologique. Nagoya, 29 octobre 2010

Ratification : Sénégal 299

N° 30795. Finlande et Suisse :

Convention entre la confédération suisse et la République de Finlande en vue d'éviter les doubles impositions en matière d'impôts sur le revenu et sur la fortune. Helsinki, 16 décembre 1991

Protocole entre la République de Finlande et la Confédération suisse modifiant la Convention en vue d'éviter les doubles impositions en matière d'impôts sur le revenu et sur la fortune et le Protocole, signés à Helsinki le 16 décembre 1991, tels que modifiés par les Protocoles signés à Helsinki le 19 avril 2006 et le 22 septembre 2009. Helsinki, 18 septembre 2012

Entrée en vigueur 300

N° 32888. Multilatéral :

Accord portant création de la Commission des thons de l'océan Indien. Rome, 25 novembre 1993

Retrait : Guinée 309

N° 34028. Multilatéral :

Convention sur l'évaluation de l'impact sur l'environnement dans un contexte transfrontière. Espoo (Finlande), 25 février 1991

Protocole à la Convention sur l'évaluation de l'impact sur l'environnement dans un contexte transfrontière, relatif à l'évaluation stratégique environnementale. Kiev, 21 mai 2003

Ratification : Lettonie 310

Amendement à la Convention sur l'évaluation de l'impact sur l'environnement dans un contexte transfrontière. Sofia, 27 février 2001

Ratification : Lettonie 311

Acceptation : République de Moldova 311

Ratification : Serbie 311

N° 34380. Pays-Bas et Chili :

Convention sur la sécurité sociale (avec Accord administratif du 4 décembre 1996). Santiago, 10 janvier 1996

Accord sur la sécurité sociale entre le Royaume des Pays-Bas et la République du Chili portant amendement de la Convention sur la sécurité sociale entre le Royaume des Pays-Bas et la République du Chili signé à Santiago le 10 janvier 1996. La Haye, 15 juin 2005

Entrée en vigueur 312

Nº 37794. Autriche et Finlande :

Accord entre la République d'Autriche et la République de Finlande tendant à éviter la double imposition et à prévenir l'évasion fiscale en matière d'impôts sur le revenu et sur la fortune. Vienne, 26 juillet 2000

Protocole et Protocole additionnel entre la République de Finlande et la République d'Autriche amendant l'Accord tendant à éviter la double imposition et à prévenir l'évasion fiscale en matière d'impôts sur le revenu et sur la fortune signé à Vienne le 26 juillet 2000. Helsinki, 4 mars 2011

Entrée en vigueur 325

Nº 38544. Multilatéral :

Statut de Rome de la Cour pénale internationale. Rome, 17 juillet 1998

Adhésion (avec déclaration) : El Salvador 342

Amendement à l'article 8 du Statut de Rome de la Cour pénale internationale. Kampala, 10 juin 2010

Ratification : El Salvador 343

Ratification : ex-République yougoslave de Macédoine 343

Amendements au Statut de Rome de la Cour pénale internationale relatifs au crime d'agression. Kampala, 11 juin 2010

Ratification : El Salvador 344

Ratification : ex-République yougoslave de Macédoine 344

Nº 39126. Pays-Bas et Philippines :

Accord entre le Royaume des Pays-Bas et la République des Philippines relatif à l'exportation des prestations d'assurance sociale. Manille, 10 avril 2001

Protocole amendant l'Accord entre le Royaume des Pays-Bas et la République des Philippines relatif à l'exportation des prestations d'assurance sociale. Manille, 21 avril 2015

Entrée en vigueur 345

N° 40214. Multilatéral :

Convention de Stockholm sur les polluants organiques persistants. Stockholm, 22 mai 2001

Adhésion : Iraq 348

N° 40879. Finlande et Singapour :

Accord entre la République de Finlande et la République de Singapour tendant à éviter la double imposition et à prévenir l'évasion fiscale en matière d'impôts sur le revenu. Singapour, 7 juin 2002

Protocole modifiant l'Accord entre la République de Finlande et la République de Singapour tendant à éviter la double imposition et à prévenir l'évasion fiscale en matière d'impôts sur le revenu, signé à Singapour le 7 juin 2002. Singapour, 16 novembre 2009

Entrée en vigueur 349

N° 42632. Multilatéral :

Accord sur la conservation des oiseaux d'eau migrateurs d'Afrique-Eurasie. La Haye, 15 août 1996

Amendements aux Annexes 2 et 3 et au Tableau 1 de l'Accord sur la conservation des oiseaux d'eau migrateurs d'Afrique-Eurasie (avec annexes). Bonn, 14 novembre 2015

Réserve : République tchèque 355

N° 42671. Multilatéral :

Convention pour la sauvegarde du patrimoine culturel immatériel. Paris, 17 octobre 2003

Acceptation : Guinée-Bissau 356

N° 43345. Multilatéral :

Traité international sur les ressources phytogénétiques pour l'alimentation et l'agriculture. Rome, 3 novembre 2001

Ratification : Chili 357

Adhésion : Guyana 357

Nº 43977. Multilatéral :

Convention sur la protection et la promotion de la diversité des expressions culturelles. Paris, 20 octobre 2005

Adhésion : Soudan du Sud 358

Nº 44004. Multilatéral :

Convention internationale pour la répression des actes de terrorisme nucléaire. New York, 13 avril 2005

Ratification : Nouvelle-Zélande 359

Exclusion territoriale : Nouvelle-Zélande 359

Ratification : Uruguay 360

Nº 44910. Multilatéral :

Convention relative aux droits des personnes handicapées. New York, 13 décembre 2006

Protocole facultatif se rapportant à la Convention relative aux droits des personnes handicapées. New York, 13 décembre 2006

Objection à la déclaration formulée par la Turquie lors de la ratification : Autriche 361

Objection à la déclaration formulée par la Turquie lors de la ratification : Grèce 362

Nº 45694. Multilatéral :

Convention sur la protection du patrimoine culturel subaquatique. Paris, 2 novembre 2001

Acceptation : Guinée-Bissau 364

Nº 46241. Multilatéral :

Convention sur la protection internationale des adultes. La Haye, 13 janvier 2000

Ratification : Monaco 365

Nº 48455. Multilatéral :

Protocole relatif à la gestion intégrée des zones côtières (GIZC) de la Méditerranée. Madrid, 21 janvier 2008

Ratification : Israël 366

Nº 52481. Allemagne et Ouzbékistan :

Accord entre la République fédérale d'Allemagne et la République d'Ouzbékistan tendant à éviter les doubles impositions en matière d'impôts sur le revenu et sur la fortune. Berlin, 7 septembre 1999

Protocole amendant et complétant l'Accord du 7 septembre 1999 entre la République fédérale d'Allemagne et la République d'Ouzbékistan tendant à éviter les doubles impositions en matière d'impôts sur le revenu et sur la fortune. Berlin, 14 octobre 2014

Entrée en vigueur 367

Nº 53490. Multilatéral :

Accord sur la création du Centre d'excellence en finances (CEF). Bled, 3 septembre 2013

Ratification : Monténégro 404

Ratification : République de Moldova 404

Ratification : Roumanie 404

Nº 53511. Multilatéral :

Accord relatif au Groupe Eurasie pour la lutte contre le blanchiment de capitaux et le financement du terrorisme. Moscou, 16 juin 2011

Ratification : Chine 405

Ratification : Kazakhstan 405

Ratification : Kirghizistan 406

Notification : Fédération de Russie 406

N° 53515. Autriche et Chine :

Accord entre la République d'Autriche et la République populaire de Chine sur la promotion et la protection réciproque des investissements. Beijing, 12 septembre 1985

Échange de notes constituant un Protocole amendant l'Accord entre la République d'Autriche et la République populaire de Chine sur la promotion et la protection réciproque des investissements. Pékin, 4 septembre 2012 et 17 septembre 2012

Entrée en vigueur 407

N° 53553. Multilatéral :

Accord portant création de la Facilité africaine de soutien juridique. Tunis, 19 juin 2008

Adhésion : Banque africaine de développement 418

Adhésion : Union africaine 418

Ratification : Burkina Faso 418

Approbation : Tchad 419

Adhésion : Comores 419

Adhésion : Congo 419

Adhésion : Égypte 419

Adhésion : France 420

Ratification : Gambie 420

Adhésion : Banque islamique de développement 420

Adhésion : Mali 420

Adhésion : Maurice 421

Adhésion : Maroc 421

Adhésion (avec réserve) : Pays-Bas 421

Adhésion : Niger 422

Adhésion : Organisation pour l'harmonisation en Afrique du droit des affaires .. 423

Ratification : Rwanda 423

Adhésion : Sierra Leone 423

Ratification (avec déclaration) : Tunisie 424

Adhésion (avec réserve) : Royaume-Uni 425

Adhésion : Banque ouest-africaine de développement 426

Résolution ALSF/GC/2012/01 du Conseil de gouvernance concernant l'amendement de l'article VIII et de l'article XXVI de l'Accord portant création de la Facilité africaine de soutien juridique. Arusha, 29 mai 2012

Entrée en vigueur 426

ANNEXE C

Ratifications, adhésions, etc.,
concernant les traités et accords internationaux de la Société des Nations
enregistré en mars 2016 au Secrétariat de l'Organisation des Nations Unies

Nº 2623. Multilatéral :

Convention internationale pour la répression du faux monnayage. Genève, 20 avril 1929

Succession : Serbie 436

Protocole à la Convention internationale pour la répression du faux monnayage. Genève, 20 avril 1929

Succession : Serbie 436

NOTE BY THE SECRETARIAT

Under Article 102 of the Charter of the United Nations, every treaty and every international agreement entered into by any Member of the United Nations after the coming into force of the Charter shall, as soon as possible, be registered with the Secretariat and published by it. Furthermore, no party to a treaty or international agreement subject to registration which has not been registered may invoke that treaty or agreement before any organ of the United Nations. The General Assembly, by resolution 97 (I), established regulations to give effect to Article 102 of the Charter (see text of the regulations, vol. 859, p. VIII; https://treaties.un.org/Pages/Resource.aspx?path=Publication/Regulation/Page1_en.xml).

The terms "treaty" and "international agreement" have not been defined either in the Charter or in the regulations, and the Secretariat follows the principle that it acts in accordance with the position of the Member State submitting an instrument for registration that, so far as that party is concerned, the instrument is a treaty or an international agreement within the meaning of Article 102. Registration of an instrument submitted by a Member State, therefore, does not imply a judgement by the Secretariat on the nature of the instrument, the status of a party or any similar question. It is the understanding of the Secretariat that its acceptance for registration of an instrument does not confer on the instrument the status of a treaty or an international agreement if it does not already have that status, and does not confer upon a party a status which it would not otherwise have.

*

* *

Disclaimer: All authentic texts in the present Series are published as submitted for registration by a party to the instrument. Unless otherwise indicated, the translations of these texts have been made by the Secretariat of the United Nations, for information.

NOTE DU SECRÉTARIAT

Aux termes de l'Article 102 de la Charte des Nations Unies, tout traité ou accord international conclu par un Membre des Nations Unies après l'entrée en vigueur de la Charte sera, le plus tôt possible, enregistré au Secrétariat et publié par lui. De plus, aucune partie à un traité ou accord international qui aurait dû être enregistré mais ne l'a pas été ne pourra invoquer ledit traité ou accord devant un organe de l'Organisation des Nations Unies. Par sa résolution 97 (I), l'Assemblée générale a adopté un règlement destiné à mettre en application l'Article 102 de la Charte (voir texte du règlement, vol. 859, p. IX; https://treaties.un.org/Pages/Resource.aspx?path=Publication/Regulation/Page1_fr.xml).

Les termes « traité » et « accord international » n'ont été définis ni dans la Charte ni dans le règlement, et le Secrétariat a pris comme principe de s'en tenir à la position adoptée à cet égard par l'État Membre qui a présenté l'instrument à l'enregistrement, à savoir que, en ce qui concerne cette partie, l'instrument constitue un traité ou un accord international au sens de l'Article 102. Il s'ensuit que l'enregistrement d'un instrument présenté par un État Membre n'implique, de la part du Secrétariat, aucun jugement sur la nature de l'instrument, le statut d'une partie ou toute autre question similaire. Le Secrétariat considère donc que son acceptation pour enregistrement d'un instrument ne confère pas audit instrument la qualité de traité ou d'accord international si ce dernier ne l'a pas déjà, et qu'il ne confère pas à une partie un statut que, par ailleurs, elle ne posséderait pas.

*

* *

Déni de responsabilité : Tous les textes authentiques du présent Recueil sont publiés tels qu'ils ont été soumis pour enregistrement par l'une des parties à l'instrument. Sauf indication contraire, les traductions de ces textes ont été établies par le Secrétariat de l'Organisation des Nations Unies, à titre d'information.

I

Treaties and international agreements

registered in

March 2016

Nos. 53560 to 53563

Traités et accords internationaux

enregistrés en

mars 2016

N°s 53560 à 53563

No. 53560

Finland
and
United States of America

Agreement between the Government of the Republic of Finland and the Government of the United States of America to improve international tax compliance and to implement FATCA (with annexes and memorandum of understanding). Helsinki, 5 March 2014

Entry into force: *20 February 2015 by notification, in accordance with article 10*

Authentic text: *English*

Registration with the Secretariat of the United Nations: *Finland, 9 March 2016*

Finlande
et
États-Unis d'Amérique

Accord entre le Gouvernement de la République de Finlande et le Gouvernement des États-Unis d'Amérique relatif au renforcement du respect des obligations fiscales internationales et à la mise en œuvre de la loi FATCA (avec annexes et mémorandum d'entente). Helsinki, 5 mars 2014

Entrée en vigueur : *20 février 2015 par notification, conformément à l'article 10*

Texte authentique : *anglais*

Enregistrement au Secrétariat de l'Organisation des Nations Unies : *Finlande, 9 mars 2016*

[TEXT IN ENGLISH – TEXTE EN ANGLAIS]

Agreement between the Government of the Republic of Finland and the Government of the United States of America to Improve International Tax Compliance and to Implement FATCA

Whereas, the Government of the Republic of Finland and the Government of the United States of America (each, a "Party," and together, the "Parties") have a longstanding and close relationship with respect to mutual assistance in tax matters and desire to conclude an agreement to improve international tax compliance by further building on that relationship;

Whereas, Article 26 of the Convention between the Government of the Republic of Finland and the Government of the United States of America for the Avoidance of Double Taxation and the Prevention of Fiscal Evasion with Respect to Taxes on Income and on Capital, as amended by the Protocol, signed at Helsinki on September 21, 1989, as amended by the Protocol done at Helsinki on May 1, 2006 (the "Convention") authorizes exchange of information for tax purposes, including on an automatic basis;

Whereas, the United States of America enacted provisions commonly known as the Foreign Account Tax Compliance Act ("FATCA"), which introduce a reporting regime for financial institutions with respect to certain accounts;

Whereas, the Government of the Republic of Finland is supportive of the underlying policy goal of FATCA to improve tax compliance;

Whereas, FATCA has raised a number of issues, including that Finnish financial institutions may not be able to comply with certain aspects of FATCA due to domestic legal impediments;

Whereas, the Government of the United States of America collects information regarding certain accounts maintained by U.S. financial institutions held by residents of Finland and is committed to exchanging such information with the Government of the Republic of Finland and pursuing equivalent levels of exchange;

Whereas, the Parties are committed to working together over the longer term towards achieving common reporting and due diligence standards for financial institutions;

Whereas, the Government of the United States of America acknowledges the need to coordinate the reporting obligations under FATCA with other U.S. tax reporting obligations of Finnish financial institutions to avoid duplicative reporting;

Whereas, an intergovernmental approach to FATCA implementation would address legal impediments and reduce burdens for Finnish financial institutions;

Whereas, the Parties desire to conclude an agreement to improve international tax compliance and provide for the implementation of FATCA based on domestic reporting and reciprocal automatic exchange pursuant to the Convention and subject to the confidentiality and other protections provided for therein, including the provisions limiting the use of the information exchanged under the Convention;

Now, therefore, the Parties have agreed as follows:

Article 1
Definitions

1. For purposes of this agreement and any annexes thereto ("Agreement"), the following terms shall have the meanings set forth below:

a) The term **"United States"** means the United States of America, including the States thereof, but does not include the U.S. Territories. Any reference to a **"State"** of the United States includes the District of Columbia.

b) The term **"U.S. Territory"** means American Samoa, the Commonwealth of the Northern Mariana Islands, Guam, the Commonwealth of Puerto Rico, or the U.S. Virgin Islands.

c) The term **"IRS"** means the U.S. Internal Revenue Service.

d) The term **"Finland"** means the Republic of Finland.

e) The term **"Partner Jurisdiction"** means a jurisdiction that has in effect an agreement with the United States to facilitate the implementation of FATCA. The IRS shall publish a list identifying all Partner Jurisdictions.

f) The term **"Competent Authority"** means:

(1) in the case of the United States, the Secretary of the Treasury or his delegate; and

(2) in the case of Finland, the Ministry of Finance or its authorized representative.

g) The term **"Financial Institution"** means a Custodial Institution, a Depository Institution, an Investment Entity, or a Specified Insurance Company.

h) The term **"Custodial Institution"** means any Entity that holds, as a substantial portion of its business, financial assets for the account of others. An entity holds financial assets for the account of others as a substantial portion of its business if the entity's gross income attributable to the holding of financial assets and related financial services equals or exceeds 20 percent of the entity's gross income during the shorter of: (i) the three-year period that ends on December 31 (or the final day of a non-calendar year accounting period) prior to the year in which the determination is being made; or (ii) the period during which the entity has been in existence.

i) The term **"Depository Institution"** means any Entity that accepts deposits in the ordinary course of a banking or similar business.

j) The term **"Investment Entity"** means any Entity that conducts as a business (or is managed by an entity that conducts as a business) one or more of the following activities or operations for or on behalf of a customer:

(1) trading in money market instruments (cheques, bills, certificates of

deposit, derivatives, etc.); foreign exchange; exchange, interest rate and index instruments; transferable securities; or commodity futures trading;

(2) individual and collective portfolio management; or

(3) otherwise investing, administering, or managing funds or money on behalf of other persons.

This subparagraph 1(j) shall be interpreted in a manner consistent with similar language set forth in the definition of "financial institution" in the Financial Action Task Force Recommendations.

k) The term **"Specified Insurance Company"** means any Entity that is an insurance company (or the holding company of an insurance company) that issues, or is obligated to make payments with respect to, a Cash Value Insurance Contract or an Annuity Contract.

l) The term **"Finnish Financial Institution"** means (i) any Financial Institution resident in Finland, but excluding any branch of such Financial Institution that is located outside Finland, and (ii) any branch of a Financial Institution not resident in Finland, if such branch is located in Finland.

m) The term **"Partner Jurisdiction Financial Institution"** means (i) any Financial Institution established in a Partner Jurisdiction, but excluding any branch of such Financial Institution that is located outside the Partner Jurisdiction, and (ii) any branch of a Financial Institution not established in the Partner Jurisdiction, if such branch is located in the Partner Jurisdiction.

n) The term **"Reporting Financial Institution"** means a Reporting Finnish Financial Institution or a Reporting U.S. Financial Institution, as the context requires.

o) The term **"Reporting Finnish Financial Institution"** means any Finnish Financial Institution that is not a Non-Reporting Finnish Financial Institution.

p) The term **"Reporting U.S. Financial Institution"** means (i) any Financial Institution that is resident in the United States, but excluding any branch of such Financial Institution that is located outside the United States, and (ii) any branch of a Financial Institution not resident in the United States, if such branch is located in the United States, provided that the Financial Institution or branch has control, receipt, or custody of income with respect to which information is required to be exchanged under subparagraph (2)(b) of Article 2 of this Agreement.

q) The term **"Non-Reporting Finnish Financial Institution"** means any Finnish Financial Institution, or other Entity resident in Finland, that is described in Annex II as a Non-Reporting Finnish Financial Institution or that otherwise qualifies as a deemed-compliant FFI or an exempt beneficial owner under relevant U.S. Treasury Regulations.

r) The term **"Nonparticipating Financial Institution"** means a nonparticipating FFI, as that term is defined in relevant U.S. Treasury Regulations, but does not include a Finnish Financial Institution or other Partner Jurisdiction Financial Institution other than a Financial Institution treated as a Nonparticipating Financial Institution pursuant to subparagraph 2(b) of Article 5 of this Agreement or the corresponding provision in an agreement between the United States and a Partner Jurisdiction.

s) The term **"Financial Account"** means an account maintained by a Financial Institution, and includes:

(1) in the case of an Entity that is a Financial Institution solely because it is an Investment Entity, any equity or debt interest (other than interests that are regularly traded on an established securities market) in the Financial Institution;

(2) in the case of a Financial Institution not described in subparagraph 1(s)(1) of this Article, any equity or debt interest in the Financial Institution (other than interests that are regularly traded on an established securities market), if (i) the value of the debt or equity interest is determined, directly or indirectly, primarily by reference to assets that give rise to U.S. Source Withholdable Payments, and (ii) the class of interests was established with a purpose of avoiding reporting in accordance with this Agreement; and

(3) any Cash Value Insurance Contract and any Annuity Contract issued or maintained by a Financial Institution, other than a noninvestment-linked, nontransferable immediate life annuity that is issued to an individual and monetizes a pension or disability benefit provided under an account that is excluded from the definition of Financial Account in Annex II.

Notwithstanding the foregoing, the term "Financial Account" does not include any account that is excluded from the definition of Financial Account in Annex II. For purposes of this Agreement, interests are "regularly traded" if there is a meaningful volume of trading with respect to the interests on an ongoing basis, and an "established securities market" means an exchange that is officially recognized and supervised by a governmental authority in which the market is located and that has a meaningful annual value of shares traded on the exchange. For purposes of this subparagraph 1(s), an interest in a Financial Institution is not "regularly traded" and shall be treated as a Financial Account if the holder of the interest (other than a Financial Institution acting as an intermediary) is registered on the books of such Financial Institution. The preceding sentence will not apply to interests first registered on the books of such Financial Institution prior to July 1, 2014, and with respect to interests first registered on the books of such Financial Institution on or after July 1, 2014, a Financial Institution is not required to apply the preceding sentence prior to January 1, 2016.

t) The term **"Depository Account"** includes any commercial, checking, savings, time, or thrift account, or an account that is evidenced by a certificate of deposit, thrift certificate, investment certificate, certificate of indebtedness, or other similar instrument maintained by a Financial Institution in the ordinary course of a banking or similar business. A Depository Account also includes an amount held by an insurance company pursuant to a guaranteed investment contract or similar agreement to pay or credit interest thereon.

u) The term **"Custodial Account"** means an account (other than an Insurance Contract or Annuity Contract) for the benefit of another person that holds any financial instrument or contract held for investment (including, but not limited to, a share or stock in a corporation, a note, bond, debenture, or other evidence of indebtedness, a currency or commodity transaction, a credit default swap, a swap based upon a nonfinancial index, a notional principal contract, an Insurance Contract or Annuity Contract, and any option or other derivative instrument).

v) The term **"Equity Interest"** means, in the case of a partnership that is a Financial Institution, either a capital or profits interest in the partnership. In the case of a trust that is a Financial Institution, an Equity Interest is considered to be held by any person treated as a settlor or beneficiary of all or a portion of the trust, or any other natural person exercising ultimate effective control over the trust. A Specified U.S. Person shall be treated as being a beneficiary of a foreign trust if such Specified U.S. Person has the right to receive directly or indirectly (for example, through a nominee) a mandatory distribution or may receive, directly or indirectly, a discretionary distribution from the trust.

w) The term **"Insurance Contract"** means a contract (other than an Annuity Contract) under which the issuer agrees to pay an amount upon the occurrence of a specified contingency involving mortality, morbidity, accident, liability, or property risk.

x) The term **"Annuity Contract"** means a contract under which the issuer agrees to make payments for a period of time determined in whole or in part by reference to the life expectancy of one or more individuals. The term also includes a contract that is considered to be an Annuity Contract in accordance with the law, regulation, or practice of the jurisdiction in which the contract was issued, and under which the issuer agrees to make payments for a term of years.

y) The term **"Cash Value Insurance Contract"** means an Insurance Contract (other than an indemnity reinsurance contract between two insurance companies) that has a Cash Value greater than $50,000.

z) The term **"Cash Value"** means the greater of (i) the amount that the policyholder is entitled to receive upon surrender or termination of the contract (determined without reduction for any surrender charge or policy loan), and (ii) the amount the policyholder can borrow under or with regard to the contract. Notwithstanding the foregoing, the term "Cash Value" does not include an amount payable under an Insurance Contract as:

(1) a personal injury or sickness benefit or other benefit providing

indemnification of an economic loss incurred upon the occurrence of the event insured against;

(2) a refund to the policyholder of a previously paid premium under an Insurance Contract (other than under a life insurance contract) due to policy cancellation or termination, decrease in risk exposure during the effective period of the Insurance Contract, or arising from a redetermination of the premium due to correction of posting or other similar error; or

(3) a policyholder dividend based upon the underwriting experience of the contract or group involved.

aa) The term **"Reportable Account"** means a U.S. Reportable Account or a Finnish Reportable Account, as the context requires.

bb) The term **"Finnish Reportable Account"** means a Financial Account maintained by a Reporting U.S. Financial Institution if: (i) in the case of a Depository Account, the account is held by an individual resident in Finland and more than $10 of interest is paid to such account in any given calendar year; or (ii) in the case of a Financial Account other than a Depository Account, the Account Holder is a resident of Finland, including an Entity that certifies that it is resident in Finland for tax purposes, with respect to which U.S. source income that is subject to reporting under chapter 3 of subtitle A or chapter 61 of subtitle F of the U.S. Internal Revenue Code is paid or credited.

cc) The term **"U.S. Reportable Account"** means a Financial Account maintained by a Reporting Finnish Financial Institution and held by one or more Specified U.S. Persons or by a Non-U.S. Entity with one or more Controlling Persons that is a Specified U.S. Person. Notwithstanding the foregoing, an account shall not be treated as a U.S. Reportable Account if such account is not identified as a U.S. Reportable Account after application of the due diligence procedures in Annex I.

dd) The term **"Account Holder"** means the person listed or identified as the holder of a Financial Account by the Financial Institution that maintains the account. A person, other than a Financial Institution, holding a Financial Account for the benefit or account of another person as agent, custodian, nominee, signatory, investment advisor, or intermediary, is not treated as holding the account for purposes of this Agreement, and such other person is treated as holding the account. For purposes of the immediately preceding sentence, the term "Financial Institution" does not include a Financial Institution organized or incorporated in a U.S. Territory. In the case of a Cash Value Insurance Contract or an Annuity Contract, the Account Holder is any person entitled to access the Cash Value or change the beneficiary of the contract. If no person can access the Cash Value or change the beneficiary, the Account Holder is any person named as the owner in the contract and any person with a vested entitlement to payment under the terms of the contract. Upon the maturity of a Cash Value Insurance Contract or an Annuity Contract, each person entitled to receive a payment under the contract is treated as an Account Holder.

ee) The term **"U.S. Person"** means a U.S. citizen or resident individual, a partnership or corporation organized in the United States or under the laws of the United States or any State thereof, a trust if (i) a court within the United States would have authority under applicable law to render orders or judgments concerning substantially all issues regarding administration of the trust, and (ii) one or more U.S. persons have the authority to control all substantial decisions of the trust, or an estate of a decedent that is a citizen or resident of the United States. This subparagraph 1(ee) shall be interpreted in accordance with the U.S. Internal Revenue Code.

ff) The term **"Specified U.S. Person"** means a U.S. Person, other than: (i) a corporation the stock of which is regularly traded on one or more established securities markets; (ii) any corporation that is a member of the same expanded affiliated group, as defined in section 1471(e)(2) of the U.S. Internal Revenue Code, as a corporation described in clause (i); (iii) the United States or any wholly owned agency or instrumentality thereof; (iv) any State of the United States, any U.S. Territory, any political subdivision of any of the foregoing, or any wholly owned agency or instrumentality of any one or more of the foregoing; (v) any organization exempt from taxation under section 501(a) of the U.S. Internal Revenue Code or an individual retirement plan as defined in section 7701(a)(37) of the U.S. Internal Revenue Code; (vi) any bank as defined in section 581 of the U.S. Internal Revenue Code; (vii) any real estate investment trust as defined in section 856 of the U.S. Internal Revenue Code; (viii) any regulated investment company as defined in section 851 of the U.S. Internal Revenue Code or any entity registered with the U.S. Securities and Exchange Commission under the Investment Company Act of 1940 (15 U.S.C. 80a-64); (ix) any common trust fund as defined in section 584(a) of the U.S. Internal Revenue Code; (x) any trust that is exempt from tax under section 664(c) of the U.S. Internal Revenue Code or that is described in section 4947(a)(1) of the U.S. Internal Revenue Code; (xi) a dealer in securities, commodities, or derivative financial instruments (including notional principal contracts, futures, forwards, and options) that is registered as such under the laws of the United States or any State; (xii) a broker as defined in section 6045(c) of the U.S. Internal Revenue Code; or (xiii) any tax-exempt trust under a plan that is described in section 403(b) or section 457(g) of the U.S. Internal Revenue Code.

gg) The term **"Entity"** means a legal person or a legal arrangement such as a trust.

hh) The term **"Non-U.S. Entity"** means an Entity that is not a U.S. Person.

ii) The term **"U.S. Source Withholdable Payment"** means any payment of interest (including any original issue discount), dividends, rents, salaries, wages, premiums, annuities, compensations, remunerations, emoluments, and other fixed or determinable annual or periodical gains, profits, and income, if such payment is from sources within the United States. Notwithstanding the foregoing, a U.S. Source Withholdable Payment does not include any payment that is not treated as a withholdable payment in relevant U.S. Treasury Regulations.

jj) An Entity is a **"Related Entity"** of another Entity if either Entity controls the other Entity, or the two Entities are under common control. For this purpose control includes direct or indirect ownership of more than 50 percent of the vote or value in an Entity. Notwithstanding the foregoing, Finland may treat an Entity as not a Related Entity of another Entity if the two Entities are not members of the same expanded affiliated group as defined in section 1471(e)(2) of the U.S. Internal Revenue Code.

kk) The term **"U.S. TIN"** means a U.S. federal taxpayer identifying number.

ll) The term **"Finnish TIN"** means a Finnish taxpayer identifying number.

mm) The term **"Controlling Persons"** means the natural persons who exercise control over an Entity. In the case of a trust, such term means the settlor, the trustees, the protector (if any), the beneficiaries or class of beneficiaries, and any other natural person exercising ultimate effective control over the trust, and in the case of a legal arrangement other than a trust, such term means persons in equivalent or similar positions. The term "Controlling Persons" shall be interpreted in a manner consistent with the Financial Action Task Force Recommendations.

2. Any term not otherwise defined in this Agreement shall, unless the context otherwise requires or the Competent Authorities agree to a common meaning (as permitted by domestic law), have the meaning that it has at that time under the law of the Party applying this Agreement, any meaning under the applicable tax laws of that Party prevailing over a meaning given to the term under other laws of that Party.

Article 2
Obligations to Obtain and Exchange Information with Respect to Reportable Accounts

1. Subject to the provisions of Article 3 of this Agreement, each Party shall obtain the information specified in paragraph 2 of this Article with respect to all Reportable Accounts and shall annually exchange this information with the other Party on an automatic basis pursuant to the provisions of Article 26 of the Convention.

2. The information to be obtained and exchanged is:

a) In the case of Finland with respect to each U.S. Reportable Account of each Reporting Finnish Financial Institution:

(1) the name, address, and U.S. TIN of each Specified U.S. Person that is an Account Holder of such account and, in the case of a Non-U.S. Entity that, after application of the due diligence procedures set forth in Annex I, is identified as having one or more Controlling Persons that is a Specified U.S. Person, the name, address, and U.S. TIN (if any) of such entity and each such Specified U.S. Person;

(2) the account number (or functional equivalent in the absence of an account number);

(3) the name and identifying number of the Reporting Finnish Financial Institution;

(4) the account balance or value (including, in the case of a Cash Value Insurance Contract or Annuity Contract, the Cash Value or surrender value) as of the end of the relevant calendar year or other appropriate reporting period or, if the account was closed during such year, immediately before closure;

(5) in the case of any Custodial Account:

(A) the total gross amount of interest, the total gross amount of dividends, and the total gross amount of other income generated with respect to the assets held in the account, in each case paid or credited to the account (or with respect to the account) during the calendar year or other appropriate reporting period; and

(B) the total gross proceeds from the sale or redemption of property paid or credited to the account during the calendar year or other appropriate reporting period with respect to which the Reporting Finnish Financial Institution acted as a custodian, broker, nominee, or otherwise as an agent for the Account Holder;

(6) in the case of any Depository Account, the total gross amount of interest paid or credited to the account during the calendar year or other appropriate reporting period; and

(7) in the case of any account not described in subparagraph 2(a)(5) or 2(a)(6) of this Article, the total gross amount paid or credited to the Account Holder with respect to the account during the calendar year or other appropriate reporting period with respect to which the Reporting Finnish Financial Institution is the obligor or debtor, including the aggregate amount of any redemption payments made to the Account Holder during the calendar year or other appropriate reporting period.

b) In the case of the United States, with respect to each Finnish Reportable Account of each Reporting U.S. Financial Institution:

(1) the name, address, and Finnish TIN of any person that is a resident of Finland and is an Account Holder of the account;

(2) the account number (or the functional equivalent in the absence of an account number);

(3) the name and identifying number of the Reporting U.S. Financial Institution;

(4) the gross amount of interest paid on a Depository Account;

(5) the gross amount of U.S. source dividends paid or credited to the account; and

(6) the gross amount of other U.S. source income paid or credited to the account, to the extent subject to reporting under chapter 3 of subtitle A or chapter 61 of subtitle F of the U.S. Internal Revenue Code.

Article 3
Time and Manner of Exchange of Information

1. For purposes of the exchange obligation in Article 2 of this Agreement, the amount and characterization of payments made with respect to a U.S. Reportable Account may be determined in accordance with the principles of Finland's tax laws, and the amount and characterization of payments made with respect to a Finnish Reportable Account may be determined in accordance with principles of U.S. federal income tax law.

2. For purposes of the exchange obligation in Article 2 of this Agreement, the information exchanged shall identify the currency in which each relevant amount is denominated.

3. With respect to paragraph 2 of Article 2 of this Agreement, information is to be obtained and exchanged with respect to 2014 and all subsequent years, except that:

a) In the case of Finland:

(1) the information to be obtained and exchanged with respect to 2014 is only the information described in subparagraphs 2(a)(1) through 2(a)(4) of Article 2 of this Agreement;

(2) the information to be obtained and exchanged with respect to 2015 is the information described in subparagraphs 2(a)(1) through 2(a)(7) of Article 2 of this Agreement, except for gross proceeds described in subparagraph 2(a)(5)(B) of Article 2 of this Agreement; and

(3) the information to be obtained and exchanged with respect to 2016 and subsequent years is the information described in subparagraphs 2(a)(1) through 2(a)(7) of Article 2 of this Agreement;

b) In the case of the United States, the information to be obtained and exchanged with respect to 2014 and subsequent years is all of the information identified in subparagraph 2(b) of Article 2 of this Agreement.

4. Notwithstanding paragraph 3 of this Article, with respect to each Reportable Account that is maintained by a Reporting Financial Institution as of June 30, 2014, and subject to paragraph 4 of Article 6 of this Agreement, the Parties are not required to obtain and include in the exchanged information the Finnish TIN or the U.S. TIN, as applicable, of any relevant person if such taxpayer identifying number is not in the records of the Reporting Financial Institution. In such a case, the Parties shall obtain and include in the exchanged information the date of birth of the relevant person, if the Reporting Financial Institution has such date of birth in its records.

5. Subject to paragraphs 3 and 4 of this Article, the information described in Article 2 of this Agreement shall be exchanged within nine months after the end of the calendar year to which the information relates.

6. The Competent Authorities of Finland and the United States shall enter into an agreement or arrangement under the mutual agreement procedure provided for in Article 25 of the Convention, which shall:

a) establish the procedures for the automatic exchange obligations described in Article 2 of this Agreement;

b) prescribe rules and procedures as may be necessary to implement Article 5 of this Agreement; and

c) establish as necessary procedures for the exchange of the information reported under subparagraph 1(b) of Article 4 of this Agreement.

7. All information exchanged shall be subject to the confidentiality and other protections provided for in the Convention, including the provisions limiting the use of the information exchanged.

Article 4
Application of FATCA to Finnish Financial Institutions

1. **Treatment of Reporting Finnish Financial Institutions.** Each Reporting Finnish Financial Institution shall be treated as complying with, and not subject to withholding under, section 1471 of the U.S. Internal Revenue Code if Finland complies with its obligations under Articles 2 and 3 of this Agreement with respect to such Reporting Finnish Financial Institution, and the Reporting Finnish Financial Institution:

a) identifies U.S. Reportable Accounts and reports annually to the Finnish Competent Authority the information required to be reported in subparagraph 2(a) of Article 2 of this Agreement in the time and manner described in Article 3 of this Agreement;

b) for each of 2015 and 2016, reports annually to the Finnish Competent Authority the name of each Nonparticipating Financial Institution to which it has made payments and the aggregate amount of such payments;

c) complies with the applicable registration requirements on the IRS FATCA registration website;

d) to the extent that a Reporting Finnish Financial Institution is (i) acting as a qualified intermediary (for purposes of section 1441 of the U.S. Internal Revenue Code) that has elected to assume primary withholding responsibility under chapter 3 of subtitle A of the U.S. Internal Revenue Code, (ii) a foreign partnership that has elected to act as a withholding foreign partnership (for purposes of both sections 1441 and 1471 of the U.S. Internal Revenue Code), or (iii) a foreign trust that has elected to act as a withholding foreign trust (for purposes of both sections 1441 and 1471 of the U.S. Internal Revenue Code), withholds 30 percent of any U.S. Source Withholdable Payment to any Nonparticipating Financial Institution; and

e) in the case of a Reporting Finnish Financial Institution that is not described in subparagraph 1(d) of this Article and that makes a payment of, or acts as an intermediary with respect to, a U.S. Source Withholdable Payment to any Nonparticipating Financial Institution, the Reporting Finnish Financial Institution provides to any immediate payor of such U.S. Source Withholdable Payment the information required for withholding and reporting to occur with respect to such payment.

Notwithstanding the foregoing, a Reporting Finnish Financial Institution with respect to which the conditions of this paragraph 1 are not satisfied shall not be subject to withholding under section 1471 of the U.S. Internal Revenue Code unless such Reporting Finnish Financial Institution is treated by the IRS as a Nonparticipating Financial Institution pursuant to subparagraph 2(b) of Article 5 of this Agreement.

2. **Suspension of Rules Relating to Recalcitrant Accounts.** The United States shall not require a Reporting Finnish Financial Institution to withhold tax under section 1471 or 1472 of the U.S. Internal Revenue Code with respect to an account held by a recalcitrant account holder (as defined in section 1471(d)(6) of the U.S. Internal Revenue Code), or to close such account, if the U.S. Competent Authority receives the information set forth in subparagraph 2(a) of Article 2 of this Agreement, subject to the provisions of Article 3 of this Agreement, with respect to such account.

3. **Specific Treatment of Finnish Retirement Plans.** The United States shall treat as deemed-compliant FFIs or exempt beneficial owners, as appropriate, for purposes of sections 1471 and 1472 of the U.S. Internal Revenue Code, Finnish retirement plans described in Annex II. For this purpose, a Finnish retirement plan includes an Entity established or located in, and regulated by, Finland, or a predetermined contractual or legal arrangement, operated to provide pension or retirement benefits or earn income for providing such benefits under the laws of Finland and regulated with respect to contributions, distributions, reporting, sponsorship, and taxation.

4. **Identification and Treatment of Other Deemed-Compliant FFIs and Exempt Beneficial Owners.** The United States shall treat each Non-Reporting Finnish Financial Institution as a deemed-compliant FFI or as an exempt beneficial owner, as appropriate, for purposes of section 1471 of the U.S. Internal Revenue Code.

5. **Special Rules Regarding Related Entities and Branches That Are Nonparticipating Financial Institutions.** If a Finnish Financial Institution, that otherwise meets the requirements described in paragraph 1 of this Article or is described in paragraph 3 or 4 of this Article, has a Related Entity or branch that operates in a jurisdiction that prevents such Related Entity or branch from fulfilling the requirements of a participating FFI or deemed-compliant FFI for purposes of section 1471 of the U.S. Internal Revenue Code or has a Related Entity or branch that is treated as a Nonparticipating Financial Institution solely due to the expiration of the transitional rule for limited FFIs and limited branches under relevant U.S. Treasury Regulations, such Finnish Financial Institution shall continue to be in compliance with the terms of this Agreement and shall continue to be treated as a deemed-compliant FFI or exempt beneficial owner, as appropriate, for purposes of section 1471 of the U.S. Internal Revenue Code, provided that:

a) the Finnish Financial Institution treats each such Related Entity or branch as a separate Nonparticipating Financial Institution for purposes of all the reporting and withholding requirements of this Agreement and each such Related Entity or branch identifies itself to withholding agents as a Nonparticipating Financial Institution;

b) each such Related Entity or branch identifies its U.S. accounts and reports the information with respect to those accounts as required under section 1471 of the U.S. Internal Revenue Code to the extent permitted under the relevant laws pertaining to the Related Entity or branch; and

c) such Related Entity or branch does not specifically solicit U.S. accounts held by persons that are not resident in the jurisdiction where such Related Entity or branch is located or accounts held by Nonparticipating Financial Institutions that are not established in the jurisdiction where such branch or Related Entity is located, and such branch or Related Entity is not used by the Finnish Financial Institution or any other Related Entity to circumvent the obligations under this Agreement or under section 1471 of the U.S. Internal Revenue Code, as appropriate.

6. **Coordination of Timing.** Notwithstanding paragraphs 3 and 5 of Article 3 of this Agreement:

a) Finland shall not be obligated to obtain and exchange information with respect to a calendar year that is prior to the calendar year with respect to which similar information is required to be reported to the IRS by participating FFIs pursuant to relevant U.S. Treasury Regulations;

b) Finland shall not be obligated to begin exchanging information prior to the date by which participating FFIs are required to report similar information to the IRS under relevant U.S. Treasury Regulations;

c) the United States shall not be obligated to obtain and exchange information with respect to a calendar year that is prior to the first calendar year with respect to which Finland is required to obtain and exchange information; and

d) the United States shall not be obligated to begin exchanging information prior to the date by which Finland is required to begin exchanging information.

7. **Coordination of Definitions with U.S. Treasury Regulations.** Notwithstanding Article 1 of this Agreement and the definitions provided in the Annexes to this Agreement, in implementing this Agreement, Finland may use, and may permit Finnish Financial Institutions to use, a definition in relevant U.S. Treasury Regulations in lieu of a corresponding definition in this Agreement, provided that such application would not frustrate the purposes of this Agreement.

Article 5
Collaboration on Compliance and Enforcement

1. **Minor and Administrative Errors.** A Competent Authority shall notify the Competent Authority of the other Party when the first-mentioned Competent Authority has

reason to believe that administrative errors or other minor errors may have led to incorrect or incomplete information reporting or resulted in other infringements of this Agreement. The Competent Authority of such other Party shall apply its domestic law (including applicable penalties) to obtain corrected and/or complete information or to resolve other infringements of this Agreement.

2. **Significant Non-Compliance.**

a) A Competent Authority shall notify the Competent Authority of the other Party when the first-mentioned Competent Authority has determined that there is significant non-compliance with the obligations under this Agreement with respect to a Reporting Financial Institution in the other jurisdiction. The Competent Authority of such other Party shall apply its domestic law (including applicable penalties) to address the significant non-compliance described in the notice.

b) If, in the case of a Reporting Finnish Financial Institution, such enforcement actions do not resolve the non-compliance within a period of 18 months after notification of significant non-compliance is first provided, the United States shall treat the Reporting Finnish Financial Institution as a Nonparticipating Financial Institution pursuant to this subparagraph 2(b).

3. **Reliance on Third Party Service Providers.** Each Party may allow Reporting Financial Institutions to use third party service providers to fulfill the obligations imposed on such Reporting Financial Institutions by a Party, as contemplated in this Agreement, but these obligations shall remain the responsibility of the Reporting Financial Institutions.

4. **Prevention of Avoidance.** The Parties shall implement as necessary requirements to prevent Financial Institutions from adopting practices intended to circumvent the reporting required under this Agreement.

Article 6
Mutual Commitment to Continue to Enhance the Effectiveness of Information Exchange and Transparency

1. **Reciprocity.** The Government of the United States acknowledges the need to achieve equivalent levels of reciprocal automatic information exchange with Finland. The Government of the United States is committed to further improve transparency and enhance the exchange relationship with Finland by pursuing the adoption of regulations and advocating and supporting relevant legislation to achieve such equivalent levels of reciprocal automatic information exchange.

2. **Treatment of Passthru Payments and Gross Proceeds.** The Parties are committed to work together, along with Partner Jurisdictions, to develop a practical and effective alternative approach to achieve the policy objectives of foreign passthru payment and gross proceeds withholding that minimizes burden.

3. **Development of Common Reporting and Exchange Model.** The Parties are committed to working with Partner Jurisdictions, the Organisation for Economic Co-operation and Development, and the European Union, on adapting the terms of this

Agreement and other agreements between the United States and Partner Jurisdictions to a common model for automatic exchange of information, including the development of reporting and due diligence standards for financial institutions.

4. **Documentation of Accounts Maintained as of June 30, 2014**. With respect to Reportable Accounts maintained by a Reporting Financial Institution as of June 30, 2014:

a) The United States commits to establish, by January 1, 2017, for reporting with respect to 2017 and subsequent years, rules requiring Reporting U.S. Financial Institutions to obtain and report the Finnish TIN of each Account Holder of a Finnish Reportable Account as required pursuant to subparagraph 2(b)(1) of Article 2 of this Agreement; and

b) Finland commits to establish, by January 1, 2017, for reporting with respect to 2017 and subsequent years, rules requiring Reporting Finnish Financial Institutions to obtain the U.S. TIN of each Specified U.S. Person as required pursuant to subparagraph 2(a)(1) of Article 2 of this Agreement.

Article 7
Consistency in the Application of FATCA to Partner Jurisdictions

1. Finland shall be granted the benefit of any more favorable terms under Article 4 or Annex I of this Agreement relating to the application of FATCA to Finnish Financial Institutions afforded to another Partner Jurisdiction under a signed bilateral agreement pursuant to which the other Partner Jurisdiction commits to undertake the same obligations as Finland described in Articles 2 and 3 of this Agreement, and subject to the same terms and conditions as described therein and in Articles 5 through 9 of this Agreement.

2. The United States shall notify Finland of any such more favorable terms and such more favorable terms shall apply automatically under this Agreement as if such terms were specified in this Agreement and effective as of the date of signing of the agreement incorporating the more favorable terms, unless Finland declines in writing the application thereof.

Article 8
Consultations and Amendments

1. In case any difficulties in the implementation of this Agreement arise, either Party may request consultations to develop appropriate measures to ensure the fulfillment of this Agreement.

2. This Agreement may be amended by written mutual agreement of the Parties. Unless otherwise agreed upon, such an amendment shall enter into force through the same procedures as set forth in paragraph 1 of Article 10 of this Agreement.

Article 9
Annexes

The Annexes form an integral part of this Agreement.

Article 10
Term of Agreement

This Agreement shall enter into force on the date of Finland's written notification to the United States that Finland has completed its necessary internal procedures for entry into force of this Agreement.

2. Either Party may terminate this Agreement by giving notice of termination in writing to the other Party. Such termination shall become effective on the first day of the month following the expiration of a period of 12 months after the date of the notice of termination.

The Parties shall, prior to December 31, 2016, consult in good faith to amend this Agreement as necessary to reflect progress on the commitments set forth in Article 6 of this Agreement.

In witness whereof, the undersigned, being duly authorized thereto by their respective Governments, have signed this Agreement.

Done at Helsinki, in duplicate, in the English language, this 5 day of March, 2014.

FOR THE GOVERNMENT OF THE REPUBLIC OF FINLAND:

FOR THE GOVERNMENT OF THE UNITED STATES OF AMERICA:

ANNEX I

DUE DILIGENCE OBLIGATIONS FOR IDENTIFYING AND REPORTING ON U.S. REPORTABLE ACCOUNTS AND ON PAYMENTS TO CERTAIN NONPARTICIPATING FINANCIAL INSTITUTIONS

I. **General**

A. Finland shall require that Reporting Finnish Financial Institutions apply the due diligence procedures contained in this Annex I to identify U.S. Reportable Accounts and accounts held by Nonparticipating Financial Institutions.

B. For purposes of the Agreement,

1. All dollar amounts are in U.S. dollars and shall be read to include the equivalent in other currencies.

2. Except as otherwise provided herein, the balance or value of an account shall be determined as of the last day of the calendar year or other appropriate reporting period.

3. Where a balance or value threshold is to be determined as of June 30, 2014, under this Annex I, the relevant balance or value shall be determined as of that day or the last day of the reporting period ending immediately before June 30, 2014, and where a balance or value threshold is to be determined as of the last day of a calendar year under this Annex I, the relevant balance or value shall be determined as of the last day of the calendar year or other appropriate reporting period.

4. Subject to subparagraph E(1) of section II of this Annex I, an account shall be treated as a U.S. Reportable Account beginning as of the date it is identified as such pursuant to the due diligence procedures in this Annex I.

5. Unless otherwise provided, information with respect to a U.S. Reportable Account shall be reported annually in the calendar year following the year to which the information relates.

C. As an alternative to the procedures described in each section of this Annex I, Finland may permit Reporting Finnish Financial Institutions to rely on the procedures described in relevant U.S. Treasury Regulations to establish whether an account is a U.S. Reportable Account or an account held by a Nonparticipating Financial Institution. Finland may permit Reporting Finnish Financial Institutions to make such election separately for each section of this Annex I either with respect to all relevant Financial Accounts or, separately, with respect to any clearly identified group of such accounts (such as by line of business or the location of where the account is maintained).

II. **Preexisting Individual Accounts.** The following rules and procedures apply for purposes of identifying U.S. Reportable Accounts among Preexisting Accounts held by individuals ("Preexisting Individual Accounts").

A. **Accounts Not Required to Be Reviewed, Identified, or Reported**. Unless the Reporting Finnish Financial Institution elects otherwise, either with respect to all Preexisting Individual Accounts or, separately, with respect to any clearly identified group of such accounts, where the implementing rules in Finland provide for such an election, the following Preexisting Individual Accounts are not required to be reviewed, identified, or reported as U.S. Reportable Accounts:

1. Subject to subparagraph E(2) of this section, a Preexisting Individual Account with a balance or value that does not exceed $50,000 as of June 30, 2014.

2. Subject to subparagraph E(2) of this section, a Preexisting Individual Account that is a Cash Value Insurance Contract or an Annuity Contract with a balance or value of $250,000 or less as of June 30, 2014.

3. A Preexisting Individual Account that is a Cash Value Insurance Contract or an Annuity Contract, provided the law or regulations of Finland or the United States effectively prevent the sale of such a Cash Value Insurance Contract or an Annuity Contract to U.S. residents (*e.g.*, if the relevant Financial Institution does not have the required registration under U.S. law, and the law of Finland requires reporting or withholding with respect to insurance products held by residents of Finland).

4. A Depository Account with a balance of $50,000 or less.

B. **Review Procedures for Preexisting Individual Accounts With a Balance or Value as of June 30, 2014, that Exceeds $50,000 ($250,000 for a Cash Value Insurance Contract or Annuity Contract), But Does Not Exceed $1,000,000 ("Lower Value Accounts")**.

1. **Electronic Record Search**. The Reporting Finnish Financial Institution must review electronically searchable data maintained by the Reporting Finnish Financial Institution for any of the following U.S. indicia:

a) Identification of the Account Holder as a U.S. citizen or resident;

b) Unambiguous indication of a U.S. place of birth;

c) Current U.S. mailing or residence address (including a U.S. post office box);

d) Current U.S. telephone number;

e) Standing instructions to transfer funds to an account maintained in the United States;

f) Currently effective power of attorney or signatory authority granted to a person with a U.S. address; or

g) An "in-care-of" or "hold mail" address that is the ***sole*** address the Reporting Finnish Financial Institution has on file for the Account Holder. In the case of a Preexisting Individual Account that is a Lower Value Account, an "in-care-of" address outside the United States or "hold mail" address shall not be treated as U.S. indicia.

2. If none of the U.S. indicia listed in subparagraph B(1) of this section are discovered in the electronic search, then no further action is required until there is a change in circumstances that results in one or more U.S. indicia being associated with the account, or the account becomes a High Value Account described in paragraph D of this section.

3. If any of the U.S. indicia listed in subparagraph B(1) of this section are discovered in the electronic search, or if there is a change in circumstances that results in one or more U.S. indicia being associated with the account, then the Reporting Finnish Financial Institution must treat the account as a U.S. Reportable Account unless it elects to apply subparagraph B (4) of this section and one of the exceptions in such subparagraph applies with respect to that account.

4. Notwithstanding a finding of U.S. indicia under subparagraph B(1) of this section, a Reporting Finnish Financial Institution is not required to treat an account as a U.S. Reportable Account if:

a) Where the Account Holder information unambiguously indicates a ***U.S. place of birth***, the Reporting Finnish Financial Institution obtains, or has previously reviewed and maintains a record of:

(1) A self-certification that the Account Holder is neither a U.S. citizen nor a U.S. resident for tax purposes (which may be on an IRS Form W-8 or other similar agreed form);

(2) A non-U.S. passport or other government-issued identification evidencing the Account Holder's citizenship or nationality in a country other than the United States; ***and***

(3) A copy of the Account Holder's Certificate of Loss of Nationality of the United States or a reasonable explanation of:

(a) The reason the Account Holder does not have such a certificate despite relinquishing U.S. citizenship; ***or***

(b) The reason the Account Holder did not obtain U.S. citizenship at birth.

b) Where the Account Holder information contains a ***current U.S. mailing or residence address, or one or more U.S. telephone numbers***

that are the only telephone numbers associated with the account, the Reporting Finnish Financial Institution obtains, or has previously reviewed and maintains a record of:

(1) A self-certification that the Account Holder is neither a U.S. citizen nor a U.S. resident for tax purposes (which may be on an IRS Form W-8 or other similar agreed form); ***and***

(2) Documentary evidence, as defined in paragraph D of section VI of this Annex I, establishing the Account Holder's non-U.S. status.

c) Where the Account Holder information contains ***standing instructions to transfer funds to an account maintained in the United States***, the Reporting Finnish Financial Institution obtains, or has previously reviewed and maintains a record of:

(1) A self-certification that the Account Holder is neither a U.S. citizen nor a U.S. resident for tax purposes (which may be on an IRS Form W-8 or other similar agreed form); ***and***

(2) Documentary evidence, as defined in paragraph D of section VI of this Annex I, establishing the Account Holder's non-U.S. status.

d) Where the Account Holder information contains ***a currently effective power of attorney or signatory authority granted to a person with a U.S. address, has an "in-care-of" address or "hold mail" address that is the sole address identified for the Account Holder, or has one or more U.S. telephone numbers (if a non-U.S. telephone number is also associated with the account)***, the Reporting Finnish Financial Institution obtains, or has previously reviewed and maintains a record of:

(1) A self-certification that the Account Holder is neither a U.S. citizen nor a U.S. resident for tax purposes (which may be on an IRS Form W-8 or other similar agreed form); ***or***

(2) Documentary evidence, as defined in paragraph D of section VI of this Annex I, establishing the Account Holder's non-U.S. status.

C. **Additional Procedures Applicable to Preexisting Individual Accounts That Are Lower Value Accounts.**

1. Review of Preexisting Individual Accounts that are Lower Value Accounts for U.S. indicia must be completed by June 30, 2016.

2. If there is a change of circumstances with respect to a Preexisting Individual Account that is a Lower Value Account that results in one or more

U.S. indicia described in subparagraph B(1) of this section being associated with the account, then the Reporting Finnish Financial Institution must treat the account as a U.S. Reportable Account unless subparagraph B(4) of this section applies.

3. Except for Depository Accounts described in subparagraph A(4) of this section, any Preexisting Individual Account that has been identified as a U.S. Reportable Account under this section shall be treated as a U.S. Reportable Account in all subsequent years, unless the Account Holder ceases to be a Specified U.S. Person.

D. **Enhanced Review Procedures for Preexisting Individual Accounts With a Balance or Value That Exceeds $1,000,000 as of June 30, 2014, or December 31 of 2015 or Any Subsequent Year ("High Value Accounts").**

1. **Electronic Record Search.** The Reporting Finnish Financial Institution must review electronically searchable data maintained by the Reporting Finnish Financial Institution for any of the U.S. indicia described in subparagraph B(1) of this section.

2. **Paper Record Search.** If the Reporting Finnish Financial Institution's electronically searchable databases include fields for and capture all of the information described in, subparagraph D(3) of this section, then no further paper record search is required. If the electronic databases do not capture all of this information, then with respect to a High Value Account, the Reporting Finnish Financial Institution must also review the current customer master file and, to the extent not contained in the current customer master file, the following documents associated with the account and obtained by the Reporting Finnish Financial Institution within the last five years for any of the U.S. indicia described in subparagraph B(1) of this section:

a) The most recent documentary evidence collected with respect to the account;

b) The most recent account opening contract or documentation;

c) The most recent documentation obtained by the Reporting Finnish Financial Institution pursuant to AML/KYC Procedures or for other regulatory purposes;

d) Any power of attorney or signature authority forms currently in effect; and

e) Any standing instructions to transfer funds currently in effect.

3. **Exception Where Databases Contain Sufficient Information.** A Reporting Finnish Financial Institution is not required to perform the paper record search described in subparagraph D(2) of this section if the Reporting Finnish Financial Institution's electronically searchable information includes the following:

a) The Account Holder's nationality or residence status;

b) The Account Holder's residence address and mailing address currently on file with the Reporting Finnish Financial Institution;

c) The Account Holder's telephone number(s) currently on file, if any, with the Reporting Finnish Financial Institution;

d) Whether there are standing instructions to transfer funds in the account to another account (including an account at another branch of the Reporting Finnish Financial Institution or another Financial Institution);

e) Whether there is a current "in-care-of" address or "hold mail" address for the Account Holder; ***and***

f) Whether there is any power of attorney or signatory authority for the account.

4. **Relationship Manager Inquiry for Actual Knowledge.** In addition to the electronic and paper record searches described above, the Reporting Finnish Financial Institution must treat as a U.S. Reportable Account any High Value Account assigned to a relationship manager (including any Financial Accounts aggregated with such High Value Account) if the relationship manager has actual knowledge that the Account Holder is a Specified U.S. Person.

5. **Effect of Finding U.S. Indicia.**

a) If none of the U.S. indicia listed in subparagraph B(1) of this section are discovered in the enhanced review of High Value Accounts described above, and the account is not identified as held by a Specified U.S. Person in subparagraph D(4) of this section, then no further action is required until there is a change in circumstances that results in one or more U.S. indicia being associated with the account.

b) If any of the U.S. indicia listed in subparagraph B(1) of this section are discovered in the enhanced review of High Value Accounts described above, or if there is a subsequent change in circumstances that results in one or more U.S. indicia being associated with the account, then the Reporting Finnish Financial Institution must treat the account as a U.S. Reportable Account unless it elects to apply subparagraph B(4) of this section and one of the exceptions in such subparagraph applies with respect to that account.

c) Except for Depository Accounts described in subparagraph A(4) of this section, any Preexisting Individual Account that has been identified as a U.S. Reportable Account under this section shall be treated as a U.S. Reportable Account in all subsequent years, unless the Account Holder ceases to be a Specified U.S. Person.

E. **Additional Procedures Applicable to High Value Accounts.**

1. If a Preexisting Individual Account is a High Value Account as of June 30, 2014, the Reporting Finnish Financial Institution must complete the enhanced review procedures described in paragraph D of this section with respect to such account by June 30, 2015. If based on this review such account is identified as a U.S. Reportable Account on or before December 31, 2014, the Reporting Finnish Financial Institution must report the required information about such account with respect to 2014 in the first report on the account and on an annual basis thereafter. In the case of an account identified as a U.S. Reportable Account after December 31, 2014 and on or before June 30, 2015, the Reporting Finnish Financial Institution is not required to report information about such account with respect to 2014, but must report information about the account on an annual basis thereafter.

2. If a Preexisting Individual Account is not a High Value Account as of June 30, 2014, but becomes a High Value Account as of the last day of 2015 or any subsequent calendar year, the Reporting Finnish Financial Institution must complete the enhanced review procedures described in paragraph D of this section with respect to such account within six months after the last day of the calendar year in which the account becomes a High Value Account. If based on this review such account is identified as a U.S. Reportable Account, the Reporting Finnish Financial Institution must report the required information about such account with respect to the year in which it is identified as a U.S. Reportable Account and subsequent years on an annual basis, unless the Account Holder ceases to be a Specified U.S. Person.

3. Once a Reporting Finnish Financial Institution applies the enhanced review procedures described in paragraph D of this section to a High Value Account, the Reporting Finnish Financial Institution is not required to re-apply such procedures, other than the relationship manager inquiry described in subparagraph D(4) of this section, to the same High Value Account in any subsequent year.

4. If there is a change of circumstances with respect to a High Value Account that results in one or more U.S. indicia described in subparagraph B(1) of this section being associated with the account, then the Reporting Finnish Financial Institution must treat the account as a U.S. Reportable Account unless it elects to apply subparagraph B(4) of this section and one of the exceptions in such subparagraph applies with respect to that account.

5. A Reporting Finnish Financial Institution must implement procedures to ensure that a relationship manager identifies any change in circumstances of an account. For example, if a relationship manager is notified that the Account Holder has a new mailing address in the United States, the Reporting Finnish Financial Institution is required to treat the new address as a change in

circumstances and, if it elects to apply subparagraph B(4) of this section, is required to obtain the appropriate documentation from the Account Holder.

F. **Preexisting Individual Accounts That Have Been Documented for Certain Other Purposes.** A Reporting Finnish Financial Institution that has previously obtained documentation from an Account Holder to establish the Account Holder's status as neither a U.S. citizen nor a U.S. resident in order to meet its obligations under a qualified intermediary, withholding foreign partnership, or withholding foreign trust agreement with the IRS, or to fulfill its obligations under chapter 61 of Title 26 of the United States Code, is not required to perform the procedures described in subparagraph B(1) of this section with respect to Lower Value Accounts or subparagraphs D(1) through D(3) of this section with respect to High Value Accounts.

III. **New Individual Accounts.** The following rules and procedures apply for purposes of identifying U.S. Reportable Accounts among Financial Accounts held by individuals and opened on or after July 1, 2014 ("New Individual Accounts").

A. **Accounts Not Required to Be Reviewed, Identified, or Reported.** Unless the Reporting Finnish Financial Institution elects otherwise, either with respect to all New Individual Accounts or, separately, with respect to any clearly identified group of such accounts, where the implementing rules in Finland provide for such an election, the following New Individual Accounts are not required to be reviewed, identified, or reported as U.S. Reportable Accounts:

1. A Depository Account unless the account balance exceeds $50,000 at the end of any calendar year or other appropriate reporting period.

2. A Cash Value Insurance Contract unless the Cash Value exceeds $50,000 at the end of any calendar year or other appropriate reporting period.

B. **Other New Individual Accounts.** With respect to New Individual Accounts not described in paragraph A of this section, upon account opening (or within 90 days after the end of the calendar year in which the account ceases to be described in paragraph A of this section), the Reporting Finnish Financial Institution must obtain a self-certification, which may be part of the account opening documentation, that allows the Reporting Finnish Financial Institution to determine whether the Account Holder is resident in the United States for tax purposes (for this purpose, a U.S. citizen is considered to be resident in the United States for tax purposes, even if the Account Holder is also a tax resident of another jurisdiction) and confirm the reasonableness of such self-certification based on the information obtained by the Reporting Finnish Financial Institution in connection with the opening of the account, including any documentation collected pursuant to AML/KYC Procedures.

C. If the self-certification establishes that the Account Holder is resident in the United States for tax purposes, the Reporting Finnish Financial Institution must treat the account as a U.S. Reportable Account and obtain a self-certification that includes the Account Holder's U.S. TIN (which may be an IRS Form W-9 or other similar agreed form).

D. If there is a change of circumstances with respect to a New Individual Account that causes the Reporting Finnish Financial Institution to know, or have reason to know, that the original self-certification is incorrect or unreliable, the Reporting Finnish Financial Institution cannot rely on the original self-certification and must obtain a valid self-certification that establishes whether the Account Holder is a U.S. citizen or resident for U.S. tax purposes. If the Reporting Finnish Financial Institution is unable to obtain a valid self-certification, the Reporting Finnish Financial Institution must treat the account as a U.S. Reportable Account.

IV. **Preexisting Entity Accounts.** The following rules and procedures apply for purposes of identifying U.S. Reportable Accounts and accounts held by Nonparticipating Financial Institutions among Preexisting Accounts held by Entities ("Preexisting Entity Accounts").

A. **Entity Accounts Not Required to Be Reviewed, Identified or Reported.** Unless the Reporting Finnish Financial Institution elects otherwise, either with respect to all Preexisting Entity Accounts or, separately, with respect to any clearly identified group of such accounts, where the implementing rules in Finland provide for such an election, a Preexisting Entity Account with an account balance or value that does not exceed $250,000 as of June 30, 2014, is not required to be reviewed, identified, or reported as a U.S. Reportable Account until the account balance or value exceeds $1,000,000.

B. **Entity Accounts Subject to Review.** A Preexisting Entity Account that has an account balance or value that exceeds $250,000 as of June 30, 2014, and a Preexisting Entity Account that does not exceed $250,000 as of June 30, 2014 but the account balance or value of which exceeds $1,000,000 as of the last day of 2015 or any subsequent calendar year, must be reviewed in accordance with the procedures set forth in paragraph D of this section.

C. **Entity Accounts With Respect to Which Reporting Is Required.** With respect to Preexisting Entity Accounts described in paragraph B of this section, only accounts that are held by one or more Entities that are Specified U.S. Persons, or by Passive NFFEs with one or more Controlling Persons who are U.S. citizens or residents, shall be treated as U.S. Reportable Accounts. In addition, accounts held by Nonparticipating Financial Institutions shall be treated as accounts for which aggregate payments as described in subparagraph 1(b) of Article 4 of the Agreement are reported to the Finnish Competent Authority.

D. **Review Procedures for Identifying Entity Accounts With Respect to Which Reporting Is Required.** For Preexisting Entity Accounts described in paragraph B of this section, the Reporting Finnish Financial Institution must apply the following review procedures to determine whether the account is held by one or more Specified U.S. Persons, by Passive NFFEs with one or more Controlling Persons who are U.S. citizens or residents, or by Nonparticipating Financial Institutions:

1. **Determine Whether the Entity Is a Specified U.S. Person.**

a) Review information maintained for regulatory or customer relationship purposes (including information collected pursuant to AML/KYC Procedures) to determine whether the information indicates that the Account Holder is a U.S. Person. For this purpose, information indicating that the Account Holder is a U.S. Person includes a U.S. place of incorporation or organization, or a U.S. address.

b) If the information indicates that the Account Holder is a U.S. Person, the Reporting Finnish Financial Institution must treat the account as a U.S. Reportable Account unless it obtains a self-certification from the Account Holder (which may be on an IRS Form W-8 or W-9, or a similar agreed form), or reasonably determines based on information in its possession or that is publicly available, that the Account Holder is not a Specified U.S. Person.

2. **Determine Whether a Non-U.S. Entity Is a Financial Institution.**

a) Review information maintained for regulatory or customer relationship purposes (including information collected pursuant to AML/KYC Procedures) to determine whether the information indicates that the Account Holder is a Financial Institution.

b) If the information indicates that the Account Holder is a Financial Institution, or the Reporting Finnish Financial Institution verifies the Account Holder's Global Intermediary Identification Number on the published IRS FFI list, then the account is not a U.S. Reportable Account.

3. **Determine Whether a Financial Institution Is a Nonparticipating Financial Institution Payments to Which Are Subject to Aggregate Reporting Under Subparagraph 1(b) of Article 4 of the Agreement.**

a) Subject to subparagraph D(3)(b) of this section, a Reporting Finnish Financial Institution may determine that the Account Holder is a Finnish Financial Institution or other Partner Jurisdiction Financial Institution if the Reporting Finnish Financial Institution reasonably determines that the Account Holder has such status on the basis of the Account Holder's Global Intermediary Identification Number on the published IRS FFI list or other information that is publicly available or in the possession of the Reporting [FATCA Partner] Financial Institution, as applicable. In such case, no further review, identification, or reporting is required with respect to the account.

b) If the Account Holder is a Finnish Financial Institution or other Partner Jurisdiction Financial Institution treated by the IRS as a Nonparticipating Financial Institution, then the account is not a U.S. Reportable Account, but payments to the Account Holder must be reported as contemplated in subparagraph 1(b) of Article 4 of the Agreement.

c) If the Account Holder is not a Finnish Financial Institution or other Partner Jurisdiction Financial Institution, then the Reporting

Finnish Financial Institution must treat the Account Holder as a Nonparticipating Financial Institution payments to which are reportable under subparagraph 1(b) of Article 4 of the Agreement, unless the Reporting Finnish Financial Institution:

(1) Obtains a self-certification (which may be on an IRS Form W-8 or similar agreed form) from the Account Holder that it is a certified deemed-compliant FFI, or an exempt beneficial owner, as those terms are defined in relevant U.S. Treasury Regulations; ***or***

(2) In the case of a participating FFI or registered deemed-compliant FFI, verifies the Account Holder's Global Intermediary Identification Number on the published IRS FFI list.

4. **Determine Whether an Account Held by an NFFE Is a U.S. Reportable Account.** With respect to an Account Holder of a Preexisting Entity Account that is not identified as either a U.S. Person or a Financial Institution, the Reporting Finnish Financial Institution must identify (i) whether the Account Holder has Controlling Persons, (ii) whether the Account Holder is a Passive NFFE, and (iii) whether any of the Controlling Persons of the Account Holder is a U.S. citizen or resident. In making these determinations the Reporting Finnish Financial Institution must follow the guidance in subparagraphs D(4)(a) through D(4)(d) of this section in the order most appropriate under the circumstances.

a) For purposes of determining the Controlling Persons of an Account Holder, a Reporting Finnish Financial Institution may rely on information collected and maintained pursuant to AML/KYC Procedures.

b) For purposes of determining whether the Account Holder is a Passive NFFE, the Reporting Finnish Financial Institution must obtain a self-certification (which may be on an IRS Form W-8 or W-9, or on a similar agreed form) from the Account Holder to establish its status, unless it has information in its possession or that is publicly available, based on which it can reasonably determine that the Account Holder is an Active NFFE.

c) For purposes of determining whether a Controlling Person of a Passive NFFE is a U.S. citizen or resident for tax purposes, a Reporting Finnish Financial Institution may rely on:

(1) Information collected and maintained pursuant to AML/KYC Procedures in the case of a Preexisting Entity Account held by one or more NFFEs with an account balance or value that does not exceed $1,000,000; ***or***

(2) A self-certification (which may be on an IRS Form W-8 or W-9, or on a similar agreed form) from the Account Holder or such Controlling Person in the case of a Preexisting Entity Account held by one or more NFFEs with an account balance or value that exceeds $1,000,000.

d) If any Controlling Person of a Passive NFFE is a U.S. citizen or resident, the account shall be treated as a U.S. Reportable Account.

E. **Timing of Review and Additional Procedures Applicable to Preexisting Entity Accounts.**

1. Review of Preexisting Entity Accounts with an account balance or value that exceeds $250,000 as of June 30, 2014 must be completed by June 30, 2016.

2. Review of Preexisting Entity Accounts with an account balance or value that does not exceed $250,000 as of June 30, 2014, but exceeds $1,000,000 as of December 31 of 2015 or any subsequent year, must be completed within six months after the last day of the calendar year in which the account balance or value exceeds $1,000,000.

3. If there is a change of circumstances with respect to a Preexisting Entity Account that causes the Reporting Finnish Financial Institution to know, or have reason to know, that the self-certification or other documentation associated with an account is incorrect or unreliable, the Reporting Finnish Financial Institution must re-determine the status of the account in accordance with the procedures set forth in paragraph D of this section.

V. **New Entity Accounts.** The following rules and procedures apply for purposes of identifying U.S. Reportable Accounts and accounts held by Nonparticipating Financial Institutions among Financial Accounts held by Entities and opened on or after July 1, 2014 ("New Entity Accounts").

A. **Entity Accounts Not Required to Be Reviewed, Identified or Reported.** Unless the Reporting Finnish Financial Institution elects otherwise, either with respect to all New Entity Accounts or, separately, with respect to any clearly identified group of such accounts, where the implementing rules in Finland provide for such election, a credit card account or a revolving credit facility treated as a New Entity Account is not required to be reviewed, identified, or reported, provided that the Reporting Finnish Financial Institution maintaining such account implements policies and procedures to prevent an account balance owed to the Account Holder that exceeds $50,000.

B. **Other New Entity Accounts.** With respect to New Entity Accounts not described in paragraph A of this section, the Reporting Finnish Financial Institution must determine whether the Account Holder is: (i) a Specified U.S. Person; (ii) a Finnish Financial Institution or other Partner Jurisdiction Financial Institution; (iii) a participating FFI, a deemed-compliant FFI, or an exempt beneficial owner, as those terms are defined in relevant U.S. Treasury Regulations; or (iv) an Active NFFE or Passive NFFE.

1. Subject to subparagraph B(2) of this section, a Reporting Finnish Financial Institution may determine that the Account Holder is an Active NFFE, a Finnish Financial Institution, or other Partner Jurisdiction Financial Institution if the Reporting Finnish Financial Institution reasonably determines that the Account Holder has such status on the basis of the Account Holder's Global Intermediary Identification Number or other information that is publicly available or in the possession of the Reporting Finnish Financial Institution, as applicable.

2. If the Account Holder is a Finnish Financial Institution or other Partner Jurisdiction Financial Institution treated by the IRS as a Nonparticipating Financial Institution, then the account is not a U.S. Reportable Account, but payments to the Account Holder must be reported as contemplated in subparagraph 1(b) of Article 4 of the Agreement.

3. In all other cases, a Reporting Finnish Financial Institution must obtain a self-certification from the Account Holder to establish the Account Holder's status. Based on the self-certification, the following rules apply:

a) If the Account Holder is ***a Specified U.S. Person***, the Reporting Finnish Financial Institution must treat the account as a U.S. Reportable Account.

b) If the Account Holder is ***a Passive NFFE***, the Reporting Finnish Financial Institution must identify the Controlling Persons as determined under AML/KYC Procedures, and must determine whether any such person is a U.S. citizen or resident on the basis of a self-certification from the Account Holder or such person. If any such person is a U.S. citizen or resident, the Reporting Finnish Financial Institution must treat the account as a U.S. Reportable Account.

c) If the Account Holder is: (i) a U.S. Person that is not a Specified U.S. Person; (ii) subject to subparagraph B(3)(d) of this section, a Finnish Financial Institution or other Partner Jurisdiction Financial Institution; (iii) a participating FFI, a deemed-compliant FFI, or an exempt beneficial owner, as those terms are defined in relevant U.S. Treasury Regulations; (iv) an Active NFFE; or (v) a Passive NFFE none of the Controlling Persons of which is a U.S. citizen or resident, then the account is not a U.S. Reportable Account, and no reporting is required with respect to the account.

d) If the Account Holder is a Nonparticipating Financial Institution (including a Finnish Financial Institution or other Partner Jurisdiction Financial Institution treated by the IRS as a Nonparticipating Financial Institution), then the account is not a U.S. Reportable Account, but payments to the Account Holder must be reported as contemplated in subparagraph 1(b) of Article 4 of the Agreement.

VI. **Special Rules and Definitions.** The following additional rules and definitions apply in implementing the due diligence procedures described above:

A. **Reliance on Self-Certifications and Documentary Evidence.** A Reporting Finnish Financial Institution may not rely on a self-certification or documentary evidence if the Reporting Finnish Financial Institution knows or has reason to know that the self-certification or documentary evidence is incorrect or unreliable.

B. **Definitions.** The following definitions apply for purposes of this Annex I.

1. **AML/KYC Procedures.** "AML/KYC Procedures" means the customer due diligence procedures of a Reporting Finnish Financial Institution pursuant to the anti-money laundering or similar requirements of Finland to which such Reporting Finnish Financial Institution is subject.

2. **NFFE.** An "NFFE" means any Non-U.S. Entity that is not an FFI as defined in relevant U.S. Treasury Regulations or is an Entity described in subparagraph B(4)(j) of this section, and also includes any Non-U.S. Entity that is established in Finland or another Partner Jurisdiction and that is not a Financial Institution.

3. **Passive NFFE.** A "Passive NFFE" means any NFFE that is not (i) an Active NFFE, or (ii) a withholding foreign partnership or withholding foreign trust pursuant to relevant U.S. Treasury Regulations.

4. **Active NFFE.** An "Active NFFE" means any NFFE that meets any of the following criteria:

   a) Less than 50 percent of the NFFE's gross income for the preceding calendar year or other appropriate reporting period is passive income and less than 50 percent of the assets held by the NFFE during the preceding calendar year or other appropriate reporting period are assets that produce or are held for the production of passive income;

   b) The stock of the NFFE is regularly traded on an established securities market or the NFFE is a Related Entity of an Entity the stock of which is regularly traded on an established securities market;

   c) The NFFE is organized in a U.S. Territory and all of the owners of the payee are bona fide residents of that U.S. Territory;

   d) The NFFE is a government (other than the U.S. government), a political subdivision of such government (which, for the avoidance of doubt, includes a state, province, county, or municipality), or a public body performing a function of such government or a political subdivision thereof, a government of a U.S. Territory, an international organization, a non-U.S. central bank of issue, or an Entity wholly owned by one or more of the foregoing;

e) Substantially all of the activities of the NFFE consist of holding (in whole or in part) the outstanding stock of, or providing financing and services to, one or more subsidiaries that engage in trades or businesses other than the business of a Financial Institution, except that an entity shall not qualify for NFFE status if the entity functions (or holds itself out) as an investment fund, such as a private equity fund, venture capital fund, leveraged buyout fund, or any investment vehicle whose purpose is to acquire or fund companies and then hold interests in those companies as capital assets for investment purposes;

f) The NFFE is not yet operating a business and has no prior operating history, but is investing capital into assets with the intent to operate a business other than that of a Financial Institution, provided that the NFFE shall not qualify for this exception after the date that is 24 months after the date of the initial organization of the NFFE;

g) The NFFE was not a Financial Institution in the past five years, and is in the process of liquidating its assets or is reorganizing with the intent to continue or recommence operations in a business other than that of a Financial Institution;

h) The NFFE primarily engages in financing and hedging transactions with, or for, Related Entities that are not Financial Institutions, and does not provide financing or hedging services to any Entity that is not a Related Entity, provided that the group of any such Related Entities is primarily engaged in a business other than that of a Financial Institution;

i) The NFFE is an "excepted NFFE" as described in relevant U.S. Treasury Regulations; ***or***

j) The NFFE meets all of the following requirements:

   i. It is established and operated in its jurisdiction of residence exclusively for religious, charitable, scientific, artistic, cultural, athletic, or educational purposes; or it is established and operated in its jurisdiction of residence and it is a professional organization, business league, chamber of commerce, labor organization, agricultural or horticultural organization, civic league or an organization operated exclusively for the promotion of social welfare;

   ii. It is exempt from income tax in its jurisdiction of residence;

iii. It has no shareholders or members who have a proprietary or beneficial interest in its income or assets;

iv. The applicable laws of the NFFE's jurisdiction of residence or the NFFE's formation documents do not permit any income or assets of the NFFE to be distributed to, or applied for the benefit of, a private person or non-charitable Entity other than pursuant to the conduct of the NFFE's charitable activities, or as payment of reasonable compensation for services rendered, or as payment representing the fair market value of property which the NFFE has purchased; ***and***

v. The applicable laws of the NFFE's jurisdiction of residence or the NFFE's formation documents require that, upon the NFFE's liquidation or dissolution, all of its assets be distributed to a governmental entity or other non-profit organization, or escheat to the government of the NFFE's jurisdiction of residence or any political subdivision thereof.

5. **Preexisting Account**. A "Preexisting Account" means a Financial Account maintained by a Reporting Financial Institution as of June 30, 2014.

C. **Account Balance Aggregation and Currency Translation Rules.**

1. **Aggregation of Individual Accounts**. For purposes of determining the aggregate balance or value of Financial Accounts held by an individual, a Reporting Finnish Financial Institution is required to aggregate all Financial Accounts maintained by the Reporting Finnish Financial Institution, or by a Related Entity, but only to the extent that the Reporting Finnish Financial Institution's computerized systems link the Financial Accounts by reference to a data element such as client number or taxpayer identification number, and allow account balances or values to be aggregated. Each holder of a jointly held Financial Account shall be attributed the entire balance or value of the jointly held Financial Account for purposes of applying the aggregation requirements described in this paragraph 1.

2. **Aggregation of Entity Accounts**. For purposes of determining the aggregate balance or value of Financial Accounts held by an Entity, a Reporting Finnish Financial Institution is required to take into account all Financial Accounts that are maintained by the Reporting Finnish Financial Institution, or by a Related Entity, but only to the extent that the Reporting Finnish Financial Institution's computerized systems link the Financial Accounts by reference to a data element such as client number or taxpayer identification number, and allow account balances or values to be aggregated.

3. **Special Aggregation Rule Applicable to Relationship Managers**. For purposes of determining the aggregate balance or value of Financial Accounts held by a person to determine whether a Financial Account is a High Value Account, a Reporting Finnish Financial Institution is also required, in

the case of any Financial Accounts that a relationship manager knows, or has reason to know, are directly or indirectly owned, controlled, or established (other than in a fiduciary capacity) by the same person, to aggregate all such accounts.

4. **Currency Translation Rule.** For purposes of determining the balance or value of Financial Accounts denominated in a currency other than the U.S. dollar, a Reporting Finnish Financial Institution must convert the U.S. dollar threshold amounts described in this Annex I into such currency using a published spot rate determined as of the last day of the calendar year preceding the year in which the Reporting Finnish Financial Institution is determining the balance or value.

D. **Documentary Evidence.** For purposes of this Annex I, acceptable documentary evidence includes any of the following:

1. A certificate of residence issued by an authorized government body (for example, a government or agency thereof, or a municipality) of the jurisdiction in which the payee claims to be a resident.

2. With respect to an individual, any valid identification issued by an authorized government body (for example, a government or agency thereof, or a municipality), that includes the individual's name and is typically used for identification purposes.

3. With respect to an Entity, any official documentation issued by an authorized government body (for example, a government or agency thereof, or a municipality) that includes the name of the Entity and either the address of its principal office in the jurisdiction (or U.S. Territory) in which it claims to be a resident or the jurisdiction (or U.S. Territory) in which the Entity was incorporated or organized.

4. With respect to a Financial Account maintained in a jurisdiction with anti-money laundering rules that have been approved by the IRS in connection with a QI agreement (as described in relevant U.S. Treasury Regulations), any of the documents, other than a Form W-8 or W-9, referenced in the jurisdiction's attachment to the QI agreement for identifying individuals or Entities.

5. Any financial statement, third-party credit report, bankruptcy filing, or U.S. Securities and Exchange Commission report.

E. **Alternative Procedures for Financial Accounts Held by Individual Beneficiaries of a Cash Value Insurance Contract.** A Reporting Finnish Financial Institution may presume that an individual beneficiary (other than the owner) of a Cash Value Insurance Contract receiving a death benefit is not a Specified U.S. Person and may treat such Financial Account as other than a U.S. Reportable Account unless the Reporting Finnish Financial Institution has actual knowledge, or reason to know, that the beneficiary is a Specified U.S. Person. A Reporting Finnish Financial Institution has reason to know that a beneficiary of a Cash Value Insurance Contract is a Specified U.S. Person if the information collected by the Reporting Finnish Financial Institution and associated with the beneficiary contains U.S. indicia as described in subparagraph (B)(1) of section II of this Annex I. If a Reporting Finnish Financial Institution has actual knowledge, or reason to know, that the beneficiary is a Specified U.S. Person, the Reporting Finnish Financial Institution must follow the procedures in subparagraph B(3) of section II of this Annex I.

F. **Reliance on Third Parties**. Regardless of whether an election is made under paragraph C of section I of this Annex I, Finland may permit Reporting Finnish Financial Institutions to rely on due diligence procedures performed by third parties, to the extent provided in relevant U.S. Treasury Regulations.

ANNEX II

The following Entities shall be treated as exempt beneficial owners or deemed-compliant FFIs, as the case may be, and the following accounts are excluded from the definition of Financial Accounts.

This Annex II may be modified by a mutual written decision entered into between the Competent Authorities of Finland and the United States: (1) to include additional Entities and accounts that present a low risk of being used by U.S. Persons to evade U.S. tax and that have similar characteristics to the Entities and accounts described in this Annex II as of the date of signature of the Agreement; or (2) to remove Entities and accounts that, due to changes in circumstances, no longer present a low risk of being used by U.S. Persons to evade U.S. tax. Any such addition or removal shall be effective on the date of signature of the mutual decision, unless otherwise provided therein. Procedures for reaching such a mutual decision may be included in the mutual agreement or arrangement described in paragraph 6 of Article 3 of the Agreement.

I. **Exempt Beneficial Owners other than Funds**. The following Entities shall be treated as Non-Reporting Finnish Financial Institutions and as exempt beneficial owners for purposes of sections 1471 and 1472 of the U.S. Internal Revenue Code, ***other than*** with respect to a payment that is derived from an obligation held in connection with a commercial financial activity of a type engaged in by a Specified Insurance Company, Custodial Institution, or Depository Institution.

A. **Governmental Entities**. The Finnish government, any political subdivision of Finland (which, for the avoidance of doubt, includes a state, province, county, or municipality), or any wholly owned agency or instrumentality of Finland or any one or more of the foregoing (each, a "Finnish Governmental Entity"). This category is comprised of the integral parts, controlled entities, and political subdivisions of Finland.

1. An integral part of Finland means any person, organization, agency, bureau, fund, instrumentality, or other body, however designated, that constitutes a governing authority of Finland. The net earnings of the governing authority must be credited to its own account or to other accounts of Finland, with no portion inuring to the benefit of any private person. An integral part does not include any individual who is a sovereign, official, or administrator acting in a private or personal capacity.

2. A controlled entity means an Entity that is separate in form from Finland or that otherwise constitutes a separate juridical entity, provided that:

(i) The Entity is wholly owned and controlled by one or more Finnish Governmental Entities directly or through one or more controlled entities;

(ii) The Entity's net earnings are credited to its own account or to the accounts of one or more Finnish Governmental Entities, with no portion of its income inuring to the benefit of any private person; and (iii)The Entity's assets vest in one or more Finnish Governmental Entities upon dissolution.

3. Income does not inure to the benefit of private persons if such persons are the intended beneficiaries of a governmental program, and the program activities are performed for the general public with respect to the common welfare or relate to the administration of some phase of government. Notwithstanding the foregoing, however, income is considered to inure to the benefit of private persons if the income is derived from the use of a governmental entity to conduct a commercial business, such as a commercial banking business, that provides financial services to private persons.

For the avoidance of doubt, each of the following shall be treated as a Non-Reporting Finnish Financial Institution and as an exempt beneficial owner for purposes of sections 1471 and 1472 of the U.S. Internal Revenue Code:

Finnvera Oyj – Finnvera plc,
Vientiluotto Oy – Finnish Export Credit Ltd, and
Kuntarahoitus Oyj - Municipality Finance plc.

B. **Central Bank.** An institution that is by law or government sanction the principal authority, other than the government of Finland itself, issuing instruments intended to circulate as currency. Such an institution may include an instrumentality that is separate from the government of Finland, whether or not owned in whole or in part by Finland.

C. **International Organizations.** Any international organization or wholly owned agency or instrumentality thereof. This category includes any intergovernmental organization (including a supranational organization) (1) that is comprised primarily of non-U.S. governments; (2) that has in effect a headquarters agreement with Finland; and (3) the income of which does not inure to the benefit of private persons.

II. **Funds that Qualify as Exempt Beneficial Owners.** The following Entities shall be treated as Non-Reporting Finnish Financial Institutions and as exempt beneficial owners for purposes of sections 1471 and 1472 of the U.S. Internal Revenue Code.

A. **Treaty-Qualified Retirement Fund.** A fund established in Finland, provided that the fund is entitled to benefits under an income tax treaty between Finland and the United States on income that it derives from sources within the United States (or would be entitled to such benefits if it derived any such income) as a resident of Finland that satisfies any applicable limitation on benefits requirement, and is operated principally to administer or provide pension or retirement benefits.

B. **Broad Participation Retirement Fund.** A fund, including a pension insurance company whether or not organized as a mutual pension insurance company, established in Finland to provide retirement, disability, or death benefits, or any combination thereof, to beneficiaries that are current or former employees (or persons designated by such employees) of one or more employers in consideration for services rendered, provided that the fund:

1. Does not have a single beneficiary with a right to more than five percent of the fund's assets;

2. Is subject to government regulation and provides annual information reporting about its beneficiaries to the relevant tax authorities in Finland; and

3. Satisfies at least one of the following requirements:

   a) The fund is generally exempt from tax in Finland on investment income under the laws of Finland due to its status as a retirement or pension plan;

   b) The fund receives at least 50 percent of its total contributions (other than transfers of assets from other plans described in paragraphs A through D of this section or from retirement and pension accounts described in subparagraph A(1) of section V of this Annex II) from the sponsoring employers;

   c) Distributions or withdrawals from the fund are allowed only upon the occurrence of specified events related to retirement, disability, or death (except rollover distributions to other retirement funds described in paragraphs A through D of this section or retirement and pension accounts described in subparagraph A(1) of section V of this Annex II), or penalties apply to distributions or withdrawals made before such specified events; or

   d) Contributions (other than certain permitted make-up contributions) by employees to the fund are limited by reference to earned income of the employee or may not exceed $50,000 annually, applying the rules set forth in Annex I for account aggregation and currency translation.

C. **Narrow Participation Retirement Fund.** A fund established in Finland to provide retirement, disability, or death benefits to beneficiaries that are current or former employees (or persons designated by such employees) of one or more employers in consideration for services rendered, provided that:

1. The fund has fewer than 50 participants;

2. The fund is sponsored by one or more employers that are not Investment Entities or Passive NFFEs;

3. The employee and employer contributions to the fund (other than transfers of assets from treaty-qualified retirement funds described in paragraph A of this section or retirement and pension accounts described in subparagraph A(1) of section V of this Annex II) are limited by reference to earned income and compensation of the employee, respectively;

4. Participants that are not residents of Finland are not entitled to more than 20 percent of the fund's assets; and

5. The fund is subject to government regulation and provides annual information reporting about its beneficiaries to the relevant tax authorities in Finland.

D. **Pension Fund of an Exempt Beneficial Owner.** A fund established in Finland by an exempt beneficial owner to provide retirement, disability, or death benefits to beneficiaries or participants that are current or former employees of the exempt beneficial owner (or persons designated by such employees), or that are not current or former employees, if the benefits provided to such beneficiaries or participants are in consideration of personal services performed for the exempt beneficial owner.

E. **Investment Entity Wholly Owned by Exempt Beneficial Owners.** An Entity that is a Finnish Financial Institution solely because it is an Investment Entity, provided that each direct holder of an Equity Interest in the Entity is an exempt beneficial owner, and each direct holder of a debt interest in such Entity is either a Depository Institution (with respect to a loan made to such Entity) or an exempt beneficial owner.

III. **Small or Limited Scope Financial Institutions that Qualify as Deemed-Compliant FFIs.** The following Financial Institutions are Non-Reporting Finnish Financial Institutions that shall be treated as deemed-compliant FFIs for purposes of section 1471 of the U.S. Internal Revenue Code.

A. **Financial Institution with a Local Client Base.**

A Finnish Financial Institution satisfying the following requirements:

1. The Financial Institution must be licensed and regulated as a financial institution under the laws of Finland;

2. The Financial Institution must have no fixed place of business outside Finland. For this purpose, a fixed place of business does not include a location that is not advertised to the public and from which the Financial Institution performs solely administrative support functions;

3. The Financial Institution must not solicit customers or Account Holders outside Finland. For this purpose, a Financial Institution shall not be considered to have solicited customers or Account Holders outside Finland merely because the Financial Institution (a) operates a website, provided that the website does not specifically indicate that the Financial Institution provides Financial Accounts or services to nonresidents, and does not otherwise target or solicit U.S. customers or Account Holders, or (b) advertises in print media or on a radio or television station that is distributed or aired primarily within Finland but is also incidentally distributed or aired in other countries, provided that the advertisement does not specifically indicate that the Financial Institution provides Financial Accounts or services to nonresidents, and does not otherwise target or solicit U.S. customers or Account Holders;

4. The Financial Institution must be required under the laws of Finland to identify resident Account Holders for purposes of either information reporting or withholding of tax with respect to Financial Accounts held by residents or for purposes of satisfying Finland's AML due diligence requirements;

5. At least 98 percent of the Financial Accounts by value maintained by the Financial Institution must be held by residents (including residents that are Entities) of Finland or a Member State of the European Union;

6. Beginning on or before July 1, 2014, the Financial Institution must have policies and procedures, consistent with those set forth in Annex I, to prevent the Financial Institution from providing a Financial Account to any Nonparticipating Financial Institution and to monitor whether the Financial Institution opens or maintains a Financial Account for any Specified U.S. Person who is not a resident of Finland (including a U.S. Person that was a resident of Finland when the Financial Account was opened but subsequently ceases to be a resident of Finland), or any Passive NFFE with Controlling Persons who are U.S. residents or U.S. citizens who are not residents of Finland;

7. Such policies and procedures must provide that if any Financial Account held by a Specified U.S. Person who is not a resident of Finland or by a Passive NFFE with Controlling Persons who are U.S. residents or U.S. citizens who are not residents of Finland is identified, the Financial Institution must report such Financial Account as would be required if the Financial Institution were a Reporting Finnish Financial Institution (including by following the applicable registration requirements on the IRS FATCA registration website) or close such Financial Account;

8. With respect to a Preexisting Account held by an individual who is not a resident of Finland or by an Entity, the Financial Institution must review those Preexisting Accounts in accordance with the procedures set forth in Annex I applicable to Preexisting Accounts to identify any U.S. Reportable Account or Financial Account held by a Nonparticipating Financial Institution, and must report such Financial Account as would be required if the Financial Institution were a Reporting Finnish Financial Institution (including by following the applicable registration requirements on the IRS FATCA registration website) or close such Financial Account;

9. Each Related Entity of the Financial Institution that is a Financial Institution must be incorporated or organized in Finland and, with the exception of any Related Entity that is a retirement fund described in paragraphs A through D of section II of this Annex II, satisfy the requirements set forth in this paragraph A; and

10. The Financial Institution must not have policies or practices that discriminate against opening or maintaining Financial Accounts for individuals who are Specified U.S. Persons and residents of Finland.

B. <u>Local Bank</u>. A Financial Institution satisfying the following requirements:

1. The Financial Institution operates solely as (and is licensed and regulated under the laws of Finland as) (a) a bank or (b) a credit union or similar cooperative credit organization that is operated without profit;

2. The Financial Institution's business consists primarily of receiving deposits from and making loans to, with respect to a bank, unrelated retail customers and, with

respect to a credit union or similar cooperative credit organization, members, provided that no member has a greater than five percent interest in such credit union or cooperative credit organization;

3. The Financial Institution satisfies the requirements set forth in subparagraphs A(2) and A(3) of this section, provided that, in addition to the limitations on the website described in subparagraph A(3) of this section, the website does not permit the opening of a Financial Account;

4. The Financial Institution does not have more than $175 million in assets on its balance sheet, and the Financial Institution and any Related Entities, taken together, do not have more than $500 million in total assets on their consolidated or combined balance sheets; and

5. Any Related Entity must be incorporated or organized in Finland, and any Related Entity that is a Financial Institution, with the exception of any Related Entity that is a retirement fund described in paragraphs A through D of section II of this Annex II or a Financial Institution with only low-value accounts described in paragraph C of this section, must satisfy the requirements set forth in this paragraph B.

C. **Financial Institution with Only Low-Value Accounts**. A Finnish Financial Institution satisfying the following requirements:

1. The Financial Institution is not an Investment Entity;

2. No Financial Account maintained by the Financial Institution or any Related Entity has a balance or value in excess of $50,000, applying the rules set forth in Annex I for account aggregation and currency translation; and

3. The Financial Institution does not have more than $50 million in assets on its balance sheet, and the Financial Institution and any Related Entities, taken together, do not have more than $50 million in total assets on their consolidated or combined balance sheets.

D. **Qualified Credit Card Issuer**. A Finnish Financial Institution satisfying the following requirements:

1. The Financial Institution is a Financial Institution solely because it is an issuer of credit cards that accepts deposits only when a customer makes a payment in excess of a balance due with respect to the card and the overpayment is not immediately returned to the customer; and

2. Beginning on or before July 1, 2014, the Financial Institution implements policies and procedures to either prevent a customer deposit in excess of $50,000, or to ensure that any customer deposit in excess of $50,000, in each case applying the rules set forth in Annex I for account aggregation and currency translation, is refunded to the customer within 60 days. For this purpose, a customer deposit does not refer to credit balances to the extent of disputed charges but does include credit balances resulting from merchandise returns.

IV. **Investment Entities that Qualify as Deemed-Compliant FFIs and Other Special Rules.** The Financial Institutions described in paragraphs A through D of this section are Non-Reporting Finnish Financial Institutions that shall be treated as deemed-compliant FFIs for purposes of section 1471 of the U.S. Internal Revenue Code. In addition, paragraph E of this section provides special rules applicable to an Investment Entity.

A. **Sponsored Investment Entity and Controlled Foreign Corporation.** A Financial Institution described in subparagraph A(1) or A(2) of this section having a sponsoring entity that complies with the requirements of subparagraph A(3) of this section.

1. A Financial Institution is a sponsored investment entity if (a) it is an Investment Entity established in Finland that is not a qualified intermediary, withholding foreign partnership, or withholding foreign trust pursuant to relevant U.S. Treasury Regulations; and (b) an Entity has agreed with the Financial Institution to act as a sponsoring entity for the Financial Institution.

2. A Financial Institution is a sponsored controlled foreign corporation if (a) the Financial Institution is a controlled foreign corporation[1] organized under the laws of Finland that is not a qualified intermediary, withholding foreign partnership, or withholding foreign trust pursuant to relevant U.S. Treasury Regulations; (b) the Financial Institution is wholly owned, directly or indirectly, by a Reporting U.S. Financial Institution that agrees to act, or requires an affiliate of the Financial Institution to act, as a sponsoring entity for the Financial Institution; and (c) the Financial Institution shares a common electronic account system with the sponsoring entity that enables the sponsoring entity to identify all Account Holders and payees of the Financial Institution and to access all account and customer information maintained by the Financial Institution including, but not limited to, customer identification information, customer documentation, account balance, and all payments made to the Account Holder or payee.

3. The sponsoring entity complies with the following requirements:

a) The sponsoring entity is authorized to act on behalf of the Financial Institution (such as a fund manager, trustee, corporate director, or managing partner) to fulfill applicable registration requirements on the IRS FATCA registration website;

b) The sponsoring entity has registered as a sponsoring entity with the IRS on the IRS FATCA registration website;

c) If the sponsoring entity identifies any U.S. Reportable Accounts with respect to the Financial Institution, the sponsoring entity registers the Financial

[1] A "controlled foreign corporation" means any foreign corporation if more than 50 percent of the total combined voting power of all classes of stock of such corporation entitled to vote, or the total value of the stock of such corporation, is owned, or is considered as owned, by "United States shareholders" on any day during the taxable year of such foreign corporation. The term a "United States shareholder" means, with respect to any foreign corporation, a United States person who owns, or is considered as owning, 10 percent or more of the total combined voting power of all classes of stock entitled to vote of such foreign corporation.

Institution pursuant to applicable registration requirements on the IRS FATCA registration website on or before the later of December 31, 2015 and the date that is 90 days after such a U.S. Reportable Account is first identified;

d) The sponsoring entity agrees to perform, on behalf of the Financial Institution, all due diligence, withholding, reporting, and other requirements that the Financial Institution would have been required to perform if it were a Reporting Finnish Financial Institution;

e) The sponsoring entity identifies the Financial Institution and includes the identifying number of the Financial Institution (obtained by following applicable registration requirements on the IRS FATCA registration website) in all reporting completed on the Financial Institution's behalf; and

f) The sponsoring entity has not had its status as a sponsor revoked.

B. Sponsored, Closely Held Investment Vehicle. A Finnish Financial Institution satisfying the following requirements:

1. The Financial Institution is a Financial Institution solely because it is an Investment Entity and is not a qualified intermediary, withholding foreign partnership, or withholding foreign trust pursuant to relevant U.S. Treasury Regulations;

2. The sponsoring entity is a Reporting U.S. Financial Institution, Reporting Model 1 FFI, or Participating FFI, is authorized to act on behalf of the Financial Institution (such as a professional manager, trustee, or managing partner), and agrees to perform, on behalf of the Financial Institution, all due diligence, withholding, reporting, and other requirements that the Financial Institution would have been required to perform if it were a Reporting Finnish Financial Institution;

3. The Financial Institution does not hold itself out as an investment vehicle for unrelated parties;

4. Twenty or fewer individuals own all of the debt interests and Equity Interests in the Financial Institution (disregarding debt interests owned by Participating FFIs and deemed-compliant FFIs and Equity Interests owned by an Entity if that Entity owns 100 percent of the Equity Interests in the Financial Institution and is itself a sponsored Financial Institution described in this paragraph B); and

5. The sponsoring entity complies with the following requirements:

   a) The sponsoring entity has registered as a sponsoring entity with the IRS on the IRS FATCA registration website;

   b) The sponsoring entity agrees to perform, on behalf of the Financial Institution, all due diligence, withholding, reporting, and other requirements that the Financial Institution would have been required to perform if it were a Reporting Finnish Financial Institution and retains documentation collected with respect to the Financial Institution for a period of six years;

c) The sponsoring entity identifies the Financial Institution in all reporting completed on the Financial Institution's behalf; and

d) The sponsoring entity has not had its status as a sponsor revoked.

C. **Investment Advisors and Investment Managers.** An Investment Entity established in Finland that is a Financial Institution solely because it (1) renders investment advice to, and acts on behalf of, or (2) manages portfolios for, and acts on behalf of, a customer for the purposes of investing, managing, or administering funds deposited in the name of the customer with a Financial Institution other than a Nonparticipating Financial Institution.

D. **Collective Investment Vehicle.** An Investment Entity established in Finland that is regulated as a collective investment vehicle, provided that all of the interests in the collective investment vehicle (including debt interests in excess of $50,000) are held by or through one or more exempt beneficial owners, Active NFFEs described in subparagraph B(4) of section VI of Annex I, U.S. Persons that are not Specified U.S. Persons, or Financial Institutions that are not Nonparticipating Financial Institutions.

E. **Special Rules.** The following rules apply to an Investment Entity:

a) With respect to interests in an Investment Entity that is a collective investment vehicle described in paragraph D of this section, the reporting obligations of any Investment Entity (other than a Financial Institution through which interests in the collective investment vehicle are held) shall be deemed fulfilled.

b) With respect to interests in:

(i) An Investment Entity established in a Partner Jurisdiction that is regulated as a collective investment vehicle, all of the interests in which (including debt interests in excess of $50,000) are held by or through one or more exempt beneficial owners, Active NFFEs described in subparagraph B(4) of section VI of Annex I, U.S. Persons that are not Specified U.S. Persons, or Financial Institutions that are not Nonparticipating Financial Institutions; or

b) An Investment Entity that is a qualified collective investment vehicle under relevant U.S. Treasury Regulations;

the reporting obligations of any Investment Entity that is a Finnish Financial Institution (other than a Financial Institution through which interests in the collective investment vehicle are held) shall be deemed fulfilled.

c) With respect to interests in an Investment Entity established in Finland that is not described in paragraph D or subparagraph E(2) of this section, consistent with paragraph 3 of Article 5 of the Agreement, the reporting obligations of all other Investment Entities with respect to such interests shall be deemed fulfilled if the information required to be reported by the first-mentioned Investment Entity pursuant to the Agreement with respect to such interests is reported by such Investment Entity or another person.

V. **<u>Accounts Excluded from Financial Accounts</u>.** The following accounts in Finland are excluded from the definition of Financial Accounts and therefore shall not be treated as U.S. Reportable Accounts.

A. **<u>Certain Savings Accounts</u>.**

1. <u>Retirement and Pension Account</u>. A retirement or pension account maintained in Finland that satisfies the following requirements under the laws of Finland.

   a) The account is subject to regulation as a personal retirement account or is part of a registered or regulated retirement or pension plan for the provision of retirement or pension benefits (including disability or death benefits);

   b) The account is tax-favored (*i.e.*, contributions to the account that would otherwise be subject to tax under the laws of Finland are deductible or excluded from the gross income of the account holder or taxed at a reduced rate, or taxation of investment income from the account is deferred or taxed at a reduced rate);

   c) Annual information reporting is required to the tax authorities in Finland with respect to the account;

   d) Withdrawals are conditioned on reaching a specified retirement age, disability, or death, or penalties apply to withdrawals made before such specified events; and

   e) Either (i) annual contributions are limited to $50,000 or less, or (ii) there is a maximum lifetime contribution limit to the account of $1,000,000 or less, in each case applying the rules set forth in Annex I for account aggregation and currency translation.

2. <u>Non-Retirement Savings Accounts</u>. An account maintained in Finland (other than an insurance or Annuity Contract) that satisfies the following requirements under the laws of Finland.

   a) The account is subject to regulation as a savings vehicle for purposes other than for retirement;

   b) The account is tax-favored (*i.e.*, contributions to the account that would otherwise be subject to tax under the laws of Finland are deductible or excluded from the gross income of the account holder or taxed at a reduced rate, or taxation of investment income from the account is deferred or taxed at a reduced rate);

   c) Withdrawals are conditioned on meeting specific criteria related to the purpose of the savings account (for example, the provision of educational or medical benefits), or penalties apply to withdrawals made before such criteria are met; and

d) Annual contributions are limited to $50,000 or less, applying the rules set forth in Annex I for account aggregation and currency translation.

B. **Certain Term Life Insurance Contracts.** A life insurance contract maintained in Finland with a coverage period that will end before the insured individual attains age 90, provided that the contract satisfies the following requirements:

1. Periodic premiums, which do not decrease over time, are payable at least annually during the period the contract is in existence or until the insured attains age 90, whichever is shorter;

2. The contract has no contract value that any person can access (by withdrawal, loan, or otherwise) without terminating the contract;

3. The amount (other than a death benefit) payable upon cancellation or termination of the contract cannot exceed the aggregate premiums paid for the contract, less the sum of mortality, morbidity, and expense charges (whether or not actually imposed) for the period or periods of the contract's existence and any amounts paid prior to the cancellation or termination of the contract; and

4. The contract is not held by a transferee for value.

C. **Account Held By an Estate.** An account maintained in Finland that is held solely by an estate if the documentation for such account includes a copy of the deceased's will or death certificate.

D. **Escrow Accounts.** An account maintained in Finland established in connection with any of the following:

1. A court order or judgment.

2. A sale, exchange, or lease of real or personal property, provided that the account satisfies the following requirements:

   a) The account is funded solely with a down payment, earnest money, deposit in an amount appropriate to secure an obligation directly related to the transaction, or a similar payment, or is funded with a financial asset that is deposited in the account in connection with the sale, exchange, or lease of the property;

   b) The account is established and used solely to secure the obligation of the purchaser to pay the purchase price for the property, the seller to pay any contingent liability, or the lessor or lessee to pay for any damages relating to the leased property as agreed under the lease;

   c) The assets of the account, including the income earned thereon, will be paid or otherwise distributed for the benefit of the purchaser, seller, lessor, or lessee (including to satisfy such person's obligation) when the property is sold, exchanged, or surrendered, or the lease terminates;

d) The account is not a margin or similar account established in connection with a sale or exchange of a financial asset; and

e) The account is not associated with a credit card account.

3. An obligation of a Financial Institution servicing a loan secured by real property to set aside a portion of a payment solely to facilitate the payment of taxes or insurance related to the real property at a later time.

4. An obligation of a Financial Institution solely to facilitate the payment of taxes at a later time.

E. **Partner Jurisdiction Accounts.** An account maintained in Finland and excluded from the definition of Financial Account under an agreement between the United States and another Partner Jurisdiction to facilitate the implementation of FATCA, provided that such account is subject to the same requirements and oversight under the laws of such other Partner Jurisdiction as if such account were established in that Partner Jurisdiction and maintained by a Partner Jurisdiction Financial Institution in that Partner Jurisdiction.

VI. **Definitions.** The following additional definitions shall apply to the descriptions above:

A. **Reporting Model 1 FFI.** The term Reporting Model 1 FFI means a Financial Institution with respect to which a non-U.S. government or agency thereof agrees to obtain and exchange information pursuant to a Model 1 IGA, other than a Financial Institution treated as a Nonparticipating Financial Institution under the Model 1 IGA. For purposes of this definition, the term Model 1 IGA means an arrangement between the United States or the Treasury Department and a non-U.S. government or one or more agencies thereof to implement FATCA through reporting by Financial Institutions to such non-U.S. government or agency thereof, followed by automatic exchange of such reported information with the IRS.

B. **Participating FFI.** The term Participating FFI means a Financial Institution that has agreed to comply with the requirements of an FFI Agreement, including a Financial Institution described in a Model 2 IGA that has agreed to comply with the requirements of an FFI Agreement. The term Participating FFI also includes a qualified intermediary branch of a Reporting U.S. Financial Institution, unless such branch is a Reporting Model 1 FFI. For purposes of this definition, the term FFI Agreement means an agreement that sets forth the requirements for a Financial Institution to be treated as complying with the requirements of section 1471(b) of the U.S. Internal Revenue Code. In addition, for purposes of this definition, the term Model 2 IGA means an arrangement between the United States or the Treasury Department and a non-U.S. government or one or more agencies thereof to facilitate the implementation of FATCA through reporting by Financial Institutions directly to the IRS in accordance with the requirements of an FFI Agreement, supplemented by the exchange of information between such non-U.S. government or agency thereof and the IRS.

**MEMORANDUM OF UNDERSTANDING
REGARDING
THE AGREEMENT BETWEEN
THE GOVERNMENT OF THE REPUBLIC OF FINLAND AND
THE GOVERNMENT OF THE UNITED STATES OF AMERICA
TO IMPROVE INTERNATIONAL TAX COMPLIANCE AND TO IMPLEMENT FATCA**

At the signing today of the Agreement between the Government of the Republic of Finland and the Government of the United States of America to Improve International Tax Compliance and to Implement FATCA (hereinafter the "Agreement"), the representatives of the Republic of Finland and the United States of America wish to confirm their understanding of the following:

In reference to paragraph 1 of Article 1 (Definitions) of the Agreement, it is understood that, in the case of securities, registered in a Finnish Central Securities Depository (Arvopaperikeskus) as defined in chapter 1 paragraph 3 of the Finnish Act on Book-Entry System and Settlement Services (Laki arvo-osuusjärjestelmästä ja selvitystoiminnasta 14.12.2012/749) that are held by or through one or more other Financial Institutions other than Nonparticipating Financial Institutions, the relevant Financial Accounts will be treated as held by such other Financial Institutions, and such other Financial Institutions will be responsible for any reporting required with respect to such Financial Accounts. Notwithstanding the foregoing, in accordance with paragraph 3 of Article 5 of the Agreement, the Finnish Central Securities Depository may report on behalf of such other Financial Institutions.

In reference to paragraph D of Section VI of the Annex I, it is understood that in case of Finland, a certificate of residence issued by an authorized government body means a certificate of fiscal residence issued by the Finnish Tax Administration.

Signed at Helsinki, in duplicate, in the English language, this 5 day of March, 2014.

FOR THE GOVERNMENT OF THE REPUBLIC OF FINLAND:

FOR THE GOVERNMENT OF THE UNITED STATES OF AMERICA:

[TRANSLATION – TRADUCTION]

ACCORD ENTRE LE GOUVERNEMENT DE LA RÉPUBLIQUE DE FINLANDE ET LE GOUVERNEMENT DES ÉTATS-UNIS D'AMÉRIQUE RELATIF AU RENFORCEMENT DU RESPECT DES OBLIGATIONS FISCALES INTERNATIONALES ET À LA MISE EN ŒUVRE DE LA LOI FATCA

Considérant que le Gouvernement de la République de Finlande et le Gouvernement des États-Unis d'Amérique (ci-après dénommés séparément une « Partie », et collectivement les « Parties ») entretiennent de longue date une relation étroite concernant l'assistance mutuelle en matière fiscale et désirent conclure un accord afin de renforcer le respect des obligations fiscales à l'échelle internationale en approfondissant cette relation,

Considérant que l'article 26, tel que modifié par le Protocole, de la Convention entre le Gouvernement de la République de Finlande et le Gouvernement des États-Unis d'Amérique tendant à éviter la double imposition et à prévenir l'évasion fiscale en matière d'impôts sur le revenu et sur la fortune signée à Helsinki le 21 septembre 1989 et modifiée par le Protocole fait à Helsinki le 1er mai 2006 (la « Convention ») autorise l'échange de renseignements à des fins fiscales, y compris de manière automatique,

Considérant que les États-Unis d'Amérique ont adopté des dispositions communément connues sous le nom de « loi relative au respect des obligations fiscales concernant les comptes étrangers » (« loi FATCA »), qui instaurent un régime déclaratif pour les institutions financières en ce qui concerne certains comptes,

Considérant que le Gouvernement de la République de Finlande soutient l'objectif stratégique fondamental de la loi FATCA, qui est de renforcer le respect des obligations fiscales,

Considérant que la loi FATCA a soulevé un certain nombre de questions, notamment le fait que les établissements financiers finlandais pourraient ne pas être en mesure de se conformer à certains aspects de la loi FATCA en raison d'obstacles juridiques internes,

Considérant que le Gouvernement des États-Unis d'Amérique recueille des renseignements sur certains comptes de résidents de Finlande auprès des institutions financières américaines et est déterminé à échanger ces renseignements avec le Gouvernement de la République de Finlande et à atteindre des niveaux équivalents d'échange,

Considérant que les Parties sont déterminées à travailler de concert sur le long terme en vue d'aboutir à des règles communes de déclaration et à des normes de diligence raisonnable pour les institutions financières,

Considérant que le Gouvernement des États-Unis d'Amérique reconnaît la nécessité de coordonner les obligations déclaratives liées à la loi FATCA et les autres obligations américaines de déclaration fiscale auxquelles sont soumises les institutions financières finlandaises afin d'éviter les doubles déclarations,

Considérant qu'une coopération intergouvernementale visant à faciliter la mise en œuvre de la loi FATCA permettrait d'aborder ces questions et de réduire les charges qui pèsent sur les institutions financières finlandaises,

Considérant que les Parties souhaitent conclure un accord afin de renforcer le respect des obligations fiscales à l'échelle internationale et de mettre en œuvre la loi FATCA sur la base d'obligations déclaratives nationales et d'échanges automatiques réciproques en application de la

Convention sous réserve de la confidentialité et des garanties prévues par celle-ci, y compris les dispositions qui limitent l'utilisation des renseignements échangés en vertu de la Convention,

Les Parties sont convenues de ce qui suit :

Article premier. Définitions

1. Aux fins du présent Accord et de ses annexes (l'« Accord »), les termes et expressions suivants ont la signification indiquée ci-dessous :

a) L'expression « États-Unis » désigne les États-Unis d'Amérique, y compris leurs États membres, mais ne comprend pas les Territoires américains. Toute référence à un « État » des États-Unis comprend le district de Columbia ;

b) L'expression « Territoire américain » désigne les Samoa américaines, le Commonwealth des Îles Mariannes septentrionales, Guam, le Commonwealth de Porto Rico ou les Îles Vierges américaines ;

c) Le sigle « IRS » désigne l'administration fiscale américaine ;

d) L'expression « Finlande » désigne la République de Finlande ;

e) L'expression « juridiction partenaire » désigne une juridiction qui a conclu un accord avec les États-Unis pour faciliter la mise en œuvre de la loi FATCA. L'IRS publie une liste énumérant toutes les juridictions partenaires ;

f) L'expression « autorité compétente » désigne :

1) Dans le cas des États-Unis, le Secrétaire au Trésor ou son représentant ; et

2) Dans le cas de la Finlande, le Ministre des finances ou son représentant autorisé ;

g) L'expression « institution financière » désigne un établissement gérant des dépôts de titres, un établissement de dépôt, une entité d'investissement ou un organisme d'assurance particulier ;

h) L'expression « établissement gérant des dépôts de titres » désigne toute entité dont une part substantielle de l'activité consiste à détenir des actifs financiers pour le compte de tiers. Une entité détient des actifs financiers pour le compte de tiers dans le cadre d'une partie substantielle de son activité si les revenus bruts de l'entité attribuables à la détention d'actifs financiers et de services financiers connexes sont égaux ou supérieurs à 20 % des revenus bruts de l'entité durant la plus courte des deux périodes suivantes : i) la période de trois ans se terminant le 31 décembre (ou le dernier jour d'un exercice comptable non civil) précédant l'année au cours de laquelle la détermination est effectuée ; ou ii) la période pendant laquelle l'entité a existé ;

i) L'expression « établissement de dépôt » désigne toute entité qui accepte des dépôts dans le cadre habituel d'une activité bancaire ou similaire ;

j) L'expression « entité d'investissement » désigne toute entité qui exerce en tant qu'entreprise (ou est gérée par une entité qui exerce en tant qu'entreprise) une ou plusieurs des activités ou opérations suivantes au nom ou pour le compte d'un client :

1) Transactions sur les instruments du marché monétaire (chèques, billets, certificats de dépôt, instruments dérivés, etc.), le marché des changes, les instruments sur devises, les produits de taux d'intérêt, les indices, les valeurs mobilières ou les marchés à terme de marchandises ;
2) Gestion individuelle ou collective de portefeuille ; ou
3) Autres opérations d'investissement, d'administration ou de gestion de fonds ou d'argent pour le compte de tiers.

Le présent alinéa j) est interprété conformément à la définition de l'expression « institution financière » qui figure dans les Recommandations du Groupe d'action financière (GAFI).

k) L'expression « organisme d'assurance particulier » désigne tout organisme d'assurance (ou la société holding d'un organisme d'assurance) qui émet un contrat d'assurance à forte valeur de rachat ou un contrat de rente ou est tenu d'effectuer des versements afférents à un tel contrat ;

l) L'expression « institution financière finlandaise » désigne : i) toute institution financière résidente de Finlande, à l'exception de toute succursale établie en dehors de Finlande ; et ii) toute succursale d'une institution financière non-résidente de Finlande si cette succursale est établie en Finlande ;

m) L'expression « institution financière de la juridiction partenaire » désigne i) toute institution financière établie dans une juridiction partenaire à l'exception de ses succursales situées en dehors du territoire de la juridiction partenaire et ii) toute succursale d'une institution financière qui n'est pas établie dans la juridiction partenaire si cette succursale est établie sur le territoire de la juridiction partenaire ;

n) L'expression « institution financière déclarante » désigne une institution financière déclarante finlandaise ou une institution financière déclarante américaine, selon le cas ;

o) L'expression « institution financière déclarante finlandaise » désigne toute institution financière finlandaise qui n'est pas une institution financière non déclarante finlandaise ;

p) L'expression « institution financière déclarante américaine » désigne : i) toute institution financière résidente des États-Unis à l'exclusion de toute succursale établie en dehors des États-Unis ; et ii) toute succursale d'une institution financière qui n'est pas résidente des États-Unis si cette succursale est située aux États-Unis, à condition que cette institution financière ou cette succursale contrôle, perçoive ou conserve un revenu à propos duquel des renseignements doivent être échangés en application de l'alinéa b) du paragraphe 2 de l'article 2 du présent Accord ;

q) L'expression « institution financière non déclarante finlandaise » désigne toute institution financière finlandaise ou autre entité résidente de Finlande décrite à l'annexe II en tant qu'institution financière non déclarante finlandaise ou qui remplit les conditions nécessaires pour être une institution financière étrangère (IFE) réputée conforme ou un bénéficiaire effectif dispensé de déclaration par la réglementation du Trésor des États-Unis ;

r) L'expression « institution financière non participante » désigne une IFE non participante au sens de la réglementation édictée par le Trésor des États-Unis, mais exclut toute institution financière finlandaise et toute institution financière d'une autre juridiction partenaire, autre qu'une institution financière considérée comme non participante en application de l'alinéa b) du paragraphe 2 de l'article 5 du présent Accord ou d'une disposition correspondante d'un accord entre les États-Unis et une juridiction partenaire ;

s) L'expression « compte financier » désigne un compte tenu par une institution financière et comprend :

1) Dans le cas d'une entité qui constitue une institution financière du seul fait qu'elle est une entité d'investissement, tout titre de participation ou de créance (autre que les titres qui font l'objet de transactions régulières sur un marché boursier réglementé) déposé auprès de l'institution financière ;

2) Dans le cas d'une institution financière non visée au point 1 de l'alinéa s) du paragraphe 1 du présent article, tout titre de participation ou de créance (autre que les titres qui font l'objet de transactions régulières sur un marché boursier réglementé) déposé auprès de l'institution financière : i) si la valeur du titre de participation ou de créance est calculée, directement ou indirectement, principalement par rapport à des actifs qui donnent lieu à des paiements de source américaine susceptibles de faire l'objet d'une retenue à la source ; et ii) si la catégorie des titres en question a été créée afin de se soustraire aux déclarations prévues par le présent Accord ;

3) Tout contrat d'assurance à forte valeur de rachat et tout contrat de rente établi ou géré par une institution financière autre qu'une rente viagère dont l'exécution est immédiate, qui est incessible et non liée à un placement, qui est versée à une personne physique et qui correspond à une pension de retraite ou d'invalidité perçue dans le cadre d'un compte, d'un produit ou d'un dispositif exclu de la définition du compte financier figurant à l'annexe II.

Nonobstant ce qui précède, l'expression « compte financier » ne comprend aucun compte qui est exclu de la définition du compte financier figurant à l'annexe II. Aux fins du présent Accord, des titres font l'objet de transactions régulières s'il y a, de façon continue, un volume significatif de transactions concernant ces titres, et un marché boursier réglementé désigne un marché officiellement reconnu et contrôlé par une autorité gouvernementale de l'État dans lequel il est situé et sur lequel est négociée annuellement une valeur significative de titres. Aux fins du présent alinéa s), une participation dans une institution financière ne fait pas l'objet de transactions régulières et doit être considérée comme un compte financier si le titulaire de cette participation (autre qu'une institution financière agissant en tant qu'intermédiaire) est inscrit dans le registre des actionnaires de cette institution financière. La phrase précédente ne s'applique pas aux participations préalablement inscrites sur le registre des actionnaires de l'institution financière avant le 1er juillet 2014, et en ce qui concerne les participations préalablement inscrites sur ce même registre à partir du 1er juillet 2014, une institution financière n'est pas tenue d'appliquer la phrase précédente avant le 1er janvier 2016.

t) L'expression « compte de dépôt » désigne tous les comptes commerciaux et comptes-chèques, d'épargne ou à terme et les comptes dont l'existence est attestée par un certificat de dépôt, un certificat d'épargne, un certificat d'investissement, un titre de créance ou un autre instrument analogue détenu auprès d'une institution financière dans le cadre habituel d'une activité bancaire ou similaire. Les comptes de dépôt comprennent également les sommes détenues par des organismes d'assurance en vertu d'un contrat de placement garanti ou d'un contrat semblable ayant pour objet de verser des intérêts ou de les porter au crédit du titulaire ;

u) L'expression « compte conservateur » désigne un compte (à l'exclusion d'un contrat d'assurance ou d'un contrat de rente) ouvert au bénéfice d'une autre personne et sur lequel figure tout instrument financier ou contrat à des fins d'investissement (notamment, mais de manière non limitative un titre de société, une obligation – garantie ou non – ou un autre titre de créance, une opération de change ou sur marchandises, un contrat d'échange sur risque de crédit, un contrat d'échange calculé en fonction d'un indice non financier, un contrat notionnel, un contrat d'assurance, un contrat de rente ou toute option ou tout autre instrument financier dérivé) ;

v) L'expression « titre de participation » désigne, dans le cas où une société de personnes est une institution financière, toute participation au capital ou aux bénéfices de la société de personnes. Dans le cas où un trust est une institution financière, un « titre de participation » est réputé détenu par toute personne considérée comme le constituant ou le bénéficiaire de tout ou partie du trust ou par toute autre personne physique exerçant en dernier lieu un contrôle effectif sur le trust. Une personne américaine déterminée est considérée comme bénéficiaire d'un trust étranger si cette personne a le droit de recevoir directement ou indirectement [par l'intermédiaire d'un prête-nom (nominee), par exemple] une distribution obligatoire ou peut recevoir, directement ou indirectement, une distribution discrétionnaire de la part du trust ;

w) L'expression « contrat d'assurance » désigne un contrat (autre qu'un contrat de rente) en vertu duquel l'assureur s'engage à verser une somme d'argent en cas de réalisation d'un risque particulier, notamment un décès, une maladie, un accident, une responsabilité civile ou un dommage matériel ;

x) L'expression « contrat de rente » désigne un contrat en vertu duquel l'assureur s'engage à effectuer des paiements pendant une certaine durée, laquelle est déterminée en tout ou partie par l'espérance de vie d'une ou plusieurs personnes physiques. L'expression comprend également tout contrat considéré comme un contrat de rente par la loi, la réglementation ou la jurisprudence de la juridiction dans laquelle ce contrat a été établi, et dans lequel l'assureur s'engage à effectuer des paiements durant plusieurs années ;

y) L'expression « contrat d'assurance à forte valeur de rachat » désigne un contrat d'assurance (autre qu'un contrat de réassurance conclu entre deux organismes d'assurance) dont la valeur de rachat est supérieure à 50 000 dollars ;

z) L'expression « valeur de rachat » désigne le plus élevé des deux montants suivants : i) le montant que le preneur d'assurance est en droit de recevoir lors du rachat ou de la résiliation du contrat (déterminé sans réduction pour les frais de rachat ou l'avance sur police) ; et ii) le montant que le preneur d'assurance peut emprunter en vertu du contrat ou eu égard à son objet. Nonobstant ce qui précède, l'expression « valeur de rachat » ne comprend pas les montants payables en vertu d'un contrat d'assurance au titre :

   1) De l'indemnisation d'un dommage corporel, d'une maladie ou d'une perte économique subie lors de la survenance d'un risque assuré ;

2) D'un remboursement au preneur d'assurance d'une prime payée antérieurement dans le cadre d'un contrat d'assurance (autre qu'un contrat d'assurance vie) en raison de l'annulation ou de la résiliation du contrat, d'une diminution de l'exposition au risque pendant la période de validité du contrat d'assurance, ou d'un nouveau calcul de la prime dû à la correction d'une erreur d'écriture ou d'une autre erreur analogue ; ou

3) De la participation au résultat due au preneur du contrat d'assurance en fonction de la couverture du risque du contrat ou du groupe concerné.

aa) L'expression « compte déclarable » désigne, selon le cas, un compte déclarable finlandais ou un compte déclarable américain ;

bb) L'expression « compte déclarable finlandais » désigne un compte financier tenu par une institution financière déclarante américaine qui remplit les conditions suivantes : i) dans le cas d'un compte de dépôt, le compte est détenu par une personne physique résidant en Finlande qui perçoit plus de 10 dollars d'intérêts sur ce compte au cours d'une année civile donnée ; ou ii) dans le cas d'un compte financier autre qu'un compte de dépôt, le titulaire du compte est un résident de Finlande, y compris une entité qui certifie qu'elle est résidente en Finlande à des fins fiscales, auquel un revenu de source américaine soumis à une obligation de déclaration en vertu du sous-titre A du chapitre 3 ou du sous-titre F du chapitre 61 de l'Internal Revenue Code (Code des impôts des États-Unis) est versé ou porté à son crédit ;

cc) L'expression « compte déclarable américain » désigne un compte financier tenu par une institution financière déclarante finlandaise et détenu par une ou plusieurs personnes américaines déterminées ou par une entité non américaine dont une ou plusieurs personnes détenant le contrôle sont des personnes américaines déterminées. Nonobstant ce qui précède, n'est pas considéré comme compte déclarable américain tout compte qui ne remplit pas les conditions d'un tel compte après application des diligences définies à l'annexe I ;

dd) L'expression « titulaire de compte » désigne la personne inscrite ou identifiée comme titulaire d'un compte financier par l'institution financière qui tient le compte. Une personne, autre qu'une institution financière, détenant un compte financier pour le compte ou le bénéfice d'une autre personne en tant que mandataire, dépositaire, prête-nom, signataire, conseiller en placement ou intermédiaire, n'est pas considérée comme détenant le compte aux fins du présent Accord, et ladite autre personne est considérée comme détenant le compte. Aux fins de la phrase précédente, l'expression « institution financière » ne comprend pas une institution financière créée ou constituée dans un Territoire américain. Dans le cas d'un contrat d'assurance à forte valeur de rachat ou d'un contrat de rente, le titulaire du compte est toute personne autorisée à tirer parti de la valeur de rachat ou à changer le nom du bénéficiaire du contrat. Si nul ne peut tirer parti de la valeur de rachat ou changer le nom du bénéficiaire, le titulaire du compte est toute personne désignée comme souscripteur de celui-ci dans le contrat ainsi que toute personne qui jouit d'un droit absolu à des paiements en vertu du contrat. À l'échéance d'un contrat d'assurance à forte valeur de rachat ou d'un contrat de rente, chaque personne ayant droit à un paiement en vertu du contrat est considérée comme un titulaire de compte ;

ee) L'expression « personne américaine » désigne une personne physique qui est un citoyen ou un résident des États-Unis, une société de personnes ou une société créée aux États-Unis ou en vertu des lois des États-Unis ou de tout État de ce pays, un trust si i) un tribunal des États-Unis était habilité, en vertu du droit applicable, à rendre des ordonnances ou des jugements concernant l'essentiel des questions relatives à l'administration du trust ; et si ii) une ou plusieurs personnes américaines sont habilitées à contrôler toutes les décisions importantes du trust, ou sur la succession d'un défunt qui était citoyen ou résident des États-Unis. Le présent point ee) est interprété conformément à l'Internal Revenue Code des États-Unis ;

ff) L'expression « personne américaine déterminée » désigne une personne américaine autre que l'une des personnes suivantes : i) une société dont les titres font l'objet de transactions régulières sur un ou plusieurs marchés boursiers réglementés ; ii) une société qui est membre du même groupe élargi de sociétés liées, au sens donné à l'expression « affiliated group » à l'article 1471 (e) (2) de l'Internal Revenue Code des États-Unis, qu'une société visée au sous-point i) ci-dessus ; iii) les États-Unis ou toute personne morale de droit public qui leur est rattachée ; iv) un État des États-Unis, un Territoire américain, une subdivision politique de ceux-ci ou toute personne morale de droit public rattachée à l'un ou plusieurs d'entre eux ; v) une organisation exonérée d'impôts en application de l'article 501 (a) de l'Internal Revenue Code des États-Unis ou un plan de retraite personnel au sens donné à l'expression « individual retirement plan » à l'article 7701 (a) (37) de l'Internal Revenue Code des États-Unis ; vi) une banque au sens donné au terme « bank » à l'article 581 de l'Internal Revenue Code des États-Unis ; vii) un fonds de placement immobilier au sens donné à l'expression « real estate investment trust » à l'article 856 de l'Internal Revenue Code des États-Unis ; viii) une société d'investissement réglementée au sens donné à l'expression « regulated investment company » à l'article 851 de l'Internal Revenue Code des États-Unis ou une entité enregistrée auprès de la Commission fédérale de contrôle des opérations de bourse en application de l'Investment Company Act de 1940 (15 U.S.C. 80a-64) ; ix) un fonds collectif de placement au sens donné à l'expression « common trust fund » à l'article 584 (a) de l'Internal Revenue Code des États-Unis ; x) un trust exonéré d'impôt en vertu de l'article 664 (c) de l'Internal Revenue Code des États-Unis ou visé à l'article 4947 (a) (1) de ce même code ; xi) un courtier en valeurs mobilières, en marchandises ou en instruments financiers dérivés (y compris les contrats notionnels, les contrats à terme et les options) qui est enregistré comme tel en vertu des lois des États-Unis ou de tout État de ce pays ; xii) un courtier au sens donné au terme « broker » à l'article 6045 (c) de l'Internal Revenue Code des États-Unis ; ou xiii) un trust exonéré d'impôt en application d'un dispositif visé à l'article 403 (b) ou 457 (g) de l'Internal Revenue Code des États-Unis ;

gg) Le terme « entité » désigne une personne morale ou une construction juridique, telle qu'un trust ;

hh) L'expression « entité non américaine » désigne une entité qui n'est pas une personne américaine ;

ii) L'expression « paiement de source américaine susceptible de faire l'objet d'une retenue à la source » désigne le paiement d'intérêts (y compris d'éventuelles primes d'émission), de dividendes, de loyers, de salaires, de traitements, de primes, de rentes, d'indemnités, de rémunérations, d'émoluments et d'autres gains, bénéfices et revenus fixes ou calculables, annuels ou périodiques, lorsque ces paiements sont de source américaine. Nonobstant ce qui précède, sont exclus des paiements de source américaine susceptibles de faire l'objet d'une retenue à la source les paiements qui ne sont pas considérés comme pouvant donner lieu à une retenue à la source selon la réglementation édictée par le Trésor des États-Unis ;

jj) Une entité est une « entité liée » à une autre entité si l'une des deux entités contrôle l'autre ou si ces deux entités sont placées sous un contrôle conjoint. À ce titre, le contrôle comprend la détention directe ou indirecte de plus de 50 % des droits de vote ou de la valeur d'une entité. Nonobstant ce qui précède, la Finlande peut considérer qu'une entité n'est pas une entité liée à une autre entité si les deux entités ne sont pas membres du même groupe élargi de sociétés liées au sens donné à l'expression « affiliated group » à l'article 1471 (e) (2) de l'Internal Revenue Code des États-Unis ;

kk) L'expression « NIF américain » désigne un numéro d'identification fiscal fédéral américain ;

ll) L'expression « NIF finlandais » désigne un numéro d'identification fiscal finlandais ;

mm) L'expression « personnes détenant le contrôle » désigne les personnes physiques qui exercent un contrôle sur une entité. Dans le cas d'un trust, cette expression désigne le constituant, les administrateurs, la personne chargée de surveiller l'administrateur le cas échéant, les bénéficiaires ou la catégorie de bénéficiaires et toute autre personne physique exerçant en dernier lieu un contrôle effectif sur le trust et, dans le cas d'une construction juridique qui n'est pas un trust, cette expression désigne les personnes dont la situation est équivalente ou analogue. L'expression « personnes détenant le contrôle » est interprétée conformément aux recommandations du GAFI.

2. Tout terme ou toute expression qui n'est pas définie dans le présent Accord a, sauf si le contexte exige une interprétation différente ou si les autorités compétentes s'entendent sur une signification commune (qui ne contrevient pas au droit national), le sens que lui attribue au moment considéré la législation de la Partie qui applique le présent Accord, toute définition figurant dans la législation fiscale applicable de cette Partie l'emportant sur une définition contenue dans une autre législation de la même Partie.

Article 2. Obligations d'obtenir et d'échanger des renseignements concernant les comptes déclarables

1. Sous réserve des dispositions de l'article 3 du présent Accord, chaque Partie obtient les renseignements visés au paragraphe 2 du présent article pour tous les comptes déclarables et échange chaque année ces renseignements avec l'autre Partie de manière automatique conformément aux dispositions de l'article 26 de la Convention.

2. Les renseignements qui doivent être obtenus et échangés sont les suivants :

a) Dans le cas de la Finlande, pour chaque compte déclarable américain de chaque institution financière déclarante finlandaise :

1) Le nom, l'adresse et le NIF américain de chaque personne américaine déterminée qui est un titulaire de ce compte et, dans le cas d'une entité non américaine pour laquelle, après application des diligences décrites à l'annexe I, il apparaît qu'une ou plusieurs personnes détenant le contrôle sont des personnes américaines déterminées, le nom, l'adresse et le NIF américain (le cas échéant) de cette entité et de chacune de ces personnes américaines déterminées ;

2) Le numéro de compte (ou son équivalent fonctionnel en l'absence de numéro de compte) ;

3) Le nom et le numéro d'identification de l'institution financière déclarante finlandaise ;

4) Le solde ou la valeur portée sur le compte (y compris, dans le cas d'un contrat d'assurance à forte valeur de rachat ou d'un contrat de rente, la valeur de rachat) à la fin de l'année civile considérée ou d'une autre période de référence adéquate ou, si le compte a été clos au cours de l'année en question, immédiatement avant la clôture ;

5) Dans le cas d'un compte conservateur :

A) Le montant brut total des intérêts, le montant brut total des dividendes et le montant brut total des autres revenus produits par les actifs détenus sur le compte, versés ou crédités sur le compte (ou au titre du compte) au cours de l'année civile ou d'une autre période de référence adéquate ; et

B) Le produit brut total de la vente ou du rachat d'un bien versé ou crédité sur le compte au cours de l'année civile ou d'une autre période de référence adéquate au titre de laquelle l'institution financière déclarante finlandaise a agi en tant que dépositaire, courtier, prête-nom ou représentant du titulaire du compte ;

6) Dans le cas d'un compte de dépôt, le montant brut total des intérêts versés ou crédités sur le compte au cours de l'année civile ou d'une autre période de référence adéquate ;

7) Dans le cas d'un compte qui n'est pas visé aux points 5) ou 6) de l'alinéa a) du paragraphe 2 du présent article, le montant brut total versé au titulaire du compte ou porté à son crédit, au cours de l'année civile ou d'une autre période de référence adéquate, dont l'institution financière déclarante finlandaise est la débitrice, y compris le montant total de toutes les sommes remboursées au titulaire au cours de l'année civile ou d'une autre période de référence adéquate ;

b) Dans le cas des États-Unis, pour chaque compte déclarable finlandais de chaque institution financière déclarante américaine :

1) Le nom, l'adresse et le NIF finlandais de toute personne qui est un résident de Finlande et qui est titulaire du compte ;

2) Le numéro de compte (ou son équivalent fonctionnel en l'absence de numéro de compte) ;

3) Le nom et le numéro d'identification de l'institution financière déclarante américaine ;

4) Le montant brut des intérêts versés sur un compte de dépôt ;

5) Le montant brut des dividendes de source américaine versés ou crédités sur le compte ;

6) Le montant brut des autres revenus de source américaine versés ou crédités sur le compte, dans la mesure où ils doivent faire l'objet d'une déclaration en vertu du chapitre 3 du sous-titre A ou du chapitre 61 du sous-titre F de l'Internal Revenue Code des États-Unis.

Article 3. Calendrier et modalités des échanges de renseignements

1. Aux fins des obligations d'échange prévues à l'article 2 du présent Accord, le montant et la qualification des versements effectués au titre d'un compte déclarable américain peuvent être déterminés conformément aux principes de la législation fiscale finlandaise et le montant et la qualification des versements effectués au titre d'un compte déclarable finlandais peuvent être déterminés conformément aux principes du droit fédéral américain en matière d'impôt sur le revenu.

2. Aux fins des obligations d'échange prévues à l'article 2 du présent Accord, les renseignements échangés indiquent la monnaie dans laquelle chaque montant concerné est libellé.

3. S'agissant du paragraphe 2 de l'article 2 du présent Accord, les renseignements doivent être obtenus et échangés pour 2014 et toutes les années suivantes, sous réserve des exceptions suivantes :

a) Dans le cas de la Finlande :

1) Les renseignements à obtenir et à échanger pour 2014 se limitent à ceux visés aux points 1 à 4 de l'alinéa a) du paragraphe 2 de l'article 2 du présent Accord ;

2) Les renseignements à obtenir et à échanger pour 2015 sont ceux visés aux points 1 à 7 de l'alinéa a) du paragraphe 2 de l'article 2 du présent Accord, à l'exception du produit brut visé à la lettre B) du point 5) de l'alinéa a) du paragraphe 2 de l'article 2 du présent Accord ; et

3) Les renseignements à obtenir et à échanger pour 2016 et les années suivantes sont ceux visés aux points 1 à 7 de l'alinéa a) du paragraphe 2 de l'article 2 du présent Accord ;

b) Dans le cas des États-Unis, les renseignements à obtenir et à échanger pour 2014 et les années suivantes sont ceux visés de l'alinéa b) du paragraphe 2 de l'article 2 du présent Accord.

4. Nonobstant le paragraphe 3 du présent article, s'agissant d'un compte déclarable ouvert auprès d'une institution financière déclarante au 30 juin 2014, et sous réserve du paragraphe 4 de l'article 6 du présent Accord, les Parties ne sont pas tenues d'obtenir et d'intégrer aux renseignements échangés le NIF finlandais ou le NIF américain, selon le cas, de toute personne concernée, si ce numéro d'identification fiscal ne figure pas dans les dossiers de l'institution financière déclarante. Dans ce cas, les Parties obtiennent et intègrent aux renseignements échangés la date de naissance de la personne concernée si une telle date figure dans les dossiers de l'institution financière déclarante.

5. Sous réserve des paragraphes 3 et 4 du présent article, les renseignements visés à l'article 2 du présent Accord sont échangés dans les neuf mois qui suivent la fin de l'année civile à laquelle ils se rattachent.

6. Les autorités compétentes de la Finlande et des États-Unis concluent un accord ou un arrangement au titre de la procédure amiable prévue à l'article 25 de la Convention qui prévoit :

a) Les procédures relatives aux obligations d'échanges automatiques visées à l'article 2 du présent Accord ;

b) Les règles et les procédures qui peuvent être nécessaires à l'application de l'article 5 du présent Accord ;

c) Au besoin, des procédures pour l'échange des renseignements déclarés en application de l'alinéa b) du paragraphe 1 de l'article 4 du présent Accord.

7. Tous les renseignements échangés sont soumis aux obligations de confidentialité et autres protections prévues par la Convention, y compris les dispositions qui limitent l'utilisation des renseignements échangés.

Article 4. Application de la loi FATCA aux institutions financières finlandaises

1. Régime des institutions financières déclarantes finlandaises. Chaque institution financière déclarante finlandaise est considérée comme étant en conformité avec l'article 1471 de l'Internal Revenue Code des États-Unis et exonérée de la retenue à la source prévue par cet article si la Finlande respecte les obligations prévues aux articles 2 et 3 du présent Accord concernant l'institution financière déclarante finlandaise en cause et si cette dernière :

a) Recense les comptes déclarables américains et fournit chaque année à l'autorité compétente finlandaise les renseignements visés à l'alinéa a) du paragraphe 2 de l'article 2 du présent Accord, dans les délais et selon les modalités prévues à l'article 3 ;

b) Fournit à l'autorité compétente finlandaise, pour chacune des années 2015 et 2016, le nom de chaque institution financière non participante à laquelle elle a fait des paiements ainsi que le montant total de ces paiements ;

c) Respecte les obligations d'enregistrement applicables figurant sur le site Web d'enregistrement de l'IRS dédié à la loi FATCA ;

d) Prélève 30 % sur tout paiement de source américaine pouvant faire l'objet d'une retenue à la source, effectué au profit d'une institution financière non participante, dans la mesure où : i) elle agit en tant qu'intermédiaire agréé (pour l'application de l'article 1441 de l'Internal Revenue Code des États-Unis) ayant choisi d'assumer la principale responsabilité en matière de retenue à la source en application du chapitre 3 du sous-titre A de l'Internal Revenue Code des États-Unis ; ii) elle est une société de personnes étrangère ayant choisi d'agir à titre de société de personnes étrangère appliquant la retenue à la source (pour l'application des articles 1441 et 1471 de l'Internal Revenue Code des États-Unis) ; ou iii) elle est un trust étranger qui a choisi d'agir comme un trust étranger appliquant la retenue à la source (pour l'application des mêmes articles de l'Internal Revenue Code des États-Unis) ;

e) Dans le cas où elle n'est pas visée par les conditions prévues à l'alinéa d) du présent paragraphe et où elle effectue au profit d'une institution financière non participante un paiement de source américaine pouvant faire l'objet d'unc retenue à la source ou agit en tant qu'intermédiaire dans le cadre d'un tel paiement, elle fournit à toute personne en amont qui procède directement à un tel versement les renseignements nécessaires pour que la retenue à la source et les déclarations concernant ce paiement puissent être effectuées.

Nonobstant ce qui précède, une institution financière déclarante finlandaise, dans le cas où les conditions du présent paragraphe ne sont pas satisfaites, ne fait pas l'objet de la retenue à la source prévue à l'article 1471 de l'Internal Revenue Code des États-Unis, à moins que cette institution financière ne soit identifiée par l'IRS comme institution financière non participante conformément à l'alinéa b) du paragraphe 2 de l'article 5 du présent Accord.

2. Suspension des règles relatives aux comptes de titulaires récalcitrants. Les États-Unis n'exigent pas d'une institution financière déclarante finlandaise d'effectuer une retenue à la source de l'impôt en application des articles 1471 ou 1472 de l'Internal Revenue Code des États-Unis pour un compte détenu par un titulaire récalcitrant (au sens donné à l'expression « recalcitrant account holder » à l'article 1471 (d) (6) de l'Internal Revenue Code des États-Unis) ou de clôturer un tel compte si l'autorité compétente américaine reçoit les renseignements visés à l'alinéa a) du paragraphe 2 de l'article 2 du présent Accord, sous réserve des dispositions de l'article 3 du présent Accord, concernant ce compte.

3. Statut particulier des régimes de retraite finlandais. Les régimes de retraite finlandais figurant à l'annexe II sont considérés par les États-Unis comme étant, selon le cas, des IFE réputées conformes ou des bénéficiaires effectifs dispensés de déclaration pour l'application des articles 1471 et 1472 de l'Internal Revenue Code des États-Unis. À cette fin, sont comprises parmi les régimes de retraite finlandais toute entité établie ou située en Finlande et régie par ses lois et toute construction contractuelle ou juridique préétablie qui est administrée dans le but de verser des prestations de pension ou de percevoir des revenus en vue du versement de ces prestations, en application de la législation finlandaise et soumises à la réglementation concernant les cotisations, les distributions, les déclarations, les parrainages et la fiscalité.

4. Identification et régime des autres IFE réputées conformes et des bénéficiaires effectifs dispensés de déclaration. Chaque institution financière non déclarante finlandaise est considérée par les États-Unis comme étant, selon le cas, une IFE réputée conforme ou un bénéficiaire effectif dispensé de déclaration pour l'application de l'article 1471 de l'Internal Revenue Code des États-Unis.

5. Règles spécifiques concernant les entités liées et succursales qui sont des institutions financières non participantes. Toute institution financière finlandaise répondant aux critères fixés au paragraphe 1 du présent article, ou visée au paragraphe 3 ou 4 du présent article, qui dispose d'une entité liée ou d'une succursale exerçant des activités dans une juridiction qui ne permet pas à cette entité liée ou à cette succursale de répondre aux critères visant les IFE participantes ou les IFE réputées conformes pour l'application de l'article 1471 de l'Internal Revenue Code des États-Unis, ou à une entité liée ou une succursale qui est considérée comme une institution financière non participante uniquement du fait de l'expiration de la période transitoire accordée aux IFE limitées et aux succursales limitées en application de la réglementation édictée par le Trésor des États-Unis, continue d'être en conformité avec les dispositions du présent Accord et d'être considérée comme une IFE réputée conforme ou un bénéficiaire effectif dispensé de déclaration, selon le cas, pour l'application de l'article 1471 précité si les conditions suivantes sont réunies :

a) L'institution financière finlandaise traite chacune de ces entités liées ou succursales comme une institution financière non participante distincte pour l'application des exigences en matière de déclaration et de retenue à la source prévues au présent Accord et chacune de ces entités liées ou succursales indique aux agents chargés d'effectuer la retenue à la source qu'elle est une institution financière non participante ;

b) Chacune de ces entités liées ou succursales établit une liste de ses comptes américains et fournit des renseignements concernant ces comptes conformément à l'article 1471 de l'Internal Revenue Code des États-Unis dans les limites autorisées par les lois qui lui sont applicables ;

c) Cette entité liée ou succursale n'effectue pas de démarches particulières concernant les comptes américains détenus par des personnes qui ne résident pas dans la juridiction où elle est située ou concernant les comptes auprès d'institutions financières non participantes qui ne sont pas établies dans cette juridiction, et cette entité liée ou succursale n'est pas utilisée par l'institution financière finlandaise ou toute autre entité liée pour contourner les obligations définies, selon le cas, dans le présent Accord ou à l'article 1471 de l'Internal Revenue Code des États-Unis.

6. Coordination du calendrier. Nonobstant les dispositions des paragraphes 3 et 5 de l'article 3 du présent Accord :

a) La Finlande n'est pas tenue d'obtenir et d'échanger des renseignements relatifs à une année civile antérieure à celle pour laquelle des IFE participantes doivent fournir à l'IRS des renseignements analogues en application de la réglementation édictée par le Trésor des États-Unis ;

b) La Finlande n'est pas tenue de commencer à échanger des renseignements avant la date à laquelle des IFE participantes doivent fournir à l'IRS des renseignements analogues dans le cadre de la réglementation édictée par le Trésor des États-Unis ;

c) Les États-Unis ne sont pas tenus d'obtenir et d'échanger des renseignements relatifs à une année civile antérieure à la première année civile au titre de laquelle la Finlande est tenue d'obtenir et d'échanger des renseignements ; et

d) Les États-Unis ne sont pas tenus de commencer à échanger des renseignements avant la date à laquelle la Finlande est tenue de le faire.

7. Coordination des définitions avec la réglementation du Trésor des États-Unis. Nonobstant l'article premier du présent Accord et les définitions figurant dans les annexes du présent Accord, lors de la mise en œuvre de celui-ci, la Finlande peut utiliser et autoriser ses institutions financières à utiliser une définition de la réglementation pertinente édictée par le Trésor des États-Unis en lieu et place de la définition correspondante du présent Accord, sous réserve que cette utilisation n'aille pas à l'encontre de l'objet du présent Accord.

Article 5. Collaboration en matière d'application et de mise en œuvre de l'Accord

1. Erreurs mineures et d'ordre administratif. Une autorité compétente transmet une notification à l'autorité compétente de l'autre Partie lorsque la première autorité compétente a des raisons de croire que des erreurs d'ordre administratif ou d'autres erreurs mineures peuvent avoir eu pour conséquence la communication de renseignements erronés ou incomplets ou d'autres formes de manquement au présent Accord. L'autorité compétente de cette autre Partie applique les dispositions de son droit interne (y compris les amendes applicables) pour obtenir des renseignements corrigés et/ou complets ou afin de résoudre d'autres formes de manquement au présent Accord.

2. Infraction significative d'une institution financière.

a) Une autorité compétente transmet une notification à l'autorité compétente de l'autre Partie lorsque la première autorité compétente établit l'existence d'une infraction significative aux obligations énoncées dans le présent Accord de la part d'une institution financière déclarante de l'autre Partie. L'autorité compétente de cette autre Partie applique les dispositions de son droit interne (y compris les amendes applicables) pour remédier à l'infraction significative décrite dans la notification.

b) Si, dans le cas d'une institution financière déclarante finlandaise, ces mesures coercitives ne mettent pas un terme à l'infraction significative constatée dans un délai de 18 mois suivant la première notification d'infraction significative, les États-Unis traitent l'institution financière déclarante finlandaise comme une institution financière non participante en vertu du présent alinéa b).

3. Recours à des tiers. Chacune des Parties peut autoriser les institutions financières déclarantes à faire appel à des prestataires tiers pour s'acquitter des obligations qu'une Partie leur impose, en application du présent Accord, ces obligations restant toutefois du domaine de la responsabilité des institutions financières déclarantes.

4. Dispositif anti-abus. Les Parties mettent en œuvre les mesures nécessaires afin d'éviter l'adoption par les institutions financières de pratiques destinées à contourner les obligations déclaratives prévues par le présent Accord.

Article 6. Engagement réciproque à poursuivre l'amélioration des échanges de renseignements et à favoriser la transparence

1. Réciprocité. Le Gouvernement des États-Unis convient de la nécessité de parvenir à des niveaux équivalents d'échanges automatiques de renseignements avec la Finlande. Le Gouvernement des États-Unis s'engage à améliorer davantage la transparence et à renforcer la relation d'échange avec la Finlande en continuant à adopter des mesures de nature réglementaire et en défendant et en soutenant l'adoption de lois appropriées afin d'atteindre ces niveaux équivalents d'échanges automatiques réciproques de renseignements.

2. Traitement des paiements indirects (Passthru payments) et des produits bruts. Les Parties s'engagent à agir de concert avec les juridictions partenaires afin d'élaborer une nouvelle méthode pratique et efficace permettant de réduire au minimum la charge de la retenue à la source pour les paiements indirects (passthru payments) et les produits bruts étrangers.

3. Élaboration de modèles de déclaration et d'échanges de renseignements communs. Les Parties s'engagent à agir de concert avec les juridictions partenaires, l'Organisation de coopération et de développement économiques et l'Union européenne pour adapter les dispositions du présent Accord et d'autres accords conclus entre les États-Unis et des juridictions partenaires afin de parvenir à un modèle commun pour les échanges automatiques de renseignements et de concevoir des modèles de déclarations et des normes de procédures de diligence raisonnable pour les institutions financières.

4. Données concernant les comptes existants au 30 juin 2014. S'agissant des comptes déclarables ouverts auprès d'une institution financière déclarante au 30 juin 2014 :

a) Les États-Unis s'engagent à adopter, d'ici au 1er janvier 2017, pour les déclarations qui concernent 2017 et les années suivantes, des règles qui imposent aux institutions financières déclarantes américaines d'obtenir et de déclarer le NIF finlandais de chaque titulaire de compte titulaire de compte d'un compte déclarable finlandais conformément au point 1) de l'alinéa b) du paragraphe 2 de l'article 2 du présent Accord ; et

b) La Finlande s'engage à adopter, d'ici au 1er janvier 2017, pour les déclarations qui concernent 2017 et les années suivantes, des règles qui imposent aux institutions financières déclarantes finlandaises d'obtenir le NIF américain de chaque personne américaine déterminée conformément au point 1) de l'alinéa a) du paragraphe 2 de l'article 2 du présent Accord.

Article 7. Cohérence dans l'application de la loi FATCA aux juridictions partenaires

1. En application de l'article 4 ou de l'annexe I du présent Accord relatifs à l'application de la loi FATCA aux institutions financières finlandaises, la Finlande bénéficie de toute clause plus favorable accordée à une autre juridiction partenaire dans le cadre d'un accord bilatéral signé en vertu duquel l'autre juridiction partenaire s'engage à respecter les mêmes obligations que la Finlande telles que visées aux articles 2 et 3 du présent Accord, sous réserve des conditions énoncées auxdits articles et aux articles 5 à 9 du présent Accord.

2. Les États-Unis informent la Finlande de toute clause plus favorable et appliquent celle-ci automatiquement en application du présent Accord comme si ladite clause était énoncée dans le présent Accord et applicable à compter de la date de signature de l'accord incluant la clause plus favorable, à moins que la Finlande n'en refuse l'application par écrit.

Article 8. Consultations et modifications

1. En cas de difficultés dans l'application du présent Accord, chaque Partie peut solliciter des consultations en vue d'élaborer des mesures appropriées pour garantir l'exécution de celui-ci.

2. Le présent Accord peut être modifié par commun accord des Parties formulé par écrit. Sauf disposition contraire, une telle modification entre en vigueur selon les mêmes procédures que celles énoncées au paragraphe 1 de l'article 10 du présent Accord.

Article 9. Annexes

Les annexes font partie intégrante du présent Accord.

Article 10. Durée de l'Accord

1. Le présent Accord entre en vigueur à la date à laquelle la Finlande notifie par écrit aux États-Unis l'accomplissement des procédures internes requises à cet effet.

2. Chacune des Parties peut dénoncer le présent Accord moyennant préavis écrit adressé à l'autre Partie. Cette dénonciation prend effet le premier jour du mois suivant l'expiration d'un délai de 12 mois suivant la date du préavis.

3. Avant le 31 décembre 2016, les Parties engagent de bonne foi des consultations afin d'apporter au présent Accord les modifications nécessaires pour refléter les progrès accomplis concernant les engagements énoncés à l'article 6 du présent Accord.

EN FOI DE QUOI, les soussignés, à ce dûment autorisés par leurs Gouvernements respectifs, ont signé le présent Accord.

FAIT à Helsinki, le 5 mars 2014, en double exemplaire, en langue anglaise.

Pour le Gouvernement de la République de Finlande :
[JUTTA URPILAINEN]

Pour le Gouvernement des États-Unis d'Amérique :
[BRUCE ORECK]

ANNEXE I.

OBLIGATIONS DE DILIGENCE EN MATIÈRE D'IDENTIFICATION ET DE DÉCLARATION DE COMPTES DÉCLARABLES AMÉRICAINS ET DE PAIEMENTS EFFECTUÉS À CERTAINES INSTITUTIONS FINANCIÈRES NON PARTICIPANTES

I. Généralités

A. La Finlande impose à toute institution financière déclarante finlandaise d'identifier les comptes déclarables américains et les comptes détenus par des institutions financières non participantes selon les procédures de diligence raisonnable énoncées dans la présente annexe I.

B. Aux fins du présent Accord :

1. Tous les montants sont exprimés en dollars des États-Unis et renvoient à leur contre-valeur en d'autres monnaies ;
2. Sauf dispositions contraires du présent Accord, le solde ou la valeur d'un compte correspond à son solde ou à sa valeur le dernier jour de l'année civile ou d'une autre période de référence pertinente ;
3. Lorsqu'un solde ou un seuil de valeur est déterminé au 30 juin 2014 en application de la présente annexe I, le solde ou le seuil de valeur considéré sera déterminé à cette date ou au dernier jour de la période de référence close immédiatement avant le 30 juin 2014, et lorsqu'un solde ou un seuil de valeur est déterminé au dernier jour d'une année civile en application de la présente annexe I, le solde ou le seuil de valeur considéré sera déterminé au dernier jour de l'année civile ou d'une autre période de référence pertinente ;
4. Sous réserve du point 1 du paragraphe E de la section II de la présente annexe I, un compte est considéré comme un compte déclarable américain à partir de la date à laquelle il est identifié comme tel en application des procédures de diligence raisonnable énoncées dans la présente annexe I ;
5. Sauf dispositions contraires, les renseignements relatifs à un compte déclarable américain sont transmis chaque année au cours de l'année civile qui suit l'année à laquelle se rattachent ces renseignements.

C. En lieu et place des procédures décrites dans chacune des sections de la présente annexe I, la Finlande peut autoriser ses institutions financières déclarantes à appliquer les procédures qui figurent dans la réglementation correspondante du Trésor des États-Unis afin d'établir si un compte est un compte déclarable américain ou un compte détenu par une institution financière non participante. La Finlande peut autoriser les institutions financières finlandaises déclarantes à faire un choix distinct en ce sens pour chaque section de la présente annexe I soit à l'égard de l'ensemble des comptes financiers en cause, soit séparément à l'égard d'un groupe de comptes financiers clairement identifié (par exemple, selon le secteur d'activité ou le lieu où le compte est tenu).

II. Comptes de personnes physiques préexistants. L'identification des comptes déclarables américains parmi les comptes préexistants détenus par des personnes physiques (les « comptes de personnes physiques préexistants ») s'effectue selon les règles et procédures suivantes.

A. Comptes non soumis à examen, identification ou déclaration. Sauf si l'institution financière déclarante finlandaise en décide autrement, soit à l'égard de tous les comptes de personnes physiques préexistants, soit séparément par rapport à un groupe clairement identifié de comptes, lorsque les règles de mise en œuvre édictées par la Finlande prévoient la possibilité d'un tel choix, il n'est pas nécessaire d'examiner, d'identifier ou de déclarer les comptes de personnes physiques préexistants suivants comme comptes déclarables américains :

1. Sous réserve du point 2 du paragraphe E de la présente section, un compte de personne physique préexistant dont le solde ou la valeur n'excède pas 50 000 dollars au 30 juin 2014 ;

2. Sous réserve du point 2 du paragraphe E de la présente section, un compte de personne physique préexistant qui est un contrat d'assurance à forte valeur de rachat ou un contrat de rente dont le solde ou la valeur n'excède pas 250 000 dollars au 30 juin 2014 ;

3. Un compte de personne physique préexistant qui est un contrat d'assurance à forte valeur de rachat ou un contrat de rente dans la mesure où la législation ou la réglementation en vigueur en Finlande ou aux États-Unis s'oppose à la vente de contrats d'assurance à forte valeur de rachat ou de contrats de rente à des personnes résidant aux États-Unis (par exemple lorsque l'institution financière concernée ne dispose pas de l'enregistrement requis en droit américain et dès lors que la législation finlandaise impose une obligation déclarative ou une retenue à la source pour les produits d'assurance détenus par des personnes résidant en Finlande) ;

4. Un compte de dépôt dont le solde n'excède pas 50 000 dollars.

B. Procédures d'examen des comptes de personnes physiques préexistants dont le solde ou la valeur au 30 juin 2014 est supérieure à 50 000 dollars (250 000 dollars pour un contrat d'assurance à forte valeur de rachat ou un contrat de rente), mais n'excède pas 1 000 000 de dollars (les « comptes de faible valeur »).

1. Examen par voie électronique. L'institution financière déclarante finlandaise est tenue d'examiner les données qu'elle détient et qui peuvent faire l'objet de recherches par voie électronique quant à la présence de l'un quelconque des indices américains suivants :

a) Identification du titulaire du compte comme citoyen ou résident américain ;

b) Indication non équivoque d'un lieu de naissance situé aux États-Unis ;

c) Adresse postale ou de résidence actuelle aux États-Unis (y compris les boîtes postales américaines) ;

d) Numéro de téléphone actuel aux États-Unis ;

e) Ordre de virement permanent sur un compte tenu aux États-Unis ;

f) Procuration ou délégation de signature en cours de validité accordée à une personne dont l'adresse est située aux États-Unis ; ou

g) Adresse portant la mention « à l'attention de » ou « poste restante » qui est l'unique adresse du titulaire du compte inscrite dans le dossier de l'institution financière déclarante finlandaise. Dans le cas d'un compte de personne physique préexistant qui est un compte de faible valeur, une adresse portant la mention « à l'attention de » située hors des États-Unis ou « poste restante » ne constitue pas un indice américain.

2. Si l'examen des données par voie électronique ne révèle aucun des indices américains énumérés au point 1 du paragraphe B de la présente section, aucune nouvelle démarche n'est requise jusqu'à ce qu'un changement de circonstances ne se produise et ait pour conséquence qu'un ou plusieurs indices américains soient associés à ce compte, ou que ce compte devienne un compte de valeur élevée décrit au paragraphe D de la présente section.

3. Si l'examen des données par voie électronique révèle l'un des indices américains énumérés au point 1 du paragraphe B de la présente section, ou si un changement de circonstances intervient qui se traduit par un ou plusieurs indices américains associés à ce compte, l'institution financière déclarante finlandaise doit considérer le compte comme un compte déclarable américain à moins qu'elle ne choisisse d'appliquer le point 4 du paragraphe B de la présente section et qu'une des exceptions qui y figure s'applique à ce compte.

4. Nonobstant la découverte d'indices américains en application du point 1 du paragraphe B de la présente section, une institution financière déclarante finlandaise n'est pas tenue de considérer un compte comme un compte déclarable américain si :

   a) Lorsque les renseignements sur le titulaire du compte comprennent sans équivoque l'indication d'un lieu de naissance situé aux États-Unis, l'institution financière déclarante finlandaise obtient, ou a auparavant examiné, et conserve une copie des documents suivants :

      1) Une autocertification qui indique que le titulaire du compte n'est ni un citoyen ni un résident américain à des fins fiscales (établie sur le formulaire W-8 de l'IRS ou un autre formulaire analogue agréé) ;

      2) Un passeport non américain ou une autre pièce d'identité délivrée par une autorité publique attestant que la nationalité ou la citoyenneté du titulaire du compte n'est pas américaine ; et

      3) Un exemplaire du certificat de perte de la nationalité américaine établi pour le titulaire du compte ou le motif pour lequel :

         a) Le titulaire du compte ne dispose pas d'un tel certificat alors qu'il a renoncé à la citoyenneté américaine ; ou

         b) Le titulaire du compte n'a pas obtenu la citoyenneté américaine à sa naissance ;

   b) Lorsque les renseignements sur le titulaire du compte comprennent une adresse postale ou de résidence actuelle aux États-Unis ou, comme seuls numéros de téléphone associés au compte, un ou plusieurs numéros de téléphone aux États-Unis, l'institution financière déclarante finlandaise obtient, ou a auparavant examiné, et conserve une copie des documents suivants :

1) Une autocertification qui indique que le titulaire du compte n'est ni un citoyen ni un résident américain à des fins fiscales (établie sur le formulaire W-8 de l'IRS ou un autre formulaire analogue agréé) ;

2) Une preuve documentaire visée au paragraphe D de la section VI de la présente annexe I, qui établit le statut non américain du titulaire du compte ;

c) Lorsque les renseignements sur le titulaire du compte comprennent un ordre de virement permanent sur un compte tenu aux États-Unis, l'institution financière déclarante finlandaise obtient ou a auparavant examiné, et conserve une copie des documents suivants :

1) Une autocertification qui indique que le titulaire du compte n'est ni un citoyen ni un résident américain à des fins fiscales (établie sur le formulaire W-8 de l'IRS ou un autre formulaire analogue agréé) ; et

2) Une preuve documentaire visée au paragraphe D de la section VI de la présente annexe I, qui établit le statut non américain du titulaire du compte ;

d) Lorsque les renseignements sur le titulaire du compte comprennent une procuration ou une délégation de signature en cours de validité accordée à une personne dont l'adresse est située aux États-Unis ou une adresse portant la mention « à l'attention de » ou « poste restante » comme seule adresse connue pour le titulaire du compte ou encore un ou plusieurs numéros de téléphone aux États-Unis (outre un numéro de téléphone non américain associé au compte), l'institution financière déclarante finlandaise obtient, ou a auparavant examiné, et conserve une copie des documents suivants :

1) Une autocertification qui indique que le titulaire du compte n'est ni un citoyen ni un résident américain à des fins fiscales (établie sur le formulaire W-8 de l'IRS ou un autre formulaire analogue agréé) ; ou

2) Une preuve documentaire visée au paragraphe D de la section VI de la présente annexe I, qui établit le statut non américain du titulaire du compte.

C. Procédures supplémentaires applicables aux comptes de personnes physiques préexistants de faible valeur.

1. L'examen des comptes des personnes physiques préexistants qui sont des comptes de faible valeur en vue de rechercher des indices américains doit être achevé le 30 juin 2016 au plus tard.

2. Si un changement de circonstances concernant un compte d'une personne physique préexistant de faible valeur se produit et a pour conséquence qu'un ou plusieurs des indices américains visés au point 1 du paragraphe B de la présente section soient associés à ce compte, l'institution financière déclarante finlandaise doit considérer le compte comme un compte déclarable américain sauf si le point 4 du paragraphe B de la présente section s'applique.

3. À l'exception des comptes de dépôt visés au point 4 du paragraphe A de la présente section, tout compte d'une personne physique préexistant qui a été

identifié comme compte déclarable américain conformément à la présente section est considéré comme un compte déclarable américain les années suivantes, sauf si le titulaire du compte cesse d'être une personne américaine déterminée.

D. Procédures d'examen approfondi pour les comptes de personnes physiques préexistants dont le solde ou la valeur excède 1 000 000 de dollars au 30 juin 2014 ou au 31 décembre 2015 ou de toute année suivante (les « comptes de valeur élevée »).

1. Examen par voie électronique. L'institution financière déclarante finlandaise est tenue d'examiner les données qu'elle détient et qui peuvent faire l'objet de recherches par voie électronique quant à la présence de l'un quelconque des indices américains décrits au point 1 du paragraphe B de la présente section.

2. Examen des dossiers papier. Si les données de l'institution financière déclarante finlandaise susceptibles d'être examinées par voie électronique contiennent des champs comprenant tous les renseignements décrits au point 3 du paragraphe D de la présente section et permettent d'en appréhender le contenu, aucun examen des dossiers papier n'est requis. Si ces données ne contiennent pas tous ces renseignements, l'institution financière déclarante finlandaise est également tenue, pour un compte de valeur élevée, d'examiner le dossier principal actuel du client et, dans la mesure où ces renseignements n'y figurent pas, les documents suivants associés au compte et obtenus par l'institution financière déclarante finlandaise au cours des cinq années précédentes en vue de rechercher l'un des indices américains décrits au point 1 du paragraphe B de la présente section :

   a) Les preuves documentaires collectées le plus récemment concernant le compte ;

   b) La convention ou la documentation d'ouverture de compte la plus récente ;

   c) La documentation la plus récente obtenue par l'institution financière déclarante finlandaise en application des mesures de connaissance de la clientèle et de lutte contre le blanchiment d'argent (AML/KYC) ou à d'autres fins réglementaires ;

   d) Toute procuration ou délégation de signature en cours de validité ; et

   e) Tout ordre de virement permanent en cours de validité.

3. Exception lorsque les données électroniques contiennent suffisamment de renseignements. Une institution financière déclarante finlandaise n'est pas tenue d'effectuer l'examen des dossiers papier décrit au point 2 du paragraphe D de la présente section si les renseignements susceptibles d'être examinés par voie électronique qu'elle détient comprennent les éléments suivants :

   a) La nationalité ou le pays de résidence du titulaire du compte ;

   b) L'adresse de résidence et l'adresse postale du titulaire du compte qui figurent au dossier de l'institution financière déclarante finlandaise ;

   c) Le ou les numéros de téléphone du titulaire du compte qui figurent éventuellement au dossier de l'institution financière déclarante finlandaise ;

d) Un éventuel ordre de virement permanent depuis le compte vers un autre compte (y compris un compte auprès d'une autre succursale de l'institution financière déclarante finlandaise ou d'une autre institution financière) ;

e) Une éventuelle adresse du titulaire du compte portant la mention « à l'attention de » ou « poste restante » ; et

f) Une éventuelle procuration ou délégation de signature sur le compte.

4. Prise de renseignements auprès du chargé de clientèle en vue d'une connaissance réelle du compte. Outre l'examen des dossiers informatiques et papier décrit ci-dessus, l'institution financière déclarante finlandaise est tenue de traiter comme compte déclarable américain tout compte de valeur élevée confié à un chargé de clientèle (y compris les éventuels comptes financiers qui sont groupés avec un tel compte de valeur élevée) si ce chargé de clientèle sait que le titulaire du compte est une personne américaine déterminée.

5. Conséquences de la découverte d'indices américains.

a) Si l'examen approfondi des comptes de valeur élevée décrit ci-dessus ne révèle aucun des indices américains énumérés au point 1 du paragraphe B de la présente section et si l'application du point 4 du paragraphe D de la présente section ne permet pas d'établir que le compte est détenu par une personne américaine déterminée, aucune nouvelle démarche n'est requise jusqu'à ce qu'un changement de circonstances intervienne qui se traduise par un ou plusieurs indices américains associés à ce compte.

b) Si l'examen approfondi des comptes de valeur élevée décrit ci-dessus révèle l'un des indices américains énumérés au point 1 du paragraphe B de la présente section ou en cas de changement ultérieur de circonstances qui a pour conséquence d'associer au compte un ou plusieurs indices américains liés au compte, l'institution financière déclarante finlandaise doit considérer le compte comme un compte déclarable américain, sauf si elle choisit d'appliquer le point 4 du paragraphe B de la présente section et que l'une des exceptions à celui-ci s'applique à ce compte.

c) À l'exception des comptes de dépôt visés au point 4 du paragraphe A de la présente section, tout compte d'une personne physique préexistant qui a été identifié comme compte déclarable américain conformément à la présente section est considéré comme un compte déclarable américain les années suivantes, sauf si le titulaire du compte cesse d'être une personne américaine déterminée.

E. Procédures supplémentaires applicables aux comptes de valeur élevée.

1. Si, au 30 juin 2014, un compte d'une personne physique préexistant est un compte de valeur élevée, l'institution financière déclarante finlandaise doit accomplir pour ce compte les procédures d'examen approfondi décrites au paragraphe D de la présente section le 30 juin 2015 au plus tard. Si, à la suite de cet examen, ce compte est identifié comme compte déclarable américain le 31 décembre 2014 ou avant cette date, l'institution financière déclarante finlandaise doit inclure les renseignements requis pour l'année 2014 dans la première déclaration concernant le compte et ensuite sur une base annuelle. Dans le cas d'un compte identifié comme compte déclarable américain après le

31 décembre 2014, et au 30 juin 2015 ou avant cette date, l'institution financière déclarante finlandaise n'a pas à fournir de renseignements relatifs à ce compte pour 2014, mais doit ensuite fournir des renseignements relatifs à ce compte sur une base annuelle.

2. Si, au 30 juin 2014, un compte d'une personne physique préexistant n'est pas un compte de valeur élevée, mais le devient au dernier jour de 2015 ou de toute année civile ultérieure, l'institution financière déclarante finlandaise doit appliquer à ce compte les procédures d'examen approfondi décrites au paragraphe D de la présente section dans les six mois qui suivent le dernier jour de l'année civile au cours de laquelle le compte devient un compte de valeur élevée. Si, à la suite de cet examen, il apparaît que ce compte est un compte déclarable américain, l'institution financière déclarante finlandaise doit fournir les renseignements requis pour ce compte pour l'année durant laquelle il est identifié comme compte déclarable américain ainsi que pour les années suivantes sur une base annuelle, à moins que le titulaire du compte ne cesse d'être une personne américaine déterminée.

3. Après qu'une institution financière déclarante finlandaise a appliqué les procédures d'examen approfondi décrites au paragraphe D de la présente section à un compte de valeur élevée, elle n'est plus tenue de renouveler l'application de ces procédures les années suivantes, à l'exception de la prise de renseignements auprès du chargé de clientèle décrite au point 4 du paragraphe D de la présente section.

4. Si un changement de circonstances concernant un compte de valeur élevée se produit et a pour conséquence qu'un ou plusieurs des indices américains visés au point 1 du paragraphe B de la présente section sont associés à ce compte, l'institution financière déclarante finlandaise doit considérer le compte comme un compte déclarable américain sauf si elle choisit d'appliquer le point 4 du paragraphe B de la présente section et si l'une des exceptions à celui-ci s'applique à ce compte.

5. Une institution financière déclarante finlandaise est tenue de mettre en œuvre des procédures garantissant que les chargés de clientèle détectent tout changement de circonstances en relation avec un compte. Si, par exemple, un chargé de clientèle est informé que le titulaire du compte dispose d'une nouvelle adresse postale aux États-Unis, l'institution financière déclarante finlandaise doit considérer cette nouvelle adresse comme un changement de circonstances et, si elle choisit d'appliquer le point 4 du paragraphe B de la présente section, obtenir les documents pertinents auprès du titulaire du compte.

F. Comptes de personnes physiques préexistants documentés à d'autres fins. Une institution financière déclarante finlandaise qui a déjà obtenu d'un titulaire de compte des documents attestant que celui-ci n'est ni un citoyen ni un résident américain afin de respecter ses obligations résultant d'un accord avec l'IRS en tant qu'intermédiaire qualifié, société de personnes étrangère procédant à la retenue à la source ou trust étranger procédant à la retenue à la source, ou afin de s'acquitter de ses obligations en application du chapitre 61 du titre 26 de l'United States Code, n'est pas tenue de suivre les procédures décrites au point 1 du paragraphe B de la présente section en ce qui concerne les comptes de faible valeur ni celles décrites aux points 1 à 3 du paragraphe D de la présente section en ce qui concerne les comptes de valeur élevée.

III. Nouveaux comptes des personnes physiques. Les règles et procédures suivantes s'appliquent pour l'identification des comptes déclarables américains parmi les comptes financiers détenus par des personnes physiques et ouverts à partir du 1er juillet 2014 (les « nouveaux comptes des personnes physiques »).

A. Comptes non soumis à examen, identification ou déclaration. Sauf si l'institution financière déclarante finlandaise en décide autrement, soit à l'égard de tous les nouveaux comptes de personnes physiques, soit séparément par rapport à un groupe clairement identifié de comptes, lorsque les règles de mise en œuvre édictées par la Finlande prévoient la possibilité d'un tel choix, il n'est pas nécessaire d'examiner, d'identifier ou de déclarer les nouveaux comptes de personnes physiques suivants comme comptes déclarables américains :

1. Un compte de dépôt, sauf si le solde du compte excède 50 000 dollars à la fin de l'année civile ou de toute autre période de référence appropriée ;

2. Un contrat d'assurance, sauf si sa valeur de rachat excède 50 000 dollars à la fin de l'année civile ou de toute autre période de référence appropriée.

B. Autres nouveaux comptes de personnes physiques. S'agissant des nouveaux comptes des personnes physiques qui ne sont pas visés au paragraphe A de la présente section, l'institution financière déclarante finlandaise doit obtenir lors de l'ouverture du compte (ou dans les 90 jours suivant la fin de l'année civile durant laquelle le compte cesse de répondre aux conditions prévues au paragraphe A de la présente section) une autocertification, laquelle peut faire partie de la documentation d'ouverture de compte, qui lui permette de déterminer si le titulaire du compte réside aux États-Unis à des fins fiscales (à cette fin, un citoyen américain est considéré comme résident fiscal aux États-Unis, même si le titulaire du compte est également un résident fiscal d'une autre juridiction) et confirmer la vraisemblance de l'autocertification en s'appuyant sur les renseignements obtenus dans le cadre de l'ouverture du compte, y compris les documents recueillis en application des mesures de connaissance de la clientèle et de lutte contre le blanchiment d'argent.

C. Si l'autocertification établit que le titulaire du compte réside aux États-Unis à des fins fiscales, l'institution financière déclarante finlandaise est tenue de traiter le compte comme un compte déclarable américain et d'obtenir une autocertification (établie en utilisant le formulaire W-9 de l'IRS ou un autre formulaire analogue agréé) sur laquelle figure le NIF américain du titulaire du compte.

D. Si un changement de circonstances concernant un nouveau compte d'une personne physique se produit et a pour conséquence que l'institution financière déclarante finlandaise constate ou a des raisons de présumer que l'autocertification initiale est inexacte ou n'est pas fiable, cette Institution ne peut utiliser cette autocertification et doit obtenir une autocertification valide qui précise si le titulaire du compte est un citoyen ou un résident américain à des fins fiscales. Si l'institution financière déclarante finlandaise ne peut obtenir d'autocertification valide, elle doit considérer le compte comme un compte déclarable américain.

IV. Comptes d'entités préexistants. Les règles et procédures suivantes s'appliquent pour l'identification des comptes déclarables américains et des comptes détenus par des institutions financières non participantes parmi les comptes préexistants détenus par des entités (les « comptes d'entités préexistants »).

A. Comptes d'entités non soumis à examen, identification ou déclaration. Sauf si l'institution financière déclarante finlandaise en décide autrement, soit à l'égard de tous les comptes d'entités préexistants ou, séparément, par rapport à un groupe clairement identifié de tels comptes, lorsque les règles de mise en œuvre édictées par la Finlande prévoient la possibilité d'un tel choix, un compte d'entité préexistant dont le solde ou la valeur n'excède pas 250 000 dollars au 30 juin 2014 n'a pas à être examiné, identifié ou déclaré comme compte déclarable américain tant que son solde ou sa valeur n'excède pas 1 000 000 de dollars.

B. Comptes d'entités soumis à examen. Un compte d'entité préexistant dont le solde ou la valeur excède 250 000 dollars au 30 juin 2014 et un compte d'entité préexistant dont le solde n'excède pas 250 000 dollars au 30 juin 2014, mais dépasse le seuil de 1 000 000 de dollars au dernier jour de 2015 ou de toute année civile ultérieure doit être examiné en appliquant les procédures décrites au paragraphe D de la présente section.

C. Comptes d'entités pour lesquels une déclaration est requise. S'agissant des comptes d'entités préexistants visés au paragraphe B de la présente section, seuls les comptes détenus par une ou plusieurs entités qui sont des personnes américaines déterminées ou par des entités étrangères non financières (EENF) passives dont une ou plusieurs des personnes qui en détiennent le contrôle sont des citoyens ou des résidents américains sont considérés comme des comptes déclarables américains. En outre, les comptes détenus par des institutions financières non participantes sont considérés comme des comptes pour lesquels les versements totaux décrits à l'alinéa b) du paragraphe 1 de l'article 4 du présent Accord doivent être déclarés aux autorités compétentes finlandaises.

D. Procédures d'examen relatives à l'identification des comptes d'entités pour lesquels des déclarations sont requises. Pour les comptes d'entités préexistants décrits au paragraphe B de la présente section, l'institution financière déclarante finlandaise doit appliquer les procédures d'examen suivantes afin de déterminer si le compte est détenu par une ou plusieurs personnes américaines déterminées, par des EENF passives dont une ou plusieurs des personnes qui en détiennent le contrôle sont des citoyens ou des résidents américains ou par des institutions financières non participantes :

   1. Déterminer si l'entité est une personne américaine déterminée :

      a) Sont à examiner les renseignements obtenus à des fins réglementaires ou de relations avec le client (y compris les renseignements collectés dans le cadre des mesures de connaissance de la clientèle et de lutte contre le blanchiment d'argent afin de déterminer si ces renseignements indiquent que le titulaire du compte est une personne américaine. À cette fin, le lieu de constitution ou de création ou une adresse aux États-Unis font partie des renseignements indiquant que le titulaire du compte est une personne américaine ;

      b) Si les renseignements obtenus indiquent que le titulaire du compte est une personne américaine, l'institution financière déclarante finlandaise est tenue de traiter le compte comme un compte déclarable américain sauf si elle obtient une autocertification du titulaire du compte (établie sur le formulaire W-8 ou W-9 de l'IRS ou un formulaire analogue agréé) ou si elle détermine avec une certitude suffisante sur la base de renseignements en sa possession ou qui sont accessibles au public que le titulaire du compte n'est pas une personne américaine déterminée.

2. Déterminer si une entité non américaine est une institution financière :

   a) Sont à examiner les renseignements obtenus à des fins réglementaires ou de relations avec le client (y compris les renseignements collectés dans le cadre des mesures de connaissance de la clientèle et de lutte contre le blanchiment d'argent afin de déterminer si ces renseignements indiquent que le titulaire du compte est une institution financière ;

   b) Si les renseignements obtenus indiquent que le titulaire du compte est une institution financière, ou si l'institution financière déclarante finlandaise vérifie le numéro d'identification du titulaire du compte (Global Intermediary Identification Number – GIIN) sur la liste des IFE publiée par l'IRS, le compte n'est pas un compte déclarable américain.

3. Déterminer si une institution financière est une institution financière non participante pour laquelle les paiements qu'elle a perçus sont soumis aux déclarations agrégées prévues à l'alinéa b) du paragraphe 1 de l'article 4 du présent Accord :

   a) Sous réserve du point b) du point 3 du paragraphe D de la présente section, une institution financière déclarante finlandaise [partenaire dans le cadre de la loi FATCA] peut déterminer que le titulaire du compte est une institution financière finlandaise ou une institution financière d'une juridiction partenaire si elle détermine avec une certitude suffisante que le titulaire du compte a ce statut sur la base du numéro d'identification du titulaire du compte (GIIN) sur la liste des IFE publiée par l'IRS ou de tout autre renseignement publiquement accessible ou en sa possession. Dans ce cas, aucun autre examen, identification ou déclaration n'est requis en ce qui concerne le compte ;

   b) Si le titulaire du compte est une institution financière finlandaise ou une institution financière d'une autre juridiction partenaire considérée par l'IRS comme une institution financière non participante, le compte n'est pas un compte déclarable américain, mais les paiements effectués au titulaire du compte doivent être déclarés conformément à ce qui est prévu à l'alinéa b) du paragraphe 1 de l'article 4 du présent Accord ;

   c) Si le titulaire du compte n'est pas une institution financière finlandaise ni une institution financière d'une autre juridiction partenaire, l'institution financière déclarante finlandaise est tenue de traiter le titulaire du compte comme une institution financière non participante pour laquelle les paiements qu'elle a perçus sont déclarables en application de l'alinéa b) du paragraphe 1 de l'article 4 du présent Accord, sauf si l'institution financière déclarante finlandaise :

      1) Obtient une autocertification (établie sur le formulaire W-8 de l'IRS ou un formulaire analogue agréé) du titulaire du compte attestant qu'il est une IFE réputée conforme certifiée ou un bénéficiaire effectif dispensé

de déclaration, selon le sens donné à ces termes dans la réglementation pertinente du Trésor des États-Unis ; ou

2) Vérifie le numéro d'identification du titulaire du compte (GIIN) sur la liste des IFE publiée par l'IRS, dans le cas d'une IFE participante ou d'une IFE enregistrée réputée conforme.

4. Déterminer si un compte détenu par une EENF est un compte déclarable américain. S'agissant d'un titulaire de compte d'un compte d'entité préexistant qui n'est ni une personne américaine ni une institution financière, l'institution financière déclarante finlandaise doit déterminer : i) si le titulaire du compte est une entité contrôlée par des personnes détenant le contrôle ; ii) si le titulaire du compte est une EENF passive ; et iii) si l'une des personnes détenant le contrôle de l'entité titulaire du compte est un citoyen ou un résident américain. À cette fin, l'institution financière déclarante finlandaise doit suivre les orientations mentionnées ci-dessous aux sous-points a) à d) dans l'ordre qui convient le mieux à la situation :

a) Pour identifier les personnes détenant le contrôle d'une entité titulaire de compte, l'institution financière déclarante finlandaise peut se fonder sur des renseignements recueillis et conservés dans le cadre des mesures de connaissance de la clientèle et de lutte contre le blanchiment d'argent ;

b) Pour déterminer si un titulaire de compte est une EENF passive, l'institution financière déclarante finlandaise doit obtenir une autocertification (établie sur le formulaire W-8 ou W-9 de l'IRS ou un formulaire analogue agréé) du titulaire du compte afin de déterminer son statut, sauf si, à partir de renseignements en sa possession ou qui sont accessibles au public, elle peut établir avec une certitude suffisante que le titulaire de compte est une EENF active ;

c) Pour déterminer si une personne détenant le contrôle d'une EENF passive est un citoyen ou un résident américain à des fins fiscales, une institution financière déclarante finlandaise peut se fonder :

1) Sur des renseignements recueillis et collectés en application des mesures de connaissance de la clientèle et de lutte contre le blanchiment d'argent dans le cas d'un compte d'entité préexistant détenu par une ou plusieurs EENF et dont le solde ou la valeur n'excède pas 1 000 000 de dollars ; ou

2) Sur une autocertification (établie sur le formulaire W-8 ou W-9 de l'IRS ou un formulaire analogue agréé) du titulaire du compte ou d'une personne détenant le contrôle dans le cas d'un compte d'entité préexistant détenu par une ou plusieurs EENF et dont le solde ou la valeur est supérieur à 1 000 000 de dollars ;

d) Si une personne détenant le contrôle d'une EENF passive est un citoyen ou un résident américain, le compte doit être traité comme un compte déclarable américain.

E. Calendrier de mise en œuvre de l'examen et procédures supplémentaires applicables aux comptes d'entités préexistants.

1. L'examen des comptes d'entités préexistants dont le solde ou la valeur est supérieure à 250 000 dollars au 30 juin 2014 doit être achevé au plus tard le 30 juin 2016.
2. L'examen des comptes d'entités préexistants dont le solde ou la valeur n'excède pas 250 000 dollars au 30 juin 2014, mais est supérieur à 1 000 000 de dollars au 31 décembre 2015 ou de toute année ultérieure doit être achevé dans les six mois qui suivent le dernier jour de l'année civile au cours de laquelle le solde ou la valeur du compte a été supérieur à 1 000 000 de dollars.
3. Si un changement de circonstances concernant un compte d'entité préexistant se produit et a pour conséquence que l'institution financière déclarante finlandaise sait ou a de bonnes raisons de présumer que l'autocertification ou un autre document associé au compte est inexact ou n'est pas fiable, celle-ci doit déterminer à nouveau le statut du compte en appliquant les procédures décrites au paragraphe D de la présente section.

V. Nouveaux comptes d'entités. Les règles et procédures suivantes s'appliquent dans le but d'identifier les comptes déclarables américains ainsi que les comptes détenus par des institutions financières non participantes parmi les comptes financiers détenus par des entités et ouverts à compter ou après le 1er juillet 2014 (les « nouveaux comptes d'entités »).

A. Comptes d'entités non soumis à examen, identification ou déclaration. Sauf si l'institution financière déclarante finlandaise en décide autrement, soit à l'égard de tous les nouveaux comptes d'entités, soit séparément par rapport à un groupe clairement identifié de comptes, lorsque les règles de mise en œuvre édictées par la Finlande prévoient la possibilité d'un tel choix, un compte utilisé pour une carte de crédit ou un crédit permanent considéré comme un nouveau compte d'entité n'a pas à être examiné, identifié ou déclaré, à condition que l'institution financière déclarante finlandaise qui détient un tel compte mette en œuvre des règles et des procédures afin d'éviter que le solde dû au titulaire du compte n'excède 50 000 dollars.

B. Autres nouveaux comptes d'entités. En ce qui concerne les nouveaux comptes d'entités non décrits au paragraphe A de la présente section, l'institution financière déclarante finlandaise doit déterminer si le titulaire du compte est : i) une personne américaine déterminée ; ii) une institution financière finlandaise ou d'une autre juridiction partenaire ; iii) une IFE participante, une IFE réputée conforme ou un bénéficiaire effectif dispensé de déclaration au sens donné à ces termes dans la réglementation applicable du Trésor des États-Unis ; ou iv) une EENF active ou passive.

1. Sous réserve du point 2 du paragraphe B de la présente section, une institution financière déclarante finlandaise peut établir que le titulaire du compte est une EENF active, une institution financière finlandaise ou d'une autre juridiction partenaire si elle détermine avec une certitude suffisante que tel est le statut du titulaire du compte à partir du numéro d'identification (GIIN) du titulaire du compte ou d'autres renseignements accessibles au public ou en sa possession.
2. Si le titulaire du compte est une institution financière finlandaise ou une institution financière d'une autre juridiction partenaire considérée par l'IRS comme une institution financière non participante, le compte n'est pas un compte déclarable américain, mais les paiements effectués au titulaire de ce

compte doivent être déclarés conformément à l'alinéa b) du paragraphe 1 de l'article 4 du présent Accord.

3. Dans tous les autres cas, l'institution financière déclarante finlandaise doit obtenir une autocertification du titulaire du compte afin d'établir son statut. Sur la base de l'autocertification, les règles suivantes s'appliquent :

   a) Si le titulaire du compte est une personne américaine déterminée, l'institution financière déclarante finlandaise doit considérer le compte comme un compte déclarable américain ;

   b) Si le titulaire du compte est une EENF passive, l'institution financière déclarante finlandaise doit identifier les personnes détenant le contrôle conformément aux mesures de connaissance de la clientèle et de lutte contre le blanchiment d'argent et déterminer si l'une de ces personnes est un citoyen ou un résident américain à partir d'une autocertification fournie par le titulaire du compte ou l'une de ces personnes. Si l'une de ces personnes est un citoyen ou un résident américain, l'institution financière déclarante finlandaise doit traiter le compte comme un compte déclarable américain ;

   c) Si le titulaire du compte est : i) une personne américaine non déterminée, ii) sous réserve du sous-point d) du point 3 du paragraphe B de la présente section, une institution financière finlandaise ou d'une autre juridiction partenaire ; iii) une IFE participante, une IFE réputée conforme ou un bénéficiaire effectif dispensé de déclaration au sens donné à ces termes dans la réglementation applicable du Trésor des États-Unis ; iv) une EENF active ; ou v) une EENF passive dont aucune des personnes détenant le contrôle n'est citoyen ou résident des États-Unis, le compte n'est pas un compte déclarable américain et aucune déclaration n'est requise pour ce compte ;

   d) Si le titulaire du compte est une institution financière non participante (y compris une institution financière finlandaise ou d'une autre juridiction partenaire qui est traitée par l'IRS comme une institution financière non participante), ce compte n'est pas un compte déclarable américain, mais les paiements effectués au titulaire de ce compte doivent être déclarés conformément à l'alinéa b) du paragraphe 1 de l'article 4 du présent Accord.

VI. Règles particulières et définitions. Pour la mise en œuvre des diligences raisonnables décrites ci-dessus, les règles et définitions supplémentaires suivantes s'appliquent :

A. Recours aux autocertifications et aux preuves documentaires. Une institution financière déclarante finlandaise ne peut pas se fier à une autocertification ou à une preuve documentaire si elle sait ou a de bonnes raisons de présumer que cette autocertification ou cette preuve documentaire est inexacte ou n'est pas fiable.

B. Définitions. Les définitions suivantes s'appliquent aux fins de la présente annexe I :

   1. Mesures de connaissance de la clientèle et de lutte contre le blanchiment d'argent. L'expression « mesures de connaissance de la clientèle et de lutte contre le blanchiment d'argent » désigne les obligations de diligence raisonnable qu'une institution financière déclarante finlandaise est tenue d'observer en vertu des dispositions de lutte contre le blanchiment d'argent ou de règles analogues

finlandaises auxquelles cette institution financière déclarante finlandaise est soumise.

2. EENF. Le sigle « EENF » désigne toute entité non américaine qui n'est pas une IFE au sens donné à ce sigle dans la réglementation pertinente du Trésor des États-Unis ou est une entité décrite au sous-point j) du point 4 du paragraphe B de la présente section, ainsi que toute entité non américaine qui est établie sur le territoire finlandais ou d'une autre juridiction partenaire et qui n'est pas une institution financière.
3. EENF passive. L'expression « EENF passive » désigne toute EENF qui n'est pas : i) une EENF active ; ni ii) une société de personnes étrangère susceptible de faire l'objet d'une retenue à la source ou un trust étranger susceptible de faire l'objet d'une retenue à la source conformément à la réglementation pertinente du Trésor des États-Unis.
4. EENF active. L'expression « EENF active » désigne toute EENF qui satisfait à l'un des critères suivants :
   a) Moins de 50 % des revenus bruts de l'EENF au titre de l'année civile précédente ou d'une autre période de référence comptable pertinente sont des revenus passifs, et moins de 50 % des actifs détenus par l'EENF au cours de l'année civile précédente ou d'une autre période de référence comptable pertinente sont des actifs qui produisent ou qui sont détenus pour obtenir des revenus passifs ;
   b) Les actions de l'EENF font l'objet de transactions régulières sur un marché boursier réglementé ou l'EENF est une entité liée à une entité dont les actions font l'objet de transactions régulières sur un marché boursier réglementé ;
   c) L'EENF est constituée sur un Territoire américain et tous les propriétaires du bénéficiaire sont des résidents de ce Territoire américain ;
   d) L'EENF est un gouvernement (autre que le Gouvernement des États-Unis), une subdivision politique d'un tel gouvernement (terme qui, pour éviter toute ambiguïté, comprend un État, une province, un comté ou une municipalité), ou un organisme public exerçant une fonction d'un gouvernement ou d'une subdivision politique, le Gouvernement d'un Territoire américain, une organisation internationale, une banque centrale non américaine ou une entité détenue à 100 % par une ou plusieurs des structures précitées ;
   e) Les activités de l'EENF consistent pour l'essentiel à détenir (en tout ou en partie) les actions émises par une ou plusieurs filiales dont les activités ne sont pas celles d'une institution financière ou à proposer des financements ou des services à ces filiales. Toutefois, une entité ne peut prétendre au statut d'EENF si elle opère (ou se présente) comme un fonds de placement, tel qu'un fonds de capital-investissement, un fonds de capital-risque, un fonds de rachat d'entreprise par endettement ou tout autre organisme de placement dont l'objet est d'acquérir ou de financer des sociétés puis d'y détenir des participations à des fins de placement ;

f) L'EENF n'exerce pas encore d'activité et n'en a jamais exercé précédemment, mais investit des capitaux dans des actifs en vue d'exercer une activité autre que celle d'une institution financière, étant entendu que cette exception ne saurait s'appliquer à l'EENF après l'expiration d'un délai de 24 mois suivant la date de sa constitution initiale ;

g) L'EENF n'était pas une institution financière durant les cinq années précédentes et procède à la liquidation de ses actifs ou est en cours de restructuration afin de poursuivre ou de reprendre des transactions ou des activités qui ne sont pas celles d'une institution financière ;

h) L'EENF se livre principalement au financement d'entités liées qui ne sont pas des institutions financières et à des transactions de couverture avec ou pour le compte de celles-ci et ne fournit pas de services de financement ou de couverture à des entités qui ne sont pas des entités liées, à condition que le groupe auquel appartiennent ces entités liées se consacre principalement à une activité qui n'est pas celle d'une institution financière ;

i) L'EENF est une « EENF exclue » telle que décrite dans la réglementation du Trésor des États-Unis correspondante ; ou

j) L'EENF remplit toutes les conditions suivantes :

   i. Elle est établie et exploitée dans sa juridiction de résidence exclusivement à des fins religieuses, caritatives, scientifiques, artistiques, culturelles, sportives ou éducatives, ou elle est établie et exploitée dans sa juridiction de résidence et est une fédération professionnelle, une organisation patronale, une chambre de commerce, une organisation syndicale, agricole ou horticole, ou civique ou un organisme dont l'objet exclusif est de promouvoir le bien-être social ;

   ii. Elle est exonérée d'impôt sur les sociétés dans sa juridiction de résidence ;

   iii. Elle n'a aucun actionnaire ni aucun membre disposant d'un droit de propriété ou de jouissance sur ses recettes ou ses actifs ;

   iv. Le droit applicable dans la juridiction de résidence de l'EENF ou les documents constitutifs de celle-ci excluent que les recettes ou les actifs de l'EENF soient distribués à des personnes physiques ou des organismes à but lucratif ou utilisés à leur bénéfice, à moins que cette utilisation ne soit en relation avec les activités caritatives de l'EENF ou à titre de rémunération raisonnable, au prix du marché, pour les biens et services rendus, acquis ou souscrits par l'EENF ; et

   v. Le droit applicable dans la juridiction de résidence de l'EENF ou les documents constitutifs de celle-ci imposent que, lors de la liquidation ou de la dissolution de l'EENF, tous ses actifs soient distribués à une entité publique ou à une autre organisation à but non lucratif ou soient dévolus au Gouvernement de l'État de résidence de l'EENF ou à l'une de ses subdivisions politiques.

5. Comptes préexistants. L'expression « compte préexistant » désigne un compte financier ouvert auprès d'une institution financière déclarante au 30 juin 2014.

C. Agrégation des soldes de compte et règles de conversion monétaire.

1. Agrégation des comptes de personnes physiques. Pour déterminer le solde ou la valeur globale des comptes financiers détenus par une personne physique, une institution financière déclarante finlandaise doit agréger tous les comptes financiers détenus auprès d'elle ou auprès d'une entité liée dans la mesure où ses systèmes informatiques établissent un lien entre les comptes grâce à une donnée telle que le numéro de client ou le numéro d'identification fiscal et permettent d'agréger les soldes ou valeurs des comptes. Chaque titulaire d'un compte financier joint se voit attribuer le solde ou la valeur totale de ce compte aux fins de l'application des obligations d'agrégation décrites au présent point 1.

2. Agrégation des comptes d'entités. Pour déterminer le solde ou la valeur globale des comptes financiers détenus par une entité, une institution financière déclarante finlandaise doit prendre en compte tous les comptes financiers détenus auprès d'elle ou auprès d'une entité liée dans la mesure où ses systèmes informatiques établissent un lien entre les comptes grâce à une donnée telle que le numéro de client ou le numéro d'identification fiscal et permettent d'agréger les soldes ou valeurs des comptes.

3. Règles d'agrégation spécifiques applicables aux chargés de clientèle. Pour déterminer le solde ou la valeur globale des comptes financiers détenus par une personne dans le but d'établir si un compte financier est un compte de valeur élevée, une institution financière déclarante finlandaise doit également agréger ces comptes, dans le cas des comptes financiers dont un chargé de clientèle sait ou a de bonnes raisons de présumer qu'ils sont, directement ou indirectement, détenus, contrôlés ou créés (à un titre autre que celui d'administrateur des biens d'autrui) par la même personne.

4. Règles de conversion monétaire. Pour déterminer le solde ou la valeur des comptes financiers libellés dans une monnaie autre que le dollar des États-Unis, une institution financière déclarante finlandaise doit convertir les seuils exprimés en dollars de la présente annexe I dans la monnaie susmentionnée en utilisant le cours déterminé le dernier jour de l'année civile qui précède l'année où elle calcule le solde ou la valeur d'un compte.

D. Preuve documentaire. Aux fins de la présente annexe I, sont réputées acceptables les preuves documentaires suivantes :

1. Une attestation de résidence délivrée par un organisme public autorisé à le faire (par exemple un État, une agence de celui-ci ou une municipalité) de la juridiction dont le bénéficiaire affirme être résident ;

2. Dans le cas d'une personne physique, toute pièce d'identité en cours de validité délivrée par un organisme public autorisé à le faire (par exemple un État, une agence de celui-ci ou une municipalité), sur laquelle figure le nom de la personne et qui est généralement utilisée à des fins d'identification ;

3. Dans le cas d'une entité, tout document officiel délivré par un organisme public autorisé à le faire (par exemple un État, une agence de celui-ci ou une municipalité) sur lequel figure la dénomination de l'entité et l'adresse de son établissement principal dans la juridiction (ou le Territoire américain) dont elle

affirme être résidente ou dans la juridiction (ou le Territoire américain) dans laquelle l'entité a été constituée ou dont le droit la régit ;

4. Dans le cas d'un compte financier ouvert dans une juridiction soumise à des règles de lutte contre le blanchiment (AML) qui ont été approuvées par l'IRS dans le cadre d'un accord avec un intermédiaire éligible (au sens donné à ces accords dans la réglementation du Trésor des États-Unis), l'un des documents autres qu'un formulaire W-8 ou W-9 référencés par cette juridiction dans les pièces jointes à l'accord avec un intermédiaire éligible (qualified intermediary – QI) servant à identifier des personnes physiques ou des entités ;
5. Tout état financier, tout rapport de solvabilité établi par un tiers, toute déclaration de cessation des paiements ou tout rapport de la Commission fédérale de contrôle des opérations de bourse.

E. Procédures alternatives pour les comptes financiers détenus par une personne physique bénéficiaire d'un contrat d'assurance à forte valeur de rachat. Une institution financière déclarante finlandaise peut présumer que le bénéficiaire d'un contrat d'assurance à forte valeur de rachat (autre que le souscripteur) qui perçoit un capital à la suite d'un décès n'est pas une personne américaine déterminée et peut considérer que ce compte financier n'est pas un compte déclarable américain à moins que l'institution financière déclarante finlandaise sache ou ait des raisons de savoir que le bénéficiaire du capital est une personne américaine déterminée. Une institution financière déclarante finlandaise a des raisons de savoir que le bénéficiaire du capital d'un contrat d'assurance à forte valeur de rachat est une personne américaine déterminée si les renseignements associés au bénéficiaire qu'elle a recueillis comprennent des indices américains conformément au point 1 du paragraphe B de la section II de la présente annexe I. Si une institution financière déclarante finlandaise sait ou a des raisons de savoir que le bénéficiaire est une personne américaine déterminée, elle doit suivre les procédures énoncées au point 3 du paragraphe B de la section II de la présente annexe I.

F. Recours à des tiers. Sans présumer du choix qui pourrait être fait en application des dispositions du paragraphe C de la section I de la présente annexe I, la Finlande peut autoriser les institutions financières déclarantes finlandaises à s'appuyer sur des procédures d'examen effectuées par des tiers, dans la mesure de ce qui est prévu dans la réglementation pertinente du Trésor des États-Unis.

ANNEXE II

Les entités ci-après sont considérées, selon le cas, soit comme des bénéficiaires effectifs dispensés de déclaration, soit comme des IFE réputées conformes, et les comptes ci-après sont exclus de la définition des comptes financiers.

La présente annexe II peut être modifiée par entente mutuelle écrite entre les autorités compétentes de la Finlande et des États-Unis en vue : 1) de l'ajout d'autres entités et comptes qui présentent un faible risque d'être utilisés par des personnes américaines pour frauder le fisc américain et dont les caractéristiques sont similaires à celles des entités et comptes énumérés dans la présente annexe II à la date de la signature du présent Accord ; ou 2) de la suppression d'entités et de comptes qui, par suite d'un changement de circonstances, ne présentent plus un faible risque d'être utilisés par des personnes américaines pour frauder le fisc américain. Tout ajout ou toute suppression de cet ordre entre en vigueur à la date de la signature de l'entente mutuelle, sauf disposition contraire prévue dans cette entente. Les procédures en vue de parvenir à cette entente mutuelle peuvent être incluses dans l'accord ou l'arrangement visé au paragraphe 6 de l'article 3 du présent Accord.

I. Bénéficiaires effectifs dispensés autres que des Fonds. Les catégories suivantes d'entités doivent être considérées comme des institutions financières non déclarantes finlandaises et comme des bénéficiaires effectifs dispensés de déclaration aux fins des articles 1471 et 1472 de l'Internal Revenue Code des États-Unis, sauf en ce qui concerne un paiement découlant d'une obligation en relation avec une activité financière commerciale dont la nature est celle des activités d'un organisme d'assurance particulier, d'un établissement gérant des dépôts de titres, ou d'un établissement de dépôt.

A. Entités publiques. Le Gouvernement finlandais, une subdivision politique de la Finlande (terme qui, pour éviter toute ambiguïté, comprend un État, une province, un comté ou une municipalité), ou tout établissement ou organisme détenu intégralement par les entités précitées (chacun constituant une « entité publique finlandaise »). Cette catégorie englobe les parties intégrantes, entités contrôlées et subdivisions politiques de la Finlande.

1. Une partie intégrante de la Finlande désigne toute personne, toute organisation, toute agence, tout bureau, tout fonds, toute personne morale ou autre organisation, quelle que soit sa désignation, qui constitue une autorité dirigeante de la Finlande. Le revenu net de l'autorité dirigeante doit être porté au crédit de son propre compte ou d'autres comptes de la Finlande, et aucune fraction de ce revenu ne peut échoir à une personne privée. Une partie intégrante exclut toute personne qui est un dirigeant, un responsable ou un administrateur agissant à titre privé ou personnel.

2. Une entité contrôlée désigne une entité de forme distincte de la Finlande ou qui constitue une entité juridiquement séparée, dès lors que :

i) L'entité est possédée et contrôlée exclusivement par une ou plusieurs entités publiques finlandaises, directement ou par le biais d'une ou de plusieurs entités contrôlées ;

ii) Le revenu net de l'entité est porté au crédit de son propre compte ou des comptes d'une ou plusieurs entités publiques finlandaises, et aucune fraction de ce revenu ne peut échoir à une personne privée ;

iii) Les actifs de l'entité reviennent à une ou plusieurs entités publiques finlandaises en cas de dissolution.

3. Le revenu n'échoit pas à des personnes privées si ces personnes sont les bénéficiaires prévus d'un programme public, et si les activités couvertes par ce programme sont accomplies à l'intention du grand public dans l'intérêt général ou se rapportent à l'administration d'une partie du gouvernement. Nonobstant ce qui précède, le revenu est considéré comme perçu par des personnes privées s'il provient du recours à une entité publique dans le but d'exercer une activité commerciale, comme des services bancaires aux entreprises, par laquelle des prestations financières sont fournies à des personnes privées.

Pour éviter toute ambiguïté, chacune des catégories suivantes d'entités sont considérées comme des institutions financières non déclarantes finlandaises et comme des bénéficiaires effectifs dispensés de déclaration aux fins des articles 1471 et 1472 de l'Internal Revenue Code des États-Unis :

- Finnvera Oyj – Finnvera plc ;
- Vientiluotto Oy - Finnish Export Credit Ltd ; et
- Kuntarahoitus Oyj – Municipality Finance plc.

B. Banque centrale. Banque qui, en vertu de la loi ou d'une décision publique, est l'autorité principale, autre que le Gouvernement de Finlande proprement dit, qui émet des instruments destinés à être utilisés comme monnaie. Cette banque peut inclure un organisme distinct du Gouvernement de Finlande, qu'il soit ou non détenu en tout ou partie par la Finlande.

C. Organisations internationales. Toute organisation internationale ou tout établissement ou organisme détenu intégralement par cette organisation. Cette catégorie englobe toute organisation intergouvernementale (y compris une organisation supranationale) : 1) qui se compose principalement de gouvernements non américains ; 2) qui a conclu un accord de siège avec la Finlande ; et 3) dont les revenus n'échoient pas à des personnes privées.

II. Fonds ayant qualité de bénéficiaires effectifs dispensés de déclaration. Les catégories suivantes d'entités sont considérées comme des institutions financières non déclarantes finlandaises et comme des bénéficiaires effectifs dispensés de déclaration aux fins des articles 1471 et 1472 de l'Internal Revenue Code des États-Unis.

A. Caisse de retraite faisant l'objet d'une convention. Caisse établie en Finlande, à condition qu'elle ait droit à des avantages aux termes d'une convention fiscale entre la Finlande et les États-Unis à l'égard de revenus qu'elle reçoit de sources américaines (ou aurait droit à ces avantages si elle recevait ce type de revenu) à titre de résidente de Finlande, qui satisfait aux critères applicables en matière de limitation des avantages, et s'occupe principalement de l'administration ou du versement de prestations de pension ou de retraite.

B. Caisse de retraite à large participation. Caisse, y compris un organisme de retraite prenant ou non la forme d'une mutuelle, établie en Finlande en vue de verser des prestations de retraite, d'invalidité ou de décès, ou une combinaison d'entre elles, à des bénéficiaires qui sont des salariés actuels ou d'anciens salariés (ou des personnes désignées par ces salariés) d'un ou de plusieurs employeurs en contrepartie de services rendus, dès lors que cette caisse :

1. N'est pas caractérisée par l'existence d'un bénéficiaire unique détenant un droit sur plus de 5 % des actifs de la caisse ;
2. Est soumise à la réglementation publique et communique chaque année des informations sur ses bénéficiaires aux autorités fiscales finlandaises compétentes ; et
3. Satisfait à au moins à l'une des exigences suivantes :
   a) La caisse est généralement dispensée, en Finlande, de l'impôt sur les revenus d'investissement en vertu de la loi finlandaise, en vertu de son statut de régime de retraite ou de pension ;
   b) La caisse reçoit au moins 50 % du total de ses cotisations (à l'exception des transferts d'actifs d'autres régimes visés aux paragraphes A à D de la présente section ou aux comptes de retraite et de pension décrits au point 1 du paragraphe A de la section V de la présente annexe II) des employeurs qui la financent ;
   c) Les versements ou retraits de la caisse sont autorisés uniquement lorsque surviennent les événements prévus en lien avec le départ en retraite, l'invalidité ou le décès (à l'exception des versements périodiques à d'autres caisses de retraite visées aux paragraphes A à D de la présente section ou aux comptes de retraite et de pension décrits au point 1 du paragraphe A de la section V de la présente annexe II), ou des pénalités s'appliquent aux versements ou aux retraits effectués avant la survenue de ces événements ; ou
   d) Les cotisations (à l'exception de certaines cotisations autorisées) des salariés à la caisse sont limitées par référence au revenu d'activité ou ne peuvent dépasser 50 000 dollars par an, en appliquant les règles exposées à l'annexe I relatives à l'agrégation des soldes des comptes et à la conversion monétaire.

C. Caisse de retraite à participation étroite. Caisse établie en Finlande en vue de verser des prestations de retraite, d'invalidité ou de décès à des bénéficiaires qui sont des salariés actuels ou d'anciens salariés (ou des personnes désignées par ces salariés) d'un ou de plusieurs employeurs en contrepartie de services rendus, dès lors que :

1. La caisse compte moins de 50 membres ;
2. La caisse est financée par un ou plusieurs employeurs qui ne sont pas des entités d'investissement ou des EENF passives ;
3. Les cotisations salariales et patronales à la caisse (à l'exception des transferts d'actifs à partir des fonds d'épargne-retraite faisant l'objet d'une convention décrits au paragraphe A de la présente section ou de comptes de retraite et de pension visés au point 1 du paragraphe A de la section V de la présente annexe II) sont limitées par référence, respectivement, au revenu d'activité et à la rémunération du salarié ;

4. Les membres qui ne sont pas établis en Finlande où se situe la caisse ne peuvent pas détenir plus de 20 % des actifs de la caisse ; et
5. La caisse est soumise à la réglementation publique et communique chaque année des informations sur ses bénéficiaires aux autorités fiscales finlandaises compétentes.

D. Caisse de retraite ayant qualité de bénéficiaire effectif dispensé de déclaration. Caisse constituée en Finlande par un bénéficiaire effectif dispensé de déclaration en vue de verser des prestations de retraite, d'invalidité ou de décès à des bénéficiaires ou des membres qui sont des salariés actuels ou d'anciens salariés du bénéficiaire effectif dispensé de déclaration (ou des personnes désignées par ces salariés), ou qui ne sont pas des salariés actuels ou d'anciens salariés, si les prestations versées à ces bénéficiaires ou membres le sont en contrepartie de services personnels rendus au bénéficiaire effectif dispensé de déclaration.

E. Entité d'investissement détenue intégralement par des bénéficiaires effectifs dispensés de déclaration. Entité qui constitue une institution financière finlandaise du seul fait qu'elle est une entité d'investissement, à condition que chaque titulaire direct d'un titre de participation soit un bénéficiaire effectif dispensé de déclaration et que chaque titulaire direct d'un titre de créance dans cette entité soit un établissement de dépôt (par rapport à un prêt fait auprès de cette entité) ou un bénéficiaire effectif dispensé de déclaration.

III. Institutions financières de portée limitée qui remplissent les conditions pour être des IFE réputées conformes. Les institutions financières suivantes sont des institutions financières non déclarantes finlandaises qui sont considérées comme des IFE réputées conformes aux fins de l'article 1471 de l'Internal Revenue Code des États-Unis.

A. Institutions financières disposant d'une base de clientèle locale.

Institution financière finlandaise qui satisfait aux critères suivants :

1. L'institution financière doit être agréée et régie en tant qu'institution financière en vertu de la législation finlandaise ;
2. L'institution financière ne doit pas avoir d'installation fixe d'affaires en dehors du territoire finlandais. À cette fin, une installation fixe d'affaires ne comprend pas un endroit qui n'est pas signalé au public et à partir duquel l'institution financière exerce exclusivement un rôle de soutien administratif ;
3. L'institution financière ne doit pas démarcher des clients ou des titulaires de compte en dehors du territoire finlandais. À cette fin, une institution financière n'est pas réputée avoir sollicité des clients ou des titulaires de comptes en dehors du territoire finlandais au simple motif que l'institution financière : a) exploite un site Web, sous réserve que ledit site n'indique pas expressément que l'institution financière fournit des comptes financiers ou des services à des non-résidents, et ne cible pas ou ne sollicite pas d'une quelconque autre manière des clients américains ou des titulaires de compte américains, ou b) effectue de la publicité dans la presse écrite, sur une station de radio ou de télévision et que ce média est distribué ou diffusé principalement en Finlande, mais est aussi accessoirement distribué ou diffusé dans d'autres pays, sous réserve que la publicité n'indique pas expressément que l'institution financière fournit des comptes financiers ou des services à des non-résidents, et ne cible pas ou ne

sollicite pas d'une quelconque autre manière des clients américains ou des titulaires de comptes américains ;

4. L'institution financière est tenue, en application de la législation finlandaise, d'identifier des titulaires de comptes résidents afin de fournir des renseignements, d'effectuer une retenue à la source de l'impôt concernant des comptes détenus par des résidents de Finlande ou afin de remplir les procédures finlandaises mises en œuvre pour lutter contre le blanchiment (AML) ;
5. Au moins 98 % de la valeur des comptes financiers gérés par l'institution financière doivent être détenus par des résidents (y compris des résidents qui sont des entités) de Finlande ou d'un autre État membre de l'Union européenne ;
6. À compter du 1er juillet 2014 ou avant cette date, l'institution financière doit avoir des règles et des procédures, conformes à celles énoncées à l'annexe I, afin de ne pas détenir un compte financier d'institution financière non participante et de vérifier si l'institution financière ouvre ou tient un compte financier pour toute personne américaine déterminée qui n'est pas un résident de Finlande (y compris une personne américaine qui était un résident de Finlande à la date d'ouverture du compte financier, mais a perdu ensuite cette qualité), ou toute EENF passive dont les personnes détenant le contrôle sont des citoyens américains qui ne sont ni des résidents finlandais ni des résidents américains ;
7. Ces règles et ces procédures doivent prévoir que si un compte financier détenu par une personne américaine déterminée qui n'est pas un résident de Finlande ou par une EENF passive dont les personnes détenant le contrôle sont des résidents américains ou des citoyens américains qui ne sont pas des résidents finlandais est identifié, l'institution financière doit déclarer ledit compte financier comme si elle était une institution financière déclarante finlandaise (y compris les obligations d'enregistrement applicables figurant sur le site Web d'enregistrement de l'IRS consacré à la loi FATCA) ou clôturer ce compte ;
8. Tout compte préexistant détenu par une personne physique qui n'est pas résident de Finlande ou par une entité doit être examiné par ladite institution financière conformément aux procédures visées à l'annexe I applicables aux comptes préexistants afin d'identifier tout compte déclarable américain ou tout compte financier détenu par une institution financière non participante. Si un tel compte est découvert, l'institution financière doit le déclarer comme si elle était une institution financière déclarante finlandaise (y compris les obligations d'enregistrement applicables figurant sur le site Web d'enregistrement de l'IRS consacré à la loi FATCA) ou le clôturer ;
9. Toute entité liée à l'institution financière qui est une institution financière doit être constituée ou régie selon la législation finlandaise et, à l'exception des caisses de retraite décrites aux paragraphes A à D de la section II de la présente annexe II, répondre aux critères définis au présent paragraphe A ; et
10. L'institution financière ne doit pas se doter de directives ou de pratiques discriminatoires dans le cadre de l'ouverture ou de la gestion de comptes financiers pour des personnes physiques qui sont des résidents de Finlande et des personnes américaines déterminées.

B. Banque locale. Institution financière qui satisfait aux critères suivants :

1. L'institution financière fonctionne uniquement en tant que (et est agréée et régie en vertu du droit finlandais en tant que) : a) banque ; ou b) caisse de crédit mutuel ou coopérative de crédit similaire à but non lucratif ;
2. L'activité de l'institution financière consiste principalement à recevoir des dépôts et à accorder des prêts, s'agissant d'une banque, à des clients finaux non liés et, en ce qui concerne une caisse de crédit mutuel ou une coopérative de crédit similaire, à des membres, à condition qu'aucun membre ne détienne une participation de plus de 5 % dans cette caisse ou coopérative ;
3. L'institution financière satisfait aux exigences exposées aux points 2 et 3 du paragraphe A de la présente section, à condition que, outre les limites imposées au site Web décrites au point 3 du paragraphe A de la présente section, le site Web ne permette pas l'ouverture d'un compte financier ;
4. L'institution financière n'a pas plus de 175 millions de dollars d'actifs à son bilan et l'institution financière et toutes les entités liées, globalement, n'ont pas plus de 500 millions de dollars d'actifs totaux à leurs bilans consolidés ou combinés ;
5. Toute entité liée doit être constituée ou régie en vertu de la législation finlandaise, et toute entité liée qui est une institution financière, à l'exception d'une entité liée qui est un fonds de pension visé aux paragraphes A à D de la section II de la présente annexe II ou une institution financière tenant uniquement des comptes de faible valeur décrits au paragraphe C de la présente section, doit répondre aux critères définis au présent paragraphe B.

C. Institution financière tenant uniquement des comptes de faible valeur. Institution financière finlandaise qui satisfait aux critères suivants :

1. L'institution financière n'est pas une entité d'investissement ;
2. Aucun compte financier tenu par l'institution financière ou par toute entité liée n'a un solde ou une valeur supérieur à 50 000 dollars lorsque l'on applique les règles énoncées à l'annexe I relatives à l'agrégation de comptes et à la conversion monétaire ; et
3. L'institution financière n'a pas plus de 50 millions de dollars d'actifs à son bilan et l'institution financière et toutes les entités liées, globalement, n'ont pas plus de 50 millions de dollars d'actifs totaux à leurs bilans consolidés ou combinés.

D. Émetteur de carte de crédit homologué. Institution financière finlandaise qui satisfait aux critères suivants :

1. L'institution financière jouit de ce statut uniquement parce qu'elle est un émetteur de cartes de crédit qui accepte les dépôts à la seule condition qu'un client procède à un paiement dont le montant dépasse le solde dû au titre de la carte et que cet excédent ne soit pas immédiatement restitué au client ; et
2. À compter du 1er juillet 2014 ou avant cette date, l'institution financière met en œuvre des règles et des procédures visant à empêcher un client de procéder à un dépôt supérieur à 50 000 dollars ou à faire en sorte que tout dépôt supérieur à 50 000 dollars, en appliquant dans les deux cas les règles énoncées à l'annexe I concernant l'agrégation des soldes de comptes et la conversion monétaire, soit remboursé au client dans un délai de 60 jours. À cette fin, le dépôt d'un client

exclut les soldes créditeurs imputables à des frais contestés, mais inclut les soldes créditeurs résultant de retours de marchandises.

IV. Entités d'investissement pouvant prétendre au statut d'IFE réputées conformes et autres règles spéciales. Les institutions financières décrites aux paragraphes A à D de la présente section sont des institutions financières non déclarantes finlandaises qui sont considérées comme des IFE réputées conformes aux fins de l'article 1471 de l'Internal Revenue Code des États-Unis. En outre, le paragraphe E de la présente section énonce des règles spécifiques applicables aux entités d'investissement.

A. Entité d'investissement parrainée et société étrangère contrôlée[1]. Institution financière décrite au point 1 ou au point 2 du paragraphe A de la présente section et parrainée par une entité qui satisfait aux critères du point 3 du paragraphe A de la présente section.

1. Une institution financière est une entité d'investissement parrainée : a) s'il s'agit d'une entité d'investissement établie en Finlande qui n'est ni un intermédiaire qualifié, ni une société de personnes étrangère susceptible de faire l'objet d'une retenue à la source ni un trust étranger susceptible de faire l'objet d'une retenue à la source conformément à la réglementation du Trésor des États-Unis ; b) si une entité a convenu avec l'institution financière d'agir en tant qu'entité parrain pour l'institution financière.

2. Une institution financière est une société étrangère contrôlée parrainée : a) si l'institution financière est une société étrangère contrôlée constituée en vertu de la législation finlandaise qui n'est ni un intermédiaire qualifié, ni une société de personnes étrangère susceptible de faire l'objet d'une retenue à la source ni un trust étranger susceptible de faire l'objet d'une retenue à la source conformément à la réglementation du Trésor des États-Unis ; b) si l'institution financière est détenue exclusivement, directement ou indirectement, par une institution financière déclarante américaine qui accepte d'agir ou exige d'une entité affiliée de l'institution financière qu'elle agisse comme une entité parrain pour l'institution financière ; c) si l'institution financière partage un système de comptes électronique commun avec l'entité parrain qui permet à cette dernière d'identifier tous les titulaires de compte et les bénéficiaires de l'institution financière et d'accéder à tous les renseignements sur les comptes et les clients conservés par l'institution financière, notamment les données d'identification des clients, les documents relatifs aux clients, les soldes de compte et tous les paiements effectués aux titulaires de compte ou aux bénéficiaires.

3. L'entité parrain se conforme aux exigences suivantes :

a) L'entité parrain est autorisée à agir pour le compte de l'institution financière (par exemple à titre de gestionnaire de fonds, d'administrateur, de directeur ou d'associé gérant) pour respecter les obligations d'enregistrement

[1] Une « société étrangère contrôlée » désigne toute société étrangère si plus de 50 % du total des droits de vote combinés de toutes les catégories d'actions de cette société ayant droit de vote, ou la valeur totale des actions de cette société, est détenu ou est considéré comme détenu, par des « actionnaires américains » à n'importe quel jour de l'année d'imposition de cette société étrangère. Aux fins du présent paragraphe, l'expression « actionnaire américain » désigne, en ce qui concerne toute société étrangère, une personne américaine qui détient, ou est considérée comme détenant, 10 % ou plus du total combiné des droits de vote de toutes les catégories d'actions avec droit de vote de cette société étrangère.

applicables figurant sur le site Web d'enregistrement de l'IRS dédié à la loi FATCA ;

b) L'entité parrain est enregistrée en tant que telle auprès de l'IRS sur le site Web d'enregistrement de l'IRS dédié à la loi FATCA ;

c) Si l'entité parrain identifie un compte déclarable américain par rapport à l'institution financière, elle enregistre l'institution financière conformément aux obligations d'enregistrement applicables figurant sur le site Web d'enregistrement de l'IRS dédié à la loi FATCA au plus tard le dernier en date des jours suivants : le 31 décembre 2015 ou à la date tombant 90 jours après la première identification d'un tel compte déclarable américain ;

d) L'entité parrain s'engage à effectuer, pour le compte de l'institution financière, toutes les obligations de diligence raisonnable, de retenue à la source, de déclaration et autres que l'institution financière aurait été tenue d'effectuer si elle était une institution financière déclarante finlandaise ;

e) L'entité parrain identifie l'institution financière et inclut le numéro d'identification de l'institution financière (obtenu en respectant les obligations d'enregistrement applicables figurant sur le site Web d'enregistrement de l'IRS dédié à la loi FATCA) dans toutes les déclarations faites pour le compte de l'institution financière ;

f) Le statut d'entité parrain de l'entité n'a pas été révoqué.

B. Organisme de placement parrainé ayant peu d'actionnaires. Institution financière finlandaise qui satisfait aux critères suivants :

1. L'institution financière jouit de ce statut uniquement parce qu'il s'agit d'une entité d'investissement et qu'elle n'est ni un intermédiaire qualifié, ni une société de personnes étrangère susceptible de faire l'objet d'une retenue à la source ni un trust étranger susceptible de faire l'objet d'une retenue à la source conformément à la réglementation pertinente du Trésor des États-Unis ;

2. L'entité parrain est une institution financière déclarante américaine, une IFE déclarante de modèle 1 ou une IFE participante, est autorisée à agir pour le compte de l'institution financière (par exemple à titre de gestionnaire professionnel, d'administrateur ou d'associé gérant) et s'engage à effectuer, pour le compte de l'institution financière, toutes les obligations de diligence raisonnable, de retenue à la source, de déclaration et autres que l'institution financière aurait été tenue d'effectuer si elle était une institution financière déclarante finlandaise ;

3. L'institution financière ne se présente pas comme un organisme de placement pour des parties non associées ;

4. Trente personnes au maximum détiennent l'ensemble des titres de créances et des titres de participation dans l'institution financière (compte non tenu des titres de créances détenus par des IFE participantes et des IFE réputées conformes et des titres de participation détenus par une entité si l'entité détient 100 % des titres de participation dans l'institution financière et est elle-même une institution financière parrainée décrite dans le présent paragraphe B) ; et

5. L'entité parrain se conforme aux exigences suivantes :

a) L'entité parrain est enregistrée en tant que telle auprès de l'IRS sur le site Web d'enregistrement de l'IRS dédié à la loi FATCA ;

b) L'entité parrain s'engage à effectuer, pour le compte de l'institution financière, toutes les obligations de diligence raisonnable, de retenue à la source, de déclaration et autres que l'institution financière aurait été tenue d'effectuer si elle était une institution financière déclarante finlandaise, et conserve la documentation collectée en ce qui concerne l'institution financière pendant une période de six ans ;

c) L'entité parrain identifie l'institution financière dans toutes les déclarations effectuées pour le compte de cette dernière ; et

d) Le statut d'entité parrain de l'entité n'a pas été révoqué.

C. Conseillers en placement et gestionnaires de portefeuilles. Entité d'investissement établie en Finlande qui est une institution financière du seul fait : i) qu'elle donne des conseils en investissement à un client et agit pour le compte de ce dernier ; ou ii) qu'elle gère des portefeuilles pour un client et agit pour le compte de ce dernier, aux fins d'investir, de gérer ou d'administrer des fonds déposés au nom du client auprès d'une institution financière autre qu'une institution financière non participante.

D. Organisme de placement collectif. Entité d'investissement établie en Finlande et réglementée en tant qu'organisme de placement collectif, sous réserve que toutes les participations dans cet organisme de placement collectif (y compris les titres de créances supérieurs à 50 000 dollars) sont détenues directement ou indirectement par un ou plusieurs bénéficiaires effectifs dispensés de déclaration, par des EENF actives visées au point 4 du paragraphe B de la section VI de l'annexe I, des personnes américaines qui ne sont pas des personnes américaines déterminées ou des institutions financières qui ne sont pas des institutions financières non participantes.

E. Règles spéciales. Les règles suivantes s'appliquent aux entités d'investissement :

a) En ce qui concerne les participations dans une entité d'investissement qui est un organisme de placement collectif décrit au paragraphe D de la présente section, les obligations déclaratives de toute entité d'investissement (autre qu'une institution financière par l'intermédiaire de laquelle des participations dans l'organisme de placement collectif sont détenues) sont considérées comme remplies ;

b) En ce qui concerne les participations dans :

i) Une entité d'investissement établie dans une juridiction partenaire qui est réglementée en tant qu'organisme de placement collectif et dont toutes les participations (y compris les titres de créances supérieurs à 50 000 dollars) sont détenues directement ou indirectement par un ou plusieurs bénéficiaires effectifs dispensés de déclaration, des EENF actives visées au point 4 du paragraphe B de la section VI de l'annexe I, des personnes américaines qui ne sont pas des personnes américaines déterminées ou des institutions financières qui ne sont pas des institutions financières non participantes ; ou

ii) Une entité d'investissement qui est un organisme de placement collectif en application de la réglementation du Trésor des États-Unis ;

Les obligations déclaratives de toute entité d'investissement qui est une institution financière finlandaise (autre qu'une institution financière par l'intermédiaire de laquelle des participations dans un organisme de placement collectif sont détenues) sont considérées comme remplies.

c) En ce qui concerne les participations dans une entité d'investissement établie en Finlande qui n'est pas visée au paragraphe D ni au point 2 du paragraphe E de la présente section, conformément au paragraphe 3 de l'article 5 du présent Accord, les obligations déclaratives des autres entités d'investissement concernant ces participations sont considérées comme remplies si les renseignements devant être déclarés par la première entité d'investissement en vertu du présent Accord et à l'égard de ces participations sont déclarés par cette entité d'investissement ou par une autre personne.

V. Produits exclus de la définition des comptes financiers. Les comptes suivants sont exclus de la définition des comptes financiers et, en conséquence, ne sont pas considérés comme des comptes déclarables américains.

A. Certains comptes d'épargne.

1. Compte de retraite ou de pension. Compte de retraite ou de pension géré en Finlande qui répond aux critères suivants en vertu du droit finlandais :

a) Le compte est réglementé en tant que compte de retraite personnel ou fait partie d'un régime de retraite ou de pension agréé ou réglementé qui prévoit le versement de prestations de retraite ou de pension (y compris d'invalidité ou de décès) ;

b) Le compte bénéficie d'un traitement fiscal favorable (les versements qui seraient normalement soumis à l'impôt en vertu du droit finlandais sont déductibles ou exclus du revenu brut du titulaire du compte ou sont imposés à taux réduit, ou l'imposition du revenu d'investissement généré par le compte est différée ou minorée) ;

c) Des renseignements relatifs au compte doivent être communiqués chaque année aux autorités fiscales finlandaises ;

d) Les retraits sont possibles uniquement à partir de l'âge fixé pour le départ en retraite, de la survenue d'une invalidité ou d'un décès, ou les retraits effectués avant de tels événements sont soumis à des pénalités ; et

e) Soit i) les cotisations annuelles sont limitées à 50 000 dollars ou moins, soit ii) un plafond de 1 000 000 de dollars ou moins s'applique au total des cotisations versées au cours de la vie du souscripteur, en suivant à chaque fois les règles définies à l'annexe I concernant l'agrégation des soldes de comptes et la conversion monétaire.

2. Comptes d'épargne hors retraite. Compte géré en Finlande (autre qu'un contrat d'assurance ou un contrat de rente) qui répond aux critères suivants en vertu de la législation de la Finlande :

a) Le compte est réglementé en tant qu'instrument d'épargne à des fins autres que la retraite ;

b) Le compte bénéficie d'un traitement fiscal favorable (les versements qui seraient normalement soumis à l'impôt en vertu du droit finlandais sont déductibles ou exclus du revenu brut du titulaire du compte ou sont imposés à taux réduit, ou l'imposition du revenu d'investissement généré par le compte est différée ou minorée) ;

c) Les retraits sont conditionnés au respect de certains critères liés à l'objectif du compte d'épargne (par exemple, le versement de prestations d'éducation ou médicales), ou des pénalités s'appliquent aux retraits effectués avant que ces critères ne soient remplis ;

d) Les cotisations annuelles sont plafonnées à 50 000 dollars ou moins, en appliquant les règles définies en annexe I concernant l'agrégation des soldes de comptes et la conversion monétaire.

B. Certains contrats d'assurance vie à échéance prédéterminée. Contrat d'assurance vie géré en Finlande dont la période de couverture s'achève avant que l'assuré n'atteigne l'âge de 90 ans, à condition que le contrat réponde aux critères suivants :

1. Des primes périodiques, dont le montant reste constant dans le temps, sont dues au moins une fois par an au cours de la durée d'existence du contrat ou jusqu'à ce que l'assuré atteigne l'âge de 90 ans, si cette période est plus courte ;

2. Il n'est pas possible pour quiconque de bénéficier des prestations contractuelles (par retrait, prêt ou autre) sans résilier le contrat ;

3. La somme (autre qu'une prestation de décès) payable en cas d'annulation ou de résiliation du contrat ne peut pas dépasser le total des primes acquittées au titre du contrat, moins l'ensemble des frais de mortalité, de morbidité et d'exploitation (qu'ils soient ou non imposés) pour la période ou les périodes d'existence du contrat et toute somme payée avant l'annulation ou la résiliation du contrat ;

4. Le contrat n'est pas conservé par un cessionnaire à titre onéreux.

C. Compte détenu par une succession. Compte géré en Finlande qui est détenu uniquement par une succession si la documentation de ce compte comprend une copie du testament du défunt ou du certificat de décès.

D. Compte séquestre. Compte géré en Finlande ouvert en lien avec l'un des éléments suivants :

1. Une ordonnance ou un jugement d'un tribunal.

2. La vente, l'échange ou la location d'un bien immobilier ou personnel, à condition que le compte réponde aux exigences suivantes :

a) Le compte est financé uniquement par un acompte versé à titre d'arrhes d'un montant suffisant pour garantir une obligation directement liée à la transaction, ou par un paiement similaire, ou est financé par un actif financier inscrit au compte en lien avec la vente, l'échange ou la location du bien ;

b) Le compte est ouvert et utilisé uniquement pour garantir l'obligation impartie à l'acheteur de payer le prix d'achat du bien, au vendeur de payer tout passif éventuel, ou au bailleur ou au locataire de prendre en charge tout dommage lié au bien loué selon les dispositions du bail ;

c) Les avoirs du compte, y compris le revenu qu'il génère, seront payés ou versés à l'acheteur, au vendeur, au bailleur ou au locataire (y compris pour couvrir ses obligations) au moment de la vente, de l'échange ou de la cession du bien, ou à l'expiration du bail ;

d) Le compte n'est pas un compte sur marge ou similaire ouvert en lien avec une vente ou un échange d'un actif financier ;

e) Le compte n'est pas associé à un compte de carte de crédit.

3. L'obligation pour une institution financière qui octroie un prêt garanti par un bien immobilier de réserver une partie d'un paiement uniquement pour faciliter à l'avenir le paiement d'impôts ou de primes d'assurance liés au bien immobilier.

4. L'obligation pour une institution financière de faciliter le paiement d'impôts à l'avenir.

E. Comptes de juridictions partenaires. Compte géré en Finlande et exclu de la définition du compte financier en vertu d'un accord entre les États-Unis et une autre juridiction partenaire pour faciliter la mise en œuvre de la loi FATCA, à condition que ledit compte soit soumis aux mêmes exigences et à la même surveillance en vertu du droit de ladite autre juridiction partenaire comme si ce compte était établi dans ladite juridiction partenaire et géré par une institution financière de la juridiction partenaire dans ladite juridiction partenaire.

VI. Définitions. Les définitions supplémentaires suivantes s'appliquent aux éléments décrits ci-dessus :

A. IFE déclarante selon le modèle 1. L'expression « IFE déclarante selon le modèle 1 » désigne une institution financière à l'égard de laquelle un gouvernement autre que celui des États-Unis ou une agence dudit gouvernement s'engage à obtenir et à échanger des renseignements en application de l'accord intergouvernemental de modèle 1 et qui n'est pas une institution financière considérée comme une institution financière non participante selon l'accord intergouvernemental de Modèle 1. Aux fins de la présente définition, l'expression « accord intergouvernemental de modèle 1 » désigne un accord entre les États-Unis ou le Département du Trésor et un gouvernement autre que celui des États-Unis ou une ou plusieurs agences de ce gouvernement pour la mise en œuvre de la loi FATCA moyennant la déclaration par les institutions financières au gouvernement étranger ou à ses agences, suivie par la transmission automatique des renseignements déclarés à l'IRS.

B. IFE participante. L'expression « IFE participante » désigne une institution financière qui s'est engagée à se conformer aux exigences d'un accord d'IFE, y compris une institution financière décrite dans un accord intergouvernemental de modèle 2 qui s'est engagée à se conformer aux exigences d'un accord d'IFE. L'expression englobe également la succursale intermédiaire agréée d'une institution financière déclarante américaine, sauf si cette succursale est une IFE déclarante selon le modèle 1. Aux fins de la présente définition, l'expression « accord d'IFE » désigne un accord qui énonce les exigences pour qu'une institution financière soit traitée comme se conformant aux exigences de l'article 1471 (b) de l'Internal Revenue Code des États-Unis. En outre, aux fins de la présente définition, l'expression « accord intergouvernemental de modèle 2 » désigne un accord entre les États-Unis ou le Département du Trésor et un gouvernement autre que celui des États-Unis ou une ou plusieurs agences de ce gouvernement pour la mise en œuvre de la loi FATCA moyennant la déclaration par les institutions financières directement à l'IRS conformément aux exigences d'un accord d'IFE, complétée par l'échange de renseignements entre le gouvernement étranger ou l'agence du gouvernement étranger en question et l'IRS.

MÉMORANDUM D'ENTENTE CONCERNANT L'ACCORD ENTRE LE GOUVERNEMENT DE LA RÉPUBLIQUE DE FINLANDE ET LE GOUVERNEMENT DES ÉTATS-UNIS D'AMÉRIQUE RELATIF AU RENFORCEMENT DU RESPECT DES OBLIGATIONS FISCALES INTERNATIONALES ET À LA MISE EN ŒUVRE DE LA LOI FATCA

Ce jour, au moment de la signature de l'Accord entre le Gouvernement de la République de Finlande et le Gouvernement des États-Unis d'Amérique relatif au renforcement du respect des obligations fiscales internationales et à la mise en œuvre de la loi FATCA (ci-après l'« Accord »), les représentants de la République de Finlande et des États-Unis d'Amérique souhaitent confirmer leur accord sur les points suivants :

En ce qui concerne le paragraphe 1 de l'article premier (Définitions) de l'Accord, il est entendu que, dans le cas de valeurs enregistrées auprès d'un dépositaire central de titres finlandais (Arvopaperikeskus) tel que défini au paragraphe 3 du chapitre I de la loi finlandaise sur les systèmes de comptes courants de titres et les services de règlement (Laki arvo-osuusjärjestelmästä ja selvitystoiminnasta 14.12.2012/749) qui sont détenues par une ou plusieurs autres institutions financières autres que des institutions financières non participantes, ou par leur intermédiaire, les comptes financiers concernés seront considérés comme étant détenus par ces autres institutions financières, et ces dernières seront responsables de toute obligation déclarative à l'égard de ces comptes financiers. Nonobstant ce qui précède, conformément au paragraphe 3 de l'article 5 de l'Accord, le dépositaire central de titres finlandais peut faire la déclaration au nom de ces autres institutions financières.

En ce qui concerne le paragraphe D de la section VI de l'annexe I, il est entendu que dans le cas de la Finlande, un certificat de résidence délivré par un organisme gouvernemental autorisé désigne un certificat de résidence fiscale délivré par l'administration fiscale finlandaise.

SIGNÉ à Helsinki, le 5 mars 2014, en double exemplaire, en langue anglaise.

Pour le Gouvernement de la République de Finlande :
[JUTTA URPILAINEN]

Pour le Gouvernement des États-Unis d'Amérique :
[BRUCE ORECK]

No. 53561

Finland and Turkey

Agreement between the Republic of Finland and the Republic of Turkey for the avoidance of double taxation with respect to taxes on income (with protocol). Istanbul, 6 October 2009

Entry into force: *4 May 2012, in accordance with article 28*

Authentic texts: *English, Finnish and Turkish*

Registration with the Secretariat of the United Nations: *Finland, 9 March 2016*

Finlande et Turquie

Accord entre la République de Finlande et la République turque tendant à éviter les doubles impositions en matière d'impôts sur le revenu (avec protocole). Istanbul, 6 octobre 2009

Entrée en vigueur : *4 mai 2012, conformément à l'article 28*

Textes authentiques : *anglais, finnois et turc*

Enregistrement au Secrétariat de l'Organisation des Nations Unies : *Finlande, 9 mars 2016*

[TEXT IN ENGLISH – TEXTE EN ANGLAIS]

AGREEMENT

BETWEEN

THE REPUBLIC OF FINLAND AND THE REPUBLIC OF TURKEY

FOR THE AVOIDANCE OF DOUBLE TAXATION

WITH RESPECT TO TAXES ON INCOME

THE GOVERNMENT OF THE REPUBLIC OF FINLAND

AND

THE GOVERNMENT OF THE REPUBLIC OF TURKEY

Desiring to conclude an agreement for the avoidance of double taxation with respect to taxes on income,

HAVE AGREED AS FOLLOWS:

Article 1

PERSONS COVERED

This Agreement shall apply to persons who are residents of one or both of the Contracting States.

Article 2

TAXES COVERED

1. This Agreement shall apply to taxes on income imposed on behalf of a Contracting State or of its local authorities, irrespective of the manner in which they are levied.

2. There shall be regarded as taxes on income all taxes imposed on total income, or on elements of income, including taxes on gains from the alienation of movable or immovable property, taxes on the total amounts of wages or salaries paid by enterprises, as well as taxes on capital appreciation.

3. The existing taxes to which the Agreement shall apply are:

a) in Turkey:

i) the income tax (gelir vergisi); and
ii) the corporation tax (kurumlar vergisi) ;

(hereinafter referred to as "Turkish tax");

b) in Finland:

i) the state income taxes (valtion tuloverot; de statliga inkomstskatterna);
ii) the corporate income tax (yhteisöjen tulovero; inkomstskatten för samfund);
iii) the communal tax (kunnallisvero; kommunalskatten);
iv) the church tax (kirkollisvero; kyrkoskatten);
v) the tax withheld at source from interest (korkotulon lähdevero; källskatten på ränteinkomst) and
vi) the tax withheld at source from non-residents' income (rajoitetusti verovelvollisen lähdevero; källskatten för begransat skattskyldig);

(hereinafter referred to as "Finnish tax").

4. The Agreement shall apply also to any identical or substantially similar taxes which are imposed after the date of signature of the Agreement in addition to, or in place of, the existing taxes. The competent authorities of the Contracting States shall notify each other of any significant changes that have been made in their respective taxation laws.

Article 3

GENERAL DEFINITIONS

1. For the purposes of this Agreement, unless the context otherwise requires:

a) i) the term "Turkey" means the Turkish territory including territorial sea and air space above it, as well as the maritime areas over which it has jurisdiction or sovereign rights for the purpose of exploration, exploitation and conservation of natural resources, pursuant to international law;

ii) the term "Finland" means the Republic of Finland and, when used in a geographical sense, means the territory of the Republic of Finland, and any area adjacent to the territorial waters of the Republic of Finland within which, under the laws of Finland and in accordance with international law, the rights of Finland with respect to the exploration for and exploitation of the natural resources of the sea bed and its sub-soil and of the superjacent waters may be exercised;

b) the terms "a Contracting State" and "the other Contracting State" mean Turkey or Finland as the context requires;

c) the term "person" includes an individual, a company and any other body of persons;

d) the term "company" means any body corporate or any entity that is treated as a body corporate for tax purposes;

e) the term "place of incorporation" means the legal head office of a company registered under the Turkish Code of Commerce or the place of registration of a company under Finnish law, as the case may be;

f) the term "national" in relation to a Contracting State, means:

i) any individual possessing the nationality or citizenship of that Contracting State; and

ii) any legal person, partnership or association deriving its status as such from the laws in force in that Contracting State;

g) the terms "enterprise of a Contracting State" and "enterprise of the other Contracting State" mean respectively an enterprise carried on by a resident of a Contracting State and an enterprise carried on by a resident of the other Contracting State;

h) the term "competent authority" means:

i) in Turkey, the Minister of Finance or his authorised representative; and

ii) in Finland, the Ministry of Finance, its authorised representative or the authority which, by the Ministry of Finance, is designated as competent authority;

i) the term "international traffic" means any transport by a ship, an aircraft or a road vehicle operated by an enterprise of a Contracting State, except when the ship, aircraft or road vehicle is operated solely between places in the other Contracting State.

2. As regards the application of the Agreement at any time by a Contracting State any term not defined therein shall, unless the context otherwise requires, have the meaning that it has at that time under the law of that State for the purposes of the taxes to which the Agreement applies, any meaning under the applicable tax laws of that State prevailing over a meaning given to the term under other laws of that State.

Article 4

RESIDENT

1. For the purposes of this Agreement, the term "resident of a Contracting State" means any person who, under the laws of that State, is liable to tax therein by reason of his domicile, residence, place of incorporation, place of management or any other criterion of a similar nature, and also includes that State and any statutory body or local authority thereof. This term, however, does not include any person who is liable to tax in that State in respect only of income from sources in that State.

2. Where by reason of the provisions of paragraph 1 an individual is a resident of both Contracting States, then his status shall be determined as follows:

a) he shall be deemed to be a resident only of the State in which he has a permanent home available to him; if he has a permanent home available to him in both States, he shall be deemed to be a resident only of the State with which his personal and economic relations are closer (centre of vital interests);

b) if the State in which he has his centre of vital interests cannot be determined, or if he has not a permanent home available to him in either State, he shall be deemed to be a resident only of the State in which he has an habitual abode;

c) if he has an habitual abode in both States or in neither of them, he shall be deemed to be a resident only of the State of which he is a national;

d) if he is a national of both States or of neither of them, the competent authorities of the Contracting States shall settle the question by mutual agreement.

3. Where by reason of the provisions of paragraph 1 a person other than an individual is a resident of both Contracting States, then it shall be deemed to be a resident only of the State in which it has been incorporated.

Article 5

PERMANENT ESTABLISHMENT

1. For the purposes of this Agreement, the term "permanent establishment" means a fixed place of business through which the business of an enterprise is wholly or partly carried on.

2. The term "permanent establishment" includes especially:

a) a place of management;

b) a branch;

c) an office;

d) a factory;

e) a workshop; and

f) a mine, an oil or gas well, a quarry or any other place of extraction of natural resources.

3. A building site, construction, assembly or installation project or supervisory activities in connection therewith constitute a permanent establishment only if such site, project or activities continue for a period of more than six months.

4. Notwithstanding the preceding provisions of this Article, the term "permanent establishment" shall be deemed not to include:

a) the use of facilities solely for the purpose of storage, display or delivery of goods or merchandise belonging to the enterprise;

b) the maintenance of a stock of goods or merchandise belonging to the enterprise solely for the purpose of storage, display or delivery;

c) the maintenance of a stock of goods or merchandise belonging to the enterprise solely for the purpose of processing by another enterprise;

d) the maintenance of a fixed place of business solely for the purpose of purchasing goods or merchandise or of collecting information, for the enterprise;

e) the maintenance of a fixed place of business solely for the purpose of carrying on, for the enterprise, any other activity of a preparatory or auxiliary character;

f) the maintenance of a fixed place of business solely for any combination of activities mentioned in sub-paragraphs a) to e), provided that the overall activity of the fixed place of business resulting from this combination is of a preparatory or auxiliary character.

5. Notwithstanding the provisions of paragraphs 1 and 2, where a person - other than an agent of an independent status to whom paragraph 6 applies - is acting in a Contracting State on behalf of an enterprise of the other Contracting State, that enterprise shall be deemed to have a

permanent establishment in the first-mentioned Contracting State in respect of any activities which that person undertakes for the enterprise, if such a person:

a) has and habitually exercises in that State an authority to conclude contracts in the name of the enterprise, unless the activities of such person are limited to those mentioned in paragraph 4 which, if exercised through a fixed place of business would not make this fixed place of business a permanent establishment under the provisions of that paragraph; or

b) has no such authority, but habitually maintains in the first-mentioned State a stock of goods or merchandise from which he regularly delivers goods or merchandise on behalf of the enterprise.

6. An enterprise shall not be deemed to have a permanent establishment in a Contracting State merely because it carries on business in that State through a broker, general commission agent or any other agent of an independent status, provided that such persons are acting in the ordinary course of their business.

7. The fact that a company which is a resident of a Contracting State controls or is controlled by a company which is a resident of the other Contracting State, or which carries on business in that other State (whether through a permanent establishment or otherwise), shall not of itself constitute either company a permanent establishment of the other.

Article 6

INCOME FROM IMMOVABLE PROPERTY

1. Income derived by a resident of a Contracting State from immovable property (including income from agriculture or forestry) situated in the other Contracting State may be taxed in that other State.

2. The term "immovable property" shall have the meaning which it has under the law of the Contracting State in which the property in question is situated. The term shall in any case include property accessory to immovable property, livestock and equipment used in agriculture (including the breeding and cultivation of fish) and forestry, rights to which the provisions of general law respecting landed property apply, usufruct of immovable property and rights to variable or fixed payments as consideration for the working of, or the right to work, mineral deposits, sources and other natural resources; ships and aircraft shall not be regarded as immovable property.

3. The provisions of paragraph 1 shall apply to income derived from the direct use, letting or use in any other form of immovable property.

4. Where the ownership of shares or other corporate rights in a company entitles the owner of such shares or corporate rights to the enjoyment of immovable property held by the company, the income from the direct use, letting, or use in any other form of such right to enjoyment may be taxed in the Contracting State in which the immovable property is situated.

5. The provisions of paragraphs 1 and 3 shall also apply to the income from immovable property of an enterprise and to income from immovable property used for the performance of independent personal services.

Article 7

BUSINESS PROFITS

1. The profits of an enterprise of a Contracting State shall be taxable only in that State unless the enterprise carries on business in the other Contracting State through a permanent establishment situated therein. If the enterprise carries on business as aforesaid, the profits of the enterprise may be taxed in the other State but only so much of them as is attributable to that permanent establishment.

2. Subject to the provisions of paragraph 3, where an enterprise of a Contracting State carries on business in the other Contracting State through a permanent establishment situated therein, there shall in each Contracting State be attributed to that permanent establishment the profits which it might be expected to make if it were a distinct and separate enterprise engaged in the same or similar activities under the same or similar conditions and dealing wholly independently with the enterprise of which it is a permanent establishment.

3. In determining the profits of a permanent establishment, there shall be allowed as deductions expenses which are incurred for the purposes of the permanent establishment, including executive and general administrative expenses so incurred, whether in the State in which the permanent establishment is situated or elsewhere. However, no such deduction will be allowed in respect of participations to the expenses and losses of the head office or other permanent establishments situated abroad and likewise, the amounts paid by the permanent establishment to the head office of the enterprise or any of its other offices, by way of royalties, interests, commissions or other similar payments.

4. No profits shall be attributed to a permanent establishment by reason of the mere purchase by that permanent establishment of goods or merchandise for the enterprise.

5. Where profits include items of income which are dealt with separately in other Articles of this Agreement, then the provisions of those Articles shall not be affected by the provisions of this Article.

Article 8

SHIPPING, AIR AND ROAD TRANSPORT

1. Profits of an enterprise of a Contracting State from the operation of ships, aircraft or road vehicles in international traffic shall be taxable only in that State.

2.The provisions of paragraph 1 shall also apply to profits from the participation in a pool, a joint business or an international operating agency.

Article 9

ASSOCIATED ENTERPRISES

1. Where

a) an enterprise of a Contracting State participates directly or indirectly in the management, control or capital of an enterprise of the other Contracting State, or

b) the same persons participate directly or indirectly in the management, control or capital of an enterprise of a Contracting State and an enterprise of the other Contracting State,

and in either case conditions are made or imposed between the two enterprises in their commercial or financial relations which differ from those which would be made between independent enterprises, then any profits which would, but for those conditions, have accrued to one of the enterprises, but, by reason of those conditions, have not so accrued, may be included in the profits of that enterprise and taxed accordingly.

2. Where a Contracting State includes in the profits of an enterprise of that State - and taxes accordingly - profits on which an enterprise of the other Contracting State has been charged to tax in that other State and the profits so included are by the first-mentioned State claimed to be profits which would have accrued to the enterprise of the first-mentioned State if the conditions made between the two enterprises had been those which would have been made between independent enterprises, then that other State shall make an appropriate adjustment to the amount of the tax charged therein on those profits, where that other State considers the adjustment justified. In determining such adjustment, due regard shall be had to the other provisions of this Agreement and the competent authorities of the Contracting States shall if necessary consult each other.

Article 10

DIVIDENDS

1. Dividends paid by a company which is a resident of a Contracting State to a resident of the other Contracting State may be taxed in that other State.

2. However, such dividends may also be taxed in the Contracting State of which the company paying the dividends is a resident and according to the laws of that State, but if the beneficial owner of the dividends is a resident of the other Contracting State, the tax so charged shall not exceed:

a) 5 per cent of the gross amount of the dividends if the beneficial owner is a company (other than a partnership) which holds directly at least 25 per cent of the capital of the company paying the dividends;

b) 15 per cent of the gross amount of the dividends in all other cases.

This paragraph shall not affect the taxation of the company in respect of the profits out of which the dividends are paid.

3. The term "dividends" as used in this Article means income from shares, "jouissance" shares or "jouissance" rights, founders' shares or other rights, not being debt-claims, participating in profits, as well as income from other corporate rights which is subjected to the same taxation treatment as income from shares by the laws of the State of which the company making the distribution is a resident.

4. Profits of a company which is resident of a Contracting State carrying on business in the other Contracting State through a permanent establishment situated therein may, after having been taxed under Article 7, be taxed on the remaining amount in the Contracting State in which the permanent establishment is situated, but the rate of tax so charged shall not exceed:

a) 5 per cent of the remaining amount provided that such profits are exempt from tax in the Contracting State in which the company is a resident;

b) 15 per cent of the remaining amount in all other cases.

5. The provisions of paragraphs 1 and 2 shall not apply if the beneficial owner of the dividends, being a resident of a Contracting State, carries on business in the other Contracting State of which the company paying the dividends is a resident, through a permanent establishment situated therein or performs in that other State independent personal services from a fixed base situated therein and the holding in respect of which the dividends are paid is effectively connected with such permanent establishment or fixed base. In such case the provisions of Article 7 or Article 14, as the case may be, shall apply.

6. Subject to the provisions of paragraph 4 of this Article, where a company which is a resident of a Contracting State derives profits or income from the other Contracting State, that other State may not impose any tax on the dividends paid by the company, except insofar as such dividends are paid to a resident of that other State or insofar as the holding in respect of which the dividends are paid is effectively connected with a permanent establishment or a fixed base situated in that other State, nor subject the company's undistributed profits to a tax on the company's undistributed profits, even if the dividends paid or the undistributed profits consist wholly or partly of profits or income arising in such other State.

Article 11

INTEREST

1. Interest arising in a Contracting State and paid to a resident of the other Contracting State may be taxed in that other State.

2. However, such interest may also be taxed in the Contracting State in which it arises and according to the laws of that State, but if the beneficial owner of the interest is a resident of the other Contracting State, the tax so charged shall not exceed:

a) 5 per cent of the gross amount of the interest in respect of a loan or credit made, guaranteed or insured for the purposes of promoting export by the Finnish Export Credit or the FINNVERA or similar Turkish public entities the objective of which are to promote the export;

b) 10 per cent of the gross amount of the interest if the interest is derived by a bank;

c) 15 per cent of the gross amount of the interest in all other cases.

3. Notwithstanding the provisions of paragraph 2, interest arising in:

a) Finland and paid to the Government of Turkey or to the Central Bank of Turkey (Türkiye Cumhuriyet Merkez Bankası) shall be exempted from Finnish tax;

b) Turkey and paid to the Government of Finland or to the Bank of Finland (Suomen Pankki) shall be exempted from Turkish tax.

4. The term "interest" as used in this Article means income from debt-claims of every kind, whether or not secured by mortgage and whether or not carrying a right to participate in the debtor's profits, and in particular, income from government securities and income from bonds or debentures, including premiums and prizes attaching to such securities, bonds or debentures, as well as all other income treated as income from money lent by the laws, relating to tax, of the Contracting State in which the income arises.

5. The provisions of paragraphs 1 and 2 shall not apply if the beneficial owner of the interest, being a resident of a Contracting State, carries on business in the other Contracting State in which the interest arises, through a permanent establishment situated therein or performs in that other State independent personal services from a fixed base situated therein, and the debt-claim in respect of which the interest is paid is effectively connected with such permanent establishment or fixed base. In such case the provisions of Article 7 or Article 14, as the case may be, shall apply.

6. Interest shall be deemed to arise in a Contracting State when the payer is that State itself, a local authority or a resident of that State. Where, however, the person paying the interest, whether he is a resident of a Contracting State or not, has in a Contracting State a permanent establishment or a fixed base in connection with which the indebtedness on which the interest is paid was incurred, and such interest is borne by such permanent establishment or fixed base, then such interest shall be deemed to arise in the State in which the permanent establishment or fixed base is situated.

7. Where, by reason of a special relationship between the payer and the beneficial owner or between both of them and some other person, the amount of the interest, having regard to the debt-claim for which it is paid, exceeds the amount which would have been agreed upon by the payer and the beneficial owner in the absence of such relationship, the provisions of this Article shall apply only to the last mentioned amount. In such case, the excess part of the payments shall remain taxable according to the laws of each Contracting State, due regard being had to the other provisions of this Agreement.

Article 12

ROYALTIES

1. Royalties arising in a Contracting State and paid to a resident of the other Contracting State may be taxed in that other State.

2. However, such royalties may also be taxed in the Contracting State in which they arise and according to the laws of that State, but if the beneficial owner of the royalties is a resident of the other Contracting State, the tax so charged shall not exceed 10 per cent of the gross amount of the royalties.

3. The term "royalties" as used in this Article means payments of any kind received as a consideration for the use of, or the right to use, any copyright of literary, artistic or scientific work including cinematograph films, and recordings for radio and television broadcasting, any patent, trade mark, design or model, plan, secret formula or process, or for information concerning industrial, commercial or scientific experience, or for the use of, or the right to use, industrial, commercial or scientific equipment.

4.The provisions of paragraphs 1 and 2 shall not apply if the beneficial owner of the royalties, being a resident of a Contracting State, carries on business in the other Contracting State in which the royalties arise, through a permanent establishment situated therein or performs in that other State independent personal services from a fixed base situated therein and the right or property in respect of which the royalties are paid is effectively connected with such permanent establishment or fixed base. In such case the provisions of Article 7 or Article 14, as the case may be, shall apply.

5. Royalties shall be deemed to arise in a Contracting State when the payer is that State itself, a local authority or a resident of that State. Where, however, the person paying the royalties, whether he is a resident of a Contracting State or not, has in a Contracting State a permanent establishment or fixed base, in connection with which the right or property giving rise to the royalties is effectively connected, and such royalties are borne by such permanent establishment or fixed base, then such royalties shall be deemed to arise in the State in which the permanent establishment or fixed base is situated.

6. Where, by reason of a special relationship between the payer and the beneficial owner or between both of them and some other person, the amount of the royalties, having regard to the use, right or information for which they are paid, exceeds the amount which would have been agreed upon by the payer and the beneficial owner in the absence of such relationship, the provisions of this Article shall apply only to the last-mentioned amount. In such case, the excess part of the payments shall remain taxable according to the laws of each Contracting State, due regard being had to the other provisions of this Agreement.

Article 13

CAPITAL GAINS

1. Gains derived by a resident of a Contracting State from the alienation of immovable property referred to in Article 6 and situated in the other Contracting State may be taxed in that other State.

2. Gains from the alienation of movable property forming part of the business property of a permanent establishment which an enterprise of a Contracting State has in the other Contracting State or of movable property pertaining to a fixed base available to a resident of a Contracting State in the other Contracting State for the purpose of performing independent personal services, including such gains from the alienation of such a permanent establishment (alone or with the whole enterprise) or of such a fixed base, may be taxed in that other State.

3. Gains derived by a resident of a Contracting State from the alienation of ships, aircraft or road vehicle operated in international traffic, or movable property pertaining to the operation of such ships, aircraft or road vehicle, shall be taxable only in that State.

4. Gains derived by a resident of a Contracting State from the alienation of shares or other corporate rights in a company of whose assets more than 50 per cent consist, directly or indirectly, of immovable property situated in the other Contracting State may be taxed in that other State.

5. Gains from the alienation of any property other than that referred to in paragraphs 1, 2, 3 and 4, shall be taxable only in the Contracting State of which the alienator is a resident. However, the capital gains mentioned in the foregoing sentence and derived from the other Contracting State, may be taxed in the other Contracting State if the time period does not exceed one year between acquisition and alienation.

Article 14

INDEPENDENT PERSONAL SERVICES

1. Income derived by an individual who is a resident of a Contracting State in respect of professional services or other activities of an independent character shall be taxable only in that State. However, such income may also be taxed in the other Contracting State if such services or activities are performed in that other State and if:

a) the individual has a fixed base regularly available to him in that other State for the purpose of performing those services or activities; or

b) the individual is present in that other State for the purpose of performing those services or activities for a period or periods amounting in the aggregate to 183 days or more in any continuous period of 12 months.

In such circumstances, only so much of the income as is attributable to that fixed base or is derived from the services or activities performed during the individual's presence in that other State, as the case may be, may be taxed in that other State.

2. Income derived by an enterprise of a Contracting State in respect of professional services or other activities of a similar character shall be taxable only in that State. However, such income may also be taxed in the other Contracting State if such services or activities are performed in that other State and if:

a) the enterprise has a permanent establishment in that other State through which the services or activities are performed; or

b) the period or periods during which the services or activities are performed exceed in the aggregate 183 days in any continuous period of 12 months.

In such circumstances only so much of the income as is attributable to that permanent establishment or to the services or activities performed in that other State, as the case may be, may be taxed in that other State. In either case, the enterprise may elect to be taxed in that other State in respect of such income in accordance with the provisions of Article 7 of this Agreement as if the income were attributable to a permanent establishment of the enterprise situated in that other State. This election shall not affect the right of other State to impose a withholding tax on such income.

3. The term "professional services" includes especially independent scientific, literary, artistic, educational or teaching activities as well as the independent activities of physicians, lawyers, engineers, architects, dentists and accountants and other activities requiring specific professional skill.

Article 15

INCOME FROM EMPLOYMENT

1. Subject to the provisions of Articles 16, 18, 19 and 20, salaries, wages and other similar remuneration derived by a resident of a Contracting State in respect of an employment shall be taxable only in that State unless the employment is exercised in the other Contracting State. If the employment is so exercised, such remuneration as is derived therefrom may be taxed in that other State.

2. Notwithstanding the provisions of paragraph 1, remuneration derived by a resident of a Contracting State in respect of an employment exercised in the other Contracting State shall be taxable only in the first-mentioned State if:

a) the recipient is present in the other State for a period or periods not exceeding in the aggregate 183 days in any twelve month period commencing or ending in the calendar year concerned, and

b) the remuneration is paid by, or on behalf of, an employer who is not a resident of the other State, and

c) the remuneration is not borne by a permanent establishment or a fixed base which the employer has in the other State.

3. Notwithstanding the preceding provisions of this Article, remuneration derived in respect of an employment exercised aboard a ship, aircraft or road vehicle operated in international traffic by an enterprise of a Contracting State may be taxed in that Contracting State.

Article 16

DIRECTORS' FEES

Directors' fees and other similar payments derived by a resident of a Contracting State in his capacity as a member of the board of directors or any other similar organ of a company which is a resident of the other Contracting State may be taxed in that other State.

Article 17

ARTISTES AND SPORTSMEN

1. Notwithstanding the provisions of Articles 14 and 15, income derived by a resident of a Contracting State as an entertainer, such as a theatre, motion picture, radio or television artiste, or a musician, or as a sportsman, from his personal activities as such exercised in the other Contracting State, may be taxed in that other State.

2. Where income in respect of personal activities exercised by an entertainer or a sportsman in his capacity as such accrues not to the entertainer or sportsman himself but to another person, that income may, notwithstanding the provisions of Articles 7, 14 and 15, be taxed in the Contracting State in which the activities of the entertainer or sportsman are exercised.

Article 18

PENSIONS

1. Pensions and other similar remuneration paid to a resident of a Contracting State in consideration of past employment shall be taxable only in that State.

2. Notwithstanding the provisions of paragraph 1, any pension paid by, or out of funds created by, a Contracting State or a statutory body or a local authority thereof to an individual in respect of services rendered to that State or body or authority, or any pension paid and other payments made under the social security legislation of a Contracting State shall be taxable only in that State. However, such pensions and other payments shall be taxable only in the Contracting State of which the individual is a resident if he is a national of that State.

Article 19

GOVERNMENT SERVICE

1. a) Salaries, wages and other similar remuneration, paid by a Contracting State or a statutory body or a local authority thereof to an individual in respect of services rendered to that State or body or authority shall be taxable only in that State.

b) However, such salaries, wages and other similar remuneration shall be taxable only in the Contracting State of which the individual is a resident if the services are rendered in that State and the individual:

i) is a national of that State; or

ii) did not become a resident of that State solely for the purpose of rendering the services.

2. The provisions of Articles 15, 16 and 17 shall apply to salaries, wages and other similar remuneration in respect of services rendered in connection with a business carried on by a Contracting State or a statutory body or a local authority thereof.

Article 20

STUDENTS AND TRAINEES

1. Payments which a student, or an apprentice or business, technical, agricultural or forestry trainee, who is or was immediately before visiting a Contracting State a resident of the other Contracting State and who is present in the first-mentioned State solely for the purpose of his education or training receives for the purpose of his maintenance, education or training shall not be taxed in that State, provided that such payments arise from sources outside that State.

2. A student at a university or other institution for higher education in a Contracting State, or an apprentice or business, technical, agricultural or forestry trainee, who is or was immediately before visiting the other Contracting State a resident of the first-mentioned State and who is present in the other Contracting State for a continuous period not exceeding 183 days, shall not be taxed in that other State in respect of remuneration for services rendered in that State, provided that the services are in connection with his studies or training and the remuneration constitutes earnings necessary for his maintenance.

Article 21

OTHER INCOME

1. Items of income of a resident of a Contracting State, wherever arising, not dealt with in the foregoing Articles of this Agreement shall be taxable only in that State.

2. The provisions of paragraph 1 shall not apply to income, other than income from immovable property as defined in paragraph 2 of Article 6, if the recipient of such income, being a resident of a Contracting State, carries on business in the other Contracting State through a permanent establishment situated therein, or performs in that other State independent personal services from a fixed base situated therein, and the right or property in respect of which the income is paid is effectively connected with such permanent establishment or fixed base. In such case the provisions of Article 7 or Article 14, as the case may be, shall apply.

3. Notwithstanding the provisions of paragraphs 1 and 2, items of income of a resident of a Contracting State not dealt with in the foregoing Articles of this Agreement and arising in the other Contracting State may also be taxed in that other State.

Article 22

ELIMINATION OF DOUBLE TAXATION

1. Double taxation for the residents of Turkey shall be eliminated as follows:

a) Subject to the provisions of the laws of Turkey regarding the allowance as a credit against Turkish tax of tax payable in a territory outside Turkey (as they may be amended from time to time without changing the general principles hereof), Finnish tax payable under the laws of Finland and in accordance with this Agreement in respect of income (including profits and chargeable gains) derived by a resident of Turkey from sources within Finland shall be allowed as a deduction from the Turkish tax on such income. Such deduction, however, shall not exceed the amount of Turkish tax, as computed before the deduction is made, attributable to such income.

b) Where in accordance with any provision of the Agreement income derived by a resident of Turkey is exempt from tax in Turkey, Turkey may nevertheless, in calculating the amount of tax on the remaining income of such resident, take into account the exempted income.

2. Subject to the provisions of Finnish law regarding the elimination of international double taxation (which shall not affect the general principle hereof), double taxation shall be eliminated in Finland as follows:

a) Where a resident of Finland derives income which, in accordance with the provisions of this Agreement, may be taxed in Turkey, Finland shall, subject to the provisions of sub-paragraph b), allow as a deduction from the Finnish tax of that person, an amount equal to the Turkish tax paid under Turkish law and in accordance with the Agreement, as computed by reference to the same income by reference to which the Finnish tax is computed.

b) Dividends paid by a company being a resident of Turkey to a company which is a resident of Finland and which controls directly at least 10 per cent of the voting power in the company paying the dividends shall be exempt from Finnish tax.

c) Where in accordance with any provision of the Agreement income derived by a resident of Finland is exempt from tax in Finland, Finland may nevertheless, in calculating the amount of tax on the remaining income of such person, take into account the exempted income.

d) For the purposes of sub-paragraph a), the term "tax, on income paid in Turkey" shall be deemed to include any amount of Turkish tax which would have been payable under Turkish taxation law but for any reduction or exemption of Turkish tax granted under the provisions concerning special incentive measures to promote economic development in Turkey.

Notwithstanding the preceding sentence, the tax on income paid in Turkey shall be calculated,

i) in the case of dividends referred to in sub-paragraph b) of paragraph 2 of Article 10, at a rate of 15 percent;

ii) in the case of interest referred to in sub-paragraph a) of paragraph 2 of Article 11, at a rate of 5 percent, in the case of interest referred to in sub-paragraph b) of paragraph 2 of Article 11, at a rate of 10 per cent and in the case of interest referred to in sub-paragraph c) of paragraph 2 of Article 11, at a rate of 15 per cent;

iii) in the case of royalties and other payments referred to in paragraph 2 of Article 12, at a rate of 10 per cent.

However, if the tax rates under Turkish taxation law applicable to dividends, interest and royalties derived by persons who are not residents of Turkey are reduced below those mentioned in this sub-paragraph, these lower rates shall apply for the purposes of this sub-paragraph.

Article 23

NON-DISCRIMINATION

1. Nationals of a Contracting State shall not be subjected in the other Contracting State to any taxation or any requirement connected therewith, which is other or more burdensome than the taxation and connected requirements to which nationals of that other State in the same circumstances, in particular with respect to residence, are or may be subjected. This provision shall, notwithstanding the provisions of Article 1, also apply to persons who are not residents of one or both of the Contracting States.

2. Subject to the provisions of paragraph 4 of Article 10, the taxation on a permanent establishment which an enterprise of a Contracting State has in the other Contracting State shall not be less favourably levied in that other State than the taxation levied on enterprises of that other State carrying on the same activities.

3. Enterprises of a Contracting State, the capital of which is wholly or partly owned or controlled, directly or indirectly, by one or more residents of the other Contracting State, shall not be subjected in the first-mentioned State to any taxation or any requirement connected therewith which is other or more burdensome than the taxation and connected requirements to which other similar enterprises of the first-mentioned State are or may be subjected.

4. Except where the provisions of paragraph 1 of Article 9, paragraph 7 of Article 11, or paragraph 6 of Article 12, apply, interest, royalties and other disbursements paid by an enterprise of a Contracting State to a resident of the other Contracting State shall, for the purpose of determining the taxable profits of such enterprise, be deductible under the same conditions as if they had been paid to a resident of the first-mentioned State.

5. These provisions shall not be construed as obliging a Contracting State to grant to residents of the other Contracting State any personal allowances, reliefs and reductions for taxation purposes on account of civil status or family responsibilities which it grants to its own residents.

6. The provisions of this Article shall apply only to the taxes which are covered by Article 2.

Article 24

MUTUAL AGREEMENT PROCEDURE

1. Where a person considers that the actions of one or both of the Contracting States result or will result for him in taxation not in accordance with the provisions of this Agreement, he may, irrespective of the remedies provided by the domestic law of those States, present his case to the competent authority of the Contracting State of which he is a resident or, if his case comes under paragraph 1 of Article 23, to that of the Contracting State of which he is a national. The case must be presented within three years from the first notification of the action resulting in taxation not in accordance with the provisions of the Agreement.

2. The competent authority shall endeavour, if the objection appears to it to be justified and if it is not itself able to arrive at a satisfactory solution, to resolve the case by mutual agreement with the competent authority of the other Contracting State, with a view to the avoidance of taxation which is not in accordance with the Agreement. Any agreement reached shall be implemented notwithstanding any time limits in the domestic law of the Contracting States.

3. The competent authorities of the Contracting States shall endeavour to resolve by mutual agreement any difficulties or doubts arising as to the interpretation or application of the Agreement. They may also consult together for the elimination of double taxation in cases not provided for in the Agreement.

4. The competent authorities of the Contracting States may communicate with each other directly including through a joint commission consisting of themselves or their representatives, for the purpose of reaching an agreement in the sense of the preceding paragraphs.

Article 25

EXCHANGE OF INFORMATION

1. The competent authorities of the Contracting States shall exchange such information as is foreseeably relevant for carrying out the provisions of this Agreement or to the administration or enforcement of the domestic laws concerning taxes of every kind and description imposed on behalf of the Contracting States, or of their political subdivisions or local authorities, insofar as the taxation thereunder is not contrary to the Agreement. The exchange of information is not restricted by Articles 1 and 2.

2. Any information received under paragraph 1 by a Contracting State shall be treated as secret in the same manner as information obtained under the domestic laws of that State and shall be disclosed only to persons or authorities (including courts and administrative bodies) concerned with the assessment or collection of, the enforcement or prosecution in respect of, the determination of appeals in relation to the taxes referred to in paragraph 1, or the oversight of the above. Such persons or authorities shall use the information only for such purposes. They may disclose the information in public court proceedings or in judicial decisions.

3. In no case shall the provisions of paragraphs 1 and 2 be construed so as to impose on a Contracting State the obligation:

a) to carry out administrative measures at variance with the laws and administrative practice of that or of the other Contracting State;

b) to supply information which is not obtainable under the laws or in the normal course of the administration of that or of the other Contracting State;

c) to supply information which would disclose any trade, business, industrial, commercial or professional secret or trade process, or information the disclosure of which would be contrary to public policy (ordre public).

4. If information is requested by a Contracting State in accordance with this Article, the other Contracting State shall use its information gathering measures to obtain the requested information, even though that other State may not need such information for its own tax purposes. The obligation contained in the preceding sentence is subject to the limitations of paragraph 3 but in no case shall such limitations be construed to permit a Contracting State to decline to supply information solely because it has no domestic interest in such information.

5. In no case shall the provisions of paragraph 3 be construed to permit a Contracting State to decline to supply information solely because the information is held by a bank, other financial institution, nominee or person acting in an agency or a fiduciary capacity or because it relates to ownership interests in a person.

Article 26

ASSISTANCE IN THE COLLECTION OF TAXES

1. The Contracting States shall lend assistance to each other in the collection of revenue claims. This assistance is not restricted by Articles 1 and 2. The competent authorities of the Contracting States may by mutual agreement settle the mode of application of this Article.

2. The term "revenue claim" as used in this Article means an amount owed in respect of taxes of every kind and description imposed on behalf of the Contracting States, or of their political subdivisions or local authorities, insofar as the taxation thereunder is not contrary to this Agreement or any other instrument to which the Contracting States are parties, as well as interest, administrative penalties and costs of collection or conservancy related to such amount.

3. When a revenue claim of a Contracting State is enforceable under the laws of that State and is owed by a person who, at that time, cannot, under the laws of that State, prevent its collection, that revenue claim shall, at the request of the competent authority of that State, be accepted for purposes of collection by the competent authority of the other Contracting State. That revenue claim shall be collected by that other State in accordance with the provisions of its laws applicable to the enforcement and collection of its own taxes as if the revenue claim were a revenue claim of that other State.

4. When a revenue claim of a Contracting State is a claim in respect of which that State may, under its law, take measures of conservancy with a view to ensure its collection, that revenue claim shall, at the request of the competent authority of that State, be accepted for purposes of taking measures of conservancy by the competent authority of the other Contracting State. That other State shall take measures of conservancy in respect of that revenue claim in accordance with the provisions of its laws as if the revenue claim were a revenue claim of that other State even if, at the time when such measures are applied, the revenue claim is not enforceable in the first-mentioned State or is owed by a person who has a right to prevent its collection.

5. Notwithstanding the provisions of paragraphs 3 and 4, a revenue claim accepted by a Contracting State for purposes of paragraph 3 or 4 shall not, in that State, be subject to the time limits or accorded any priority applicable to a revenue claim under the laws of that State by reason of its nature as such. In addition, a revenue claim accepted by a Contracting State for the purposes of paragraph 3 or 4 shall not, in that State, have any priority applicable to that revenue claim under the laws of the other Contracting State.

6. Proceedings with respect to the existence, validity or the amount of a revenue claim of a Contracting State shall not be brought before the courts or administrative bodies of the other Contracting State.

7. Where, at any time after a request has been made by a Contracting State under paragraph 3 or 4 and before the other Contracting State has collected and remitted the relevant revenue claim to the first-mentioned State, the relevant revenue claim ceases to be

a) in the case of a request under paragraph 3, a revenue claim of the first-mentioned State that is enforceable under the laws of that State and is owed by a person who, at that time, cannot, under the laws of that State, prevent its collection, or

b) in the case of a request under paragraph 4, a revenue claim of the first-mentioned State in respect of which that State may, under its laws, take measures of conservancy with a view to ensure its collection

the competent authority of the first-mentioned State shall promptly notify the competent authority of the other State of that fact and, at the option of the other State, the first-mentioned State shall either suspend or withdraw its request.

8. In no case shall the provisions of this Article be construed so as to impose on a Contracting State the obligation:

a) to carry out administrative measures at variance with the laws and administrative practice of that or of the other Contracting State;

b) to carry out measures which would be contrary to public policy (ordre public);

c) to provide assistance if the other Contracting State has not pursued all reasonable measures of collection or conservancy, as the case may be, available

under its laws or administrative practice;

d) to provide assistance in those cases where the administrative burden for that State is clearly disproportionate to the benefit to be derived by the other Contracting State.

Article 27

MEMBERS OF DIPLOMATIC MISSIONS AND CONSULAR POSTS

Nothing in this Agreement shall affect the fiscal privileges of members of diplomatic missions and consular posts under the general rules of international law or under the provisions of special agreements.

Article 28

ENTRY INTO FORCE

1. Each of the Contracting States shall notify to the other, through the diplomatic channels the completion of the procedures required by its domestic law for the bringing into force of this Agreement. The Agreement shall enter into force thirty days after the date of the later of the notifications and its provisions shall have effect:

a) in Turkey, for taxes with respect to every taxable period beginning on or after the first day of January of the year following that of entry into force of the Agreement;

b) in Finland:

i) in respect of taxes withheld at source, on income derived on or after 1January in the calendar year next following the year in which the Agreement enters into force;

ii) in respect of other taxes on income for taxes chargeable for any tax year beginning on or after 1 January in the calendar year next following the year in which the Agreement enters into force.

2. "The Agreement between the Republic of Finland and the Republic of Turkey for the Avoidance of Double Taxation With Respect to Taxes on Income", signed in Ankara on 09 May 1986, (hereinafter referred to as "the 1986 Agreement") shall cease to have effect from the date on which this Agreement becomes effective in accordance with the provisions of paragraph 1. The 1986 Agreement shall terminate on the last date on which it has effect in accordance with the foregoing provisions of this paragraph.

Article 29
TERMINATION

This Agreement shall remain in force until terminated by a Contracting State. Either Contracting State may terminate the Agreement, through diplomatic channels, by giving notice of termination at least six months before the end of any calendar year following after the period of five years from the date on which the Agreement enters into force. In such event, the Agreement shall cease to have effect:

a) in Turkey, for taxes with respect to every taxable period beginning on or after the first day of January of the year following that in which the notice is given;

b) in Finland:

i) in respect of taxes withheld at source, on income derived on or after 1 January in the calendar year next following the year in which the notice is given;

ii) in respect of other taxes on income for taxes chargeable for any tax year beginning on or after 1 January in the calendar year next following the year in which the notice is given.

IN WITNESS WHEREOF, the undersigned duly authorized hereto, have signed this Agreement.

Done in duplicate at Istanbul this day of October 2009, in the Finnish, Turkish and English languages, all three texts being equally authentic, in the case of divergence of interpretation the English text shall prevail.

FOR THE GOVERNMENT OF THE REPUBLIC OF FINLAND

FOR THE GOVERNMENT OF THE REPUBLIC OF TURKEY

PROTOCOL

At the moment of the signing of the Agreement between the Republic of Finland and the Republic of Turkey for the avoidance of double taxation with respect to taxes on income the undersigned have agreed upon the following provisions which shall constitute an integral part of the Agreement.

1. With reference to Article 7, paragraph 1.

It is understood that where an enterprise of a Contracting State has a permanent establishment in the other State and the enterprise

a) effects sales in that other State of goods or merchandise of the same or similar kind as those sold through that permanent establishment, or

b) carries on other business activities in that other State of the same or similar kind as those effected in that permanent establishment;

the sales and the business activities shall be taxed in that other Contracting State as part of the permanent establishment's profits if it is proved that such sales or activities have been effected through the permanent establishment; this taxation cannot be excluded by artificial sales arrangements.

2. With reference to Article 10, paragraph 3.

It is understood that the term "dividend" in the case of Turkey shall also include income derived from an investment fund and investment trust.

3. With reference to Articles 12 and 13.

It is understood that in the case of any payment received as a consideration for the sale of the property as meant in paragraph 3 of Article 12, the provisions of Article 12 shall apply, unless it is proved that the payment in question is a payment for a genuine alienation of the said property. In such case, the provisions of Article 13 shall apply.

4. With reference to Article 15, paragraph 2.

It is understood that paragraph 2 of Article 15 shall not apply to remuneration derived by a resident of a Contracting State ("the employee"), and paid by or on behalf of an employer who is a resident of that State in respect of an employment exercised in the other Contracting State where:

a) the employee renders services in the course of that employment to a person other than the employer who, directly or indirectly, supervises, directs or controls the manner in which those services are performed; and

b) the employer is not responsible for the outcome of the work performed by the recipient.

5. With reference to Articles 4, 18 and 19.

It is understood that the term "statutory body" means:

a) in the case of Turkey
(i) the Central Bank of Turkey (Türkiye Cumhuriyeti Merkez Bankasi);
(ii) the obligatory Turkish social insurance institutions; and
(iii) universities and other similar institutions for higher education;

b) in the case of Finland
(i) the Bank of Finland (Suomen Pankki);
(ii) the Social Insurance Institution (Kansaneläkelaitos); and
(iii) the University of Helsinki (Helsingin yliopisto).

For the purposes of Articles 18 and 19 the term "statutory body" includes,

in the case of Turkey: the Presidency of Religious Affairs; and

in the case of Finland: the Evangelical-Lutheran and Orthodox Churches and the local communities thereof.

6. With reference to Article 22, paragraph 2, subparagraph d).

The provisions of subparagraph d) of paragraph 2 of Article 22 shall apply only for the first five years for which the Agreement is effective.

7. With reference to Article 24, paragraph 2.

It is understood that with respect to paragraph 2 of Article 24 the taxpayer must in the case of Turkey claim the refund resulting from such mutual agreement within a period of one year after the tax administration has notified the taxpayer of the result of the mutual agreement.

IN WITNESS WHEREOF, the undersigned duly authorized hereto, have signed this Protocol.

Done in duplicate at Istanbul this day of October 2009, in the Finnish, Turkish and English languages, all three texts being equally authentic, in the case of divergence of interpretation the English text shall prevail.

FOR THE GOVERNMENT OF THE REPUBLIC OF FINLAND	FOR THE GOVERNMENT OF THE REPUBLIC OF TURKEY
[signature]	[signature]

[TEXT IN FINNISH – TEXTE EN FINNOIS]

SOPIMUS
SUOMEN TASAVALLAN JA TURKIN TASAVALLAN VÄLILLÄ TULOVEROJA KOSKEVAN KAKSINKERTAISEN VEROTUKSEN VÄLTTÄMISEKSI

SUOMEN TASAVALLAN HALLITUS JA TURKIN TASAVALLAN HALLITUS

jotka haluavat tehdä sopimuksen tuloveroja koskevan kaksinkertaisen verotuksen välttämiseksi,

OVAT SOPINEET SEURAAVASTA:

1 artikla
Sopimuksen piiriin kuuluvat henkilöt

Tätä sopimusta sovelletaan henkilöihin, jotka asuvat sopimusvaltiossa tai molemmissa sopimusvaltioissa.

2 artikla
Sopimuksen piiriin kuuluvat verot

1. Tätä sopimusta sovelletaan tulon perusteella suoritettaviin veroihin, jotka määrätään sopimusvaltion tai sen paikallisviranomaisten lukuun, riippumatta siitä, millä tavoin verot kannetaan.

2. Tulon perusteella suoritettavina veroina pidetään kaikkia kokonaistulon tai tulon osan perusteella suoritettavia veroja, niihin luettuina irtaimen tai kiinteän omaisuuden luovutuksesta saadun voiton perusteella suoritettavat verot, yrityksen maksamien palkkojen yhteenlasketun määrän perusteella suoritettavat verot sekä arvonnousun perusteella suoritettavat verot.

3. Tällä hetkellä suoritettavat verot, joihin sopimusta sovelletaan, ovat:

a) Turkissa:

1) tulovero (gelir vergisi); ja

2) yhtiövero (kurumlar vergisi);

(jäljempänä "Turkin vero");

b) Suomessa:

1) valtion tuloverot;

2) yhteisöjen tulovero;

3) kunnallisvero;

4) kirkollisvero;

5) korkotulon lähdevero; ja

6) rajoitetusti verovelvollisen lähdevero;

(jäljempänä "Suomen vero").

4. Sopimusta sovelletaan myös kaikkiin samanlaisiin tai pääasiallisesti samanluonteisiin veroihin, joita on sopimuksen allekirjoittamisen jälkeen suoritettava tällä hetkellä suoritettavien verojen ohella tai asemesta. Sopimusvaltioiden toimivaltaisten viranomaisten on ilmoitettava toisilleen verolainsäädäntöönsä tehdyistä merkittävistä muutoksista.

3 artikla

Yleiset määritelmät

1. Jollei asiayhteydestä muuta johdu, tätä sopimusta sovellettaessa:

a) 1) "Turkki" tarkoittaa Turkin aluetta mukaan lukien aluemeri ja sen yläpuolinen ilmatila samoin kuin merialueet, joilla Turkilla kansainvälisen oikeuden mukaisesti on tuomiovalta tai suvereenit oikeudet tutkia, käyttää hyväksi ja suojella luonnonveroja;

2) "Suomi" tarkoittaa Suomen tasavaltaa ja, maantieteellisessä merkityksessä käytettynä, Suomen tasavallan aluetta ja Suomen tasavallan aluevesiin rajoittuvia alueita, joilla Suomi lainsäädäntönsä mukaan ja kansainvälisen oikeuden mukaisesti saa käyttää oikeuksiaan merenpohjan ja sen sisustan sekä niiden yläpuolella olevien vesien luonnonvarojen tutkimiseen ja hyväksikäyttöön;

b) "sopimusvaltio" ja "toinen sopimusvaltio" tarkoittavat Turkkia tai Suomea sen mukaan kuin asiayhteys edellyttää;

c) "henkilö" käsittää luonnollisen henkilön, yhtiön ja muun yhteenliittymän;

d) "yhtiö" tarkoittaa oikeushenkilöä tai muuta, jota verotuksessa käsitellään oikeushenkilönä;

e) "perustamispaikka" tarkoittaa Turkin kauppalainsäädännön (Turkish Code of Commerce) mukaisesti rekisteröidyn yhtiön laillista pääkonttoria tai Suomen lainsäädännön mukaista yhtiön rekisteröintipaikkaa;

f) "kansalainen" tarkoittaa sopimusvaltion osalta:

1) luonnollista henkilöä, jolla on tämän sopimusvaltion kansalaisuus tai kansallisuus; ja

2) oikeushenkilöä, yhtymää tai muuta yhteenliittymää, joka on muodostettu tässä sopimusvaltiossa voimassa olevan lainsäädännön mukaan;

g) "sopimusvaltiossa oleva yritys" ja "toisessa sopimusvaltiossa oleva yritys" tarkoittavat yritystä, jota sopimusvaltiossa asuva henkilö harjoittaa, ja vastaavasti yritystä, jota toisessa sopimusvaltiossa asuva henkilö harjoittaa;

h) "toimivaltainen viranomainen" tarkoittaa:

1) Turkissa the Minister of Finance tai hänen valtuuttamaansa edustaja; ja

2) Suomessa valtiovarainministeriötä, sen valtuuttamaa edustajaa tai sitä viranomaista, jonka valtiovarainministeriö määrää toimivaltaiseksi viranomaiseksi;

i) "kansainvälinen liikenne" tarkoittaa kuljetusta laivalla, ilma-aluksella tai maantiekulkuneuvolla, jota sopimusvaltiossa oleva yritys käyttää, paitsi milloin laivaa, ilma-alusta tai maantiekulkuneuvoa käytetään ainoastaan toisessa sopimusvaltiossa olevien paikkojen välillä.

2. Kun sopimusvaltio jonakin ajankohtana soveltaa sopimusta, katsotaan, jollei asiayhteydestä muuta johdu, jokaisella sanonnalla, jota ei ole sopimuksessa määritelty, olevan se merkitys, joka sillä tänä ajankohtana on tämän valtion niitä veroja koskevan lainsäädännön mukaan, joihin sopimusta sovelletaan, ja tässä valtiossa sovellettavan verolainsäädännön mukaisella merkityksellä on etusija sanonnalle tämän valtion muussa lainsäädännössä annettuun merkitykseen nähden.

4 artikla

Sopimusvaltiossa asuva henkilö

1. Tätä sopimusta sovellettaessa ilmaisulla "sopimusvaltiossa asuva henkilö" tarkoitetaan henkilöä, joka tämän valtion lainsäädännön mukaan on siellä verovelvollinen domisiilin, asumisen, perustamispaikan, johdon sijaintipaikan tai muun sellaisen seikan nojalla, ja ilmaisu käsittää myös tämän valtion ja sen julkisyhteisön tai paikallisviranomaisen. Ilmaisu ei kuitenkaan käsitä henkilöä, joka on tässä valtiossa verovelvollinen vain tässä valtiossa olevista lähteistä saadun tulon perusteella.

2. Milloin luonnollinen henkilö 1 kappaleen määräysten mukaan asuu molemmissa sopimusvaltioissa, hänen kotipaikkansa määritetään seuraavasti:

a) hänen katsotaan asuvan vain siinä valtiossa, jossa hänen käytettävänään on vakinainen asunto; jos hänen käytettävänään on vakinainen asunto molemmissa valtioissa, hänen katsotaan asuvan vain siinä valtiossa, johon hänen henkilökohtaiset ja taloudelliset suhteensa ovat kiinteämmät (elinetujen keskus);

b) jos ei voida ratkaista, kummassa valtiossa hänen elinetujensa keskus on, tai jos hänen käytettävänään ei ole vakinaista asuntoa kummassakaan valtiossa, hänen katsotaan asuvan vain siinä valtiossa, jossa hän oleskelee pysyvästi;

c) jos hän oleskelee pysyvästi kummassakin valtiossa tai ei oleskele pysyvästi kummassakaan niistä, hänen katsotaan asuvan vain siinä valtiossa, jonka kansalainen hän on;

d) jos hän on kummankin valtion kansalainen tai ei ole kummankaan valtion kansalainen, sopimusvaltioiden toimivaltaisten viranomaisten on ratkaistava asia keskinäisin sopimuksin.

3. Milloin muu kuin luonnollinen henkilö 1 kappaleen määräysten mukaan asuu molemmissa sopimusvaltioissa, sen katsotaan asuvan vain siinä valtiossa, jossa se on perustettu.

5 artikla

Kiinteä toimipaikka

1. Tätä sopimusta sovellettaessa sanonnalla "kiinteä toimipaikka" tarkoitetaan kiinteää liikepaikkaa, josta yrityksen toimintaa kokonaan tai osaksi harjoitetaan.

2. Ilmaisu "kiinteä toimipaikka" käsittää erityisesti:

a) johdon sijaintipaikan;

b) sivuliikkeen;

c) toimiston;

d) tehtaan;

e) työpajan; ja

f) kaivoksen, öljy- tai kaasulähteen, louhoksen tai muun paikan, josta luonnonvaroja otetaan.

3. Paikka, jossa harjoitetaan rakennus-, kokoonpano- tai asennustoimintaa taikka siihen liittyvää valvontatoimintaa, muodostaa kiinteän toimipaikan vain, jos toiminta kestää yli kuusi kuukautta.

4. Tämän artiklan edellä olevien määräysten estämättä ilmaisun "kiinteä toimipaikka" ei katsota käsittävän:

a) järjestelyjä, jotka on tarkoitettu ainoastaan yritykselle kuuluvien tavaroiden varastoimista, näytteillä pitämistä tai luovuttamista varten;

b) yritykselle kuuluvan tavaravaraston pitämistä ainoastaan varastoimista, näytteillä pitämistä tai luovuttamista varten;

c) yritykselle kuuluvan tavaravaraston pitämistä ainoastaan toisen yrityksen toimesta tapahtuvaa muokkaamista tai jalostamista varten;

d) kiinteän liikepaikan pitämistä ainoastaan tavaroiden ostamiseksi tai tietojen keräämiseksi yritykselle;

e) kiinteän liikepaikan pitämistä ainoastaan muun luonteeltaan valmistelevan tai avustavan toiminnan harjoittamiseksi yritykselle;

f) kiinteän liikepaikan pitämistä ainoastaan a)–e) kohdassa mainittujen toimintojen yhdistämiseksi, edellyttäen, että koko se kiinteästä liikepaikasta harjoitettava toiminta, joka perustuu tähän yhdistämiseen, on luonteeltaan valmistelevaa tai avustavaa.

5. Jos henkilö, joka ei ole sellainen itsenäinen edustaja, johon 6 kappaletta sovelletaan, toimii sopimusvaltiossa toisessa sopimusvaltiossa olevan yrityksen puolesta, tällä yrityksellä katsotaan 1 ja 2 kappaleen määräysten estämättä olevan kiinteä toimipaikka ensiksi mainitussa valtiossa kaiken sen toiminnan osalta, jota tämä henkilö harjoittaa yrityksen lukuun, jos tällä henkilöllä:

a) on tässä valtiossa valtuus tehdä sopimuksia yrityksen nimissä ja hän käyttää valtuuttaan siellä tavanomaisesti. Tätä ei kuitenkaan noudateta, jos tämän henkilön toiminta rajoittuu sellaiseen, joka mainitaan 4 kappaleessa ja joka, jos sitä harjoitettaisiin kiinteästä liikepaikasta, ei tekisi tätä kiinteää liikepaikkaa kiinteäksi toimipaikaksi mainitun kappaleen määräysten mukaan; tai

b) ei ole sellaista valtuutta, mutta hän pitää tavanomaisesti ensiksi mainitussa valtiossa tavaravarastoa, josta hän säännöllisesti luovuttaa tavaroita yrityksen puolesta.

6. Yrityksellä ei katsota olevan kiinteää toimipaikkaa sopimusvaltiossa pelkästään sen vuoksi, että se harjoittaa liiketoimintaa siinä valtiossa välittäjän, komissionäärin tai muun itsenäisen edustajan välityksellä, edellyttäen, että tämä henkilö toimii säännönmukaisen liiketoimintansa rajoissa.

7. Se seikka, että sopimusvaltiossa asuvalla yhtiöllä on määräämisvalta yhtiössä – tai siinä on määräämisvalta yhtiöllä –, joka asuu toisessa sopimusvaltiossa taikka joka tässä toisessa valtiossa harjoittaa liiketoimintaa (joko kiinteästä toimipaikasta tai muulla tavoin), ei itsestään tee kumpaakaan yhtiötä toisen kiinteäksi toimipaikaksi.

6 artikla
Kiinteästä omaisuudesta saatu tulo

1. Tulosta, jonka sopimusvaltiossa asuva henkilö saa toisessa sopimusvaltiossa olevasta kiinteästä omaisuudesta (siihen luettuna maataloudesta tai metsätaloudesta saatu tulo), voidaan verottaa tässä toisessa valtiossa.

2. Ilmaisulla "kiinteä omaisuus" on sen sopimusvaltion lainsäädännön mukainen merkitys, jossa omaisuus on. Ilmaisu käsittää kuitenkin aina kiinteän omaisuuden tarpeiston, maataloudessa ja metsätaloudessa käytetyn elävän ja elottoman irtaimiston (mukaan lukien kalankasvatus ja -viljely), oikeudet, joihin sovelletaan yksityisoikeuden kiinteää omaisuutta koskevia määräyksiä, kiinteän omaisuuden käyttöoikeuden sekä oikeudet määrältään muuttuviin tai kiinteisiin korvauksiin, jotka saadaan kivennäisesiintymien, lähteiden ja muiden luonnonvarojen hyväksikäytöstä tai oikeudesta niiden hyväksikäyttöön; laivoja ja ilma-aluksia ei pidetä kiinteänä omaisuutena.

3. Tämän artiklan 1 kappaleen määräyksiä sovelletaan tuloon, joka saadaan kiinteän omaisuuden välittömästä käytöstä, sen vuokralle antamisesta tai muusta käytöstä.

4. Jos osakkeiden tai muiden yhtiöosuuksien omistus oikeuttaa osakkeiden tai yhtiöosuuksien omistajan hallitsemaan yhtiölle kuuluvaa kiinteää omaisuutta, voidaan tulosta, joka saadaan tällaisen hallintaoikeuden välittömästä käytöstä, sen vuokralle antamisesta tai muusta käytöstä, verottaa siinä sopimusvaltiossa, jossa kiinteä omaisuus on.

5. Tämän artiklan 1 ja 3 kappaleen määräyksiä sovelletaan myös yrityksen kiinteästä omaisuudesta saatuun tuloon ja itsenäisessä ammatinharjoittamisessa käytetystä kiinteästä omaisuudesta saatuun tuloon.

7 artikla
Liiketulo

1. Sopimusvaltion yrityksen saamasta tulosta verotetaan vain siinä valtiossa, paitsi jos yritys harjoittaa toisessa sopimusvaltiossa liiketoimintaa siellä olevasta kiinteästä toimipaikasta. Jos yritys harjoittaa liiketoimintaa edellä sanotuin tavoin, voidaan toisessa valtiossa verottaa yrityksen saamasta tulosta, mutta vain niin suuresta tulon osasta, joka on luettava kiinteään toimipaikkaan kuuluvaksi.

2. Jos sopimusvaltion yritys harjoittaa liiketoimintaa toisessa sopimusvaltiossa siellä olevasta kiinteästä toimipaikasta, luetaan, jollei 3 kappaleen määräyksistä muuta johdu, kummassakin sopimusvaltiossa kiinteään toimipaikkaan kuuluvaksi se tulo, jonka toimipaikan olisi voitu olettaa tuottavan, jos se olisi ollut erillinen yritys, joka harjoittaa samaa tai samanlaista toimintaa samojen tai samanlaisten edellytysten vallitessa ja itsenäisesti päättää liiketoimista sen yrityksen kanssa, jonka kiinteä toimipaikka se on.

3. Kiinteän toimipaikan tuloa määrättäessä on vähennykseksi hyväksyttävä kiinteästä toimipaikasta johtuneet menot, niihin luettuina yrityksen johtamisesta ja yleisestä hallinnosta johtuneet menot, riippumatta siitä, ovatko ne syntyneet siinä valtiossa, jossa kiinteä toimipaikka on, vai muualla. Vähennystä ei kuitenkaan myönnetä siltä osin kuin kyseessä ovat osuudet ulkomailla sijaitsevien pääkonttorin tai muiden kiinteiden toimipaikkojen kuluista ja tappioista eikä myöskään kiinteän toimipaikan yrityksen pääkonttorille tai muulle konttorille rojaltin, koron, provision tai muun samankaltaisen suorituksen muodossa maksamien määrien osalta.

4. Tuloa ei lueta kiinteään toimipaikkaan kuuluvaksi pelkästään sen perusteella, että kiinteä toimipaikka ostaa tavaroita yrityksen lukuun.

5. Milloin liiketuloon sisältyy tulolajeja, joita käsitellään erikseen tämän sopimuksen muissa artikloissa, tämän artiklan määräykset eivät vaikuta sanottujen artiklojen määräyksiin.

8 artikla
Merenkulku, ilma- ja maantiekuljetus

1. Tulosta, jonka sopimusvaltiossa oleva yritys saa laivan, ilma-aluksen tai maantiekulkuneuvon käyttämisestä kansainväliseen liikenteeseen, verotetaan vain tässä valtiossa.

2. Kappaleen 1 määräyksiä sovelletaan myös tuloon, joka saadaan osallistumisesta pooliin, yhteiseen liiketoimintaan tai kansainväliseen kuljetusjärjestöön.

9 artikla
Etuyhteydessä keskenään olevat yritykset

1. Milloin

a) sopimusvaltion yritys välittömästi tai välillisesti osallistuu toisen sopimusvaltion yrityksen johtoon tai valvontaan tahi omistaa osan sen pääomasta, taikka

b) samat henkilöt välittömästi tai välillisesti osallistuvat sekä sopimusvaltion yrityksen että toisen sopimusvaltion yrityksen johtoon tai valvontaan tahi omistavat osan niiden pääomasta,

noudatetaan seuraavaa:

Jos jommassakummassa tapauksessa yritysten välillä kauppa- tai rahoitussuhteissa sovitaan ehdoista tai määrätään ehtoja, jotka poikkeavat siitä, mistä riippumattomien yritysten välillä olisi sovittu, voidaan kaikki tulo, joka ilman näitä ehtoja olisi kertynyt toiselle näistä yrityksistä, mutta näiden ehtojen vuoksi ei ole kertynyt yritykselle, lukea tämän yrityksen tuloon ja verottaa siitä tämän mukaisesti.

2. Milloin sopimusvaltio tässä valtiossa olevan yrityksen tuloon lukee – ja tämän mukaisesti verottaa – tulon, josta toisessa sopimusvaltiossa olevaa yritystä on verotettu tässä toisessa valtiossa, sekä siten mukaan luettu tulo on tuloa, joka olisi kertynyt ensiksi mainitussa valtiossa olevalle yritykselle, jos yritysten välillä sovitut ehdot olisivat olleet sellaisia, joista riippumattomien yritysten välillä olisi sovittu, tämän toisen valtion on asianmukaisesti oikaistava tästä tulosta siellä määrätyn veron määrä, jos tämä toinen valtio pitää oikaisua oikeutettuna. Tällaista oikaisua tehtäessä on otettava huomioon tämän sopimuksen muut määräykset, ja sopimusvaltioiden toimivaltaisten viranomaisten on tarvittaessa neuvoteltava keskenään.

10 artikla
Osinko

1. Sopimusvaltiossa asuvan yhtiön toisessa sopimusvaltiossa asuvalle henkilölle maksamasta osingosta voidaan verottaa tässä toisessa valtiossa.

2. Osingosta voidaan kuitenkin verottaa myös siinä sopimusvaltiossa, jossa osingon maksava yhtiö asuu ja tämän valtion lainsäädännön mukaisesti, mutta jos osinkoetuuden omistaja on toisessa sopimusvaltiossa asuva henkilö, vero ei saa olla suurempi kuin:

a) 5 prosenttia osingon kokonaismäärästä, jos etuuden omistaja on yhtiö (lukuun ottamatta yhtymää), joka välittömästi omistaa vähintään 25 prosenttia osingon maksavan yhtiön pääomasta;

b) 15 prosenttia osingon kokonaismäärästä kaikissa muissa tapauksissa.

Tämän kappale ei vaikuta yhtiön verottamiseen siitä voitosta, josta osinko maksetaan.

3. Ilmaisulla "osinko" tarkoitetaan tässä artiklassa tuloa, joka on saatu osakkeista, osuustodistuksista tai muista samanlaisista voitto-osuuteen oikeuttavista ["jouissance"-] todistuksista, perustajaosuuksista tai muista osuuksista, jotka eivät ole saamisia ja jotka oikeuttavat voitto-osuuteen, samoin kuin muista yhtiöosuuksista saatavaa tuloa, jota voi-

ton jakavan yhtiön asuinvaltion lainsäädännön mukaan kohdellaan verotuksessa samalla tavoin kuin osakkeista saatua tuloa.

4. Sopimusvaltiossa asuvan ja liiketoimintaa toisessa sopimusvaltiossa siellä olevasta kiinteästä toimipaikasta harjoittavan yhtiön tuloa voidaan, sen jälkeen kun tulosta on verotettu 7 artiklan perusteella, verottaa jäljelle jääneestä määrästä siinä sopimusvaltiossa, jossa kiinteä toimipaikka on, mutta näin kannetun veron verokanta ei saa olla suurempi kuin:

a) 5 prosenttia jäljelle jääneestä määrästä edellyttäen, että tulo on vapautettu verosta siinä sopimusvaltiossa, jossa yhtiö asuu;

b) 15 prosenttia jäljelle jääneestä määrästä kaikissa muissa tapauksissa.

5. Tämän artiklan 1 ja 2 kappaleen määräyksiä ei sovelleta, jos sopimusvaltiossa asuva osinkoetuuden omistaja harjoittaa toisessa sopimusvaltiossa, jossa osingon maksava yhtiö asuu, liiketoimintaa siellä olevasta kiinteästä toimipaikasta tai harjoittaa tässä toisessa valtiossa itsenäistä ammattitoimintaa siellä olevasta kiinteästä paikasta, ja osingon maksamisen perusteena oleva osuus tosiasiallisesti liittyy tähän kiinteään toimipaikkaan tai kiinteään paikkaan. Tässä tapauksessa sovelletaan 7 tai 14 artiklan määräyksiä.

6. Jollei tämän artiklan 4 kappaleen määräyksistä muuta johdu, jos sopimusvaltiossa asuva yhtiö saa tuloa toisesta sopimusvaltiosta, tämä toinen valtio ei saa verottaa yhtiön maksamasta osingosta, paitsi mikäli osinko maksetaan tässä toisessa valtiossa asuvalle henkilölle tai mikäli osingon maksamisen perusteena oleva osuus tosiasiallisesti liittyy tässä toisessa valtiossa olevaan kiinteään toimipaikkaan tai kiinteään paikkaan, eikä myöskään määrätä yhtiön jakamattomasta voitosta tällaisesta voitosta suoritettavaa veroa, vaikka maksettu osinko tai jakamaton voitto kokonaan tai osaksi koostuisi tässä toisessa valtiossa kertyneestä tulosta.

11 artikla
Korko

1. Sopimusvaltiosta kertyvästä, toisessa sopimusvaltiossa asuvalle henkilölle maksetusta korosta voidaan verottaa tässä toisessa valtiossa.

2. Korosta voidaan kuitenkin verottaa myös siinä sopimusvaltiossa, josta se kertyy ja tämän valtion lainsäädännön mukaan, mutta jos korkoetuuden omistaja on toisessa sopimusvaltiossa asuva henkilö, näin määrätty vero ei saa olla suurempi kuin:

a) 5 prosenttia koron kokonaismäärästä sellaisen lainan tai luoton osalta, jonka on myöntänyt, taannut tai vakuuttanut viennin edistämistä varten Suomen Vientiluotto tai FINNVERA tai samanlaiset turkkilaiset julkiset yksiköt, joiden tarkoitus on viennin edistäminen;

b) 10 prosenttia koron kokonaismäärästä, jos koron saa pankki;

c) 15 prosenttia koron kokonaismäärästä kaikissa muissa tapauksissa.

3. Kappaleen 2 määräysten estämättä, korko, joka kertyy:

a) Suomesta ja maksetaan Turkin hallitukselle tai the Central Bank of Turkey:lle (Türkiye Cumhuriyet Merkez Bankası), on vapautettu Suomen verosta;

b) Turkista ja maksetaan Suomen valtiolle tai Suomen Pankille, on vapautettu Turkin verosta.

4. Ilmaisulla "korko" tarkoitetaan tässä artiklassa tuloa, joka saadaan kaikenlaatuisista saamisista riippumatta siitä, onko ne turvattu kiinteistökiinnityksin vai ei, ja liittyykö niihin oikeus osuuteen velallisen voitosta vai ei, ja erityisesti tuloa, joka saadaan valtion antamista arvopapereista, ja tuloa, joka saadaan obligaatioista tai debentuureista, mukaan lukien tällaisiin arvopapereihin, obligaatioihin tai debentuureihin liittyvät agiot ja voitot, samoin kuin kaikkea muuta tuloa, jota käsitellään lainaksi annetun rahan tuottamana tulona sen sopimusvaltion verolainsäädännössä, josta tulo kertyy.

5. Tämän artiklan 1 ja 2 kappaleen määräyksiä ei sovelleta, jos sopimusvaltiossa asuva korkoetuuden omistaja harjoittaa toisessa sopimusvaltiossa, josta korko kertyy, liiketoimintaa siellä olevasta kiinteästä toimipaikasta tai harjoittaa tässä toisessa valtiossa itsenäistä ammattitoimintaa siellä olevasta kiinteästä paikasta, ja koron maksamisen perusteena oleva saaminen tosiasiallisesti liittyy tähän kiinteään toimipaikkaan tai kiinteään paikkaan. Tässä tapauksessa sovelletaan 7 tai 14 artiklan määräyksiä.

6. Koron katsotaan kertyvän sopimusvaltiosta silloin, kun sen maksaja on tämä valtio, sen paikallisviranomainen tai tässä valtiossa asuva henkilö. Jos kuitenkin koron maksajalla, siitä riippumatta, asuuko hän sopimusvaltiossa vai ei, on sopimusvaltiossa kiinteä toimipaikka tai kiinteä paikka, jonka yhteydessä koron maksamisen perusteena oleva velka on syntynyt, ja korko rasittaa tätä kiinteää toimipaikkaa tai kiinteää paikkaa, koron katsotaan kertyvän siitä valtiosta, jossa kiinteä toimipaikka tai kiinteä paikka on.

7. Jos koron määrä maksajan ja korkoetuuden omistajan tai heidän molempien ja muun henkilön välisen erityisen suhteen vuoksi ylittää koron maksamisen perusteena olevaan saamiseen nähden määrän, josta maksaja ja korkoetuuden omistaja olisivat sopineet, jollei tällaista suhdetta olisi, tämän artiklan määräyksiä sovelletaan vain viimeksi mainittuun määrään. Tässä tapauksessa verotetaan tämän määrän ylittävästä maksun osasta kummankin sopimusvaltion lainsäädännön mukaan, ottaen huomioon tämän sopimuksen muut määräykset.

12 artikla
Rojalti

1. Rojaltista, joka kertyy sopimusvaltiosta ja maksetaan toisessa sopimusvaltiossa asuvalle henkilölle, voidaan verottaa tässä toisessa valtiossa.

2. Rojaltista voidaan kuitenkin verottaa myös siinä sopimusvaltiossa, josta se kertyy, tämän valtion lainsäädännön mukaan, mutta jos rojaltietuuden omistaja on toisessa sopimusvaltiossa asuva henkilö, vero ei saa olla suurempi kuin 10 prosenttia rojaltin kokonaismäärästä.

3. Ilmaisulla "rojalti" tarkoitetaan tässä artiklassa kaikkia suorituksia, jotka saadaan korvauksena kirjallisen, taiteellisen tai tieteellisen teoksen mukaan lukien elokuvafilmi sekä tallenne televisio- ja radiolähetyksiä varten, tekijänoikeuden, patentin, tavaramerkin, mallin tai muotin, piirustuksen, salaisen kaavan tai valmistusmenetelmän käytöstä tai käyttöoikeudesta, tai kokemusperäisestä teollis-, kaupallis- tai tieteellisluonteisesta tiedosta tai teollisen, kaupallisen tai tieteellisen välineistön käytöstä tai käyttöoikeudesta.

4. Tämän artiklan 1 ja 2 kappaleen määräyksiä ei sovelleta, jos sopimusvaltiossa asuva rojaltietuuden omistaja harjoittaa toisessa sopimusvaltiossa, josta rojalti kertyy, liiketoimintaa siellä olevasta kiinteästä toimipaikasta tai harjoittaa tässä toisessa valtiossa itsenäistä ammattitoimintaa siellä olevasta kiinteästä paikasta, ja rojaltin maksamisen perusteena oleva oikeus tai omaisuus tosiasiallisesti liittyy tähän kiinteään toimipaikkaan tai kiinteään paikkaan. Tässä tapauksessa sovelletaan 7 tai 14 artiklan määräyksiä.

5. Rojaltin katsotaan kertyvän sopimusvaltiosta silloin, kun sen maksaja on tämä valtio, sen paikallisviranomainen tai tässä valtiossa asuva henkilö. Jos kuitenkin rojaltin maksajalla riippumatta siitä, asuuko hän sopimusvaltiossa vai ei, on sopimusvaltiossa kiinteä toimipaikka tai kiinteä paikka, johon rojaltin tuottava oikeus tai omaisuus tosiasiallisesti liittyy, ja rojalti rasittaa tätä kiinteää toimipaikkaa tai kiinteää paikkaa, rojaltin katsotaan kertyvän siitä valtiosta, jossa kiinteä toimipaikka tai kiinteä paikka on.

6. Jos rojaltin määrä maksajan ja rojaltietuuden omistajan tai heidän molempien ja muun henkilön välisen erityisen suhteen vuoksi ylittää rojaltin maksamisen perusteena olevaan käyttöön, oikeuteen tai tietoon nähden määrän, josta maksaja ja rojaltietuuden omistaja olisivat sopineet, jollei tällaista suhdetta olisi, tämän artiklan määräyksiä sovelletaan vain viimeksi mainittuun määrään. Tässä tapauksessa verotetaan tämän määrän ylittävästä maksun osasta kummankin sopimusvaltion lainsäädännön mukaan, ottaen huomioon tämän sopimuksen muut määräykset.

13 artikla

Luovutusvoitto

1. Voitosta, jonka sopimusvaltiossa asuva henkilö saa 6 artiklassa tarkoitetun, toisessa sopimusvaltiossa olevan kiinteän omaisuuden luovutuksesta, voidaan verottaa tässä toisessa valtiossa.

2. Voitosta, joka saadaan sopimusvaltiossa olevan yrityksen toisessa sopimusvaltiossa olevan kiinteän toimipaikan liikeomaisuuteen kuuluvan irtaimen omaisuuden tai sopimusvaltiossa asuvan henkilön toisessa sopimusvaltiossa itsenäistä ammatinharjoittamista varten käytettävänä olevaan kiinteään paikkaan kuuluvan irtaimen omaisuuden luovutuksesta, voidaan verottaa tässä toisessa valtiossa. Sama koskee voittoa, joka saadaan tällaisen kiinteän toimipaikan luovutuksesta (erillisenä tai koko yrityksen mukana) tai kiinteän paikan luovutuksesta.

3. Voitosta, jonka sopimusvaltiossa asuva henkilö saa kansainväliseen liikenteeseen käytetyn laivan, ilma-aluksen tai maantiekulkuneuvon taikka tällaisen laivan, ilma-aluksen tai maantiekulkuneuvon käyttämiseen liittyvän irtaimen omaisuuden luovutuksesta, verotetaan vain tässä valtiossa.

4. Voitosta, jonka sopimusvaltiossa asuva henkilö saa sellaisen yhtiön osakkeen tai muun osuuden luovutuksesta, jonka varoista enemmän kuin 50 prosenttia välittömästi tai välillisesti koostuu toisessa sopimusvaltiossa olevasta kiinteästä omaisuudesta, voidaan verottaa tässä toisessa valtiossa.

5. Voitosta, joka saadaan muun kuin tämän artiklan 1, 2, 3 ja 4 kappaleissa tarkoitetun omaisuuden luovutuksesta, verotetaan vain siinä sopimusvaltiossa, jossa luovuttaja asuu. Edellisessä lauseessa mainitusta ja toisesta sopimusvaltiosta saadusta luovutusvoitosta voidaan kuitenkin verottaa toisessa sopimusvaltiossa, jos hankinnan ja luovutuksen välinen aika ei ole yhtä vuotta pidempi.

14 artikla

Itsenäinen ammatinharjoittaminen

1. Tulosta, jonka sopimusvaltiossa asuva luonnollinen henkilö saa vapaan ammatin tai muun itsenäisen toiminnan harjoittamisesta, verotetaan vain tässä valtiossa. Tällaisesta tulosta voidaan kuitenkin verottaa myös toisessa sopimusvaltiossa, jos tällaista ammattia tai toimintaa harjoitetaan tässä toisessa valtiossa ja jos:

a) luonnollisella henkilöllä on tässä toisessa valtiossa kiinteä paikka, joka on vakinaisesti hänen käytettävänään tämän ammatin tai toiminnan harjoittamista varten; tai

b) luonnollinen henkilö oleskelee tässä toisessa valtiossa tämän ammatin tai toiminnan harjoittamista varten yhdessä jaksossa, tai useassa jaksossa yhteensä, 183 päivää tai kauemmin yhtäjaksoisen kahdentoista kuukauden ajanjakson aikana.

Tässä toisessa valtiossa voidaan silloin verottaa vain siitä tulon osasta, joka on luettava kuuluvaksi tähän kiinteään paikkaan tai joka saadaan ammatin tai toiminnan harjoittamisesta aikana, jolloin luonnollisesti henkilö oleskelee tässä toisessa valtiossa.

2. Tulosta, jonka sopimusvaltiossa oleva yritys saa vapaan ammatin tai muun itsenäisen toiminnan harjoittamisesta, verotetaan vain tässä valtiossa. Tällaisesta tulosta voidaan kuitenkin verottaa myös toisessa sopimusvaltiossa, jos tällaista ammattia tai toimintaa harjoitetaan tässä toisessa valtiossa ja jos:

a) yrityksellä on tässä toisessa valtiossa kiinteä toimipaikka, josta ammattia tai toimintaa harjoitetaan; tai

b) ajanjakso tai -jaksot, joiden aikana ammattia tai toimintaa harjoitetaan, ylittävät yhteensä 183 päivää yhtäjaksoisen kahdentoista kuukauden ajanjakson aikana.

Tässä toisessa valtiossa voidaan silloin verottaa vain siitä tulon osasta, joka on luettava kuuluvaksi tähän kiinteään toimipaikkaan tai tässä toisessa valtiossa harjoitettuun ammattiin tai toimintaan. Kummassakin tapauksessa yritys voi valita sen vaihtoehdon, että sitä verotetaan tästä tulosta tässä toisessa valtiossa tämän sopimuksen 7 artiklan määräysten mukaisesti ikään kuin tulo olisi luettava kuuluvaksi yrityksellä tässä toisessa valtiossa olevaan kiinteään toimipaikkaan. Tämä valinta ei vaikuta toisen valtion oikeuteen kantaa tällaisesta tulosta lähdeveroa.

3. Ilmaisu "vapaa ammatti" käsittää erityisesti itsenäisen tieteellisen, kirjallisen ja taiteellisen toiminnan, kasvatus- ja opetustoiminnan sekä sellaisen itsenäisen toiminnan, jota lääkäri, asianajaja, insinööri, arkkitehti, hammaslääkäri ja tilintarkastaja harjoittavat, ja muun erityistä ammattitaitoa vaativan toiminnan.

15 artikla
Työtulo

1. Jollei 16, 18, 19 ja 20 artiklan määräyksistä muuta johdu, verotetaan palkasta ja muusta sellaisesta hyvityksestä, jonka sopimusvaltiossa asuva henkilö saa epäitsenäisestä työstä, vain tässä valtiossa, jollei työtä tehdä toisessa sopimusvaltiossa. Jos työ tehdään tässä toisessa valtiossa, työstä saadusta hyvityksestä voidaan verottaa siellä.

2. Tämän artiklan 1 kappaleen määräysten estämättä verotetaan hyvityksestä, jonka sopimusvaltiossa asuva henkilö saa toisessa sopimusvaltiossa tekemästään epäitsenäisestä työstä, vain ensiksi mainitussa valtiossa, jos:

a) saaja oleskelee toisessa valtiossa yhdessä jaksossa, tai useassa jaksossa yhteensä, enintään 183 päivää kahdentoista kuukauden ajanjakson aikana, joka alkaa tai päättyy kyseisen kalenterivuoden aikana, ja

b) hyvityksen maksaa työnantaja tai se maksetaan työnantajan puolesta, joka ei asu toisessa valtiossa, ja

c) hyvityksellä ei rasiteta kiinteää toimipaikkaa tai kiinteää paikkaa, joka työnantajalla on toisessa valtiossa.

3. Tämän artiklan edellä olevien määräysten estämättä voidaan hyvityksestä, joka saadaan sopimusvaltiossa olevan yrityksen kansainväliseen liikenteeseen käyttämässä laivassa, ilma-aluksessa tai maantiekulkuneuvossa tehdystä epäitsenäisestä työstä, verottaa tässä sopimusvaltiossa.

16 artikla
Johtajanpalkkio

Johtajanpalkkiosta ja muusta sellaisesta suorituksesta, jonka sopimusvaltiossa asuva henkilö saa toisessa sopimusvaltiossa asuvan yhtiön johtokunnan tai muun sellaisen toimielimen jäsenenä, voidaan verottaa tässä toisessa valtiossa.

17 artikla
Taiteilijat ja urheilijat

1. Tämän sopimuksen 14 ja 15 artiklan määräysten estämättä voidaan tulosta, jonka sopimusvaltiossa asuva henkilö saa viihdetaiteilijana, kuten teatteri- tai elokuvanäyttelijänä, radio- tai televisiotaiteilijana tahi muusikkona, taikka urheilijana, toisessa sopimus-

valtiossa harjoittamastaan henkilökohtaisesta toiminnasta, verottaa tässä toisessa valtiossa.

2. Milloin tulo, joka saadaan viihdetaiteilijan tai urheilijan tässä ominaisuudessaan harjoittamasta henkilökohtaisesta toiminnasta, ei tule viihdetaiteilijalle tai urheilijalle itselleen, vaan toiselle henkilölle, voidaan tästä tulosta, 7, 14 ja 15 artiklan määräysten estämättä, verottaa siinä sopimusvaltiossa, jossa viihdetaiteilija tai urheilija harjoittaa toimintaansa.

18 artikla
Eläkkeet

1. Eläkkeestä ja muusta samanluonteisesta hyvityksestä, joka maksetaan sopimusvaltiossa asuvalle henkilölle aikaisemman epäitsenäisen työn perusteella, verotetaan vain tässä valtiossa.

2. Tämän artiklan 1 kappaleen määräysten estämättä, verotetaan eläkkeestä, jonka sopimusvaltio, sen julkisyhteisö tai paikallisviranomainen maksaa, tai joka maksetaan niiden perustamista rahastoista, luonnolliselle henkilölle työstä, joka on tehty tämän valtion, sen julkisyhteisön tai paikallisviranomaisen palveluksessa, tai eläkkeestä, joka maksetaan sopimusvaltion sosiaaliturvaa koskevan lainsäädännön mukaan, ja muusta suorituksesta, joka tapahtuu tämän lainsäädännön mukaan, vain tässä valtiossa. Tällaisesta eläkkeestä ja muusta suorituksesta verotetaan kuitenkin vain siinä sopimusvaltiossa, jossa tämä luonnollinen henkilö asuu, jos hän on tämän valtion kansalainen.

19 artikla
Julkinen palvelus

1. a) Palkasta ja muusta sellaisesta hyvityksestä, jonka sopimusvaltio, sen julkisyhteisö tai paikallisviranomainen maksaa luonnolliselle henkilölle työstä, joka tehdään tämän valtion, yhteisön tai viranomaisen palveluksessa, verotetaan vain tässä valtiossa.

b) Tällaisesta palkasta ja muusta sellaisesta hyvityksestä verotetaan kuitenkin vain siinä sopimusvaltiossa, jossa tämä henkilö asuu, jos työ tehdään tässä valtiossa ja:

1) henkilö on tämän valtion kansalainen; tai

2) hänestä ei tullut tässä valtiossa asuvaa ainoastaan tämän työn tekemiseksi.

2. Tämän sopimuksen 15, 16 ja 17 artiklan määräyksiä sovelletaan palkkaan ja muuhun sellaiseen hyvitykseen, jotka maksetaan sopimusvaltion tai sen julkisyhteisön tai paikallisviranomaisen harjoittaman liiketoiminnan yhteydessä tehdystä työstä.

20 artikla

Opiskelijat ja harjoittelijat

1. Rahamääristä, jotka opiskelija, ammattioppilas tai liikealan, teollisuuden, maatalouden tai metsätalouden harjoittelija, joka asuu tai välittömästi ennen oleskeluaan sopimusvaltiossa asui toisessa sopimusvaltiossa ja joka oleskelee ensiksi mainitussa valtiossa yksinomaan koulutuksensa tai harjoittelunsa vuoksi, saa elatustaan, koulutustaan tai harjoitteluaan varten, ei tässä valtiossa veroteta, edellyttäen, että nämä rahamäärät kertyvät tämän valtion ulkopuolella olevista lähteistä.

2. Sopimusvaltiossa olevan yliopiston, korkeakoulun tai muun ylemmän oppilaitoksen opiskelijaa tai ammattioppilasta tai liikealan, teollisuuden, maatalouden tai metsätalouden harjoittelijaa, joka asuu tai välittömästi ennen oleskeluaan toisessa sopimusvaltiossa asui ensiksi mainitussa valtiossa ja joka yhtäjaksoisesti oleskelee toisessa sopimusvaltiossa enintään 183 päivää, ei veroteta tässä toisessa valtiossa hyvityksestä, joka saadaan tässä valtiossa tehdystä työstä, jos työ liittyy hänen opintoihinsa tai harjoitteluunsa ja hyvitys koostuu hänen elatustaan varten välttämättömistä ansioista.

21 artikla

Muu tulo

1. Tulosta, jonka sopimusvaltiossa asuva henkilö saa ja jota ei käsitellä tämän sopimuksen edellisissä artikloissa, verotetaan vain tässä valtiossa, riippumatta siitä, mistä tulo kertyy.

2. Tämän artiklan 1 kappaleen määräyksiä ei sovelleta tuloon, joka on muuta kuin 6 artiklan 2 kappaleessa tarkoitettua kiinteästä omaisuudesta saatua tuloa, jos sopimusvaltiossa asuva tulon saaja harjoittaa toisessa sopimusvaltiossa liiketoimintaa siellä olevasta kiinteästä toimipaikasta tai harjoittaa tässä toisessa valtiossa itsenäistä ammattitoimintaa siellä olevasta kiinteästä paikasta, ja tulon maksamisen perusteena oleva oikeus tai omaisuus tosiasiallisesti liittyy tähän kiinteään toimipaikkaan tai kiinteään paikkaan. Tässä tapauksessa sovelletaan 7 artiklan tai 14 artiklan määräyksiä.

3. Tulosta, jonka sopimusvaltiossa asuva henkilö saa ja jota ei käsitellä tämän sopimuksen edellä olevissa artikloissa ja joka kertyy toisesta sopimusvaltiosta, voidaan 1 ja 2 kappaleen määräysten estämättä verottaa myös tässä toisessa valtiossa.

22 artikla

Kaksinkertaisen verotuksen poistaminen

1. Turkissa asuvien henkilöiden kaksinkertainen verotus poistetaan seuraavasti:

a) Jollei Turkin lainsäädännön niistä säännöksistä (sellaisina kuin ne kulloinkin ovat muutettuina ilman että näitä yleisiä periaatteita on muutettu), jotka koskevat Turkin ulkopuolisella alueella maksettavan veron hyvittämistä Turkin veroa vastaan, muuta johdu, Suomen vero, joka Suomen lainsäädännön mukaan ja tämän sopimuksen mukaisesti on maksettava Turkissa asuvan henkilön Suomessa olevasta lähteestä saamasta tulosta (mukaan lukien liiketulo ja veronalainen luovutusvoitto), on vähennettävä tästä tulosta suoritettavasta

Turkin verosta. Vähennys ei kuitenkaan saa ylittää sitä ennen vähennyksen tekemistä laskettua Turkin veron määrää, joka johtuu tästä tulosta.

b) Jos Turkissa asuvan henkilön saama tulo on sopimuksen määräyksen mukaan vapautettu verosta Turkissa, Turkki voi kuitenkin tämän henkilön muusta tulosta suoritettavan veron määrää määrätessään ottaa lukuun verosta vapautetun tulon.

2. Jollei Suomen lainsäädännöstä, joka koskee kansainvälisen kaksinkertaisen verotuksen poistamista, muuta johdu (sikäli kuin tämä lainsäädäntö ei vaikuta tässä esitettyyn yleiseen periaatteeseen), kaksinkertainen verotus poistetaan Suomessa seuraavasti:

a) Milloin Suomessa asuva henkilö saa tuloa, josta tämän sopimuksen määräysten mukaan voidaan verottaa Turkissa, Suomen on, jollei jäljempänä olevan b) kohdan määräyksistä muuta johdu, vähennettävä tämän henkilön Suomen verosta Turkin lainsäädännön mukaan ja sopimuksen mukaisesti maksettua Turkin veroa vastaava määrä, joka lasketaan saman tulon perusteella kuin minkä perusteella Suomen vero lasketaan.

b) Osinko, jonka Turkissa asuva yhtiö maksaa Suomessa asuvalle yhtiölle, vapautetaan Suomen verosta, jos saaja välittömästi hallitsee vähintään 10 prosenttia osingon maksavan yhtiön äänimäärästä.

c) Jos Suomessa asuvan henkilön tulo on sopimuksen määräyksen mukaan vapautettu verosta Suomessa, Suomi voi kuitenkin määrätessään tämän henkilön muusta tulosta suoritettavan veron määrää ottaa lukuun verosta vapautetun tulon.

d) Tämän kappaleen a) kohtaa sovellettaessa ilmaisun "Turkissa tulosta maksettu vero" katsotaan käsittävän Turkin veron määrän, joka Turkin verolainsäädännön mukaan olisi ollut maksettava, jollei Turkin veroa olisi alennettu tai siitä olisi myönnetty vapautusta Turkin taloudellisen kehityksen edistämistä erityiskannustintoimenpitein koskevien määräysten mukaan.

Edellisen lauseen estämättä Turkissa tulosta maksettu vero määrätään

1) 10 artiklan 2 kappaleen b) kohdassa tarkoitetun osingon osalta 15 prosentin verokannan mukaan;

2) 11 artiklan 2 kappaleen a) kohdassa tarkoitetun koron osalta 5 prosentin verokannan mukaan, 11 artiklan 2 kappaleen b) kohdassa tarkoitetun koron osalta 10 prosentin verokannan mukaan ja 11 artiklan 2 kappaleen c) kohdassa tarkoitetun koron osalta 15 prosentin verokannan mukaan;

3) 12 artiklan 2 kappaleessa tarkoitetun rojaltin ja muun suorituksen osalta 10 prosentin verokannan mukaan.

Jos henkilöiden, jotka eivät asu Turkissa, saamaan osinkoon, korkoon ja rojaltiin Turkin verolainsäädännön mukaan sovellettavia verokantoja kuitenkin alennetaan tässä kohdassa mainittuja verokantoja alemmiksi, näitä alempia verokantoja on käytettävä tätä kohtaa sovellettaessa.

23 artikla

Syrjintäkielto

1. Sopimusvaltion kansalainen ei toisessa sopimusvaltiossa saa joutua sellaisen verotuksen tai siihen liittyvän velvoituksen kohteeksi, joka on muunlainen tai raskaampi kuin verotus tai siihen liittyvä velvoitus, jonka kohteeksi tämän toisen valtion kansalainen samoissa, erityisesti asuinpaikkaa koskevissa olosuhteissa joutuu tai saattaa joutua. Tämän sopimuksen 1 artiklan määräysten estämättä tätä määräystä sovelletaan myös henkilöön, joka ei asu sopimusvaltiossa tai molemmissa sopimusvaltioissa.

2. Jollei 10 artiklan 4 kappaleen määräyksistä muuta johdu, verotus, joka kohdistuu sopimusvaltiossa olevan yrityksen toisessa sopimusvaltiossa olevaan kiinteään toimipaikkaan, ei tässä toisessa valtiossa saa olla epäedullisempi kuin verotus, joka kohdistuu tässä toisessa valtiossa olevaan samanlaista toimintaa harjoittavaan yritykseen.

3. Sopimusvaltiossa oleva yritys, jonka pääoman toisessa sopimusvaltiossa asuva henkilö tai siellä asuvat henkilöt välittömästi tai välillisesti joko kokonaan tai osaksi omistavat tai joista he tällä tavoin määräävät, ei ensiksi mainitussa valtiossa saa joutua sellaisen verotuksen tai siihen liittyvän velvoituksen kohteeksi, joka on muunlainen tai raskaampi kuin verotus tai siihen liittyvä velvoitus, jonka kohteeksi ensiksi mainitussa valtiossa oleva muu samanluonteinen yritys joutuu tai saattaa joutua.

4. Muussa kuin sellaisessa tapauksessa, jossa 9 artiklan 1 kappaleen, 11 artiklan 7 kappaleen tai 12 artiklan 6 kappaleen määräyksiä sovelletaan, ovat korko, rojalti ja muu maksu, jotka sopimusvaltiossa oleva yritys suorittaa toisessa sopimusvaltiossa asuvalle henkilölle, vähennyskelpoisia tämän yrityksen verotettavaa tuloa määrättäessä samoin ehdoin kuin maksu ensiksi mainitussa valtiossa asuvalle henkilölle.

5. Näiden määräysten ei katsota velvoittavan sopimusvaltiota myöntämään toisessa sopimusvaltiossa asuville henkilöille sellaista henkilökohtaista verovähennystä, -vapautusta ja veronalennusta siviilisäädyn taikka perheen huoltovelvollisuuden perusteella, jonka se myöntää siinä valtiossa asuville henkilöille.

6. Tämän artiklan määräyksiä sovelletaan vain 2 artiklan piiriin kuuluviin veroihin.

24 artikla

Keskinäinen sopimusmenettely

1. Jos henkilö katsoo, että sopimusvaltion tai molempien sopimusvaltioiden toimenpiteet ovat johtaneet tai johtavat hänen osaltaan verotukseen, joka on tämän sopimuksen määräysten vastainen, hän voi saattaa asiansa sen sopimusvaltion toimivaltaisen viranomaisen käsiteltäväksi, jossa hän asuu tai, jos kysymyksessä on 23 artiklan 1 kappaleen soveltaminen, jonka kansalainen hän on, ilman että tämä vaikuttaa hänen oikeuteensa käyttää näiden valtioiden sisäisessä oikeusjärjestyksessä olevia oikeussuojakeinoja. Asia on saatettava käsiteltäväksi kolmen vuoden kuluessa siitä kun henkilö sai ensimmäisen kerran tiedon toimenpiteestä, joka on aiheuttanut sopimuksen määräysten vastaisen vero-

tuksen.

2. Jos toimivaltainen viranomainen havaitsee huomautuksen perustelluksi, mutta ei itse voi saada aikaan tyydyttävää ratkaisua, viranomaisen on pyrittävä toisen sopimusvaltion toimivaltaisen viranomaisen kanssa keskinäisin sopimuksin ratkaisemaan asia siinä tarkoituksessa, että vältetään verotus, joka on sopimuksen vastainen. Tehty sopimus pannaan täytäntöön sopimusvaltioiden sisäisessä lainsäädännössä olevista aikarajoista riippumatta.

3. Sopimusvaltioiden toimivaltaisten viranomaisten on pyrittävä keskinäisin sopimuksin ratkaisemaan sopimuksen tulkinnassa tai soveltamisessa syntyvät vaikeudet tai epätietoisuutta aiheuttavat kysymykset. Ne voivat myös neuvotella keskenään kaksinkertaisen verotuksen poistamiseksi sellaisissa tapauksissa, joita ei säännellä sopimuksessa.

4. Sopimusvaltioiden toimivaltaiset viranomaiset voivat olla suoraan yhteydessä toisiinsa, myös sellaisessa yhteisessä toimikunnassa, johon ne itse kuuluvat tai johon kuuluu niiden edustajia, päästäkseen sopimukseen siinä merkityksessä kuin edellä olevissa kappaleissa tarkoitetaan.

25 artikla
Tietojen vaihtaminen

1. Sopimusvaltioiden toimivaltaisten viranomaisten on vaihdettava keskenään sellaisia tietoja, jotka ovat ennalta katsoen olennaisia tämän sopimuksen määräysten soveltamiseksi tai sopimusvaltioiden tai niiden valtiollisten osien tai paikallisviranomaisten lukuun määrättäviä kaikenlaatuisia veroja koskevan sisäisen lainsäädännön hallinnoimiseksi tai toimeenpanemiseksi, mikäli tämän lainsäädännön perusteella tapahtuva verotus ei ole tämän sopimuksen vastainen. Sopimuksen 1 ja 2 artikla eivät rajoita tietojen vaihtamista.

2. Sopimusvaltion 1 kappaleen perusteella vastaanottamia tietoja on käsiteltävä salaisina samalla tavalla kuin tämän valtion sisäisen lainsäädännön perusteella saatuja tietoja ja niitä saadaan ilmaista vain henkilöille tai viranomaisille (niihin luettuina tuomioistuimet ja hallintoelimet), jotka määräävät, kantavat tai perivät 1 kappaleessa mainittuja veroja tai käsittelevät näitä veroja koskevia syytteitä tai valituksia, taikka valvovat edellä mainittuja toimia. Näiden henkilöiden tai viranomaisten on käytettävä tietoja vain tällaisiin tarkoituksiin. He saavat ilmaista tietoja julkisessa oikeudenkäynnissä tai tuomioistuimen ratkaisuissa.

3. Tämän artiklan 1 ja 2 kappaleen määräysten ei katsota velvoittavan sopimusvaltiota:

a) ryhtymään hallintotoimiin, jotka poikkeavat tämän sopimusvaltion tai toisen sopimusvaltion lainsäädännöstä ja hallintokäytännöstä;

b) antamaan tietoja, joita tämän sopimusvaltion tai toisen sopimusvaltion lainsäädännön mukaan tai säännönmukaisen hallintomenettelyn puitteissa ei voida hankkia;

c) antamaan tietoja, jotka paljastaisivat liikesalaisuuden taikka teollisen, kaupallisen tai ammatillisen salaisuuden tai elinkeinotoiminnassa käytetyn menettelytavan, taikka tietoja, joiden paljastaminen olisi vastoin yleistä järjestystä (ordre public).

4. Jos sopimusvaltio pyytää tietoja tämän artiklan mukaisesti, toisen sopimusvaltion on käytettävä tietojenhankintakeinojaan pyydettyjen tietojen hankkimiseksi, vaikka tämä toinen valtio ei ehkä tarvitsekaan näitä tietoja omiin verotuksellisiin tarkoituksiinsa. Edelliseen lauseeseen sisältyvää velvollisuutta koskevat 3 kappaleen rajoitukset, mutta näiden rajoitusten ei milloinkaan voida katsoa sallivan sitä, että sopimusvaltio kieltäytyy antamasta tietoja vain sen vuoksi, että ne eivät sen osalta koske kansallista etua.

5. Tämän artiklan 3 kappaleen määräysten ei voida milloinkaan katsoa sallivan sitä, että sopimusvaltio kieltäytyy antamasta tietoja vain sen vuoksi, että tiedot ovat pankin, muun rahoituslaitoksen, välittäjän tai edustajan tai uskotun miehen hallussa tai ne koskevat omistusosuuksia henkilössä.

26 artikla

Virka-apu verojen perimisessä

1. Sopimusvaltioiden on annettava toisilleen virka-apua verosaamisten perimisessä. Sopimuksen 1 ja 2 artikla eivät rajoita tätä virka-apua. Sopimusvaltioiden toimivaltaiset viranomaiset voivat keskinäisellä sopimuksella sopia tämän artiklan soveltamistavasta.

2. Ilmaisulla "verosaaminen" tarkoitetaan tässä artiklassa sopimusvaltioiden tai niiden valtiollisten osien tai paikallisviranomaisten puolesta määrättyjen kaikenlaatuisten verojen velkana olevaa määrää, mikäli niitä koskeva verotus ei ole vastoin tätä sopimusta tai muuta asiakirjaa, jonka osapuolia sopimusvaltiot ovat, samoin kuin tähän määrään liittyvää korkoa, hallinnollisia rangaistuksia ja perimis- tai turvaamiskuluja.

3. Kun sopimusvaltion verosaaminen on tämän valtion lainsäädännön mukaan täytäntöönpanokelpoinen ja velallinen on henkilö, joka sinä ajankohtana ei tämän valtion lainsäädännön mukaan voi estää verosaamisen perimistä, toisen valtion toimivaltaisen viranomaisen on tämän valtion toimivaltaisen viranomaisen pyynnöstä hyväksyttävä verosaaminen perittäväksi. Tämän toisen valtion on perittävä tämä verosaaminen omien verojensa täytäntöönpanoon ja perimiseen sovellettavan lainsäädäntönsä mukaan ikään kuin verosaaminen olisi tämän toisen valtion verosaaminen.

4. Kun sopimusvaltion verosaaminen on sellainen saaminen, jonka osalta tämä valtio voi lainsäädäntönsä mukaan ryhtyä turvaamistoimiin sen perimisen turvaamiseksi, toisen sopimusvaltion toimivaltaisen viranomaisen on tämän valtion toimivaltaisen viranomaisen pyynnöstä hyväksyttävä tämä verosaaminen turvaamistoimiin ryhtymistä varten. Tämän toisen valtion on ryhdyttävä tämän verosaamisen osalta turvaamistoimiin lainsäädäntönsä mukaan ikään kuin verosaaminen olisi tämän toisen valtion verosaaminen, vaikka silloin kun nämä toimet suoritetaan, verosaaminen ei ole täytäntöönpanokelpoinen ensiksi mainitussa valtiossa tai velallinen on henkilö, jolla on oikeus estää sen periminen.

5. Tämän artiklan 3 ja 4 kappaleen estämättä, sopimusvaltion 3 tai 4 kappaleen soveltamista varten hyväksymää verosaamista eivät siinä valtiossa koske ne määräajat eikä niille myönnetä sitä etuoikeutta, joita sovelletaan tämän valtion lainsäädännön mukaisesti verosaamiseen sellaisenaan sen luonteen perusteella. Sopimusvaltion 3 tai 4 kappaleen soveltamista varten hyväksymällä verosaamisella ei ole tässä valtiossa myöskään toisen sopimusvaltion lakeihin perustuvaa tähän verosaamiseen sovellettavaa etuoikeutta.

6. Sopimusvaltion verosaamisen olemassaolosta, pätevyydestä tai määrästä ei voida käydä oikeutta toisen sopimusvaltion tuomioistuimissa tai hallintoelimissä.

7. Milloin jonakin ajankohtana sen jälkeen kun sopimusvaltio on tehnyt 3 tai 4 kappaleen mukaisen pyynnön ja ennen kuin toinen sopimusvaltio on perinyt ja siirtänyt kyseisen verosaamisen ensiksi mainitulle valtiolle, tämä verosaaminen lakkaa olemasta

a) kun kyseessä on 3 kappaleeseen perustuva pyyntö, sellainen ensiksi mainitun valtion verosaaminen, joka on tämän valtion lakien mukaan täytäntöönpanokelpoinen ja jonka velallinen on henkilö, joka sinä ajankohtana ei voi tämän valtion lakien mukaan estää sen perimistä, tai

b) kun kyseessä on 4 kappaleeseen perustuva pyyntö, ensiksi mainitun valtion sellainen verosaaminen, jonka osalta tämä valtio voi lakiensa mukaan suorittaa turvaamistoimia sen perimisen turvaamiseksi,

ensiksi mainitun valtion toimivaltaisen viranomaisen on viipymättä ilmoitettava tästä toisen sopimusvaltion toimivaltaiselle viranomaiselle ja ensiksi mainitun valtion on, toisen valtion valinnan mukaan, lykättävä pyyntöään tai peruutettava se.

8. Tämän artiklan 1 kappaleen määräysten ei missään tapauksessa katsota velvoittavan sopimusvaltiota:

a) ryhtymään hallintotoimiin, jotka poikkeavat sen tai toisen sopimusvaltion lainsäädännöstä ja hallintokäytännöstä;

b) suorittamaan toimia, jotka olisivat vastoin yleistä järjestystä (ordre public);

c) antamaan virka-apua, jos toinen sopimusvaltio ei ole käyttänyt kaikkia kohtuullisia perimis- tai turvaamistoimia, jotka ovat käytettävissä sen lainsäädännön tai hallintokäytännön mukaan;

d) antamaan virka-apua tapauksissa, joissa hallinnollinen rasitus tällä valtiolle on selvästi suhteettoman suuri verrattuna siihen etuun, jonka toinen sopimusvaltio voi saada.

27 artikla
Diplomaattisen edustuston ja konsuliedustuston jäsenet

Tämä sopimus ei vaikuta niihin verotuksellisiin erioikeuksiin, jotka kansainvälisen oikeuden yleisten sääntöjen tai erityisten sopimusten määräysten mukaan myönnetään diplomaattisille edustajille tai konsulivirkamiehille.

28 artikla
Voimaantulo

1. Kumpikin sopimusvaltio ilmoittaa toiselle sopimusvaltiolle diplomaattista tietä täyttäneensä kansallisessa lainsäädännössään tämän sopimuksen voimaantulolle asetetut edellytykset. Sopimus tulee voimaan kolmenkymmenen päivän kuluttua myöhemmän ilmoituksen päivämäärästä, ja sen määräyksiä sovelletaan:

a) Turkissa, veroihin kaikilta niiltä verokausilta, jotka alkavat sopimuksen voimaantulovuotta seuraavan vuoden tammikuun 1 päivänä tai sen jälkeen;

b) Suomessa:

1) lähteellä pidätettävien verojen osalta, tuloon, joka saadaan sopimuksen voimaantulovuotta lähinnä seuraavan kalenterivuoden tammikuun 1 päivänä tai sen jälkeen;

2) muiden tulosta suoritettavien verojen osalta, veroihin, jotka määrätään sopimuksen voimaantulovuotta lähinnä seuraavan kalenterivuoden tammikuun 1 päivänä tai sen jälkeen alkavilta verovuosilta.

2. Ankarassa 9 päivänä toukokuuta 1986 allekirjoitettua "sopimusta Turkin tasavallan ja Suomen tasavallan välillä tuloveroja koskevan kaksinkertaisen verotuksen välttämiseksi" (jäljempänä "vuoden 1986 sopimus") lakataan soveltamasta ajankohdasta, jolloin tätä sopimusta 1 kappaleen määräysten mukaan aletaan soveltaa. Vuoden 1986 sopimus lakkaa olemasta voimassa sinä viimeisenä ajankohtana, jona sitä tämän kappaleen edellä olevien määräysten mukaan sovelletaan.

29 artikla
Päättyminen

Tämä sopimus on voimassa, kunnes jompikumpi sopimusvaltio sen irtisanoo. Kumpikin sopimusvaltio voi viiden vuoden kuluttua sopimuksen voimaantulopäivästä irtisanoa sopimuksen diplomaattista tietä antamalla irtisanomisilmoituksen vähintään kuusi kuukautta ennen jonkin kalenterivuoden päättymistä. Tässä tapauksessa sopimusta lakataan soveltamasta:

a) Turkissa, veroihin niiltä verokausilta, jotka alkavat irtisanomisilmoituksen antamisvuotta seuraavan vuoden tammikuun 1 päivänä tai sen jälkeen;

b) Suomessa:

1) lähteellä pidätettävien verojen osalta, tuloon, joka saadaan irtisanomisilmoituksen antamisvuotta lähinnä seuraavan kalenterivuoden tammikuun 1 päivänä tai sen jälkeen;

2) muiden tulosta suoritettavien verojen osalta, veroihin, jotka määrätään irtisanomisilmoituksen antamisvuotta lähinnä seuraavan kalenterivuoden tammikuun 1 päivänä tai sen jälkeen alkavilta verovuosilta.

Tämän vakuudeksi ovat allekirjoittaneet, asianmukaisesti siihen valtuutettuina, allekirjoittaneet tämän sopimuksen.

Tehty Istanbulissa päivänä lokakuuta 2009, kahtena suomen-, turkin- ja englanninkielisenä kappaleena kaikkien tekstien ollessa yhtä todistusvoimaiset. Tulkintaerimielisyyden sattuessa englanninkielinen on teksti ratkaiseva.

SUOMEN TASAVALLAN HALLITUKSEN PUOLESTA:

TURKIN TASAVALLAN HALLITUKSEN PUOLESTA:

PÖYTÄKIRJA

Allekirjoitettaessa sopimusta Suomen tasavallan ja Turkin tasavallan välillä tuloveroja koskevan kaksinkertaisen verotuksen välttämiseksi allekirjoittaneet ovat sopineet seuraavista määräyksistä, jotka ovat sopimuksen olennainen osa.

1. Sopimuksen 7 artiklan 1 kappale.

Milloin sopimusvaltiossa olevalla yrityksellä on kiinteä toimipaikka toisessa valtiossa ja yritys

a) myy tässä toisessa valtiossa samanlaisia tai samankaltaisia tavaroita kuin ne, joita myydään tästä kiinteästä toimipaikasta, tai

b) harjoittaa tässä toisessa valtiossa muuta liiketoimintaa, joka on samanlaista tai samankaltaista kuin tässä kiinteässä toimipaikassa harjoitettu liiketoiminta,

myynnistä ja liiketoiminnasta verotetaan tässä toisessa sopimusvaltiossa osana kiinteän toimipaikan tuloa, jos osoitetaan, että tällaista myyntiä tai toimintaa on harjoitettu kiinteästä toimipaikasta. Tätä verotusta ei voida sulkea pois keinotekoisilla myyntijärjestelyillä.

2. Sopimuksen 10 artiklan 3 kappale.

Ilmaisun "osinko" katsotaan Turkin osalta käsittävän myös investointirahastosta ja -trustista saadun tulon.

3. Sopimuksen 12 ja 13 artikla.

Kaikkien 12 artiklan 3 kappaleessa tarkoitetun omaisuuden myynnistä korvauksena saatujen suoritusten osalta on sovellettava 12 artiklan määräyksiä, paitsi jos osoitetaan, että kyseinen suoritus on suoritus aidosta mainitun omaisuuden luovutuksesta. Silloin on sovellettava 13 artiklan määräyksiä.

4. Sopimuksen 15 artiklan 2 kappale.

Sopimuksen 15 artiklan 2 kappaletta ei sovelleta hyvitykseen, jonka sopimusvaltiossa asuva henkilö ("työntekijä") saa ja jonka maksaa siinä valtiossa asuva työnantaja tai joka maksetaan siinä valtiossa asuvan työnantajan puolesta, toisessa sopimusvaltiossa tehdystä työstä, jos:

a) työntekijä suorittaa tämän työn aikana palveluja muulle henkilölle kuin työnantajalle ja tämä henkilö suoraan tai välillisesti valvoo, ohjaa tai kontrolloi tapaa, jolla nämä palvelut suoritetaan; ja

b) työnantaja ei vastaa saajan suorittaman työn lopputuloksesta.

5. Sopimuksen 4, 18 ja 19 artikla.

Ilmaisun "julkisyhteisö" katsotaan tarkoittavan:

a) Turkin osalta

1) the Central Bank of Turkey (Türkiye Cumhuriyeti Merkez Bankasi);

2) Turkin pakollisia sosiaalivakuutuslaitoksia; ja

3) yliopistoja ja muita samanlaisia korkeamman koulutuksen laitoksia;

b) Suomen osalta

1) Suomen Pankkia;

2) Kansaneläkelaitosta; ja

3) Helsingin Yliopistoa.

Artiklojen 18 ja 19 osalta "julkisyhteisö" käsittää,

Turkin osalta: uskonnolliset laitokset; ja

Suomen osalta: evankelis-luterilaisen ja ortodoksisen kirkon ja niiden paikallisyhteisöt.

6. Sopimuksen 22 artiklan 2 kappaleen d)kohta.

Sopimuksen 22 artiklan 2 kappaleen d) kohdan määräyksiä sovelletaan vain sopimuksen viideltä ensimmäiseltä soveltamisvuodelta.

7. Sopimuksen 24 artiklan 2 kappale.

Verovelvollisen on Turkin kyseessä ollen vaadittava 24 artiklan 2 kappaleen osalta tällaisesta keskinäisestä sopimuksesta johtuvaa palautusta vuoden kuluessa siitä, kun verohallinto on antanut verovelvolliselle tiedoksi keskinäisen sopimuksen tuloksen.

Tämän vakuudeksi ovat allekirjoittaneet, asianmukaisesti siihen valtuutettuina, allekirjoittaneet tämän pöytäkirjan.

Tehty Istanbulissa 6 päivänä lokakuuta 2009, kahtena suomen-, turkin- ja englanninkielisenä kappaleena kaikkien tekstien ollessa yhtä todistusvoimaiset. Tulkintaerimielisyyden sattuessa englanninkielinen teksti on ratkaiseva.

SUOMEN TASAVALLAN HALLITUKSEN PUOLESTA:	TURKIN TASAVALLAN HALLITUKSEN PUOLESTA:

[TEXT IN TURKISH – TEXTE EN TURC]

FİNLANDİYA CUMHURİYETİ

İLE

TÜRKİYE CUMHURİYETİ

ARASINDA

GELİR ÜZERİNDEN ALINAN VERGİLERDE

ÇİFTE VERGİLENDİRMEYİ ÖNLEME

ANLAŞMASI

FİNLANDİYA CUMHURİYETİ HÜKÜMETİ

VE

TÜRKİYE CUMHURİYETİ HÜKÜMETİ

Gelir üzerinden alınan vergilerde çifte vergilendirmeyi önleyen bir Anlaşma yapmak isteğiyle,

AŞAĞIDAKİ ANLAŞMAYA VARMIŞLARDIR:

Madde 1

KAPSANAN KİŞİLER

Bu Anlaşma Akit Devletlerden birinin veya her ikisinin mukimi olan kişilere uygulanacaktır.

Madde 2

KAPSANAN VERGİLER

1. Bu Anlaşma, ne şekilde alındığına bakılmaksızın, bir Akit Devlet veya mahalli idareleri adına gelir üzerinden alınan vergilere uygulanacaktır.

2. Menkul veya gayrimenkul varlıkların devrinden doğan kazançlara uygulanan vergiler ile teşebbüsler tarafından ödenen ücret veya maaşların toplam tutarı üzerinden alınan vergiler ve bunun yanı sıra sermaye değer artışlarına uygulanan vergiler de dahil olmak üzere, toplam gelir veya gelirin unsurları üzerinden alınan tüm vergiler, gelirden alınan vergiler olarak kabul edilecektir.

3. Anlaşmanın uygulanacağı mevcut vergiler:

a) Türkiye'de:

i) gelir vergisi; ve

ii) kurumlar vergisi;

(bundan böyle "Türk vergisi" olarak bahsedilecektir);

b) Finlandiya'da:

i) devlet gelir vergileri (valtion tuloverot; de statliga inkomstskatterna);

ii) kurumlar vergisi (yhteisöjen tulovero; inkomstskatten för samfund);

iii) mahalli vergi (kunnallisvero; kommunalskatten);

iv) kilise vergisi (kirkollisvero; kyrkoskatten);

v) Faiz üzerinden kaynakta tevkif edilen vergi (korkotulon lähdevero; källskatten på ränteinkomst) ve

vi) Dar mükelleflerin gelirleri üzerinden kaynakta tevkif edilen vergi (rajoitetusti verovelvollisen lähdevero; källskatten för begransat skattskyldig);

(bundan böyle "Fin vergisi" olarak bahsedilecektir).

4. Anlaşma aynı zamanda, Anlaşmanın imza tarihinden sonra mevcut vergilerin yerine veya onlara ilave olarak alınacak ve mevcut vergilerle aynı nitelikte olan veya onlara önemli ölçüde benzeyen vergilere de uygulanacaktır. Akit Devletlerin yetkili makamları, ilgili vergi kanunlarında yapılan önemli değişiklikleri birbirlerine bildireceklerdir.

Madde 3

GENEL TANIMLAR

1. Bu Anlaşmanın amaçları yönünden, metin aksini gerektirmedikçe:

a) i) "Türkiye" terimi, kara suları ve üzerindeki hava sahası da dahil olmak üzere, Türkiye'nin egemenlik alanını, bunun yanı sıra uluslararası hukuka uygun olarak doğal kaynakların aranması, işletilmesi ve korunması amacıyla yargı yetkisi veya egemenlik haklarına sahip olduğu deniz alanlarını ifade eder:

ii) "Finlandiya" terimi, Finlandiya Cumhuriyeti'ni ifade eder ve coğrafi anlamda kullanıldığında, Finlandiya Cumhuriyeti'nin egemenlik alanı ile Finlandiya Cumhuriyeti kara sularına bitişik olup, Finlandiya kanunları ve uluslararası hukuk uyarınca deniz yatağı, onun toprak altı ve üzerindeki sularda doğal kaynakları arama ve işletme hakkının Finlandiya'ya ait olduğu alanları ifade eder;

b) "Bir Akit Devlet" ve "diğer Akit Devlet" terimleri metnin gereğine göre, Türkiye veya Finlandiya anlamına gelir;

c) "Kişi" terimi, bir gerçek kişiyi, bir şirketi ve kişilerin oluşturduğu diğer herhangi bir kuruluşu kapsamına alır;

d) "Şirket" terimi, herhangi bir kurum veya vergileme yönünden kurum olarak muamele gören herhangi bir kuruluş anlamına gelir;

e) "Kuruluş yeri" terimi, duruma göre, Türk Ticaret Kanunu'na göre tescil edilen bir şirketin kanuni merkezi veya Fin mevzuatına göre bir şirketin kayıtlı olduğu yer anlamına gelir;

f) bir Akit Devlete ilişkin "vatandaş" terimi:

i) o Akit Devletin vatandaşlığına veya uyrukluğuna sahip herhangi bir gerçek kişiyi; ve

ii) o Akit Devlette yürürlükte olan mevzuata göre statü kazanan herhangi bir hükmi şahsı, ortaklığı veya derneği

ifade eder.

g) "Bir Akit Devletin teşebbüsü" ve "diğer Akit Devletin teşebbüsü" terimleri sırasıyla, bir Akit Devletin mukimi tarafından işletilen bir teşebbüs ve diğer Akit Devletin mukimi tarafından işletilen bir teşebbüs anlamına gelir;

h) "Yetkili makam" terimi:

i) Türkiye'de, Maliye Bakanı'nı veya onun yetkili temsilcisini; ve

ii) Finlandiya'da, Maliye Bakanlığını, onun yetkili temsilcisini veya Maliye Bakanlığı tarafından yetkili makam olarak belirtilen makamı

ifade eder;

i) "Uluslararası trafik" terimi, yalnızca diğer Akit Devletin sınırları içinde gerçekleştirilen gemi, uçak veya kara yolu nakil vasıtası işletmeciliği hariç olmak üzere, bir Akit Devlet teşebbüsü tarafından gemi, uçak veya kara yolu nakil vasıtası işletilerek yapılan taşımacılığı ifade eder.

2. Anlaşmanın bir Akit Devlet tarafından herhangi bir tarihte uygulanmasına ilişkin olarak, Anlaşmada tanımlanmamış herhangi bir terim, metin aksini gerektirmedikçe, Anlaşmanın uygulanacağı vergilerin amaçları bakımından, o tarihte bu Devletin mevzuatında sahip olduğu anlamı taşıyacak ve bu Devletin yürürlükteki vergi mevzuatında yer alan bir anlam, bu Devletin diğer mevzuatında bu terime verilen anlama göre üstünlük taşıyacaktır.

Madde 4

MUKİM

1. Bu Anlaşmanın amaçları bakımından, "bir Akit Devletin mukimi" terimi, bu Devlet, statüye sahip herhangi bir kuruluşu veya mahalli idaresi de dahil olmak üzere, o Devletin mevzuatı gereğince ev, ikametgah, kuruluş yeri, yönetim yeri veya benzer yapıda diğer herhangi bir kriter nedeniyle vergi mükellefiyeti altına giren kişi anlamına

gelir. Ancak bu terim, yalnızca o Devletteki kaynaklardan elde edilen gelir nedeniyle o Devlette vergiye tabi tutulan herhangi bir kişiyi kapsamaz.

2. 1 inci fıkra hükümleri dolayısıyla bir gerçek kişi her iki Akit Devletin de mukimi olduğunda, bu kişinin durumu aşağıdaki şekilde belirlenecektir:

a) bu kişi, yalnızca daimi olarak kalabileceği bir evin bulunduğu Devletin mukimi kabul edilecektir; eğer bu kişinin her iki Devlette de daimi olarak kalabileceği bir evi varsa, bu kişi yalnızca kişisel ve ekonomik ilişkilerinin daha yakın olduğu (hayati menfaatlerin merkezi) Devletin mukimi kabul edilecektir;

b) eğer kişinin hayati menfaatlerinin merkezinin yer aldığı Devlet saptanamazsa veya her iki Devlette de daimi olarak kalabileceği bir evi yoksa, bu kişi yalnızca kalmayı adet edindiği evin bulunduğu Devletin mukimi kabul edilecektir;

c) eğer kişinin her iki Devlette de kalmayı adet edindiği bir ev varsa veya her iki Devlette de böyle bir ev söz konusu değilse, bu kişi vatandaşı olduğu Devletin mukimi kabul edilecektir;

d) eğer kişi her iki Devletin de vatandaşıysa veya her iki Devletin de vatandaşı değilse, Akit Devletlerin yetkili makamları sorunu karşılıklı anlaşmayla çözeceklerdir.

3. 1 inci fıkra hükümleri dolayısıyla gerçek kişi dışındaki bir kişi her iki Akit Devletin de mukimi olduğunda, bu kişi yalnızca kurulmuş olduğu Devletin bir mukimi olarak kabul edilecektir.

Madde 5

İŞ YERİ

1. Bu Anlaşmanın amaçları bakımından "iş yeri" terimi, bir teşebbüsün işinin tamamen veya kısmen yürütüldüğü işe ilişkin sabit bir yer anlamına gelir.

2. "İş yeri" terimi özellikle şunları kapsamına alır:

a) yönetim yeri;

b) şube;

c) büro;

d) fabrika;

e) atölye; ve

f) maden ocağı, petrol veya doğal gaz kuyusu, taş ocağı veya doğal kaynakların çıkarıldığı diğer herhangi bir yer.

3. Bir inşaat şantiyesi, yapım, montaj veya kurma projesi veya bunlara ilişkin gözetim faaliyetleri, altı ayı aşan bir süre devam etmesi durumunda bir iş yeri oluşturur.

4. Bu maddenin daha önceki hükümlerine bakılmaksızın, "iş yeri" teriminin aşağıdaki hususları kapsamadığı kabul edilecektir:

a) tesislerin, teşebbüse ait malların veya ticari eşyanın yalnızca depolanması, teşhiri veya teslimi amacıyla kullanılması;

b) teşebbüse ait mal veya ticari eşya stoklarının yalnızca depolama, teşhir veya teslim amacıyla elde tutulması;

c) teşebbüse ait mal veya ticari eşya stoklarının yalnızca bir başka teşebbüse işlettirilmesi amacıyla elde tutulması;

d) işe ilişkin sabit bir yerin yalnızca teşebbüse mal veya ticari eşya satın alma veya bilgi toplama amacıyla elde tutulması;

e) işe ilişkin sabit bir yerin teşebbüs için yalnızca hazırlayıcı veya yardımcı karakter taşıyan diğer herhangi bir faaliyetin yürütülmesi amacıyla elde tutulması;

f) işe ilişkin sabit yerdeki bütün faaliyetlerin bir arada yürütülmesi sonucunda oluşan faaliyetin hazırlayıcı veya yardımcı nitelikte olması şartıyla, işe ilişkin sabit bir yerin yalnızca (a) ila (e) bentlerinde bahsedilen faaliyetlerin birini veya birkaçını bir arada yürütmek amacıyla elde tutulması.

5. 1 inci ve 2 nci fıkra hükümlerine bakılmaksızın, bir kişi -6 ncı fıkranın uygulanacağı bağımsız nitelikteki bir acente dışında- bir Akit Devlette, diğer Akit Devletin bir teşebbüsü adına hareket ederse, aşağıdaki şartlarla bu teşebbüs, ilk bahsedilen Devlette, bu kişinin teşebbüs için gerçekleştirdiği her türlü faaliyet dolayısıyla bir iş yerine sahip kabul edilecektir:

a) kişinin faaliyetleri 4 üncü fıkrada belirtilen ve işe ilişkin sabit bir yerden yapılması durumunda bu yeri, o fıkra hükümlerine göre iş yeri haline getirmeyen nitelikteki faaliyetlerle sınırlı olmadıkça, bu kişi, o Devlette teşebbüs adına mukavele akdetme yetkisine sahip olur ve bu yetkisini mutaden kullanırsa; veya

b) eğer bu kişi, böyle bir yetkisi olmamasına rağmen, teşebbüs adına düzenli olarak sevk ettiği mallardan veya ticari eşyadan ilk bahsedilen Devlette mutaden mal veya ticari eşya stoku bulundurursa.

6. Bir teşebbüs, bir Akit Devlette işlerini yalnızca bir simsar, bir genel komisyon acentesi veya bağımsız statüde diğer herhangi bir acente vasıtasıyla yürüttüğü için bu Devlette bir iş yerine sahip kabul olunmayacaktır; şu kadar ki, bu kişilerin kendi işlerine olağan şekilde devam etmeleri şarttır.

7. Bir Akit Devletin mukimi olan bir şirket, diğer Akit Devletin mukimi olan veya bu diğer Akit Devlette ticari faaliyette bulunan (bir iş yeri vasıtasıyla veya diğer bir şekilde) bir şirketi kontrol eder ya da onun tarafından kontrol edilirse, bu şirketlerden herhangi biri, diğeri için bir iş yeri oluşturmayacaktır.

Madde 6

GAYRİMENKUL VARLIKLARDAN ELDE EDİLEN GELİR

1. Bir Akit Devlet mukiminin diğer Akit Devlette bulunan gayrimenkul varlıklardan elde ettiği gelir (tarım veya ormancılıktan elde edilen gelir dahil), bu diğer Devlette vergilendirilebilir.

2. "Gayrimenkul varlık" terimi, söz konusu varlığın bulunduğu Akit Devletin mevzuatına göre tanımlanacaktır. Terim her halükarda gayrimenkul varlığa müteferri varlıkları, tarım (balık üretimi ve yetiştiriciliği dahil) ve ormancılıkta kullanılan araçları ve hayvanları, gayrimenkule ilişkin özel hukuk hükümlerinin uygulanacağı hakları, gayrimenkul intifa haklarını ve maden ocaklarının, kaynakların ve diğer doğal kaynakların işletme hakkından veya işletilmesinden doğan sabit ya da değişken ödemeler üzerindeki hakları kapsayacak; gemiler ve uçaklar gayrimenkul varlık olarak kabul edilmeyecektir.

3. 1 inci fıkra hükümleri, gayrimenkul varlığın doğrudan kullanımından, kiralanmasından veya diğer herhangi bir şekilde kullanımından elde edilen gelire uygulanacaktır.

4. Bir şirketin hisseleri veya diğer şirket haklarına sahip olmak, bu hisse veya şirket haklarının sahibine, şirketin mülkiyetinde bulunan gayrimenkul varlıklardan yararlanma hakkını sağlıyorsa, söz konusu yararlanma hakkının doğrudan kullanımından, kiralanmasından veya diğer herhangi bir şekilde kullanımından elde edilen gelir, gayrimenkul varlığın bulunduğu Akit Devlette vergilendirilebilir.

5. 1 inci ve 3 üncü fıkra hükümleri aynı zamanda, bir teşebbüsün gayrimenkul varlıklarından elde edilen gelir ile serbest meslek faaliyetlerinin icrasında kullanılan

gayrimenkul varlıklardan elde edilen gelire de uygulanacaktır.

Madde 7

TİCARİ KAZANÇLAR

1. Bir Akit Devlet teşebbüsüne ait kazanç, söz konusu teşebbüs diğer Akit Devlette yer alan bir iş yeri vasıtasıyla ticari faaliyette bulunmadıkça, yalnızca bu Devlette vergilendirilecektir. Eğer teşebbüs yukarıda bahsedilen şekilde ticari faaliyette bulunursa, teşebbüsün kazancı, yalnızca iş yerine atfedilebilen miktarla sınırlı olmak üzere bu diğer Devlette vergilendirilebilir.

2. 3 üncü fıkra hükümleri saklı kalmak üzere, bir Akit Devlet teşebbüsü diğer Akit Devlette yer alan bir iş yeri vasıtasıyla ticari faaliyette bulunduğunda, her iki Akit Devlette de bu iş yerine atfedilecek kazanç, bu iş yeri aynı veya benzer koşullar altında aynı veya benzer faaliyetlerde bulunan, ayrı ve bağımsız bir teşebbüs olsaydı ve iş yerini oluşturduğu teşebbüsten tamamen bağımsız bir nitelik kazansaydı ne kazanç elde edecek ise aynı miktarda bir kazanç olacaktır.

3. İş yerinin kazancı belirlenirken, iş yerinin bulunduğu Devlette veya başka bir yerde yapılan, yönetim ve genel idare giderleri de dahil, iş yerinin amaçlarına uygun olan giderlerin indirilmesine müsaade edilecektir. Bununla beraber, ana merkezin veya yurt dışında bulunan diğer işyerlerinin gider ve zararlarına katılım ve aynı şekilde, iş yeri tarafından teşebbüsün ana merkezine veya diğer herhangi bir bürosuna yapılan gayrimaddi hak bedeli, faiz, komisyon veya diğer benzeri ödemelerin gider olarak indirilmesine müsaade edilmeyecektir.

4. İş yerine, bu iş yeri tarafından teşebbüs adına yalnızca mal veya ticari eşya satın alınması dolayısıyla hiç bir kazanç atfedilmeyecektir.

5. Kazanç, bu Anlaşmanın diğer maddelerinde ayrı olarak düzenlenen gelir unsurlarını da kapsamına aldığında, o maddelerin hükümleri bu madde hükümlerinden etkilenmeyecektir.

Madde 8

DENİZ, HAVA VE KARA YOLU TAŞIMACILIĞI

1. Bir Akit Devlet teşebbüsünün uluslararası trafikte gemi, uçak veya kara yolu nakil vasıtası işletmeciliğinden elde ettiği kazançlar, yalnızca bu Devlette vergilendirilecektir.

2. 1 inci fıkra hükümleri aynı zamanda, bir ortaklığa, bir ortak teşebbüse veya uluslararası işletilen bir acenteye iştirak dolayısıyla elde edilen kazançlara da uygulanacaktır.

Madde 9

BAĞIMLI TEŞEBBÜSLER

1. a) Bir Akit Devlet teşebbüsü doğrudan veya dolaylı olarak diğer Akit Devlet teşebbüsünün yönetim, kontrol veya sermayesine katıldığında; veya

   b) Aynı kişiler doğrudan veya dolaylı olarak bir Akit Devlet teşebbüsünün ve diğer Akit Devlet teşebbüsünün yönetim, kontrol veya sermayesine katıldığında,

ve her iki halde de, iki teşebbüs arasındaki ticari ve mali ilişkilerde oluşan veya empoze edilen koşullar, bağımsız teşebbüsler arasında oluşması gereken koşullardan farklılaştığında, teşebbüslerden birinde olması gereken, fakat bu koşullar dolayısıyla kendini göstermeyen kazanç, o teşebbüsün kazancına eklenip buna göre vergilendirilebilir.

2. Bir Akit Devletin kendi teşebbüsünün kazancına dahil edip vergilendirdiği kazanç, bu diğer Akit Devlette vergilendirilen diğer Devlet teşebbüsünün kazancını içermesi ve aynı zamanda, ilk bahsedilen Devletin kavradığı bu kazancın, iki bağımsız teşebbüs arasında olması gereken koşullar göz önünde tutularak, bu ilk bahsedilen Devletçe yürütülen hesaplamalar sonucunda belirlenen kazanç olması durumunda, diğer Devlet bu belirlemenin yerinde olduğu kanaatine varırsa, söz konusu kazanç üzerinden alınan verginin miktarında gerekli düzeltmeleri yapacaktır. Bu düzeltme yapılırken, bu Anlaşmanın diğer hükümleri göz önünde tutulacak ve gerektiğinde Akit Devletlerin yetkili makamları birbirlerine danışacaklardır.

Madde 10

TEMETTÜLER

1. Bir Akit Devletin mukimi olan bir şirket tarafından diğer Akit Devletin bir mukimine ödenen temettüler, bu diğer Devlette vergilendirilebilir.

2. Bununla beraber söz konusu temettüler, temettüleri ödeyen şirketin mukim olduğu Akit Devlette ve o Devletin mevzuatına göre de vergilendirilebilir; ancak, temettünün gerçek lehdarı diğer Akit Devletin bir mukimi ise, bu şekilde alınacak vergi aşağıdaki oranları aşmayacaktır:

a) gerçek lehdar, temettüyü ödeyen şirketin sermayesinin doğrudan doğruya en az yüzde 25 ini elinde tutan bir şirket ise (ortaklık hariç) gayrisafi temettü tutarının yüzde 5 i,

b) diğer tüm durumlarda gayrisafi temettü tutarının yüzde 15 i.

Bu fıkra, temettülerin ödendiği kazançlar yönünden şirketin vergilendirilmesini etkilemeyecektir.

3. Bu maddede kullanılan "temettü" terimi, hisse senetlerinden, intifa senetlerinden veya intifa haklarından, kurucu hisse senetlerinden veya alacak niteliğinde olmayıp kazanca katılmayı sağlayan diğer haklardan elde edilen gelirler ile dağıtımı yapan şirketin mukim olduğu Devletin mevzuatına göre, vergileme yönünden hisse senetlerinden elde edilen gelirle aynı muameleyi gören diğer şirket haklarından elde edilen gelirleri ifade eder.

4. Diğer Akit devlette yer alan bir iş yeri vasıtasıyla ticari faaliyette bulunan bir Akit Devlet şirketinin kazancı, 7 nci maddeye göre vergilendirildikten sonra, kalan kısım iş yerinin bulunduğu Akit Devlette vergilendirilebilir. Ancak, bu şekilde alınacak vergi aşağıdaki oranları aşmayacaktır:

a) bu kazançların, şirketin mukim olduğu Akit Devlette vergiden istisna edilmesi koşuluyla kalan kısmın yüzde 5 i,

b) diğer tüm durumlarda kalan kısmın yüzde 15 i.

5. Bir Akit Devlet mukimi olan temettünün gerçek lehdarı, temettüyü ödeyen şirketin mukim olduğu diğer Akit Devlette yer alan bir iş yeri vasıtasıyla ticari faaliyette bulunursa veya bu diğer Devlette yer alan sabit bir yer vasıtasıyla serbest meslek faaliyetinde bulunursa ve söz konusu temettü elde ediş olayı ile bu iş yeri veya sabit yer arasında etkin bir bağ bulunmaktaysa, 1 inci ve 2 nci fıkra hükümleri uygulanmayacaktır. Bu durumda, olayına göre 7 nci veya 14 üncü madde hükümleri uygulanacaktır.

6. Bu maddenin 4 üncü fıkra hükümleri saklı kalmak üzere, bir Akit Devlet mukimi olan bir şirket, diğer Akit Devletten kazanç veya gelir elde ettiğinde, bu diğer Devlet, temettülerin kendi mukimlerinden birine ödenmesi veya temettü elde edilmesi ile bu diğer Devlette bulunan bir iş yeri veya sabit yer arasında etkin bir bağ bulunması durumları hariç olmak üzere, bu şirket tarafından ödenen temettüler üzerinden herhangi bir vergi alamayacağı gibi, ödenen temettülerin veya dağıtılmamış kazancın tamamen veya kısmen bu diğer Devlette elde edilen kazanç veya gelirden oluşması durumunda bile, bu şirketin dağıtılmayan kazançları üzerinden dağıtılmayan kazanç vergisi alamaz.

Madde 11

FAİZ

1. Bir Akit Devlette doğan ve diğer Akit Devletin bir mukimine ödenen faiz, bu diğer Devlette vergilendirilebilir.

2. Bununla beraber bu faiz, elde edildiği Akit Devlette ve o Devletin mevzuatına göre de vergilendirilebilir; ancak, faizin gerçek lehdarı diğer Akit Devletin bir mukimi ise, bu şekilde alınacak vergi aşağıdaki oranları aşmayacaktır:

a) Finlandiya İhracat Kredi Kurumu (Finnish Export Credit) veya FINNVERA ile amacı ihracatı teşvik olan benzeri Türk kamu kurumları tarafından ihracatı teşvik amacıyla verilen, garanti edilen veya sigortalanan borç veya krediler yönünden, faizin gayrisafi tutarının yüzde 5 i,

b) faizin bir banka tarafından elde edilmesi durumda, faizin gayrisafi tutarının yüzde 10 u,

c) tüm diğer durumlarda faizin gayrisafi tutarının yüzde 15 i.

3. 2 nci fıkra hükümlerine bakılmaksızın:

a) Finlandiya'da doğan ve Türkiye Hükümeti'ne veya Türkiye Cumhuriyet Merkez Bankası'na ödenen faizler, Fin vergisinden istisna edilecektir,

b) Türkiye'de doğan ve Finlandiya Hükümeti'ne veya Finlandiya Bankası'na (Suomen Pankki) ödenen faizler, Türk vergisinden istisna edilecektir

4. Bu maddede kullanılan "faiz" terimi, ipotek garantisine bağlı olsun olmasın ve borçlunun kazancına katılma hakkı tanısın tanımasın, her nevi alacaktan doğan gelirleri ve özellikle kamu menkul kıymetleri ile tahvil veya borç senetlerine ilişkin prim ve ikramiyeler dahil olmak üzere, söz konusu menkul kıymet, tahvil veya borç senetlerinden elde edilen gelirler ile gelirin elde edildiği Akit Devletin vergi mevzuatına göre ikrazat geliri sayılan diğer bütün gelirleri ifade eder.

5. Bir Akit Devlet mukimi olan faizin gerçek lehdarı, faizin elde edildiği diğer Akit Devlette bulunan bir iş yeri vasıtasıyla ticari faaliyette bulunursa veya bu diğer Devlette yer alan sabit bir yer vasıtasıyla serbest meslek faaliyetinde bulunursa ve söz konusu faizin ödendiği alacak ile bu iş yeri veya sabit yer arasında etkin bir bağ bulunmaktaysa, 1 inci ve 2 nci fıkra hükümleri uygulanmayacaktır. Bu durumda, olayına göre, 7 nci veya 14 üncü madde hükümleri uygulanacaktır.

6. Bir Akit Devletin kendisi, mahalli idaresi veya bir mukimi tarafından ödenen

faizin, o Devlette elde edildiği kabul olunacaktır. Bununla beraber, faiz ödeyen kişi, bir Akit Devletin mukimi olsun veya olmasın, bir Akit Devlette faiz ödemeye neden olan borç-alacak ilişkisiyle bağlantılı bir iş yerine veya sabit yere sahip olduğunda ve faiz bu iş yerinden veya sabit yerden kaynaklandığında, söz konusu faizin iş yerinin veya sabit yerin bulunduğu Devlette elde edildiği kabul olunacaktır.

7. Alacak karşılığında ödenen faizin miktarı, ödeyici ile gerçek lehdar arasında veya her ikisi ile bir başka kişi arasında var olan özel ilişki nedeniyle, böyle bir ilişkinin olmadığı durumlarda ödeyici ve gerçek lehdar arasında kararlaştırılacak miktarı aştığında, bu madde hükümleri yalnızca en son bahsedilen miktara uygulanacaktır. Bu durumda ödemelerin aşan kısmı, bu Anlaşmanın diğer hükümleri de dikkate alınarak, her bir Akit Devletin mevzuatına göre vergilendirilecektir.

Madde 12

GAYRİMADDİ HAK BEDELLERİ

1. Bir Akit Devlette doğan ve diğer Akit Devletin bir mukimine ödenen gayrimaddi hak bedelleri, bu diğer Devlette vergilendirilebilir.

2. Bununla beraber, söz konusu gayrimaddi hak bedelleri elde edildikleri Akit Devlette ve o Devletin mevzuatına göre de vergilendirilebilir; ancak gayrimaddi hak bedelinin gerçek lehdarı diğer Akit Devletin bir mukimi ise, bu şekilde alınacak vergi gayrimaddi hak bedelinin gayrisafi tutarının yüzde 10 unu aşmayacaktır.

3. Bu maddede kullanılan "gayrimaddi hak bedelleri" terimi, sinema filmleri ile radyo ve televizyon yayınlarında kullanılan kayıtlar dahil olmak üzere edebi, sanatsal veya bilimsel her nevi telif hakkının, her nevi patentin, alâmeti farikanın, desen veya modelin, planın, gizli formül veya üretim yönteminin kullanımı veya kullanım hakkı karşılığında veya sınai, ticari veya bilimsel tecrübeye dayalı bilgi birikimi için veya sınai, ticari veya bilimsel teçhizatın kullanımı ya da kullanım hakkı karşılığında yapılan her türlü ödemeyi ifade eder.

4. Bir Akit Devlet mukimi olan gayrimaddi hak bedelinin gerçek lehdarı, gayrimaddi hak bedelinin elde edildiği diğer Akit Devlette yer alan bir iş yeri vasıtasıyla ticari faaliyette bulunursa veya bu diğer Devlette yer alan sabit bir yer vasıtasıyla serbest meslek faaliyetinde bulunursa ve söz konusu bedelin ödendiği hak veya varlık ile bu iş yeri veya sabit yer arasında etkin bir bağ bulunmaktaysa, 1 inci ve 2 nci fıkra hükümleri uygulanmayacaktır. Bu durumda, olayına göre, 7 nci veya 14 üncü madde hükümleri uygulanacaktır.

5. Bir Akit Devletin kendisi, mahalli idaresi veya bir mukimi tarafından ödenen gayrimaddi hak bedelinin, o Devlette elde edildiği kabul olunacaktır. Bununla beraber, gayrimaddi hak bedelini ödeyen kişi, bir Akit Devletin mukimi olsun ya da olmasın, bir

Akit Devlette gayrimaddi hak bedelini ödemeye neden olan hak veya varlık ile bağlantılı bir iş yerine veya sabit yere sahip olduğunda ve gayrimaddi hak bedeli bu iş yeri veya sabit yerden kaynaklandığında, söz konusu gayrimaddi hak bedelinin, iş yerinin veya sabit yerin bulunduğu Devlette elde edildiği kabul olunacaktır.

6. Kullanım, hak veya bilgi karşılığında ödenen gayrimaddi hak bedelinin miktarı, ödeyici ile gerçek lehdar arasında veya her ikisi ile bir başka kişi arasında var olan özel ilişki nedeniyle, böyle bir ilişkinin olmadığı durumlarda ödeyici ile gerçek lehdar arasında kararlaştırılacak miktarı aştığında, bu madde hükümleri yalnızca en son bahsedilen miktara uygulanacaktır. Bu durumda ödemelerin aşan kısmı, bu Anlaşmanın diğer hükümleri de dikkate alınarak, her bir Akit Devletin mevzuatına göre vergilendirilecektir.

Madde 13

SERMAYE DEĞER ARTIŞ KAZANÇLARI

1. Bir Akit Devlet mukimince, diğer Akit Devlette yer alan ve 6 ncı maddede belirtilen gayrimenkul varlıkların elden çıkarılmasından sağlanan kazançlar, bu diğer Devlette vergilendirilebilir.

2. Bir Akit Devlet teşebbüsünün diğer Akit Devlette sahip olduğu bir iş yerinin ticari varlığına dahil menkul varlıkların veya bir Akit Devlet mukiminin diğer Akit Devlette serbest meslek faaliyeti icra etmek üzere kullandığı sabit bir yere ait menkul varlıkların elden çıkarılmasından doğan kazançlar, bu iş yerinin (tek olarak veya tüm teşebbüsle birlikte) veya sabit yerin elden çıkarılmasından doğan kazanç da dahil olmak üzere, bu diğer Devlette vergilendirilebilir.

3. Bir Akit Devlet mukimince uluslararası trafikte işletilen gemi, uçak veya kara yolu nakil vasıtalarının veya söz konusu gemi, uçak veya kara yolu nakil vasıtalarının işletilmesiyle ilgili menkul varlıkların elden çıkarılmasından sağlanan kazançlar, yalnızca bu Devlette vergilendirilecektir.

4. Bir Akit Devlet mukimince, aktifinin % 50 sinden fazlası doğrudan veya dolaylı olarak diğer Akit Devlette bulunan gayrimenkul varlıklardan oluşan bir şirketteki hisselerin veya diğer şirket haklarının elden çıkarılmasından sağlanan kazançlar, bu diğer Devlette vergilendirilebilir.

5. 1, 2, 3 ve 4 üncü fıkralarda belirtilenlerin dışında kalan varlıkların elden çıkarılmasından doğan kazançlar, yalnızca elden çıkaranın mukim olduğu Akit Devlette vergilendirilecektir. Bununla beraber, diğer Akit Devlette elde edilen ve bundan önceki cümlede bahsedilen sermaye değer artış kazançları, iktisap ve elden çıkarma arasındaki süre bir yılı aşmadığı takdirde, diğer Akit Devlette vergilendirilebilir.

Madde 14

SERBEST MESLEK FAALİYETLERİ

1. Bir Akit Devletin mukimi olan bir gerçek kişinin, serbest meslek faaliyetleri veya bağımsız nitelikteki diğer faaliyetleri dolayısıyla elde ettiği gelir, yalnızca bu Devlette vergilendirilecektir. Bununla beraber, bu hizmet veya faaliyetler diğer Akit Devlette icra edilirse ve eğer:

a) gerçek kişi, bu diğer Devlette, söz konusu hizmet veya faaliyetleri icra etmek amacıyla sürekli kullanabileceği sabit bir yere sahip ise; veya

b) gerçek kişi, bu diğer Devlette, söz konusu hizmet veya faaliyetleri icra etmek amacıyla, 12 aylık herhangi bir kesintisiz dönemde, bir veya birkaç seferde toplam 183 gün veya daha fazla kalırsa

söz konusu gelir aynı zamanda diğer Akit Devlette de vergilendirilebilir.

Böyle bir durumda, olayına göre yalnızca söz konusu sabit yere atfedilebilen gelir ya da yalnızca gerçek kişinin bu diğer Devlette bulunduğu süre içerisinde icra ettiği hizmet veya faaliyetlerden elde ettiği gelir, bu diğer Devlette vergilendirilebilir.

2. Bir Akit Devlet teşebbüsünün serbest meslek faaliyetleri veya benzer nitelikteki diğer faaliyetleri dolayısıyla elde ettiği gelir, yalnızca bu Devlette vergilendirilecektir. Bununla beraber, bu hizmet veya faaliyetler diğer Devlette icra edilirse ve eğer:

a) teşebbüs, söz konusu hizmet veya faaliyetleri icra etmek üzere bu diğer Devlette bir iş yerine sahip olursa; veya

b) hizmet veya faaliyetlerin icra edildiği süre veya süreler 12 aylık herhangi bir kesintisiz dönemde toplam 183 günü aşarsa

söz konusu gelir aynı zamanda bu diğer Akit Devlette de vergilendirilebilir.

Böyle bir durumda, olayına göre yalnızca söz konusu iş yerine ya da bu diğer Devlette icra edilen hizmet veya faaliyetlere atfedilebilen gelir, bu diğer Devlette vergilendirilebilir. Her iki durumda da bu teşebbüs, söz konusu gelir bu teşebbüsün diğer Devlette bulunan iş yerine atfedilebilen bir gelirmiş gibi, bu diğer Devlette, bu Anlaşmanın 7 nci maddesi hükümleri göre vergilendirilmeyi tercih edebilir. Bu tercih, diğer Devletin, söz konusu gelir üzerinden tevkifat suretiyle vergi alma hakkını etkilemeyecektir.

3. "Serbest meslek faaliyetleri" terimi, özellikle bağımsız olarak yürütülen bilimsel,

edebi, sanatsal, eğitici veya öğretici faaliyetleri, bunun yanısıra, doktorların, avukatların, mühendislerin, mimarların, dişçilerin ve muhasebecilerin bağımsız faaliyetleri ile özel mesleki yetenek gerektiren diğer faaliyetleri kapsamına alır.

Madde 15

ÜCRET GELİRLERİ

1. 16, 18, 19 ve 20 nci maddelerin hükümleri saklı kalmak üzere, bir Akit Devlet mukiminin bir hizmet akdi dolayısıyla elde ettiği maaş, ücret ve diğer benzeri gelirler, bu hizmet diğer Akit Devlette ifa edilmedikçe, yalnızca bu Devlette vergilendirilecektir. Hizmet diğer Devlette ifa edilirse, buradan elde edilen söz konusu gelir bu diğer Devlette vergilendirilebilir.

2. 1 inci fıkra hükümlerine bakılmaksızın, bir Akit Devlet mukiminin diğer Akit Devlette ifa ettiği bir hizmet dolayısıyla elde ettiği gelir, eğer:

a) gelir elde eden kişi, diğer Devlette, ilgili takvim yılı içinde başlayan veya sona eren herhangi bir on iki aylık dönemde bir veya birkaç seferde toplam 183 günü aşmamak üzere kalırsa, ve

b) ödeme, diğer Devletin mukimi olmayan bir işveren tarafından veya böyle bir işveren adına yapılırsa, ve

c) ödeme, işverenin diğer Devlette sahip olduğu bir iş yerinden veya sabit yerden yapılmazsa

yalnızca ilk bahsedilen Devlette vergilendirilecektir.

3. Bu maddenin bundan önceki hükümlerine bakılmaksızın, bir Akit Devlet teşebbüsü tarafından uluslararası trafikte işletilen bir gemi, uçak veya kara yolu nakil vasıtasında ifa edilen bir hizmet dolayısıyla elde edilen gelir, bu Akit Devlette vergilendirilebilir.

Madde 16

YÖNETİCİLERE YAPILAN ÖDEMELER

Bir Akit Devlet mukiminin, diğer Akit Devlet mukimi olan bir şirketin yönetim kurulu üyesi veya benzeri diğer herhangi bir organın üyesi olması dolayısıyla elde ettiği ücret ve diğer benzeri ödemeler, bu diğer Devlette vergilendirilebilir.

Madde 17

SANATÇI VE SPORCULAR

1. 14 ve 15 inci madde hükümlerine bakılmaksızın, bir Akit Devlet mukimi olan tiyatro, sinema, radyo veya televizyon sanatçısı gibi bir sanatçının ya da bir müzisyenin veya bir sporcunun diğer Akit Devlette icra ettiği bu nitelikteki şahsi faaliyetleri dolayısıyla elde ettiği gelir, bu diğer Devlette vergilendirilebilir.

2. Bir sanatçının ya da sporcunun icra ettiği şahsi faaliyetlerden doğan gelir, sanatçının veya sporcunun kendisi adına değil de bir başkası adına tahakkuk ederse, bu gelir 7, 14 ve 15 inci madde hükümlerine bakılmaksızın, sanatçı ya da sporcunun faaliyetlerinin icra edildiği Akit Devlette vergilendirilebilir.

Madde 18

EMEKLİ MAAŞLARI

1. Bir Akit Devlet mukimine geçmiş çalışmalarının karşılığında ödenen emekli maaşları ve diğer benzeri ödemeler, yalnızca bu Devlette vergilendirilecektir.

2. 1 inci fıkra hükümlerine bakılmaksızın, bir Akit Devletin kendisine, statüye sahip kuruluşuna veya mahalli idaresine, bir gerçek kişi tarafından verilen hizmetler karşılığında, bu Devlet, kuruluş veya idare tarafından veya bunlarca oluşturulan fonlardan ödenen emekli maaşları veya bir Akit Devletin sosyal güvenlik mevzuatı çerçevesinde ödenen emekli maaşları ile yapılan diğer ödemeler, yalnızca bu Devlette vergilendirilecektir. Bununla beraber, söz konusu emekli maaşları ve diğer ödemeler, gerçek kişinin, mukimi olduğu Akit Devletin vatandaşı olması halinde, yalnızca bu Devlette vergilendirilecektir.

Madde 19

KAMU HİZMETİ

1. a) Bir Akit Devletin kendisine, statüye sahip bir kuruluşuna veya mahalli idaresine bir gerçek kişi tarafından verilen hizmetler karşılığında, bu Devlet, kuruluş veya idare tarafından ödenen maaş, ücret ve diğer benzeri ödemeler yalnızca bu Devlette vergilendirilecektir.

   b) Bununla beraber, hizmet bir Akit Devlette ifa edildiğinde ve gerçek kişinin:

i) bu Devletin vatandaşı; veya

ii) yalnızca bu hizmeti ifa etmek için bu Devletin mukimi durumuna geçmemiş

olması halinde, söz konusu maaş, ücret ve diğer benzeri ödemeler, yalnızca gerçek kişinin mukim olduğu bu Devlette vergilendirilecektir.

2. Bir Akit Devletin kendisi, statüye sahip bir kuruluşu veya mahalli idaresi tarafından yürütülen ticari faaliyetlerle bağlantılı hizmetler karşılığında yapılan maaş, ücret ve diğer benzeri ödemelere 15, 16 ve 17 nci madde hükümleri uygulanacaktır.

Madde 20

ÖĞRENCİ VE STAJYERLER

1. Bir Akit Devleti ziyareti sırasında veya hemen öncesinde diğer Akit Devletin mukimi durumunda olan ve ilk bahsedilen Devlette yalnızca öğrenim veya mesleki eğitim amacıyla bulunan bir öğrenci, stajyer veya ticaret, teknik, tarım veya ormancılık alanında mesleki eğitim gören kişiye geçimini, öğrenimini veya mesleki eğitimini sağlayabilmesi için bu Devletin dışındaki kaynaklardan yapılan ödemeler, bu Devlette vergilendirilmeyecektir.

2. Bir Akit Devletteki bir üniversite veya yüksek öğrenim kurumundaki bir öğrenci, stajyer veya ticaret, teknik, tarım veya ormancılık alanlarında mesleki eğitim gören ve diğer Akit Devleti ziyareti sırasında veya hemen öncesinde ilk bahsedilen Devletin mukimi durumunda olup, 183 günü aşmayan kesintisiz bir dönemde diğer Akit Devlette bulunan kişilerin, öğrenim veya mesleki eğitimleriyle ilgili olarak bu diğer Devlette ifa ettikleri hizmetler karşılığında elde ettikleri ve zorunlu geçim giderlerine yetecek miktardaki gelirleri, bu diğer Devlette vergilendirilmeyecektir.

Madde 21

DİĞER GELİRLER

1. Bir Akit Devlet mukiminin, nerede doğarsa doğsun, bu Anlaşmanın önceki maddelerinde ele alınmayan gelir unsurları, yalnızca bu Devlette vergilendirilecektir.

2. 6 ncı maddenin 2 nci fıkrasında tanımlanan gayrimenkul varlıklardan elde edilen gelir hariç olmak üzere, bir Akit Devlet mukimi olan söz konusu gelirin lehdarı, diğer Akit Devlette bulunan bir iş yeri vasıtasıyla ticari faaliyette veya bu diğer Devlette yer alan sabit bir yer vasıtasıyla serbest meslek faaliyetinde bulunursa ve gelirin ödendiği hak veya varlık ile bu iş yeri veya sabit yer arasında etkin bir bağ bulunmaktaysa, bu gelire 1 inci fıkra hükümleri uygulanmayacaktır. Bu durumda, olayına göre 7 nci veya 14 üncü madde hükümleri uygulanacaktır.

3. 1 inci ve 2 nci fıkra hükümlerine bakılmaksızın, bir Akit Devlet mukiminin, bu Anlaşmanın daha önceki maddelerinde belirtilmeyen ve diğer Akit Devlette doğan gelir unsurları, bu diğer Devlette de vergilendirilebilir.

Madde 22

ÇİFTE VERGİLENDİRMENİN ÖNLENMESİ

1. Türkiye mukimleri için çifte vergilendirme aşağıdaki şekilde önlenecektir:

a) Türkiye dışındaki bir ülkede ödenen verginin Türk vergisinden mahsubunu düzenleyen Türk mevzuatı hükümleri saklı kalmak üzere, (bu hükümler buradaki genel prensipleri değiştirmeksizin zaman zaman tadil edilebilir) bir Türkiye mukimince Finlandiya'daki kaynaklardan elde edilen gelir (kazançlar ve vergiye tabi gelirler dahil) üzerinden Finlandiya mevzuatı ve bu Anlaşmaya uygun olarak ödenen Fin vergisinin, söz konusu gelir üzerinden alınacak Türk vergisinden mahsubuna müsaade edilecektir. Bununla beraber bu mahsup, söz konusu gelire atfedilebilen, mahsuptan önce hesaplanan Türk vergisi tutarını aşmayacaktır.

b) bir Türkiye mukimi tarafından elde edilen gelir Anlaşmanın herhangi bir hükmü uyarınca Türkiye'de vergiden istisna edilirse, Türkiye, bu mukimin geriye kalan gelirleri üzerinden alınacak vergi miktarını hesaplarken, istisna edilmiş olan geliri de dikkate alabilir.

2. Uluslararası çifte vergilendirmenin önlenmesine ilişkin Fin mevzuatı hükümleri saklı kalmak üzere (bu hükümler, Anlaşmanın genel prensiplerini etkilemeyecektir), Finlandiya'da çifte vergilendirme aşağıdaki şekilde önlenecektir:

a) Bir Finlandiya mukimi, bu Anlaşma hükümlerine göre Türkiye'de vergilendirilebilen bir gelir elde ettiğinde, Finlandiya, (b) bendi hükümleri saklı kalmak üzere, bu kişinin Fin vergisinden, Türk mevzuatı uyarınca ve bu Anlaşmaya uygun olarak ödediği, Fin vergisinin hesaplandığı aynı gelire ilişkin olarak hesaplanan Türk vergisine eşit bir tutarın mahsubuna müsaade edecektir.

b) Türkiye'de mukim bir şirket tarafından Finlandiya'da mukim olan ve temettüleri ödeyen şirketteki oy gücünün doğrudan en az % 10 unu kontrol eden bir şirkete ödenen temettüler Fin vergisinden istisna edilecektir.

c) Bir Finlandiya mukimince, Anlaşmanın herhangi bir hükmüne uygun olarak Finlandiya'da vergiden istisna edilen bir gelir elde edilmesi durumunda, Finlandiya, bu kişinin geriye kalan gelirine ilişkin vergiyi hesaplarken, istisna edilen geliri de dikkate alabilir.

d) (a) bendinin amaçları bakımından, "Türkiye'de gelir üzerinden ödenen vergi" teriminin, Türk vergi mevzuatı gereğince ödenmesi gereken, fakat Türkiye'deki ekonomik kalkınmayı hızlandırmaya yönelik özel teşvik tedbirleri hükümleri çerçevesinde Türk vergisinden indirilen veya istisna edilen tutarları kapsadığı kabul edilecektir.

Bundan önceki cümleye bakılmaksızın, Türkiye'de gelir üzerinden ödenen vergi aşağıdaki şekilde hesaplanacaktır:

i) 10 uncu maddenin 2 nci fıkrasının (b) bendinde bahsedilen temettüler bakımından % 15 oranında;

ii) 11 inci maddenin 2 nci fıkrasının (a) bendinde bahsedilen faizler bakımından % 5, 11 inci maddenin 2 nci fıkrasının (b) bendinde bahsedilen faizler bakımında % 10 ve 11 inci maddenin 2 nci fıkrasının (c) bendinde bahsedilen faizler bakımından % 15 oranında;

iii) 12 nci maddenin 2 nci fıkrasında bahsedilen gayrimaddi hak bedelleri ve diğer ödemeler bakımından % 10 oranında.

Bununla beraber, Türkiye mukimi olmayan kişiler tarafından elde edilen temettü, faiz ve gayrimaddi hak bedellerine Türk vergi mevzuatı uyarınca uygulanan vergi oranları, bu bentte belirtilen oranların altına indirilirse, bu bendin amaçları yönünden, bu düşük oranlar uygulanacaktır.

MADDE 23

AYRIM YAPILMAMASI

1.Bir Akit Devletin vatandaşları, diğer Akit Devlette, bu diğer Devletin vatandaşlarının aynı koşullarda, özellikle mukimlik yönünden, karşı karşıya kaldıkları veya kalabilecekleri vergilemeden ve buna bağlı mükellefiyetlerden değişik veya daha ağır bir vergilemeye ve buna bağlı mükellefiyetlere tabi tutulmayacaklardır. Bu hüküm, 1 inci madde hükümlerine bakılmaksızın, Akit Devletlerden birinin veya her ikisinin mukimi olmayan kişilere de uygulanacaktır.

2. 10 uncu maddenin 4 üncü fıkrası hükümleri saklı kalmak üzere, bir Akit Devlet teşebbüsünün diğer Akit Devlette sahip olduğu bir iş yeri, diğer Devlette, bu diğer Devletin aynı faaliyetleri yürüten teşebbüslerine göre daha az lehe bir vergilemeyle karşı karşıya kalmayacaktır.

3. Bir Akit Devletin, diğer Akit Devletin bir veya birkaç mukimi tarafından, doğrudan veya dolaylı olarak, kısmen veya tamamen sermayesine sahip olunan veya kontrol edilen teşebbüsleri, ilk bahsedilen Devlette, bu Devletin diğer benzeri teşebbüslerinin tabi oldukları veya olabilecekleri vergilemeden ve buna bağlı mükellefiyetlerden değişik veya daha ağır bir vergilemeye ve buna bağlı mükellefiyetlere tabi tutulmayacaklardır.

4. 9 uncu maddenin 1 inci fıkrası, 11 inci maddenin 7 nci fıkrası veya 12 nci maddenin 6 ncı fıkrası hükümlerinin uygulanacağı durumlar hariç olmak üzere, bir Akit Devlet teşebbüsünün diğer Akit Devletin bir mukimine yaptığı faiz, gayrimaddi hak bedeli ve diğer ödemeler, söz konusu teşebbüsün vergilendirilebilir kazancının belirlenmesi amacıyla, bu ödemeler ilk bahsedilen Devletin bir mukimine yapılmış gibi, aynı koşullarda indirilebilecektir.

5. Bu hükümler, bir Akit Devletin kendi mukimlerine şahsi veya ailevi durumları dolayısıyla uyguladığı şahsi indirimleri, vergi ve matrah indirimlerini, diğer Akit Devletin mukimlerine de uygulamak zorunda olduğu yönünde anlaşılmayacaktır.

6. Bu madde hükümleri, yalnızca 2 nci maddede kapsanan vergilere uygulanacaktır.

MADDE 24

KARŞILIKLI ANLAŞMA USULÜ

1. Bir kişi, Akit Devletlerden birinin veya her ikisinin işlemlerinin kendisi için bu Anlaşma hükümlerine uygun olmayan bir vergileme yarattığı veya yaratacağı kanaatine vardığında, bu Devletlerin iç mevzuatlarında öngörülen müracaat usulleriyle bağlı kalmaksızın, durumu mukimi olduğu Akit Devletin yetkili makamına veya durumu 23 üncü maddenin 1 inci fıkrasına uygunsa, vatandaşı olduğu Akit Devletin yetkili makamına arz edebilir. Söz konusu müracaat, Anlaşma hükümlerine aykırı düşen bir vergilemeyle sonuçlanan eylemin ilk bildiriminden itibaren üç yıl içerisinde yapılmalıdır.

2. Söz konusu yetkili makam, itirazı haklı bulur ancak kendisi tatminkar bir çözüme ulaşamaz ise, Anlaşmaya ters düşen vergilemeyi önlemek amacıyla, diğer Akit Devletin yetkili makamıyla karşılıklı anlaşma yoluyla konuyu çözmeye gayret sarf edecektir. Anlaşmaya varılan her husus, Akit Devletlerin iç mevzuatlarında öngörülen zamanaşımı sürelerine bakılmaksızın uygulanacaktır.

3. Akit Devletlerin yetkili makamları, Anlaşmanın yorumundan veya uygulanmasından kaynaklanan her türlü güçlüğü veya tereddüdü karşılıklı anlaşmayla çözmek için gayret göstereceklerdir. Yetkili makamlar aynı zamanda, Anlaşmada ele alınmayan durumlardan kaynaklanan çifte vergilemenin ortadan kaldırılması için de birbirlerine danışabilirler.

4. Akit Devletlerin yetkili makamları, bundan önceki fıkralarda belirtilen hususlarda anlaşmaya varabilmek için, birbirleriyle, kendilerinden veya temsilcilerinden oluşan bir komisyon kanalı da dahil olmak üzere, doğrudan haberleşebilirler.

MADDE 25

BİLGİ DEĞİŞİMİ

1. Akit Devletlerin yetkili makamları, bu Anlaşma hükümlerinin uygulanmasıyla ilgili bilgileri veya Anlaşma ile uyumsuzluk göstermediği sürece Akit Devletler, politik alt bölümleri veya mahalli idareleri adına alınan her tür ve tanımdaki vergilerle ilgili iç mevzuat hükümlerinin uygulanması ile ilgili olduğu düşünülen bilgileri değişime tabi tutacaklardır. Bilgi değişimi 1 inci ve 2 nci maddelerle sınırlı değildir.

2. Bir Akit Devlet tarafından 1 inci fıkra kapsamında alınan her türlü bilgi, o Devletin kendi iç mevzuatı çerçevesinde elde ettiği bilgiler gibi gizli tutulacak ve yalnızca 1 inci fıkrada bahsedilen vergilerin tahakkuk veya tahsilleri veya cebri icra ya da kovuşturmasıyla veya bu hususlardaki itirazlara bakmakla görevli kişi veya makamlara (adli makamlar ve idari kuruluşlar dahil) veya bunları denetlemekle görevli olan kişilere verilebilecektir. Bu kişi veya makamlar, söz konusu bilgileri yalnızca bu amaçlar doğrultusunda kullanacaklardır. Bu kişi veya makamlar söz konusu bilgileri mahkeme duruşmalarında veya adli kararlar alınırken açıklayabilirler.

3. 1 inci ve 2 nci fıkra hükümleri, hiçbir surette bir Akit Devleti:

a) kendisinin veya diğer Akit Devletin mevzuatına ve idari uygulamalarına aykırı idari önlemler alma;

b) kendisinin veya diğer Akit Devletin mevzuatı veya normal idari işlemleri çerçevesinde elde edilemeyen bilgileri sunma;

c) herhangi bir ticari, sınai, mesleki sırrı veya ticari işlemi aleni hale getiren bilgileri veya aleniyeti kamu düzenine aykırı düşen bilgileri verme

yükümlülüğü altına sokacak şekilde yorumlanamaz.

4. Bir Akit Devlet tarafından bu madde uyarınca bilgi talep edilmesi durumunda,

diğer Akit Devlet, kendi vergi amaçları yönünden bu bilgilere ihtiyacı olmasa bile, talep edilen bilgiyi sağlamak için kendi bilgi toplama yöntemlerini kullanacaktır. Önceki cümlede yer alan yükümlülük, 3 üncü fıkradaki sınırlamalara tabi olmakla birlikte, bu sınırlamalar hiç bir surette bir Akit Devlete, sadece ulusal menfaati olmadığı gerekçesiyle bilgi sağlamayı reddetme hakkı verecek şekilde yorumlanmayacaktır.

5. 3 üncü fıkra hükümleri hiç bir surette, bir Akit Devlete, bilginin bir banka, diğer finansal kurum, temsilci veya bir acente ya da yediemin gibi hareket eden bir kişide bulunması veya bir kişinin sermaye payları ile ilgili olması nedeniyle bu bilgiyi sağlamayı reddetme hakkı verecek şekilde yorumlanmayacaktır.

MADDE 26

VERGİLERİN TAHSİLATINDA YARDIMLAŞMA

1. Akit Devletler, alacaklarının tahsilatında birbirlerine yardım edeceklerdir. Bu yardım 1 inci ve 2 nci maddelerle sınırlı değildir. Akit Devletlerin yetkili makamları, bu maddenin uygulama biçimini karşılıklı anlaşma yoluyla belirleyebilirler.

2. Bu maddede kullanılan "alacak" terimi, bu Anlaşmaya veya Akit Devletlerin taraf olduğu diğer herhangi bir hukuki belgeye aykırı olmadığı sürece, Akit Devletler, politik alt bölümleri ya da mahalli idareleri adına alınan her tür ve tanımdaki vergiler dolayısıyla borçlanılan bir tutarı, bunun yanı sıra faiz, idari cezalar ve bu tutara ilişkin tahsilat veya koruma masraflarını ifade eder.

3. Bir Akit Devletin alacağının, bu Devletin mevzuatı uyarınca icra yoluyla istenebildiği ve borçlunun, o esnada bu Devletin mevzuatı uyarınca alacağın tahsilatını engelleyemediği durumda, söz konusu alacak, bu Devletin yetkili makamının talebi üzerine diğer Akit Devletin yetkili makamınca tahsil edilmek amacıyla kabul edilecektir. Bu alacak, diğer Devlet tarafından, kendi alacağıymış gibi, kendi vergilerinin icrası ve tahsilatına uyguladığı mevzuat hükümlerine göre tahsil edilecektir.

4. Bir Akit Devlet alacağının, bu Devletin kendi mevzuatı uyarınca tahsilatını sağlamak için koruma tedbirleri alabileceği bir alacak olması durumunda, söz konusu alacak, bu Devletin yetkili makamının talebi üzerine, koruma önlemleri almak amacıyla diğer Akit Devletin yetkili makamınca kabul edilecektir. Bu diğer Devlet, bu tür tedbirlerin uygulandığı sırada, alacağın ilk bahsedilen Devlette icra yoluyla alınamayacak veya borçlunun tahsilatı önleme hakkının bulunduğu durumlarda bile, kendi mevzuatı hükümleri uyarınca, bu alacak kendi alacağıymış gibi koruma tedbirleri alacaktır.

5. 3 üncü ve 4 üncü fıkra hükümlerine bakılmaksızın, 3 üncü veya 4 üncü fıkranın amaçları yönünden bir Akit Devlet tarafından kabul edilen bir alacak, bu Devlette zaman aşımına tabi olmayacak veya niteliği gereği, bu Devletin mevzuatı uyarınca bir alacağa

tanınan herhangi bir öncelik, bu alacağa tanınmayacaktır. Bunun yanı sıra, 3 üncü veya 4 üncü fıkranın amaçları bakımından, bir Akit Devlet tarafından kabul edilen bir alacak, bu Devlette, diğer Akit Devletin mevzuatı uyarınca bu alacağa tanınan herhangi bir önceliğe sahip olmayacaktır.

6. Bir Akit Devlet alacağının varlığı, geçerliliği veya tutarıyla ilgili davalar, diğer Akit Devletin mahkemeleri veya idari kuruluşlarına getirilemez.

7. Bir Akit Devletin, 3 üncü veya 4 üncü fıkra uyarınca bir talepte bulunmasından sonra ve diğer Akit Devletin alacağı tahsil ederek ilk bahsedilen Devlete göndermesinden önceki herhangi bir zamanda, ilgili alacağın,

a) 3 üncü fıkraya göre talepte bulunulması durumunda, ilk bahsedilen Devletin alacağının, bu Devletin mevzuatı uyarınca icra yoluyla istenebilen ve borçlusunun o esnada bu Devletin mevzuatı uyarınca tahsilatını engelleyemediği, veya

b) 4 üncü fıkraya göre talepte bulunulması durumunda, ilk bahsedilen Devletin alacağının, alacağın tahsilatını sağlamak amacıyla kendi mevzuatı uyarınca koruma tedbirleri alabileceği

bir alacak olmaktan çıkması durumunda, ilk bahsedilen Devletin yetkili makamı, diğer Devletin yetkili makamını derhal durumdan haberdar edecek ve ilk bahsedilen Devlet, diğer Devletin tercihi doğrultusunda talebini ya askıya alacak ya da geri çekecektir.

8. Bu madde hükümleri hiçbir şekilde bir Akit Devleti:

a) kendisinin veya diğer Akit Devletin mevzuatına ve idari uygulamalarına aykırı idari önlemler alma;

b) kamu düzenine aykırı önlemleri alma;

c) diğer Akit Devletin, olayına göre, kendi mevzuatı ve idari uygulamaları gereğince tahsilat ve korumaya ilişkin gerekli önlemlerin hiç birini almaması durumunda, yardım sağlama;

d) bu Devletin idari külfetinin, diğer Akit Devletin elde edeceği faydadan açık bir şekilde fazla olduğu durumlarda, yardım sağlama

yükümlülüğü altına sokacak şekilde yorumlanamaz.

MADDE 27

DİPLOMATİK TEMSİLCİLER VE KONSOLOSLUK MEMURLARI

Bu Anlaşma hükümleri, diplomatik temsilciler veya konsolosluk memurlarının uluslararası hukukun genel kuralları veya özel anlaşma hükümleri uyarınca yararlandıkları mali ayrıcalıkları etkilemeyecektir.

MADDE 28

YÜRÜRLÜĞE GİRME

1. Her bir Akit Devlet, bu Anlaşmanın yürürlüğe girmesi için kendi iç mevzuatında öngörülen işlemlerin tamamlandığını diplomatik yollardan diğerine bildirecektir. Bu Anlaşma, bu bildirimlerden sonuncusunun yapıldığı tarihten 30 gün sonra yürürlüğe girecek ve hükümleri:

a) Türkiye'de, Anlaşmanın yürürlüğe girmesini izleyen yılın Ocak ayının birinci günü veya daha sonra başlayan her vergilendirme dönemine ilişkin vergiler için;

b) Finlandiya'da:

i) kaynakta tevkif edilen vergiler bakımından, Anlaşmanın yürürlüğe girdiği yılı izleyen takvim yılının 1 Ocak günü veya daha sonra elde edilen gelirler için;

ii) gelir üzerinden alınan diğer vergiler bakımından, Anlaşmanın yürürlüğe girdiği yılı izleyen takvim yılının 1 Ocak günü veya daha sonra başlayan her vergi yılına ilişkin vergiler için

hüküm ifade edecektir.

2. 9 Mayıs 1986 tarihinde Ankara'da imzalanan "Türkiye Cumhuriyeti ile Finlandiya Cumhuriyeti Arasında Gelir Üzerinden Alınan Vergilerde Çifte Vergilendirmeyi Önleme Anlaşması" (bundan böyle "1986 Anlaşması" olarak bahsedilecektir), bu Anlaşma'nın, 1 inci fıkra hükümlerine uygun olarak yürürlüğe girdiği tarihten itibaren hüküm ifade etmeyecektir. 1986 Anlaşması, bu fıkranın önceki hükümleri uyarınca yürürlükte kaldığı son tarihte, yürürlükten kalkacaktır.

MADDE 29

YÜRÜRLÜKTEN KALKMA

Bu Anlaşma, bir Akit Devlet tarafından feshedilinceye kadar yürürlükte kalacaktır. Her bir Akit Devlet, Anlaşmanın yürürlüğe girdiği tarihten itibaren beş yıllık dönem sonrasını izleyen herhangi bir takvim yılının bitiminden en az altı ay önce, diplomatik yollardan fesih ihbarnamesi vermek suretiyle Anlamayı feshedebilir. Bu durumda Anlaşma:

a) Türkiye'de, fesih ihbarnamesinin verilmesini izleyen yılın Ocak ayının birinci günü veya daha sonra başlayan her vergilendirme dönemine ilişkin vergiler için;

b) Finlandiya'da:

i) kaynakta tevkif edilen vergiler bakımından, fesih ihbarnamesinin verildiği yılı izleyen takvim yılının 1 Ocak günü veya daha sonra elde edilen gelirler için;

ii) gelir üzerinden alınan diğer vergiler bakımından, fesih ihbarnamesinin verildiği yılı izleyen takvim yılının 1 Ocak günü veya daha sonra başlayan her vergi yılına ilişkin vergiler için

hüküm ifade etmeyecektir.

BU HUSUSLARI TEYİDEN, aşağıda imzaları bulunan tam yetkili temsilciler, bu Anlaşmayı imzaladılar.

Fin, Türk ve İngiliz dillerinde, ikişer nüsha halinde, her üç metin de aynı derecede geçerli olmak üzere, ... Ekim 2009 tarihinde İstanbul'da düzenlenmiştir. Yorumda farklılık olması halinde İngilizce metin geçerli olacaktır.

FİNLANDİYA CUMHURİYETİ HÜKÜMETİ ADINA

TÜRKİYE CUMHURİYETİ HÜKÜMETİ ADINA

PROTOKOL

Finlandiya Cumhuriyeti ile Türkiye Cumhuriyeti arasında Gelir Üzerinden Alınan Vergilerde Çifte Vergilendirmeyi Önleme Anlaşmasının imzalanması sırasında imzalayan taraflar, aşağıdaki hükümlerin Anlaşmanın ayrılmaz bir parçasını oluşturduğu hususunda anlaşmaya varmışlardır.

1. 7 nci maddenin 1 inci fıkrası ile ilgili olarak

Bir Akit Devlet teşebbüsünün diğer Akit Devlette bir iş yerinin olması ve bu teşebbüsün;

a) bu diğer Devlette, bu iş yeri vasıtasıyla satılan mal veya ticari eşya ile aynı veya benzer nitelikte mal veya ticari eşya satışı gerçekleştirmesi, veya

b) bu diğer Devlette, söz konusu iş yeri vasıtasıyla yürütülenlerle aynı veya benzer nitelikli diğer ticari faaliyetlerde bulunması

durumunda, söz konusu satış veya ticari faaliyetlerin bu iş yeri vasıtasıyla gerçekleştirildiği ispatlanırsa, bu satış veya faaliyetlerin, iş yeri kazancının bir parçası olarak diğer Akit Devlette vergilendirileceği anlaşılmaktadır. Bu vergileme, sahte satış sözleşmeleri ile engellenemez.

2. 10 uncu maddenin 3 üncü fıkrası ile ilgili olarak

Türkiye yönünden "temettü" teriminin, yatırım fonu ve yatırım ortaklığından elde edilen gelirleri de kapsadığı anlaşılmaktadır.

3. 12 ve 13 üncü maddeler ile ilgili olarak

12 nci maddenin 3 üncü fıkrasında belirtilen bir varlığın satışı karşılığında yapılan ödemelere, bu ödemelerin, söz konusu varlığın gerçekten elden çıkarılması karşılığında yapıldığı ispat edilmediği sürece 12 nci madde hükümlerinin uygulanacağı anlaşılmaktadır. Bu husus ispat edilirse 13 üncü madde hükümleri uygulanacaktır.

4. **15 inci maddenin 2 nci fıkrası ile ilgili olarak**

Bir Akit Devlet mukimine (işçi), bu Devletin bir mukimi tarafından veya onun adına, diğer Akit Devlette ifa edilen bir hizmet dolayısıyla yapılan ödemelere;

a) işçinin bu görev esnasında, ifa edilen hizmetleri doğrudan ya da dolaylı olarak gözetim, yönetim veya kontrol altında tutan bir işveren dışındaki bir kişiye hizmet sunması; ve

b) işverenin, ödemeyi alan kişi tarafından gerçekleştirilen işlerin sonuçlarından sorumlu olmaması

durumunda 15 inci maddenin 2 nci fıkrasının uygulanmayacağı anlaşılmaktadır.

5. **4, 18 ve 19 uncu maddeler ile ilgili olarak**

"Statüye sahip kuruluş" terimi:

a) Türkiye yönünden:

i) Türkiye Cumhuriyet Merkez Bankası;
ii) Zorunlu Türk sosyal sigorta kurumları; ve
iii) Üniversiteler ve diğer benzeri yüksek öğretim kurumları;

b) Finlandiya yönünden:

i) Finlandiya Bankası (Suomen Pankki);
ii) Sosyal Sigorta Kurumu (Kansanelakelaitos); ve
iii) Helsinki Üniversitesi (Helsingin yliopisto)

anlamına gelmektedir.

18 ve 19 uncu maddeler yönünden "statüye sahip kuruluş" terimi,

Türkiye yönünden: Diyanet İşleri Başkanlığını; ve

Finlandiya yönünden: Evangelical- Lutheren ve Ortodoks Kiliseleri ile bunların mahalli topluluklarını

kapsamaktadır.

6. **<u>22 nci maddenin 2 nci fıkrasının (d) bendi ile ilgili olarak</u>**

22 nci maddenin 2 nci fıkrasının (d) bendi hükümleri, yalnızca bu Anlaşmanın yürürlükte olduğu ilk beş yıl için uygulanacaktır.

7. **<u>24 üncü maddenin 2 nci fıkrası ile ilgili olarak</u>**

24 üncü maddenin 2 nci fıkrasına ilişkin olarak, Türkiye yönünden mükellefin, karşılıklı anlaşma sonucunun vergi idaresi tarafından kendisine bildirilmesinden sonraki 1 yıllık süre içerisinde, söz konusu karşılıklı anlaşmadan kaynaklanan iadeyi talep etmek zorunda olduğu anlaşılmaktadır.

BU HUSUSLARI TEYİDEN, aşağıda imzaları bulunan tam yetkili temsilciler, bu Protokolü imzaladılar.

Fin, Türk ve İngiliz dillerinde, ikişer nüsha halinde, her üç metin de aynı derecede geçerli olmak üzere, ... Ekim 2009 tarihinde, İstanbul'da düzenlenmiştir. Yorumda farklılık olması halinde İngilizce metin geçerli olacaktır.

FİNLANDİYA CUMHURİYETİ HÜKÜMETİ ADINA	TÜRKİYE CUMHURİYETİ HÜKÜMETİ ADINA

[TRANSLATION – TRADUCTION]

ACCORD ENTRE LA RÉPUBLIQUE DE FINLANDE ET LA RÉPUBLIQUE TURQUE EN TENDANT À ÉVITER LES DOUBLES IMPOSITIONS EN MATIÈRE D'IMPÔTS SUR LE REVENU

Le Gouvernement de la République de Finlande et le Gouvernement de la République turque,

Désireux de conclure un accord tendant à éviter les doubles impositions en matière d'impôts sur le revenu,

Sont convenus de ce qui suit :

Article premier. Personnes visées

Le présent Accord s'applique aux personnes qui sont des résidents d'un État contractant ou des deux États contractants.

Article 2. Impôts visés

1. Le présent Accord s'applique aux impôts sur le revenu prélevés pour le compte d'un État contractant ou d'une de ses collectivités locales, quel que soit le système de perception.

2. Sont considérés comme impôts sur le revenu les impôts perçus sur le revenu total ou sur des éléments du revenu, y compris les impôts sur les gains provenant de la cession de biens mobiliers ou immobiliers, les impôts sur le montant global des salaires payés par les entreprises, ainsi que les impôts sur les gains en capital.

3. Les impôts actuels auxquels s'applique le présent Accord sont, notamment :

a) En Turquie :

i) L'impôt sur le revenu (gelir vergisi) ; et

ii) L'impôt sur les sociétés (kurumlar vergisi) ;

(ci-après dénommés l'« impôt turc ») ;

b) En Finlande :

i) L'impôt sur le revenu (valtion tuloverot ; de statliga inkomstskatterna) ;

ii) L'impôt sur les sociétés (yhteisöjen tulovero ; inkomstskatten för samfund) ;

iii) L'impôt communal (kunnallisvero ; kommunalskatten) ;

iv) L'impôt ecclésiastique (kirkollisvero ; kyrkoskatten) ;

v) L'impôt retenu à la source sur les intérêts (korkotulon lähdevero ; källskatten pá ränteinkomst) ; et

vi) L'impôt retenu à la source sur le revenu des non-résidents (rajoitetusti verovelvollisen lähdevero ; källskatten för begransat skattskyldig) ;

(ci-après dénommés l'« impôt finlandais »).

4. L'Accord s'applique également aux impôts de nature identique ou analogue qui seraient établis après la date de signature de l'Accord et qui s'ajouteraient aux impôts actuels ou qui les

remplaceraient. Les autorités compétentes des États contractants se communiquent les modifications significatives apportées à leurs législations fiscales respectives.

Article 3. Définitions générales

1. Aux fins du présent Accord, à moins que le contexte n'exige une interprétation différente :

a) i) Le terme « Turquie » désigne le territoire turc, y compris les eaux territoriales et l'espace aérien situé au-dessus, ainsi que les zones maritimes sur lesquelles la Turquie exerce ses droits juridictionnels ou souverains aux fins de l'exploration, de l'exploitation et de la conservation des ressources naturelles, en application du droit international ;

ii) Le terme « Finlande » désigne la République de Finlande et, lorsqu'il est employé dans un sens géographique, désigne le territoire de la République de Finlande et toute zone adjacente aux eaux territoriales de la République de Finlande où, en vertu de la législation de la Finlande et conformément au droit international, la Finlande peut exercer ses droits en matière d'exploration et d'exploitation des ressources naturelles des fonds marins et de son sous-sol et des eaux surjacentes ;

b) Les expressions « un État contractant » et « l'autre État contractant » désignent, suivant le contexte, la Turquie ou la Finlande ;

c) Le terme « personne » comprend les personnes physiques, les sociétés et autres groupements de personnes ;

d) Le terme « société » désigne toute personne morale ou toute entité qui est considérée comme une personne morale aux fins d'imposition ;

e) L'expression « siège de direction » désigne le siège social légal d'une société enregistrée conformément au Code de commerce turc ou le lieu d'immatriculation d'une société conformément au droit finlandais, selon le cas ;

f) Le terme « ressortissant », en ce qui concerne un État contractant, désigne :

i) Toute personne physique qui possède la nationalité ou la citoyenneté de cet État contractant ; et

ii) Toute personne morale, société de personnes ou association constituée conformément à la législation en vigueur dans cet État contractant ;

g) Les expressions « entreprise d'un État contractant » et « entreprise de l'autre État contractant » désignent respectivement une entreprise exploitée par un résident d'un État contractant et une entreprise exploitée par un résident de l'autre État contractant ;

h) L'expression « autorité compétente » désigne :

i) En Turquie, le Ministre des finances ou son représentant autorisé ; et

ii) En Finlande, le Ministère des finances, son représentant autorisé ou l'autorité qui est désignée par le Ministère des finances comme autorité compétente ;

i) L'expression « trafic international » désigne tout transport effectué par un navire, un aéronef ou un véhicule routier exploité par une entreprise d'un État contractant, sauf lorsque le navire, l'aéronef ou le véhicule routier n'est exploité qu'entre des points situés dans l'autre État contractant.

2. Pour l'application de l'Accord à un moment donné par un État contractant, tout terme ou toute expression qui n'y est pas défini a, sauf si le contexte exige une interprétation différente, le sens que lui attribue, à ce moment, le droit de cet État concernant les impôts auxquels s'applique l'Accord, le sens attribué à ce terme ou à cette expression par le droit fiscal de cet État prévalant sur le sens que lui attribuent les autres branches du droit de cet État.

Article 4. Résident

1. Aux fins du présent Accord, l'expression « résident d'un État contractant » désigne toute personne qui, en vertu de la législation de cet État, est assujettie à l'impôt dans cet État en raison de son domicile, de sa résidence, de son lieu d'établissement, de son siège de direction ou de tout autre critère de nature analogue et s'applique aussi à cet État ainsi qu'à tous ses organismes de droit public ou à toutes ses collectivités locales. Toutefois, cette expression ne comprend pas les personnes qui ne sont assujetties à l'impôt dans cet État que pour les revenus de sources situées dans cet État.

2. Lorsque, selon les dispositions du paragraphe 1, une personne physique est un résident des deux États contractants, sa situation est réglée de la manière suivante :

a) Cette personne est considérée comme résidente seulement de l'État dans lequel elle dispose d'un foyer d'habitation permanent ; si elle dispose d'un foyer d'habitation permanent dans les deux États, elle est considérée comme résidente seulement de l'État avec lequel ses liens personnels et économiques sont les plus étroits (centre des intérêts vitaux) ;

b) Si l'État où cette personne a ses intérêts vitaux ne peut pas être déterminé, ou si elle ne dispose d'un foyer d'habitation permanent dans aucun des États, elle est considérée comme résidente seulement de l'État où elle séjourne de façon habituelle ;

c) Si cette personne séjourne habituellement dans les deux États ou si elle ne séjourne de façon habituelle dans aucun d'eux, elle est considérée comme résidente seulement de l'État dont elle possède la nationalité ;

d) Si cette personne est un ressortissant des deux États ou si elle n'est un ressortissant d'aucun d'eux, les autorités compétentes des États contractants tranchent la question d'un commun accord.

3. Lorsque, selon les dispositions du paragraphe 1, une personne autre qu'une personne physique est résidente des deux États contractants, elle est alors considérée comme résidente seulement de l'État où son lieu d'immatriculation est situé.

Article 5. Établissement stable

1. Au sens du présent Accord, l'expression « établissement stable » désigne une installation fixe d'affaires par l'intermédiaire de laquelle une entreprise exerce tout ou partie de son activité.

2. L'expression « établissement stable » comprend notamment :

a) Un siège de direction ;

b) Une succursale ;

c) Un bureau ;

d) Une usine ;

e) Un atelier ; et

f) Une mine, un puits de pétrole ou de gaz, une carrière ou tout autre lieu d'extraction de ressources naturelles.

3. Un chantier de construction, un projet de montage ou d'installation ou des activités de supervision liées à ce projet constituent un établissement stable, mais seulement si ce chantier de construction, ce projet ou ces activités durent plus de six mois.

4. Nonobstant les dispositions précédentes du présent article, l'expression « établissement stable » ne comprend pas :

a) L'utilisation d'installations aux seules fins de stockage, d'exposition ou de livraison de biens ou de marchandises appartenant à l'entreprise ;

b) L'exploitation d'un stock de biens ou de marchandises appartenant à l'entreprise aux seules fins de stockage, d'exposition ou de livraison ;

c) L'exploitation d'un stock de biens ou de marchandises appartenant à l'entreprise aux seules fins de transformation par une autre entreprise ;

d) L'exploitation d'une installation fixe d'affaires aux seules fins d'acheter des biens ou des marchandises ou de réunir des renseignements pour l'entreprise ;

e) L'exploitation d'une installation fixe d'affaires aux seules fins d'exercice, pour l'entreprise, de toute autre activité de caractère préparatoire ou auxiliaire ;

f) L'exploitation d'une installation fixe d'affaires aux seules fins d'exercice cumulé d'activités visées aux alinéas a) à e), à condition que l'activité d'ensemble de l'installation fixe d'affaires résultant de ce cumul garde un caractère préparatoire ou auxiliaire.

5. Nonobstant les dispositions des paragraphes 1 et 2, lorsqu'une personne, autre qu'un agent jouissant d'un statut indépendant auquel s'applique le paragraphe 6, agit dans un État contractant pour le compte d'une entreprise de l'autre État contractant, cette entreprise est considérée comme ayant un établissement stable dans le premier État contractant pour toutes les activités que cette personne entreprend pour l'entreprise, si cette personne :

a) Dispose dans cet État du pouvoir qu'elle y exerce habituellement lui permettant de conclure des contrats au nom de l'entreprise, à moins que les activités de cette personne ne soient limitées à celles qui sont énumérées au paragraphe 4 et qui, si elles étaient exercées par l'intermédiaire d'une installation fixe d'affaires, ne permettraient pas de considérer cette installation comme un établissement stable selon les dispositions de ce paragraphe ; ou

b) Ne dispose pas de tels pouvoirs, mais exploite habituellement dans le premier État d'un stock de biens ou de marchandises à partir duquel il livre régulièrement des biens ou des marchandises pour le compte de l'entreprise.

6. Une entreprise n'est pas considérée comme ayant un établissement stable dans un État contractant du seul fait qu'elle y exerce son activité par l'entremise d'un courtier, d'un commissionnaire général ou de tout autre agent jouissant d'un statut indépendant, à condition que ces personnes agissent dans le cadre ordinaire de leur activité.

7. Le fait qu'une société qui est résidente d'un État contractant contrôle ou est contrôlée par une société qui est résidente de l'autre État contractant ou qui exerce son activité dans cet autre État (que ce soit par l'intermédiaire d'un établissement stable ou non) ne suffit pas, en lui-même, à faire de l'une quelconque de ces sociétés un établissement stable de l'autre.

Article 6. Revenus immobiliers

1. Les revenus qu'un résident d'un État contractant tire de biens immobiliers (y compris les revenus des exploitations agricoles ou forestières) situés dans l'autre État contractant sont imposables dans cet autre État.

2. L'expression « biens immobiliers » a le sens que lui attribue le droit de l'État contractant où les biens considérés sont situés. L'expression comprend en tout cas les accessoires et les équipements utilisés dans les exploitations agricoles (y compris la reproduction et l'élevage des poissons) et forestières, les droits auxquels s'appliquent les dispositions du droit foncier concernant la propriété foncière, l'usufruit des biens immobiliers et les droits à des paiements variables ou fixes pour l'exploitation ou la concession de l'exploitation de gisements minéraux, sources et autres ressources naturelles. Les navires et aéronefs ne sont pas considérés comme des biens immobiliers.

3. Les dispositions du paragraphe 1 s'appliquent aux revenus provenant de l'exploitation directe, de la location ou de l'affermage, ainsi que de toute autre forme d'exploitation de biens immobiliers.

4. Quand la propriété d'actions ou d'autres parts sociales d'une société donne le droit au propriétaire de ces actions ou parts sociales de jouir des biens immobiliers appartenant à la société, les revenus provenant de l'exploitation directe, de la location ou de l'affermage, ainsi que de toute autre forme d'exploitation de ce droit de jouissance sont imposables dans l'État contractant où les biens immobiliers sont situés.

5. Les dispositions des paragraphes 1 et 3 s'appliquent également aux revenus des biens immobiliers d'une entreprise ainsi qu'aux revenus des biens immobiliers servant à l'exercice d'une profession indépendante.

Article 7. Bénéfices des entreprises

1. Les bénéfices d'une entreprise d'un État contractant ne sont imposables que dans cet État, sauf si l'entreprise exerce son activité dans l'autre État contractant par l'intermédiaire d'un établissement stable qui y est situé. Si l'entreprise exerce son activité d'une telle façon, les bénéfices de l'entreprise sont imposables dans l'autre État, mais uniquement dans la mesure où ils sont imputables audit établissement stable.

2. Sous réserve des dispositions du paragraphe 3, lorsqu'une entreprise d'un État contractant exerce son activité dans l'autre État contractant par l'intermédiaire d'un établissement stable qui y est situé, il est imputé à cet établissement stable, dans chaque État contractant, les bénéfices qu'il aurait pu réaliser s'il avait constitué une entreprise distincte exerçant des activités identiques ou analogues dans des conditions identiques ou analogues et traitant en toute indépendance avec l'entreprise dont il constitue un établissement stable.

3. Pour déterminer les bénéfices d'un établissement stable, sont admises en déduction les dépenses relatives aux fins poursuivies par cet établissement stable, y compris les dépenses de

direction et les frais généraux d'administration ainsi enregistrés, soit dans l'État où est situé cet établissement stable, soit ailleurs. Toutefois, aucune déduction n'est admise au titre des participations aux dépenses et pertes du siège social ou d'autres établissements stables situés à l'étranger, ainsi qu'aux sommes versées par l'établissement stable au siège central de l'entreprise ou à l'un quelconque de ses autres bureaux, comme redevances, intérêts, commissions ou autres paiements similaires.

4. Aucun bénéfice n'est imputé à un établissement stable du simple fait qu'il a acheté des biens ou des marchandises pour l'entreprise.

5. Lorsque les bénéfices englobent des éléments de revenu qui sont traités séparément dans d'autres articles du présent Accord, les dispositions de ces articles ne sont pas affectées par les dispositions du présent article.

Article 8. Transports maritimes, aériens et routiers

1. Les bénéfices d'une entreprise d'un État contractant issus de l'exploitation en trafic international de navires, d'aéronefs ou de véhicules routiers ne sont imposables que dans cet État.

2. Les dispositions du paragraphe 1 s'appliquent également aux bénéfices issus de la participation à un consortium, une coentreprise ou un organisme international d'exploitation.

Article 9. Entreprises associées

1. Lorsque :

a) Une entreprise d'un État contractant participe directement ou indirectement à la direction, au contrôle ou au capital d'une entreprise de l'autre État contractant ; ou que

b) Les mêmes personnes participent directement ou indirectement à la direction, au contrôle ou au capital d'une entreprise d'un État contractant et d'une entreprise de l'autre État contractant ;

et que, dans l'un et l'autre cas, les deux entreprises sont, dans leurs relations commerciales ou financières, liées par des conditions convenues ou imposées qui diffèrent de celles qui seraient convenues entre des entreprises indépendantes, les bénéfices qui, sans ces conditions, auraient été réalisés par l'une des entreprises mais n'ont pu l'être en fait à cause de ces conditions, peuvent être inclus dans les bénéfices de cette entreprise et imposés en conséquence.

2. Lorsqu'un État contractant inclut dans les bénéfices d'une entreprise de cet État, et impose en conséquence, des bénéfices sur lesquels une entreprise de l'autre État contractant a été imposée dans cet autre État, et que les bénéfices ainsi inclus sont des bénéfices qui auraient été réalisés par l'entreprise du premier État si les conditions convenues entre les deux entreprises avaient été celles qui auraient été convenues entre des entreprises indépendantes, alors cet autre État procède à un ajustement approprié du montant de l'impôt qui y a été perçu sur ces bénéfices. Pour déterminer cet ajustement, il est dûment tenu compte des autres dispositions du présent Accord et, si nécessaire, les autorités compétentes des deux États contractants se consultent.

Article 10. Dividendes

1. Les dividendes payés par une société résidente d'un État contractant à un résident de l'autre État contractant sont imposables dans cet autre État.

2. Toutefois, ces dividendes sont aussi imposables dans l'État contractant dont la société qui paie les dividendes est résident et selon la législation de cet État, mais si le bénéficiaire effectif des dividendes est un résident de l'autre État contractant, l'impôt ainsi établi ne peut excéder :

a) 5 % du montant brut des dividendes si le bénéficiaire effectif est une société (autre qu'une société de personnes) qui détient directement au moins 25 % du capital de la société qui paie les dividendes ;

b) 15 % du montant brut des dividendes dans tous les autres cas.

Le présent paragraphe n'affecte pas l'imposition de la société au titre des bénéfices qui servent au paiement des dividendes.

3. Le terme « dividendes » employé dans le présent article désigne les revenus provenant d'actions, actions ou bons de jouissance, parts de fondateur ou autres parts bénéficiaires à l'exception des créances, ainsi que les revenus d'autres parts sociales soumis au même régime fiscal que les revenus d'actions par la législation de l'État dont la société distributrice est un résident.

4. Les bénéfices d'une société résidente d'un État contractant qui exerce dans l'autre État contractant une activité industrielle ou commerciale par l'intermédiaire d'un établissement stable qui y est situé peuvent, après avoir été imposés au titre de l'article 7, être soumis à imposition sur le montant restant dans l'État contractant où l'établissement stable est situé. Toutefois l'impôt ainsi exigé ne doit pas dépasser :

a) 5 % du montant restant, à condition que ces bénéfices soient exonérés d'impôt dans l'État contractant dont la société est un résident ;

b) 15 % du montant restant dans tous les autres cas.

5. Les dispositions des paragraphes 1 et 2 ne s'appliquent pas lorsque le bénéficiaire effectif des dividendes, résident d'un État contractant, exerce dans l'autre État contractant dont la société qui paie les dividendes est un résident, soit une activité industrielle ou commerciale par l'intermédiaire d'un établissement stable qui y est situé, soit une profession indépendante au moyen d'une base fixe qui y est située, et que la participation génératrice des dividendes s'y rattache effectivement. Dans ce cas, les dispositions de l'article 7 ou de l'article 14, selon le cas, sont applicables.

6. Lorsque, selon les dispositions du paragraphe 4 du présent article, une société qui est résidente d'un État contractant tire des bénéfices ou des revenus de l'autre État contractant, cet autre État contractant ne peut percevoir aucun impôt sur les dividendes payés par la société, sauf dans la mesure où ces dividendes sont payés à un résident de cet autre État ou dans la mesure où la participation génératrice des dividendes se rattache effectivement à un établissement stable ou à une base fixe situés dans cet autre État, ni prélever aucun impôt, au titre de l'impôt sur les bénéfices non distribués de la société, sur les bénéfices non distribués de la société, même si les dividendes versés ou les bénéfices non distribués consistent en tout ou en partie en bénéfices ou revenus provenant de cet autre État.

Article 11. Intérêts

1. Les intérêts provenant d'un État contractant et payés à un résident de l'autre État contractant sont imposables dans cet autre État.

2. Toutefois, ces intérêts sont aussi imposables dans l'État contractant d'où ils proviennent et selon la législation de cet État, mais si le bénéficiaire effectif des intérêts est un résident de l'autre État contractant, l'impôt ainsi établi ne peut excéder :

a) 5 % du montant brut des intérêts versés en raison d'un prêt ou d'un crédit consenti, garanti ou assuré aux fins de la promotion des exportations par la Finnish Export Credit, par FINNVERA ou par une entité publique turque similaire dont l'objectif est de promouvoir les exportations ;

b) 10 % du montant brut des intérêts s'ils sont perçus par une banque ;

c) 15 % du montant brut des intérêts dans tous les autres cas.

3. Nonobstant les dispositions du paragraphe 2, les intérêts provenant :

a) De Finlande et versés au Gouvernement de la Turquie ou à la Banque centrale de Turquie (Türkiye Cumhuriyet Merkez Bankasi) sont exonérés de l'impôt finlandais ;

b) De Turquie et versés au Gouvernement de la Finlande ou à la Banque de Finlande (Suomen Pankki) sont exonérés de l'impôt turc.

4. Le terme « intérêts » employé dans le présent article désigne les revenus des créances de toute nature, assorties ou non de garanties hypothécaires ou d'une clause de participation aux bénéfices du débiteur, et notamment les revenus des fonds publics et des obligations d'emprunts, y compris les primes et lots attachés à ces titres, de même que tout autre revenu considéré comme un revenu de l'argent prêté, par la législation fiscale de l'État contractant dans lequel les revenus sont générés.

5. Les dispositions des paragraphes 1 et 2 ne s'appliquent pas lorsque le bénéficiaire effectif des intérêts, résident d'un État contractant, exerce dans l'autre État contractant d'où proviennent les intérêts, soit une activité industrielle ou commerciale par l'intermédiaire d'un établissement stable qui y est situé, soit une profession indépendante au moyen d'une base fixe qui y est située, et que la créance génératrice des intérêts se rattache effectivement à l'établissement stable ou à la base fixe en question. Dans ces cas, les dispositions de l'article 7 ou de l'article 14, selon le cas, sont applicables.

6. Les intérêts sont considérés comme provenant d'un État contractant lorsque le débiteur est cet État ou l'une des autorités locales ou des résidents de cet État. Toutefois, lorsque le débiteur des intérêts, qu'il soit ou non résident d'un État contractant, a dans un État contractant un établissement stable ou une base fixe pour lesquels la dette donnant lieu au paiement des intérêts a été contractée et qui supportent la charge de ces intérêts, ceux-ci sont considérés comme provenant de l'État où l'établissement stable, ou la base fixe, est situé.

7. Lorsque, en raison de relations spéciales entre le débiteur et le bénéficiaire effectif ou entre l'un et l'autre et quelque autre personne, le montant des intérêts, compte tenu de la créance pour laquelle ils sont payés, excède celui dont seraient convenus le débiteur et le bénéficiaire effectif en l'absence de pareilles relations, les dispositions du présent article ne s'appliquent qu'à ce dernier montant. Dans ce cas, la partie excédentaire des paiements reste imposable selon la législation de chaque État contractant et compte tenu des autres dispositions du présent Accord.

Article 12. Redevances

1. Les redevances provenant d'un État contractant et payées à un résident de l'autre État contractant sont imposables dans cet autre État.

2. Toutefois, ces redevances sont aussi imposables dans l'État contractant d'où elles proviennent et selon la législation de cet État, mais si le bénéficiaire effectif des redevances est un résident de l'autre État contractant, l'impôt ainsi établi ne peut excéder 10 % du montant brut des redevances.

3. Le terme « redevances » employé dans le présent article désigne les rémunérations de toute nature payées pour l'usage ou la concession de l'usage d'un droit d'auteur sur une œuvre littéraire, artistique ou scientifique, y compris les films cinématographiques, et les enregistrements pour les émissions radiophoniques ou télévisées, d'un brevet, d'une marque de fabrique ou de commerce, d'un dessin ou d'un modèle, d'un plan, d'une formule ou d'un procédé secrets et pour des renseignements ayant trait à une expérience acquise dans le domaine industriel, commercial ou scientifique, ainsi que pour l'usage ou la concession de l'usage d'un équipement industriel, commercial ou scientifique.

4. Les dispositions des paragraphes 1 et 2 ne s'appliquent pas lorsque le bénéficiaire effectif des redevances, résident d'un État contractant, exerce dans l'autre État contractant source des redevances soit une activité industrielle ou commerciale par l'intermédiaire d'un établissement stable qui y est situé, soit une profession indépendante au moyen d'une base fixe qui y est située, et que le droit ou le bien générateur des redevances se rattache effectivement à l'établissement stable ou à la base fixe en question. Dans ces cas, les dispositions de l'article 7 ou de l'article 14, suivant le cas, sont applicables.

5. Les redevances sont considérées comme provenant d'un État contractant lorsque le débiteur est cet État, l'une de ses collectivités locales ou l'un de ses résidents. Toutefois, lorsque le débiteur des redevances, qu'il soit ou non résident d'un État contractant, a dans un État contractant un établissement stable ou une base fixe pour lesquels le droit ou le bien générateur des redevances est effectivement rattaché, et que lesdites redevances sont imputées audit établissement stable ou à ladite base fixe, celles-ci sont considérées comme provenant de l'État où l'établissement stable, ou la base fixe, est situé.

6. Lorsque, en raison de relations spéciales existant entre le débiteur et le bénéficiaire effectif ou que l'un et l'autre entretiennent avec des tiers, le montant des redevances, compte tenu de la prestation pour laquelle elles sont payées, excède celui dont seraient convenus le débiteur et le bénéficiaire effectif en l'absence de pareilles relations, les dispositions du présent article ne s'appliquent qu'à ce dernier montant. Dans ce cas, la partie excédentaire des paiements reste imposable selon la législation de chaque État contractant et compte tenu des autres dispositions du présent Accord.

Article 13. Gains en capital

1. Les gains qu'un résident d'un État contractant tire de l'aliénation de biens immobiliers visés à l'article 6 et situés dans l'autre État contractant sont imposables dans cet autre État.

2. Les gains provenant de l'aliénation de biens mobiliers qui font partie de l'actif d'un établissement stable qu'une entreprise d'un État contractant a dans l'autre État contractant, ou de biens mobiliers qui appartiennent à une base fixe dont un résident d'un État contractant dispose

dans l'autre État contractant pour l'exercice d'une profession indépendante, y compris de tels gains dégagés par l'aliénation de cet établissement stable (seul ou avec l'ensemble de l'entreprise) ou de cette base fixe, sont imposables dans cet autre État.

3. Les gains qu'un résident d'un État contractant tire de l'aliénation de navires, d'aéronefs ou de véhicules routiers exploités en trafic international, ou de biens mobiliers affectés à l'exploitation de ces navires, aéronefs ou véhicules routiers, ne sont imposables que dans cet État.

4. Les gains qu'un résident d'un État contractant tire de l'aliénation d'actions ou d'autres parts sociales d'une société dont l'actif est composé, directement ou indirectement, de plus de 50 % de biens immobiliers situés dans l'autre État contractant sont imposables dans cet autre État.

5. Les gains provenant de l'aliénation de tous biens autres que ceux visés aux paragraphes 1, 2, 3 et 4 ne sont imposables que dans l'État contractant dont le cédant est un résident. Toutefois, les gains en capital mentionnés dans la phrase précédente et provenant de l'autre État contractant sont imposables dans cet autre État contractant si le délai écoulé entre l'acquisition et la cession n'excède pas un an.

Article 14. Professions indépendantes

1. Les revenus qu'une personne physique qui est un résident d'un État contractant tire d'une profession libérale ou d'autres activités de caractère indépendant ne sont imposables que dans cet État. Toutefois, ces revenus sont également imposables dans l'autre État contractant si les services ou les activités sont exercés dans cet autre État et si :

a) La personne physique dispose de façon habituelle dans cet autre État d'une base fixe pour la réalisation de ces services ou de ces activités ; ou

b) La personne physique séjourne dans cet autre État aux fins de l'exercice de ces services ou activités pendant une période ou des périodes d'une durée totale égale ou supérieure à 183 jours au cours de toute période ininterrompue de 12 mois.

En pareil cas, seule la part des revenus qui est imputable à cette base fixe ou qui provient des services fournis ou des activités exercées pendant le séjour de l'intéressé dans cet autre État, selon le cas, est imposable dans cet autre État.

2. Les revenus qu'une entreprise d'un État contractant tire d'une profession indépendante ou d'autres activités de caractère analogue ne sont imposables que dans cet État. Toutefois, ces revenus sont également imposables dans l'autre État contractant si ces services ou ces activités sont exercés dans cet autre État et si :

a) L'entreprise dispose d'un établissement stable dans cet autre État par l'intermédiaire duquel les services ou les activités sont exercés ; ou

b) La période ou les périodes pendant lesquelles les services ou les activités sont exercés totalisent plus de 183 jours au cours de toute période ininterrompue de 12 mois.

En pareil cas, seule la part des revenus qui est imputable à cet établissement stable ou qui provient des services fournis ou des activités exercées dans cet autre État, selon le cas, est imposable dans cet autre État. Dans un cas comme dans l'autre, l'entreprise peut décider d'être imposée dans cet autre État pour ces revenus conformément aux dispositions de l'article 7 du présent Accord, comme si les revenus étaient imputables à un établissement stable de l'entreprise situé dans cet autre État. Cette décision n'a pas d'effet sur le droit de l'autre État d'exiger un impôt retenu à la source sur ces revenus.

3. L'expression « profession indépendante » se rapporte notamment aux activités indépendantes d'ordre scientifique, littéraire, artistique, éducatif ou pédagogique, ainsi qu'aux activités indépendantes des médecins, avocats, ingénieurs, architectes, dentistes et comptables et d'autres activités nécessitant une compétence professionnelle particulière.

Article 15. Revenus d'emploi

1. Sous réserve des dispositions des articles 16, 18, 19 et 20, les salaires, traitements et autres rémunérations similaires qu'un résident d'un État contractant reçoit au titre d'un emploi salarié ne sont imposables que dans cet État, à moins que l'emploi ne soit exercé dans l'autre État contractant. Si l'emploi y est exercé, les rémunérations reçues à ce titre sont imposables dans cet autre État.

2. Nonobstant les dispositions du paragraphe 1, les rémunérations qu'un résident d'un État contractant reçoit au titre d'un emploi salarié exercé dans l'autre État contractant ne sont imposables que dans le premier État si :

a) Le bénéficiaire séjourne dans l'autre État pendant une période ou des périodes n'excédant pas au total 183 jours pendant toute période de 12 mois commençant ou s'achevant pendant l'année civile considérée ; et

b) Les rémunérations sont versées par un employeur ou pour le compte d'un employeur qui n'est pas un résident de l'autre État ; et

c) La charge des rémunérations n'est pas supportée par un établissement stable ou une base fixe que l'employeur a dans l'autre État.

3. Nonobstant les dispositions précédentes du présent article, les rémunérations reçues au titre d'un emploi salarié exercé à bord d'un navire, d'un aéronef ou d'un véhicule routier exploité en trafic international par une entreprise d'un État contractant sont imposables dans cet État contractant.

Article 16. Tantièmes

Les tantièmes et autres rétributions similaires qu'un résident d'un État contractant reçoit en sa qualité de membre du conseil d'administration ou de tout autre organe analogue d'une société qui est résidente de l'autre État contractant sont imposables dans cet autre État.

Article 17. Artistes du spectacle et athlètes

1. Nonobstant les dispositions des articles 14 et 15, les revenus qu'un résident d'un État contractant tire de ses activités personnelles exercées dans l'autre État contractant en tant qu'artiste du spectacle, tel qu'un artiste de théâtre, de cinéma, de la radio ou de la télévision, ou un musicien, ou en tant qu'athlète, sont imposables dans cet autre État.

2. Lorsque les revenus d'activités qu'un artiste du spectacle ou un athlète exerce personnellement en cette qualité sont attribués non pas à l'artiste du spectacle ou à l'athlète lui-même mais à une autre personne, ces revenus sont, nonobstant les dispositions des

articles 7, 14 et 15, imposables dans l'État contractant où les activités de l'artiste du spectacle ou de l'athlète sont exercées.

Article 18. Pensions

1. Les pensions et autres rémunérations similaires versées à un résident d'un État contractant au titre d'un emploi antérieur ne sont imposables que dans cet État.

2. Nonobstant les dispositions du paragraphe 1, les pensions payées par un État contractant ou par l'un de ses organismes de droit public ou l'une de ses collectivités locales, soit directement soit par prélèvement sur des fonds qu'ils ont constitués, à une personne physique au titre de services fournis à cet État ou à cet organisme ou à cette collectivité, ou les pensions payées et d'autres paiements versés en vertu de la législation relative à la sécurité sociale d'un État contractant ne sont imposables que dans cet État. Toutefois, ces pensions et autres paiements ne sont imposables que dans l'État contractant dont la personne physique est un résident si elle est un ressortissant de cet État.

Article 19. Fonction publique

1. a) Les salaires, traitements et autres rémunérations similaires versés par un État contractant, l'un de ses organismes de droit public ou l'une de ses collectivités locales à une personne physique au titre de services fournis à cet État, à cet organisme ou à cette collectivité ne sont imposables que dans cet État ;

   b) Toutefois, ces salaires, traitements et autres rémunérations similaires ne sont imposables que dans l'État contractant dont la personne physique est un résident si les services sont exécutés dans cet État et si la personne physique :

      i) Est un ressortissant de cet État ; ou

      ii) N'est pas devenue résidente de cet État à seule fin d'exécuter les services en question.

2. Les dispositions des articles 15, 16 et 17 s'appliquent aux salaires, traitements et autres rémunérations similaires versés au titre de services fournis dans le cadre d'une activité industrielle ou commerciale exercée par un État contractant ou par l'un de ses organismes de droit public ou l'une de ses collectivités locales.

Article 20. Étudiants et stagiaires

1. Les sommes qu'un étudiant, un apprenti ou un stagiaire d'un établissement commercial, technique, agricole ou forestier qui est ou qui était, immédiatement avant d'aller vivre dans un État contractant un résident de l'autre État contractant et qui séjourne dans le premier État à seule fin d'y poursuivre ses études ou sa formation reçoit pour couvrir ses frais d'entretien, d'études ou de formation ne sont pas imposables dans cet État, à condition qu'elles proviennent de sources situées en dehors de cet État.

2. Un étudiant d'une université ou d'un autre établissement d'enseignement supérieur d'un État contractant, ou un apprenti ou un stagiaire d'un établissement commercial, technique, agricole ou forestier, qui est ou qui était immédiatement avant d'aller vivre dans l'autre État contractant, un résident du premier État contractant et qui séjourne dans l'autre État contractant pendant une

période continue ne dépassant pas 183 jours, n'est pas imposé dans cet autre État sur la rémunération des services exécutés dans cet État, à condition que ces services soient en rapport avec ses études ou sa formation et que la rémunération constitue un revenu nécessaire à sa subsistance.

Article 21. Autres revenus

1. Les éléments du revenu d'un résident d'un État contractant, d'où qu'ils proviennent, qui ne sont pas traités dans les articles précédents du présent Accord ne sont imposables que dans cet État.

2. Les dispositions du paragraphe 1 ne s'appliquent pas aux revenus autres que les revenus provenant de biens immobiliers, tels qu'ils sont définis au paragraphe 2 de l'article 6, lorsque le bénéficiaire de tels revenus, résident d'un État contractant, exerce dans l'autre État contractant soit une activité industrielle ou commerciale par l'intermédiaire d'un établissement stable qui y est situé, soit une profession indépendante au moyen d'une base fixe qui y est située, et que le droit ou le bien générateur des revenus se rattache effectivement à cet établissement stable ou à cette base fixe. Dans ces cas, les dispositions de l'article 7 ou de l'article 14, selon le cas, sont applicables.

3. Nonobstant les dispositions des paragraphes 1 et 2, les éléments du revenu d'un résident d'un État contractant qui ne sont pas traités dans les articles précédents du présent Accord et qui proviennent de l'autre État contractant sont également imposables dans cet autre État.

Article 22. Élimination des doubles impositions

1. La double imposition des résidents de Turquie est éliminée de la manière suivante :

   a) Sous réserve des dispositions de la législation de la Turquie concernant la possibilité de déduire de l'impôt turc tout impôt dû dans un territoire extérieur à la Turquie (et de toute modification qui pourrait être apportée à la législation sans pour autant changer les principes généraux ici posés), l'impôt finlandais dû en vertu de la législation finlandaise et conformément au présent Accord au regard du revenu (y compris les bénéfices et les gains en capital) qu'un résident de la Turquie tire de sources situées en Finlande peut être déduit de l'impôt turc sur ce revenu. Cette déduction ne peut toutefois excéder la fraction de l'impôt turc, calculé avant déduction, correspondant à ce revenu ;

   b) Lorsque, conformément à une disposition quelconque de l'Accord, les revenus qu'un résident de la Turquie reçoit sont exonérés de l'impôt turc, la Turquie peut néanmoins, pour calculer le montant de l'impôt sur le reste des revenus de ce résident, tenir compte des revenus exonérés.

2. Sous réserve des dispositions de la législation finlandaise concernant l'élimination de la double imposition internationale (qui n'affecte pas le principe général ici posé), la double imposition est éliminée comme suit en Finlande :

   a) Lorsqu'un résident de la Finlande perçoit des revenus qui, conformément aux dispositions du présent Accord, sont imposables en Turquie, la Finlande, sous réserve des dispositions de l'alinéa b) accorde, en tant que déduction de l'impôt sur le revenu de cette personne, un montant égal à l'impôt effectivement payé en

Turquie calculé sur la base du même revenu à partir duquel l'impôt finlandais est calculé ;

b) Les dividendes payés par une société qui est résidente de la Turquie à une société qui est résidente de la Finlande et détient directement au moins 10 % des droits de vote de la société qui paie les dividendes sont exonérés de l'impôt finlandais ;

c) Lorsque, conformément à une disposition quelconque du présent Accord, les revenus qu'un résident de la Finlande reçoit sont exonérés de l'impôt finlandais, la Finlande peut néanmoins, pour calculer le montant de l'impôt sur le reste des revenus de cette personne, tenir compte des revenus exonérés ;

d) Aux fins de l'alinéa a), l'expression « impôt sur le revenu payé en Turquie » est réputée inclure tout montant de l'impôt turc qui aurait été exigible en vertu de la législation fiscale turque, mais pour tout dégrèvement ou toute exonération de l'impôt turc accordé en vertu de dispositions relatives aux mesures spéciales d'encouragement visant à promouvoir le développement économique en Turquie.

Nonobstant la disposition précédente, l'impôt sur le revenu payé en Turquie est calculé :

i) Dans le cas de dividendes visés à l'alinéa b) du paragraphe 2 de l'article 10, à un taux de 15 % ;

ii) Dans le cas des intérêts visés à l'alinéa a) du paragraphe 2 de l'article 11, à un taux de 5 %, dans le cas des intérêts visés à l'alinéa b) du paragraphe 2 de l'article 11, à un taux de 10 %, et dans le cas des intérêts visés à l'alinéa c) du paragraphe 2 de l'article 11, à un taux de 15 % ;

iii) Dans le cas des redevances et autres paiements visés au paragraphe 2 de l'article 12, à un taux de 10 %.

Toutefois, si les taux d'imposition établis en vertu de la législation fiscale turque applicable aux dividendes, intérêts et redevances reçus par des personnes qui ne sont pas des résidents de la Turquie sont réduits par rapport aux niveaux indiqués dans le présent alinéa, ces taux réduits seraient applicables aux fins du présent alinéa.

Article 23. Non-discrimination

1. Les ressortissants d'un État contractant ne sont soumis dans l'autre État contractant à aucune imposition ou obligation correspondante qui est autre ou plus lourde que celles auxquelles sont ou pourront être assujettis les ressortissants de cet autre État qui se trouvent dans la même situation, notamment au regard de la résidence. La présente disposition s'applique aussi, nonobstant les dispositions de l'article premier, aux personnes qui ne sont pas des résidents d'un État contractant ou des deux États contractants.

2. Sous réserve des dispositions du paragraphe 4 de l'article 10, l'imposition d'un établissement stable qu'une entreprise d'un État contractant a dans l'autre État contractant n'est pas établie dans cet autre État d'une façon moins favorable que l'imposition des entreprises de cet autre État qui exercent la même activité.

3. Les entreprises d'un État contractant dont le capital est en totalité ou en partie, directement ou indirectement, détenu ou contrôlé par un ou plusieurs résidents de l'autre État contractant, ne sont soumises dans le premier État à aucune imposition ou obligation

correspondante qui est autre ou plus lourde que celles auxquelles sont ou pourront être assujetties les autres entreprises similaires du premier État.

4. À moins que les dispositions du paragraphe 1 de l'article 9, du paragraphe 7 de l'article 11 ou du paragraphe 6 de l'article 12 ne soient applicables, les intérêts, redevances et autres dépenses payés par une entreprise d'un État contractant à un résident de l'autre État contractant sont déductibles, pour la détermination des bénéfices imposables de cette entreprise, dans les mêmes conditions que s'ils avaient été payés à un résident du premier État.

5. Ces dispositions ne peuvent être interprétées comme obligeant un État contractant à accorder aux résidents de l'autre État contractant les déductions personnelles, abattements et réductions d'impôt en fonction de la situation ou des charges de famille qu'il accorde à ses propres résidents.

6. Les dispositions du présent article ne s'appliquent qu'aux impôts relevant de l'article 2.

Article 24. Procédure amiable

1. Lorsqu'une personne estime que les mesures prises par un État contractant ou par les deux États contractants entraînent ou entraîneront pour elle une imposition non conforme aux dispositions du présent Accord, elle peut, indépendamment des recours prévus par le droit interne de ces États, soumettre son cas à l'autorité compétente de l'État contractant dont elle est résidente ou, si son cas relève du paragraphe 1 de l'article 23, à celle de l'État contractant dont elle possède la nationalité. Le cas doit être soumis dans un délai de trois ans à partir de la première notification des mesures qui entraînent une imposition non conforme aux dispositions de l'Accord.

2. L'autorité compétente s'efforce, si la réclamation lui paraît fondée et si elle n'est pas elle-même en mesure d'y apporter une solution satisfaisante, de résoudre le cas par voie amiable avec l'autorité compétente de l'autre État contractant, en vue d'éviter une imposition non conforme à l'Accord. Tout accord conclu est appliqué quels que soient les délais prévus par le droit interne des États contractants.

3. Les autorités compétentes des États contractants s'efforcent, par voie d'accord amiable, de résoudre les difficultés ou de dissiper les doutes auxquels peuvent donner lieu l'interprétation ou l'application de l'Accord. Elles peuvent aussi se concerter en vue d'éliminer les doubles impositions dans les cas non prévus par l'Accord.

4. Les autorités compétentes des États contractants peuvent communiquer directement entre elles, notamment par l'intermédiaire d'une commission mixte constituée d'elles-mêmes ou de leurs représentants, en vue de parvenir à un accord au sens des paragraphes précédents.

Article 25. Échange de renseignements

1. Les autorités compétentes des États contractants échangent les renseignements vraisemblablement pertinents pour appliquer les dispositions du présent Accord ou celles de la législation interne des États contractants relative aux impôts de toute nature ou dénomination perçus pour le compte d'un État contractant, de leurs subdivisions politiques ou de leurs collectivités locales, dans la mesure où l'imposition qu'elle prévoit n'est pas contraire à l'Accord. L'échange de renseignements n'est pas restreint par les articles premier et 2.

2. Les renseignements reçus par un État contractant en vertu du paragraphe 1 sont tenus secrets de la même manière que les renseignements obtenus en application de la législation interne

de cet État, et ils ne sont communiqués qu'aux personnes ou autorités (y compris les tribunaux et organes administratifs) concernées par l'établissement ou le recouvrement des impôts visés au paragraphe 1, par les procédures ou poursuites concernant ces impôts, par les décisions sur les recours relatifs à ces impôts, ou par le contrôle de ce qui précède. Ces personnes ou autorités n'utilisent les renseignements qu'à ces fins, mais peuvent en faire état au cours d'audiences publiques de tribunaux ou dans les jugements.

3. Les dispositions des paragraphes 1 et 2 ne peuvent en aucun cas être interprétées comme imposant à un État contractant l'obligation :

a) De prendre des mesures administratives dérogeant à sa législation et à sa pratique administrative ou à celles de l'autre État contractant ;

b) De fournir des renseignements qui ne pourraient être obtenus sur la base de sa législation ou dans le cadre de sa pratique administrative normale ou de celles de l'autre État contractant ;

c) De fournir des renseignements qui révéleraient un secret commercial, industriel, professionnel ou un procédé commercial ou des renseignements dont la communication serait contraire à l'ordre public.

4. Si des renseignements sont demandés par un État contractant conformément au présent article, l'autre État contractant utilise ses mesures de collecte de renseignements pour obtenir les renseignements demandés quand bien même cet autre État contractant n'aurait pas besoin de ces renseignements à ses propres fins fiscales. L'obligation contenue dans la phrase précédente est subordonnée aux limitations du paragraphe 3, mais en aucun cas ces limitations ne doivent être interprétées comme autorisant un État contractant à refuser de fournir des renseignements pour la seule raison qu'il ne détient aucun intérêt national dans de tels renseignements.

5. Les dispositions du paragraphe 3 ne doivent en aucun cas être interprétées comme autorisant un État contractant à refuser de fournir des renseignements pour la seule raison que les renseignements sont tenus par une banque, une autre institution financière, un mandataire ou une personne agissant en qualité d'agent ou à titre fiduciaire ou parce que cela concerne les intérêts fonciers d'une personne.

Article 26. Assistance en matière de recouvrement des impôts

1. Les États contractants se prêtent mutuellement assistance pour le recouvrement de leurs créances fiscales. Cette assistance n'est pas limitée par les articles premier et 2. Les autorités compétentes des États contractants peuvent régler d'un commun accord les modalités d'application du présent article.

2. L'expression « créance fiscale » utilisée dans le présent article désigne une somme due au titre d'impôts de toute nature ou dénomination perçus pour le compte des États contractants, de leurs subdivisions politiques ou collectivités locales, dans la mesure où l'imposition qu'elle prévoit n'est pas contraire au présent Accord ou à tout autre instrument auquel ces États contractants sont parties, ainsi que les intérêts, pénalités administratives et coûts de recouvrement ou de conservation afférents à ce montant.

3. Lorsqu'une créance fiscale d'un État contractant qui est recouvrable en vertu des lois de cet État est due par une personne qui, à cette date, ne peut, en vertu de ces lois, empêcher son recouvrement, cette créance fiscale est, à la demande des autorités compétentes de cet État, acceptée en vue de son recouvrement par les autorités compétentes de l'autre État contractant.

Cette créance fiscale est recouvrée par cet autre État conformément aux dispositions de sa législation applicable en matière de recouvrement de ses propres impôts comme si la créance en question était une créance fiscale de cet autre État.

4. Lorsqu'une créance fiscale d'un État contractant est une créance à l'égard de laquelle cet État peut, en vertu de sa législation, prendre des mesures conservatoires pour assurer son recouvrement, cette créance doit, à la demande des autorités compétentes de cet État, être acceptée aux fins d'adoption de mesures conservatoires par les autorités compétentes de l'autre État contractant. Cet autre État doit prendre des mesures conservatoires à l'égard de cette créance fiscale conformément aux dispositions de sa législation comme s'il s'agissait d'une créance fiscale de cet autre État même si, au moment où ces mesures sont appliquées, la créance fiscale n'est pas recouvrable dans le premier État ou est due par une personne qui a le droit d'empêcher son recouvrement.

5. Nonobstant les dispositions des paragraphes 3 et 4, les délais de prescription et la priorité applicables, en vertu de la législation d'un État contractant, à une créance fiscale en raison de sa nature en tant que telle ne s'appliquent pas à une créance fiscale acceptée par cet État aux fins du paragraphe 3 ou 4. En outre, une créance fiscale acceptée par un État contractant aux fins du paragraphe 3 ou 4 ne peut se voir appliquer aucune priorité dans cet État en vertu de la législation de l'autre État contractant.

6. Les procédures concernant l'existence, la validité ou le montant d'une créance fiscale d'un État contractant ne sont pas soumises aux tribunaux ou organes administratifs de l'autre État contractant.

7. Quand à tout moment après qu'une demande a été formulée par un État contractant en vertu du paragraphe 3 ou 4 et avant que l'autre État ait recouvré et transmis le montant de la créance fiscale en question au premier État, cette créance fiscale cesse d'être :

a) Dans le cas d'une demande présentée en vertu du paragraphe 3, une créance fiscale du premier État qui est recouvrable en vertu des lois de cet État et est due par une personne qui, à ce moment, ne peut, en vertu des lois de cet État, empêcher son recouvrement ; ou

b) Dans le cas d'une demande présentée en vertu du paragraphe 4, une créance fiscale du premier État à l'égard de laquelle cet État peut, en vertu de sa législation, prendre des mesures conservatoires pour assurer son recouvrement ;

les autorités compétentes du premier État notifient promptement ce fait aux autorités compétentes de l'autre État et le premier État, au choix de l'autre État, suspend ou retire sa demande.

8. Les dispositions du présent article ne peuvent en aucun cas être interprétées comme imposant à un État contractant l'obligation :

a) De prendre des mesures administratives dérogeant à sa législation et à sa pratique administrative ou à celles de l'autre État contractant ;

b) De prendre des mesures qui seraient contraires à l'ordre public ;

c) De prêter assistance si l'autre État contractant n'a pas pris toutes les mesures raisonnables de recouvrement ou de conservation, selon le cas, qui sont disponibles en vertu de sa législation ou de sa pratique administrative ;

d) De prêter assistance dans les cas où la charge administrative qui en résulte pour cet État est nettement disproportionnée par rapport aux avantages que peut en tirer l'autre État contractant.

Article 27. Membres de missions diplomatiques et de postes consulaires

Rien dans la présente Convention ne porte atteinte aux privilèges fiscaux dont bénéficient les agents diplomatiques ou les fonctionnaires consulaires en vertu soit des règles générales du droit international, soit des dispositions d'accords particuliers.

Article 28. Entrée en vigueur

1. Les États contractants se notifient mutuellement, par la voie diplomatique, l'accomplissement des formalités internes requises pour l'entrée en vigueur du présent Accord. Le présent Accord entre en vigueur le trentième jour qui suit la date de réception de la dernière de ces notifications et ses dispositions sont applicables :

a) En Turquie : aux impôts relatifs à tout exercice fiscal commençant le 1er janvier de l'année suivant celle de l'entrée en vigueur du présent Accord ou après cette date ;

b) En Finlande :

i) En ce qui concerne les impôts retenus à la source, aux revenus perçus le 1er janvier de l'année civile qui suit celle au cours de laquelle l'Accord est entré en vigueur ou après cette date ;

ii) En ce qui concerne les autres impôts sur le revenu, aux impôts à recouvrer pour tout exercice fiscal commençant le 1er janvier de l'année civile qui suit celle au cours de laquelle l'Accord est entré en vigueur ou après cette date.

2. « L'Accord entre la République de Finlande et la République turque tendant à éviter la double imposition en matière d'impôts sur le revenu », signé à Ankara le 9 mai 1986 (ci-après dénommé « l'Accord de 1986 ») cesse d'être applicable à la date à laquelle le présent Accord prendra effet conformément aux dispositions du paragraphe 1. L'Accord de 1986 prend fin à la dernière des dates à laquelle il est applicable conformément aux dispositions précédentes du présent paragraphe.

Article 29. Dénonciation

Le présent Accord demeure en vigueur tant qu'il n'a pas été dénoncé par un État contractant. Chaque État contractant peut dénoncer l'Accord par la voie diplomatique moyennant un préavis minimal de six mois avant la fin de chaque année civile après l'expiration d'une période de cinq ans à compter de la date d'entrée en vigueur de l'Accord. Dans ce cas, l'Accord cesse d'être applicable :

a) En Turquie : pour les impôts relatifs à tout exercice fiscal commençant le 1er janvier de l'année suivant celle au cours de laquelle la dénonciation est notifiée ou après cette date ;

b) En Finlande :

i) En ce qui concerne les impôts retenus à la source, pour les revenus perçus le 1er janvier de l'année civile suivant celle au cours de laquelle la dénonciation est notifiée ou après cette date ;

ii) En ce qui concerne les autres impôts sur le revenu, pour les impôts à recouvrer pour tout exercice fiscal commençant le 1er janvier de l'année civile suivant celle au cours de laquelle la dénonciation est notifiée ou après cette date.

EN FOI DE QUOI, les soussignés, à ce dûment autorisés, ont signé le présent Accord.

FAIT à Istanbul, le 6 octobre 2009, en double exemplaire, en langues finnoise, turque et anglaise, les trois textes faisant également foi. En cas de divergence d'interprétation, le texte anglais prévaut.

Pour le Gouvernement de la République de Finlande :
[MATTI VANHANEN]

Pour le Gouvernement de la République turque :
[RECEP TAYYIP ERDOĞAN]

PROTOCOLE

Lors de la signature de l'Accord entre la République de Finlande et la République turque tendant à éviter les doubles impositions en matière d'impôts sur le revenu, les soussignés sont convenus des dispositions suivantes qui font partie intégrante de l'Accord.

1. En ce qui concerne le paragraphe 1 de l'article 7.

Il est entendu que lorsqu'une entreprise d'un État contractant possède un établissement stable dans l'autre État contractant et que cette entreprise :

a) Procède dans cet autre État à la vente de marchandises de même nature ou semblables à celles qui sont vendues par l'intermédiaire de cet établissement stable ; ou

b) Exerce dans cet autre État une activité commerciale ou industrielle de même nature ou semblable à celle exercée dans cet établissement stable ;

les ventes et les activités commerciales ou industrielles sont imposables dans cet autre État contractant au titre des bénéfices de l'établissement stable s'il est prouvé que ces ventes ou activités ont été effectuées par l'intermédiaire de l'établissement stable ; cette imposition ne peut être exclue par des arrangements de vente factices.

2. En ce qui concerne le paragraphe 3 de l'article 10.

Il est entendu que le terme « dividendes » comprend également, dans le cas de la Turquie, les revenus provenant de fonds d'investissement et de sociétés d'investissement.

3. En ce qui concerne les articles 12 et 13.

Il est entendu que, si un paiement est reçu pour la vente des biens au sens du paragraphe 3 de l'article 12, les dispositions de l'article 12 s'appliquent, à moins qu'il ne soit prouvé que le paiement en question est un paiement pour la cession effective desdits biens. Dans ce cas, les dispositions de l'article 13 s'appliquent.

4. En ce qui concerne le paragraphe 2 de l'article 15.

Il est entendu que le paragraphe 2 de l'article 15 ne s'applique pas aux rémunérations qu'un résident d'un État contractant (« travailleur salarié ») reçoit et qui sont payées par un employeur ou pour le compte d'un employeur qui est un résident de cet État au titre d'un emploi salarié exercé dans l'autre État contractant lorsque :

a) Le travailleur salarié fournit, dans le cadre de cet emploi, des services à une personne autre que l'employeur et qui, directement ou indirectement, supervise, dirige ou contrôle la manière dont lesdits services sont fournis ; et

b) L'employeur n'est pas responsable du résultat du travail effectué par le bénéficiaire.

5. En ce qui concerne les articles 4, 18 et 19.

Il est entendu que l'expression « organisme de droit public » désigne :

a) Dans le cas de la Turquie :

   i) La Banque centrale de Turquie (Türkiye Cumhuriyeti Merkez Bankasi) ;

   ii) Des organismes d'assurance sociale à participation obligatoire ; et

   iii) Des universités et d'autres établissements d'enseignement supérieur ;

b) Dans le cas de la Finlande :

i) La Banque de Finlande (Suomen Pankki) ;

ii) Des organismes d'assurance sociale (Kansaneläkelaitos) ; et

iii) L'Université d'Helsinki (Helsingin yliopisto).

Aux fins des articles 18 et 19, l'expression « organisme de droit public » comprend :

- Dans le cas de la Turquie : la Présidence des affaires religieuses ; et
- Dans le cas de la Finlande : les églises évangéliques luthériennes et orthodoxes et leurs communautés locales.

6. En ce qui concerne l'alinéa d) du paragraphe 2 de l'article 22.

Les dispositions de l'alinéa d) du paragraphe 2 de l'article 22 ne s'appliquent que pendant les cinq premières années d'application de l'Accord.

7. En ce qui concerne le paragraphe 2 de l'article 24.

Il est entendu qu'en ce qui concerne le paragraphe 2 de l'article 24, le contribuable doit, dans le cas de la Turquie, demander le remboursement résultant de cet accord amiable dans un délai d'un an après la notification de l'administration fiscale au contribuable du résultat de l'accord amiable.

EN FOI DE QUOI, les soussignés, à ce dûment autorisés, ont signé le présent Protocole.

FAIT à Istanbul, le 6 octobre 2009, en double exemplaire, en langues finnoise, turque et anglaise, les trois textes faisant également foi. En cas de divergence d'interprétation, le texte anglais prévaut.

Pour le Gouvernement de la République de Finlande :

[MATTI VANHANEN]

Pour le Gouvernement de la République turque :

[RECEP TAYYIP ERDOĞAN]

No. 53562

United Nations and Netherlands (in respect of Aruba)

Exchange of letters constituting an Agreement between the Government of the Kingdom of the Netherlands, on behalf of the Government of Aruba, and the United Nations regarding the hosting the Aruba Public-Private Partnerships Conference, to be held in Oranjestad, Aruba, from 22 to 24 March 2016. New York, 18 March 2016

Entry into force: *18 March 2016, in accordance with the provisions of the said letters*

Authentic text: *English*

Registration with the Secretariat of the United Nations: *ex officio, 18 March 2016*

Not published in print, in accordance with article 12(2) of the General Assembly regulations to give effect to Article 102 of the Charter of the United Nations, as amended, and the publication practice of the Secretariat.

Organisation des Nations Unies et Pays-Bas (à l'égard d'Aruba)

Échange de lettres constituant un Accord entre le Gouvernement du Royaume des Pays-Bas, à l'égard du Gouvernement d'Aruba, et l'Organisation des Nations Unies concernant l'organisation de la conférence sur les partenariats public-privé d'Aruba, qui se tiendra à Oranjestad, Aruba, du 22 au 24 mars 2016. New York, 18 mars 2016

Entrée en vigueur : *18 mars 2016, conformément aux dispositions desdites lettres*

Texte authentique : *anglais*

Enregistrement au Secrétariat de l'Organisation des Nations Unies : *d'office, 18 mars 2016*

Non disponible en version imprimée, conformément au paragraphe 2 de l'article 12 du règlement de l'Assemblée générale destiné à mettre en application l'Article 102 de la Charte des Nations Unies, tel qu'amendé, et à la pratique du Secrétariat en matière de publication.

No. 53563

Turkey
and
Bosnia and Herzegovina

Agreement between the Government of the Republic of Turkey and the Council of Ministers of Bosnia and Herzegovina on cooperation in the field of health. Ankara, 11 May 2010

Entry into force: *14 September 2015 by notification, in accordance with article 7*

Authentic texts: *Bosnian, Croatian, English, Serbian and Turkish*

Registration with the Secretariat of the United Nations: *Turkey, 1 March 2016*

Turquie
et
Bosnie-Herzégovine

Accord entre le Gouvernement de la République turque et le Conseil des ministres de la Bosnie-Herzégovine relatif à la coopération dans le domaine de la santé. Ankara, 11 mai 2010

Entrée en vigueur : *14 septembre 2015 par notification, conformément à l'article 7*

Textes authentiques : *bosniaque, croate, anglais, serbe et turc*

Enregistrement au Secrétariat de l'Organisation des Nations Unies : *Turquie, 1er mars 2016*

[TEXT IN BOSNIAN – TEXTE EN BOSNIAQUE]

SPORAZUM IZMEĐU VLADE REPUBLIKE TURSKE I VIJEĆA MINISTARA BOSNE I HERCEGOVINE O SARADNJI U OBLASTI ZDRAVSTVA

Vlada Republike Turske i Vijeće ministara Bosne i Hercegovine (u daljnjem tekstu Ugovorne strane);

Vođene željom da unaprijede saradnju između dvije zemlje u oblasti zdravstva i medicinskih nauka;

Prepoznajući da će ta saradnja doprinijeti unaprjeđenju zdravlja njihovih naroda,

Usaglasile su se o sljedećem:

Član 1.

Ugovorne strane, na osnovu principa ravnopravnosti i uzajamnosti, te u skladu sa međusobnom dobrobiti za svaku od zemalja, će promovirati saradnju na polju zdravstva i medicinskih nauka. Konkretne oblasti saradnje bit će utvrđene u odnosu na interese obje Ugovorne strane i uz uzajamno odobravanje.

Član 2.

Ugovorne strane će sarađivati na polju zdravstva i medicinskih nauka, uz uzajamno odobravanje, posredstvom:

a) razmjene informacija,
b) razmjene delegacija i specijalista u oblasti zdravstva,
c) podsticanja učešća specijalista na konferencijama i naučnim skupovima, koje organizira bilo koja od dviju Ugovornih strana,
d) drugih vrsta saradnje na polju zdravstva i medicinskih nauka uz međusobni sporazum.

Član 3.

a) Ugovorne strane ustanovljavaju Zajedničku radnu komisiju s ciljem utvrđivanja i ocjene aktivnosti saradnje među njima. Komisija se sastaje jednom godišnje na naizmjeničnoj osnovi.

b) Članove iz Bosne i Hercegovine za Zajedničku radnu komisiju će imenovati Ministarstvo civilnih poslova u saradnji sa Ministarstvom zdravlja i socijalne zaštite Republike Srpske, Federalnim ministarstvom zdravstva i Odjelom za zdravstvo i ostale usluge Brčko Distrikta Bosne i Hercegovine.

Član 4.

Pri posjetama eksperata i drugog personala obiju zemalja u okviru ovog Sporazuma:

Kamuran ÖZDEN
Daire Başkanı

a) Ugovorna strana-pošiljalac pokriva troškove povratnih karata za putovanje.
b) Ugovorna strana-domaćin za posjetioca pokriva smještaj, obroke i putovanje u okviru svoje zemlje (po potrebi).

Ovaj period neće biti duži od 1 do 2 mjeseca.

Član 5.

a) Ministarstvo zdravlja Republike Turske i Ministarstvo civilnih poslova Bosne i Hercegovine u saradnji sa Federalnim ministarstvom zdravstva, Ministarstvom zdravlja i socijalne zaštite Republike Srpske i Odjelom za zdravstvo i ostale usluge Distrikta Brčko će osigurati provedbu ovog Sporazuma.

b) Polja saradnje predviđena u Sporazumu i uvjeti ostvarivanja saradnje biti će utvrđeni u Akcionim planovima i Provedbenim programima, koji se trebaju pripremiti u rokovima i broju neophodnom za Ugovorne strane.

Član 6.

Od datuma stupanja na snagu ovog Sporazuma, Ugovorne strane su se složile da se poništi važenje „Sporazuma o saradnji na polju zdravstva između Ministarstva zdravlja Republike Turske i Ministarstva zdravlja Republike Bosne i Hercegovine" od 25. oktobra 1994. godine.

Član 7.

a) Ugovorne strane će ratificirati ovaj Sporazum u skladu s domaćim pravilima i propisima Ugovornih strana.

b) Ovaj Sporazum stupa na snagu od datuma obavljanja razmjene diplomatskih nota o ratifikaciji svake od Ugovornih strana i od tada on ostaje na snazi u periodu od pet godina.

c) Ako nijedna od Ugovornih strana ne obavijesti drugu o namjeri da raskine Sporazum šest mjeseci prije datuma njegovog isteka, Sporazum će se obnavljati svaki put na dodatni jednogodišnji period.

d) Zaključeno u Ankari, dana 11/05/2010, u dva originalna primjerka na turskom, službenim jezicima Bosne i Hercegovine i engleskom jeziku, s tim da su svi tekstovi jednako autentični. U slučaju sumnje, mjerodavan će biti tekst na engleskom jeziku.

U ime Vlade Republike Turske	U ime Vijeća Ministara Bosne i Hercegovine
Ministar zdravstva	Ministar civilnih poslova
prof.dr Recep Akdağ	mr Sredoje Nović

ASLI GİBİDİR
Kamuran ÖZDEN
Daire Başkanı

[TEXT IN CROATIAN – TEXTE EN CROATE]

SPORAZUM IZMEĐU VLADE REPUBLIKE TURSKE I VIJEĆA MINISTARA BOSNE I HERCEGOVINE O SURADNJI U PODRUČJU ZDRAVSTVA

Vlada Republike Turske i Vijeće ministara Bosne i Hercegovine (u daljnjem tekstu Ugovorne strane);

Vođene željom da unaprijede suradnju između dvije zemalje u području zdravstva i medicinskih znanosti;

Prepoznajući da će ta suradnja doprinijeti unaprjeđenju zdravlja njihovih naroda;

Usuglasile su se o sljedećem:

Članak 1.

Ugovorne strane, na temelju principa ravnopravnosti i uzajamnosti, te sukladno međusobnoj dobrobiti za svaku od zemalja, će promovirati suradnju na polju zdravstva i medicinskih znanosti. Konkretna područja suradnje bit će utvrđena u odnosu na interese obje Ugovorne strane i uz uzajamno odobravanje.

Članak 2.

Ugovorne strane će surađivati na polju zdravstva i medicinskih znanosti, uz uzajamno odobravanje, posredstvom:

a) razmjene informacija,
b) razmjene delegacija i specijalista u području zdravstva,
c) poticanja sudjelovanja specijalista na konferencijama i znanstvenim skupovima, koje organizira bilo koja od dviju Ugovornih strana,
d) drugih vrsta suradnje na polju zdravstva i medicinskih znanosti uz međusobni sporazum.

Članak 3.

a) Ugovorne strane ustanovljavaju Zajedničko radno povjerenstvo s ciljem utvrđivanja i ocjene aktivnosti suradnje među njima. Povjerenstvo se sastaje jednom godišnje na naizmjeničnoj osnovi.

b) Članove iz Bosne i Hercegovine za Zajedničko radno povjerenstvo će imenovati Ministarstvo civilnih poslova u suradnji sa Ministarstvom zdravlja i socijalne zaštite Republike Srpske, Federalnim ministarstvom zdravstva i Odjelom za zdravstvo i ostale usluge Brčko Distrikta Bosne i Hercegovine.

Članak 4.

Pri posjetu eksperata i drugog personala obiju zemalja u okviru ovog Sporazuma:

a) Ugovorna strana-pošiljatelj pokriva troškove povratnih karata za putovanje.
b) Ugovorna strana-domaćin za posjetitelja pokriva smještaj, obroke i putovanje u okviru svoje zemlje (po potrebi).

Ovo razdoblje neće biti duže od 1do 2 mjeseca.

Članak 5.

a) Ministarstvo zdravlja Republike Turske i Ministarstvo civilnih poslova Bosne i Hercegovine u suradnji sa Federalnim ministarstvom zdravstva, Ministarstvom zdravlja i socijalne zaštite Republike Srpske i Odjelom za zdravstvo i ostale usluge Distrikta Brčko će osigurati provedbu ovog Sporazuma.

b) Polja suradnje predviđena u Sporazumu i uvjeti ostvarivanja suradnje biti će utvrđeni u Akcionim planovima i Provedbenim programima, koji se trebaju pripremiti u rokovima i broju neophodnom za Ugovorne strane.

Članak 6.

Od datuma stupanja na snagu ovog Sporazuma, Ugovorne strane su se složile da se poništi važenje „Sporazuma o suradnji na polju zdravstva između Ministarstva zdravlja Republike Turske i Ministarstva zdravlja Republike Bosne i Hercegovine" od 25. listopada 1994. godine.

Članak 7.

a) Ugovorne strane će ratificirati ovaj Sporazum sukladno domaćim pravilima i propisima Ugovornih strana.

b) Ovaj Sporazum stupa na snagu od datuma obavljanja razmjene diplomatskih nota o ratifikaciji svake od Ugovornih strana i od tada on ostaje na snazi u razdoblju od pet godina.

c) Ako nijedna od Ugovornih strana ne obavijesti drugu o namjeri da raskine Sporazum šest mjeseci prije datuma njegovog isteka, Sporazum će se obnavljati svaki put na dodano jednogodišnje razdoblje.

d) Zaključeno u Ankari, dana 11/05/2010, u dva originalna primjerka na turskom, službenim jezicima Bosne i Hercegovine i engleskom jeziku, s tim da su svi tekstovi jednako autentični. U slučaju sumnje, mjerodavan će biti tekst na engleskom jeziku.

U ime Vlade Republike Turske Ministar zdravst va prof.dr Recep Akdağ	**U ime Vijeća Ministara Bosne i Hercegovine Ministar civilnih poslova mr Sredoje Nović**

[TEXT IN ENGLISH – TEXTE EN ANGLAIS]

AGREEMENT BETWEEN THE GOVERNMENT OF THE REPUBLIC OF TURKEY AND THE COUNCIL OF MINISTERS OF BOSNIA AND HERZEGOVINA ON COOPERATION IN THE FIELD OF HEALTH

The Government of the Republic of Turkey and the Council of Ministers of Bosnia and Herzegovina (hereinafter referred to as the "Parties"),

Guided by the wish to enhance the cooperation between the two countries in the fields of health and medical sciences,

Recognizing that this cooperation will contribute to the improvement of the health of their people,

have agreed as follows:

ARTICLE 1

The Parties, based on the principles of equality and reciprocity, and in conformity with their mutual benefits, shall promote cooperation in the fields of health and medical sciences. The specific areas of cooperation will be determined with respect to the interests of both Parties upon mutual approval.

ARTICLE 2

The Parties, will cooperate in the fields of health and medical sciences, upon mutual approval, by means of:

a) Exchange of information.
b) Exchange of delegations and health specialists.
c) Encouraging the participation of specialists at conferences and scientific meetings to be organized by either of the Parties.
d) Other types of cooperation in the fields of health and medical sciences upon mutual agreement.

ARTICLE 3

a) The Parties shall establish a Joint Working Committee with a view to determining and evaluating cooperation activities between them. The Committee shall meet once a year on alternating basis.
b) Members from Bosnia and Herzegovina for the Joint Working Committee will be appointed by the Ministry of Civil Affairs, in cooperation with the Ministry of Health and Social Welfare of Republika Srpska, the Federal Ministry of Health and the Department for Health and Other Services of Brcko District of Bosnia and Herzegovina.

ARTICLE 4

For visits of experts and other personnel of both countries within the framework this Agreement:

a) The Sending Party will cover round-trip travel expenses.
b) The Hosting Party will cover board, lodging and domestic travel (if necessary) expenses of the visitor.

This period shall not be longer than 1-2 months.

ARTICLE 5

a) The Ministry of Health of the Republic of Turkey and the Ministry of Civil Affairs of Bosnia and Herzegovina in cooperation with the Federal Ministry of Health, Ministry of Health and Social Welfare of Republika Srpska and the Department for Health and Other Services of Brcko District shall provide for the implementation of this Agreement.
b) Cooperation fields envisaged by this Agreement and conditions of the realization of the cooperation will be determined by Action Plans and Implementation Programmes to be prepared in periods and numbers as deemed necessary by the Parties.

ARTICLE 6

The Parties, from the date of this Agreement's entry into force, have agreed upon the termination of validity period of the "Agreement on Cooperation in the Field of Health between the Ministry of Health of the Republic of Turkey and the Ministry of Health of the Republic of Bosnia and Herzegovina" dated 25 October 1994.

ARTICLE 7

This Agreement will be ratified by the Contracting Parties in accordance with the domestic rules and regulations of the Parties.

This Agreement shall enter into force from the date of the completion of exchange of diplomatic notes on ratification of each Party and thereafter it shall remain in force for a period of five years.

If none of the Contracting Parties notifies the other of its intention to terminate the Agreement six months before its expiration date, the Agreement will be renewed each time for a further period of one year.

Done in Ankara, on 11 May 2010, in two original copies in Turkish, in official languages of Bosnia and Hercegovine and in English, all texts being equally authentic. In case of doubt, the English text shall prevail.

On behalf of the Government of the Republic of Turkey	On behalf of the Council of Ministers of Bosnia and Herzegovina
Prof.Dr. Recep Akdağ Minister of Health	Sredoje Nović M.A. Minister of Civil Affairs

ASLI GİBİDİR
Kamuran ÖZDEN
Daire Başkanı

[TEXT IN SERBIAN – TEXTE EN SERBE]

СПОРАЗУМ ИЗМЕЂУ ВЛАДЕ РЕПУБЛИКЕ ТУРСКЕ И САВЈЕТА МИНИСТАРА БОСНЕ И ХЕРЦЕГОВИНЕ О САРАДЊИ У ОБЛАСТИ ЗДРАВСТВА

Влада Републике Турске и Савјет министара Босне и Херцеговине (у даљем тексту Уговорне стране);

Вођене жељом да унаприједе сарадњу између двије земаље у области здравства и медицинских наука;

Препознајући да ће та сарадња допринијети унапрјеђењу здравља њихових народа;

Усагласиле су се о сљедећем:

Члан 1.

Уговорне стране, на основу принципа равноправности и узајамности, те у складу са међусобном добробити за сваку од земаља, ће промовисати сарадњу на пољу здравства и медицинских наука. Конкретне области сарадње биће утврђене у односу на интересе обје Уговорне стране и уз узајамно одобравање.

Члан 2.

Уговорне стране ће сарађивати на пољу здравства и медицинских наука, уз узајамно одобравање, посредством:

а) размјене информација,
б) размјене делегација и специјалиста у области здравства,
ц) подстицања учешћа специјалиста на конференцијама и научним скуповима, које организује било која од двију Уговорних страна,
д) других врста сарадње на пољу здравства и медицинских наука уз међусобни споразум.

Члан 3.

а) Уговорне стране установљавају Заједничку радну комисију с циљем утврђивања и оцјене активности сарадње међу њима. Комисија се састаје једном годишње на наизмјеничној основи.

б) Чланове из Босне и Херцеговине за Заједничку радну комисију ће именовати Министарство цивилних послова у сарадњи са Министарством здравља и социјалне заштите Републике Српске, Федералним министарством здравства и Одјељењем за здравство и остале услуге Брчко Дистрикта Босне и Херцеговине.

Члан 4.

При посјетама експерата и другог персонала обију земаља у оквиру овог Споразума:

T.C. Kamuran ÖZDEN Daire Başkanı

а) Уговорна страна-пошиљалац покрива трошкове повратних карата за путовање.

б) Уговорна страна-домаћин за посјетиоца покрива смјештај, оброке и путовање у оквиру своје земље (по потреби).

Овај период неће бити дужи од 1 до 2 мјесеца.

Члан 5.

а) Министарство здравља Републике Турске и Министарство цивилних послова Босне и Херцеговине у сарадњи са Федералним министарством здравства, Министарством здравља и социјалне заштите Републике Српске и Одјељењем за здравство и остале услуге Дистрикта Брчко ће обезбиједити спровођење овог Споразума.

б) Поља сарадње предвиђена у Споразуму и услови остваривања сарадње биће утврђени у Акционим плановима и Програмима спровођења, који се требају припремити у роковима и броју неопходном за Уговорне стране.

Члан 6.

Од датума ступања на снагу овог Споразума, Уговорне стране су се сложиле да се поништи важење „Споразума о сарадњи на пољу здравства између Министарства здравља Републике Турске и Министарства здравља Републике Босне и Херцеговине" од 25. октобра 1994. године.

Члан 7.

а) Уговорне стране ће ратификовати овај Споразум у складу с домаћим правилима и прописима Уговорних страна.

б) Овај Споразум ступа на снагу од датума обављања размјене дипломатских нота о ратификацији сваке од Уговорних страна и од тада он остаје на снази у периоду од пет година.

ц) Ако ниједна од Уговорних страна не обавијести другу о намјери да раскине Споразум шест мјесеци прије датума његовог истека, Споразум ће се обнављати сваки пут на додатни једногодишњи период.

д) Закључено у Анкари, дана 11/05/2010, у два оригинална примјерка на турском, службеним језицима Босне и Херцеговине и енглеском језику, с тим да су сви текстови једнако аутентични. У случају сумње, мјеродаван ће бити текст на енглеском језику.

У име Владе Републике Турске Министар здравства Проф.др Рецеп Акдаг	**У име Савјета Министара Босне и Херцеговине Министар цивилних послова мр Средоје Новић**

[TEXT IN TURKISH – TEXTE EN TURC]

TÜRKİYE CUMHURİYETİ HÜKÜMETİ İLE BOSNA VE HERSEK BAKANLAR KONSEYİ ARASINDA SAĞLIK ALANINDA İŞBİRLİĞİ ANLAŞMASI

Türkiye Cumhuriyeti Hükümeti ile Bosna ve Hersek Bakanlar Konseyi (bundan sonra "Taraflar" olarak anılacaklardır),

İki ülke arasında sağlık ve tıp bilimleri alanlarında işbirliğini geliştirme arzusunun rehberliğinde,

Bu işbirliğinin halklarının sağlığının gelişmesine katkıda bulanacağına inanarak,

Aşağıdaki hususlarda anlaşmaya varmışlardır:

MADDE 1

Taraflar, eşitlik ve karşılıklılık ilkeleri temelinde ve karşılıklı faydalarına uygunluk içinde, sağlık ve tıp bilimleri alanında işbirliğini teşvik edeceklerdir. Özel işbirliği alanları her iki tarafın çıkarları dikkate alınarak, karşılıklı mutabakat ile belirlenecektir.

MADDE 2

Taraflar, sağlık ve tıp bilimleri alanlarında karşılıklı mutabakat ile aşağıdaki yöntemlerle işbirliği yapacaklardır:

a) Bilgi değişimi.
b) Heyetlerin ve sağlık uzmanlarının değişimi.
c) Taraflardan biri tarafından düzenlenecek konferanslara ve bilimsel toplantılara uzmanların katılımının teşvik edilmesi.
d) Sağlık ve tıp bilimleri alanlarında karşılıklı mutabakat ile belirlenecek diğer şekillerde işbirliği.

MADDE 3

a) Taraflar aralarındaki işbirliği faaliyetlerini belirlemek ve değerlendirmek üzere bir Ortak Çalışma Komitesi kuracaklardır. Bu Komite yılda bir kez dönüşümlü olarak toplanacaktır.
b) Ortak Çalışma Komitesi için Bosna Hersek'in üyeleri Sivil İşler Bakanlığı tarafından Sırp Cumhuriyeti Sağlık ve Sosyal Refah Bakanlığı, Federal Sağlık Bakanlığı ve Bosna Hersek Brcko Bölgesi Sağlık ve Diğer Hizmetler Dairesi ile işbirliği içerisinde atanacaktır.

MADDE 4

İşbu Anlaşma çerçevesinde her iki ülkenin uzman ve diğer personellerinin ziyaretlerinde:

a) Gönderen Taraf gidiş-dönüş seyahat masraflarını karşılayacaktır.
b) Evsahibi Taraf ziyaretçinin iaşe ve ibate giderleri ile ülke içi yolculuk giderlerini (gerekli olduğu takdirde) karşılayacaktır.

Bu süre 1-2 aydan fazla olmayacaktır.

MADDE 5

a) İşbu Anlaşma'nın yürütülmesini Türkiye Cumhuriyeti Sağlık Bakanlığı ve Federal Sağlık Bakanlığı, Sırp Cumhuriyeti Sağlık ve Sosyal Refah Bakanlığı ve Brcko Bölgesi Sağlık ve Diğer Hizmetler Dairesi ile işbirliği içerisinde Bosna ve Hersek Sivil İşler Bakanlığı sağlayacaklardır.
b) İşbu Anlaşma ile öngörülen işbirliği alanları ile işbirliğinin hayata geçirilme şartları, Taraflarca gerekli görülecek dönemlerde ve sayılarda hazırlanacak Eylem Planları ve Uygulama Programları ile belirlenecektir.

MADDE 6

Taraflar, bu Anlaşma'nın yürürlüğe girdiği tarihten itibaren, 25 Ekim 1994 tarihli "Türkiye Cumhuriyeti Hükümeti Sağlık Bakanlığı ile Bosna ve Hersek Cumhuriyeti Hükümeti Sağlık Bakanlığı Arasında Sağlık Alanında İşbirliği Anlaşması"nın geçerlilik süresinin sona ermesi hususunda mutabık kalmışlardır.

MADDE 7

İşbu Anlaşma Akit Taraflarca, Tarafların iç usul ve mevzuatlarına uygun olarak onaylanacaktır.

İşbu Anlaşma, Taraflarca onaylandığının diplomatik yoldan nota teatisi ile bildiriminin tamamlandığı tarihte yürürlüğe girecek ve bundan sonra beş yıllık bir süre için yürürlükte kalacaktır.

Akit taraflardan biri, yürürlülük süresi bitiminden 6 ay önce, Anlaşmayı sona erdirmek istediğini yazılı olarak bildirmedikçe, işbu Anlaşma her defasında birer yıllık süreler için yenilenmiş olacaktır.

İşbu Anlaşma, Ankara'da, 11 Mayıs 2010 tarihinde, Türkçe, Bosna ve Hersek'in resmi dillerinde ve İngilizce iki orijinal nüsha halinde ve bütün metinler eşit geçerlikte olmak üzere imzalanmıştır. Tereddüt halinde İngilizce metin esas kabul alınacaktır.

Türkiye Cumhuriyeti Hükümeti Adına	Bosna ve Hersek Bakanlar Konseyi Adına
Prof.Dr. Recep Akdağ Sağlık Bakanı	Sredoje Nović Sivil İşler Bakanı

[TRANSLATION – TRADUCTION]

ACCORD ENTRE LE GOUVERNEMENT DE LA RÉPUBLIQUE TURQUE ET LE CONSEIL DES MINISTRES DE BOSNIE-HERZÉGOVINE RELATIF À LA COOPÉRATION DANS LE DOMAINE DE LA SANTÉ

Le Gouvernement de la République turque et le Conseil des ministres de la Bosnie-Herzégovine (ci-après dénommés les « Parties »),

Guidés par le désir de renforcer la coopération entre les deux pays dans les domaines de la santé et des sciences médicales,

Conscients que cette coopération contribuera à améliorer la santé de leurs populations,

Sont convenus de ce qui suit :

Article premier

Les Parties, en se fondant sur les principes d'égalité et de réciprocité, et selon leurs intérêts mutuels, favorisent la coopération dans les domaines de la santé et des sciences médicales. Les domaines spécifiques de coopération sont déterminés d'un commun accord en fonction des intérêts des deux Parties.

Article 2

Les Parties coopèrent dans les domaines de la santé et des sciences médicales, d'un commun accord :

a) En s'échangeant des renseignements ;

b) En échangeant des délégations et des spécialistes de la santé ;

c) En encourageant la participation de spécialistes aux conférences et réunions scientifiques organisées par l'une ou l'autre Partie ;

d) Par d'autres moyens de coopération dans les domaines de la santé et des sciences médicales, définis d'un commun accord.

Article 3

a) Les Parties mettent en place un Comité de travail mixte chargé de déterminer et d'évaluer les activités de coopération entre elles. Le Comité se réunit une fois par an en alternance.

b) Les membres du Comité de travail mixte issus de la Bosnie-Herzégovine sont nommés par le Ministère des affaires civiles, en coopération avec le Ministère de la santé et de la protection sociale de la Republika Srpska, le Ministère fédéral de la santé et le Département de la santé et d'autres services du district de Brcko en Bosnie-Herzégovine.

Article 4

Pour ce qui est des visites d'experts et d'autres agents des deux pays dans le cadre du présent Accord :

a) La Partie d'envoi prend en charge les frais de voyage aller-retour ;

b) La Partie d'accueil prend en charge les frais de séjour, d'hébergement et de déplacement des visiteurs à l'intérieur du pays (le cas échéant).

Cette période n'excède pas un à deux mois.

Article 5

a) Le Ministère de la santé de la République turque et le Ministère des affaires civiles de Bosnie-Herzégovine, en coopération avec le Ministère fédéral de la santé, le Ministère de la santé et de la protection sociale de la Republika Srpska et le Département de la santé et d'autres services du district de Brcko, sont chargés de la mise en œuvre du présent Accord.

b) Les domaines de coopération visés par le présent Accord et les conditions de réalisation de la coopération sont déterminés par des plans d'action et des programmes de mise en œuvre, qui sont élaborés lorsque les Parties l'estiment nécessaire et en nombre qu'elles jugent utile.

Article 6

Les Parties, à compter de la date d'entrée en vigueur du présent Accord, conviennent que la période de validité de l'Accord de coopération dans le domaine de la santé entre le Ministère de la santé de la République turque et le Ministère de la santé de la République de Bosnie-Herzégovine du 25 octobre 1994 prend fin.

Article 7

Le présent Accord est ratifié par les Parties contractantes conformément aux lois et règlements internes des Parties.

Le présent Accord entre en vigueur à la date de la conclusion de l'échange de notes diplomatiques de ratification des Parties et reste ensuite en vigueur pour une durée de cinq ans.

Si aucune des Parties contractantes ne notifie à l'autre son intention de dénoncer le présent Accord six mois avant sa date d'expiration, l'Accord est renouvelé chaque fois pour une nouvelle période d'un an.

FAIT à Ankara, le 11 mai 2010, en deux exemplaires originaux, en langue turque, dans les langues officielles de la Bosnie-Herzégovine et en langue anglaise, tous les textes faisant également foi. En cas de doute, le texte anglais prévaut.

Pour le Gouvernement de la République turque :

RECEP AKDAĞ
Ministre de la santé

Pour le Conseil des ministres de Bosnie-Herzégovine :

SREDOJE NOVIĆ
Ministre des affaires civiles

II

Treaties and international agreements

filed and recorded in

March 2016

No. 1378

Traités et accords internationaux

classés et inscrits au répertoire en

mars 2016

N° 1378

No. 1378

United Nations and World Tourism Organization

Agreement between the United Nations and the World Tourism Organization (with Protocol). Beijing, 24 October 2003, and New York, 23 December 2003

Entry into force: *23 December 2013, in accordance with article 21*

Authentic texts: *English and French*

Registration with the Secretariat of the United Nations: *ex officio, 1 March 2016*

Organisation des Nations Unies et Organisation mondiale du tourisme

Accord entre l'Organisation des Nations Unies et l'Organisation mondiale du tourisme (avec Protocole). Beijing, 24 octobre 2003, et New York, 23 décembre 2003

Entrée en vigueur : *23 décembre 2013, conformément à l'article 21*

Textes authentiques : *anglais et français*

Enregistrement au Secrétariat de l'Organisation des Nations Unies : *d'office, 1er mars 2016*

[TEXT IN ENGLISH – TEXTE EN ANGLAIS]

Agreement between the United Nations and the World Tourism Organization

Recalling resolutions 2529 (XXIV) of 5 December 1969 and 32/156 of 19 December 1977 of the General Assembly of the United Nations,

In consideration of the Charter of the United Nations and the Statutes of the World Tourism Organization,

In further consideration of the provisions of Article 57 of the Charter of the United Nations and of article 3, paragraph 3, and article 31 of the Statutes of the World Tourism Organization,

The United Nations and the World Tourism Organization agree as follows:

Article 1
Recognition

1. The United Nations recognizes the World Tourism Organization as a specialized agency of the United Nations responsible for taking such action as may be appropriate under its Statutes for the accomplishment of the objectives set forth therein.

2. The United Nations recognizes the decisive and central role of the World Tourism Organization, as an intergovernmental organization, in world tourism, as enshrined in its Statutes.

3. Convinced that tourism can contribute significantly to the pursuit of the shared objectives of achieving sustainable development and poverty eradication, the United Nations notes that, in accordance with its Statutes, the World Tourism Organization shall pay particular attention to the interests of the developing countries in the field of tourism.

Article 2
Coordination and cooperation

1. In its relations with the United Nations, its organs and the agencies of the United Nations system, the World Tourism Organization recognizes the coordinating role, as well as the comprehensive responsibilities in promoting economic and social development, of the General Assembly and the Economic and Social Council under the Charter of the United Nations.

2. In exercise of its central coordinating role in the field of tourism undertaken in accordance with its Statutes and with a view to contributing to economic and social development, in particular opportunities for poverty eradication and employment creation in the least developed countries, the World Tourism Organization recognizes the need for effective coordination and cooperation with the United Nations, its organs and the agencies of the United Nations system.

3. The World Tourism Organization, accordingly, agrees to cooperate with the United Nations in whatever measure may be necessary to effect the required coordination of policies and activities.

4. The World Tourism Organization agrees further to participate in, and to cooperate with, any body or bodies that have been established or may be established by the United Nations for the purpose of facilitating such cooperation and coordination, in particular through membership in the United Nations System Chief Executives Board for Coordination, and to furnish such information as may be required for the carrying out of this purpose.

5. The World Tourism Organization shall inform the Economic and Social Council of matters of inter-agency concern within its competence and of any formal agreement on such matters to be concluded between the World Tourism Organization and another agency within the United Nations system.

Article 3
Reciprocal representation

1. Representatives of the United Nations shall be invited to attend the meetings of the General Assembly and the Executive Council of the World Tourism Organization and their subsidiary organs, and to participate, without the right to vote, in the deliberations of these bodies. Written statements presented by the United Nations shall be distributed by the secretariat of the World Tourism Organization to the members of the above-mentioned bodies, in accordance with the relevant rules of procedure.

2. Representatives of the World Tourism Organization shall be invited to attend meetings and to participate, without the right to vote and in accordance with the relevant rules of procedure, in the deliberations of the Economic and Social Council, its commissions and its committees, of the Main Committees and other organs of the General Assembly and of the conferences and meetings of the United Nations, with respect to items on their agenda relating to matters within the scope of the activities of the World Tourism Organization and other matters of mutual interest. Written statements presented by the World Tourism Organization shall be distributed by the Secretariat of the United Nations to the members of the above-mentioned bodies, in accordance with the relevant rules of procedure.

3. Representatives of the World Tourism Organization shall be invited, for purposes of consultation, to attend meetings of the General Assembly when matters defined in paragraph 2 of the present article are under consideration.

Article 4
Proposals of agenda items

1. After such preliminary consultations as may be necessary, the World Tourism Organization shall arrange for the inclusion in the agenda of its General Assembly, the Executive Council or their subsidiary bodies, as appropriate, items proposed by the United Nations.

2. After such preliminary consultations as may be necessary, the United Nations shall arrange for the inclusion in the agenda of the Economic and Social Council or, as appropriate and in accordance with the relevant rules of procedure, of other organs or bodies of the United Nations of items proposed by the World Tourism Organization.

Article 5
Recommendations of the United Nations

1. Having regard to the obligations of the United Nations to promote the objectives set forth in Article 55 of the Charter of the United Nations and the functions and powers of the Economic and Social Council, under Article 62 of the Charter, to make or initiate studies and reports with respect to international economic, social, cultural, educational, health and related matters and to make recommendations concerning these matters to the specialized agencies concerned, and having regard also to the responsibility of the United Nations, under Articles 58 and 63 of the Charter, to make recommendations for the coordination of the policies and activities of such specialized agencies, the World Tourism Organization agrees to arrange for the submission, as soon as possible, to the appropriate organ of the World Tourism Organization of all formal recommendations which the United Nations may make to it.

2. The World Tourism Organization agrees to enter into consultations with the United Nations upon request with respect to such recommendations, and in due course to report to the United Nations on the action taken by the World Tourism Organization or by its members to give effect to such recommendations, or on the other results of their consideration.

Article 6
Assistance to the United Nations

In accordance with the Charter of the United Nations and the Statutes of the World Tourism Organization, the World Tourism Organization shall cooperate with the United Nations by furnishing to it to the fullest extent possible such special information or studies, and by rendering such assistance to it as the United Nations may request.

Article 7
Regular reports

The World Tourism Organization shall submit to the United Nations regular reports on its activities.

Article 8
Exchange of information and documents

Subject to such arrangements as may be necessary for the safeguarding of confidential material, full and prompt exchange of appropriate information and documents shall be made between the United Nations and the World Tourism Organization.

Article 9
Public information

Having regard to the aim of the World Tourism Organization, as defined in article 3, paragraph 1, of its Statutes, and with a view to coordinating the activities of the World Tourism Organization in this field with the operations of the information services of the United Nations, supplementary arrangements regarding these matters shall be concluded between the United Nations and the World Tourism Organization.

Article 10
Relations with the International Court of Justice

1. The World Tourism Organization agrees to furnish any information which may be requested by the International Court of Justice in pursuance of Article 34 of the Statute of the Court.

2. The General Assembly of the United Nations authorizes the World Tourism Organization to request advisory opinions of the International Court of Justice on legal questions arising within the scope of its competence other than questions concerning the mutual relationships between the United Nations and the World Tourism Organization or other specialized agencies.

3. Such requests may be addressed to the International Court of Justice by the General Assembly or by the Executive Council of the World Tourism Organization acting in pursuance of an authorization by the General Assembly of the World Tourism Organization.

4. When requesting the International Court of Justice to give an advisory opinion, the World Tourism Organization shall inform the Economic and Social Council of the request.

Article 11
Non-Self-Governing and other Territories

The World Tourism Organization agrees to cooperate within the fields of its competence with the United Nations in giving effect to the principles and obligations set forth in Chapters XI, XII and XIII of the Charter of the United Nations and other internationally recognized principles and obligations regarding colonial countries and peoples, and taking into account the relevant resolutions of the General Assembly of the United Nations, with regard to matters affecting the well-being and development of the peoples of the Non-Self-Governing and other Territories.

Article 12
Technical assistance

The United Nations and the World Tourism Organization undertake to work together in the provision of technical assistance in the field of tourism and tourism development. In particular, they undertake to avoid undesirable duplication of activities and services and agree to take such measures as may be required to achieve effective coordination within the framework of existing coordinating machinery in the field of technical assistance, taking into account the respective roles and responsibilities of the United Nations and the World Tourism Organization under their constituent instruments, as well as those of other organizations participating in technical assistance activities. To this end, the World Tourism Organization recognizes the overall responsibilities of the resident coordinators for operational activities for development, as formulated in the relevant General Assembly resolutions. As one of the smaller specialized agencies without field representation, the World Tourism Organization may use resident coordinators to ensure its representation and promote its role.

Article 13
Statistical services

1. The United Nations and the World Tourism Organization agree to strive for the maximum cooperation, the elimination of all undesirable duplication between them and the most efficient use of personnel in their respective collection, analysis, publication and dissemination of statistical information. They agree to combine their efforts to secure the greatest possible usefulness and utilization of statistical information, to guarantee close coordination in their respective statistical initiatives and to minimize the burden placed upon Governments and other organizations from which such information may be collected.

2. The World Tourism Organization recognizes that the United Nations is the central agency for the collection, analysis, publication, standardization and improvement of tourism statistics serving the general purposes of international organizations.

3. The United Nations recognizes the World Tourism Organization as the appropriate organization to collect, to analyse, to publish, to standardize and to improve the statistics of tourism and to promote the integration of these statistics within the sphere of the United Nations system.

Article 14
Administrative cooperation

1. The United Nations and the World Tourism Organization recognize the desirability of cooperation in administrative matters of mutual interest.

2. Accordingly, the United Nations and the World Tourism Organization undertake to consult together, and with other agencies concerned within the United Nations system, from time to time concerning these matters, particularly the most efficient and harmonized use of facilities, staff and services and appropriate methods of avoiding the establishment and operation of competitive or overlapping facilities and services with a view to securing as much uniformity in these matters as possible.

3. The consultations referred to in the present article shall be utilized to establish the most equitable manner in which any special services or assistance furnished, on request, by the World Tourism Organization to the United Nations or by the United Nations to the World Tourism Organization shall be financed subject to supplementary arrangements to be concluded for that purpose.

4. The consultations referred to in the present article shall also explore the possibility of continuing or establishing common facilities or services in specific areas, including the possibility of one organization providing such facilities or services to one or several other organizations, and establish the most equitable manner in which such facilities or services shall be financed subject to supplementary arrangements to be concluded for that purpose.

Article 15
Regional and branch offices

Any regional or branch offices which the World Tourism Organization may establish shall closely cooperate with the regional or branch offices which the United Nations has established or may establish, in particular the offices of the regional commissions and of the resident coordinators.

Article 16
Personnel arrangements

1. The United Nations and the World Tourism Organization agree to develop, in the interests of uniform standards of international employment and to the extent feasible, common personnel standards, methods and arrangements designed to avoid unjustified differences in terms and conditions of employment, to avoid competition in recruitment of personnel and to facilitate any mutually desirable and beneficial

interchange of personnel. For this purpose the World Tourism Organization agrees to accept the Statute of the International Civil Service Commission and participate in the United Nations Joint Staff Pension Fund in accordance with the Regulations of the Fund and accept the jurisdiction of the United Nations Administrative Tribunal in matters involving applications alleging non-observance of those Regulations.

2. The United Nations and the World Tourism Organization agree to cooperate to the fullest extent possible in achieving these ends, and in particular they agree:

(*a*) To consult together from time to time concerning matters of mutual interest relating to the terms and conditions of employment of the officers and staff, with a view to securing as much uniformity in these matters as may be feasible;

(*b*) To cooperate in the interchange of personnel when desirable, on a temporary or a permanent basis, making due provision for the retention of seniority and pension rights;

(*c*) To cooperate with the agencies of the United Nations system in the establishment and operation of suitable machinery for the settlement of disputes arising in connection with the employment of personnel and related matters.

3. The terms and conditions under which any facilities or services of the United Nations or the World Tourism Organization in connection with the matters referred to in the present article are to be extended to the other shall, where necessary, be the subject of supplementary arrangements concluded for this purpose pursuant to article 20 of the present Agreement.

Article 17
Budgetary and financial matters

1. The World Tourism Organization recognizes the desirability of establishing close budgetary and financial relationships with the United Nations in order that the administrative operations of the United Nations and the agencies within the United Nations system shall be carried out in the most efficient and economic manner possible, and that the maximum measure of coordination and uniformity with respect to these operations shall be secured.

2. The World Tourism Organization agrees to accept the Statute of the Joint Inspection Unit.

3. The World Tourism Organization agrees to conform, as far as may be practicable and appropriate, to standard practices and forms recommended by the United Nations.

4. Financial and budgetary arrangements that may be entered into between the United Nations and the World Tourism Organization shall be approved in accordance with their respective constitutive instruments.

5. In the preparation of the budget of the World Tourism Organization, the Secretary-General of the World Tourism Organization shall consult with the Secretary-General of the United Nations with a view to achieving, insofar as practicable, uniformity in presentation of the budgets of the United Nations and of the agencies within the United Nations system for the purposes of providing a basis for comparison of the several budgets without precluding the use by each organization of different currencies to formulate its budget.

6. The World Tourism Organization agrees to transmit its proposed budgets to the United Nations not later than when the said budgets are transmitted to its members so as to enable the General Assembly of the United Nations to examine them and make recommendations, in accordance with Article 17, paragraph 3, of the Charter of the United Nations.

7. Representatives of the World Tourism Organization shall be entitled to participate, without vote, in the deliberations of the General Assembly or any committee thereof established by it, at all times when the budget of the World Tourism Organization or general administrative or financial questions concerning the World Tourism Organization are under consideration.

Article 18
United Nations laissez-passer

Officials of the World Tourism Organization shall be entitled, in accordance with such special arrangements as may be concluded between the Secretary-General of the United Nations and the Secretary-General of the World Tourism Organization, to use laissez-passer of the United Nations.

Article 19
Implementation of the Agreement

The Secretary-General of the United Nations and the Secretary-General of the World Tourism Organization may enter into such supplementary arrangements for the implementation of the present Agreement as may be found desirable.

Article 20
Amendment and revision

The present Agreement may be amended or revised by agreement between the United Nations and the World Tourism Organization, and any such amendment or revision shall come into force on its approval by the General Assembly of the United Nations and the General Assembly of the World Tourism Organization.

Article 21
Entry into force

The present Agreement enters into force on its approval by the General Assembly of the United Nations and the General Assembly of the World Tourism Organization.

PROTOCOL CONCERNING THE ENTRY INTO FORCE OF THE AGREEMENT BETWEEN THE UNITED NATIONS AND THE WORLD TOURISM ORGANIZATION

Article 57 of the Charter of the United Nations provides that specialized agencies established by intergovernmental agreement and having wide international responsibilities as defined in their basic instruments in economic, social, cultural, educational, health and related fields shall be bought into relationship with the United Nations. Article 63 of the Charter provides that the Economic and Social Council may enter into agreements with any of the agencies referred to in Article 57, defining the terms on which the agency concerned shall be brought into relationship with the United Nations, and specifies that such agreements shall be subject to approval by the General Assembly.

Article 3, paragraph 3, of the Statutes of the World Tourism Organization of 27 September 1970 provides that, in order to establish its central role in the field of tourism, the World Tourism Organization shall establish and maintain effective collaboration with the appropriate organs of the United Nations and its specialized agencies.

At its fourteenth session held in Seoul, Republic of Korea, and Osaka, Japan, from 24 to 29 September 2001, the General Assembly of the World Tourism Organization adopted resolution 420(XIV) in which it stated that steps should be taken to study the possibility of transforming the World Tourism Organization into a specialized agency of the United Nations system.

By a letter dated 21 December 2001 (E/2002/5), the Secretary-General of the World Tourism Organization requested the Secretary-General of the United Nations the inclusion in the draft provisional agenda of the next session of the Economic and Social Council an item relative to the transformation of the World Tourism Organization into a specialized agency of the United Nations.

On 30 April 2002, at its 5th plenary meeting, the Economic and Social Council decided to include in the agenda of its substantive session of 2002 an item entitled "Consideration of the request for conversion of the World Tourism Organization, an intergovernmental organization with observer status with the Economic and Social Council, to a specialized agency of the United Nations system" (Economic and Social Council decision 2002/214).

At its sixty-eighth session held in Petra, Jordan, from 18 to 19 June 2002, the Executive Council of the World Tourism Organization adopted decision 11(LXVIII) by which it decided, without pre-empting the outcome of the consideration of the request for conversion by the Economic and Social Council, to establish, on its side and on a contingency basis, a Committee on the negotiation with the United Nations.

On 24 July 2002, at its 37th plenary meeting, the Economic and Social Council adopted resolution 2002/24 entitled "Arrangements for the negotiation of an agreement between the United Nations and the World Tourism Organization" in which it authorized the President of the Economic and Social Council to appoint the members of the Committee on Negotiations with Intergovernmental Agencies. The Economic and Social Council also requested the Committee to negotiate with the World Tourism Organization a relationship agreement between the United Nations and the World Tourism Organization, on the basis of proposals submitted by the Secretary-General, and to submit a draft relationship agreement for the consideration of the Economic and Social Council at its substantive session of 2003.

At its sixty-ninth session held in Saint Petersburg, Russian Federation, from 2 to 4 October 2002, the Executive Council of the World Tourism Organization adopted decision 10 (LXIX) in which it confirmed its earlier decision 11(LXVIII) regarding the creation of the Committee of the World Tourism Organization in charge of negotiating with the United Nations and decided that the current Chairman of the Executive Council should chair the Committee.

On 26 March and on 7, 10, 15, 16 and 17 April 2003, the Committee on Negotiations with Intergovernmental Agencies established by the Economic and Social Council considered the text of the draft relationship agreement between the United Nations and World Tourism Organization as submitted by the Secretary-General (E/C.1/2003/1), and approved it with a number of amendments. On 17 April 2003, the Committee agreed to transmit the text of the draft agreement to the Committee on Negotiations of the World Tourism Organization for its consideration (E/2003/60).

On 29 April 2003, the World Tourism Organization's Committee on Negotiations for the Conversion of the Organization into a Specialized Agency of the United Nations approved the text of the draft agreement as prepared by the Economic and Social Council's Committee on Negotiations with Intergovernmental Agencies without making any changes to it, and recommended that the Executive Council of the World Tourism Organization approve it in the same way (E/C.1/2003/2).

On 4 June 2003, at the seventieth session held in Madrid, Spain, the Executive Council of the World Tourism Organization adopted decision 4(LXX) in which it noted with satisfaction the text of the draft agreement as submitted to it by the negotiating groups of the Economic and Social Council and the World Tourism Organization, and decided to submit it without modifications to the next session of the General Assembly of the World Tourism Organization for its approval.

On 10 July 2003, at the 29th plenary meeting, the Economic and Social Council adopted resolution 2003/2 by which it recommended that the General Assembly of the United Nations approve the agreement at its fifty-eighth session.

On 24 October 2003, at its fifteenth session held in Beijing, China, the General Assembly of the World Tourism Organization adopted resolution 453(XV) by which the General Assembly approved the draft agreement without modifications.

On 23 December 2003, at the 78th plenary meeting of its fifty-eighth session, the General Assembly of the United Nations adopted resolution 58/232, by which it approved the Agreement between the United Nations and World Tourism Organization.

Article 21 of the Agreement provides that the Agreement enters into force on its approval by the General Assembly of the United Nations and the General Assembly of the World Tourism Organization.

The Agreement accordingly came into force on 23 December 2003.

A copy of the text of the Agreement in English and French is attached hereto, both the English and French texts being equally authentic.

IN FAITH WHEREOF we have appended our signatures this 18th day of December 2015 at New York, and 14th day of January 2016 at Madrid, to two original copies of the present Protocol, the text of which consists of versions in the English and French languages which are equally authentic. One of the original copies will be kept by the Secretariat of the United Nations and the other will be kept by the Secretariat of the World Tourism Organization.

Ban Ki-moon
Secretary-General of the United Nations

Taleb Rifai
Secretary-General of the World Tourism Organization

[TEXT IN FRENCH – TEXTE EN FRANÇAIS]

Accord entre l'Organisation des Nations Unies et l'Organisation mondiale du tourisme

Rappelant les résolutions 2529 (XXIV) du 5 décembre 1969 et 32/156 du 19 décembre 1977 de l'Assemblée générale des Nations Unies,

Conformément à la Charte des Nations Unies et aux Statuts de l'Organisation mondiale du tourisme,

Conformément, en particulier, aux dispositions de l'Article 57 de la Charte des Nations Unies ainsi que du paragraphe 3 de l'article 3 et de l'article 31 des Statuts de l'Organisation mondiale du tourisme,

L'Organisation des Nations Unies et l'Organisation mondiale du tourisme conviennent de ce qui suit :

Article premier
Reconnaissance

1. L'Organisation des Nations Unies reconnaît l'Organisation mondiale du tourisme comme étant une institution spécialisée du système des Nations Unies investie de la responsabilité de prendre des mesures appropriées, conformément à ses Statuts aux fins de la réalisation des objectifs énoncés dans le présent Accord.

2. L'Organisation des Nations Unies reconnaît que l'Organisation mondiale du tourisme joue, en tant qu'organisation intergouvernementale, un rôle décisif et central dans le tourisme mondial, comme énoncé dans ses Statuts.

3. Convaincue que le tourisme peut largement contribuer à la réalisation d'objectifs communs, notamment à l'instauration d'un développement durable et à l'élimination de la pauvreté, l'Organisation des Nations Unies note que, conformément à ses Statuts, l'Organisation mondiale du tourisme se souciera tout particulièrement des intérêts des pays en développement dans le domaine du tourisme.

Article 2
Coordination et coopération

1. Dans ses relations avec l'Organisation des Nations Unies, ses organes et les organismes des Nations Unies, l'Organisation mondiale du tourisme reconnaît le rôle de coordonnateur ainsi que les responsabilités générales qui incombent en matière de promotion du développement économique et social à l'Assemblée générale des Nations Unies et au Conseil économique et social en vertu de la Charte des Nations Unies.

2. Dans l'exercice du rôle central de coordination qu'elle joue, conformément à ses Statuts, dans le secteur du tourisme en vue de contribuer au développement économique et social, notamment en créant des débouchés et des emplois pour

éradiquer la pauvreté dans les pays les moins avancés, l'Organisation mondiale du tourisme reconnaît la nécessité d'une coordination et d'une coopération effectives avec l'Organisation des Nations Unies, ses organes et les autres organismes des Nations Unies.

3. En conséquence, l'Organisation mondiale du tourisme convient de coopérer avec l'Organisation des Nations Unies à toute mesure nécessaire en vue d'assurer la coordination voulue des politiques et activités.

4. L'Organisation mondiale du tourisme convient en outre de collaborer et de coopérer avec tout organe qui aura été ou pourra être institué par l'Organisation des Nations Unies en vue de faciliter cette coopération et cette coordination, en particulier en devenant membre du Conseil des chefs de secrétariat des organismes des Nations Unies pour la coordination et en communiquant toute information nécessaire à la réalisation de cet objectif.

5. L'Organisation mondiale du tourisme informe le Conseil économique et social de toute question de sa compétence pouvant présenter un intérêt pour les autres organismes et de la conclusion de tout accord formel sur ces questions entre elle et un autre organisme des Nations Unies.

Article 3
Représentation réciproque

1. Des représentants de l'Organisation des Nations Unies sont invités à assister aux réunions de l'Assemblée générale et du Conseil exécutif de l'Organisation mondiale du tourisme et de leurs organes subsidiaires et à participer, sans droit de vote, aux délibérations de ces organes. Le secrétariat de l'Organisation mondiale du tourisme assure la distribution aux membres des organes susmentionnés, conformément aux dispositions applicable du règlement intérieur, des communications écrites présentées par l'Organisation des Nations Unies.

2. Des représentants de l'Organisation mondiale du tourisme sont invités à assister aux réunions et à participer, sans droit de vote et conformément au dispositions applicables du règlement intérieur, aux délibérations du Conseil économique et social, de ses commissions et comités, des grandes commissions et autres organes de l'Assemblée générale des Nations Unies, ainsi que des conférences et réunions de l'Organisation des Nations Unies portant sur des points de leur ordre du jour qui relèvent du domaine d'activité de l'Organisation mondiale du tourisme et sur d'autres questions d'intérêt mutuel. Le Secrétariat de l'Organisation des Nations Unies assure la distribution aux membres des organes susmentionnés, conformément aux dispositions applicables du règlement intérieur, des communications écrites présentées par l'Organisation mondiale du tourisme.

3. Des représentants de l'Organisation mondiale du tourisme sont invités à assister, à titre consultatif, aux réunions de l'Assemblée générale des Nations Unies

au cours desquelles il doit être débattu de questions visées au paragraphe 2 du présent article.

Article 4
Inscription de questions à l'ordre du jour

1. Après les consultations préliminaires qui pourraient être nécessaires, l'Organisation mondiale du tourisme prendra des dispositions pour inscrire à l'ordre du jour de son Assemblée générale, de son Conseil exécutif ou de leurs organes subsidiaires, selon le cas, les questions proposées par l'Organisation des Nations Unies.

2. Après les consultations préalables qui pourraient être nécessaires, l'Organisation des Nations Unies prendra des dispositions pour inscrire à l'ordre du jour du Conseil économique et social ou, selon le cas et conformément aux dispositions applicables du règlement intérieur, d'autres organes ou organismes des Nations Unies, des questions proposées par l'Organisation mondiale du tourisme.

Article 5
Recommandations de l'Organisation des Nations Unies

1. Tenant compte de l'obligation de l'Organisation des Nations Unies de favoriser la réalisation des objectifs prévus à l'Article 55 de la Charte des Nations Unies et l'exercice des fonctions et pouvoirs du Conseil économique et social, prévus à l'Article 62 de la Charte, de faire ou de susciter des études et des rapports sur des questions internationales dans les domaines économique, social, de la culture, de l'éducation et de la santé publique et autres domaines connexes et d'adresser ses recommandations sur ces questions aux institutions spécialisées intéressées, et tenant compte également de la responsabilité de l'Organisation des Nations Unies, aux termes des Articles 58 et 63 de la Charte, de faire des recommandations en vue de coordonner les programmes et activités des institutions spécialisées, l'Organisation mondiale du tourisme convient de prendre des mesures afin de soumettre dès que possible à ses organes compétents respectifs toutes les recommandations formelles que l'Organisation des Nations Unies pourrait lui adresser.

2. L'Organisation mondiale du tourisme convient d'engager des consultations avec l'Organisation des Nations Unies, à la demande de cette dernière, et de lui rendre compte en temps opportun des mesures qu'elle ou ses membres auront prises en vue de donner effet à ces recommandations, ou de tout autre résultat auquel auraient abouti leurs délibérations.

Article 6
Assistance à l'Organisation des Nations Unies

L'Organisation mondiale du tourisme coopère avec l'Organisation des Nations Unies, conformément à la Charte des Nations Unies et à ses propres Statuts, en lui fournissant, autant que possible, toute information ou études particulières ainsi que toute assistance que celle-ci peut lui demander.

Article 7
Rapports périodiques

L'Organisation mondiale du tourisme présente à l'Organisation des Nations Unies des rapports périodiques sur ses activités.

Article 8
Échange d'informations et de documents

Sous réserve des mesures qui pourraient être nécessaires pour préserver le caractère confidentiel de certains documents, l'Organisation des Nations Unies et l'Organisation mondiale du tourisme procèdent à un échange complet et rapide des informations et documents susceptibles de présenter un intérêt.

Article 9
Information

Compte tenu de l'objectif de l'Organisation mondiale du tourisme, tel qu'énoncé au paragraphe 1 de l'article 3 de ses Statuts, et aux fins de la coordination des activités de l'Organisation dans ce domaine avec celles des services d'information de l'Organisation des Nations Unies, l'Organisation mondiale du tourisme et l'Organisation des Nations Unies conviennent de conclure des arrangements complémentaires à cet égard.

Article 10
Relations avec la Cour internationale de Justice

1. L'Organisation mondiale du tourisme convient de fournir toute information qui lui serait demandée par la Cour internationale de Justice, conformément à l'article 34 du Statut de la Cour.

2. L'Assemblée générale des Nations Unies autorise l'Organisation mondiale du tourisme à demander des avis consultatifs à la Cour internationale de Justice sur les questions juridiques qui se poseraient dans le cadre des activités relevant de sa compétence, à l'exception de celles concernant les relations entre l'Organisation des Nations Unies et l'Organisation mondiale du tourisme ou d'autres institutions spécialisées.

3. La demande peut être adressée à la Cour internationale de Justice par l'Assemblée générale ou par le Conseil exécutif de l'Organisation mondiale du tourisme agissant sur autorisation de l'Assemblée générale de l'Organisation mondiale du tourisme.

4. Lorsqu'elle présente à la Cour internationale de Justice une demande d'avis consultatif, l'Organisation mondiale du tourisme en informe le Conseil économique et social.

Article 11
Territoires non autonomes et autres territoires

L'Organisation mondiale du tourisme convient de coopérer, dans le domaine de sa compétence, avec l'Organisation des Nations Unies à la mise en œuvre des principes et obligations prévus aux Chapitres XI, XII et XIII de la Charte des Nations Unies, ainsi que des autres principes et obligations internationalement reconnus relatifs aux pays et aux peuples coloniaux ainsi qu'à la prise en considération des résolutions pertinentes de l'Assemblée générale des Nations Unies s'agissant des questions touchant au bien-être et au développement des peuples des territoires non autonomes et des autres territoires.

Article 12
Coopération technique

L'Organisation des Nations Unies et l'Organisation mondiale du tourisme s'engagent à coopérer en vue de la fourniture d'une assistance technique dans le domaine du tourisme et du développement touristique. Elles s'engagent, en particulier, à éviter tout double emploi inopportun de leurs activités et services et conviennent de prendre les mesures nécessaires pour coordonner efficacement lesdites activités dans le cadre du système actuel de coordination de l'assistance technique, compte tenu des responsabilités et des rôles propres à l'une et l'autre organisations aux termes de leurs instruments constitutifs, aussi bien que de ceux d'autres organisations participant à des activités d'assistance technique. À cette fin, l'Organisation mondiale du tourisme convient de reconnaître les responsabilités générales des coordonnateurs résidents en ce qui concerne les activités opérationnelles de développement telles qu'elles sont énoncées dans les résolutions pertinentes de l'Assemblée générale des Nations Unies. En tant que l'une des plus petites institutions spécialisées sans représentation sur le terrain, l'Organisation mondiale du tourisme peut utiliser les coordonnateurs résidents pour assurer sa représentation et promouvoir ses activités.

Article 13
Services de statistique

1. L'Organisation des Nations Unies et l'Organisation mondiale du tourisme conviennent de s'efforcer de coopérer, dans toute la mesure possible, afin d'éviter tout double emploi inopportun et d'utiliser avec la plus grande efficacité leur personnel technique dans leurs activités respectives visant à recueillir, analyser, publier et diffuser l'information statistique. Les deux organisations conviennent de joindre leurs efforts en vue d'assurer le meilleur usage et la plus large utilisation possibles de leurs données statistiques, de garantir une coordination étroite dans le cadre de leurs activités statistiques respectives et de réduire au minimum la charge

imposée aux gouvernements et aux autres organisations auprès desquelles ces données pourront être recueillies.

2. L'Organisation mondiale du tourisme reconnaît que l'Organisation des Nations Unies constitue l'organisme central chargé de recueillir, d'analyser, de publier, d'unifier et d'améliorer les statistiques touristiques servant les buts généraux des organisations internationales.

3. L'Organisation des Nations Unies reconnaît en l'Organisation mondiale du tourisme l'organisme approprié pour recueillir, analyser, publier, unifier et améliorer les statistiques touristiques et promouvoir l'intégration de ces statistiques à l'échelle du système des Nations Unies.

Article 14
Coopération administrative

1. L'Organisation des Nations Unies et l'Organisation mondiale du tourisme jugent souhaitable de coopérer en ce qui concerne les questions administratives d'intérêt commun.

2. En conséquence, l'Organisation des Nations Unies et l'Organisation mondiale du tourisme s'engagent à se consulter, de temps à autre, et à consulter les autres organismes intéressés des Nations Unies sur ces questions, notamment en ce qui concerne l'utilisation la plus efficace et la plus rationnelle des installations et moyens, du personnel et des services, ainsi que les méthodes permettant d'éviter la mise en place et l'entretien de moyens matériels et de services qui entreraient en concurrence ou feraient double emploi, en vue d'assurer toute l'uniformité possible dans les domaines considérés.

3. Les consultations visées au présent article auront également pour objet de déterminer la manière la plus équitable de financer l'assistance ou les services spéciaux fournis, sur leur demande, par l'Organisation mondiale du tourisme à l'Organisation des Nations Unies et réciproquement, sous réserve de la conclusion d'arrangements complémentaires à cet effet.

4. Les consultations visées au présent article serviront aussi à explorer la possibilité de maintenir ou mettre en place des facilités ou services communs dans certains domaines, y compris la possibilité pour une organisation de fournir ces facilités ou services à une ou plusieurs autres organisations, et à déterminer la manière la plus équitable de financer ceux-ci, sous réserve de la conclusion d'arrangements complémentaires à cet effet.

Article 15
Bureaux régionaux et locaux

Les bureaux régionaux ou locaux que l'Organisation mondiale du tourisme pourra créer coopéreront étroitement avec les bureaux régionaux ou locaux que l'Organisation des Nations Unies a créés ou pourra créer, en particulier les bureaux des commissions régionales et des coordonnateurs résidents.

Article 16
Arrangements concernant le personnel

1. L'Organisation des Nations Unies et l'Organisation mondiale du tourisme conviennent, dans l'intérêt de l'uniformité des normes en matière d'emploi sur le plan international, de mettre au point, dans toute la mesure possible, des normes communes concernant le personnel et des méthodes et arrangements destinés à éviter des différences injustifiées dans les clauses et conditions d'emploi, à éviter qu'elles ne se fassent concurrence dans le recrutement du personnel et à faciliter les échanges de personnel souhaitables et profitables pour les deux organisations. À cette fin l'Organisation mondiale du tourisme reconnaît le statut de la Commission de la fonction publique internationale, accepte de participer à la Caisse commune des pensions du personnel des Nations Unies conformément aux Statuts de celle-ci et reconnaît la compétence du Tribunal administratif des Nations Unies pour connaître de toute plainte relative au non-respect de ces Statuts.

2. L'Organisation des Nations Unies et l'Organisation mondiale du tourisme conviennent de coopérer, autant que possible, en vue de la réalisation de ces objectifs et notamment de :

a) Se consulter de temps à autre sur les questions d'intérêt commun concernant les clauses et conditions d'emploi des fonctionnaires et du personnel, afin d'assurer autant d'uniformité que possible dans ce domaine ;

b) Coopérer dans les échanges de personnel lorsque cela est souhaitable, sur une base soit temporaire soit permanente, en prenant soin de garantir le respect de l'ancienneté et les droits à pension ;

c) Collaborer avec les autres organismes des Nations Unies en vue de la création et du fonctionnement d'un mécanisme approprié pour le règlement de litiges concernant l'emploi du personnel et des questions connexes.

3. Les termes et conditions auxquels les moyens et installations ou services de l'Organisation des Nations Unies ou de l'Organisation mondiale du tourisme sont mis à la disposition de l'autre organisation, en rapport avec les questions visées dans le présent article, font l'objet, le cas échéant, d'accords subsidiaires qui seront conclus spécialement à cet effet conformément à l'article 20 du présent Accord.

Article 17
Questions budgétaires et financières

1. L'Organisation mondiale du tourisme reconnaît qu'il est souhaitable qu'elle établisse avec l'Organisation des Nations Unies d'étroites relations budgétaires et financières afin que les activités administratives de l'Organisation des Nations Unies

et des autres organismes des Nations Unies soient menées de la manière la plus efficace et la plus économique possible et que soit assuré le maximum de coordination et d'uniformité dans ces activités.

2. L'Organisation mondiale du tourisme convient d'accepter le statut du Corps commun d'inspection.

3. L'Organisation mondiale du tourisme convient de se conformer, dans toute la mesure possible, aux pratiques et procédures uniformes recommandées par l'Organisation des Nations Unies.

4. Les arrangements budgétaires et financiers conclus entre l'Organisation des Nations Unies et l'Organisation mondiale du tourisme sont approuvés conformément à leurs instruments constitutifs respectifs.

5. En établissant le budget de l'Organisation mondiale du tourisme, le Secrétaire général de l'Organisation procédera à un échange de vues avec le Secrétaire général de l'Organisation des Nations Unies en vue d'assurer, dans toute la mesure possible, l'uniformité dans la présentation des budgets de l'Organisation des Nations Unies et des autres organismes des Nations Unies, afin de permettre la comparaison entre les divers budgets, sans exclure pour autant la possibilité pour chaque organisation d'établir son budget dans ses devises respectives.

6. L'Organisation mondiale du tourisme convient de communiquer ses projets de budget à l'Organisation des Nations Unies au plus tard à la date à laquelle lesdits projets de budget sont communiqués à ses membres afin de permettre à l'Assemblée générale des Nations Unies de les examiner et de faire des recommandations, conformément au paragraphe 3 de l'Article 17 de la Charte des Nations Unies.

7. Des représentants de l'Organisation mondiale du tourisme sont autorisés à participer, sans droit de vote, aux délibérations de l'Assemblée générale des Nations Unies ou de toute commission de celle-ci, au moment où sont examinés le budget de l'Organisation mondiale du tourisme ou des questions administratives ou financières générales intéressant cette dernière.

Article 18
Laissez-passer des Nations Unies

Les fonctionnaires de l'Organisation mondiale du tourisme ont le droit d'utiliser le laissez-passer des Nations Unies conformément aux accords spéciaux conclus par le Secrétaire général de l'Organisation des Nations Unies et le Secrétaire général de l'Organisation mondiale du tourisme.

Article 19
Exécution de l'Accord

Le Secrétaire général de l'Organisation des Nations Unies et le Secrétaire général de l'Organisation mondiale du tourisme peuvent conclure les arrangements complémentaires qui peuvent paraître souhaitables aux fins d'exécution du présent Accord.

Article 20
Modification et révision

Le présent Accord peut être modifié ou révisé par entente entre l'Organisation des Nations Unies et l'Organisation mondiale du tourisme, et toute modification ou révision entrera en vigueur dès qu'elle aura été approuvée par l'Assemblée générale des Nations Unies et par l'Assemblée générale de l'Organisation mondiale du tourisme.

Article 21
Entrée en vigueur

Le présent Accord entrera en vigueur dès qu'il aura été approuvé par l'Assemblée générale des Nations Unies et par l'Assemblée générale de l'Organisation mondiale du tourisme.

PROTOCOLE RELATIF A L'ENTREE EN VIGUEUR DE L'ACCORD ENTRE L'ORGANISATION DES NATIONS UNIES ET L'ORGANISATION MONDIALE DU TOURISME

Conformément aux dispositions de l'Article 57 de la Charte des Nations Unies, les institutions spécialisées créées par accords intergouvernementaux et pourvues, aux termes de leurs statuts, d'attributions internationales étendues dans les domaines économique, social, de la culture intellectuelle et de l'éducation, de la santé publique et autres domaines connexes, sont reliées à l'Organisation des Nations Unies. L'Article 63 de la Charte dispose que le Conseil économique et social peut conclure, avec toute institution visée à l'Article 57, des accords fixant les conditions dans lesquelles cette institution sera reliée à l'Organisation, et précise que ces accords sont soumis à l'approbation de l'Assemblée générale.

Le paragraphe 3 de l'article 3 des Statuts de l'Organisation mondiale du tourisme, adoptés le 27 septembre 1970, dispose qu'afin d'affirmer le rôle central qu'elle est appelée à jouer dans le domaine du tourisme, l'Organisation établira et maintiendra une coopération efficace avec les organes compétents des Nations Unies et ses institutions spécialisées.

À sa quatorzième session, tenue du 24 au 29 septembre 2001 à Séoul (République de Corée) et à Osaka (Japon), l'Assemblée générale de l'Organisation mondiale du tourisme a adopté la résolution 420(XIV), dans laquelle elle a déclaré que des mesures devraient être prises pour étudier la possibilité de transformer l'Organisation mondiale du tourisme en une institution spécialisée des Nations Unies.

Dans une lettre datée du 21 décembre 2001 (E/2002/5), le Secrétaire général de l'Organisation mondiale du tourisme a demandé au Secrétaire général de l'Organisation des Nations Unies d'inscrire dans le projet d'ordre du jour provisoire de la session suivante du Conseil économique et social un point relatif à la transformation de l'Organisation mondiale du tourisme en institution spécialisée des Nations Unies.

Le 30 avril 2002, à sa 5ᵉ séance plénière, le Conseil économique et social a décidé d'inscrire à l'ordre du jour de sa session de fond de 2002 un point intitulé : « Examen de la demande de transformation de l'Organisation mondiale du tourisme, organisation intergouvernementale dotée du statut consultatif auprès du Conseil économique et social, en institution spécialisée des Nations Unies » (décision du Conseil économique et social 2002/214).

À sa soixante-huitième session, tenue à Petra (Jordanie) les 18 et 19 juin 2002, le Conseil exécutif de l'Organisation mondiale du tourisme a adopté la décision 11(LXVIII), par laquelle il a décidé, sans préjuger le résultat de l'examen par le Conseil économique et social de la demande de transformation, de mettre en place, de son côté et à titre provisoire, un Comité de négociation avec l'Organisation des Nations Unies.

Le 24 juillet 2002, à sa 37e séance plénière, le Conseil économique et social a adopté la résolution 2002/24 intitulée « Modalités de la négociation d'un accord entre l'Organisation des Nations Unies et l'Organisation mondiale du tourisme », par laquelle il a autorisé son président à nommer les membres du Comité chargé des négociations avec les institutions intergouvernementales. Il a aussi invité ce comité à négocier avec l'Organisation mondiale du tourisme un accord sur les relations entre cette organisation et l'Organisation des Nations Unies, sur la base des propositions présentées par le Secrétaire général, et de lui soumettre, pour qu'il l'examine à sa session de fond de 2003, un projet d'accord sur les relations entre les deux organisations.

À sa soixante-neuvième session, tenue à Saint-Pétersbourg (Fédération de Russie) du 2 au 4 octobre 2002, le Conseil exécutif de l'Organisation mondiale du tourisme a adopté la décision 10(LXIX), par laquelle il a confirmé sa décision 11(LXVIII) concernant la création du Comité de négociation avec l'Organisation des Nations Unies, et a décidé que le Président en exercice du Conseil exécutif présiderait ce comité.

Le 26 mars ainsi que les 7, 10, 15, 16 et 17 avril 2003, le Comité chargé des négociations avec les institutions intergouvernementales, créé par le Conseil économique et social, a examiné le texte du projet d'accord sur les relations entre l'Organisation des Nations Unies et l'Organisation mondiale du tourisme soumis par le Secrétaire général (E/C.1/2003/1) et l'a approuvé avec plusieurs modifications. Le 17 avril 2003, le Comité est convenu de transmettre le texte du projet d'accord au Comité de négociation de l'Organisation mondiale du tourisme pour examen (E/2003/60).

Le 29 avril 2003, le Comité de négociation de l'Organisation mondiale du tourisme en vue de la transformation de l'Organisation en institution spécialisée des Nations Unies a approuvé sans changement le texte du projet d'accord, tel que préparé par le Comité chargé des négociations avec les institutions intergouvernementales du Conseil économique et social, et a recommandé au Conseil exécutif de l'Organisation mondiale du tourisme de l'approuver de la même manière (E/C.1/2003/2).

Le 4 juin 2003, à sa soixante-dixième session, tenue à Madrid (Espagne), le Conseil exécutif de l'Organisation mondiale du tourisme a adopté la décision 4(LXX) dans laquelle il a pris note avec satisfaction du texte du projet d'accord tel que présenté par les comités de négociation du Conseil économique et social et de l'Organisation mondiale du tourisme, et a décidé de le soumettre sans modifications à la session suivante de l'Assemblée générale de l'Organisation mondiale du tourisme, pour approbation.

Le 10 juillet 2003, à sa 29e séance plénière, le Conseil économique et social a adopté la résolution 2003/2, par laquelle il a recommandé que l'Assemblée générale des Nations Unies approuve l'Accord à sa cinquante-huitième session.

Le 24 octobre 2003, à sa quinzième session, tenue à Beijing (Chine), l'Assemblée générale de l'Organisation mondiale du tourisme a adopté la résolution 453(XV), par laquelle elle a approuvé sans modifications le projet d'accord.

Le 23 décembre 2003, à la 78e séance plénière de sa cinquante-huitième session, l'Assemblée générale de l'Organisation des Nations Unies a adopté la résolution 58/232, par laquelle elle a approuvé l'Accord entre l'Organisation des Nations Unies et l'Organisation mondiale du tourisme.

L'article 21 de l'Accord dispose que l'Accord entrera en vigueur dès qu'il aura été approuvé par l'Assemblée générale de l'Organisation des Nations Unies et par l'Assemblée générale de l'Organisation mondiale du tourisme.

L'accord est ainsi entré en vigueur le 23 décembre 2003.

Une copie des textes en anglais et en français de l'Accord est jointe au présent document, les deux textes faisant également foi.

EN FOI DE QUOI nous avons signé, ce 18 décembre 2015 à New York, et ce 14 janvier 2016 à Madrid, deux exemplaires originaux du présent Protocole, dont les versions anglaise et française font également foi. L'un des exemplaires originaux sera conservé par le Secrétariat de l'Organisation des Nations Unies et l'autre par le Secrétariat de l'Organisation mondiale du tourisme.

BAN Ki-moon
Le Secrétaire général de l'Organisation
des Nations Unies

Taleb Rifai
Le Secrétaire général de l'Organisation mondiale
du tourisme

ANNEX A

Ratifications, accessions, subsequent agreements, etc., concerning treaties and international agreements registered in March 2016 with the Secretariat of the United Nations

ANNEXE A

Ratifications, adhésions, accords ultérieurs, etc., concernant des traités et accords internationaux enregistrés en mars 2016 au Secrétariat de l'Organisation des Nations Unies

No. 2997. Multilateral

STATUTE OF THE HAGUE CONFERENCE ON PRIVATE INTERNATIONAL LAW (REVISED TEXT). THE HAGUE, 9 OCTOBER 1951 AND 31 OCTOBER 1951 [*United Nations, Treaty Series, vol. 220, I-2997.*]

ACCEPTANCE

Republic of Moldova

Deposit of instrument with the Government of the Netherlands: 16 March 2016

Date of effect: 16 March 2016

Registration with the Secretariat of the United Nations: Netherlands, 23 March 2016

N° 2997. Multilatéral

STATUT DE LA CONFÉRENCE DE LA HAYE DE DROIT INTERNATIONAL PRIVÉ (TEXTE RÉVISÉ). LA HAYE, 9 OCTOBRE 1951 ET 31 OCTOBRE 1951 [*Nations Unies, Recueil des Traités, vol. 220, I-2997.*]

ACCEPTATION

République de Moldova

Dépôt de l'instrument auprès du Gouvernement néerlandais : 16 mars 2016

Date de prise d'effet : 16 mars 2016

Enregistrement au Secrétariat de l'Organisation des Nations Unies : Pays-Bas, 23 mars 2016

No. 9464. Multilateral

INTERNATIONAL CONVENTION ON THE ELIMINATION OF ALL FORMS OF RACIAL DISCRIMINATION. NEW YORK, 7 MARCH 1966 [*United Nations, Treaty Series, vol. 660, I-9464.*]

DECLARATION UNDER ARTICLE 14 (1)

El Salvador

Notification deposited with the Secretary-General of the United Nations: 23 March 2016

Registration with the Secretariat of the United Nations: ex officio, 23 March 2016

Nº 9464. Multilatéral

CONVENTION INTERNATIONALE SUR L'ÉLIMINATION DE TOUTES LES FORMES DE DISCRIMINATION RACIALE. NEW YORK, 7 MARS 1966 [*Nations Unies, Recueil des Traités, vol. 660, I-9464.*]

DÉCLARATION EN VERTU DU PARAGRAPHE 1 DE L'ARTICLE 14

El Salvador

Dépôt de la notification auprès du Secrétaire général de l'Organisation des Nations Unies : 23 mars 2016

Enregistrement au Secrétariat de l'Organisation des Nations Unies : d'office, 23 mars 2016

[TEXT IN SPANISH – TEXTE EN ESPAGNOL]

el Gobierno de la República de El Salvador reconoce la competencia del Comité para la Eliminación de la Discriminación Racial, para recibir y examinar las comunicaciones de personas o grupos de personas, comprendidas dentro de la jurisdicción del Estado Parte que aleguen ser víctimas de violaciones por parte de ese Estado, de cualquiera de los derechos estipulados en la Convención Internacional sobre la Eliminación de todas las formas de Discriminación Racial, según lo establecido en el Artículo 14 de la referida Convención.

[TRANSLATION – TRADUCTION]

... the Government of the Republic of El Salvador recognizes the competence of the Committee on the Elimination of Racial Discrimination to receive and consider communications from individuals or groups of individuals within the jurisdiction of a State Party who claim to be victims of violations by that State of any of the rights set forth in the International Convention on the Elimination of All Forms of Racial Discrimination, as provided for in article 14 of the said Convention.

[TRANSLATION – TRADUCTION]

… le Gouvernement de la République d'El Salvador reconnaît la compétence du Comité pour l'élimination de la discrimination raciale pour recevoir et examiner des communications émanant de personnes ou groupes de personnes relevant de la juridiction d'un État partie qui se plaignent d'être victimes de violations, par cet État, de l'un quelconque des droits énoncés dans la Convention internationale sur l'élimination de toutes les formes de discrimination raciale, comme prévu à l'article 14 de ladite Convention.

No. 14668. Multilateral

INTERNATIONAL COVENANT ON CIVIL AND POLITICAL RIGHTS. NEW YORK, 16 DECEMBER 1966 [*United Nations, Treaty Series, vol. 999, I-14668.*]

NOTIFICATION UNDER ARTICLE 4 (3)

Peru

Notification deposited with the Secretary-General of the United Nations: 17 March 2016

Registration with the Secretariat of the United Nations: ex officio, 17 March 2016

Nº 14668. Multilatéral

PACTE INTERNATIONAL RELATIF AUX DROITS CIVILS ET POLITIQUES. NEW YORK, 16 DÉCEMBRE 1966 [*Nations Unies, Recueil des Traités, vol. 999, I-14668.*]

NOTIFICATION EN VERTU DU PARAGRAPHE 3 DE L'ARTICLE 4

Pérou

Dépôt de la notification auprès du Secrétaire général de l'Organisation des Nations Unies : 17 mars 2016

Enregistrement au Secrétariat de l'Organisation des Nations Unies : d'office, 17 mars 2016

[TEXT IN SPANISH – TEXTE EN ESPAGNOL]

Misión Permanente del Perú ante las Naciones Unidas

Permanent Mission of Peru to the United Nations

7-1-SG/14

La Misión Permanente del Perú ante las Naciones Unidas presenta sus atentos saludos a la Secretaría General de las Naciones Unidas – Sección de Tratados de la Oficina de Asuntos Jurídicos, y en cumplimiento de lo dispuesto por el Artículo 4º del Pacto Internacional de Derechos Civiles y Políticos tiene a honra informar que, mediante Decreto Supremo Nº 003-2016-PCM publicado el pasado 15 de enero, cuya copia se acompaña, se prorrogó por sesenta días, a partir del 21 de enero de 2016, el Estado de Emergencia declarado en el distrito de Echarate, ubicado en la provincia de La Convención del departamento del Cusco.

Cabe recordar que oportunamente esta Misión Permanente ha cumplido con informar a esa Secretaría General sobre prórrogas anteriores al Estado de Emergencia declarado en la localidad indicada, siendo la última comunicada mediante Nota 7-1-SG/64 de fecha 11 de diciembre de 2015.

Durante el Estado de Emergencia quedan suspendidos los derechos relativos a la libertad y seguridad personales, la inviolabilidad de domicilio y la libertad de reunión y de tránsito en el territorio, contemplados en los incisos 9, 11, 12 y 24(f) del Artículo 2º de la Constitución Política del Perú, y en los Artículos 17º, 12º, 21º y 9º del Pacto Internacional de Derechos Civiles y Políticos, respectivamente, con el motivo de consolidar la pacificación de la zona y del país.

La Misión Permanente del Perú ante las Naciones Unidas aprovecha la oportunidad para renovar a la Secretaría General de las Naciones Unidas las seguridades de su más alta y distinguida consideración.

Nueva York, 16 de marzo de 2016

Prórroga de Estado de Emergencia declarado en el distrito de Echarate, provincia de La Convención, departamento del Cusco

DECRETO SUPREMO
Nº 003-2016-PCM

EL PRESIDENTE DE LA REPÚBLICA

CONSIDERANDO:

Que, mediante Decreto Supremo Nº 079-2015-PCM publicado el 12 de noviembre de 2015, se prorrogó por el término de SESENTA (60) días calendario, a partir del 22 de noviembre de 2015, el Estado de Emergencia en el distrito de Echarate, ubicado en la provincia de La Convención del departamento de Cusco;

Que, mediante Decreto Supremo Nº 085-2015-PCM de fecha 10 de diciembre de 2015, se delimitó el ámbito de actuación de las Fuerzas Armadas y Policía Nacional del Perú en las zonas del VRAEM que se encuentran en Estado de Emergencia, orientando su misionamiento en contrarrestar los remanentes terroristas, así como la lucha frontal contra el tráfico ilícito de Drogas y otras actividades ilícitas, respectivamente;

Que, estando por vencer el plazo de vigencia del Estado de Emergencia referido en el considerando precedente, y de acuerdo con lo manifestado por el Director General de la Policía Nacional del Perú, mediante el Oficio Nº 07-2016-DIRGEN PNP/SA, de fecha 04 de enero de 2016, aún subsisten las condiciones que determinaron la declaratoria del Estado de Emergencia en la provincia y distrito indicado, por lo que es necesario prorrogar el mismo, a fin que la presencia de la Policía Nacional del Perú, con su acertado accionar permita que la población se identifique con los fines u objetivos que busca el Gobierno Nacional, esto es, la consolidación de la pacificación de la zona y del país;

Que, el numeral 1) del artículo 137º de la Constitución Política del Perú, establece que la prórroga del Estado de Emergencia requiere de un nuevo Decreto Supremo;

Que, mediante Decreto Legislativo Nº 1186, Decreto Legislativo que regula el uso de la fuerza por parte de la Policía Nacional del Perú, se precisa el uso de la fuerza en el ejercicio de la función policial, los niveles del uso de la fuerza y las circunstancias y reglas de conducta en el uso de la fuerza;

Que, mediante Decreto Legislativo Nº 1095, se estableció el marco legal que regula los principios, formas, condiciones y límites para el empleo y uso de la fuerza por parte de las Fuerzas Armadas en el territorio nacional y en su Título II se establecen las normas del uso de la fuerza en otras situaciones de violencia, en zonas declaradas en Estado de Emergencia con el control del orden interno a cargo de la Policía Nacional del Perú, en cumplimiento de su función constitucional, mediante el empleo de su potencialidad y capacidad coercitiva para la protección de la sociedad, en defensa del Estado de Derecho;

De conformidad con lo establecido en los numerales 4) y 14) del artículo 118º de la Constitución Política del Perú; y,

Con el voto aprobatorio del Consejo de Ministros y con cargo a dar cuenta al Congreso de la República.

DECRETA:

Artículo 1.- Prórroga de Estado de Emergencia

Prorrogar por el término de SESENTA (60) días calendario, a partir del 21 de enero de 2016, el Estado de Emergencia en el distrito de Echarate, ubicado en la provincia de La Convención, del departamento de Cusco.

Artículo 2.- Suspensión del ejercicio de Derechos Constitucionales

Durante el Estado de Emergencia a que se refiere el artículo anterior y en la circunscripción señalada en el mismo, quedan suspendidos los derechos constitucionales relativos a la libertad y seguridad personales, la inviolabilidad de domicilio y la libertad de reunión y de tránsito en el territorio, comprendidos en los incisos 9), 11), 12) y 24), apartado f) del artículo 2º de la Constitución Política del Perú.

Artículo 3.- Control del Orden Interno

Disponer que la Policía Nacional del Perú asuma el control del Orden Interno en tanto dure el Estado de Emergencia declarado en el artículo 1º del presente Decreto Supremo.

Las Fuerzas Armadas apoyarán a la Policía Nacional del Perú para el logro de dicho objetivo en el distrito de Echarate, ubicado en la provincia de La Convención, del departamento de Cusco.

Artículo 4.- De la Intervención de las Fuerzas Armadas y Policía Nacional del Perú

La intervención de las Fuerzas Armadas y de la Policía Nacional del Perú, se efectuará conforme a lo dispuesto en el Decreto Legislativo Nº 1095 y Decreto Legislativo Nº 1186, respectivamente; así como a lo dispuesto en el Decreto Supremo Nº 085-2015-PCM, que dispone que las Fuerzas Armadas orientan su misionamiento en contrarrestar el accionar de los remanentes terroristas y la Policía Nacional del Perú en su lucha frontal contra el tráfico ilícito de Drogas y otras actividades ilícitas.

Artículo 5.- Refrendo

El presente Decreto Supremo será refrendado por el Presidente del Consejo de Ministros, el Ministro de Defensa, el Ministro del Interior y el Ministro de Justicia y Derechos Humanos.

Dado en la Casa de Gobierno, en Lima, a los catorce días del mes de enero del año dos mil dieciséis.

OLLANTA HUMALA TASSO
Presidente de la República

ANA MARÍA SÁNCHEZ DE RÍOS
Ministra de Relaciones Exteriores
Encargada del Despacho de la Presidencia del Consejo de Ministros

JAKKE VALAKIVI ÁLVAREZ
Ministro de Defensa

JOSÉ LUIS PÉREZ GUADALUPE
Ministro del Interior y
Encargado del Despacho del Ministerio de Justicia y Derechos Humanos

[TRANSLATION – TRADUCTION]

The Permanent Mission of Peru to the United Nations presents its compliments to the Treaty Section of the Office of Legal Affairs, United Nations Secretariat, and, in accordance with article 4 of the International Covenant on Civil and Political Rights, has the honour to inform it that, by Supreme Decree No. 003-2016-PCM, issued on 15 January 2016 (copy attached), the state of emergency declared in the District of Echarate in the Province of La Convención, Department of Cusco, has been extended for 60 days, with effect from 21 January 2016.

It should be recalled that the Permanent Mission has duly reported to the Secretariat previous extensions of the state of emergency in the aforementioned place, the most recent communication being note No. 7-1-SG/64 of 11 December 2015.

During the state of emergency, the rights relating to liberty and security of person, inviolability of the home, freedom of assembly and freedom of movement within the territory, recognized in article 2, paragraphs 9, 11, 12 and 24 (f), of the Political Constitution of Peru and in articles 17, 12, 21 and 9 of the International Covenant on Civil and Political Rights, respectively, are suspended in order to consolidate peace in the area and in the country.

The Permanent Mission of Peru to the United Nations takes this opportunity to convey to the Secretariat the renewed assurances of its highest consideration.

New York, 16 March 2016

Extension of the state of emergency declared in the District of Echarate in the Province of La Convención, Department of Cusco

Supreme Decree No. 003-2016-PCM

The President of the Republic

Considering:

That, by Supreme Decree No. 079-2015-PCM, issued on 12 November 2015, the state of emergency in the District of Echarate in the Province of La Convención, Department of Cusco, was extended for a period of sixty (60) calendar days, with effect from 22 November 2015;

That Supreme Decree No. 085-2015-PCM dated 10 December 2015 defined the scope of action of the armed forces and the National Police of Peru in the VRAEM regions which are currently under a state of emergency, directing their mission towards resisting remaining terrorists and directly combatting illegal drug trafficking and other illicit activities, respectively;

That, while the state of emergency referred to in the preceding paragraph is about to expire, the Director General of the National Police of Peru has reported, in note No. 07-2016-DIRGEN PNP/SA of 4 January 2016, that the circumstances that gave rise to the declaration of a state of emergency still prevail in the above-mentioned province and district; and that it is therefore necessary to extend the state of emergency in order to enable the population, through the presence and appropriate action of the National Police of Peru, to identify with the ends or objectives sought by the national Government, namely the consolidation of peace in the area and in the country as a whole;

That article 137, paragraph 1, of the Political Constitution of Peru provides that the extension of a state of emergency requires a new Supreme Decree;

That by Legislative Decree No. 1186, which regulates the use of force by the National Police of Peru, the use of force in the exercise of police functions, the levels of the use of force and the circumstances and rules of conduct concerning the use of force are defined;

That Legislative Decree No. 1095 establishes the legal framework governing the principles, forms, conditions and limits concerning the use of force by the armed forces within the national territory when discharging their constitutional duties by using their powers and enforcement capabilities to protect society and defend the rule of law in areas where a state of emergency has been declared in which the National Police of Peru is responsible for maintaining public order and that Part II thereof establishes the norms on the use of force by the armed forces in other violent situations;

In accordance with article 118, paragraphs 4 and 14, of the Political Constitution of Peru; and

With the approval of the Council of Ministers and subject to notification of the Congress of the Republic;

Hereby decrees:

Article 1: Extension of the state of emergency

The state of emergency in the District of Echarate in the Province of La Convención, Department of Cusco, is hereby extended for a period of sixty (60) calendar days, with effect from 21 January 2016.

Article 2: Suspension of constitutional rights

During the state of emergency and in the location referred to in the preceding article, the constitutional rights relating to liberty and security of person, inviolability of the home and freedom of assembly and of movement within the territory, recognized in article 2, paragraphs 9, 11, 12 and 24 (f) of the Political Constitution of Peru, shall be suspended.

Article 3: Maintenance of public order

The National Police of Peru shall be responsible for maintaining public order during the state of emergency declared in article 1 hereof.

The armed forces shall assist the National Police of Peru in achieving this objective in the District of Echarate in the Province of La Convención, Department of Cusco.

Article 4: Parameters of action by the armed forces and the National Police of Peru

The armed forces and the National Police of Peru shall act in accordance with Legislative Decree No. 1095 and Legislative Decree No. 1186, respectively, and in accordance with Supreme Decree No. 085-2015-PCM which stipulates that the armed forces focus their mission on combatting the activities of remaining terrorists and that the National Police of Peru focus their mission on combatting illegal drug trafficking and other illicit activities.

Article 5: Endorsement

The present Supreme Decree shall be endorsed by the President of the Council of Ministers, the Minister of Defence, the Minister of the Interior and the Minister of Justice and Human Rights.

Done at Government House, Lima, on 14 January 2016.

Ollanta Humala Tasso
Constitutional President of the Republic

Ana María Sánchez de Ríos
Minister for Foreign Affairs
Acting President of the Council of Ministers

Jakke Valakivi Álvarez
Minister of Defence

José Luis Pérez Guadalupe
Minister of the Interior and
Acting Minister of Justice and Human Rights

[TRANSLATION – TRADUCTION]

La Mission permanente du Pérou auprès de l'Organisation des Nations Unies présente ses compliments à la Section des traités du Bureau des affaires juridiques du Secrétariat de l'Organisation et, en application des dispositions de l'article 4 du Pacte international relatif aux droits civils et politiques, a l'honneur de l'informer que le décret suprême n° 003-2016-PCM, publié le 15 janvier 2016 et dont le texte est joint à la présente, proroge, pour une durée de 60 jours commençant le 21 janvier 2016, l'état d'urgence déclaré dans le district d'Echarate, situé dans la province de La Convención (département de Cusco).

Il convient de rappeler que la Mission permanente a dûment informé le Secrétariat des précédentes prorogations de l'état d'urgence dans le lieu indiqué, la dernière communication en la matière résultant de la note 7-1-SG/64 du 11 décembre 2015.

Est suspendu, pendant la durée de l'état d'urgence et afin de consolider la pacification de la zone considérée et du pays, l'exercice des droits relatifs à la liberté et à la sécurité de la personne, à l'inviolabilité du domicile et à la liberté de réunion et de circulation sur le territoire, consacrés aux paragraphes 9, 11, 12 et 24 f) de l'article 2 de la Constitution politique du Pérou et aux articles 17, 12, 21 et 9 du Pacte international relatif aux droits civils et politiques, respectivement.

La Mission permanente du Pérou auprès de l'Organisation des Nations Unies saisit cette occasion pour renouveler au Secrétariat de l'Organisation les assurances de sa très haute considération.

New York, le 16 mars 2016

Prorogation de l'état d'urgence déclaré dans le district d'Echarate de la province de La Convención (département de Cusco)

Décret suprême n° 003-2016-PCM

Le Président de la République,

Considérant :

Que, par le décret suprême n° 079-2015-PCM, publié le 12 novembre 2015, l'état d'urgence a été prorogé pour une durée de soixante (60) jours calendaires commençant le 22 novembre 2015 dans le district d'Echarate, situé dans la province de La Convención (département de Cusco);

Que, le décret suprême n° 085-2015-PCM du 10 décembre 2015 définit le domaine d'intervention des forces armées et de la Police nationale péruvienne dans la région de VRAEM qui se trouve actuellement en état d'urgence, et oriente leur mission vers la lutte contre les terroristes et contre le trafic de drogues et d'autres activités illicites, respectivement;

Qu'alors que le délai d'application de l'état d'urgence mentionné à l'alinéa précédent vient à expiration, que, selon la communication n° 07-2016-DIRGEN PNP/SA du 4 janvier 2016 du Directeur général de la Police nationale du Pérou, les circonstances ayant dicté la proclamation de l'état d'urgence dans la province et le district précités persistent, et qu'il y a donc lieu de le proroger afin de permettre à la Police nationale péruvienne, par sa présence et son intervention appropriée, de faire le nécessaire pour favoriser l'adhésion de la population aux buts et objectifs recherchés par le Gouvernement central, à savoir la consolidation de la paix dans la zone considérée et dans le pays;

Qu'aux termes du paragraphe 1 de l'article 137 de la Constitution politique du Pérou, l'état d'urgence se proroge par décret suprême;

Que par le décret législatif n° 1186, le décret législatif qui régit l'emploi de la force par la Police nationale péruvienne, l'emploi de la force dans l'exercice des fonctions policières ainsi que les niveaux, les circonstances et règles de conduite de l'emploi de la force sont définis;

Que le décret législatif n° 1095 définit les principes, formes, conditions et limites de l'emploi de la force par les forces armées dans les zones sous régime d'état d'urgence, la force coercitive devant être mise au service de l'exécution de leur mission constitutionnelle de protection de la société et de sauvegarde de l'état de droit sur le territoire national; et que Partie II établit les normes de l'emploi de la force dans d'autres situations violentes;

Conformément aux dispositions énoncées aux paragraphes 4 et 14 de l'article 118 de la Constitution politique du Pérou; et

Après avis favorable du Conseil des ministres, le Congrès de la République devant en être informé;

Décrète :

Article premier – Prorogation de l'état d'urgence

Est prorogé pour une durée de soixante (60) jours calendaires commençant le 21 janvier 2016 l'état d'urgence déclaré dans le district d'Echarate, situé dans la province de La Convención (département de Cusco).

Article 2 – Suspension de l'exercice des droits constitutionnels

Est suspendu, pendant la durée de l'état d'urgence déclaré à l'article premier et dans la circonscription y visée, l'exercice des droits constitutionnels relatifs à la liberté et à la sécurité de la personne, à l'inviolabilité du domicile et à la liberté de réunion et de circulation sur le territoire, garantis aux paragraphes 9, 11, 12 et 24 f) de l'article 2 de la Constitution politique du Pérou.

Article 3 – Maintien de l'ordre public

La Police nationale péruvienne assure le maintien de l'ordre public pendant toute la durée de l'état d'urgence prorogé à l'article premier du présent décret.

Les forces armées contribuent à la réalisation de cet objectif dans le district d'Echarate, situé dans la province de La Convención (département de Cusco).

Article 4 – De l'intervention des forces armées et de la Police nationale du Pérou

L'intervention des forces armées et de la Police nationale péruvienne obéit aux conditions prévues par le décret législatif n° 1095 et le décret législatif n° 1186, respectivement, ainsi que par le décret suprême n° 085-2015-PCM qui oriente leur mission vers la lutte contre les terroristes et contre le trafic de drogues et d'autres activités illicites.

Article 5 – Contreseing

Le présent décret suprême est contresigné par le Président du Conseil des ministres, le Ministre de la défense, le Ministre de l'intérieur et le Ministre de la justice et des droits de l'homme.

Fait au Palais présidentiel, à Lima, le 14 janvier deux mille seize.

Le Président de la République
Ollanta Humala Tasso

Pour le Président du Conseil des ministres,
La Ministre des relations extérieures
Ana María Sánchez De Ríos

Le Ministre de la défense
Jakke Valakivi Álvarez

Le Ministre de l'intérieur et
Pour le Ministre de la justice et des droits de l'homme
José Luis Pérez Guadalupe

NOTIFICATION UNDER ARTICLE 4 (3)

Peru

Notification deposited with the Secretary-General of the United Nations: 17 March 2016

Registration with the Secretariat of the United Nations: ex officio, 17 March 2016

NOTIFICATION EN VERTU DU PARAGRAPHE 3 DE L'ARTICLE 4

Pérou

Dépôt de la notification auprès du Secrétaire général de l'Organisation des Nations Unies : 17 mars 2016

Enregistrement au Secrétariat de l'Organisation des Nations Unies : d'office, 17 mars 2016

[TEXT IN SPANISH – TEXTE EN ESPAGNOL]

Misión Permanente del Perú ante las Naciones Unidas

Permanent Mission of Peru to the United Nations

7-1-SG/15

La Misión Permanente del Perú ante las Naciones Unidas presenta sus atentos saludos a la Secretaría General de las Naciones Unidas – Sección de Tratados de la Oficina de Asuntos Jurídicos, y en cumplimiento de lo dispuesto por el Artículo 4° del Pacto Internacional de Derechos Civiles y Políticos tiene a honra informar que, mediante Decreto Supremo N° 004-2016-PCM publicado el pasado 16 de enero, cuya copia se acompaña, se prorrogó por cuarenta y cinco días, a partir del 18 de enero de 2016, el Estado de Emergencia declarado en la Provincia Constitucional del Callao.

Cabe recordar que oportunamente esta Misión Permanente ha cumplido con informar a esa Secretaría General sobre la declaración del Estado de Emergencia en la localidad indicada, mediante Nota 7-1-SG/67 de fecha 11 de diciembre de 2015.

Durante el Estado de Emergencia quedan suspendidos los derechos relativos a la libertad y seguridad personales y la inviolabilidad de domicilio, contemplados en los incisos 9 y 24(f) del Artículo 2° de la Constitución Política del Perú, y en los Artículos 17° y 9° del Pacto Internacional de Derechos Civiles y Políticos, respectivamente, con el motivo de consolidar la pacificación de la zona y del país.

La Misión Permanente del Perú ante las Naciones Unidas aprovecha la oportunidad para renovar a la Secretaría General de las Naciones Unidas las seguridades de su más alta y distinguida consideración.

Nueva York, 16 de marzo de 2016

Prórroga de Estado de Emergencia declarado en la Provincia Constitucional del Callao

DECRETO SUPREMO
Nº 004-2016-PCM

EL PRESIDENTE DE LA REPÚBLICA

CONSIDERANDO:

Que, el artículo 44 de la Constitución Política del Perú, prevé que son deberes primordiales del Estado garantizar la plena vigencia de los derechos fundamentales, proteger a la población de las amenazas contra su seguridad y promover el bienestar general que se fundamenta en la justicia y en el desarrollo integral y equilibrado de la Nación;

Que, asimismo, el artículo 137 de la Carta Magna establece que el Presidente de la República, con acuerdo del Consejo de Ministros, puede decretar, por plazo determinado, en todo el territorio nacional o en parte de él, y dando cuenta al Congreso o a la Comisión Permanente, los estados de excepción señalados en dicho artículo, entre los cuales se encuentra el Estado de Emergencia, decretado en caso de perturbación de la paz o del orden interno, de catástrofe o de graves circunstancias que afecten la vida de la Nación, pudiendo restringirse o suspenderse el ejercicio de los derechos constitucionales relativos a la libertad y la seguridad personales, la inviolabilidad de domicilio, y la libertad de reunión y de tránsito en el territorio;

Que, es obligación del Gobierno Constitucional garantizar el derecho de los ciudadanos al orden, a la tranquilidad pública y a la seguridad;

Que, mediante Decreto Supremo N° 083-2015-PCM, publicado el 4 de diciembre de 2015, se declara por el término de cuarenta y cinco (45) días calendario, computado a partir de la fecha de publicación del acotado dispositivo, el Estado de Emergencia en la Provincia Constitucional del Callao, disponiendo que la Policía Nacional del Perú mantendrá el control del orden interno;

Que, mediante Oficio Nº 16-2016-DIRGEN PNP/SA, el Director General de la Policía Nacional del Perú recomienda que se prorrogue el Estado de Emergencia declarado por Decreto Supremo N° 083-2015-PCM, en la Provincia Constitucional del Callao, sustentando dicha petición en el Oficio Nº 002-2016-REGPOL-CALLAO/JEM-UNIPLO, del Jefe de la Región Policial Callao y en el Informe Nº 001-2016-REGPOL-CALLAO/JEM-UNIPLO, a fin de consolidar la lucha contra la inseguridad ciudadana y el crimen organizado en todas sus modalidades;

Que, el numeral 1) del artículo 137 de la Constitución Política del Perú establece que la prórroga del Estado de Emergencia requiere nuevo Decreto;

De conformidad con lo establecido en los numerales 4) y 14) del artículo 118, el numeral 1) del artículo 137 de la Constitución Política del Perú, y los literales b) y d) del numeral 2) del artículo 4 de la Ley Nº 29158, Ley Orgánica del Poder Ejecutivo; y,

Con el voto aprobatorio del Consejo de Ministros, y con cargo a dar cuenta al Congreso de la República;

DECRETA:

Artículo 1.- Prórroga del Estado de Emergencia
Prorrogar el Estado de Emergencia por el plazo de cuarenta y cinco (45) días calendario, a partir del 18 de enero de 2016, en la Provincia Constitucional del Callao. La Policía Nacional del Perú mantendrá el control del orden interno.

Artículo 2.- Suspensión del ejercicio de Derechos Constitucionales
Durante el Estado de Emergencia a que se refiere el artículo anterior y en la circunscripción señalada en el mismo, quedan suspendidos los derechos constitucionales relativos a la libertad y seguridad personales y la inviolabilidad de domicilio, comprendidos en los incisos 9) y 24) apartado f) del artículo 2 de la Constitución Política del Perú.

Artículo 3.- Refrendo
El presente Decreto Supremo será refrendado por el Presidente del Consejo de Ministros, el Ministro

del Interior y el Ministro de Justicia y Derechos Humanos.

Dado en la Casa de Gobierno, en Lima, a los quince días del mes de enero del año dos mil dieciséis.

OLLANTA HUMALA TASSO
Presidente de la República

ANA MARÍA SÁNCHEZ DE RÍOS
Ministra de Relaciones Exteriores
Encargada del Despacho de la
Presidencia del Consejo de Ministros

JOSÉ LUIS PÉREZ GUADALUPE
Ministro del Interior y
Encargado del Despacho del Ministerio
de Justicia y Derechos Humanos

1334805-1

[TRANSLATION – TRADUCTION]

The Permanent Mission of Peru to the United Nations presents its compliments to the Treaty Section of the Office of Legal Affairs, United Nations Secretariat, and, in accordance with article 4 of the International Covenant on Civil and Political Rights, has the honour to inform it that, by Supreme Decree No. 004-2016-PCM issued on 16 January 2016 (copy attached), the state of emergency declared in the Constitutional Province of Callao has been extended for 45 days, with effect from 18 January 2016.

It should be recalled that the Permanent Mission has duly reported to the Secretariat the declaration of a state of emergency in the aforementioned locality though note No. 7-1-SG/67 dated 11 December 2015.

During the state of emergency, the rights relating to liberty and security of person and the inviolability of the home, recognized in article 2, paragraphs 9 and 24 (f), of the Political Constitution of Peru and in articles 17 and 9 of the International Covenant on Civil and Political Rights, respectively, are suspended in order to consolidate peace in the area and in the country.

The Permanent Mission of Peru to the United Nations takes this opportunity to convey to the Secretariat the renewed assurances of its highest consideration.

New York, 16 March 2016

Extension of the state of emergency declared in the Constitutional Province of Callao

Supreme Decree No. 004-2016-PCM

The President of the Republic

Considering:

That article 44 of the Political Constitution of Peru provides that the primary duties of the State include guaranteeing the full enjoyment of fundamental rights, protecting the population from security threats and promoting the general welfare based on justice and the comprehensive and balanced development of the nation;

That, furthermore, article 137 of the Constitution provides that the President of the Republic may, with the consent of the Council of Ministers and upon notifying Congress or the Standing Committee, declare the states of emergency stipulated therein, for a fixed duration and throughout the national territory or in a part thereof, including a state of emergency declared in the event of a disturbance of the peace or public order, a disaster, or serious circumstances affecting the life of the nation, during which time the exercise of the constitutional rights of liberty and security of person, inviolability of the home, freedom of assembly and freedom of movement in the territory may be restricted or suspended;

That the constitutional Government has an obligation to guarantee the right of citizens to order, public peace and security;

That, by Supreme Decree No. 083-2015-PCM, issued on 4 December 2015, a state of emergency was declared in the Constitutional Province of Callao for a period of forty-five (45) calendar days, with effect from the date of issuance of that instrument, which provides that the National Police of Peru shall maintain control of public order.

That, by means of note No. 16-2016-DIRGEN PNP/SA, the Director General of the National Police of Peru recommended that the state of emergency declared by Supreme Decree No. 083-2015-PCM in the Constitutional Province of Callao be extended, basing that request on note No. 002-2016-REGPOL-CALLAO/JEM-UNIPLO, from the chief of the Callao Police Region, and report No. 001-2016-REGPOL-CALLAO/JEM-UNIPLO, in order to strengthen efforts against public insecurity and organized crimes in all its forms;

That article 137, paragraph 1, of the Political Constitution of Peru provides that the extension of a state of emergency requires a new decree;

In accordance with article 118, paragraphs 4 and 14, and article 137, paragraph 1, of the Political Constitution of Peru, and article 4, paragraphs 2 (b) and 2 (d), of Act No. 29158, Organic Law of the Executive Branch; and

With the approval of the Council of Ministers and subject to notification of the Congress of the Republic;

Hereby decrees:

Article 1: Extension of the state of emergency

The state of emergency in the Constitutional Province of Callao is hereby extended for a period of forty-five (45) calendar days, with effect from 18 January 2016. The National Police of Peru shall maintain public order.

Article 2: Suspension of constitutional rights

During the state of emergency and in the location referred to in the preceding article, the constitutional rights relating to liberty and security of person and the inviolability of the home, recognized in article 2, paragraphs 9 and 24 (f), of the Political Constitution of Peru, shall be suspended.

Article 3: Endorsement

The present Supreme Decree shall be endorsed by the President of the Council of Ministers, the Minister of the Interior and the Minister of Justice and Human Rights.

Done at Government House, Lima, on 15 January 2016.

Ollanta Humala Tasso
Constitutional President of the Republic

Ana María Sánchez de Ríos
Minister for Foreign Affairs
Acting President of the Council of Ministers

José Luis Pérez Guadalupe
Minister of the Interior and
Acting Minister of Justice and Human Rights

[TRANSLATION – TRADUCTION]

La Mission permanente du Pérou auprès de l'Organisation des Nations Unies présente ses compliments à la Section des traités du Bureau des affaires juridiques du Secrétariat de l'Organisation et, en application des dispositions de l'article 4 du Pacte international relatif aux droits civils et politiques, a l'honneur de l'informer que le décret suprême n° 004-2016-PCM, publié le 16 janvier 2016 et dont le texte est joint à la présente, proroge, pour une durée de 45 jours commençant le 18 janvier 2016, l'état d'urgence déclaré dans la province constitutionnelle du Callao.

Il convient de rappeler que la Mission permanente a dûment informé le Secrétariat de la déclaration de l'état d'urgence dans le lieu indiqué par note 7-1-SG/67 du 11 décembre 2015.

Est suspendu, pendant la durée de l'état d'urgence et afin de consolider la pacification de la zone considérée et du pays, l'exercice des droits relatifs à la liberté et à la sécurité de la personne et à l'inviolabilité du domicile consacrés aux paragraphes 9 et 24 f) de l'article 2 de la Constitution politique du Pérou et aux articles 17 et 9 du Pacte international relatif aux droits civils et politiques, respectivement.

La Mission permanente du Pérou auprès de l'Organisation des Nations Unies saisit cette occasion pour renouveler au Secrétariat de l'Organisation les assurances de sa très haute considération.

New York, le 16 mars 2016

Prorogation de l'état d'urgence déclaré dans la province constitutionnelle du Callao

Décret suprême n° 004-2016-PCM

Le Président de la République,

Considérant :

Que l'article 44 de la Constitution politique du Pérou dispose que l'État est tenu de garantir la pleine jouissance des droits fondamentaux, de protéger la population des risques menaçant sa sécurité et de veiller au bien-être général, fondé sur la justice et le développement intégral et équilibré de la nation;

Que l'article 137 de la Constitution dispose que le Président de la République peut décréter, avec l'accord du Conseil des ministres et l'obligation d'en informer le Congrès et la Commission permanente, pour une durée déterminée, dans la totalité ou une partie du territoire national, les régimes d'exception y visés, notamment l'état d'urgence, décrété en cas de perturbation de la paix ou de l'ordre public, de catastrophe ou de situation grave troublant la vie de la nation, durant lequel peut être restreint ou suspendu l'exercice des droits constitutionnels relatifs à la liberté et à la sécurité de la personne, à l'inviolabilité du domicile et à la liberté de réunion et de circulation sur le territoire;

Que le Gouvernement est tenu de garantir le droit des citoyens à l'ordre, la tranquillité publique et la sécurité.

Que, par le décret suprême n° 083-2015-PCM publié le 4 décembre 2015, un état d'urgence a été déclaré dans la province constitutionnelle du Callao pour une durée de quarante-cinq (45) jours calendaires à compter du jour de la publication dudit instrument, disposant que la Police nationale du Pérou maintiendra le contrôle de l'ordre public;

Que, par sa communication n° 16-2016-DIRGEN PNP/SA, le Directeur général de la Police nationale du Pérou a recommandé que soit prorogé l'état d'urgence déclaré par décret suprême n° 083-2015-PCM dans la province constitutionnelle du Callao afin de renforcer la lutte contre l'insécurité des citoyens et la criminalité organisée sous toute ses formes, fondant sa demande sur la communication n° 002-2016-REGPOL-CALLAO-JEM-UNIPLO du chef de la police de la région du Callao et sur le rapport n° 001-2016-REGPOL-CALLAO/JEM-UNIPLO;

Qu'aux termes du paragraphe 1 de l'article 137 de la Constitution politique du Pérou, l'état d'urgence se proroge par décret;

Conformément aux dispositions énoncées aux paragraphes 4 et 14 de l'article 118 et au paragraphe 1 de l'article 137 de la Constitution politique du Pérou, et aux alinéas b) et d) du paragraphe 2 de l'article 4 de la loi n° 29158 (loi relative à l'organisation du pouvoir exécutif); et

Après avis favorable du Conseil des ministres, le Congrès de la République devant en être informé;

Décrète :

Article premier - Prorogation de l'état d'urgence

Est prorogé pour une durée de quarante-cinq (45) jours calendaires, à compter du 18 janvier 2016, l'état d'urgence dans la province constitutionnelle du Callao. La Police nationale péruvienne maintiendra l'ordre public.

Article 2 -Suspension de l'exercice des droits constitutionnels

Est suspendu, pendant la durée de l'état d'urgence déclaré à l'article premier et dans la circonscription y visée, l'exercice des droits constitutionnels relatifs à la liberté et à la sécurité de la personne et à l'inviolabilité du domicile, garantis aux paragraphes 9 et 24 f) de l'article 2 de la Constitution politique du Pérou.

Article 3 - Contreseing

Le présent décret suprême est contresigné par le Président du Conseil des ministres, le Ministre de l'intérieur et le Ministre de la justice et des droits de l'homme.

Fait au Palais présidentiel, à Lima, le quinze janvier deux mille seize.

Le Président de la République
Ollanta Humala Tasso

Pour le Président du Conseil des ministres,
La Ministre des relations extérieures
Ana María Sánchez De Ríos

Le Ministre de l'intérieur et
Pour le Ministre de la justice et des droits de l'homme
José Luis Pérez Guadalupe

NOTIFICATION UNDER ARTICLE 4 (3)

Peru

Notification deposited with the Secretary-General of the United Nations: 21 March 2016

Registration with the Secretariat of the United Nations: ex officio, 21 March 2016

NOTIFICATION EN VERTU DU PARAGRAPHE 3 DE L'ARTICLE 4

Pérou

Dépôt de la notification auprès du Secrétaire général de l'Organisation des Nations Unies : 21 mars 2016

Enregistrement au Secrétariat de l'Organisation des Nations Unies : d'office, 21 mars 2016

[TEXT IN SPANISH – TEXTE EN ESPAGNOL]

Misión Permanente del Perú
ante las Naciones Unidas

Permanent Mission of Peru to
the United Nations

7-1-SG/17

La Misión Permanente del Perú ante las Naciones Unidas presenta sus atentos saludos a la Secretaría General de las Naciones Unidas – Sección de Tratados de la Oficina de Asuntos Jurídicos, y en cumplimiento de lo dispuesto por el Artículo 4° del Pacto Internacional de Derechos Civiles y Políticos tiene a honra informar que, mediante Decreto Supremo N° 013-2016-PCM publicado el pasado 2 de marzo, cuya copia se acompaña, se prorrogó por cuarenta y cinco días, a partir del 3 de marzo del 2016, el Estado de Emergencia declarado en la Provincia Constitucional del Callao.

Cabe recordar que oportunamente esta Misión Permanente ha cumplido con informar a esa Secretaría General sobre la prórroga al Estado de Emergencia declarado en la localidad indicada, mediante Nota 7-1-SG/15 de fecha 16 de marzo de 2015.

Durante el Estado de Emergencia quedan suspendidos los derechos relativos a la libertad y seguridad personales y la inviolabilidad de domicilio, contemplados en los incisos 9 y 24(f) del Artículo 2° de la Constitución Política del Perú, y en los Artículos 17° y 9° del Pacto Internacional de Derechos Civiles y Políticos, respectivamente, con el motivo de consolidar la pacificación de la zona y del país.

La Misión Permanente del Perú ante las Naciones Unidas aprovecha la oportunidad para renovar a la Secretaría General de las Naciones Unidas las seguridades de su más alta y distinguida consideración.

Nueva York, 21 de marzo de 2016

Prórroga de Estado de Emergencia declarado en la Provincia Constitucional del Callao

DECRETO SUPREMO
Nº 013-2016-PCM

EL PRESIDENTE DE LA REPÚBLICA

CONSIDERANDO:

Que, el artículo 44 de la Constitución Política del Perú, prevé que son deberes primordiales del Estado garantizar la plena vigencia de los derechos fundamentales, proteger a la población de las amenazas contra su seguridad y promover el bienestar general que se fundamenta en la justicia y en el desarrollo integral y equilibrado de la Nación;

Que, asimismo, el artículo 137 de la Carta Magna establece que el Presidente de la República, con acuerdo del Consejo de Ministros, puede decretar, por plazo determinado, en todo el territorio nacional o en parte de él, y dando cuenta al Congreso o a la Comisión Permanente, los estados de excepción señalados en dicho artículo, entre los cuales se encuentra el Estado de Emergencia, decretado en caso de perturbación de la paz o del orden interno, de catástrofe o de graves circunstancias que afecten la vida de la Nación, pudiendo restringirse o suspenderse el ejercicio de los derechos constitucionales relativos a la libertad y la seguridad personales, la inviolabilidad de domicilio, y la libertad de reunión y de tránsito en el territorio;

Que, es obligación del Gobierno Constitucional garantizar el derecho de los ciudadanos al orden, a la tranquilidad pública y a la seguridad;

Que, mediante Decreto Supremo Nº 083-2015-PCM, publicado el 4 de diciembre de 2015, se declara por el término de cuarenta y cinco (45) días calendario, computado a partir de la fecha de publicación del acotado dispositivo, el Estado de Emergencia en la Provincia Constitucional del Callao, disponiendo que la Policía Nacional del Perú mantendrá el control del orden interno;

Que, posteriormente con Decreto Supremo Nº004-2016-PCM, publicado el 16 de enero de 2016, se prorrogó el estado de emergencia declarado en la Provincia Constitucional del Callao Provincia Constitucional del Callao, por cuarenta y cinco (45) días calendario adicionales, a partir del 18 de enero de 2016;

Que, mediante Oficio Nº 146-2016-DGPNP/SA, el Director General de la Policía Nacional del Perú recomienda que se prorrogue el Estado de Emergencia declarado por Decreto Supremo Nº 083-2015-PCM, en la Provincia Constitucional del Callao, sustentando dicha petición en el Oficio Nº 52-2016-REGPOL-CALLAO/JEM-UNIPLO, del Jefe de la Región Policial Callao y en el Informe Nº 023-2016-REGPOL-CALLAO/JEM-UNIPLO, a fin de consolidar la lucha contra la inseguridad ciudadana y el crimen organizado en todas sus modalidades;

Que, el numeral 1) del artículo 137 de la Constitución Política del Perú establece que la prórroga del Estado de Emergencia requiere nuevo Decreto;

De conformidad con lo establecido en los numerales 4) y 14) del artículo 118, el numeral 1) del artículo 137 de la Constitución Política del Perú, y los literales b) y d) del numeral 2) del artículo 4 de la Ley Nº 29158, Ley Orgánica del Poder Ejecutivo; y,

Con el voto aprobatorio del Consejo de Ministros, y con cargo a dar cuenta al Congreso de la República,

DECRETA:

Artículo 1.- Prórroga del Estado de Emergencia

Prorrogar el Estado de Emergencia por el plazo de cuarenta y cinco (45) días calendario, a partir del 3 de marzo de 2016, en la Provincia Constitucional del Callao. La Policía Nacional del Perú mantendrá el control del orden interno.

Artículo 2.- Suspensión del ejercicio de Derechos Constitucionales

Durante el Estado de Emergencia a que se refiere el artículo anterior y en la circunscripción señalada en el mismo, quedan suspendidos los derechos constitucionales relativos a la libertad y seguridad personales y la inviolabilidad de domicilio, comprendidos en los incisos 9) y 24) apartado f) del artículo 2 de la Constitución Política del Perú.

Artículo 3.- Refrendo

El presente Decreto Supremo será refrendado por el Presidente del Consejo de Ministros, el Ministro del Interior y el Ministro de Justicia y Derechos Humanos.

Dado en la Casa de Gobierno, en Lima, al primer día del mes de marzo del año dos mil dieciséis.

OLLANTA HUMALA TASSO
Presidente de la República

PEDRO CATERIANO BELLIDO
Presidente del Consejo de Ministros

JOSÉ LUIS PÉREZ GUADALUPE
Ministro del Interior

ALDO VÁSQUEZ RÍOS
Ministro de Justicia y Derechos Humanos

[TRANSLATION – TRADUCTION]

The Permanent Mission of Peru to the United Nations presents its compliments to the Treaty Section of the Office of Legal Affairs, United Nations Secretariat, and, in accordance with article 4 of the International Covenant on Civil and Political Rights, has the honour to inform it that, by Supreme Decree No. 013-2016-PCM issued on 2 March 2016 (copy attached), the state of emergency declared in the Constitutional Province of Callao has been extended for 45 days, with effect from 3 March 2016.

It should be recalled that the Permanent Mission has duly reported to the Secretariat the extension of the state of emergency in the aforementioned locality though note No. 7-1-SG/15 dated 16 March 2016.

During the state of emergency, the rights relating to liberty and security of person and the inviolability of the home, recognized in article 2, paragraphs 9 and 24 (f), of the Political Constitution of Peru and in articles 17 and 9 of the International Covenant on Civil and Political Rights, respectively, are suspended in order to consolidate peace in the area and in the country.

The Permanent Mission of Peru to the United Nations takes this opportunity to convey to the Secretariat the renewed assurances of its highest consideration.

New York, 21 March 2016

Extension of the state of emergency declared in the Constitutional Province of Callao

Supreme Decree No. 013-2016-PCM

The President of the Republic

Considering:

That article 44 of the Political Constitution of Peru provides that the primary duties of the State include guaranteeing the full enjoyment of fundamental rights, protecting the population from security threats and promoting the general welfare based on justice and the comprehensive and balanced development of the nation;

That, furthermore, article 137 of the Constitution provides that the President of the Republic may, with the consent of the Council of Ministers and upon notifying Congress or the Standing Committee, declare the states of emergency stipulated therein, for a fixed duration and throughout the national territory or in a part thereof, including a state of emergency declared in the event of a disturbance of the peace or public order, a disaster, or serious circumstances affecting the life of the nation, during which time the exercise of the constitutional rights of liberty and security of person, inviolability of the home, freedom of assembly and freedom of movement in the territory may be restricted or suspended;

That the constitutional Government has an obligation to guarantee the right of citizens to order, public peace and security;

That, by Supreme Decree No. 083-2015-PCM, issued on 4 December 2015, a state of emergency was declared in the Constitutional Province of Callao for a period of forty-five (45) calendar days, with effect from the date of issuance of that instrument, which provides that the National Police of Peru shall maintain control of public order.

That, subsequently by Supreme Decree No. 004-2016-PCM, issued on 16 January 2016, the state of emergency declared in the Constitutional Province of Callao was extended for an additional period of forty-five (45) calendar days, with effect from 18 January 2016.

That, by means of note No. 146-2016-DGPNP/SA, the Director General of the National Police of Peru recommended that the state of emergency declared by Supreme Decree No. 083-2015-PCM in the Constitutional Province of Callao be extended, basing that request on note No. 52-2016-REGPOL-CALLAO/JEM-UNIPLO, from the chief of the Callao Police Region, and report No. 023-2016-REGPOL-CALLAO/JEM-UNIPLO, in order to strengthen efforts against public insecurity and organized crimes in all its forms;

That article 137, paragraph 1, of the Political Constitution of Peru provides that the extension of a state of emergency requires a new decree;

In accordance with article 118, paragraphs 4 and 14, and article 137, paragraph 1, of the Political Constitution of Peru, and article 4, paragraphs 2 (b) and 2 (d), of Act No. 29158, Organic Law of the Executive Branch; and

With the approval of the Council of Ministers and subject to notification of the Congress of the Republic;

Hereby decrees:

Article 1: Extension of the state of emergency

The state of emergency in the Constitutional Province of Callao is hereby extended for a period of forty-five (45) calendar days, with effect from 3 March 2016. The National Police of Peru shall maintain public order.

Article 2: Suspension of constitutional rights

During the state of emergency and in the location referred to in the preceding article, the constitutional rights relating to liberty and security of person and the inviolability of the home, recognized in article 2, paragraphs 9 and 24 (f), of the Political Constitution of Peru, shall be suspended.

Article 3: Endorsement

The present Supreme Decree shall be endorsed by the President of the Council of Ministers, the Minister of the Interior and the Minister of Justice and Human Rights.

Done at Government House, Lima, on 1 March 2016.

Ollanta Humala Tasso
Constitutional President of the Republic

Pedro Cateriano Bellido
President of the Council of Ministers

José Luis Pérez Guadalupe
Minister of the Interior

Aldo Vásquez Ríos
Minister of Justice and Human Rights

[TRANSLATION – TRADUCTION]

La Mission permanente du Pérou auprès de l'Organisation des Nations Unies présente ses compliments à la Section des traités du Bureau des affaires juridiques du Secrétariat de l'Organisation et, en application des dispositions de l'article 4 du Pacte international relatif aux droits civils et politiques, a l'honneur de l'informer que le décret suprême n° 013-2016-PCM, publié le 2 mars 2016 et dont le texte est joint à la présente, proroge, pour une durée de 45 jours commençant le 3 mars 2016, l'état d'urgence déclaré dans la province constitutionnelle du Callao.

Il convient de rappeler que la Mission permanente a dûment informé le Secrétariat de la prorogation de l'état d'urgence dans le lieu indiqué par note 7-1-SG/15 du 16 mars 2016.

Est suspendu, pendant la durée de l'état d'urgence et afin de consolider la pacification de la zone considérée et du pays, l'exercice des droits relatifs à la liberté et à la sécurité de la personne et à l'inviolabilité du domicile consacrés aux paragraphes 9 et 24 f) de l'article 2 de la Constitution politique du Pérou et aux articles 17 et 9 du Pacte international relatif aux droits civils et politiques, respectivement.

La Mission permanente du Pérou auprès de l'Organisation des Nations Unies saisit cette occasion pour renouveler au Secrétariat de l'Organisation les assurances de sa très haute considération.

New York, le 21 mars 2016

Prorogation de l'état d'urgence déclaré dans la province constitutionnelle du Callao

Décret suprême n° 013-2016-PCM

Le Président de la République,

Considérant :

Que l'article 44 de la Constitution politique du Pérou dispose que l'État est tenu de garantir la pleine jouissance des droits fondamentaux, de protéger la population des risques menaçant sa sécurité et de veiller au bien-être général, fondé sur la justice et le développement intégral et équilibré de la nation;

Que l'article 137 de la Constitution dispose que le Président de la République peut décréter, avec l'accord du Conseil des ministres et l'obligation d'en informer le Congrès et la Commission permanente, pour une durée déterminée, dans la totalité ou une partie du territoire national, les régimes d'exception y visés, notamment l'état d'urgence, décrété en cas de perturbation de la paix ou de l'ordre public, de catastrophe ou de situation grave troublant la vie de la nation, durant lequel peut être restreint ou suspendu l'exercice des droits constitutionnels relatifs à la liberté et à la sécurité de la personne, à l'inviolabilité du domicile et à la liberté de réunion et de circulation sur le territoire;

Que le Gouvernement est tenu de garantir le droit des citoyens à l'ordre, la tranquillité publique et la sécurité.

Que, par le décret suprême n° 083-2015-PCM publié le 4 décembre 2015, un état d'urgence a été déclaré dans la province constitutionnelle du Callao pour une durée de quarante-cinq (45) jours calendaires à compter du jour de la publication dudit instrument, disposant que la Police nationale du Pérou maintiendra le contrôle de l'ordre public;

Que, par la suite, par décret suprême n° 004-2016-PCM publié le 16 janvier 2016, l'état d'urgence dans la province constitutionnelle du Callao a été prorogé pour une durée supplémentaire de quarante-cinq (45) jours calendaires à compter du 18 janvier 2016;

Que, par sa communication n° 146-2016-DGPNP/SA, le Directeur général de la Police nationale du Pérou a recommandé que soit prorogé l'état d'urgence déclaré par décret suprême n° 083-2015-PCM dans la province constitutionnelle du Callao afin de renforcer la lutte contre l'insécurité des citoyens et la criminalité organisée sous toute ses formes, fondant sa demande sur la communication n° 52-2016-REGPOL-CALLAO/JEM-UNIPLO du chef de la police de la région du Callao et sur le rapport n° 023-2016-REGPOL-CALLAO/JEM-UNIPLO;

Qu'aux termes du paragraphe 1 de l'article 137 de la Constitution politique du Pérou, l'état d'urgence se proroge par décret;

Conformément aux dispositions énoncées aux paragraphes 4 et 14 de l'article 118 et au paragraphe 1 de l'article 137 de la Constitution politique du Pérou, et aux alinéas b) et d) du paragraphe 2 de l'article 4 de la loi n° 29158 (loi relative à l'organisation du pouvoir exécutif); et

Après avis favorable du Conseil des ministres, le Congrès de la République devant en être informé;

Décrète :

Article premier - Prorogation de l'état d'urgence

Est prorogé pour une durée de quarante-cinq (45) jours calendaires, à compter du 3 mars 2016, l'état d'urgence dans la province constitutionnelle du Callao. La Police nationale péruvienne maintiendra l'ordre public.

Article 2 -Suspension de l'exercice des droits constitutionnels

Est suspendu, pendant la durée de l'état d'urgence déclaré à l'article premier et dans la circonscription y visée, l'exercice des droits constitutionnels relatifs à la liberté et à la sécurité de la personne et à l'inviolabilité du domicile, garantis aux paragraphes 9 et 24 f) de l'article 2 de la Constitution politique du Pérou.

Article 3 - Contreseing

Le présent décret suprême est contresigné par le Président du Conseil des ministres, le Ministre de l'intérieur et le Ministre de la justice et des droits de l'homme.

Fait au Palais présidentiel, à Lima, le 1er mars deux mille seize.

Le Président de la République
Ollanta Humala Tasso

Le Président du Conseil des ministres
Pedro Cateriano Bellido

Le Ministre de l'intérieur
José Luis Pérez Guadalupe

Le Ministre de la justice et des droits de l'homme
Aldo Vásquez Ríos

No. 15705. Multilateral

CONVENTION ON ROAD TRAFFIC. VIENNA, 8 NOVEMBER 1968
[*United Nations, Treaty Series, vol. 1042, I-15705.*]

AMENDMENTS TO ARTICLES 8 AND 39 OF THE CONVENTION ON ROAD TRAFFIC. GENEVA, 23 SEPTEMBER 2015

Entry into force: 23 March 2016

Authentic texts: English and French

Registration with the Secretariat of the United Nations: ex officio, 23 March 2016

Not published in print, in accordance with article 12(2) of the General Assembly regulations to give effect to Article 102 of the Charter of the United Nations, as amended, and the publication practice of the Secretariat.

Nº 15705. Multilatéral

CONVENTION SUR LA CIRCULATION ROUTIÈRE. VIENNE, 8 NOVEMBRE 1968
[*Nations Unies, Recueil des Traités, vol. 1042, I-15705.*]

AMENDEMENTS AUX ARTICLES 8 ET 39 DE LA CONVENTION SUR LA CIRCULATION ROUTIÈRE. GENÈVE, 23 SEPTEMBRE 2015

Entrée en vigueur : 23 mars 2016

Textes authentiques : anglais et français

Enregistrement au Secrétariat de l'Organisation des Nations Unies : d'office, 23 mars 2016

Non disponible en version imprimée, conformément au paragraphe 2 de l'article 12 du règlement de l'Assemblée générale destiné à mettre en application l'Article 102 de la Charte des Nations Unies, tel qu'amendé, et à la pratique du Secrétariat en matière de publication.

No. 16908. Multilateral

CONVENTION FOR THE PROTECTION OF THE MEDITERRANEAN SEA AGAINST POLLUTION (WITH ANNEX AND PROTOCOL FOR THE PREVENTION OF POLLUTION OF THE MEDITERRANEAN SEA BY DUMPING FROM SHIPS AND AIRCRAFT AND PROTOCOL CONCERNING CO-OPERATION IN COMBATING POLLUTION OF THE MEDITERRANEAN SEA BY OIL AND OTHER HARMFUL SUBSTANCES IN CASES OF EMERGENCY). BARCELONA, 16 FEBRUARY 1976 [*United Nations, Treaty Series, vol. 1102, I-16908.*]

AMENDMENTS TO THE CONVENTION FOR THE PROTECTION OF THE MEDITERRANEAN SEA AGAINST POLLUTION (WITH FINAL ACT). BARCELONA, 10 JUNE 1995 [*United Nations, Treaty Series, vol. 2942, A-16908.*]

RATIFICATION

Lebanon

Deposit of instrument with the Government of Spain: 22 April 2009

Date of effect: 22 May 2009

Registration with the Secretariat of the United Nations: Spain, 29 March 2016

Nº 16908. Multilatéral

CONVENTION POUR LA PROTECTION DE LA MER MÉDITERRANÉE CONTRE LA POLLUTION (AVEC ANNEXE ET PROTOCOLE RELATIF À LA PRÉVENTION DE LA POLLUTION DE LA MER MÉDITERRANÉE PAR LES OPÉRATIONS D'IMMERSION EFFECTUÉES PAR LES NAVIRES ET AÉRONEFS ET PROTOCOLE RELATIF À LA COOPÉRATION EN MATIÈRE DE LUTTE CONTRE LA POLLUTION DE LA MER MÉDITERRANÉE PAR LES HYDROCARBURES ET AUTRES SUBSTANCES NUISIBLES EN CAS DE SITUATION CRITIQUE). BARCELONE, 16 FÉVRIER 1976 [*Nations Unies, Recueil des Traités, vol. 1102, I-16908.*]

AMENDEMENTS À LA CONVENTION POUR LA PROTECTION DE LA MER MÉDITERRANÉE CONTRE LA POLLUTION (AVEC ACTE FINAL). BARCELONE, 10 JUIN 1995 [*Nations Unies, Recueil des Traités, vol. 2942, A-16908.*]

RATIFICATION

Liban

Dépôt de l'instrument auprès du Gouvernement espagnol : 22 avril 2009

Date de prise d'effet : 22 mai 2009

Enregistrement au Secrétariat de l'Organisation des Nations Unies : Espagne, 29 mars 2016

No. 20337. Federal Republic of Germany and France

AGREEMENT BETWEEN THE GOVERNMENT OF THE FEDERAL REPUBLIC OF GERMANY AND THE GOVERNMENT OF THE FRENCH REPUBLIC ON EXEMPTION FROM CERTAIN PRIOR EDUCATIONAL REQUIREMENTS FOR ADMISSION TO UNIVERSITY COURSES IN THE HUMANITIES AND NATURAL SCIENCES IN THE PARTNER COUNTRY. BONN, 10 JULY 1980 [*United Nations, Treaty Series, vol. 1247, I-20337.*]

Termination in accordance with:

53539. Agreement between the Government of the Federal Republic of Germany and the Government of the French Republic concerning the recognition of qualifications, degrees and periods of study in the higher education sector (with annex). Berlin, 31 March 2015 [*United Nations, Treaty Series, vol. 3114, I-53539.*]

Entry into force: 27 October 2015

Registration with the Secretariat of the United Nations: Germany, 4 March 2016

Information provided by the Secretariat of the United Nations: 4 March 2016

N° 20337. République fédérale d'Allemagne et France

ACCORD ENTRE LE GOUVERNEMENT DE LA RÉPUBLIQUE FRANÇAISE ET LE GOUVERNEMENT DE LA RÉPUBLIQUE FÉDÉRALE D'ALLEMAGNE SUR LES DISPENSES DE SCOLARITÉ, D'EXAMENS ET DE DIPLÔMES POUR L'ADMISSION AUX ÉTUDES UNIVERSITAIRES DANS LE PAYS PARTENAIRE EN SCIENCES, LETTRES ET SCIENCES HUMAINES. BONN, 10 JUILLET 1980 [*Nations Unies, Recueil des Traités, vol. 1247, I-20337.*]

Abrogation conformément à :

53539. Accord entre le Gouvernement de la République fédérale d'Allemagne et le Gouvernement de la République française sur la reconnaissance des diplômes, des grades et des périodes d'études de l'enseignement supérieur (avec annexe). Berlin, 31 mars 2015 [*Nations Unies, Recueil des Traités, vol. 3114, I-53539.*]

Entrée en vigueur : 27 octobre 2015

Enregistrement au Secrétariat de l'Organisation des Nations Unies : Allemagne, 4 mars 2016

Information fournie par le Secrétariat de l'Organisation des Nations Unies : 4 mars 2016

No. 20378. Multilateral

CONVENTION ON THE ELIMINATION OF ALL FORMS OF DISCRIMINATION AGAINST WOMEN. NEW YORK, 18 DECEMBER 1979 [*United Nations, Treaty Series, vol. 1249, I-20378.*]

TERRITORIAL APPLICATION IN RESPECT OF ANGUILLA AND THE CAYMAN ISLANDS (WITH RESERVATION)

United Kingdom of Great Britain and Northern Ireland

Notification deposited with the Secretary-General of the United Nations: 16 March 2016

Registration with the Secretariat of the United Nations: ex officio, 16 March 2016

N° 20378. Multilatéral

CONVENTION SUR L'ÉLIMINATION DE TOUTES LES FORMES DE DISCRIMINATION À L'ÉGARD DES FEMMES. NEW YORK, 18 DÉCEMBRE 1979 [*Nations Unies, Recueil des Traités, vol. 1249, I-20378.*]

APPLICATION TERRITORIALE À L'ÉGARD D'ANGUILLA ET DES ÎLES CAÏMANES (AVEC RÉSERVE)

Royaume-Uni de Grande-Bretagne et d'Irlande du Nord

Dépôt de la notification auprès du Secrétaire général de l'Organisation des Nations Unies : 16 mars 2016

Enregistrement au Secrétariat de l'Organisation des Nations Unies : d'office, 16 mars 2016

Reservation:

Réserve :

[TEXT IN ENGLISH – TEXTE EN ANGLAIS]

"The Cayman Islands reserves the right to continue to apply such immigration legislation governing entry into, stay in, and departure from, the Cayman Islands as it may deem necessary from time to time and, accordingly, its acceptance of Article 15 (4) and of the other provisions of the Convention is subject to the provisions of any such legislation as regards persons not at the time having the right under the laws of the Cayman Islands to enter and remain in the Cayman Islands."

[TRANSLATION – TRADUCTION]

Les Îles Caïmanes se réservent le droit de continuer d'appliquer les lois sur l'immigration régissant l'admission et le séjour aux Îles Caïmanes et le départ des Îles Caïmanes qu'ils pourront juger nécessaires et, en conséquence, acceptent la disposition énoncée au paragraphe 4 de l'article 15 et les autres dispositions de la Convention, sous réserve des dispositions desdites lois applicables aux personnes qui, au moment considéré, n'ont pas le droit d'entrer et de demeurer aux Îles Caïmanes en vertu de la législation du pays.

No. 21934. Finland and Luxembourg

Nº 21934. Finlande et Luxembourg

CONVENTION FOR THE AVOIDANCE OF DOUBLE TAXATION WITH RESPECT TO TAXES ON INCOME AND ON CAPITAL. LUXEMBOURG, 1 MARCH 1982 [*United Nations, Treaty Series, vol. 1317, I-21934.*]

CONVENTION TENDANT À ÉVITER LES DOUBLES IMPOSITIONS EN MATIÈRE D'IMPÔTS SUR LE REVENU ET SUR LA FORTUNE. LUXEMBOURG, 1ER MARS 1982 [*Nations Unies, Recueil des Traités, vol. 1317, I-21934.*]

PROTOCOL BETWEEN FINLAND AND LUXEMBOURG FOR AMENDING THE AGREEMENT FOR THE AVOIDANCE OF DOUBLE TAXATION WITH RESPECT TO TAXES ON INCOME. LUXEMBOURG, 1 JULY 2009

AVENANT EN VUE DE MODIFIER LA CONVENTION ENTRE LA FINLANDE ET LE LUXEMBOURG TENDANT À ÉVITER LES DOUBLES IMPOSITIONS EN MATIÈRE D'IMPÔTS SUR LE REVENU ET SUR LA FORTUNE. LUXEMBOURG, 1ER JUILLET 2009

Entry into force: 12 April 2010, in accordance with article 26

Authentic texts: Finnish and French

Registration with the Secretariat of the United Nations: Finland, 9 March 2016

Entrée en vigueur : 12 avril 2010, conformément à l'article 26

Textes authentiques : finnois et français

Enregistrement au Secrétariat de l'Organisation des Nations Unies : Finlande, 9 mars 2016

[TEXT IN FINNISH – TEXTE EN FINNOIS]

PÖYTÄKIRJA
SUOMEN JA LUXEMBURGIN VÄLILLÄ TULO- JA VARALLISUUSVEROJA (OSKEVAN KAKSINKERTAISEN VEROTUKSEN VÄLTTÄMISEKSI TEHDYN SOPIMUKSEN MUUTTAMISESTA

Suomen tasavallan hallitus ja Luxemburgin suurherttuakunnan hallitus,

jotka haluavat tehdä pöytäkirjan Suomen ja Luxemburgin välillä Luxemburgissa 1 ıivänä maaliskuuta 1982 tulo- ja varallisuusveroja koskevan kaksinkertaisen verotuksen .lttämiseksi tehdyn sopimuksen (jäljempänä "Sopimus"), sellaisena kuin se on muutettuna ıxemburgissa 24 päivänä tammikuuta 1990 tehdyllä pöytäkirjalla, muuttamisesta, ovat sonect seuraavasta:

I artikla

Sopimuksen 26 artikla (Tietojen vaihtaminen) poistetaan ja korvataan seuraavalla:

"26 artikla
Tietojen vaihtaminen

1. Sopimusvaltioiden toimivaltaisten viranomaisten on vaihdettava keskenään sellaisia tietoja, jotka ovat ennalta katsottuna olennaisia tämän sopimuksen määräysten soveltamiseksi tai sopimusvaltioiden tai niiden paikallisviranomaisten lukuun määrättäviä kaikenlaatuisia veroja koskevan sisäisen lainsäädännön hallinnoimiseksi tai toimeenpanemiseksi, mikäli tämän lainsäädännön perusteella tapahtuva verotus ei ole tämän sopimuksen vastainen. Sopimuksen 1 ja 2 artikla eivät rajoita tietojen vaihtamista.

2. Sopimusvaltion 1 kappaleen perusteella vastaanottamia tietoja on käsiteltävä salaisina samalla tavalla kuin tämän valtion sisäisen lainsäädännön perusteella saatuja tietoja ja niitä saadaan ilmaista vain henkilöille tai viranomaisille (niihin luettuina tuomioistuimet ja hallintoelimet), jotka määräävät, kantavat tai perivät 1 kappaleessa mainittuja veroja tai käsittelevät näitä veroja koskevia syytteitä tai valituksia, taikka valvovat edellä mainittuja toimia. Näiden henkilöiden tai viranomaisten on käytettävä tietoja vain tällaisiin tarkoituksiin. He saavat ilmaista tietoja julkisessa oikeudenkäynnissä tai tuomioistuimen ratkaisuissa.

3. Tämän artiklan 1 ja 2 kappaleiden määräysten ei katsota velvoittavan sopimusvaltiota:

a) ryhtymään hallintotoimiin, jotka poikkeavat tämän sopimusvaltion tai toisen sopimusvaltion lainsäädännöstä ja hallintokäytännöstä;

b) antamaan tietoja, joita tämän sopimusvaltion tai toisen sopimusvaltion lainsäädännön mukaan tai säännönmukaisen hallintomenettelyn puitteissa ei voida hankkia;

c) antamaan tietoja, jotka paljastaisivat liikesalaisuuden taikka teollisen, kaupallisen tai ammatillisen salaisuuden tai elinkeinotoiminnassa käytetyn menettelytavan, taikka tietoja, joiden ilmaiseminen olisi vastoin yleistä järjestystä (ordre public).

4. Jos sopimusvaltio pyytää tietoja tämän artiklan mukaisesti, toisen sopimusvaltion on käytettävä tiedonhankintakeinojaan pyydettyjen tietojen hankkimiseksi, vaikka tämä toinen valtio ei ehkä tarvitse näitä tietoja omiin verotuksellisiin tarkoituksiinsa. Edelliseen lauseeseen sisältyvän velvollisuuden osalta sovelletaan 3 kappaleen rajoituksia, mutta näiden rajoitusten ei voida milloinkaan katsoa sallivan sitä, että sopimusvaltio kieltäytyy antamasta tietoja vain sen vuoksi, että ne eivät sen osalta koske kansallista etua.

5. Tämän artiklan 3 kappaleen määräysten ei voida milloinkaan katsoa sallivan sitä, että sopimusvaltio kieltäytyy antamasta tietoja pyynnön perusteella vain sen vuoksi, että tiedot ovat pankin, muun rahoituslaitoksen, välittäjän tai edustajan tai uskotun miehen hallussa tai ne koskevat omistusosuuksia henkilössä."

1. Sopimusvaltiot ilmoittavat toisilleen kirjallisesti diplomaattista tietä täyttäneensä valtiosäännössään tämän pöytäkirjan voimaantulolle asetetut edellytykset.

2. Pöytäkirja tulee voimaan sinä päivänä, jona myöhempi 1 kappaleessa tarkoitetuista ilmoituksista on tehty. Tämän pöytäkirjan määräyksiä sovelletaan niiltä verovuosilta, jotka alkavat tämän pöytäkirjan voimaantulovuotta lähinnä seuraavan kalenterivuoden tammikuun 1 päivänä tai sen jälkeen.

Tämän vakuudeksi ovat allekirjoittaneet, asianmukaisesti siihen valtuutettuina, allekirjoittaneet tämän pöytäkirjan.

Tehty Luxemburgissa 1 päivänä heinäkuuta 2009 kahtena suomen- ja ranskankielisenä kappaleena kummankin tekstin ollessa yhtä todistusvoimaiset.

SUOMEN TASAVALLAN HALLITUKSEN PUOLESTA:

Tarja Laitiainen

LUXEMBURGIN SUURHERTTUAKUNNAN HALLITUKSEN PUOLESTA:

Luc Frieden

[TEXT IN FRENCH – TEXTE EN FRANÇAIS]

AVENANT
EN VUE DE MODIFIER LA CONVENTION ENTRE LA FINLANDE ET LE LUXEMBOURG TENDANT A EVITER LES DOUBLES IMPOSITIONS EN MATIERE D'IMPOTS SUR LE REVENU ET SUR LA FORTUNE

Le Gouvernement de la République de Finlande et le Gouvernement du Grand-Duché xembourg,

désireux de conclure un Avenant en vue de modifier la Convention entre la Finlande et cembourg tendant à éviter les doubles impositions en matière d'impôts sur le revenu et fortune, signée à Luxembourg le 1er mars 1982, telle que modifiée par l'Avenant signé embourg le 24 janvier 1990, (ci-après dénommée "la Convention"), sont convenus de suit:

ARTICLE I

L'article 26 (Échange de Renseignements) de la Convention est supprimé et remplacé par celui qui suit:

"ARTICLE 26

Échange de Renseignements

1. Les autorités compétentes des États contractants échangent les renseignements vraisemblablement pertinents pour appliquer les dispositions de la présente Convention ou pour l'administration ou pour l'application de la législation interne relative aux impôts de toute nature ou dénomination perçus pour le compte des États contractants ou de leurs collectivités locales dans la mesure où l'imposition qu'elle prévoit n'est pas contraire à la Convention. L'échange de renseignements n'est pas restreint par les articles 1 et 2.

2. Les renseignements reçus en vertu du paragraphe 1 par un État contractant sont tenus secrets de la même manière que les renseignements obtenus en application de la législation interne de cet État et ne sont communiqués qu'aux personnes ou autorités (y compris les tribunaux et organes administratifs) concernées par l'établissement ou le recouvrement des impôts mentionnés au paragraphe 1, par les procédures ou poursuites concernant ces impôts, par les décisions sur les recours relatifs à ces impôts, ou par le contrôle de ce qui précède. Ces personnes ou autorités n'utilisent ces renseignements qu'à ces fins. Elles peuvent révéler ces renseignements au cours d'audiences publiques de tribunaux ou dans des jugements.

3. Les dispositions des paragraphes 1 et 2 ne peuvent en aucun cas être interprétées comme imposant à un État contractant l'obligation:

a) de prendre des mesures administratives dérogeant à sa législation et à sa pratique administrative ou à celles de l'autre État contractant;

b) de fournir des renseignements qui ne pourraient être obtenus sur la base de sa législation ou dans le cadre de sa pratique administrative ou de celles de l'autre État contractant;

c) de fournir des renseignements qui révéleraient un secret commercial, industriel, professionnel ou un procédé commercial ou des renseignements dont la communication serait contraire à l'ordre public.

4. Si des renseignements sont demandés par un État contractant conformément à cet article, l'autre État contractant utilise les pouvoirs dont il dispose pour obtenir les renseignements demandés, même s'il n'en a pas besoin à ses propres fins fiscales. L'obligation qui figure dans la phrase précédente est soumise aux limitations prévues au paragraphe 3 sauf si ces limitations sont susceptibles d'empêcher un État contractant de communiquer des renseignements uniquement parce que ceux-ci ne présentent pas d'intérêt pour lui dans le cadre national.

5. En aucun cas, les dispositions du paragraphe 3 ne peuvent être interprétées comme permettant à un État contractant de refuser de communiquer des renseignements sur demande uniquement parce que ceux-ci sont détenus par une banque, un autre établissement financier, un mandataire ou une personne agissant en tant qu'agent ou fiduciaire ou parce que ces renseignements se rattachent aux droits de propriété d'une personne."

ARTICLE II

1. Chacun des États contractants notifiera à l'autre par écrit, par la voie diplomatique, que les exigences constitutionnelles pour l'entrée en vigueur du présent Avenant ont été remplies.

2. L'Avenant entrera en vigueur à la date de la dernière des notifications visées au paragraphe 1. Les dispositions du présent Avenant seront applicables aux années d'imposition commençant le ou après le 1er janvier de l'année civile suivant immédiatement l'année de l'entrée en vigueur du présent Avenant.

EN FOI DE QUOI, les soussignés, dûment autorisés à cet effet, ont signé le présent Avenant.

Fait en deux exemplaires à Luxembourg, le 1 juillet 2009 en langues finlandaise et française, les deux textes faisant également foi.

Pour le Gouvernement de la République de Finlande	Pour le Gouvernement du Grand-Duché de Luxembourg
Tarja Laitiainen	Luc Frieden

[TRANSLATION – TRADUCTION]

PROTOCOL AMENDING THE CONVENTION BETWEEN FINLAND AND LUXEMBOURG FOR THE AVOIDANCE OF DOUBLE TAXATION WITH RESPECT TO TAXES ON INCOME AND ON CAPITAL

The Government of the Republic of Finland and the Government of the Grand Duchy of Luxembourg,

Desiring to conclude a Protocol to amend the Convention between Finland and Luxembourg for the Avoidance of Double Taxation with Respect to Taxes on Income and on Capital, signed at Luxembourg on 1 March 1982, as amended by the Protocol signed at Luxembourg on 24 January 1990 (hereafter called "the Convention"), have agreed as follows:

Article I

Article 26 (Exchange of information) of the Convention shall be abrogated and replaced by the following:

"Article 26. Exchange of information

1. The competent authorities of the Contracting States shall exchange such information as is foreseeably relevant for carrying out the provisions of this Convention or for the administration or enforcement of the domestic laws concerning taxes of every kind and description imposed on behalf of the Contracting States or their local authorities, insofar as the taxation thereunder is not contrary to the Convention. The exchange of information is not restricted by articles 1 and 2.

2. Any information received under paragraph 1 by a Contracting State shall be treated as secret in the same manner as information obtained under the domestic laws of that State and shall be disclosed only to persons or authorities (including courts and administrative bodies) involved in the assessment or collection of, the enforcement or prosecution in respect of, the determination of appeals in relation to the taxes referred to in paragraph 1, or the oversight of the above. Such persons or authorities shall use the information only for such purposes. These persons or authorities may disclose the information in public court proceedings or in judicial decisions.

3. In no case shall the provisions of paragraphs 1 and 2 be construed so as to impose on a Contracting State the obligation:

(a) To carry out administrative measures at variance with the laws or the administrative practice of that or of the other Contracting State;

(b) To supply information which is not obtainable under the laws or in the normal course of the administration of that or of the other Contracting State;

(c) To supply information which would disclose any trade, business, industrial, commercial or professional secret or trade process, or information, the disclosure of which would be contrary to public policy (ordre public).

4. If information is requested by a Contracting State in accordance with this article, the other Contracting State shall use its information gathering measures to obtain the requested information, even though that other State may not need such information for its own tax purposes.

The obligation contained in the preceding sentence is subject to the limitations of paragraph 3, but in no case shall such limitations be construed to permit a Contracting State to decline to supply information solely because it has no domestic interest in such information.

5. In no case shall the provisions of paragraph 3 be construed to permit a Contracting State to decline to supply information solely because the information is held by a bank, other financial institution, nominee or person acting in an agency or a fiduciary capacity or because it relates to a person's ownership rights."

Article II

1. The Contracting Parties shall notify each other in writing, through diplomatic channels, that the constitutional requirements for the entry into force of the present Protocol have been fulfilled.

2. This Protocol shall enter into force on the date of the last of the notifications referred to in paragraph 1. The provisions of this Protocol shall be effective in respect of the tax years starting on or after 1 January of the calendar year immediately following the entry into force of the present Protocol.

IN WITNESS WHEREOF, the undersigned, being duly authorized for such purpose, have signed this Protocol.

Done in duplicate at Luxembourg on 1 July 2009 in the Finnish and French languages, both texts being equally authentic.

For the Government of the Republic of Finland:

TARJA LAITIAINEN

For the Government of the Grand Duchy of Luxembourg:

LUC FRIEDEN

No. 22495. Multilateral

CONVENTION ON PROHIBITIONS OR RESTRICTIONS ON THE USE OF CERTAIN CONVENTIONAL WEAPONS WHICH MAY BE DEEMED TO BE EXCESSIVELY INJURIOUS OR TO HAVE INDISCRIMINATE EFFECTS (WITH PROTOCOLS I, II AND III). GENEVA, 10 OCTOBER 1980 [*United Nations, Treaty Series, vol. 1342, I-22495.*]

ACCESSION

Bahrain

Deposit of instrument with the Secretary-General of the United Nations: 11 March 2016

Date of effect: 11 September 2016

Registration with the Secretariat of the United Nations: ex officio, 11 March 2016

N° 22495. Multilatéral

CONVENTION SUR L'INTERDICTION OU LA LIMITATION DE L'EMPLOI DE CERTAINES ARMES CLASSIQUES QUI PEUVENT ÊTRE CONSIDÉRÉES COMME PRODUISANT DES EFFETS TRAUMATIQUES EXCESSIFS OU COMME FRAPPANT SANS DISCRIMINATION (AVEC PROTOCOLES I, II ET III). GENÈVE, 10 OCTOBRE 1980 [*Nations Unies, Recueil des Traités, vol. 1342, I-22495.*]

ADHÉSION

Bahreïn

Dépôt de l'instrument auprès du Secrétaire général de l'Organisation des Nations Unies : 11 mars 2016

Date de prise d'effet : 11 septembre 2016

Enregistrement au Secrétariat de l'Organisation des Nations Unies : d'office, 11 mars 2016

ADDITIONAL PROTOCOL TO THE CONVENTION ON PROHIBITIONS OR RESTRICTIONS ON THE USE OF CERTAIN CONVENTIONAL WEAPONS WHICH MAY BE DEEMED TO BE EXCESSIVELY INJURIOUS OR TO HAVE INDISCRIMINATE EFFECTS (PROTOCOL IV, ENTITLED PROTOCOL ON BLINDING LASER WEAPONS). VIENNA, 13 OCTOBER 1995 [*United Nations, Treaty Series, vol. 2024, A-22495.*]

CONSENT TO BE BOUND

Bahrain

Notification effected with the Secretary-General of the United Nations: 11 March 2016

Date of effect: 11 September 2016

Registration with the Secretariat of the United Nations: ex officio, 11 March 2016

PROTOCOLE ADDITIONNEL À LA CONVENTION SUR L'INTERDICTION OU LA LIMITATION DE L'EMPLOI DE CERTAINES ARMES CLASSIQUES QUI PEUVENT ÊTRE CONSIDÉRÉES COMME PRODUISANT DES EFFETS TRAUMATIQUES EXCESSIFS OU COMME FRAPPANT SANS DISCRIMINATION (PROTOCOLE IV, INTITULÉ PROTOCOLE RELATIF AUX ARMES À LASER AVEUGLANTES). VIENNE, 13 OCTOBRE 1995 [*Nations Unies, Recueil des Traités, vol. 2024, A-22495.*]

CONSENTEMENT À ÊTRE LIÉ

Bahreïn

Notification effectuée auprès du Secrétaire général de l'Organisation des Nations Unies : 11 mars 2016

Date de prise d'effet : 11 septembre 2016

Enregistrement au Secrétariat de l'Organisation des Nations Unies : d'office, 11 mars 2016

PROTOCOL ON EXPLOSIVE REMNANTS OF WAR TO THE CONVENTION ON PROHIBITIONS OR RESTRICTIONS ON THE USE OF CERTAIN CONVENTIONAL WEAPONS WHICH MAY BE DEEMED TO BE EXCESSIVELY INJURIOUS OR TO HAVE INDISCRIMINATE EFFECTS (PROTOCOL V). GENEVA, 28 NOVEMBER 2003 [*United Nations, Treaty Series, vol. 2399, A-22495.*]

CONSENT TO BE BOUND

Bahrain

Notification effected with the Secretary-General of the United Nations: 11 March 2016

Date of effect: 11 September 2016

Registration with the Secretariat of the United Nations: ex officio, 11 March 2016

PROTOCOLE RELATIF AUX RESTES EXPLOSIFS DE GUERRE À LA CONVENTION SUR L'INTERDICTION OU LA LIMITATION DE L'EMPLOI DE CERTAINES ARMES CLASSIQUES QUI PEUVENT ÊTRE CONSIDÉRÉES COMME PRODUISANT DES EFFETS TRAUMATIQUES EXCESSIFS OU COMME FRAPPANT SANS DISCRIMINATION (PROTOCOLE V). GENÈVE, 28 NOVEMBRE 2003 [*Nations Unies, Recueil des Traités, vol. 2399, A-22495.*]

CONSENTEMENT À ÊTRE LIÉ

Bahreïn

Notification effectuée auprès du Secrétaire général de l'Organisation des Nations Unies : 11 mars 2016

Date de prise d'effet : 11 septembre 2016

Enregistrement au Secrétariat de l'Organisation des Nations Unies : d'office, 11 mars 2016

No. 22514. Multilateral

CONVENTION ON THE CIVIL ASPECTS OF INTERNATIONAL CHILD ABDUCTION. THE HAGUE, 25 OCTOBER 1980 [*United Nations, Treaty Series, vol. 1343, I-22514.*]

ACCEPTANCE OF ACCESSION OF KAZAKHSTAN

Switzerland

Notification effected with the Government of the Netherlands: 1 March 2016

Date of effect: 1 June 2016

Registration with the Secretariat of the United Nations: Netherlands, 23 March 2016

ACCEPTANCE OF ACCESSION OF GUINEA

Ukraine

Notification effected with the Government of the Netherlands: 12 February 2016

Date of effect: 1 May 2016

Registration with the Secretariat of the United Nations: Netherlands, 23 March 2016

ACCEPTANCE OF ACCESSION OF IRAQ

Ukraine

Notification effected with the Government of the Netherlands: 24 February 2016

Date of effect: 1 May 2016

Registration with the Secretariat of the United Nations: Netherlands, 23 March 2016

N° 22514. Multilatéral

CONVENTION SUR LES ASPECTS CIVILS DE L'ENLÈVEMENT INTERNATIONAL D'ENFANTS. LA HAYE, 25 OCTOBRE 1980 [*Nations Unies, Recueil des Traités, vol. 1343, I-22514.*]

ACCEPTATION D'ADHÉSION DU KAZAKHSTAN

Suisse

Notification effectuée auprès du Gouvernement néerlandais : 1er mars 2016

Date de prise d'effet : 1er juin 2016

Enregistrement au Secrétariat de l'Organisation des Nations Unies : Pays-Bas, 23 mars 2016

ACCEPTATION D'ADHÉSION DE LA GUINÉE

Ukraine

Notification effectuée auprès du Gouvernement néerlandais : 12 février 2016

Date de prise d'effet : 1er mai 2016

Enregistrement au Secrétariat de l'Organisation des Nations Unies : Pays-Bas, 23 mars 2016

ACCEPTATION D'ADHÉSION DE L'IRAK

Ukraine

Notification effectuée auprès du Gouvernement néerlandais : 24 février 2016

Date de prise d'effet : 1er mai 2016

Enregistrement au Secrétariat de l'Organisation des Nations Unies : Pays-Bas, 23 mars 2016

ACCEPTANCE OF ACCESSION OF KAZAKHSTAN

Ukraine

Notification effected with the Government of the Netherlands: 12 February 2016

Date of effect: 1 May 2016

Registration with the Secretariat of the United Nations: Netherlands, 23 March 2016

ACCEPTATION D'ADHÉSION DU KAZAKHSTAN

Ukraine

Notification effectuée auprès du Gouvernement néerlandais : 12 février 2016

Date de prise d'effet : 1er mai 2016

Enregistrement au Secrétariat de l'Organisation des Nations Unies : Pays-Bas, 23 mars 2016

ACCEPTANCE OF ACCESSION OF LESOTHO

Ukraine

Notification effected with the Government of the Netherlands: 24 February 2016

Date of effect: 1 May 2016

Registration with the Secretariat of the United Nations: Netherlands, 23 March 2016

ACCEPTATION D'ADHÉSION DU LESOTHO

Ukraine

Notification effectuée auprès du Gouvernement néerlandais : 24 février 2016

Date de prise d'effet : 1er mai 2016

Enregistrement au Secrétariat de l'Organisation des Nations Unies : Pays-Bas, 23 mars 2016

ACCEPTANCE OF ACCESSION OF THE REPUBLIC OF KOREA

Ukraine

Notification effected with the Government of the Netherlands: 24 February 2016

Date of effect: 1 May 2016

Registration with the Secretariat of the United Nations: Netherlands, 23 March 2016

ACCEPTATION D'ADHÉSION DE LA RÉPUBLIQUE DE CORÉE

Ukraine

Notification effectuée auprès du Gouvernement néerlandais : 24 février 2016

Date de prise d'effet : 1er mai 2016

Enregistrement au Secrétariat de l'Organisation des Nations Unies : Pays-Bas, 23 mars 2016

ACCEPTANCE OF ACCESSION OF ZAMBIA

Ukraine

Notification effected with the Government of the Netherlands: 24 February 2016

Date of effect: 1 May 2016

Registration with the Secretariat of the United Nations: Netherlands, 23 March 2016

ACCEPTATION D'ADHÉSION DE LA ZAMBIE

Ukraine

Notification effectuée auprès du Gouvernement néerlandais : 24 février 2016

Date de prise d'effet : 1er mai 2016

Enregistrement au Secrétariat de l'Organisation des Nations Unies : Pays-Bas, 23 mars 2016

No. 24841. Multilateral

CONVENTION AGAINST TORTURE AND OTHER CRUEL, INHUMAN OR DEGRADING TREATMENT OR PUNISHMENT. NEW YORK, 10 DECEMBER 1984 [*United Nations, Treaty Series, vol. 1465, I-24841.*]

RATIFICATION (WITH RESERVATION)

Fiji

Deposit of instrument with the Secretary-General of the United Nations: 14 March 2016

Date of effect: 13 April 2016

Registration with the Secretariat of the United Nations: ex officio, 14 March 2016

Nº 24841. Multilatéral

CONVENTION CONTRE LA TORTURE ET AUTRES PEINES OU TRAITEMENTS CRUELS, INHUMAINS OU DÉGRADANTS. NEW YORK, 10 DÉCEMBRE 1984 [*Nations Unies, Recueil des Traités, vol. 1465, I-24841.*]

RATIFICATION (AVEC RÉSERVE)

Fidji

Dépôt de l'instrument auprès du Secrétaire général de l'Organisation des Nations Unies : 14 mars 2016

Date de prise d'effet : 13 avril 2016

Enregistrement au Secrétariat de l'Organisation des Nations Unies : d'office, 14 mars 2016

Reservation:

Réserve :

[TEXT IN ENGLISH – TEXTE EN ANGLAIS]

"The Government of the Republic of Fiji does not recognize the definition of Torture as provided for in article 1 of the Convention therefore shall not be bound by these provisions. The definition of Torture in the Convention is only applicable to the extent as expressed in the Fijian Constitution.

The Government of the Republic of Fiji recognizes the article 14 of the Convention only to the extent that the right to award compensation to victims of an act of torture shall be subject to the determination of a Court of law.

The Government of the Republic of Fiji does not recognize the competence of the Committee against Torture as provided for in article(s) 20, 21 and 22 of the Convention and therefore shall not be bound by these provisions.

The Government of the Republic of Fiji does not recognize paragraph 1 of article 30 of the Convention and therefore shall not be bound by this provision."

The Convention will enter into force for Fiji on 13 April 2016 in accordance with its article 27(2), which reads as follows:

"For each State ratifying this Convention or acceding to it after the deposit of the twentieth instrument of ratification or accession, the Convention shall enter into force on the thirtieth day after the date of the deposit of its own instrument of ratification or accession."

[TRANSLATION – TRADUCTION]

Le Gouvernement de la République des Fidji ne reconnaît pas la définition de la torture telle qu'elle est énoncée à l'article premier de la Convention et n'est donc pas lié pas ces dispositions. La définition de la torture qui figure dans la Convention n'est applicable que dans la mesure où elle est compatible avec la Constitution fidjienne.

Le Gouvernement de la République des Fidji ne reconnaît l'article 14 de la Convention que dans la mesure où le droit à indemnisation des victimes d'un acte de torture est soumis à la décision d'une cour de justice.

Le Gouvernement de la République des Fidji ne reconnaît pas la compétence accordée au Comité contre la torture aux termes des articles 20, 21 et 22 de la Convention et n'est donc pas lié par ces dispositions.

Le Gouvernement de la République des Fidji ne reconnaît pas le paragraphe 1 de l'article 30 de la Convention et n'est donc pas lié par cette disposition.

La Convention entrera en vigueur pour les Fidji le 13 avril 2016 conformément au paragraphe 2 de son article 27 qui stipule:

« Pour tout Etat qui ratifiera la présente Convention ou y adhérera après le dépôt du vingtième instrument de ratification ou d'adhésion, la Convention entrera en vigueur le trentième jour après la date du dépôt par cet Etat de son instrument de ratification ou d'adhésion. »

No. 27531. Multilateral

CONVENTION ON THE RIGHTS OF THE CHILD. NEW YORK, 20 NOVEMBER 1989 [*United Nations, Treaty Series, vol. 1577, I-27531.*]

OBJECTION TO THE RESERVATIONS MADE BY SOMALIA UPON RATIFICATION

Austria

Notification deposited with the Secretary-General of the United Nations: 31 March 2016

Registration with the Secretariat of the United Nations: ex officio, 31 March 2016

Nº 27531. Multilatéral

CONVENTION RELATIVE AUX DROITS DE L'ENFANT. NEW YORK, 20 NOVEMBRE 1989 [*Nations Unies, Recueil des Traités, vol. 1577, I-27531.*]

OBJECTION AUX RÉSERVES FORMULÉES PAR LA SOMALIE LORS DE LA RATIFICATION

Autriche

Dépôt de la notification auprès du Secrétaire général de l'Organisation des Nations Unies : 31 mars 2016

Enregistrement au Secrétariat de l'Organisation des Nations Unies : d'office, 31 mars 2016

[TEXT IN ENGLISH – TEXTE EN ANGLAIS]

"The Government of Austria has examined the reservation made by the Federal Republic of Somalia upon ratification of the United Nations Convention on the Rights of the Child.

Austria considers that by referring to the General Principles of Islamic Sharia Somalia has made a reservation of a general and indeterminate scope. This reservation does not clearly define for the other States Parties to the Convention the extent to which the reserving State has accepted the obligations of the Convention.

Austria therefore considers the reservation to be incompatible with the object and purpose of the Convention and objects to it.

This objection shall not preclude the entry into force of the Convention between the Republic of Austria and the Federal Republic of Somalia."

[TRANSLATION – TRADUCTION]

Le Gouvernement de l'Autriche a examiné la réserve formulée par la République fédérale de Somalie lors de sa ratification de la Convention relative aux droits de l'enfant.

L'Autriche estime que la Somalie, en invoquant les principes généraux de la charia islamique, a formulé une réserve d'une portée générale et indéterminée. Cette réserve ne définit pas clairement, pour les autres Etats parties à la Convention, dans quelle mesure l'Etat qui a formulé la réserve a accepté les obligations découlant de la Convention.

L'Autriche estime en conséquence que la réserve est incompatible avec l'objet et le but de la Convention et s'y oppose.

La présente objection n'empêche pas l'entrée en vigueur de la Convention entre la République de l'Autriche et la République fédérale de Somalie.

OBJECTION TO THE RESERVATIONS MADE BY SOMALIA UPON RATIFICATION

Latvia

Notification deposited with the Secretary-General of the United Nations: 23 March 2016

Registration with the Secretariat of the United Nations: ex officio, 23 March 2016

OBJECTION AUX RÉSERVES FORMULÉES PAR LA SOMALIE LORS DE LA RATIFICATION

Lettonie

Dépôt de la notification auprès du Secrétaire général de l'Organisation des Nations Unies : 23 mars 2016

Enregistrement au Secrétariat de l'Organisation des Nations Unies : d'office, 23 mars 2016

[TEXT IN ENGLISH – TEXTE EN ANGLAIS]

"... The Government of the Republic of Latvia has carefully examined the reservations made by the Federal Republic of Somalia upon ratification of the Convention on the Rights of the Child.

The Republic of Latvia considers that Article 14 of the Convention forms the very basis of the Convention and thereof International Human Rights Law, thus no derogations from those obligations can be made. Moreover, the Republic of Latvia emphasises that para 3 of Article 14 contains the particular provisions related to the possible limitations of the right to manifest child's religious beliefs. Therefore, the Republic of Latvia considers that general reservation to Article 14 of the Convention cannot be considered in line with object and purpose of the Convention.

Regarding the reservation to Articles 20 and 21 of the Convention that address the issues of the removal of child from family environment and matters of adoption, the Government of Latvia draws attention that Articles provide only general principles, leaving the issues of practical implementation up to the State Parties. Consequently, the reservation stipulating that the State Party to the Convention is not bound by Articles establishing the principle that the child can be removed from family environment and that the adoption shall be performed in the best interests of child, cannot be considered in line with aim and purpose of the Convention.

Moreover, the reservation subjecting any of provision of the Convention to the General Principles of Islamic Sharia does not allow evaluate to what extent the Federal Republic of Somalia considers itself bound by the provisions of the Convention.

Therefore, the Government of the Republic of Latvia referring to para 2 of Article 51 of the Convention setting out that reservation incompatible with the object and purpose of the Convention shall not be permitted, objects to the aforesaid reservations made by the Federal Republic of Somalia to the Convention on the Rights of the Child.

However, this objection shall not preclude the entry into force of the Convention between the Republic of Latvia and the Federal Republic of Somalia. Thus, the Convention will become operative without the Federal Republic of Somalia benefiting from its reservation..."

[TRANSLATION – TRADUCTION]

... Le Gouvernement de la République de Lettonie a examiné attentivement les réserves formulées par la République fédérale de Somalie en ratifiant la Convention relative aux droits de l'enfant.

La République de Lettonie considère que l'article 14 de la Convention en forme la base même et ainsi la base du droit international des droits de l'homme, raison pour laquelle aucune dérogation aux obligations correspondantes ne peut être faite. En outre, la République de Lettonie souligne que le paragraphe 3 de l'article 14 contient les dispositions spécifiques relatives aux limitations possibles au droit de manifester les croyances religieuses de l'enfant. Par conséquent, la République de Lettonie estime que la réserve générale à l'article 14 de la Convention ne peut être considérée comme étant en conformité avec l'objet et le but de la Convention.

En ce qui concerne la réserve aux articles 20 et 21 de la Convention, qui ont trait aux questions relatives à la situation où l'enfant est privé du milieu familial et à l'adoption, le Gouvernement de Lettonie observe que ces articles ne font que poser des principes généraux, laissant les questions relatives à leur exécution pratique aux États parties. Il s'ensuit que la réserve selon laquelle l'État partie à la Convention n'est pas lié par les articles établissant le principe que l'enfant peut être privé du milieu familial et que l'adoption doit s'effectuer dans l'intérêt supérieur de l'enfant ne peut être considérée comme étant en conformité avec l'objet et le but de la Convention.

En outre, la réserve qui subordonne toute disposition de la Convention aux principes généraux de la sharia islamique ne permet pas d'évaluer dans quelle mesure la République fédérale de Somalie se considère comme liée par les dispositions de la Convention.

Dès lors, le Gouvernement de la République de Lettonie, se référant au paragraphe 2 de l'article 51 de la Convention, paragraphe selon lequel aucune réserve incompatible avec l'objet et le but de la Convention n'est autorisée, fait objection aux réserves formulées par la République fédérale de Somalie à la Convention relative aux droits de l'enfant.

Toutefois, la présente objection n'empêche pas l'entrée en vigueur de la Convention entre la République de Lettonie et la République fédérale de Somalie. Ainsi la Convention s'appliquera sans que la République fédérale de Somalie bénéficie de la réserve...

OBJECTION TO THE RESERVATIONS MADE BY SOMALIA UPON RATIFICATION

Netherlands

Notification deposited with the Secretary-General of the United Nations: 8 March 2016

Registration with the Secretariat of the United Nations: ex officio, 8 March 2016

OBJECTION AUX RÉSERVES FORMULÉES PAR LA SOMALIE LORS DE LA RATIFICATION

Pays-Bas

Dépôt de la notification auprès du Secrétaire général de l'Organisation des Nations Unies : 8 mars 2016

Enregistrement au Secrétariat de l'Organisation des Nations Unies : d'office, 8 mars 2016

[TEXT IN ENGLISH – TEXTE EN ANGLAIS]

"The Government of the Kingdom of the Netherlands has carefully examined the reservations made by the Government of the Federal Republic of Somalia with respect to the Convention on the Rights of the Child.

The Government of the Kingdom of the Netherlands considers that the reservations regarding articles 14, 20 and 21 of the Convention on the Rights of the Child are incompatible with the object and purpose of the Convention.

Furthermore, the Government of the Kingdom of the Netherlands notes that the Federal Republic of Somalia subjects application of the Convention to the beliefs and principles of Islam.

The Government of the Kingdom of the Netherlands considers that such reservations, which seek to limit the responsibilities of the reserving State under the Convention by general reference to religious laws, raises doubts as to the commitment of that State to the object and purpose of the Convention.

The Government of the Kingdom of the Netherlands recalls that according to Article 51, paragraph 2 of the Convention, a reservation incompatible with the object and purpose of the Convention shall not be permitted. The Government of the Kingdom of the Netherlands therefore objects to these reservations.

This objection shall not preclude the entry into force of the Convention between the Kingdom of the Netherlands and the Federal Republic of Somalia."

[TRANSLATION – TRADUCTION]

Le Gouvernement du Royaume des Pays-Bas a examiné attentivement les réserves formulées par le Gouvernement de la République fédérale de Somalie à la Convention relative aux droits de l'enfant.

Le Gouvernement du Royaume des Pays-Bas estime que les réserves concernant les articles 14, 20 et 21 de la Convention relative aux droits de l'enfant sont incompatibles avec l'objet et le but de la Convention.

Le Gouvernement du Royaume des Pays-Bas note en outre que la République fédérale de Somalie subordonne l'application de la Convention aux croyances et principes de l'Islam.

Le Gouvernement du Royaume des Pays-Bas considère que de telles réserves, par lesquelles un État limite les responsabilités qui lui incombent en vertu de la Convention en invoquant, de façon générale, des lois religieuses, autorisent à douter de l'engagement de cet État envers l'objet et le but de la Convention.

Le Gouvernement du Royaume des Pays-Bas rappelle le paragraphe 2 de l'article 51 de la Convention, selon lequel aucune réserve incompatible avec l'objet et le but de la Convention n'est autorisée. En conséquence, il fait objection aux réserves formulées.

La présente objection n'empêche pas l'entrée en vigueur de la Convention entre le Royaume des Pays-Bas et la République fédérale de Somalie.

OPTIONAL PROTOCOL TO THE CONVENTION ON THE RIGHTS OF THE CHILD ON THE SALE OF CHILDREN, CHILD PROSTITUTION AND CHILD PORNOGRAPHY. NEW YORK, 25 MAY 2000 [*United Nations, Treaty Series, vol. 2171, A-27531.*]

ACCESSION (WITH RESERVATION)

United Arab Emirates

Deposit of instrument with the Secretary-General of the United Nations: 2 March 2016

Date of effect: 2 April 2016

Registration with the Secretariat of the United Nations: ex officio, 2 March 2016

Reservation:

PROTOCOLE FACULTATIF À LA CONVENTION RELATIVE AUX DROITS DE L'ENFANT, CONCERNANT LA VENTE D'ENFANTS, LA PROSTITUTION DES ENFANTS ET LA PORNOGRAPHIE METTANT EN SCÈNE DES ENFANTS. NEW YORK, 25 MAI 2000 [*Nations Unies, Recueil des Traités, vol. 2171, A-27531.*]

ADHÉSION (AVEC RÉSERVE)

Émirats arabes unis

Dépôt de l'instrument auprès du Secrétaire général de l'Organisation des Nations Unies : 2 mars 2016

Date de prise d'effet : 2 avril 2016

Enregistrement au Secrétariat de l'Organisation des Nations Unies : d'office, 2 mars 2016

Réserve :

[TEXT IN ARABIC – TEXTE EN ARABE]

مع التحفظ على الفقرة (5) من المادة

(3) من البروتوكول المشار إليه أعلاه.

[TRANSLATION – TRADUCTION]

... with a reservation regarding article 3, paragraph 5.

[TRANSLATION – TRADUCTION]

... avec une réserve relative au paragraphe 5 de l'article 3.

No. 30619. Multilateral

CONVENTION ON BIOLOGICAL DIVERSITY. RIO DE JANEIRO, 5 JUNE 1992 [*United Nations, Treaty Series, vol. 1760, I-30619.*]

NAGOYA PROTOCOL ON ACCESS TO GENETIC RESOURCES AND THE FAIR AND EQUITABLE SHARING OF BENEFITS ARISING FROM THEIR UTILIZATION TO THE CONVENTION ON BIOLOGICAL DIVERSITY. NAGOYA, 29 OCTOBER 2010 [*United Nations, Treaty Series, vol. 3008, A-30619.*]

RATIFICATION

Senegal

Deposit of instrument with the Secretary-General of the United Nations: 3 March 2016

Date of effect: 1 June 2016

Registration with the Secretariat of the United Nations: ex officio, 3 March 2016

N° 30619. Multilatéral

CONVENTION SUR LA DIVERSITÉ BIOLOGIQUE. RIO DE JANEIRO, 5 JUIN 1992 [*Nations Unies, Recueil des Traités, vol. 1760, I-30619.*]

PROTOCOLE DE NAGOYA SUR L'ACCÈS AUX RESSOURCES GÉNÉTIQUES ET LE PARTAGE JUSTE ET ÉQUITABLE DES AVANTAGES DÉCOULANT DE LEUR UTILISATION RELATIF À LA CONVENTION SUR LA DIVERSITÉ BIOLOGIQUE. NAGOYA, 29 OCTOBRE 2010 [*Nations Unies, Recueil des Traités, vol. 3008, A-30619.*]

RATIFICATION

Sénégal

Dépôt de l'instrument auprès du Secrétaire général de l'Organisation des Nations Unies : 3 mars 2016

Date de prise d'effet : 1er juin 2016

Enregistrement au Secrétariat de l'Organisation des Nations Unies : d'office, 3 mars 2016

No. 30795. Finland and Switzerland

AGREEMENT BETWEEN THE SWISS CONFEDERATION AND THE REPUBLIC OF FINLAND FOR THE AVOIDANCE OF DOUBLE TAXATION WITH RESPECT TO TAXES ON INCOME AND ON CAPITAL. HELSINKI, 16 DECEMBER 1991 [*United Nations, Treaty Series, vol. 1770, I-30795.*]

PROTOCOL BETWEEN THE REPUBLIC OF FINLAND AND THE SWISS CONFEDERATION AMENDING THE AGREEMENT FOR THE AVOIDANCE OF DOUBLE TAXATION WITH RESPECT TO TAXES ON INCOME AND ON CAPITAL AND THE PROTOCOL, SIGNED AT HELSINKI ON DECEMBER 16, 1991, AS AMENDED BY THE PROTOCOLS SIGNED AT HELSINKI ON APRIL 19, 2006 AND 22 SEPTEMBER 2009. HELSINKI, 18 SEPTEMBER 2012

Entry into force: 3 February 2013, in accordance with article II

Authentic texts: English, Finnish and German

Registration with the Secretariat of the United Nations: Finland, 9 March 2016

N° 30795. Finlande et Suisse

CONVENTION ENTRE LA CONFÉDÉRATION SUISSE ET LA RÉPUBLIQUE DE FINLANDE EN VUE D'ÉVITER LES DOUBLES IMPOSITIONS EN MATIÈRE D'IMPÔTS SUR LE REVENU ET SUR LA FORTUNE. HELSINKI, 16 DÉCEMBRE 1991 [*Nations Unies, Recueil des Traités, vol. 1770, I-30795.*]

PROTOCOLE ENTRE LA RÉPUBLIQUE DE FINLANDE ET LA CONFÉDÉRATION SUISSE MODIFIANT LA CONVENTION EN VUE D'ÉVITER LES DOUBLES IMPOSITIONS EN MATIÈRE D'IMPÔTS SUR LE REVENU ET SUR LA FORTUNE ET LE PROTOCOLE, SIGNÉS À HELSINKI LE 16 DÉCEMBRE 1991, TELS QUE MODIFIÉS PAR LES PROTOCOLES SIGNÉS À HELSINKI LE 19 AVRIL 2006 ET LE 22 SEPTEMBRE 2009. HELSINKI, 18 SEPTEMBRE 2012

Entrée en vigueur : 3 février 2013, conformément à l'article II

Textes authentiques : anglais, finnois et allemand

Enregistrement au Secrétariat de l'Organisation des Nations Unies : Finlande, 9 mars 2016

[TEXT IN ENGLISH – TEXTE EN ANGLAIS]

PROTOCOL BETWEEN THE REPUBLIC OF FINLAND AND THE SWISS CONFEDERATION AMENDING THE AGREEMENT FOR THE AVOIDANCE OF DOUBLE TAXATION WITH RESPECT TO TAXES ON INCOME AND ON CAPITAL AND THE PROTOCOL, SIGNED AT HELSINKI ON DECEMBER 16, 1991, AS AMENDED BY THE PROTOCOLS SIGNED AT HELSINKI ON APRIL 19, 2006 AND SEPTEMBER 22, 2009

The Government of the Republic of Finland and the Swiss Federal Council acting through the Federal Department of Finance

desiring to amend the Agreement for the avoidance of double taxation with respect to taxes on income and on capital and the Protocol signed at Helsinki on December 16, 1991 as amended by the Protoools signed at Helsinki on April 19, 2006 and September 22, 2009 (hereinafter referred to as "the Agreement" and "the Protocol to the Agreement", respectively),

have agreed as follows:

ARTICLE I

1. Subparagraph b of Paragraph 4 of the Protocol to the Agreement shall be deleted and replaced by the following subparagraph:

> "b) The reference to "foreseeable relevance" is intended to provide for exchange of information in tax matters to the widest possible extent and, at the same time, to clarify that the Contracting States are not at liberty to engage in "fishing expeditions" or to request information that is unlikely to be relevant to the tax affairs of a given taxpayer. While the details to be given when making a request for information are important procedural requirements that are intended to ensure that «fishing expeditions» do not occur, they nevertheless need to be interpreted in order not to frustrate effective exchange of information.

2. Subsubparagraphs (i) and (v) of Subparagraph c of Paragraph 4 of the Protocol to the Agreement shall be deleted and replaced by the following subsubparagraphs:

> "(i) the identification of the person under examination or investigation; such identification may be provided by other means than by indicating the name and address of the person concerned;
>
> (v) to the extent known, the name and address of any person believed to be in possession of the requested information."

ARTICLE II

1. The Governments of the Contracting States shall notify each other through diplomatic channels that the constitutional requirements for the entry into force of this Protocol have been complied with.

2. This Protocol, which shall form an integral part of the Agreement and the Protocol, shall enter into force thirty days after the date of the latter of the notifications referred to in paragraph 1 and its provisions shall have effect in both States from the date of entry into force of the Protocol signed at Helsinki on September 22, 2009 amending the Agreement.

In witness whereof the undersigned, duly authorized thereto by their respective Governments, have signed this Protocol.

Done in duplicate at Helsinki this 18th of September 2012 in the Finnish, German and English languages. In case of any divergence of interpretation, the English text shall prevail.

For the Government of the Republic of Finland:	For the Swiss Federal Council:

[TEXT IN FINNISH – TEXTE EN FINNOIS]

**PÖYTÄKIRJA
SUOMEN TASAVALLAN JA SVEITSIN VALALIITON VÄLILLÄ
HELSINGISSÄ 16 PÄIVÄNÄ JOULUKUUTA 1991 TULO- JA
VARALLISUUSVEROJA KOSKEVAN KAKSINKERTAISEN
VEROTUKSEN VÄLTTÄMISEKSI TEHDYN SOPIMUKSEN
JA PÖYTÄKIRJAN MUUTTAMISESTA, SELLAISENA
KUIN NE OVAT MUUTETTUNA HELSINGISSÄ 19
PÄIVÄNÄ HUHTIKUUTA 2006 JA 22 PÄIVÄNÄ
SYYSKUUTA 2009 TEHDYILLÄ
PÖYTÄKIRJOILLA**

Suomen tasavallan hallitus ja Sveitsin liittoneuvosto Federal Department of Financen edustamana

jotka haluavat muuttaa Helsingissä 16 päivänä joulukuuta 1991 tulo- ja varallisuusveroja koskevan kaksinkertaisen verotuksen välttämiseksi tehtyä sopimusta ja pöytäkirjaa, sellaisena kuin ne ovat muutettuna Helsingissä 19 päivänä huhtikuuta 2006 ja 22 päivänä syyskuuta 2009 tehdyillä pöytäkirjoilla (jäljempänä "sopimus" ja vastaavasti "sopimuksen pöytäkirja"),

ovat sopineet seuraavasta:

I ARTIKLA

1. Sopimuksen pöytäkirjan 4 kappaleen b kohta poistetaan ja korvataan seuraavalla kohdalla:

> "b) Viittauksella "ennalta katsoen olennaiseen" on tarkoitus määrätä mahdollisimman laajasta tiedonvaihdosta veroasioissa ja samanaikaisesti selventää, että sopimusvaltioiden ei ole lupa ryhtyä "tietojen kalasteluun" tai pyytää tietoja, jotka todennäköisesti eivät ole olennaisia tietyn verovelvollisen veroasioissa. Vaikka pyyntöä tehtäessä annettavat yksityiskohdat ovat tärkeitä menettelyä koskevia vaatimuksia, joilla on tarkoitus varmistaa, ettei "tietojen kalastelua" tapahdu, niitä on kuitenkin tulkittava, jotta tehokasta tiedonvaihtoa ei tehdä tyhjäksi."

2. Sopimuksen pöytäkirjan 4 kappaleen c kohdan 1 ja 5 alakohta poistetaan ja korvataan seuraavilla alakohdilla:

> "1) tarkastuksen tai tutkinnan kohteena olevan henkilön tunnistamistiedot; tunnistaminen voi tapahtua myös muilla keinoilla kuin ilmoittamalla kyseisen henkilön nimi ja osoite;
>
> 5) sikäli kuin ne ovat tunnetut, sellaisen henkilön nimi ja osoite, jonka uskotaan pitävän pyydettyjä tietoja hallussaan."

II ARTIKLA

1. Sopimusvaltioiden hallitusten on ilmoitettava toisilleen diplomaattista tietä täyttäneensä valtiosäännössään tämän pöytäkirjan voimaantulolle asetetut edellytykset.

2. Tämä pöytäkirja, joka on sopimuksen ja pöytäkirjan olennainen osa, tulee voimaan kolmantenakymmenentenä päivänä siitä päivästä, jona myöhempi 1 kappaleessa tarkoitetuista ilmoituksista on tehty, ja sen määräyksiä sovelletaan molemmissa valtioissa Helsingissä 22 päivänä syyskuuta 2009 sopimuksen muuttamisesta tehdyn pöytäkirjan voimaantulopäivästä alkaen.

Tämän vakuudeksi ovat allekirjoittaneet, hallitustensa asianmukaisesti siihen valtuuttamina, allekirjoittaneet tämän pöytäkirjan.

Tehty Helsingissä päivänä 5 Heinäkuuta 2012 kahtena suomen,- saksan- ja englanninkielisenä kappaleena. Tulkintaerimielisyyksien esiintyessä englanninkielinen teksti on ratkaiseva.

Suomen tasavallan hallituksen puolesta:	Sveitsin liittoneuvoston puolesta:

[TEXT IN GERMAN – TEXTE EN ALLEMAND]

PROTOKOLL
ZWISCHEN DER REPUBLIK FINNLAND UND DER SCHWEIZERISCHEN EIDGENOSSENSCHAFT ZUR ÄNDERUNG DES ABKOMMENS ZUR VERMEIDUNG DER DOPPELBESTEUERUNG AUF DEM GEBIET DER STEUERN VOM EINKOMMEN UND VOM VERMÖGEN SOWIE DES PROTOKOLLS, UNTERZEICHNET IN HELSINKI AM 16. DEZEMBER 1991, GEÄNDERT DURCH DIE AM 19. APRIL 2006 UND 22. SEPTEMBER 2009 IN HELSINKI UNTERZEICHNETEN PROTOKOLLE

Die Regierung der Republik Finnland und der Schweizerische Bundesrat handelnd durch das Eidgenössische Finanzdepartement

vom Wunsch geleitet, das Abkommen zur Vermeidung der Doppelbesteuerung auf dem Gebiet der Steuern vom Einkommen und vom Vermögen und das dazugehörige Protokoll, unterzeichnet in Helsinki am 16. Dezember 1991, geändert durch die am 19. April 2006 und 22. September 2009 in Helsinki unterzeichneten Protokolle (nachfolgend «das Abkommen» beziehungsweise «das Protokoll zum Abkommen» genannt) zu ändern,

haben Folgendes vereinbart:

Art. I

1. Absatz 4 Buchstabe b des Protokolls zum Abkommen wird gelöscht und durch folgenden Buchstaben ersetzt:

"b) Der Zweck der Verweisung auf Informationen, die voraussichtlich erheblich sind, besteht darin, einen möglichst weit gehenden Informationsaustausch in Steuerbelangen zu gewährleisten, ohne den Vertragsstaaten zu erlauben, «fishing expeditions» zu betreiben oder um Informationen zu ersuchen, deren Erheblichkeit hinsichtlich der Steuerbelange einer bestimmten steuerpflichtigen Person unwahrscheinlich ist. Die im Amtshilfeersuchen zu liefernden Angaben sind zwar wichtige verfahrenstechnische Voraussetzungen für die Vermeidung von «fishing expeditions»; sie sind jedoch nicht so auszulegen, dass sie einen wirksamen Informationsaustausch behindern."

2. Absatz 4 Buchstabe c Unterabsätze (i) und (v) des Protokolls zum Abkommen werden gelöscht und durch folgende Unterabsätze ersetzt:

"(i) die Identifikation der steuerpflichtigen Person, wobei diese Identifikation auch auf andere Weise als durch Angabe des Namens und der Adresse erfolgen kann;

(v) den Namen und die Adresse des mutmasslichen Informationsinhabers, soweit sie bekannt sind."

Art. II

1. Die Regierungen der Vertragsstaaten notifizieren sich gegenseitig auf diplomatischem Weg, dass die verfassungsrechtlichen Erfordernisse für das Inkrafttreten dieses Protokolls erfüllt sind.

2. Dieses Protokoll, das integrierender Bestandteil des Abkommens und des Protokolls ist, tritt dreissig Tage nach dem Datum der späteren der in Absatz 1 erwähnten Notifikationen in Kraft, und seine Bestimmungen finden in beiden Staaten ab dem Datum des Inkrafttretens des am 22. September 2009 in Helsinki unterzeichneten Protokolls Anwendung.

Zu Urkund dessen haben die hierzu von ihren Regierungen gehörig bevollmächtigten Unterzeichneten dieses Protokoll unterschrieben.

Geschehen zu Helsinki, am 18. September 2012, im Doppel in finnischer, deutscher und englischer Sprache. Bei unterschiedlicher Auslegung soll der englische Wortlaut massgebend sein.

Für die Regierung der Republik Finnland:	Für den Schweizerischen Bundesrat:

[TRANSLATION – TRADUCTION]

PROTOCOLE ENTRE LA RÉPUBLIQUE DE FINLANDE ET LA CONFÉDÉRATION SUISSE MODIFIANT LA CONVENTION EN VUE D'ÉVITER LES DOUBLES IMPOSITIONS EN MATIÈRE D'IMPÔTS SUR LE REVENU ET SUR LA FORTUNE ET LE PROTOCOLE, SIGNÉS À HELSINKI LE 16 DÉCEMBRE 1991, TELS QUE MODIFIÉS PAR LES PROTOCOLES SIGNÉS À HELSINKI LE 19 AVRIL 2006 ET LE 22 SEPTEMBRE 2009

Le Gouvernement de la République de Finlande et le Conseil fédéral suisse agissant par l'intermédiaire du Département fédéral des finances,

Désireux de modifier la Convention en vue d'éviter les doubles impositions en matière d'impôts sur le revenu et sur la fortune et le Protocole, signés le 16 décembre 1991 à Helsinki, tels que modifiés par les Protocoles signés à Helsinki le 19 avril 2006 et le 22 septembre 2009 (ci-après dénommés respectivement la « Convention » et le « Protocole à la Convention »),

Sont convenus de ce qui suit :

Article premier

1. L'alinéa b) du paragraphe 4 du Protocole à la Convention est abrogé et remplacé par le paragraphe suivant :

« b) La référence aux renseignements "vraisemblablement pertinents" a pour but d'assurer un échange de renseignements en matière fiscale qui soit le plus large possible, sans qu'il soit pour autant loisible aux États contractants d'aller à la "pêche aux renseignements" ou de demander des renseignements dont il est peu probable qu'ils soient pertinents pour élucider les affaires fiscales d'un contribuable déterminé. Si les détails à fournir lors de la présentation d'une demande de renseignements sont des exigences procédurales importantes qui visent à éviter la "pêche aux renseignements", ils doivent néanmoins être interprétés de manière à ne pas entraver l'échange effectif de renseignements. »

2. Les sous-alinéas (i) et (v) de l'alinéa c) du paragraphe 4 du Protocole à la Convention sont abrogés et remplacés par les sous-alinéas suivants :

« (i) l'identité de la personne visée par le contrôle ou l'enquête ; cette identité peut être fournie par d'autres moyens qu'en indiquant le nom et l'adresse de la personne concernée;

(v) dans la mesure où ils sont connus, le nom et l'adresse de toute personne présumée être en possession des renseignements requis. »

Article II

1. Les Gouvernements des États contractants se notifient, par la voie diplomatique, l'accomplissement des conditions constitutionnelles nécessaires à l'entrée en vigueur du présent Protocole.

2. Le présent Protocole, qui fait partie intégrante de la Convention et du Protocole, entre en vigueur 30 jours après la date de la dernière des notifications visées au paragraphe 1 et ses dispositions prennent effet dans les deux États à compter de la date d'entrée en vigueur du Protocole signé à Helsinki le 22 septembre 2009, modifiant la Convention.

EN FOI DE QUOI, les soussignés, à ce dûment autorisés par leurs Gouvernements respectifs, ont signé le présent Protocole.

FAIT à Helsinki, le 18 septembre 2012, en double exemplaire, en langues finnoise, allemande et anglaise. En cas de divergence d'interprétation, le texte anglais prévaut.

Pour le Gouvernement de la République de Finlande :
[LASSE ARVELA]

Pour le Conseil fédéral suisse :
[MAURICE DARIER]

No. 32888. Multilateral

AGREEMENT FOR THE ESTABLISHMENT OF THE INDIAN OCEAN TUNA COMMISSION. ROME, 25 NOVEMBER 1993 [*United Nations, Treaty Series, vol. 1927, I-32888.*]

WITHDRAWAL

Guinea

Notification deposited with the Director-General of the Food and Agriculture Organization of the United Nations: 22 February 2016

Date of effect: 31 December 2017

Registration with the Secretariat of the United Nations: Food and Agriculture Organization of the United Nations, 16 March 2016

N° 32888. Multilatéral

ACCORD PORTANT CRÉATION DE LA COMMISSION DES THONS DE L'OCÉAN INDIEN. ROME, 25 NOVEMBRE 1993 [*Nations Unies, Recueil des Traités, vol. 1927, I-32888.*]

RETRAIT

Guinée

Dépôt de la notification auprès du Directeur général de l'Organisation des Nations Unies pour l'alimentation et l'agriculture : 22 février 2016

Date de prise d'effet : 31 décembre 2017

Enregistrement au Secrétariat de l'Organisation des Nations Unies : Organisation des Nations Unies pour l'alimentation et l'agriculture, 16 mars 2016

No. 34028. Multilateral

CONVENTION ON ENVIRONMENTAL IMPACT ASSESSMENT IN A TRANSBOUNDARY CONTEXT. ESPOO, FINLAND, 25 FEBRUARY 1991 [*United Nations, Treaty Series, vol. 1989, I-34028.*]

PROTOCOL ON STRATEGIC ENVIRONMENTAL ASSESSMENT TO THE CONVENTION ON ENVIRONMENTAL IMPACT ASSESSMENT IN A TRANSBOUNDARY CONTEXT. KIEV, 21 MAY 2003 [*United Nations, Treaty Series, vol. 2685, A-34028.*]

RATIFICATION

Latvia

Deposit of instrument with the Secretary-General of the United Nations: 23 March 2016

Date of effect: 21 June 2016

Registration with the Secretariat of the United Nations: ex officio, 23 March 2016

Nº 34028. Multilatéral

CONVENTION SUR L'ÉVALUATION DE L'IMPACT SUR L'ENVIRONNEMENT DANS UN CONTEXTE TRANSFRONTIÈRE. ESPOO (FINLANDE), 25 FÉVRIER 1991 [*Nations Unies, Recueil des Traités, vol. 1989, I-34028.*]

PROTOCOLE À LA CONVENTION SUR L'ÉVALUATION DE L'IMPACT SUR L'ENVIRONNEMENT DANS UN CONTEXTE TRANSFRONTIÈRE, RELATIF À L'ÉVALUATION STRATÉGIQUE ENVIRONNEMENTALE. KIEV, 21 MAI 2003 [*Nations Unies, Recueil des Traités, vol. 2685, A-34028.*]

RATIFICATION

Lettonie

Dépôt de l'instrument auprès du Secrétaire général de l'Organisation des Nations Unies : 23 mars 2016

Date de prise d'effet : 21 juin 2016

Enregistrement au Secrétariat de l'Organisation des Nations Unies : d'office, 23 mars 2016

AMENDMENT TO THE CONVENTION ON ENVIRONMENTAL IMPACT ASSESSMENT IN A TRANSBOUNDARY CONTEXT. SOFIA, 27 FEBRUARY 2001 [*United Nations, Treaty Series, vol. 2999, A-34028.*]

RATIFICATION

Latvia

Deposit of instrument with the Secretary-General of the United Nations: 23 March 2016

Date of effect: 21 June 2016

Registration with the Secretariat of the United Nations: ex officio, 23 March 2016

ACCEPTANCE

Republic of Moldova

Deposit of instrument with the Secretary-General of the United Nations: 15 March 2016

Date of effect: 13 June 2016

Registration with the Secretariat of the United Nations: ex officio, 15 March 2016

RATIFICATION

Serbia

Deposit of instrument with the Secretary-General of the United Nations: 21 March 2016

Date of effect: 19 June 2016

Registration with the Secretariat of the United Nations: ex officio, 21 March 2016

AMENDEMENT À LA CONVENTION SUR L'ÉVALUATION DE L'IMPACT SUR L'ENVIRONNEMENT DANS UN CONTEXTE TRANSFRONTIÈRE. SOFIA, 27 FÉVRIER 2001 [*Nations Unies, Recueil des Traités, vol. 2999, A-34028.*]

RATIFICATION

Lettonie

Dépôt de l'instrument auprès du Secrétaire général de l'Organisation des Nations Unies : 23 mars 2016

Date de prise d'effet : 21 juin 2016

Enregistrement au Secrétariat de l'Organisation des Nations Unies : d'office, 23 mars 2016

ACCEPTATION

République de Moldova

Dépôt de l'instrument auprès du Secrétaire général de l'Organisation des Nations Unies : 15 mars 2016

Date de prise d'effet : 13 juin 2016

Enregistrement au Secrétariat de l'Organisation des Nations Unies : d'office, 15 mars 2016

RATIFICATION

Serbie

Dépôt de l'instrument auprès du Secrétaire général de l'Organisation des Nations Unies : 21 mars 2016

Date de prise d'effet : 19 juin 2016

Enregistrement au Secrétariat de l'Organisation des Nations Unies : d'office, 21 mars 2016

No. 34380. Netherlands and Chile

CONVENTION ON SOCIAL SECURITY (WITH ADMINISTRATIVE AGREEMENT OF 4 DECEMBER 1996). SANTIAGO, 10 JANUARY 1996 [*United Nations, Treaty Series, vol. 2006, I-34380.*]

AGREEMENT ON SOCIAL INSURANCE BETWEEN THE KINGDOM OF THE NETHERLANDS AND THE REPUBLIC OF CHILE, AMENDING THE CONVENTION ON SOCIAL INSURANCE BETWEEN THE KINGDOM OF THE NETHERLANDS AND THE REPUBLIC OF CHILE SIGNED IN SANTIAGO ON 10 JANUARY 1996. THE HAGUE, 15 JUNE 2005

Entry into force: 1 March 2016, in accordance with article IV

Authentic texts: Dutch and Spanish

Registration with the Secretariat of the United Nations: Netherlands, 31 March 2016

N° 34380. Pays-Bas et Chili

CONVENTION SUR LA SÉCURITÉ SOCIALE (AVEC ACCORD ADMINISTRATIF DU 4 DÉCEMBRE 1996). SANTIAGO, 10 JANVIER 1996 [*Nations Unies, Recueil des Traités, vol. 2006, I-34380.*]

ACCORD SUR LA SÉCURITÉ SOCIALE ENTRE LE ROYAUME DES PAYS-BAS ET LA RÉPUBLIQUE DU CHILI PORTANT AMENDEMENT DE LA CONVENTION SUR LA SÉCURITÉ SOCIALE ENTRE LE ROYAUME DES PAYS-BAS ET LA RÉPUBLIQUE DU CHILI SIGNÉ À SANTIAGO LE 10 JANVIER 1996. LA HAYE, 15 JUIN 2005

Entrée en vigueur : 1er mars 2016, conformément à l'article IV

Textes authentiques : néerlandais et espagnol

Enregistrement au Secrétariat de l'Organisation des Nations Unies : Pays-Bas, 31 mars 2016

[TEXT IN DUTCH – TEXTE EN NÉERLANDAIS]

Verdrag inzake sociale zekerheid tussen het Koninkrijk der Nederlanden en de Republiek Chili houdende herziening van het Verdrag inzake sociale zekerheid tussen het Koninkrijk der Nederlanden en de Republiek Chili, getekend te Santiago op 10 januari 1996

Het Koninkrijk der Nederlanden

en

de Republiek Chili,

Wensend de vriendschappelijke betrekkingen die tussen beide landen bestaan opnieuw te bevestigen, en

Voornemens de samenwerking op het terrein van de sociale zekerheid voort te zetten, en

Geleid door de wens enkele bepalingen van het Verdrag inzake sociale zekerheid tussen beide landen, ondertekend te Santiago, Chili, op 10 januari 1996, nader te noemen "het Verdrag", te herzien,

Zijn het volgende overeengekomen:

Artikel I

De volgende bepalingen van het Verdrag worden vervangen:

1. Artikel 1, letter h, door:
„h. ,uitkering': elke uitkering of elk pensioen ingevolge de wetgeving van één van beide Verdragsluitende Staten, met inbegrip van aanvullingen op en verhogingen van een uitkering of een pensioen conform de wetgeving genoemd in artikel 2."

2. Artikel 2, eerste lid, A, door:
„A. wat betreft Chili, op de wetgeving betreffende:
  a. het stelsel van ouderdoms-, invaliditeits- en nabestaandenpensioenen, gebaseerd op individuele kapitalisatie;
  b. de wettelijke regelingen met betrekking tot ouderdoms-, invaliditeits- en nabestaandenpensioenen beheerd door het Instituut voor de Normalisatie van de sociale zekerheid, en
  c. de wettelijke regelingen met betrekking tot verstrekkingen bij ziekte, alleen voor de toepassing van de artikelen 6 tot en met 12, ook op de wetgeving met betrekking tot:
  d. de overige sociale-verzekeringsregelingen, indien van toepassing."

3. Artikel 2, eerste lid, B, door:
„B. wat betreft Nederland, op de wetgeving betreffende:
  a. de invaliditeitsverzekering;
  b. de algemene ouderdomsverzekering;

c. de algemene weduwen- en wezenverzekering;
d. de kinderbijslag;
e. de ziekteverzekering (uitkeringen);
en voor de toepassing van de artikelen 6 tot en met 12, ook op de wetgeving met betrekking tot:
f. de ziekteverzekering (verstrekkingen);
g. de werkloosheidsverzekering."

Artikel II

Na artikel 21 van het Verdrag worden een nieuw artikel 21A en een nieuw artikel 21B toegevoegd, die luiden als volgt:

„Artikel 21A

Kinderbijslag

1. Het Nederlands bevoegd orgaan stelt de kinderbijslagen rechtstreeks en uitsluitend vast krachtens de Algemene Kinderbijslagwet.

2. Personen die recht hebben op, of in aanmerking komen om recht te verkrijgen op, kinderbijslag, zijn gerechtigd die uitkering te ontvangen indien zij wonen op het grondgebied van Chili.

Artikel 21B

Uitkeringen bij ziekte

1. Het Nederlands bevoegd orgaan stelt de uitkeringen bij ziekte rechtstreeks en uitsluitend vast krachtens de Ziektewet.

2. Personen die recht hebben op, of in aanmerking komen om recht te verkrijgen op, een uitkering bij ziekte, zijn gerechtigd die uitkering te ontvangen indien zij wonen op het grondgebied van Chili."

Artikel III

Aan artikel 5 van het Verdrag wordt een vierde lid toegevoegd dat als volgt luidt:

„4. Het eerste lid is, wat Nederland betreft, niet van toepassing op een uitkering op grond van de Toeslagenwet van 6 november 1986 dan wel op grond van de Wet arbeidsongeschiktheidsvoorziening jonggehandicapten van 24 april 1997."

Artikel IV

1. Beide Verdragsluitende Staten stellen elkaar schriftelijk in kennis van de voltooiing van hun respectieve interne juridische vereisten voor de inwerkingtreding van dit Verdrag. Dit Verdrag treedt in werking op

de eerste dag van de derde maand volgende op de datum van de laatste van deze kennisgevingen. Artikel II van dit Verdrag treedt voor het Koninkrijk der Nederlanden op 1 januari 2003 met terugwerkende kracht in werking.

2. Het Koninkrijk der Nederlanden past artikel II van dit Verdrag voorlopig eenzijdig toe met ingang van de eerste dag van de tweede maand volgende op de datum van ondertekening van dit Verdrag.

TEN BLIJKE WAARVAN de ondergetekenden, daartoe naar behoren gemachtigd, dit Verdrag hebben ondertekend.

GEDAAN in tweevoud te Den Haag, op 15 juni 2005, in de Nederlandse en de Spaanse taal, zijnde beide teksten gelijkelijk authentiek.

Voor het Koninkrijk der Nederlanden

B. R. BOT

Voor de Republiek Chili

I. WALKER

[TEXT IN SPANISH – TEXTE EN ESPAGNOL]

Acuerdo sobre seguridad social entre el Reino de Los Países Bajos y la República de Chile que modifica el Convenio sobre seguridad social entre el Reino de Los Países Bajos y la República de Chile, suscrito en Santiago, el 10 de enero 1996

El Reino de los Países Bajos

y

la República de Chile,

Deseando mantener las amistosas relaciones que existen entre ambos países, y

Animados de continuar la cooperación en el terreno de Seguridad Social, y

Ante la necesidad de revisar algunas disposiciones del Convenio sobre Seguridad Social entre ambos países, suscrito en Santiago de Chile el 10 de enero 1996, en adelante «El Convenio»,

Han convenido el siguiente Acuerdo:

Artículo I

Los siguientes artículos del Convenio serán remplazados por:

1. Artículo 1, párrafo h, por:
«h. ‹Beneficios›, cualquier prestación o pensión otorgada en virtud de la legislación de cualquiera de los Estados Contratantes, incluyéndose todo aumento o suma adicional que deba pagarse con una prestación o pensión conforme a la legislación mencionada en el artículo 2.»

2. Artículo 2, párrafo 1, A, por:
«A. Con respecto a Chile, a la legislación relativa a:
   a. el sistema de pensiones de vejez, invalidez y sobrevivencia, que se basa en la capitalización individual;
   b. los regímenes legales relativos a las pensiones de vejez, invalidez y sobrevivencia, administrados por el Instituto de Normalización Previsional, y
   c. los regímenes legales relativos a las prestaciones de salud, sólo para la aplicación del artículo 16; y para los efectos de la aplicación de los artículos 6 a 12, también a su legislación sobre:
   d. los otros regímenes de seguridad social, cuando corresponda»

3. Artículo 2, párrafo 1, B, por:
«B. Con respecto a los Países Bajos, a la legislación relativa a:
   a. el seguro de invalidez;
   b. el seguro general de vejez;

c. el seguro general de viudez y orfandad;
d. las asignaciones familiares;
e. el seguro de enfermedad (prestaciones monetarias);

y para los efectos de la aplicación de los artículos 6 a 12, también a su legislación sobre:

f. el seguro de enfermedad (prestaciones en especie);
g. el seguro de desempleo.»

Artículo II

A continuación del artículo 21 del Convenio agréganse, un nuevo artículo 21A y un nuevo artículo 21B, cuyo tenor es el siguente:

«Artículo 21A

Asignaciones familiares

1. La Institución Competente neerlandesa determinará las asignaciones familiares directamente y únicamente en virtud de la Ley general de ayuda familiar.

2. Una persona que tiene derecho a o está calificada para obtener derecho a asignaciones familiares, tendrá derecho a percibir esta prestación si tiene su domicilio en el territorio de Chile.

Artículo 21B

Prestaciones de enfermedad

1. La Institución Competente neerlandesa determinará las prestaciones de enfermedad directamente y únicamente en virtud de la Ley de Enfermedad.

2. Una persona que tiene derecho a o está calificada para obtener derecho a una prestación de enfermedad, tendrá derecho a percibir esta prestación si tiene su domicilio en el territorio de Chile.»

Artículo III

Al artículo 5 del Convenio se le agrega un número 4 del siguiente tenor:

«4. En lo que respecta a los Países Bajos, el apartado primero no será de aplicación a las prestaciones concedidas en virtud de la Ley de Complementos neerlandesa (‹Toeslagenwet›), ley del 6 de noviembre de 1986 o en virtud de la Ley de Incapacidad Laboral de personas jóvenes no válidas (‹Wajong›), de 24 de abril de 1997.»

Artículo IV

1. Ambos Estados Contratantes se notificarán mutuamente por escrito que han cumplido con sus respectivos requisitos jurídicos internos, necesarios para la entrada en vigencia del presente Acuerdo. Este Acuerdo

entrará en vigencia el primer día del tercer mes siguiente a la fecha de la última de estas notificaciones. El artículo II de este Acuerdo entrará en vigor para el Reino de los Países Bajos con efecto retroactivo a partir del 1 de enero de 2000.

2. El Reino de los Países Bajos aplicará unilateralmente el artículo II del presente Acuerdo con carácter provisional desde el primer día del segundo mes posterior a la fecha de la firma del presente Acuerdo.

EN TESTIMONIO DE LO CUAL, los suscritos, debidamente autorizados para ello, suscribieron el presente Acuerdo.

HECHO en duplicado en Den Haag, el quince junio 2005, en los idiomas neerlandés y español, siendo ambos textos igualmente auténticos.

Por el Reino de los Países Bajos

B. R. BOT

Por la República de Chile

I. WALKER

[TRANSLATION – TRADUCTION]

AGREEMENT ON SOCIAL INSURANCE BETWEEN THE KINGDOM OF THE NETHERLANDS AND THE REPUBLIC OF CHILE, AMENDING THE CONVENTION ON SOCIAL INSURANCE BETWEEN THE KINGDOM OF THE NETHERLANDS AND THE REPUBLIC OF CHILE SIGNED IN SANTIAGO ON 10 JANUARY 1996

The Kingdom of the Netherlands

and

the Republic of Chile,

Desiring to maintain the friendly relations between the two countries, and

Encouraged to continue cooperation in the field of social security, and

In view of the need to revise certain provisions of the Convention on social insurance between the two countries, signed at Santiago de Chile on 10 January 1996, hereinafter "the Convention",

Have agreed as follows:

Article I

The following articles of the Convention shall be replaced by:

1. Article 1, paragraph h by:

   "(h) 'Benefits' means any benefit or pension awarded under the legislation of any of the Contracting States, including supplements to and increases in a benefit or a pension under the legislation referred to in article 2."

2. Article 2, paragraph 1 A by:

   "A. In relation to Chile, to the legislation on:

   (a) The system of old-age, disability and surviving relatives' pensions, which is based on individual capitalization;

   (b) The statutory regulations governing old-age, disability and surviving relatives' pensions administered by the Institute of Social Security Standardization; and

   (c) For the implementation of article 16 only, the statutory regulations governing sickness allowances; and, for the implementation of articles 6 to 12, also to the legislation on:

   (d) The other social security schemes, as applicable."

3. Article 2, paragraph 1 B, by:

   "B. In relation to the Netherlands, to the legislation on:

   (a) Disability insurance;

   (b) General old-age pension insurance;

   (c) General widows' and orphans' insurance;

   (d) Family allowances;

(e) Health insurance (cash benefits);

and, for the implementation of articles 6 to 12, also to the legislation on:

(f) Health insurance (benefits in kind);

(g) Unemployment insurance."

Article II

Following article 21 of the Convention, a new article 21A and a new article 21B shall be added, which read:

"Article 21A. Family allowances

1. The competent Netherlands institution shall determine family allowances directly and exclusively, pursuant to the Family Allowance Act.

2. A person who is entitled or qualified to obtain the right to family allowances shall be entitled to receive this benefit if domiciled in the territory of Chile.

Article 21B. Sickness benefits

1. The competent Netherlands institution shall determine sickness benefits directly and exclusively, pursuant to the Sickness Benefits Act.

2. A person who is entitled or qualified to obtain the right to a sickness benefit shall be entitled to receive this benefit if domiciled in the territory of Chile."

Article III

A fourth paragraph shall be added to article 5 of the Convention, reading as follows:

"4. With regard to the Netherlands, paragraph 1 shall not apply to benefits granted under the Netherlands Supplementary Benefits Act ('Toeslagenwet') of 6 November 1986, or under the Invalidity Insurance Act specifically for young disabled persons ('Wajong') of 24 April 1997."

Article IV

1. Both Contracting States shall notify each other in writing that they have complied with their respective internal legal procedures required for the entry into force of this Agreement. This Agreement shall enter into force on the first day of the third month following the date of the last of these notifications. Article II of this Agreement shall enter into force for the Kingdom of the Netherlands with retroactive effect from 1 January 2000.

2. The Kingdom of the Netherlands shall unilaterally apply article II of this Agreement, provisionally, from the first day of the second month following the date of signature of this Agreement.

IN WITNESS THEREOF, the undersigned, being duly authorized thereto, have signed the present Agreement.

DONE in duplicate at The Hague on 15 June 2005, in the Dutch and Spanish languages, both texts being equally authentic.

For the Kingdom of the Netherlands:
B. R. BOT

For the Republic of Chile:
I. WALKER

[TRANSLATION – TRADUCTION]

ACCORD SUR LA SÉCURITÉ SOCIALE ENTRE LE ROYAUME DES PAYS-BAS ET LA RÉPUBLIQUE DU CHILI PORTANT AMENDEMENT DE LA CONVENTION SUR LA SÉCURITÉ SOCIALE ENTRE LE ROYAUME DES PAYS-BAS ET LA RÉPUBLIQUE DU CHILI SIGNÉE À SANTIAGO LE 10 JANVIER 1996

Le Royaume des Pays-Bas et la République du Chili,

Souhaitant maintenir les liens d'amitié qui existent entre les deux pays, et

Animés du désir de poursuivre la coopération dans le domaine de la sécurité sociale, et

Compte tenu de la nécessité de réviser certaines dispositions de la Convention sur la sécurité sociale entre les deux pays, signée à Santiago le 10 janvier 1996, ci-après dénommée la « Convention »,

Sont convenus de ce qui suit :

Article premier

Les articles suivants de la Convention sont remplacés comme suit :

1. L'alinéa h) du paragraphe 1 de l'article 1 par le texte suivant :

   « h) L'expression "allocations" désignera toute prestation ou pension servie en vertu de la législation de l'un quelconque des deux États contractants, y compris toute majoration ou tout supplément devant être versés à titre de prestation ou de pension en vertu de la législation visée à l'article 2. »

2. Le sous-paragraphe A du paragraphe 1 de l'article 2 par le texte suivant :

   « A. Pour ce qui est du Chili, à la législation concernant :

   a) Le régime des pensions de vieillesse, d'invalidité et de survivant fondé sur la capitalisation individuelle;

   b) Les régimes légaux relatifs aux pensions de vieillesse, d'invalidité et de survivant administrés par l'Institut de normalisation prévisionnelle; et

   c) Les régimes légaux relatifs aux prestations de santé, uniquement pour ce qui est de l'application de l'article 16; et, aux fins de l'application des articles 6 à 12, également aux dispositions législatives chiliennes sur :

   d) Les autres régimes de sécurité sociale, selon qu'il appartiendra. »

3. Le sous-paragraphe B du paragraphe 1 de l'article 2 par le texte suivant :

   « B. Pour ce qui est des Pays-Bas, à la législation concernant :

   a) L'assurance invalidité;

   b) L'assurance générale vieillesse;

   c) L'assurance générale veuvage et orphelinage;

   d) Les allocations familiales;

   e) L'assurance maladie (prestations monétaires);

et, aux fins de l'application des articles 6 à 12, également aux dispositions législatives chiliennes sur :

f) L'assurance maladie (prestations en espèces);

g) L'assurance chômage. »

Article II

Le nouvel article 21A et le nouvel article 21B suivants sont insérés après l'article 21 de la Convention :

« Article 21A. Allocations familiales

1. L'institution néerlandaise compétente déterminera les allocations familiales directement et exclusivement en application de la Loi générale sur l'aide aux familles.

2. Toute personne qui a droit ou est admissible à des allocations familiales aura le droit de percevoir ces allocations si elle est domiciliée sur le territoire du Chili.

Article 21B. Indemnités de maladie

1. L'institution néerlandaise compétente déterminera les indemnités de maladie directement et exclusivement en application de la Loi sur les prestations maladie.

2. Toute personne qui a droit ou est admissible à des indemnités de maladie aura le droit de recevoir ces allocations si elle est domiciliée sur le territoire du Chili. »

Article III

Un quatrième paragraphe, libellé comme suit, est ajouté à l'article 5 de la Convention :

« 4. S'agissant des Pays-Bas, le paragraphe 1 ne s'appliquera pas aux allocations accordées en vertu de la Loi néerlandaise sur les prestations complémentaires ("Toeslagenwet") du 6 novembre 1986 ou de la Loi sur les prestations d'invalidité pour les jeunes ("Wajong") du 24 avril 1997. »

Article IV

1. Les deux États contractants s'informent mutuellement par écrit de l'accomplissement des formalités juridiques internes requises pour l'entrée en vigueur du présent Accord. Le présent Accord entre en vigueur le premier jour du troisième mois suivant la date de la dernière de ces notifications. L'article II du présent Accord entre en vigueur pour le Royaume des Pays-Bas avec effet rétroactif à compter du 1er janvier 2000.

2. Le Royaume des Pays-Bas appliquera unilatéralement l'article II du présent Accord à titre provisoire à partir du premier jour du deuxième mois suivant la date de signature du présent Accord.

EN FOI DE QUOI, les soussignés, à ce dûment autorisés, ont signé le présent Accord.

FAIT à La Haye, le 15 juin 2005, en double exemplaire, en langues néerlandaise et espagnole, les deux textes faisant également foi.

Pour le Royaume des Pays-Bas :

B. R. BOT

Pour la République du Chili :

I. WALKER

No. 37794. Austria and Finland

AGREEMENT BETWEEN THE REPUBLIC OF AUSTRIA AND THE REPUBLIC OF FINLAND FOR THE AVOIDANCE OF DOUBLE TAXATION AND THE PREVENTION OF FISCAL EVASION WITH RESPECT TO TAXES ON INCOME AND ON CAPITAL. VIENNA, 26 JULY 2000 [*United Nations, Treaty Series, vol. 2164, I-37794.*]

PROTOCOL AND SUPPLEMENTARY PROTOCOL AMENDING THE AGREEMENT BETWEEN THE REPUBLIC OF AUSTRIA AND THE REPUBLIC OF FINLAND FOR THE AVOIDANCE OF DOUBLE TAXATION AND THE PREVENTION OF FISCAL EVASION WITH RESPECT TO TAXES ON INCOME AND ON CAPITAL SIGNED AT VIENNA ON 26 JULY 2000. HELSINKI, 4 MARCH 2011

Entry into force: 1 December 2011, in accordance with article 2

Authentic texts: Finnish and German

Registration with the Secretariat of the United Nations: Finland, 9 March 2016

N° 37794. Autriche et Finlande

ACCORD ENTRE LA RÉPUBLIQUE D'AUTRICHE ET LA RÉPUBLIQUE DE FINLANDE TENDANT À ÉVITER LA DOUBLE IMPOSITION ET À PRÉVENIR L'ÉVASION FISCALE EN MATIÈRE D'IMPÔTS SUR LE REVENU ET SUR LA FORTUNE. VIENNE, 26 JUILLET 2000 [*Nations Unies, Recueil des Traités, vol. 2164, I-37794.*]

PROTOCOLE ET PROTOCOLE ADDITIONNEL ENTRE LA RÉPUBLIQUE DE FINLANDE ET LA RÉPUBLIQUE D'AUTRICHE AMENDANT L'ACCORD TENDANT À ÉVITER LA DOUBLE IMPOSITION ET À PRÉVENIR L'ÉVASION FISCALE EN MATIÈRE D'IMPÔTS SUR LE REVENU ET SUR LA FORTUNE SIGNÉ À VIENNE LE 26 JUILLET 2000. HELSINKI, 4 MARS 2011

Entrée en vigueur : 1er décembre 2011, conformément à l'article 2

Textes authentiques : finnois et allemand

Enregistrement au Secrétariat de l'Organisation des Nations Unies : Finlande, 9 mars 2016

[TEXT IN FINNISH – TEXTE EN FINNOIS]

PÖYTÄKIRJA JA LISÄPÖYTÄKIRJA SUOMEN TASAVALLAN JA ITÄVALLAN TASAVALLAN VÄLILLÄ WIENISSÄ 26 PÄIVÄNÄ HEINÄKUUTA VUONNA 2000 TULO- JA VARALLISUUSVEROJA KOSKEVAN KAKSINKERTAISEN VEROTUKSEN VÄLTTÄMISEKSI JA VERON KIERTÄMISEN ESTÄMISEKSI TEHDYN SOPIMUKSEN MUUTTAMISESTA

Suomen tasavalta ja Itävallan tasavalta, jotka haluavat tehdä pöytäkirjan ja lisäpöytäkirjan Wienissä 26 päivänä heinäkuuta vuonna 2000 tulo- ja varallisuusveroja koskevan kaksinkertaisen verotuksen välttämiseksi ja veron kiertämisen estämiseksi tehdyn sopimuksen (jäljempänä "sopimus") muuttamisesta,

ovat sopineet seuraavasta:

I artikla

Sopimuksen 26 artikla poistetaan ja korvataan seuraavalla määräyksellä:

"26 artikla
Tietojen vaihtaminen

1. Sopimusvaltioiden toimivaltaisten viranomaisten on vaihdettava keskenään sellaisia tietoja, jotka ovat ennalta katsoen olennaisia tämän sopimuksen määräysten soveltamiseksi tai sopimusvaltioiden tai niiden valtiollisten osien tai paikallisviranomaisten lukuun määrättyjä kaikenlaatuisia veroja koskevan sisäisen lainsäädännön hallinnoimiseksi tai toimeenpanemiseksi, mikäli tämän lainsäädännön perusteella tapahtuva verotus ei ole vastoin tätä sopimusta. Sopimuksen 1 ja 2 artikla eivät rajoita tietojen vaihtamista.

2. Sopimusvaltion 1 kappaleen perusteella vastaanottamia tietoja on käsiteltävä salaisina samalla tavalla kuin tämän valtion sisäisen lainsäädännön perusteella saatuja tietoja ja niitä saadaan ilmaista vain henkilöille tai viranomaisille (mukaan lukien tuomioistuimet ja hallintoelimet), jotka määräävät, kantavat tai perivät 1 kappaleessa tarkoitettuja veroja tai käsittelevät näitä veroja koskevia syytteitä tai valituksia taikka valvovat edellä mainittuja toimia. Näiden henkilöiden tai viranomaisten on käytettävä tietoja vain tällaisiin tarkoituksiin. Ne saavat ilmaista tietoja julkisessa oikeudenkäynnissä tai tuomioistuimen ratkaisuissa. Sopimusvaltion saamia tietoja voidaan edellä olevan estämättä käyttää muihin tarkoituksiin, kun tällaisia tietoja voidaan kummankin valtion lainsäädännön mukaan käyttää tällaisiin muihin tarkoituksiin ja tiedot antavan valtion toimivaltainen viranomainen antaa luvan tällaiseen käyttöön.

3. Tämän artiklan 1 ja 2 kappaleen määräysten ei missään tapauksessa katsota velvoittavan sopimusvaltiota:

a) ryhtymään hallintotoimiin, jotka poikkeavat tämän sopimusvaltion tai toisen sopimusvaltion lainsäädännöstä ja hallintokäytännöstä;

b) antamaan tietoja, joita tämän sopimusvaltion tai toisen sopimusvaltion lainsäädännön mukaan tai säännönmukaisen hallintomenettelyn puitteissa ei voida hankkia;

c) antamaan tietoja, jotka paljastaisivat liikesalaisuuden taikka teollisen, kaupallisen tai ammatillisen salaisuuden tai elinkeinotoiminnassa käytetyn menettelytavan, taikka tietoja, joiden paljastaminen olisi vastoin yleistä järjestystä (ordre public).

4. Jos sopimusvaltio pyytää tietoja tämän artiklan mukaisesti, toisen sopimusvaltion on käytettävä tietojenhankintakeinojaan pyydettyjen tietojen hankkimiseksi, vaikka tämä toinen valtio ei ehkä tarvitsekaan näitä tietoja omiin verotuksellisiin tarkoituksiinsa. Edelliseen lauseeseen sisältyvän velvollisuuden osalta sovelletaan 3 kappaleen rajoituksia, mutta näiden rajoitusten ei voida milloinkaan katsoa sallivan sitä, että sopimusvaltio kieltäytyy antamasta tietoja vain sen vuoksi, että ne eivät sen osalta koske kansallista etua.

5. Tämän artiklan 3 kappaleen määräysten ei voida milloinkaan katsoa sallivan sitä, että sopimusvaltio kieltäytyy antamasta tietoja vain sen vuoksi, että tiedot ovat pankin, muun rahoituslaitoksen, välittäjän tai edustajan tai uskotun miehen hallussa tai ne koskevat omistusosuuksia henkilössä."

2 artikla

Sopimusvaltioiden on ilmoitettava toisilleen diplomaattista tietä, että kaikki oikeudelliset menettelyt tämän pöytäkirjan voimaantulemiseksi on suoritettu. Pöytäkirja tulee voimaan sen kolmannen kuukauden ensimmäisenä päivänä, joka lähinnä seuraa sen päivän jälkeen, jona myöhempi edellä tarkoitetuista ilmoituksista on vastaanotettu. Tämän pöytäkirjan määräyksiä sovelletaan verokausiin, jotka alkavat pöytäkirjan voimaantulovuotta lähinnä seuraavan kalenterivuoden tammikuun 1 päivänä tai sen jälkeen.

TÄMÄN VAKUUDEKSI kahden sopimusvaltion täysivaltaiset edustajat, asianmukaisesti siihen valtuutettuina, ovat allekirjoittaneet tämän pöytäkirjan.

Tehty Helsingissä 4 päivänä maaliskuuta 2011, kahtena suomen- ja saksankielisenä kappaleena kaikkien tekstien ollessa yhtä todistusvoimaiset.

SUOMEN TASAVALLAN PUOLESTA:

ITÄVALLAN TASAVALLAN PUOLESTA:

LISÄPÖYTÄKIRJA

Allekirjoitettaessa Suomen tasavallan ja Itävallan tasavallan välillä tänä päivänä tehtyä pöytäkirjaa Wienissä 26 päivänä heinäkuuta vuonna 2000 tulo- ja varallisuusveroja koskevan kaksinkertaisen verotuksen välttämiseksi ja veron kiertämisen estämiseksi tehdyn sopimuksen muuttamisesta, allekirjoittaneet ovat sopineet siitä, että seuraavat määräykset muodostavat pöytäkirjan olennaisen osan:

Lisäys 26 artiklaan:

1. Tietoja pyytävän valtion toimivaltaisen viranomaisen on sopimuksen mukaisen tietopyynnön tehdessään annettava pyynnön vastaanottavan valtion toimivaltaiselle viranomaiselle seuraavat tiedot sen osoittamiseksi, että pyydetyt tiedot ovat ennalta katsoen olennaisia:

a) tarkastettavana tai tutkittavana olevan henkilön henkilöllisyys;

b) selvitys etsityistä tiedoista mukaan lukien niiden luonne ja se, missä muodossa tietoja pyytävä valtio haluaa tiedot pyynnön vastaanottaneelta valtiolta saada;

c) se verotuksellinen tarkoitus, jota varten tietoja haetaan;

d) syyt, jotka antavat aiheen uskoa, että pyydetyt tiedot ovat pyynnön vastaanottaneessa valtiossa tai pyynnön vastaanottaneen valtion toimivallan piiriin kuuluvan henkilön hallussa tai hänen kontrollinsa alaisia;

e) siltä osin kuin ne ovat tunnetut, jokaisen sellaisen henkilön nimi ja osoite, jolla uskotaan olevan pyydetyt tiedot hallussaan;

f) selvitys siitä, että tietoja pyytävä valtio on käyttänyt kaikki omalla alueellaan käytettävissä olevat keinot tietojen hankkimiseksi, pois lukien keinot, jotka aiheuttaisivat suhteettoman suuria vaikeuksia.

2. Artiklassa 26 määrätyn tietojen vaihtamisen ei katsota sisältävän toimenpiteitä, jotka ovat vain todisteiden keräämistä ("tietojen kalastelua").

3. Artiklan 26 5 kappaleen ei katsota edellyttävän sitä, että sopimusvaltiot vaihtavat tietoja spontaanisti tai automaattisesti.

4. Kun 26 artiklaa tulkitaan, katsotaan, että edellä mainittujen periaatteiden lisäksi on otettava huomioon myös OECD:n kommentaareissa asetetut periaatteet.

TÄMÄN VAKUUDEKSI kahden sopimusvaltion täysivaltaiset edustajat, asianmukaisesti siihen valtuutettuina, ovat allekirjoittaneet tämän lisäpöytäkirjan.

Tehty Helsingissä 4 päivänä maaliskuuta 2011, kahtena suomen- ja saksankielisenä kappaleena kaikkien tekstien ollessa yhtä todistusvoimaiset.

SUOMEN TASAVALLAN PUOLESTA:

ITÄVALLAN TASAVALLAN PUOLESTA:

[TEXT IN GERMAN – TEXTE EN ALLEMAND]

PROTOKOLL UND ZUSATZPROTOKOLL ZWISCHEN DER REPUBLIK FINNLAND UND DER REPUBLIK ÖSTERREICH ZUR ABÄNDERUNG DES AM 26. JULI 2000 IN WIEN UNTERZEICHNETEN ABKOMMENS ZUR VERMEIDUNG DER DOPPELBESTEUERUNG UND ZUR VERHINDERUNG DER STEUERUMGEHUNG AUF DEM GEBIETE DER STEUERN VOM EINKOMMEN UND VOM VERMÖGEN

Die Republik Finnland und die Republik Österreich, von dem Wunsch geleitet, ein Protokoll und ein Zusatzprotokoll zur Abänderung des am 26. Juli 2000 in Wien unterzeichneten Abkommens zur Vermeidung der Doppelbesteuerung und zur Verhinderung der Steuerumgehung auf dem Gebiete der Steuern vom Einkommen und vom Vermögen (im Folgenden "Abkommen" genannt) abzuschließen,

Sind wie folgt übereingekommen:

Artikel 1

Artikel 26 des Abkommens wird aufgehoben und durch folgende Bestimmung ersetzt:

"Artikel 26
Informationsaustausch

1. Die zuständigen Behörden der Vertragsstaaten tauschen die Informationen aus, die zur Durchführung dieses Abkommens oder zur Anwendung oder Durchsetzung des innerstaatlichen Rechts betreffend Steuern jeder Art und Bezeichnung, die für Rechnung der Vertragsstaaten oder ihrer Gebietskörperschaften erhoben werden, voraussichtlich erheblich sind, soweit die diesem Recht entsprechende Besteuerung nicht dem Abkommen widerspricht. Der Informationsaustausch ist durch Artikel 1 und 2 nicht eingeschränkt.

2. Alle Informationen, die ein Vertragsstaat nach Absatz 1 erhalten hat, sind ebenso geheim zu halten wie die auf Grund des innerstaatlichen Rechts dieses Staates beschafften Informationen und dürfen nur den Personen oder Behörden (einschließlich der Gerichte und Verwaltungsbehörden) zugänglich gemacht werden, die mit der Veranlagung oder Erhebung, der Vollstreckung oder Strafverfolgung, oder mit der Entscheidung von Rechtsmitteln hinsichtlich der in Absatz 1 genannten Steuern oder mit der Aufsicht darüber befasst sind. Diese Personen oder Behörden dürfen die Informationen nur für diese Zwecke verwenden. Sie dürfen die Informationen in einem öffentlichen Gerichtsverfahren oder in einer Gerichtsentscheidung offen legen. Ungeachtet der vorstehenden Bestimmungen kann ein Vertragsstaat die erhaltenen Informationen für andere Zwecke verwenden, wenn solche Informationen nach dem Recht beider Staaten für solche andere Zwecke verwendet werden dürfen und die zuständige Behörde desjenigen Staates, der die Informationen erteilt hat, dieser anderen Verwendung zustimmt.

3. Die Absätze 1 und 2 sind nicht so auszulegen, als verpflichteten sie einen Vertragsstaat,

a) Verwaltungsmaßnahmen durchzuführen, die von den Gesetzen und der Verwaltungspraxis dieses oder des anderen Vertragsstaats abweichen;

b) Informationen zu erteilen, die nach den Gesetzen oder im üblichen Verwaltungsverfahren dieses oder des anderen Vertragsstaats nicht beschafft werden können;

c) Informationen zu erteilen, die ein Handels-, Industrie-, Gewerbe- oder Berufsgeheimnis oder ein Geschäftsverfahren preisgeben würden oder deren Erteilung dem Ordre public widerspräche.

4. Ersucht ein Vertragsstaat gemäß diesem Artikel um Informationen, so nutzt der andere Vertragsstaat die ihm zur Verfügung stehenden Möglichkeiten zur Beschaffung der erbetenen Informationen, selbst wenn dieser andere Staat diese Informationen für seine eigenen steuerlichen Zwecke nicht benötigt. Die im vorhergehenden Satz enthaltene Verpflichtung unterliegt den Beschränkungen nach Absatz 3, wobei diese jedoch nicht so auszulegen sind, dass ein Vertragsstaat die Erteilung von Informationen nur deshalb ablehnen kann, weil er kein innerstaatliches Interesse an solchen Informationen hat.

5. Absatz 3 ist in keinem Fall so auszulegen, als könne ein Vertragsstaat die Erteilung von Informationen nur deshalb ablehnen, weil sich die Informationen bei einer Bank, einem sonstigen Kreditinstitut, einem Bevollmächtigten, Vertreter oder Treuhänder befinden oder weil sie sich auf das Eigentum an einer Person beziehen."

Artikel 2

Die Vertragsstaaten teilen einander auf diplomatischem Weg mit, dass alle rechtlichen Voraussetzungen für das Inkrafttreten dieses Protokolls abgeschlossen sind. Das Protokoll tritt am ersten Tag des dritten Monats in Kraft, der dem Zeitpunkt des Empfanges der späteren der oben genannten Mitteilungen folgt. Die Bestimmungen des Protokolls finden Anwendung auf alle Steuerzeiträume, die am oder nach dem 1. Jänner des Kalenderjahres beginnen, das dem Zeitpunkt des Inkrafttretens dieses Protokolls folgt.

ZU URKUND DESSEN haben die hiezu gehörig Bevollmächtigten der beiden Vertragsstaaten dieses Protokoll unterzeichnet.

GESCHEHEN zu Helsinki am 4. März 2011 in zweifacher Ausfertigung, jede in finnischer und deutscher Sprache, wobei jeder Text gleichermaßen authentisch ist.

Für die Republik Finnland:

Für die Republik Österreich:

ZUSATZPROTOKOLL

Im Zeitpunkt der Unterzeichnung des Protokolls zur Abänderung des am 26. Juli 2000 in Wien unterzeichneten Abkommens zur Vermeidung der Doppelbesteuerung und zur Verhinderung der Steuerumgehung auf dem Gebiete der Steuern vom Einkommen und vom Vermögen, das heute zwischen der Republik Finnland und der Republik Österreich abgeschlossen wurde, sind die Gefertigten übereingekommen, dass die folgenden Bestimmungen einen integrierenden Bestandteil des Protokolls bilden:

Zu Artikel 26:

1. Die zuständige Behörde des ersuchenden Staates stellt der zuständigen Behörde des ersuchten Staates zur Darstellung der voraussichtlichen Erheblichkeit der Auskünfte die folgenden Informationen zur Verfügung, wenn diese ein Auskunftsersuchen gemäß dem Abkommen stellt:

   a) die Bezeichnung der Person, der die Ermittlung oder Untersuchung gilt;

   b) eine Stellungnahme betreffend die gesuchten Auskünfte einschließlich der Art und der Form, in der der ersuchende Staat die Auskünfte vorzugsweise vom ersuchten Staat erhalten möchte;

   c) den steuerlichen Zweck, für den um die Auskünfte ersucht wird;

   d) die Gründe für die Annahme, dass die erbetenen Auskünfte dem ersuchten Staat vorliegen oder sich im Besitz oder in der Verfügungsmacht einer Person im Hoheitsbereich des ersuchten Staates befinden;

   e) den Namen und die Anschrift von Personen, soweit bekannt, in deren Besitz sich die erbetenen Auskünfte vermutlich befinden;

   f) eine Erklärung, dass der ersuchende Staat alle ihm in seinem eigenen Gebiet zur Verfügung stehenden Maßnahmen zur Einholung der Auskünfte ausgeschöpft hat, ausgenommen solche, die unverhältnismäßig große Schwierigkeiten mit sich bringen würden.

2. Es besteht Einvernehmen darüber, dass die in Artikel 26 vorgesehene Amtshilfe nicht Maßnahmen einschließt, die lediglich der Beweisausforschung dienen ("fishing expeditions").

3. Es besteht Einvernehmen darüber, dass Artikel 26 Absatz 5 des Abkommens die Vertragsstaaten nicht dazu verpflichtet, Informationen auf automatischer oder spontaner Basis auszutauschen.

4. Es besteht Einvernehmen darüber, dass zur Auslegung des Artikels 26 neben den oben angeführten Grundsätzen auch die aus den Kommentaren der OECD abzuleitenden Anwendungsgrundsätze zu berücksichtigen sind.

ZU URKUND DESSEN haben die hiezu gehörig Bevollmächtigten der beiden Vertragsstaaten dieses Zusatzprotokoll unterzeichnet.

GESCHEHEN zu Helsinki am 4. März 2011 in zweifacher Ausfertigung, jede in finnischer und deutscher Sprache, wobei jeder Text gleichermaßen authentisch ist.

Für die Republik
Finnland:

Für die Republik
Österreich:

[TRANSLATION – TRADUCTION]

PROTOCOL AND SUPPLEMENTARY PROTOCOL AMENDING THE AGREEMENT BETWEEN THE REPUBLIC OF AUSTRIA AND THE REPUBLIC OF FINLAND FOR THE AVOIDANCE OF DOUBLE TAXATION AND THE PREVENTION OF FISCAL EVASION WITH RESPECT TO TAXES ON INCOME AND CAPITAL, SIGNED AT VIENNA ON 26 JULY 2000

The Republic of Finland and the Republic of Austria, desiring to conclude a Protocol and a Supplementary Protocol amending the Agreement for the avoidance of double taxation and the prevention of fiscal evasion with respect to taxes on income and capital, signed at Vienna on 26 July 2000 (hereinafter "the Agreement"),

Have agreed as follows:

Article 1

Article 26 of the Agreement shall be removed and replaced by the following provision:

"Article 26. Exchange of information

1. The competent authorities of the Contracting States shall exchange such information as is foreseeably relevant for carrying out the provisions of this Agreement or to the administration or enforcement of the domestic laws of the Contracting States concerning taxes of every kind and description imposed on behalf of the Contracting States or their political subdivisions, insofar as the taxation thereunder is not contrary to the Agreement. The exchange of information shall not be restricted by articles 1 and 2.

2. Any information received under paragraph 1 by a Contracting State shall be treated as secret in the same manner as information obtained under the domestic laws of that State and shall be disclosed only to persons or authorities (including courts and administrative bodies) concerned with the assessment or collection of, the enforcement or prosecution in respect of, or the determination of appeals in relation to, the taxes referred to in paragraph 1, or the oversight of the above. Such persons or authorities shall use the information only for such purposes. They may disclose the information in public court proceedings or in judicial decisions. Notwithstanding the foregoing provisions, the information may be used by a Contracting State for other purposes when it may be used for such other purposes under the laws of both States and the competent authority of the sending State authorizes such use.

3. In no case shall paragraphs 1 and 2 be construed so as to impose on a Contracting State the obligation:

(a) To carry out administrative measures at variance with the laws and administrative practice of that or of the other Contracting State;

(b) To supply information which is not obtainable under the laws or in the normal course of the administration of that or of the other Contracting State;

(c) To supply information that would disclose any trade, industrial, commercial or professional secret or trade process, or information, the disclosure of which would be contrary to public policy (ordre public).

4. If information is requested by a Contracting State in accordance with this article, the other Contracting State shall use its information gathering measures to obtain the requested information, even though that other State may not need such information for its own tax purposes. The obligation contained in the preceding sentence is subject to the limitations paragraph 3, but in no case shall such limitations be construed to permit a Contracting State to decline to supply information solely because it has no domestic interest in such information.

5. In no case shall the provisions of paragraph 3 be construed to permit a Contracting State to decline to supply information solely because the information is held by a bank, other financial institution, nominee, or person acting in an agency or a fiduciary capacity, or because it relates to ownership interests in a person."

Article 2

The Contracting States shall notify one another through the diplomatic channel of the completion of the legal procedures necessary for the entry into force of this Protocol. The Protocol shall enter into force on the first day of the third month following the date of receipt of the later of the aforementioned notifications. The provisions of the Protocol shall apply to all tax periods starting on or after 1 January of the calendar year following the date of entry into force of this Protocol.

IN WITNESS WHEREOF the undersigned representatives of the two Contracting States, being duly authorized thereto, have signed this Protocol.

DONE at Helsinki on 4 March 2011 in two copies, each in the Finnish and German languages, each text being equally authentic.

For the Republic of Finland:
[JYRKI KATAINEN]

For the Republic of Austria:
[JOSEF PRÖLL]

SUPPLEMENTARY PROTOCOL

At the time of signature of the Protocol amending the Agreement for the avoidance of double taxation and the prevention of fiscal evasion with respect to taxes on income and capital, signed at Vienna on 26 July 2000, which was concluded today between the Republic of Finland and the Republic of Austria, the Parties have agreed that the following provisions shall form an integral part of the Protocol:

Article 26:

1. The competent authority of the Requesting State shall provide the following information to the competent authority of the Requested State when making a request for information under the Agreement to demonstrate the foreseeable relevance of the information to the request:

   (a) The identity of the person under examination or inquiry;

   (b) A statement of the information sought including its nature and the form in which the Requesting State wishes to receive the information from the Requested State;

   (c) The tax purpose for which the information is sought;

   (d) The grounds for believing that the information requested is held in the Requested State or is in the possession or control of a person within the jurisdiction of the Requested State;

   (e) To the extent known, the names and addresses of any person believed to be in possession of the requested information;

   (f) A statement to the effect that the Requesting State has exhausted all means available in its own territory to obtain the information, except those that would give rise to disproportionate difficulties.

2. It is understood that the mutual assistance provided for in article 26 shall not include measures the aim of which is solely to trawl for evidence ("fishing expeditions").

3. It is understood that the Contracting States are not obliged by article 26 (5) of the Agreement to exchange information automatically or spontaneously.

4. It is understood that, in addition to the principles set out above, the principles regarding application contained in the OECD commentaries shall also be taken into account for the interpretation of article 26.

IN WITNESS WHEREOF the undersigned representatives of the two Contracting Parties, being duly authorized thereto, have signed this Supplementary Protocol.

DONE at Helsinki on 4 March 2011 in two copies, each in the Finnish and German languages, each text being equally authentic.

For the Republic of Finland:
[JYRKI KATAINEN]

For the Republic of Austria:
[JOSEF PRÖLL]

[TRANSLATION – TRADUCTION]

PROTOCOLE ET PROTOCOLE ADDITIONNEL ENTRE LA RÉPUBLIQUE DE FINLANDE ET LA RÉPUBLIQUE D'AUTRICHE AMENDANT L'ACCORD TENDANT À ÉVITER LA DOUBLE IMPOSITION ET À PRÉVENIR L'ÉVASION FISCALE EN MATIÈRE D'IMPÔTS SUR LE REVENU ET SUR LA FORTUNE SIGNÉ À VIENNE LE 26 JUILLET 2000

La République de Finlande et la République d'Autriche,

Désireuses de conclure un Protocole et un Protocole additionnel amendant l'Accord tendant à éviter la double imposition et à prévenir l'évasion fiscale en matière d'impôts sur le revenu et sur la fortune, signé à Vienne le 26 juillet 2000 (ci-après dénommé la « Convention »),

Sont convenues de ce qui suit :

Article premier

L'article 26 de l'Accord est supprimé et remplacé par la disposition suivante :

« Article 26. Échange de renseignements

1. Les autorités compétentes des États contractants échangent les renseignements vraisemblablement pertinents pour appliquer les dispositions du présent Accord ou celles de la législation interne des États contractants relative aux impôts de toute nature et de toute dénomination perçus pour le compte des États contractants ou de leurs subdivisions politiques, dans la mesure où l'imposition qu'elle prévoit n'est pas contraire à l'Accord. L'échange de renseignements n'est pas restreint par les articles premier et 2.

2. Les renseignements reçus par un État contractant en vertu du paragraphe 1 sont tenus secrets de la même manière que les renseignements obtenus en application de la législation interne de cet État, et ils ne sont communiqués qu'aux personnes ou autorités (y compris les tribunaux et organes administratifs) concernées par l'établissement ou le recouvrement des impôts visés au paragraphe 1, par les procédures ou poursuites concernant ces impôts, par les décisions sur les recours relatifs à ces impôts, ou par le contrôle de ce qui précède. Ces personnes ou autorités n'utilisent ces renseignements qu'à ces fins, mais peuvent en faire état au cours d'audiences publiques de tribunaux ou dans des jugements. Nonobstant les dispositions précédentes, ces renseignements peuvent être utilisés à d'autres fins par un État contractant si la législation des deux États le permet et si l'autorité compétente de l'État qui fournit les renseignements l'autorise.

3. Les paragraphes 1 et 2 ne peuvent être interprétés comme imposant à un État contractant l'obligation :

a) de prendre des mesures administratives dérogeant à sa législation et à sa pratique administrative ou à celles de l'autre État contractant;

b) de fournir des renseignements qui ne pourraient être obtenus sur la base de sa législation ou dans le cadre de sa pratique administrative normale ou de celles de l'autre État contractant;

c) de fournir des renseignements qui révéleraient un secret commercial, industriel ou professionnel ou un procédé commercial, ou des renseignements dont la divulgation serait contraire à l'ordre public.

4. Si des renseignements sont demandés par un État contractant conformément au présent article, l'autre État contractant utilise ses mesures de collecte de renseignements pour obtenir les renseignements demandés quand bien même cet autre État n'aurait pas besoin de ces renseignements à ses propres fins fiscales. L'obligation contenue dans la phrase précédente est subordonnée aux limitations du paragraphe 3, mais en aucun cas ces limitations ne doivent être interprétées comme autorisant un État contractant à refuser de fournir des renseignements pour la seule raison qu'il ne détient aucun intérêt national dans de tels renseignements.

5. Les dispositions du paragraphe 3 ne doivent en aucun cas être interprétées comme autorisant un État contractant à refuser de fournir des renseignements pour la seule raison que les renseignements sont tenus par une banque, une autre institution financière, un mandataire ou une personne agissant en qualité d'agent ou à titre fiduciaire ou parce que cela concerne les intérêts fonciers d'une personne. »

Article 2

Les États contractants se notifient, par la voie diplomatique, l'accomplissement des procédures juridiques nécessaires à l'entrée en vigueur du présent Protocole. Le Protocole entre en vigueur le premier jour du troisième mois suivant la date de réception de la dernière des notifications susmentionnées. Les dispositions du Protocole sont applicables à toutes les périodes imposables commençant le 1er janvier de l'année civile suivant la date d'entrée en vigueur du présent Protocole ou après cette date.

EN FOI DE QUOI, les représentants soussignés des deux États contractants, à ce dûment autorisés, ont signé le présent Protocole.

FAIT à Helsinki, le 4 mars 2011, en deux exemplaires, chacun en langues finnoise et allemande, tous les textes faisant également foi.

Pour la République de Finlande :

[JYRKI KATAINEN]

Pour la République d'Autriche :

[JOSEF PRÖLL]

PROTOCOLE ADDITIONNEL

Lors de la signature du Protocole amendant l'Accord tendant à éviter la double imposition et à prévenir l'évasion fiscale en matière d'impôts sur le revenu et sur la fortune, signé à Vienne le 26 juillet 2000, conclu ce jour entre la République d'Autriche et la République d'Autriche, les Parties sont convenues que les dispositions suivantes font partie intégrante du Protocole :

Article 26 :

1. L'autorité compétente de l'État requérant fournit les informations suivantes à l'autorité compétente de l'État requis lorsqu'elle soumet une demande de renseignements en vertu de l'Accord, afin de démontrer la pertinence vraisemblable des renseignements demandés :

   a) L'identité de la personne faisant l'objet d'un contrôle ou d'une enquête ;

   b) Les indications concernant les renseignements demandés, notamment leur nature et la forme sous laquelle l'État requérant souhaite recevoir les renseignements de l'État requis ;

   c) Le but fiscal dans lequel les renseignements sont demandés ;

   d) Les raisons qui donnent à penser que les renseignements demandés sont détenus par l'État requis ou sont en la possession ou sous le contrôle d'une personne relevant de la compétence de l'État requis ;

   e) Dans la mesure où ils sont connus, les nom et adresse de toute personne dont il y a lieu de penser qu'elle est en possession des renseignements demandés ;

   f) Une déclaration précisant que l'État requérant a utilisé pour obtenir les renseignements tous les moyens disponibles sur son propre territoire, hormis ceux qui susciteraient des difficultés disproportionnées.

2. Il est entendu que l'assistance mutuelle prévue à l'article 26 n'inclut pas de mesures servant exclusivement à la recherche de preuves (« pêche aux informations »).

3. Il est entendu que les dispositions du paragraphe 5 de l'article 26 de l'Accord n'obligent en aucun cas les États contractants à échanger des renseignements de manière automatique ou spontanée.

4. Il est entendu que, outre les principes énoncés ci-dessus, les principes d'application établis dans les commentaires de l'OCDE doivent également être pris en considération aux fins de l'interprétation de l'article 26.

EN FOI DE QUOI, les représentants soussignés des deux Parties contractantes, à ce dûment autorisés, ont signé le présent Protocole additionnel.

FAIT à Helsinki, le 4 mars 2011, en deux exemplaires, chacun en langues finnoise et allemande, chaque texte faisant également foi.

Pour la République de Finlande :
[JYRKI KATAINEN]

Pour la République d'Autriche :
[JOSEF PRÖLL]

No. 38544. Multilateral

ROME STATUTE OF THE INTERNATIONAL CRIMINAL COURT. ROME, 17 JULY 1998 [*United Nations, Treaty Series, vol. 2187, I-38544.*]

ACCESSION (WITH DECLARATION)

El Salvador

Deposit of instrument with the Secretary-General of the United Nations: 3 March 2016

Date of effect: 1 June 2016

Registration with the Secretariat of the United Nations: ex officio, 3 March 2016

N° 38544. Multilatéral

STATUT DE ROME DE LA COUR PÉNALE INTERNATIONALE. ROME, 17 JUILLET 1998 [*Nations Unies, Recueil des Traités, vol. 2187, I-38544.*]

ADHÉSION (AVEC DÉCLARATION)

El Salvador

Dépôt de l'instrument auprès du Secrétaire général de l'Organisation des Nations Unies : 3 mars 2016

Date de prise d'effet : 1er juin 2016

Enregistrement au Secrétariat de l'Organisation des Nations Unies : d'office, 3 mars 2016

Declaration:

Déclaration :

[TEXT IN SPANISH – TEXTE EN ESPAGNOL]

De conformidad con el artículo 87, párrafo 1 del Estatuto de Roma de la Corte Penal Internacional, la República de El Salvador declara que todas las solicitudes de cooperación deberán tramitarse por vía diplomática.

De conformidad con el artículo 87, párrafo 2 del Estatuto de Roma de la Corte Penal Internacional, declara que las solicitudes de cooperación y los documentos que las justifiquen estarán redactados en idioma español, o deberán enviarse acompañados de una traducción en este idioma.

[TRANSLATION – TRADUCTION]

In accordance with article 87 (1) of the Rome Statute of the International Criminal Court, the Republic of El Salvador declares that all requests for cooperation must be transmitted through diplomatic channel.

In accordance with article 87 (2) of the Rome Statute of the International Criminal Court, the Republic of El Salvador declares that the requests for cooperation and any documents supporting the request must be written in the Spanish language or be accompanied by a translation into Spanish.

[TRANSLATION – TRADUCTION]

Conformément au paragraphe 1 de l'article 87 du Statut de Rome de la Cour pénale internationale, la République d'El Salvador déclare que toutes les demandes de coopération doivent être transmises par voie diplomatique.

Conformément au paragraphe 2 de l'article 87 du Statut de Rome de la Cour pénale internationale, la République d'El Salvador déclare que les demandes de coopération et les pièces justificatives y afférentes doivent être rédigées en espagnol ou être accompagnées d'une traduction en espagnol.

AMENDMENT TO ARTICLE 8 OF THE ROME STATUTE OF THE INTERNATIONAL CRIMINAL COURT. KAMPALA, 10 JUNE 2010 [*United Nations, Treaty Series, vol. 2868, A-38544.*]

RATIFICATION

El Salvador

Deposit of instrument with the Secretary-General of the United Nations: 3 March 2016

Date of effect: 3 March 2017

Registration with the Secretariat of the United Nations: ex officio, 3 March 2016

RATIFICATION

The former Yugoslav Republic of Macedonia

Deposit of instrument with the Secretary-General of the United Nations: 1 March 2016

Date of effect: 1 March 2017

Registration with the Secretariat of the United Nations: ex officio, 1 March 2016

AMENDEMENT À L'ARTICLE 8 DU STATUT DE ROME DE LA COUR PÉNALE INTERNATIONALE. KAMPALA, 10 JUIN 2010 [*Nations Unies, Recueil des Traités, vol. 2868, A-38544.*]

RATIFICATION

El Salvador

Dépôt de l'instrument auprès du Secrétaire général de l'Organisation des Nations Unies : 3 mars 2016

Date de prise d'effet : 3 mars 2017

Enregistrement au Secrétariat de l'Organisation des Nations Unies : d'office, 3 mars 2016

RATIFICATION

ex-République yougoslave de Macédoine

Dépôt de l'instrument auprès du Secrétaire général de l'Organisation des Nations Unies : 1er mars 2016

Date de prise d'effet : 1er mars 2017

Enregistrement au Secrétariat de l'Organisation des Nations Unies : d'office, 1er mars 2016

AMENDMENTS ON THE CRIME OF AGGRESSION TO THE ROME STATUTE OF THE INTERNATIONAL CRIMINAL COURT. KAMPALA, 11 JUNE 2010 [*United Nations, Treaty Series, vol. 2922, A-38544.*]

RATIFICATION

El Salvador

Deposit of instrument with the Secretary-General of the United Nations: 3 March 2016

Date of effect: 3 March 2017

Registration with the Secretariat of the United Nations: ex officio, 3 March 2016

RATIFICATION

The former Yugoslav Republic of Macedonia

Date: 1 March 2016

Date of effect: 1 March 2017

Registration with the Secretariat of the United Nations: ex officio, 1 March 2016

AMENDEMENTS AU STATUT DE ROME DE LA COUR PÉNALE INTERNATIONALE RELATIFS AU CRIME D'AGRESSION. KAMPALA, 11 JUIN 2010 [*Nations Unies, Recueil des Traités, vol. 2922, A-38544.*]

RATIFICATION

El Salvador

Dépôt de l'instrument auprès du Secrétaire général de l'Organisation des Nations Unies : 3 mars 2016

Date de prise d'effet : 3 mars 2017

Enregistrement au Secrétariat de l'Organisation des Nations Unies : d'office, 3 mars 2016

RATIFICATION

ex-République yougoslave de Macédoine

Date : 1er mars 2016

Date de prise d'effet : 1er mars 2017

Enregistrement au Secrétariat de l'Organisation des Nations Unies : d'office, 1er mars 2016

No. 39126. Netherlands and Philippines

AGREEMENT BETWEEN THE KINGDOM OF THE NETHERLANDS AND THE REPUBLIC OF THE PHILIPPINES ON THE EXPORT OF SOCIAL INSURANCE BENEFITS. MANILA, 10 APRIL 2001 [*United Nations, Treaty Series, vol. 2203, I-39126.*]

PROTOCOL AMENDING THE AGREEMENT BETWEEN THE KINGDOM OF THE NETHERLANDS AND THE REPUBLIC OF THE PHILIPPINES ON THE EXPORT OF SOCIAL INSURANCE BENEFITS. MANILA, 21 APRIL 2015

Entry into force: provisionally on 1 July 2015 and definitively on 1 March 2016, in accordance with article III

Authentic text: English

Registration with the Secretariat of the United Nations: Netherlands, 31 March 2016

N° 39126. Pays-Bas et Philippines

ACCORD ENTRE LE ROYAUME DES PAYS-BAS ET LA RÉPUBLIQUE DES PHILIPPINES RELATIF À L'EXPORTATION DES PRESTATIONS D'ASSURANCE SOCIALE. MANILLE, 10 AVRIL 2001 [*Nations Unies, Recueil des Traités, vol. 2203, I-39126.*]

PROTOCOLE AMENDANT L'ACCORD ENTRE LE ROYAUME DES PAYS-BAS ET LA RÉPUBLIQUE DES PHILIPPINES RELATIF À L'EXPORTATION DES PRESTATIONS D'ASSURANCE SOCIALE. MANILLE, 21 AVRIL 2015

Entrée en vigueur : provisoirement le 1er juillet 2015 et définitivement le 1er mars 2016, conformément à l'article III

Texte authentique : anglais

Enregistrement au Secrétariat de l'Organisation des Nations Unies : Pays-Bas, 31 mars 2016

[TEXT IN ENGLISH – TEXTE EN ANGLAIS]

Protocol amending the Agreement between the Kingdom of the Netherlands and the Republic of the Philippines on the export of social insurance benefits

The Kingdom of the Netherlands

and

the Republic of the Philippines,

hereinafter "the Parties",

Wishing to amend the Agreement between the Kingdom of the Netherlands and the Republic of the Philippines on the export of social insurance benefits, signed in Manila on 10 April 2001, hereinafter referred to as the "Agreement",

Have agreed as follows:

Article I

Article 1, paragraph 1 (e) of the Agreement is hereby amended as follows:
"e) "competent institution" means in relation to the Kingdom of the Netherlands regarding the legislation referred to in Article 2, paragraph 1, under A) (i), (ii) and (iii): the "Landelijk instituut sociale verzekeringen" (National Social Insurance Institute) c/o Gak Nederland bv or its legal successor and regarding the legislation referred to in Article 2, paragraph 1, under A) (iv) and (v): the "Sociale Verzekeringsbank" (Social Insurance Bank); in relation to the Republic of the Philippines, the Social Security System for the private sector workers and the Government Service Insurance System for the public sector workers;"

Article II

1. Article 2, paragraph 1 (A) (iv and v) of the Agreement is hereby amended as follows: (iv) old age insurance: and (v) survivors' insurance.

2. Article 2, paragraph 1 (A) (vi) of the Agreement is hereby deleted.

Article III

1. In accordance with Article 13, paragraph 3 of the Agreement, this Protocol shall enter into force on the first day of the second month following the date of the last written notification, through diplomatic channels, by either Party.

2. This Protocol shall be applicable provisionally from 1 July 2015.

IN WITNESS WHEREOF the undersigned, being duly authorized thereto by their respective Governments, have affixed their signature to this Protocol.

DONE in duplicate at Manila this 21st day of April 2015, in the English language.

For the Kingdom of the Netherlands:

M.C.T. DERCKX

For the Republic of the Philippines:

E. QUIROS

[TRANSLATION – TRADUCTION]

PROTOCOLE AMENDANT L'ACCORD ENTRE LE ROYAUME DES PAYS-BAS ET LA RÉPUBLIQUE DES PHILIPPINES RELATIF À L'EXPORTATION DES PRESTATIONS D'ASSURANCE SOCIALE

Le Royaume des Pays-Bas et la République des Philippines, ci-après dénommés les « Parties »,

Désireux d'amender l'Accord entre le Royaume des Pays-Bas et la République des Philippines relatif à l'exportation des prestations d'assurance sociale, signé à Manille le 10 avril 2001, ci-après dénommé l'« Accord »,

Sont convenus de ce qui suit :

Article premier

L'alinéa e) du paragraphe 1 de l'article premier de l'Accord est amendé comme suit :

« e) L'expression "institution compétente" désigne, pour le Royaume des Pays-Bas concernant la législation mentionnée aux points i), ii) et iii) de l'alinéa A) du paragraphe 1 de l'article 2 : le "Landelijk instituut sociale verzekeringen" (Institut national d'assurance sociale) c/o Gak Nederland bv ou ses successeurs en droit, et concernant la législation mentionnée aux points iv) et v) de l'alinéa A) du paragraphe 1 de l'article 2 : la "Sociale Verzekeringsbank" (Banque d'assurance sociale); et pour la République des Philippines, la sécurité sociale pour les travailleurs du secteur privé et la Caisse d'assurance des fonctionnaires pour les travailleurs du secteur public; »

Article II

1. Les sous-alinéas iv) et v) de l'alinéa A) du paragraphe 1 de l'article 2 de l'Accord sont amendés comme suit : « iv) L'assurance vieillesse; et v) L'assurance décès. »
2. Le sous-alinéa vi) de l'alinéa A) du paragraphe 1 de l'article 2 de l'Accord est supprimé.

Article III

1. Conformément au paragraphe 3 de l'article 13 de l'Accord, le présent Protocole entre en vigueur le premier jour du deuxième mois suivant la date de la dernière des notifications écrites échangées entre les Parties par la voie diplomatique.
2. Le présent Protocole s'applique à titre provisoire à compter du 1er juillet 2015.

EN FOI DE QUOI, les soussignés, à ce dûment autorisés par leurs Gouvernements respectifs, ont signé le présent Protocole.

FAIT à Manille, le 21 avril 2015, en double exemplaire, en langue anglaise.

Pour le Royaume des Pays-Bas :

M.C.T. DERCKX

Pour la République des Philippines :

E. QUIROS

No. 40214. Multilateral

STOCKHOLM CONVENTION ON PERSISTENT ORGANIC POLLUTANTS. STOCKHOLM, 22 MAY 2001 [*United Nations, Treaty Series, vol. 2256, I-40214.*]

ACCESSION

Iraq

Deposit of instrument with the Secretary-General of the United Nations: 8 March 2016

Date of effect: 6 June 2016

Registration with the Secretariat of the United Nations: ex officio, 8 March 2016

Nº 40214. Multilatéral

CONVENTION DE STOCKHOLM SUR LES POLLUANTS ORGANIQUES PERSISTANTS. STOCKHOLM, 22 MAI 2001 [*Nations Unies, Recueil des Traités, vol. 2256, I-40214.*]

ADHÉSION

Iraq

Dépôt de l'instrument auprès du Secrétaire général de l'Organisation des Nations Unies : 8 mars 2016

Date de prise d'effet : 6 juin 2016

Enregistrement au Secrétariat de l'Organisation des Nations Unies : d'office, 8 mars 2016

No. 40879. Finland and Singapore

AGREEMENT BETWEEN THE REPUBLIC OF FINLAND AND THE REPUBLIC OF SINGAPORE FOR THE AVOIDANCE OF DOUBLE TAXATION AND THE PREVENTION OF FISCAL EVASION WITH RESPECT TO TAXES ON INCOME. SINGAPORE, 7 JUNE 2002 [*United Nations, Treaty Series, vol. 2294, I-40879.*]

PROTOCOL AMENDING THE AGREEMENT BETWEEN THE REPUBLIC OF FINLAND AND THE REPUBLIC OF SINGAPORE FOR THE AVOIDANCE OF DOUBLE TAXATION AND THE PREVENTION OF FISCAL EVASION WITH RESPECT TO TAXES ON INCOME SIGNED AT SINGAPORE ON 7 JUNE 2002. SINGAPORE, 16 NOVEMBER 2009

Entry into force: 30 April 2010, in accordance with article II

Authentic text: English

Registration with the Secretariat of the United Nations: Finland, 9 March 2016

Nº 40879. Finlande et Singapour

ACCORD ENTRE LA RÉPUBLIQUE DE FINLANDE ET LA RÉPUBLIQUE DE SINGAPOUR TENDANT À ÉVITER LA DOUBLE IMPOSITION ET À PRÉVENIR L'ÉVASION FISCALE EN MATIÈRE D'IMPÔTS SUR LE REVENU. SINGAPOUR, 7 JUIN 2002 [*Nations Unies, Recueil des Traités, vol. 2294, I-40879.*]

PROTOCOLE MODIFIANT L'ACCORD ENTRE LA RÉPUBLIQUE DE FINLANDE ET LA RÉPUBLIQUE DE SINGAPOUR TENDANT À ÉVITER LA DOUBLE IMPOSITION ET À PRÉVENIR L'ÉVASION FISCALE EN MATIÈRE D'IMPÔTS SUR LE REVENU, SIGNÉ À SINGAPOUR LE 7 JUIN 2002. SINGAPOUR, 16 NOVEMBRE 2009

Entrée en vigueur : 30 avril 2010, conformément à l'article II

Texte authentique : anglais

Enregistrement au Secrétariat de l'Organisation des Nations Unies : Finlande, 9 mars 2016

[TEXT IN ENGLISH – TEXTE EN ANGLAIS]

PROTOCOL
AMENDING THE AGREEMENT BETWEEN THE REPUBLIC OF FINLAND AND THE REPUBLIC OF SINGAPORE FOR THE AVOIDANCE OF DOUBLE TAXATION AND THE PREVENTION OF FISCAL EVASION WITH RESPECT TO TAXES ON INCOME SIGNED AT SINGAPORE ON 7 JUNE 2002

The Government of the Republic of Finland and the Government of the Republic of Singapore,

Desiring to amend the Agreement between the Republic of Finland and the Republic of Singapore for the avoidance of double taxation and the prevention of fiscal evasion with respect to taxes on income, signed at Singapore on 7 June 2002 (hereinafter referred to as "the Agreement"),

Have agreed as follows:

ARTICLE I

The text of Article 26 of the Agreement is deleted and replaced by the following:

"1. The competent authorities of the Contracting States shall exchange such information as is foreseeably relevant for carrying out the provisions of this Agreement or to the administration or enforcement of the domestic laws concerning taxes of every kind and description imposed on behalf of the Contracting States, or of their political subdivisions or local authorities, insofar as the taxation thereunder is not contrary to the Agreement. The exchange of information is not restricted by Articles 1 and 2.

2. Any information received under paragraph 1 by a Contracting State shall be treated as secret in the same manner as information obtained under the domestic laws of that State and shall be disclosed only to persons or authorities (including courts and administrative bodies) concerned with the assessment or collection of, the enforcement or prosecution in respect of, the determination of appeals in relation to the taxes referred to in paragraph 1, or the oversight of the above. Such persons or authorities shall use the information only for such purposes. They may disclose the information in public court proceedings or in judicial decisions.

3. In no case shall the provisions of paragraphs 1 and 2 be construed so as to impose on a Contracting State the obligation:

a) to carry out administrative measures at variance with the laws and administrative practice of that or of the other Contracting State;

b) to supply information which is not obtainable under the laws or in the normal course of the administration of that or of the other Contracting State;

c) to supply information which would disclose any trade, business, industrial, commercial or professional secret or trade process, or information, the disclosure of which would be contrary to public policy (ordre public).

4. If information is requested by a Contracting State in accordance with this Article, the other Contracting State shall use its information gathering measures to obtain the requested information, even though that other State may not need such information for its own tax purposes. The obligation contained in the preceding sentence is subject to the limitations of paragraph 3 but in no case shall such limitations be construed to permit a Contracting State to decline to supply information solely because it has no domestic interest in such information.

5. In no case shall the provisions of paragraph 3 be construed to permit a Contracting State to decline to supply information solely because the information is held by a bank, other financial institution, nominee or person acting in an agency or a fiduciary capacity or because it relates to ownership interests in a person."

ARTICLE II

Each of the Contracting States shall notify the other, through diplomatic channels, of the completion of the procedures required by their respective laws for the bringing into force of this Protocol. The Protocol shall enter into force 30 days after the date of the later of such notification and the Protocol shall have effect on that date.

ARTICLE III

This Protocol, which shall form an integral part of the Agreement, shall remain in force as long as the Agreement remains in force and shall apply as long as the Agreement itself is applicable.

IN WITNESS WHEREOF, the undersigned, duly authorised thereto by their respective Governments, have signed this Protocol.

DONE in duplicate at Singapore on this ..16.... day of November 2009, in the English language.

For the Government of
the Republic of Finland

[signature]

For the Government of
the Republic of Singapore

[signature]

[TRANSLATION – TRADUCTION]

PROTOCOLE AMENDANT L'ACCORD ENTRE LA RÉPUBLIQUE DE FINLANDE ET LA RÉPUBLIQUE DE SINGAPOUR TENDANT À ÉVITER LA DOUBLE IMPOSITION ET À PRÉVENIR L'ÉVASION FISCALE EN MATIÈRE D'IMPÔTS SUR LE REVENU SIGNÉ À SINGAPOUR LE 7 JUIN 2002

Le Gouvernement de la République de Finlande et le Gouvernement de la République de Singapour,

Désireux d'amender l'Accord entre la République de Finlande et la République de Singapour tendant à éviter la double imposition et à prévenir l'évasion fiscale en matière d'impôts sur le revenu, signé à Singapour le 7 juin 2002 (ci-après dénommé l'« Accord »),

Sont convenus de ce qui suit :

Article premier

Le texte de l'article 26 de l'Accord est supprimé et remplacé par ce qui suit :

« 1. Les autorités compétentes des États contractants échangent les renseignements vraisemblablement pertinents pour appliquer les dispositions du présent Accord ou celles de la législation interne relative aux impôts de toute nature ou dénomination perçus pour le compte des États contractants, de leurs subdivisions politiques ou de leurs collectivités locales, dans la mesure où l'imposition qu'il prévoit n'est pas incompatible avec l'Accord. L'échange de renseignements n'est pas restreint par les articles premier et 2.

2. Les renseignements reçus par un État contractant en vertu du paragraphe 1 sont tenus secrets de la même manière que les renseignements obtenus en application de la législation interne de cet État, et ils ne sont communiqués qu'aux personnes ou autorités (y compris les tribunaux et organes administratifs) concernées par l'établissement ou le recouvrement des impôts visés au paragraphe 1, par les procédures ou poursuites concernant ces impôts, par les décisions sur les recours relatifs à ces impôts, ou par le contrôle de ce qui précède. Ces personnes ou autorités n'utilisent ces renseignements qu'à ces fins, mais peuvent en faire état au cours d'audiences publiques des tribunaux ou dans des jugements.

3. Les dispositions des paragraphes 1 et 2 ne peuvent en aucun cas être interprétées comme imposant à un État contractant l'obligation :

a) de prendre des mesures administratives dérogeant à sa propre législation et à sa pratique administrative ou à celles de l'autre État contractant;

b) de fournir des renseignements qui ne pourraient être obtenus en vertu de sa législation ou dans le cadre de sa pratique administrative normale ou de celles de l'autre État contractant;

c) de fournir des renseignements qui révéleraient un secret commercial, industriel, professionnel ou un procédé commercial ou des renseignements dont la communication serait contraire à l'ordre public.

4. Si des renseignements sont demandés par un État contractant conformément au présent article, l'autre État contractant utilise ses mesures de collecte de renseignements pour obtenir les

renseignements demandés quand bien même cet autre État n'aurait pas besoin de ces renseignements à ses propres fins fiscales. L'obligation contenue dans la phrase précédente est subordonnée aux limitations du paragraphe 3, mais en aucun cas ces limitations ne doivent être interprétées comme autorisant un État contractant à refuser de fournir des renseignements pour la seule raison qu'il ne détient aucun intérêt national dans de tels renseignements.

5. Les dispositions du paragraphe 3 ne doivent en aucun cas être interprétées comme autorisant un État contractant à refuser de fournir des renseignements pour la seule raison que les renseignements sont tenus par une banque, une autre institution financière, un mandataire ou une personne agissant en qualité d'agent ou à titre fiduciaire ou parce que cela concerne les intérêts fonciers d'une personne. »

Article II

Chacun des États contractants notifie à l'autre, par la voie diplomatique, l'accomplissement des procédures requises par sa législation pour l'entrée en vigueur du présent Protocole. Le Protocole entre en vigueur 30 jours après la date de la dernière de ces notifications et il prend effet à cette date.

Article III

Le présent Protocole, qui fait partie intégrante de l'Accord, reste en vigueur aussi longtemps que l'Accord et s'applique tant que l'Accord lui-même est applicable.

EN FOI DE QUOI, les soussignés, à ce dûment autorisés par leurs Gouvernements respectifs, ont signé le présent Protocole.

FAIT à Singapour, le 16 novembre 2009, en double exemplaire, en langue anglaise.

Pour le Gouvernement de la République de Finlande :

[SATU MATTILA]

Pour le Gouvernement de la République de Singapour :

[PETER ONG]

No. 42632. Multilateral

AGREEMENT ON THE CONSERVATION OF AFRICAN-EURASIAN MIGRATORY WATERBIRDS. THE HAGUE, 15 AUGUST 1996 [*United Nations, Treaty Series, vol. 2365, I-42632.*]

AMENDMENTS TO ANNEXES 2 AND 3 AND TO TABLE 1 OF THE AGREEMENT ON THE CONSERVATION OF AFRICAN-EURASIAN MIGRATORY WATERBIRDS (WITH ANNEXES). BONN, 14 NOVEMBER 2015 [*United Nations, Treaty Series, vol. 3111, A-42632.*]

RESERVATION

Czech Republic

Notification deposited with the Government of the Netherlands: 11 February 2016

Registration with the Secretariat of the United Nations: Netherlands, 10 March 2016

N° 42632. Multilatéral

ACCORD SUR LA CONSERVATION DES OISEAUX D'EAU MIGRATEURS D'AFRIQUE-EURASIE. LA HAYE, 15 AOÛT 1996 [*Nations Unies, Recueil des Traités, vol. 2365, I-42632.*]

AMENDEMENTS AUX ANNEXES 2 ET 3 ET AU TABLEAU 1 DE L'ACCORD SUR LA CONSERVATION DES OISEAUX D'EAU MIGRATEURS D'AFRIQUE-EURASIE (AVEC ANNEXES). BONN, 14 NOVEMBRE 2015 [*Nations Unies, Recueil des Traités, vol. 3111, A-42632.*]

RÉSERVE

République tchèque

Dépôt de la notification auprès du Gouvernement néerlandais : 11 février 2016

Enregistrement au Secrétariat de l'Organisation des Nations Unies : Pays-Bas, 10 mars 2016

No. 42671. Multilateral

CONVENTION FOR THE SAFEGUARDING OF THE INTANGIBLE CULTURAL HERITAGE. PARIS, 17 OCTOBER 2003 [*United Nations, Treaty Series, vol. 2368, I-42671.*]

ACCEPTANCE

Guinea-Bissau

Deposit of instrument with the Director-General of the United Nations Educational, Scientific and Cultural Organization: 7 March 2016

Date of effect: 7 June 2016

Registration with the Secretariat of the United Nations: United Nations Educational, Scientific and Cultural Organization, 31 March 2016

N° 42671. Multilatéral

CONVENTION POUR LA SAUVEGARDE DU PATRIMOINE CULTUREL IMMATÉRIEL. PARIS, 17 OCTOBRE 2003 [*Nations Unies, Recueil des Traités, vol. 2368, I-42671.*]

ACCEPTATION

Guinée-Bissau

Dépôt de l'instrument auprès du Directeur général de l'Organisation des Nations Unies pour l'éducation, la science et la culture : 7 mars 2016

Date de prise d'effet : 7 juin 2016

Enregistrement au Secrétariat de l'Organisation des Nations Unies : Organisation des Nations Unies pour l'éducation, la science et la culture, 31 mars 2016

No. 43345. Multilateral

INTERNATIONAL TREATY ON PLANT GENETIC RESOURCES FOR FOOD AND AGRICULTURE. ROME, 3 NOVEMBER 2001 [*United Nations, Treaty Series, vol. 2400, I-43345.*]

RATIFICATION

Chile

Deposit of instrument with the Director-General of the Food and Agriculture Organization of the United Nations: 14 January 2016

Date of effect: 13 April 2016

Registration with the Secretariat of the United Nations: Food and Agriculture Organization of the United Nations, 16 March 2016

ACCESSION

Guyana

Deposit of instrument with the Director-General of the Food and Agriculture Organization of the United Nations: 31 December 2015

Date of effect: 30 March 2016

Registration with the Secretariat of the United Nations: Food and Agriculture Organization of the United Nations, 24 March 2016

N° 43345. Multilatéral

TRAITÉ INTERNATIONAL SUR LES RESSOURCES PHYTOGÉNÉTIQUES POUR L'ALIMENTATION ET L'AGRICULTURE. ROME, 3 NOVEMBRE 2001 [*Nations Unies, Recueil des Traités, vol. 2400, I-43345.*]

RATIFICATION

Chili

Dépôt de l'instrument auprès du Directeur général de l'Organisation des Nations Unies pour l'alimentation et l'agriculture : 14 janvier 2016

Date de prise d'effet : 13 avril 2016

Enregistrement au Secrétariat de l'Organisation des Nations Unies : Organisation des Nations Unies pour l'alimentation et l'agriculture, 16 mars 2016

ADHÉSION

Guyana

Dépôt de l'instrument auprès du Directeur général de l'Organisation des Nations Unies pour l'alimentation et l'agriculture : 31 décembre 2015

Date de prise d'effet : 30 mars 2016

Enregistrement au Secrétariat de l'Organisation des Nations Unies : Organisation des Nations Unies pour l'alimentation et l'agriculture, 24 mars 2016

No. 43977. Multilateral

CONVENTION ON THE PROTECTION AND PROMOTION OF THE DIVERSITY OF CULTURAL EXPRESSIONS. PARIS, 20 OCTOBER 2005 [*United Nations, Treaty Series, vol. 2440, I-43977.*]

ACCESSION

South Sudan

Deposit of instrument with the Director-General of the United Nations Educational, Scientific and Cultural Organization: 9 March 2016

Date of effect: 9 June 2016

Registration with the Secretariat of the United Nations: United Nations Educational, Scientific and Cultural Organization, 31 March 2016

N° 43977. Multilatéral

CONVENTION SUR LA PROTECTION ET LA PROMOTION DE LA DIVERSITÉ DES EXPRESSIONS CULTURELLES. PARIS, 20 OCTOBRE 2005 [*Nations Unies, Recueil des Traités, vol. 2440, I-43977.*]

ADHÉSION

Soudan du Sud

Dépôt de l'instrument auprès du Directeur général de l'Organisation des Nations Unies pour l'éducation, la science et la culture : 9 mars 2016

Date de prise d'effet : 9 juin 2016

Enregistrement au Secrétariat de l'Organisation des Nations Unies : Organisation des Nations Unies pour l'éducation, la science et la culture, 31 mars 2016

No. 44004. Multilateral

INTERNATIONAL CONVENTION FOR THE SUPPRESSION OF ACTS OF NUCLEAR TERRORISM. NEW YORK, 13 APRIL 2005 [*United Nations, Treaty Series, vol. 2445, I-44004.*]

RATIFICATION

New Zealand

Deposit of instrument with the Secretary-General of the United Nations: 18 March 2016

Date of effect: 17 April 2016

Registration with the Secretariat of the United Nations: ex officio, 18 March 2016

TERRITORIAL EXCLUSION

New Zealand

Notification deposited with the Secretary-General of the United Nations: 18 March 2016

Registration with the Secretariat of the United Nations: ex officio, 18 March 2016

Nº 44004. Multilatéral

CONVENTION INTERNATIONALE POUR LA RÉPRESSION DES ACTES DE TERRORISME NUCLÉAIRE. NEW YORK, 13 AVRIL 2005 [*Nations Unies, Recueil des Traités, vol. 2445, I-44004.*]

RATIFICATION

Nouvelle-Zélande

Dépôt de l'instrument auprès du Secrétaire général de l'Organisation des Nations Unies : 18 mars 2016

Date de prise d'effet : 17 avril 2016

Enregistrement au Secrétariat de l'Organisation des Nations Unies : d'office, 18 mars 2016

EXCLUSION TERRITORIALE

Nouvelle-Zélande

Dépôt de la notification auprès du Secrétaire général de l'Organisation des Nations Unies : 18 mars 2016

Enregistrement au Secrétariat de l'Organisation des Nations Unies : d'office, 18 mars 2016

[TEXT IN ENGLISH – TEXTE EN ANGLAIS]

"... consistent with the constitutional status of Tokelau and taking into account the commitment of the Government of New Zealand to the development of self-government for Tokelau through an act of self-determination under the Charter of the United Nations, [the ratification by New Zealand of this Convention] shall not extend to Tokelau unless and until a Declaration to this effect is lodged by the Government of New Zealand with the Depositary on the basis of appropriate consultation with that territory..."

[TRANSLATION – TRADUCTION]

... conformément au statut constitutionnel des Tokélaou et compte tenu de l'engagement du Gouvernement néo-zélandais à œuvrer à l'avènement de l'autonomie des Tokélaou par un acte d'autodétermination conformément à la Charte des Nations Unies, la ratification de la présente Convention par la Nouvelle Zélande ne s'appliquera aux Tokélaou que lorsque le Gouvernement néo-zélandais aura déposé une déclaration à ce sujet auprès du dépositaire à la suite d'une consultation appropriée avec ce territoire...

RATIFICATION

Uruguay

Deposit of instrument with the Secretary-General of the United Nations: 4 March 2016

Date of effect: 3 April 2016

Registration with the Secretariat of the United Nations: ex officio, 4 March 2016

RATIFICATION

Uruguay

Dépôt de l'instrument auprès du Secrétaire général de l'Organisation des Nations Unies : 4 mars 2016

Date de prise d'effet : 3 avril 2016

Enregistrement au Secrétariat de l'Organisation des Nations Unies : d'office, 4 mars 2016

No. 44910. Multilateral

CONVENTION ON THE RIGHTS OF PERSONS WITH DISABILITIES. NEW YORK, 13 DECEMBER 2006 [*United Nations, Treaty Series, vol. 2515, I-44910.*]

OPTIONAL PROTOCOL TO THE CONVENTION ON THE RIGHTS OF PERSONS WITH DISABILITIES. NEW YORK, 13 DECEMBER 2006 [*United Nations, Treaty Series, vol. 2518, A-44910.*]

OBJECTION TO THE DECLARATION MADE BY TURKEY UPON RATIFICATION

Austria

Notification deposited with the Secretary-General of the United Nations: 16 March 2016

Registration with the Secretariat of the United Nations: ex officio, 16 March 2016

N° 44910. Multilatéral

CONVENTION RELATIVE AUX DROITS DES PERSONNES HANDICAPÉES. NEW YORK, 13 DÉCEMBRE 2006 [*Nations Unies, Recueil des Traités, vol. 2515, I-44910.*]

PROTOCOLE FACULTATIF SE RAPPORTANT À LA CONVENTION RELATIVE AUX DROITS DES PERSONNES HANDICAPÉES. NEW YORK, 13 DÉCEMBRE 2006 [*Nations Unies, Recueil des Traités, vol. 2518, A-44910.*]

OBJECTION À LA DÉCLARATION FORMULÉE PAR LA TURQUIE LORS DE LA RATIFICATION

Autriche

Dépôt de la notification auprès du Secrétaire général de l'Organisation des Nations Unies : 16 mars 2016

Enregistrement au Secrétariat de l'Organisation des Nations Unies : d'office, 16 mars 2016

[TEXT IN ENGLISH – TEXTE EN ANGLAIS]

"The Government of Austria has examined the declaration made by the Republic of Turkey upon ratification of the Optional Protocol to the Convention on the Rights of Persons with Disabilities adopted on 13 December 2006. It welcomes the ratification of the Optional Protocol by Turkey as a significant step for the promotion of the rights of persons with disabilities. However, as a member state of the European Union, Austria opposes the declaration made by the Republic of Turkey which describes another member state, the Republic of Cyprus, as a defunct entity."

[TRANSLATION – TRADUCTION]

Le Gouvernement autrichien a examiné la déclaration faite par la République de Turquie lors de la ratification du Protocole facultatif se rapportant à la Convention relative aux droits des personnes handicapées, adopté le 13 décembre 2006. Il se félicite de la ratification du Protocole facultatif par la Turquie, qui constitue une avancée importante dans la promotion des droits des personnes handicapées. Cependant, en tant qu'État membre de l'Union européenne, l'Autriche objecte à la déclaration faite par la République de Turquie qui qualifie un autre État Membre, en l'occurrence la République de Chypre, d'entité « défunte ».

Objection to the declaration made by Turkey upon ratification

Greece

Notification deposited with the Secretary-General of the United Nations: 16 March 2016

Registration with the Secretariat of the United Nations: ex officio, 16 March 2016

Objection à la déclaration formulée par la Turquie lors de la ratification

Grèce

Dépôt de la notification auprès du Secrétaire général de l'Organisation des Nations Unies : 16 mars 2016

Enregistrement au Secrétariat de l'Organisation des Nations Unies : d'office, 16 mars 2016

[Text in English – Texte en anglais]

"… The Government of the Hellenic Republic has examined the declaration made by the Republic of Turkey upon ratification, on 26 March 2015, of the Optional Protocol to the Convention on the Rights of Persons with Disabilities.

The Republic of Turkey declares that its ratification of the Optional Protocol to the Convention on the Rights of Persons with Disabilities should not imply any obligation on the part of Turkey to enter into any dealing with the Republic of Cyprus within the framework of the said Protocol.

In [the] view of the Government of the Hellenic Republic, the above declaration in fact amounts to a reservation, as it purports to exclude the application of the Protocol in Turkey's relations with the Republic of Cyprus. Such a reservation is incompatible with the principle that inter-State reciprocity has no place in the context of human rights treaties, which concern the endowment of individuals with rights. It is, therefore, contrary to the object and purpose of the Convention on the Rights of Persons with Disabilities and its Optional Protocol.

The Government of the Hellenic Republic recalls that, according to Article 14 paragraph 1 of the Optional Protocol to the Convention on the Rights of Persons with Disabilities, reservations incompatible with the object and purpose of this Protocol shall not be permitted.

For the above reasons, the Government of the Hellenic Republic objects to the declaration made by the Republic of Turkey upon ratification of the said Protocol.

This objection shall not preclude the entry into force of the Protocol between the Hellenic Republic and the Republic of Turkey…"

[TRANSLATION – TRADUCTION]

… Le Gouvernement de la République hellénique a examiné la déclaration faite par la République de Turquie lors de sa ratification, le 26 mars 2015, du Protocole facultatif se rapportant à la Convention relative aux droits des personnes handicapées.

La République de Turquie déclare que sa ratification du Protocole facultatif se rapportant à la Convention relative aux droits des personnes handicapées n'implique aucune obligation de sa part d'entretenir avec la République de Chypre des relations dans le cadre dudit Protocole.

De l'avis du Gouvernement de la République hellénique, cette déclaration équivaut en fait à une réserve car sa finalité est d'exclure l'application du Protocole dans les relations de la Turquie avec la République de Chypre. Une telle réserve est incompatible avec le principe selon lequel la réciprocité inter-États n'a pas sa place dans les traités relatifs aux droits de l'homme, qui visent à garantir des droits à des individus. Elle est donc contraire à l'objet et au but de la Convention relative aux droits des personnes handicapées.

Le Gouvernement de la République hellénique rappelle que, conformément au paragraphe 1 de l'article 14 du Protocole facultatif se rapportant à la Convention relative aux droits des personnes handicapées, les réserves incompatibles avec l'objet et le but du Protocole ne sont pas admises.

Pour les raisons susmentionnées, le Gouvernement de la République hellénique formule une objection à la déclaration faite par la République de Turquie lors de sa ratification dudit Protocole.

Cette objection n'empêche pas l'entrée en vigueur du Protocole entre la République hellénique et la République de Turquie…

No. 45694. Multilateral

CONVENTION ON THE PROTECTION OF THE UNDERWATER CULTURAL HERITAGE. PARIS, 2 NOVEMBER 2001 [*United Nations, Treaty Series, vol. 2562, I-45694.*]

ACCEPTANCE

Guinea-Bissau

Deposit of instrument with the Director-General of the United Nations Educational, Scientific and Cultural Organization: 7 March 2016

Date of effect: 7 June 2016

Registration with the Secretariat of the United Nations: United Nations Educational, Scientific and Cultural Organization, 31 March 2016

N° 45694. Multilatéral

CONVENTION SUR LA PROTECTION DU PATRIMOINE CULTUREL SUBAQUATIQUE. PARIS, 2 NOVEMBRE 2001 [*Nations Unies, Recueil des Traités, vol. 2562, I-45694.*]

ACCEPTATION

Guinée-Bissau

Dépôt de l'instrument auprès du Directeur général de l'Organisation des Nations Unies pour l'éducation, la science et la culture : 7 mars 2016

Date de prise d'effet : 7 juin 2016

Enregistrement au Secrétariat de l'Organisation des Nations Unies : Organisation des Nations Unies pour l'éducation, la science et la culture, 31 mars 2016

No. 46241. Multilateral

CONVENTION ON THE INTERNATIONAL PROTECTION OF ADULTS. THE HAGUE, 13 JANUARY 2000 [*United Nations, Treaty Series, vol. 2600, I-46241.*]

RATIFICATION

Monaco

Deposit of instrument with the Government of the Netherlands: 4 March 2016

Date of effect: 1 July 2016

Registration with the Secretariat of the United Nations: Netherlands, 23 March 2016

N° 46241. Multilatéral

CONVENTION SUR LA PROTECTION INTERNATIONALE DES ADULTES. LA HAYE, 13 JANVIER 2000 [*Nations Unies, Recueil des Traités, vol. 2600, I-46241.*]

RATIFICATION

Monaco

Dépôt de l'instrument auprès du Gouvernement néerlandais : 4 mars 2016

Date de prise d'effet : 1er juillet 2016

Enregistrement au Secrétariat de l'Organisation des Nations Unies : Pays-Bas, 23 mars 2016

No. 48455. Multilateral

PROTOCOL ON INTEGRATED COASTAL ZONE MANAGEMENT (ICZM) IN THE MEDITERRANEAN. MADRID, 21 JANUARY 2008 [*United Nations, Treaty Series, vol. 2742, I-48455.*]

RATIFICATION

Israel

Deposit of instrument with the Government of Spain: 1 February 2016

Date of effect: 2 March 2016

Registration with the Secretariat of the United Nations: Spain, 29 March 2016

N° 48455. Multilatéral

PROTOCOLE RELATIF À LA GESTION INTÉGRÉE DES ZONES CÔTIÈRES (GIZC) DE LA MÉDITERRANÉE. MADRID, 21 JANVIER 2008 [*Nations Unies, Recueil des Traités, vol. 2742, I-48455.*]

RATIFICATION

Israël

Dépôt de l'instrument auprès du Gouvernement espagnol : 1er février 2016

Date de prise d'effet : 2 mars 2016

Enregistrement au Secrétariat de l'Organisation des Nations Unies : Espagne, 29 mars 2016

No. 52481. Germany and Uzbekistan

CONVENTION BETWEEN THE FEDERAL REPUBLIC OF GERMANY AND THE REPUBLIC OF UZBEKISTAN FOR THE AVOIDANCE OF DOUBLE TAXATION WITH RESPECT TO TAXES ON INCOME AND CAPITAL. BERLIN, 7 SEPTEMBER 1999 [*United Nations, Treaty Series, vol. 3020, I-52481.*]

PROTOCOL AMENDING AND SUPPLEMENTING THE CONVENTION OF 7 SEPTEMBER 1999 BETWEEN THE FEDERAL REPUBLIC OF GERMANY AND THE REPUBLIC OF UZBEKISTAN FOR THE AVOIDANCE OF DOUBLE TAXATION WITH RESPECT TO TAXES ON INCOME AND CAPITAL. BERLIN, 14 OCTOBER 2014

Entry into force: 29 December 2015 by the exchange of the instruments of ratification, in accordance with article 4

Authentic texts: German, Russian and Uzbek

Registration with the Secretariat of the United Nations: Germany, 11 March 2016

N° 52481. Allemagne et Ouzbékistan

ACCORD ENTRE LA RÉPUBLIQUE FÉDÉRALE D'ALLEMAGNE ET LA RÉPUBLIQUE D'OUZBÉKISTAN TENDANT À ÉVITER LES DOUBLES IMPOSITIONS EN MATIÈRE D'IMPÔTS SUR LE REVENU ET SUR LA FORTUNE. BERLIN, 7 SEPTEMBRE 1999 [*Nations Unies, Recueil des Traités, vol. 3020, I-52481.*]

PROTOCOLE AMENDANT ET COMPLÉTANT L'ACCORD DU 7 SEPTEMBRE 1999 ENTRE LA RÉPUBLIQUE FÉDÉRALE D'ALLEMAGNE ET LA RÉPUBLIQUE D'OUZBÉKISTAN TENDANT À ÉVITER LES DOUBLES IMPOSITIONS EN MATIÈRE D'IMPÔTS SUR LE REVENU ET SUR LA FORTUNE. BERLIN, 14 OCTOBRE 2014

Entrée en vigueur : 29 décembre 2015 par l'échange des instruments de ratification, conformément à l'article 4

Textes authentiques : allemand, russe et ouzbek

Enregistrement au Secrétariat de l'Organisation des Nations Unies : Allemagne, 11 mars 2016

[TEXT IN GERMAN – TEXTE EN ALLEMAND]

Protokoll

zur

Änderung und Ergänzung des Abkommens vom 7. September 1999
zwischen
der Bundesrepublik Deutschland
und
der Republik Usbekistan
zur Vermeidung der Doppelbesteuerung
auf dem Gebiet der Steuern vom Einkommen und
vom Vermögen

Die Bundesrepublik Deutschland

und

die Republik Usbekistan,
im Folgenden als „Vertragsstaaten" bezeichnet –

in Übereinstimmung mit dem Abkommen vom 07. September 1999 zwischen der Bundesrepublik Deutschland und der Republik Usbekistan zur Vermeidung der Doppelbesteuerung auf dem Gebiet der Steuern vom Einkommen und vom Vermögen (im Folgenden als „Abkommen" bezeichnet),

von dem Wunsch geleitet, die beiderseitigen wirtschaftlichen Beziehungen weiter zu entwickeln und die Zusammenarbeit auf steuerlichem Gebiet zur Gewährleistung einer wirksamen und zutreffenden Steuererhebung zu vertiefen -

sind wie folgt übereingekommen:

Artikel 1

Artikel 26 des Abkommens erhält folgende Fassung:

„Artikel 26
Informationsaustausch

(1) Die zuständigen Behörden der Vertragsstaaten tauschen die Informationen aus, die zur Durchführung dieses Abkommens oder zur Verwaltung oder Durchsetzung des innerstaatlichen Rechts betreffend Steuern jeder Art und Bezeichnung , die für Rechnung eines Vertragsstaats oder einer seiner Gebietskörperschaften erhoben werden, voraussichtlich

erheblich sind, soweit die diesem Recht entsprechende Besteuerung nicht dem Abkommen widerspricht. Der Informationsaustausch ist durch Artikel 1 und 2 nicht eingeschränkt.

(2) Alle Informationen, die ein Vertragsstaat nach Absatz 1 erhalten hat, sind ebenso geheim zu halten wie die aufgrund des innerstaatlichen Rechts dieses Staates beschafften Informationen und dürfen nur den Personen oder Behörden (einschließlich der Gerichte und Verwaltungsbehörden) zugänglich gemacht werden, die mit der Festsetzung oder Erhebung, der Vollstreckung oder Strafverfolgung, der Entscheidung über Rechtsbehelfe hinsichtlich der in Absatz 1 genannten Steuern oder mit der Aufsicht darüber befasst sind. Diese Personen oder Behörden dürfen die Informationen nur für diese Zwecke verwenden. Für diese Zwecke dürfen die Informationen in einem verwaltungs- oder strafrechtlichen Ermittlungsverfahren, in einem öffentlichen Gerichtsverfahren oder in einer Gerichtsentscheidung offengelegt werden. Ungeachtet der vorstehenden Bestimmungen können Informationen, die ein Vertragsstaat erhalten hat, für andere Zwecke verwendet werden, wenn sie nach dem Recht beider Staaten für diese anderen Zwecke verwendet werden können und die zuständige Behörde des übermittelnden Staates dieser Verwendung zugestimmt hat.

(3) Absätze 1 und 2 sind nicht so auszulegen, als verpflichteten sie einen Vertragsstaat,

a) Verwaltungsmaßnahmen durchzuführen, die von den Gesetzen und der Verwaltungspraxis dieses oder des anderen Vertragsstaats abweichen;

b) Informationen zu erteilen, die nach den Gesetzen oder im üblichen Verwaltungsverfahren dieses oder des anderen Vertragsstaats nicht beschafft werden können;

c) Informationen zu erteilen, die ein Betriebs-, Geschäfts-, Gewerbe-, Handels- oder Berufsgeheimnis oder ein Geschäftsverfahren preisgeben würden oder deren Erteilung der öffentlichen Ordnung (ordre public) widerspräche.

(4) Ersucht ein Vertragsstaat nach diesem Artikel um Informationen, so nutzt der andere Vertragsstaat die ihm zur Verfügung stehenden Möglichkeiten zur Beschaffung der erbetenen In-

formationen, selbst wenn er diese Informationen für seine eigenen steuerlichen Zwecke nicht benötigt. Die in Satz 1 enthaltene Verpflichtung unterliegt den Beschränkungen nach Absatz 3, aber diese Beschränkungen sind nicht so auszulegen, als könne ein Vertragsstaat die Erteilung von Informationen nur deshalb ablehnen, weil er kein innerstaatliches Interesse an diesen Informationen hat.

(5) Absatz 3 ist nicht so auszulegen, als könne ein Vertragsstaat die Erteilung von Informationen nur deshalb ablehnen, weil sich die Informationen bei einer Bank, einem sonstigen Finanzinstitut, einem Bevollmächtigten, Vertreter oder Treuhänder befinden oder weil sie sich auf Eigentumsanteile an einer Person beziehen."

Artikel 2

Das Abkommen wird durch Artikel 26a mit folgendem Inhalt ergänzt:

„Artikel 26a
Amtshilfe bei der Steuererhebung

(1) Die Vertragsstaaten leisten sich gegenseitige Amtshilfe bei der Erhebung von Steueransprüchen. Diese Amtshilfe wird durch die Artikel 1 und 2 nicht eingeschränkt. Die zuständigen Behörden der Vertragsstaaten können durch Verständigung regeln, wie dieser Artikel durchzuführen ist.

(2) Der Ausdruck „Steueranspruch" im Sinne dieses Artikels bedeutet einen Betrag, der aufgrund von Steuern jeder Art und Bezeichnung, die für Rechnung eines Vertragsstaats oder einer seiner Gebietskörperschaften erhoben werden, geschuldet wird, soweit die Besteuerung nicht diesem Abkommen oder anderen völkerrechtlichen Vereinbarungen, denen die Vertragsstaaten beigetreten sind, widerspricht, sowie mit diesem Betrag zusammenhängende Zinsen, Geldbußen sowie Vollstreckungskosten und Kosten für Sicherungsmaßnahmen.

(3) Ist der Steueranspruch eines Vertragsstaats nach dem Recht dieses Staates vollstreckbar und wird er von einer Person geschuldet, die zu diesem Zeitpunkt nach dem Recht dieses Staates die Vollstreckung nicht verhindern kann, wird dieser Steueranspruch auf Ersuchen der zuständigen Behörde dieses Staates für die Zwecke der Erhebung von der zuständigen Behörde des anderen Vertragsstaats anerkannt. Der Steueranspruch wird von dem anderen Staat nach dessen Rechtsvorschriften über die Vollstreckung und Erhebung der eigenen Steuern erhoben, als handele es sich bei dem Steueranspruch um einen Steueranspruch dieses anderen Staates.

(4) Handelt es sich bei dem Steueranspruch eines Vertragsstaats um einen Anspruch, bei dem dieser Staat nach seinem Recht Maßnahmen zur Sicherung der Erhebung erlassen kann, wird dieser Steueranspruch auf Ersuchen der zuständigen Behörde dieses Staates zum Zwecke der Einleitung von Sicherungsmaßnahmen durch die zuständige Behörde des anderen Vertragsstaats anerkannt. Dieser andere Staat leitet in Übereinstimmung mit den eigenen Rechtsvorschriften Sicherungsmaßnahmen in Bezug auf diesen Steueranspruch ein, als wäre der Steueranspruch ein Steueranspruch dieses anderen Staates, selbst wenn der Steueranspruch im Zeitpunkt der Einleitung dieser Maßnahmen in dem erstgenannten Staat nicht vollstreckbar ist oder von einer Person geschuldet wird, die berechtigt ist, die Vollstreckung zu verhindern.

(5) Ungeachtet der Absätze 3 und 4 unterliegt ein von einem Vertragsstaat für die Zwecke der Absätze 3 oder 4 anerkannter Steueranspruch als solcher in diesem Staat nicht den Verjährungsfristen oder den Bestimmungen über vorrangige Behandlung eines Steueranspruchs nach dem Recht dieses Staates. Auch hat ein Steueranspruch, der von einem Vertragsstaat für die Zwecke der Absätze 3 oder 4 anerkannt wurde, in diesem Staat nicht den Vorrang, den dieser Steueranspruch nach dem Recht des anderen Vertragsstaats hat.

(6) Verfahren im Zusammenhang mit dem Bestehen, der Gültigkeit oder der Höhe des Steueranspruchs eines Vertragsstaats können nicht bei den Gerichten oder Verwaltungsbehörden des anderen Vertragsstaats eingeleitet werden.

(7) Verliert der betreffende Steueranspruch, nachdem das Ersuchen eines Vertragsstaats nach den Absätzen 3 oder 4 gestellt wurde und bevor der andere Vertragsstaat den betreffenden Steueranspruch erhoben und an den erstgenannten Staat ausgezahlt hat,

a) im Falle eines Ersuchens nach Absatz 3 seine Eigenschaft als Steueranspruch des erstgenannten Staates, der nach dem Recht dieses Staates vollstreckbar ist und von einer Person geschuldet wird, die zu diesem Zeitpunkt nach dem Recht dieses

Staates die Vollstreckung nicht verhindern kann, oder

b) im Falle eines Ersuchens nach Absatz 4 seine Eigenschaft als Steueranspruch des erstgenannten Staates, für den dieser Staat nach seinem Recht Maßnahmen zur Sicherung der Erhebung erlassen kann,

teilt die zuständige Behörde des erstgenannten Staates dies der zuständigen Behörde des anderen Staates unverzüglich mit und setzt das Ersuchen nach Wahl des anderen Staates aus oder nimmt es zurück.

(8) Die Bestimmungen dieses Artikels sind nicht so auszulegen, als ob ein Vertragsstaat verpflichtet würde,

a) Verwaltungsmaßnahmen durchzuführen, die von den Gesetzen und der Verwaltungspraxis dieses oder des anderen Vertragsstaats abweichen;

b) Maßnahmen durchzuführen, die der öffentlichen Ordnung (ordre public) widersprächen;

c) Amtshilfe zu leisten, wenn der andere Vertragsstaat nicht alle angemessenen Maßnahmen zur Erhebung oder Sicherung seines Steueranspruchs, die nach seinen Gesetzen oder seiner Verwaltungspraxis möglich sind, ausgeschöpft hat.

d) Amtshilfe zu leisten, wenn der Verwaltungsaufwand für diesen Staat im Vergleich zum sich daraus ergebenden Vorteil für den anderen Vertragsstaat unverhältnismäßig hoch ist."

Artikel 3

Nummer 6 des Protokolls zum Abkommen zwischen der Bundesrepublik Deutschland und der Republik Usbekistan zur Vermeidung der Doppelbesteuerung auf dem Gebiet der Steuern vom Einkommen und vom Vermögen erhält folgende Fassung:

„6. Zu Artikel 26:

a) Die empfangende Stelle kann die Daten in Übereinstimmung mit Artikel 26 Absatz 2 nur zu dem von der übermittelnden Stelle angegebenen Zweck verwenden und unterliegt dabei den durch die übermittelnde Stelle vorgeschriebenen und mit Artikel 26 in Einklang stehenden Bedingungen.

b) Die Informationen können für andere Zwecke ohne die in Artikel 26 Absatz 2 Satz 4 vorgesehene vorherige Zustimmung der zuständigen Behörde des übermittelnden Staates nur verwendet werden, wenn eine solche Verwendung zur Abwehr einer im Einzelfall bestehenden dringenden Gefahr für das Leben, die körperliche Unversehrtheit oder die persönliche Freiheit einer Person oder für bedeutende Vermögenswerte erforderlich ist und Gefahr im Verzug besteht. In diesem Fall ist die zuständige Behörde des übermittelnden Staates unverzüglich um nachträgliche Genehmigung der Zweckänderung zu ersuchen. Wird die Genehmigung verweigert, ist die weitere Verwendung der Informationen für den anderen Zweck unzulässig; ein durch die zweckändernde Verwendung der Informationen entstandener Schaden ist zu ersetzen.

c) Die übermittelnde Stelle ist verpflichtet, auf die Richtigkeit der zu übermittelnden Daten und ihre voraussichtliche Erheblichkeit im Sinne des Artikels 26 Absatz 1 und die Verhältnismäßigkeit in Bezug auf den mit der Übermittlung verfolgten Zweck zu achten. Voraussichtlich erheblich sind die Daten, wenn im konkreten Fall die ernstliche Möglichkeit besteht, dass der andere Vertragsstaat ein Besteuerungsrecht hat, und keine Anhaltspunkte dafür vorliegen, dass die Daten der zuständigen Behörde des anderen Vertragsstaats bereits bekannt sind oder dass die zuständige Behörde des anderen Vertragsstaats ohne die Information von dem Gegenstand des Besteuerungsrechts Kenntnis erlangt.

Erweist sich, dass unrichtige Daten oder Daten, die nicht übermittelt werden durften, übermittelt worden sind, so ist dies der empfangenden Stelle unverzüglich mitzuteilen. Diese ist verpflichtet, die Berichtigung oder Löschung solcher Daten unverzüglich vorzunehmen.

d) Auf Ersuchen unterrichtet die empfangende Stelle die übermittelnde Stelle im Einzelfall über die Verwendung der übermittelten Daten und die dadurch erzielten Ergebnisse.

e) Die empfangende Stelle hat den Betroffenen über die Datenerhebung bei der übermittelnden Stelle zu informieren. Die Information kann unterbleiben, soweit und solange eine Abwägung ergibt, dass das öffentliche Interesse an dem Unterbleiben der Information gegenüber dem Informationsinteresse des Betroffenen überwiegt.

f) Der Betroffene ist auf Antrag über die zu seiner Person übermittelten Daten sowie über deren vorgesehene Verwendung zu unterrichten. Buchstabe e Satz 2 gilt entsprechend.

g) Wird jemand im Zusammenhang mit Übermittlungen im Rahmen des Datenaustauschs nach diesem Abkommen rechtswidrig geschädigt, haftet ihm hierfür die empfangende Stelle nach Maßgabe des innerstaatlichen Rechts ihres Staates. Sie kann sich im Verhältnis zum Geschädigten zu ihrer Entlastung nicht darauf berufen, dass der Schaden durch die übermittelnde Stelle verursacht worden ist.

h) Die übermittelnde und die empfangende Stelle sind verpflichtet, die Übermittlung und den Empfang von personenbezogenen Daten aktenkundig zu machen.

i) Soweit das für die übermittelnde Stelle geltende innerstaatliche Recht in Bezug auf die übermittelten personenbezogenen Daten besondere Löschungsfristen vorsieht, weist diese Stelle die empfangende Stelle darauf hin. In jedem Fall sind die übermittelten personenbezogenen Daten zu löschen, sobald sie für den Zweck, für den sie übermittelt worden sind, nicht mehr erforderlich sind.

j) Die übermittelnde und die empfangende Stelle sind verpflichtet, die übermittelten personenbezogenen Daten wirksam gegen unbefugten Zugang, unbefugte Veränderung und unbefugte Bekanntgabe zu schützen."

Artikel 4

Dieses Protokoll bedarf der Ratifikation. Dieses Protokoll tritt am Tag des Austauschs der Ratifikationsurkunden in Kraft und ist in beiden Vertragsstaaten ab dem 1. Januar des Kalenderjahres, das auf das Kalenderjahr folgt, in dem das Protokoll in Kraft tritt, anzuwenden.

Artikel 5

Dieses Protokoll ist Bestandteil des Abkommens und tritt am selben Tag wie das Abkommen außer Kraft.

Zu Urkund dessen haben die unterzeichneten, hierzu gehörig befugten Bevollmächtigten dieses Protokoll unterschrieben.

Geschehen zu Berlin am 14. Oktober 2014, in zwei Urschriften, jede in deutscher, usbekischer und russischer Sprache, wobei jeder Wortlaut verbindlich ist. Bei unterschiedlicher Auslegung des deutschen und des usbekischen Wortlauts ist der russische Wortlaut maßgebend.

Für die Bundesrepublik Deutschland	Für die Republik Usbekistan

[TEXT IN RUSSIAN – TEXTE EN RUSSE]

Протокол

о

внесении изменений и дополнений в Соглашение

между

Федеративной Республикой Германия

и

Республикой Узбекистан

об

избежании двойного налогообложения

в отношении налогов на доходы

и имущество

от 7 сентября 1999 года

Федеративная Республика Германия

и

Республика Узбекистан,

далее именуемые «Договаривающиеся Государства»,

в соответствии с Соглашением между Федеративной Республикой Германия и Республикой Узбекистан об избежании двойного налогообложения в отношении налогов на доходы и имущество от 7 сентября 1999 года (далее именуемым «Соглашение»),

желая далее развивать двусторонние экономические отношения и углублять сотрудничество в области налогов для обеспечения действенного и верного взимания налогов,

согласились о нижеследующем:

СТАТЬЯ 1

Статью 26 Соглашения изложить в следующей редакции:

«Статья 26

Обмен информацией

(1) Компетентные органы Договаривающихся Государств обмениваются информацией, которая может считаться существенной для осуществления настоящего

Соглашения или для администрирования или реализации национального законодательства Договаривающихся Государств в отношении налогов любого вида или наименования, взимаемых от имени Договаривающегося Государства или одного из его административно-территориальных образований, в той части, в какой налогообложение по этому законодательству не противоречит настоящему Соглашению. Обмен информацией не ограничивается положениями статей 1 и 2 настоящего Соглашения.

(2) Любая информация, полученная Договаривающимся Государством согласно пункту 1 настоящей статьи, должна считаться конфиденциальной так же, как информация, получаемая на основании национального законодательства этого Государства, и может быть предоставлена только лицам или органам (включая суды и административные органы), которые занимаются начислением или взиманием налогов, упомянутых в пункте 1 настоящей статьи, принудительным взысканием или уголовным преследованием, принятием решений по возражениям и жалобам в отношении этих налогов, либо надзором за такой деятельностью. Эти лица или органы могут использовать информацию только в указанных целях. В указанных целях информация может быть раскрыта в ходе предварительного расследования по административным или уголовным делам, в ходе открытого судебного заседания или в судебном решении. Несмотря на предыдущие положения, информация, полученная одним Договаривающимся Государством, может быть использована в иных целях, если она в соответствии с законодательством обоих Государств может быть использована в этих иных целях и если компетентный орган передающего Государства выразил свое согласие с таким использованием.

(3) Положения пунктов 1 и 2 настоящей статьи не должны истолковываться как обязывающие Договаривающееся Государство:

a) проводить административные меры, противоречащие законодательству или административной практике этого или другого Договаривающегося Государства;

b) предоставлять информацию, которая в соответствии с законами или имеющейся административной практикой этого или другого Договаривающегося Государства не может быть получена;

c) предоставлять информацию, которая раскрывала бы какую-либо производственную, коммерческую, предпринимательскую, торговую или профессиональную тайну либо деловую процедуру, или предоставление которой противоречило бы общественному порядку (odre public).

(4) Если Договаривающееся Государство запрашивает информацию согласно положениям настоящей статьи, то другое Договаривающееся Государство предпринимает имеющиеся в его распоряжении меры для получения запрошенной информации даже в случае, если это другое Государство для собственных налоговых целей в такой информации не нуждается. Обязательство, предусмотренное в первом предложении настоящего пункта, подлежит ограничениям, установленным пунктом 3 настоящей статьи, но эти ограничения не должны истолковываться, как позволяющие Договаривающемуся Государству отказать в предоставлении информации только лишь на том основании, что оно само в национальных налоговых целях в такой информации не заинтересовано.

(5) Пункт 3 настоящей статьи не должен истолковываться, как позволяющий Договаривающемуся Государству отказать в предоставлении информации только лишь на том основании, что такой информацией располагает банк, иная кредитная организация, номинальный держатель, агент или доверительный управляющий или что такая информация касается долевых имущественных интересов применительно к какому-либо лицу».

СТАТЬЯ 2

Дополнить Соглашение статьей 26а следующего ссдержания:

«Статья 26а

Административная помощь при взимании налогов

(1) Договаривающиеся Государства оказывают друг другу административную помощь при взимании сумм налоговых требований. Такая административная помощь не ограничивается положениями статей 1 и 2 настоящего Соглашения. Компетентные органы Договаривающихся Государств путем согласования могут установить порядок применения настоящей статьи.

(2) Термин «налоговое требование», в смысле настоящей статьи, означает подлежащую уплате сумму налогов любого вида или наименования, взимаемых от имени Договаривающегося Государства или одного из его административно-территориальных образований, в той части, в какой такое налогообложение не противоречит настоящему Соглашению или каким-либо иным международным соглашениям, сторонами которых являются Договаривающиеся Государства, а также относящиеся к такой сумме проценты, административные штрафы, а также расходы на исполнительные или обеспечительные меры.

(3) Если налоговое требование Договаривающегося Государства по законодательству этого Государства может быть исполнено и если оно подлежит уплате лицом, которое согласно законодательству этого Государства в момент исполнения не может препятствовать его исполнению, то такое налоговое требование по запросу компетентного органа этого Государства принимается для целей взимания компетентным органом другого Договаривающегося Государства. Взимание суммы налогового требования осуществляется этим другим Государством в соответствии с положениями его законодательства о принудительном исполнении и взимании собственных налогов, как если бы это налоговое требование являлось налоговым требованием этого другого Государства.

(4) Если налоговое требование Договаривающегося Государства является требованием, в отношении которого это Государство может в соответствии с его законодательством издавать меры по обеспечению взимания, то такое налоговое требование по запросу компетентного органа этого Государства принимается для целей принятия обеспечительных мер компетентным органом другого Договаривающегося Государства. Это другое Государство принимает обеспечительные меры в отношении такого налогового требования в соответствии с положениями его законодательства, как если бы это налоговое требование являлось налоговым требованием этого другого Государства, даже в том случае, когда налоговое требование в момент принятия таких

мер в первом упомянутом Государстве не может быть исполнено или если оно подлежит уплате лицом, которое вправе препятствовать его исполнению.

(5) Несмотря на положения пунктов 3 и 4 настоящей статьи, налоговое требование, принятое Договаривающимся Государством для целей пункта 3 или 4 настоящей статьи, как таковое в этом Государстве не подлежит срокам давности или положениям о первоочередном рассмотрении налогового требования согласно законодательству этого Государства. Кроме того, налоговое требование, принятое Договаривающимся Государством для целей пункта 3 или 4 настоящей статьи, не имеет в этом Государстве того же преимущественного статуса, которым это налоговое требование отличается по законодательству другого Договаривающегося Государства.

(6) Правовые процедуры на предмет наличия, действительности или суммы налогового требования Договаривающегося Государства не могут возбуждаться в судах или административных органах другого Договаривающегося Государства.

(7) Если соответствующее налоговое требование в период с момента представления Договаривающимся Государством запроса в соответствии с пунктом 3 или 4 настоящей статьи и до осуществления другим Договаривающимся Государством взимания суммы соответствующего налогового требования и её перечисления первому упомянутому Государству:

a) применительно к запросу согласно пункту 3 настоящей статьи утрачивает характер налогового требования первого упомянутого Государства, которое по законодательству этого Государства может быть исполнено и подлежит уплате лицом, которое в момент исполнения не может препятствовать его исполнению, или

b) применительно к запросу согласно пункту 4 настоящей статьи утрачивает характер налогового требования первого упомянутого Государства, в отношении которого это Государство может согласно его законодательству принимать меры по обеспечению взимания,

компетентный орган первого упомянутого Государства незамедлительно уведомляет компетентный орган другого Государства о таком факте, и, в зависимости от выбора другого Государства, приостанавливает либо аннулирует свой запрос.

(8) Положения настоящей статьи никоим образом не должны истолковываться как налагающие на Договаривающееся Государство обязательство:

a) проводить административные меры, противоречащие законодательству или административной практике этого или другого Договаривающегося Государства;

b) проводить меры, которые бы противоречили общественному порядку (ordre public);

c) оказывать административную помощь в случаях, когда другое Договаривающееся Государство не исчерпало любые соответствующие меры по взиманию или принятию обеспечительных мер в отношении к своему налоговому требованию, возможные согласно его законодательству или административной практике;

d) оказывать административную помощь, когда административные расходы этого Государства в сопоставлении с пользой, которую получает другое Договаривающееся Государство от этой помощи являются несоразмерно высокими».

СТАТЬЯ 3

Пункт 6 Протокола к Соглашению между Федеративной Республикой Германия и Республикой Узбекистан об избежании двойного налогообложения в отношении налогов на доходы и имущество от 7 сентября 1999 года изложить в следующей редакции:

«6. К статье 26:

a) Принимающее учреждение может пользоваться сведениями в соответствии с положениями пункта 2 статьи 26 только в указанных передающим учреждением целях и подлежит при этом предусмотренным передающим учреждением и соответствующим статье 26 условиям.

b) Информация без предусмотренного предложением 4 пункта 2 статьи 26 предыдущего согласия компетентного органа передающего Государства может быть использована для иных целей лишь в тех случаях, если такое использование необходимо для предотвращения существующей в конкретном случае непосредственной опасности для жизни, физической неприкосновенности или личной свободы лица либо для значительных имущественных ценностей и в случаях, не терпящих отлагательства. В данном случае следует незамедлительно обратиться в компетентный орган передающего Государства с просьбой о последующем санкционировании изменения цели. В случае отказа санкционирования, дальнейшее использование информации для иных целей недопустимо; возникший в связи с использованием информаций для иных целей ущерб подлежит возмещению.

c) Передающее учреждение обязано следить за достоверностью передаваемых сведений и за их возможной существенностью в смысле пункта 1 статьи 26, а также за их адекватностью целям, которые преследуются передачей сведений. Сведения являются, возможно, существенными, если в конкретном случае существует серьезная возможность, что другое Договаривающееся Государство располагает правом налогообложения, и нет основания для того, что эти сведения уже известны компетентному органу другого Договаривающегося Государства и для того, что без передачи информации компетентный орган другого Договаривающегося Государства не узнает о предмете налогообложения. Если оказывается, что были переданы недостоверные сведения или сведения, не подлежащие передаче, то об этом необходимо незамедлительно известить принимающее учреждение. Оно обязано производить их исправление или уничтожение.

d) Принимающее учреждение в конкретном случае ставит в известность передавшее сведения учреждение по его просьбе об использовании переданных сведений и полученных с их помощью результатах.

e) Принимающее учреждение информирует заинтересованное лицо о сборе сведений передаваемым учреждением. Предоставление информации не обязательно, если анализ показывает, что государственная заинтересованность отказаться от выдачи информации превалирует над заинтересованностью упомянутого лица в получении информации.

f) По заявлению заинтересованному лицу выдается информация о передаче касающихся его данных, а также о предполагаемых целях их использования. Положения второго предложения пункта e) применяются соответственно.

g) Если кому-либо в связи с передачей сведений в рамках обмена информацией по настоящему Соглашению противоправно причиняется ущерб, ответственность перед ним в этой связи несет принимающее учреждение в соответствии с национальным законодательством своего государства. Оно не может в отношении понесшего ущерб лица ссылаться в оправдание на то, что ущерб был причинен передающим сведения учреждением.

h) Передающее и принимающее учреждения обязаны документально зарегистрировать передачу и получение сведений, касающихся физических лиц.

i) Если национальное законодательство, в рамках которого действует передающее учреждение, предусматривает в отношении переданных сведений, касающихся физических лиц, особые правила уничтожения, то передающее учреждение указывает на это принимающему учреждению. Во всех случаях, переданные сведения, касающиеся физических лиц, подлежат уничтожению, если они больше не требуются для целей, для которых они были переданы.

j) Передающее и принимающее учреждения обязаны охранять переданные в отношении физических лиц сведения от доступа к ним, их изменения и разглашения лицами, не имеющими на то право».

СТАТЬЯ 4

Настоящий Протокол подлежит ратификации.

Настоящий Протокол вступит в силу в день обмена ратификационными грамотами, и его положения будут применяться в обоих Договаривающихся

Государствах с 1 января календарного года, последующего за календарным годом, в котором Протокол вступил в силу.

СТАТЬЯ 5

Настоящий протокол является неотъемлемой частью Соглашения и прекратит свое действие с даты прекращения действия Соглашения.

В удостоверение чего, нижеподписавшиеся, соответствующим образом на то уполномоченные, подписали настоящий протокол.

Совершено в городе Берлин 14 октября 2014 года в двух подлинных экземплярах, каждый на немецком, узбекском и русском языках, причем все тексты имеют одинаковую силу. При различном толковании немецкого и узбекского текстов, текст на русском языке будет считаться определяющим.

За Федеративную Республику Германия

За Республику Узбекистан

[TEXT IN UZBEK – TEXTE EN OUZBEK]

Германия Федератив Республикаси ва Ўзбекистон Республикаси ўртасида даромад ва мол-мулк солиқлари юзасидан икки ёқлама солиққа тортишнинг олдини олиш тўғрисида 1999 йил 7 сентябрдаги Битимга ўзгартиш ва қўшимчалар киритиш тўғрисида
БАЁННОМА

Германия Федератив Республикаси ва Ўзбекистон Республикаси, бундан кейин «Аҳдлашувчи Давлатлар» деб аталувчилар,

Германия Федератив Республикаси ва Ўзбекистон Республикаси ўртасида даромад ва мол-мулк солиқлари юзасидан икки ёқлама солиққа тортишнинг олдини олиш тўғрисида 1999 йил 7 сентябрдаги Битимга (бундан кейинги ўринларда «Битим» деб аталувчи) мувофиқ,

келгусида икки томонлама иқтисодий муносабатларни ривожлантириш ҳамда солиқларнинг самарали ва тўғри ундирилишини таъминлаш учун солиқлар соҳасида ҳамкорликни чуқурлаштириш истагида,

қуйидагилар тўғрисида келишиб олдилар:

1-МОДДА

Битимнинг 26-моддаси қуйидаги таҳрирда баён қилинсин:

«26-модда
Маълумот алмашинуви

(1) Аҳдлашувчи Давлатларнинг ваколатли органлари мазкур Битимни амалга ошириш учун ёки Аҳдлашувчи Давлат ёхуд унинг маъмурий-ҳудудий тузилмаларидан бири номидан Аҳдлашувчи Давлатлар миллий қонунчилиги бўйича солиқ солиниши мазкур Битимга зид бўлмаган қисмига оид ундириладиган ҳар қандай кўринишдаги ва номланишдаги солиқларга нисбатан ушбу қонунчиликни қўллаш ёки унга амал қилиш учун аҳамиятли бўлиши мумкин бўлган маълумотларни алмашадилар. Маълумот алмашинуви мазкур Битимнинг 1- ва 2-моддалари қоидалари билан чекланмайди.

(2) Аҳдлашувчи Давлат томонидан мазкур модданинг 1-бандига мувофиқ олинган ҳар қандай маълумот ушбу Давлатнинг миллий қонунчилигига асосан олинган маълумот каби махфий деб ҳисобланиши лозим ҳамда фақат мазкур модданинг 1-бандида айтиб ўтилган солиқларни ҳисоблаш ёки ундириш, мажбурий ундириш ёки

жиноятни таъқиб қилиш, ушбу солиқларга нисбатан эътироз ва шикоятлар бўйича қарорлар қабул қилиш ёхуд бундай фаолиятни назорат қилиш билан шуғулланувчи шахслар ёки органларгагина (суд ва маъмурий идоралар шулар жумласидан) тақдим қилиниши мумкин. Ушбу шахслар ёки идоралар маълумотдан фақатгина кўрсатилган мақсадлардагина фойдаланишлари мумкин. Кўрсатилган мақсадларда маълумот маъмурий ёки жиноий ишлар бўйича дастлабки тергов жараёнида, очиқ суд муҳокамаси ёки суд қарорида ошкор қилиниши мумкин. Аввалги қоидалардан қатъий назар бир Аҳдлашувчи Давлат томонидан олинган маълумот бошқа мақсадларда ишлатилиши мумкин, башарти бундай маълумот ҳар икки Давлат қонунчилигига кўра бошқа мақсадларда фойдаланиши мумкин бўлса ҳамда маълумотни тақдим этаётган Давлат ваколатли органининг бундай фойдаланишга розилиги мавжуд бўлса.

(3) Мазкур модданинг 1- ва 2-бандлари қоидалари Аҳдлашувчи Давлатни қуйидагиларга мажбурловчи меъёр сифатида талқин қилинмаслиги лозим:

а) у ёки бу Аҳдлашувчи Давлатнинг қонунчилиги ёки маъмурий амалиётига зид бўлган маъмурий чораларни қўллаш;

b) у ёки бу Аҳдлашувчи Давлатнинг қонунлари ёки мавжуд маъмурий амалиётига мувофиқ олиниши мумкин бўлмаган маълумот тақдим қилиш;

с) ҳар қандай ишлаб чиқариш, тижорат, тадбиркорлик, савдо ёки касбий сирни ёхуд ишбилармонлик жараёнларини ошкор қилувчи ёки тақдим қилиниши жамоат тартибига (ordre public) зид бўлган маълумот тақдим қилиш.

(4) Агар Аҳдлашувчи Давлат мазкур модда қоидаларига мувофиқ маълумот сўраётган бўлса, унда бошқа Аҳдлашувчи Давлат ўзининг солиқ мақсадлари учун бундай маълумотга муҳтож бўлмаган ҳолда ҳам сўралаётган маълумотни олиш учун ўз ихтиёрида мавжуд бўлган чораларни кўради. Мазкур банднинг биринчи жумласида назарда тутилган мажбуриятга нисбатан ушбу модданинг 3-бандида белгиланган чекловлар қўлланилади, лекин бундай чекловлар Аҳдлашувчи Давлатга фақатгина у ўзининг миллий солиқ тизими мақсадларида бундай маълумот олишдан манфаатдор эмаслиги асосида маълумот тақдим қилишни рад этишга имконият сифатида талқин қилинмаслиги лозим.

(5) Мазкур модданинг 3-банди Аҳдлашувчи Давлатга бундай маълумот фақатгина банк, бошқа кредит ташкилоти, номинал эгаси, агент ёки ишончли бошқарувчилар ихтиёрида эканлиги ёхуд бундай маълумот бирор бир шахсга нисбатан улушли мулкий манфаатларга

таллуқлилиги асосида маълумот тақдим қилишни рад этишга имконият сифатида талқин қилинмаслиги лозим».

2-МОДДА

Битим қуйидаги мазмундаги 26а-модда билан тўлдирилсин:

«26а-модда
Солиқларни ундиришда маъмурий ёрдам

(1) Аҳдлашувчи Давлатлар солиқ талабномалари суммаларини ундиришда бир бирларига маъмурий ёрдам кўрсатадилар. Бундай маъмурий ёрдам мазкур Битимнинг 1- ва 2-моддалари қоидалари билан чекланмайди. Аҳдлашувчи Давлатларнинг ваколатли органлари мазкур моддани қўллаш тартибини келишиш йўли билан ўрнатишлари мумкин.

(2) Мазкур моддада "солиқ талабномаси" атамаси Аҳдлашувчи Давлат ёки унинг маъмурий-ҳудудий тузилмаларидан бири номидан мазкур Битимга ёки Аҳдлашувчи Давлатлар иштирокчиси бўлган бошқа бирон-бир халқаро шартномаларга зид бўлмаган қисмида ҳар қандай кўринишдаги ва номланишдаги тўланиши лозим бўлган солиқ суммасини, шунингдек, бундай суммага тегишли фоизлар, маъмурий жарималар ҳамда ижро қилиш ёки таъминлаш чораларига оид харажатларни англатади.

(3) Башарти Аҳдлашувчи Давлатнинг солиқ талабномаси ушбу Давлатнинг қонунчилиги бўйича бажарилиши мумкин бўлса ҳамда агарда ушбу Давлат конунчилигига биноан ижро этилиши пайтида унинг бажарилишига қаршилик қила олмайдиган шахс томонидан тўланиши лозим бўлса, бу ҳолда ушбу Давлатнинг ваколатли органи сўровномасига асосан бундай солиқ талабномаси бошқа Аҳдлашувчи Давлатнинг ваколатли органи томонидан ундириш мақсадида қабул қилинади. Солиқ талабномаси суммасини ундириш ушбу бошқа Давлат томонидан унинг мажбурий ижро этиш ва ўз солиқларини ундириш тўғрисидаги қонунчилиги қоидаларига мувофиқ бу солиқ талабномаси ушбу бошқа Давлатнинг солиқ талабномаси бўлгани каби амалга оширилади.

(4) Агарда Аҳдлашувчи Давлатнинг солиқ талабномаси ушбу Давлат қонунчилигига мувофиқ ундиришни таъминлаш чораларини кўришни тақозо қиладиган талабнома бўлса, бундай солиқ талабномаси ушбу Давлатнинг ваколатли органи сўровномаси асосида бошқа Аҳдлашувчи Давлатнинг ваколатли органи томонидан

таъминлаш чораларини кўриш мақсадида қабул қилинади. Ушбу бошқа Давлат бундай солиқ талабномасига нисбатан, хатто дастлабки кўрсатилган Давлатда бундай чораларни кўриш пайтида солиқ талабномаси бажарилишининг имкони бўлмаган ёки уни ижро этилишига тўсқинлик қилиш ҳуқуқига эга шахс томонидан тўланиши керак бўлган тақдирда ҳам, ўз қонунчилиги қоидаларига мувофиқ ўзининг солиқ талабномасига нисбатан белгиланган таъминлаш чораларини кўради.

(5) Мазкур модданинг 3- ва 4-бандлари қоидаларидан қатъий назар, Аҳдлашувчи Давлат томонидан мазкур модданинг 3- ёки 4-бандлари мақсадларида қабул қилинган солиқ талабномасига нисбатан ушбу Давлатдаги солиқ талабномасига бўлгани каби даъво муддатлари ёки ушбу Давлатнинг қонунчилигига мувофиқ солиқ талабномасини биринчи навбатда кўриб чиқиш тўғрисидаги қоидалар татбиқ қилинмайди. Бундан ташқари, Аҳдлашувчи Давлат томонидан мазкур модданинг 3- ёки 4-бандлари мақсадлари учун қабул қилинган солиқ талабномаси, ушбу Давлатда бошқа Аҳдлашувчи Давлатнинг қонунчилигига кўра бундай солиқ талабидан фарқ қиладиган солиқ талабномасидан устувор мақомга эга эмас.

(6) Аҳдлашувчи Давлатнинг солиқ талабномаси мавжудлиги, ҳақиқийлиги ва суммаси юзасидан ҳуқуқий жараёнлар бошқа Аҳдлашувчи Давлатнинг судлари ёки маъмурий органларида қўзғатилиши мумкин эмас.

(7) Агар тегишли солиқ талабномаси Аҳдлашувчи Давлат томонидан мазкур модданинг 3- ёки 4-бандларига мувофиқ сўровнома тақдим қилиш пайтида ҳамда бошқа Аҳдлашувчи Давлат томонидан тегишли солиқ талабномаси суммаси ундирилиши амалга оширилгунга ва уни биринчи айтиб ўтилган Давлатга ўтказилгунига қадар:

а) сўровномага нисбатан мазкур модданинг 3-бандига биноан биринчи айтиб ўтилган Аҳдлашувчи Давлатнинг солиқ талабномаси хусусиятини йўқотса ҳамда у ушбу Аҳдлашувчи Давлатнинг қонунчилигига кўра бажарилиши мумкин ва ижро этилиши пайтида уни бажаришга тўсқинлик қилиши мумкин бўлмаган шахс томонидан тўланиши лозим бўлса, ёки

b) сўровномага нисбатан мазкур модданинг 4-бандига биноан дастлабки айтиб ўтилган Аҳдлашувчи Давлатнинг солиқ талабномаси хусусиятини йўқотса ва унга нисбатан ушбу Аҳдлашувчи Давлат ўз қонунчилигига мувофиқ ундиришни таъминлаш чораларини кўриши мумкин бўлса, дастлабки таъкидлаб ўтилган Аҳдлашувчи Давлатнинг ваколатли органи бошқа Аҳдлашувчи Давлатнинг ваколатли органини бундай факт юзасидан зудлик билан хабардор қилади ва бошқа Аҳдлашувчи Давлат ваколатли органининг мурожаатига мувофиқ ўз сўровномасини тўхтатиб туради ёки бекор қилади.

(8) Мазкур модданинг қоидалари ҳеч қандай кўринишда Аҳдлашувчи Давлатга қуйидаги мажбуриятларни юклаш сифатида талқин қилинмаслиги лозим:

a) у ёки бу Аҳдлашувчи Давлатнинг қонунчилиги ёхуд маъмурий амалиётига зид бўлган маъмурий чораларни кўриш;

b) жамоат тартибига (ordre public) зид бўлиши мумкин бўлган чораларни кўриш;

c) бошқа Аҳдлашувчи Давлат унинг қонунчилиги ёки маъмурий амалиётига биноан ўзининг солиқ талабномасига нисбатан амалга оширилиши мумкин бўлган ундириш ёки таъминлаш чораларини қабул қилиши бўйича ҳар қандай тегишли чораларни батамом қўллаб бўлмаган ҳолларда маъмурий ёрдам кўрсатиш;

d) Аҳдлашувчи Давлатнинг маъмурий харажатлари бошқа Аҳдлашувчи Давлат бундай ёрдамдан оладиган фойдаси билан таққосланса номутаносиб даражада юқори бўлганда маъмурий ёрдам кўрсатиш».

3-МОДДА

Германия Федератив Республикаси ва Ўзбекистон Республикаси ўртасида даромад ва мол-мулк солиқлари юзасидан икки ёқлама солиққа тортишнинг олдини олиш тўғрисида 1999 йил 7 сентябрдаги Битим Баённомасининг 6-банди қуйидаги таҳрирда баён қилинсин:

«6. 26-моддага:

a) Қабул қилувчи муассаса маълумотлардан 26-модданинг 2-банди қоидаларига мувофиқ фақат тақдим этувчи муассаса кўрсатган мақсадларда фойдаланиши мумкин ва бунда тақдим этувчи муассаса томонидан белгиланган ҳамда 26-моддада кўрсатиб ўтилган шартлар қўлланилади.

b) Маълумот 26-модданинг 2-банди 4-жумласида назарда тутилган тақдим этувчи Давлат ваколатли органининг олдиндан олинган розилигисиз бошқа мақсадлар учун муайян вазиятда мавжуд бўлган ҳаёт, жисмоний дахлсизлик ёки шахснинг шахсий эркинлигига ёхуд кўп миқдордаги мулкий бойликларга бевосита хавфнинг олдини олиш зарурияти бўлган ҳолларда ва кечиктириб бўлмайдиган ҳолларда фойдаланилиши мумкин. Мазкур ҳолатда зудлик билан тақдим этувчи Давлат ваколатли органига мақсадни ўзгартиришга рухсат беришни сўраб кейинчалик мурожаат қилинади. Рухсат бериш рад этилган тақдирда маълумотдан кейинчалик ўзга мақсадларда фойдаланилиши мумкин эмас; маълумотдан ўзга мақсадларда фойдаланиш билан боғлиқ равишда юзага келган зарар қопланиши лозим.

c) Тақдим этувчи муассаса, берилаётган маълумотларнинг ишончлилиги ва уларнинг 26-модданинг 1-бандида назарга тутилган маънога мос эканлигини, шунингдек, маълумотларни беришдан кўзланган мақсадларга мувофиқлигини кузатиб бориши шарт. Башарти аниқ ҳолатда бошқа Аҳдлашувчи Давлат солиққа тортиш ҳуқуқига эга эканлигининг жиддий имконияти мавжуд бўлса ҳамда ушбу маълумотлар бошқа Аҳдлашувчи Давлат ваколатли органига аён эканлиги учун ҳамда бундай маълумот берилмаса бошқа Аҳдлашувчи Давлат ваколатли органи солиққа тортишнинг предмети тўғрисида билиб олиши учун асослар мавжуд бўлмаса маълумот муҳим ҳисобланиши мумкин. Агарда тақдим қилиниши мумкин бўлмаган ишончсиз маълумот берилганлиги аниқланса, бу ҳақда қабул қилувчи муассаса зудлик билан хабардор қилиниши лозим. Қабул қилувчи муассаса бу каби маълумотларни тузатиш ёки йўқ қилишга мажбур.

d) Қабул қилувчи муассаса маълумотларни тақдим этувчи муассасани унинг илтимосига кўра аниқ ҳолатда берилган маълумотларнинг қўлланилиши ва улар ёрдамида олинган натижалар ҳақида хабардор қилади.

e) Қабул қилувчи муассаса тақдим этилаётган муассаса томондан маълумотлар тўпланиши юзасидан манфаатдор шахсни хабардор қилади. Башарти давлатнинг маълумот беришни рад этишдан манфаатдорлиги кўрсатиб ўтилган шахснинг маълумот олишга бўлган манфаатдорлигидан устун бўлса маълумот бериш мажбурий ҳисобланмайди.

f) Аризага биноан манфаатдор шахсга унга тегишли маълумотларнинг юборилиши, шунингдек, ундан фойдаланишнинг тахминий мақсадлари тўғрисида хабар берилади. “e” банднинг иккинчи жумласи қоидалари тегишли тарзда қўлланилади.

g) Агарда мазкур Битим доирасида маълумот алмашинуви бўйича маълумотларни бериш билан боғлиқ ҳолда бирор кимсага ноқонуний зарар етказилса, қабул қилувчи муассаса унинг олдида ўз давлатининг миллий қонунчилигига мувофиқ жавобгар бўлади. У зарар кўрган шахсга нисбатан зарар маълумот тақдим этувчи муассаса томонидан етказилганлигига ҳавола қилиб ўзини оқлай олмайди.

h) Тақдим этувчи ва қабул қилувчи муассасалар жисмоний шахсларга таааллуқли маълумотларнинг тақдим этилиши ва қабул қилинишини ҳужжатлар асосида рўйхатдан ўтказишлари шарт.

i) Агарда тақдим этувчи муассаса фаолиятини тартибга соладиган миллий қонунчилик жисмоний шахсларга оид берилаётган маълумотларни йўқ қилиш бўйича алоҳида қоидаларни назарда тутса, тақдим этувчи муассаса қабул қилувчи муассасани бу ҳақда хабардор қилади. Ҳар қандай ҳолатда ҳам жисмоний шахсларга оид берилаётган маълумотлар, агарда улардан тақдим этишда кўзланган мақсадлар учун қайта фойдаланиш талаб қилинмаса, йўқ қилинади.

j) Тақдим этувчи ва қабул қилувчи муассасалар жисмоний шахсларга оид тақдим этилган маълумотларни улардан фойдаланиш, уларни ўзгартириш ва ошкора қилиш ҳуқуқига эга бўлмаган шахсларнинг қўлига тушишидан ҳимоя қилишга мажбурдирлар».

4-МОДДА

Мазкур Баённома ратификация қилинади.

Мазкур Баённома ратификация ёрлиқлари билан алмашилган кундан кучга киради ва унинг қоидалари ҳар иккала Аҳдлашувчи Давлатда Баённома кучга кирган календарь йилдан кейинги келадиган календарь йилнинг 1 январидан қўлланилади.

5-МОДДА

Мазкур Баённома Битимнинг ажралмас қисми ҳисобланади ва Битимнинг амал қилиш муддати тугаган санадан ўз кучини йўқотади.

Тегишли тартибда ваколат берилган қуйида имзо чекувчилар шунга гувоҳлик бериб, ушбу Баённомани имзоладилар.

Берлин шаҳрида 2014 йил 14 октябрда икки асл нусҳада ҳар бири немис, ўзбек ва рус тилларда тузилди, бунда барча матнлар бир хил кучга эга. Немис ва ўзбек тилларидаги матнларни талқин этишда келишмовчиликлар юзага келган ҳолларда рус тилидаги матн устувор ҳисобланади.

Германия Федератив Республикаси номидан	Ўзбекистон Республикаси номидан
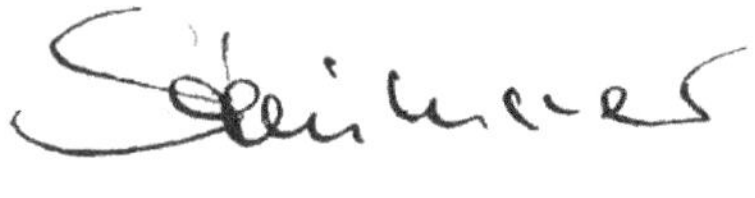	

[TRANSLATION – TRADUCTION]

PROTOCOL AMENDING AND SUPPLEMENTING THE CONVENTION OF 7 SEPTEMBER 1999 BETWEEN THE FEDERAL REPUBLIC OF GERMANY AND THE REPUBLIC OF UZBEKISTAN FOR THE AVOIDANCE OF DOUBLE TAXATION WITH RESPECT TO TAXES ON INCOME AND CAPITAL

The Federal Republic of Germany and the Republic of Uzbekistan, hereinafter referred to as the "Contracting Parties",

In accordance with the Convention of 7 September 1999 between the Federal Republic of Germany and the Republic of Uzbekistan for the avoidance of double taxation with respect to taxes on income and capital (hereinafter the Convention),

Desirous of further developing mutual economic relations and deepening cooperation in the field of taxation with a view to ensuring efficient and appropriate tax collection,

Have agreed as follows:

Article 1

Article 26 of the Agreement shall be worded as follows:

"Article 26. Exchange of information

(1) The competent authorities of the Contracting States shall exchange such information as is foreseeably relevant for carrying out the provisions of this Convention or to the administration or enforcement of the domestic laws concerning taxes of every kind and description imposed on behalf of a Contracting State, or of their political subdivisions or local authorities, insofar as the taxation thereunder is not contrary to the Convention. The exchange of information shall not be restricted by articles 1 and 2.

(2) Any information received under paragraph 1 by a Contracting State shall be treated as secret in the same manner as information obtained under the domestic laws of that State and it shall be disclosed only to persons or authorities (including courts and administrative bodies) concerned with the assessment or collection of, the enforcement or prosecution in respect of, or the determination of appeals in relation to the taxes referred to in paragraph 1, or the oversight of the above. Such persons or authorities shall use the information only for such purposes. The information may be disclosed in the course of an administrative or criminal investigation, public court proceedings or in judicial decisions. Notwithstanding the foregoing, information received by a Contracting State may be used for other purposes when such information may be used for such other purposes under the laws of both States and the competent authority of the Sending State authorizes such use.

(3) In no case shall the provisions of paragraphs 1 and 2 be construed to impose on a Contracting State the obligation:

(a) To carry out administrative measures at variance with the laws and administrative practice of that or of the other Contracting State;

(b) To supply information which is not obtainable under the laws or in the normal course of the administration of that or of the other Contracting State;

(c) To supply information which would disclose any trade, business, industrial, commercial or professional secret or trade process, or information the disclosure of which would be contrary to public policy (ordre public).

(4) If information is requested by a Contracting State in accordance with this article, the other Contracting State shall use its information gathering measures to obtain the requested information, even though that other State may not need such information for its own tax purposes. The obligation in the preceding sentence is subject to the limitations of paragraph 3 but in no case shall such limitations be construed to permit a Contracting State to decline to supply information solely because it has no domestic interest in such information.

(5) In no case shall the provisions of paragraph 3 be construed to permit a Contracting State to decline to supply information solely because the information is held by a bank, other financial institution, nominee or person acting in an agency or a fiduciary capacity, or because it relates to ownership interests in a person."

Article 2

Article 26a shall be added to the Agreement and shall be worded as follows:

"Article 26a. Assistance in the collection of taxes

(1) The Contracting States shall lend assistance to each other in the collection of revenue claims. Such assistance shall not be restricted by articles 1 and 2. The competent authorities of the Contracting States may by mutual agreement settle the mode of application of this article.

(2) The term "revenue claim" as used in this article means an amount owed in respect of taxes of every kind and description imposed on behalf of the Contracting States, or of their political subdivisions or local authorities, insofar as the taxation thereunder is not contrary to this Convention or any other instrument to which the Contracting States are parties, as well as interest, administrative penalties and costs of collection or conservancy related to such amount.

(3) When a revenue claim of a Contracting State is enforceable under the laws of that State and is owed by a person who, at that time, cannot, under the laws of that State, prevent its collection, that revenue claim shall, at the request of the competent authority of that State, be accepted for purposes of collection by the competent authority of the other Contracting State. That revenue claim shall be collected by that other State in accordance with the provisions of its laws applicable to the enforcement and collection of its own taxes as if the revenue claim were a revenue claim of that other State.

(4) When a revenue claim of a Contracting State is a claim in respect of which that State may, under its law, take measures of conservancy with a view to ensure its collection, that revenue claim shall, at the request of the competent authority of that State, be accepted for purposes of taking measures of conservancy by the competent authority of the other Contracting State. That other State shall take measures of conservancy in respect of that revenue claim in accordance with the provisions of its laws as if the revenue claim were a revenue claim of that other State even if, at the time when such measures are applied, the revenue claim is not enforceable in the first-mentioned State or is owed by a person who has a right to prevent its collection.

(5) Notwithstanding the provisions of paragraphs 3 and 4, a revenue claim accepted by a Contracting State for the purposes of paragraph 3 or 4 shall not, in that State, be subject to the time limits or accorded any priority applicable to a revenue claim under the laws of that State by reason of its nature as such. In addition, a revenue claim accepted by a Contracting State for the purposes of paragraph 3 or 4 shall not, in that State, have any priority applicable to that revenue claim under the laws of the other Contracting State.

(6) Proceedings with respect to the existence, validity or the amount of a revenue claim of a Contracting State shall not be brought before the courts or administrative bodies of the other Contracting State.

(7) Where, at any time after a request has been made by a Contracting State under paragraph 3 or 4 and before the other Contracting State has collected and remitted the relevant revenue claim to the first-mentioned State, the relevant revenue claim ceases to be:

(a) In the case of a request under paragraph 3, a revenue claim of the first-mentioned State that is enforceable under the laws of that State and is owed by a person who, at that time, cannot, under the laws of that State, prevent its collection, or

(b) In the case of a request under paragraph 4, a revenue claim of the first-mentioned State in respect of which that State may, under its laws, take measures of conservancy with a view to ensuring its collection,

the competent authority of the first-mentioned State shall promptly notify the competent authority of the other State of that fact and, at the option of the other State, the first-mentioned State shall either suspend or withdraw the request.

(8) In no case shall the provisions of this article be construed so as to impose on a Contracting State the obligation:

(a) To carry out administrative measures at variance with the laws and administrative practice of that or of the other Contracting State;

(b) To carry out measures which would be contrary to public policy (ordre public);

(c) To provide assistance if the other Contracting State has not pursued all reasonable measures of collection or conservancy, as the case may be, available under its laws or administrative practice;

(d) To provide assistance in those cases where the administrative burden for that State is clearly disproportionate to the benefit to be derived by the other Contracting State."

Article 3

Item 6 of the Protocol to the Agreement between the Federal Republic of Germany and the Republic of Uzbekistan for the avoidance of double taxation with respect to taxes on income and capital shall be worded as follows:

"6. Concerning article 26:

(a) The receiving authority may use the data in accordance with article 26 (2) only for the purpose indicated by the sending authority and subject to the conditions prescribed by the sending authority and in accordance with article 26.

(b) The information may be used for other purposes without the prior authorization of the competent authority of the Sending State provided for in the fourth sentence of article 26 (2) only if such use is necessary to prevent an urgent threat to the life, physical integrity or personal liberty of a person or to significant property in a particular case and if there is imminent danger. In such case, a request shall be made without delay to the competent authority of the Sending State to authorize the subsequent change of purpose. If authorization is denied, the further use of the information for the other purpose shall not be permitted, and compensation shall be made for any harm caused by the use of said information for other than the intended purpose.

(c) The sending authority shall be responsible for ensuring the accuracy of the data to be sent and, in accordance with article 26 (1), shall satisfy itself that the data is relevant and commensurate with the intended purpose of their transmission. Such data is likely to be relevant where, in a particular case, there is a reasonable expectation that tax is due to the other Contracting State and there is no evidence that the data is already known to the competent authority of the other Contracting State or that the competent authority of the other Contracting State might become aware that tax is due in the particular case without such information. The receiving authority shall be notified promptly of any transmission of inaccurate data or of data that should not have been sent. It shall be obliged to correct or destroy such data without delay.

(d) The receiving authority shall, upon request, inform the sending authority of any use made of the data supplied and of the results achieved thereby.

(e) The receiving authority shall notify the person concerned of the collection of the data by the sending authority. Such notification may be omitted where it is deemed that the public interest in omitting such notification outweighs that of the person concerned in being notified.

(f) The person concerned shall, upon request, be informed of the data related to him or her that has been transmitted and the intended use thereof. Paragraph 2 (e) shall apply as appropriate.

(g) If someone is unlawfully harmed as a result of the transmission of data in the context of the exchange of data under this Agreement, the receiving authority shall be liable for that with regard to the injured party in accordance with its domestic law. It shall not claim in its defence with respect to the injured party that the harm has been caused by the sending authority.

(h) The sending and receiving authorities shall be obliged to keep a record of the transmission and receipt of personal data.

(i) Insofar as the domestic law applicable to the sending authority and relating to personal data sent specifies particular deadlines by which the data must be destroyed, that authority shall notify the receiving authority thereof. In any event, the personal data transmitted shall be destroyed as soon as it is no longer required for the purpose for which it was supplied.

(j) The sending and receiving authorities shall be obliged to protect any personal data transmitted effectively against unauthorized access, unauthorized change and unauthorized disclosure."

Article 4

This Protocol shall be subject to ratification. It shall enter into force on the date of the exchange of the instruments of ratification and shall be applied in both Contracting States from 1 January of the calendar year following the calendar year in which the Protocol enters into force.

Article 5

This Protocol shall form an integral part of the Agreement and shall cease to have effect on the same date as the Agreement.

IN WITNESS WHEREOF, the undersigned plenipotentiaries, being duly authorized thereto, have signed this Protocol.

DONE at Berlin on 14 October 2014, in duplicate, in the German, Uzbek and Russian languages, all texts being equally authentic. In the case of divergence of interpretation of the German and Uzbek texts, the Russian text shall prevail.

For the Federal Republic of Germany:

[FRANK-WALTER STEINMEIER]

For the Republic of Uzbekistan:

[ABDULAZIZ KAMILOV]

[TRANSLATION – TRADUCTION]

PROTOCOLE AMENDANT ET COMPLÉTANT L'ACCORD DU 7 SEPTEMBRE 1999 ENTRE LA RÉPUBLIQUE FÉDÉRALE D'ALLEMAGNE ET LA RÉPUBLIQUE D'OUZBÉKISTAN TENDANT À ÉVITER LES DOUBLES IMPOSITIONS EN MATIÈRE D'IMPÔTS SUR LE REVENU ET SUR LA FORTUNE

La République fédérale d'Allemagne et la République d'Ouzbékistan, ci-après dénommées les « Parties contractantes »,

Conformément à l'Accord du 7 septembre 1999 entre la République fédérale d'Allemagne et la République d'Ouzbékistan tendant à éviter les doubles impositions en matière d'impôts sur le revenu et sur la fortune (ci-après dénommé l'« Accord »),

Désireuses de développer davantage les relations économiques et de renforcer la coopération en matière fiscale en vue d'assurer un recouvrement efficace et approprié des impôts,

Sont convenues de ce qui suit :

Article premier

L'article 26 de l'Accord est libellé comme suit :

« Article 26. Échange de renseignements

1. Les autorités compétentes des États contractants échangent les renseignements vraisemblablement pertinents pour appliquer les dispositions du présent Accord ou celles de la législation interne relative aux impôts de toute nature et de toute dénomination perçus pour le compte des États contractants, ou de l'une de leurs subdivisions politiques ou de leurs collectivités locales, dans la mesure où l'imposition prévue n'est pas contraire au présent Accord. L'échange de renseignements n'est pas restreint par les articles premier et 2.

2. Les renseignements reçus par un État contractant en vertu du paragraphe 1 sont tenus secrets de la même manière que les renseignements obtenus en application de la législation interne de cet État, et ils ne sont communiqués qu'aux personnes ou autorités (y compris les tribunaux et organes administratifs) concernées par l'établissement ou le recouvrement des impôts visés au paragraphe 1, par les procédures ou poursuites concernant ces impôts, par les décisions sur les recours relatifs à ces impôts, ou par le contrôle de ce qui précède. Ces personnes ou autorités n'utilisent ces renseignements qu'à ces fins, mais peuvent en faire état au cours d'enquêtes administratives et pénales, d'audiences publiques de tribunaux ou dans des jugements. Nonobstant ce qui précède, les renseignements reçus par un État contractant peuvent être utilisés à d'autres fins si la législation des deux États l'autorise et si l'autorité compétente de l'État qui fournit ces renseignements autorise cette utilisation.

3. Les dispositions des paragraphes 1 et 2 ne peuvent en aucun cas être interprétées comme imposant à un État contractant l'obligation :

a) De prendre des mesures administratives dérogeant à sa législation et à sa pratique administrative ou à celles de l'autre État contractant ;

b) De fournir des renseignements qui ne pourraient être obtenus sur la base de sa législation ou dans le cadre de sa pratique administrative normale ou de celles de l'autre État contractant ;

c) De fournir des renseignements qui révéleraient un secret commercial, industriel, professionnel ou un procédé commercial ou des renseignements dont la communication serait contraire à l'ordre public.

4. Si des renseignements sont demandés par un État contractant conformément au présent article, l'autre État contractant utilise ses mesures de collecte de renseignements pour obtenir les renseignements demandés quand bien même cet autre État n'aurait pas besoin de ces renseignements à ses propres fins fiscales. L'obligation contenue dans la phrase précédente est soumise aux limitations du paragraphe 3, mais en aucun cas ces limitations ne doivent être interprétées comme autorisant un État contractant à refuser de fournir des renseignements pour la seule raison qu'il ne détient aucun intérêt national dans de tels renseignements.

5. Les dispositions du paragraphe 3 ne doivent en aucun cas être interprétées comme autorisant un État contractant à refuser de fournir des renseignements pour la seule raison que les renseignements sont tenus par une banque, une autre institution financière, un mandataire ou une personne agissant en qualité d'agent ou titre fiduciaire ou parce que cela concerne les intérêts fonciers d'une personne. »

Article 2

L'article 26a est ajouté à l'Accord et est libellé comme suit :

« Article 26a. Assistance en matière de recouvrement des impôts

1. Les États contractants se prêtent mutuellement assistance pour le recouvrement de leurs créances fiscales. Cette assistance n'est pas limitée par les articles premier et 2. Les autorités compétentes des États contractants peuvent régler d'un commun accord les modalités d'application du présent article.

2. L'expression "créance fiscale" utilisée dans le présent article désigne une somme due au titre d'impôts de toute nature ou dénomination perçus pour le compte des États contractants, de leurs subdivisions politiques ou de leurs collectivités locales dans la mesure où l'imposition qu'elle prévoit n'est pas contraire au présent Accord ou à tout autre instrument auquel les États contractants sont parties, ainsi que les intérêts, pénalités administratives et coûts de recouvrement ou de conservation afférents à ce montant.

3. Lorsqu'une créance fiscale d'un État contractant qui est recouvrable en vertu des lois de cet État et est due par une personne qui, à cette date, ne peut, en vertu de ses lois, empêcher son recouvrement, cette créance fiscale est, à la demande des autorités compétentes de cet État, acceptée en vue de son recouvrement par l'autorité compétente de l'autre État contractant. Cette créance fiscale est recouvrée par cet autre État conformément aux dispositions de sa législation applicable en matière de recouvrement de ses propres impôts comme si la créance en question était une créance fiscale de cet autre État.

4. Lorsqu'une créance fiscale d'un État contractant est une créance à l'égard de laquelle cet État peut, en vertu de sa législation, prendre des mesures conservatoires pour assurer son recouvrement, cette créance doit, à la demande des autorités compétentes de cet État, être acceptée

aux fins d'adoption de mesures conservatoires par les autorités compétentes de l'autre État contractant. Cet autre État doit prendre des mesures conservatoires à l'égard de cette créance fiscale conformément aux dispositions de sa législation comme s'il s'agissait d'une créance fiscale de cet autre État même si, au moment où ces mesures sont appliquées, la créance fiscale n'est pas recouvrable dans le premier État ou est due par une personne qui a le droit d'empêcher son recouvrement.

5. Nonobstant les dispositions des paragraphes 3 et 4, les délais de prescription et la priorité applicables, en vertu de la législation d'un État contractant, à une créance fiscale en raison de sa nature en tant que telle ne s'appliquent pas à une créance fiscale acceptée par cet État aux fins du paragraphe 3 ou 4. En outre, une créance fiscale acceptée par un État contractant aux fins du paragraphe 3 ou 4 ne peut se voir appliquer aucune priorité dans cet État en vertu de la législation de l'autre État contractant.

6. Les procédures concernant l'existence, la validité ou le montant d'une créance fiscale d'un État contractant ne sont pas soumises aux tribunaux ou organismes administratifs de l'autre État contractant.

7. Quand à tout moment après qu'une demande a été formulée par un État contractant en vertu des paragraphes 3 ou 4 et avant que l'autre État contractant ait recouvré et transmis le montant de la créance fiscale en question au premier État, cette créance fiscale cesse d'être :

a) Dans le cas d'une demande présentée en vertu du paragraphe 3, une créance fiscale du premier État recouvrable en vertu des lois de cet État et due par une personne qui, à ce moment, ne peut, en vertu des lois de cet État, en empêcher le recouvrement ; ou

b) Dans le cas d'une demande présentée en vertu du paragraphe 4, une créance fiscale du premier État à l'égard de laquelle cet État peut, en vertu de sa législation, prendre des mesures conservatoires pour assurer son recouvrement, les autorités compétentes du premier État notifient promptement ce fait à l'autorité compétente de l'autre État et le premier État, au choix de l'autre État, suspend ou retire sa demande.

8. Les dispositions du présent article ne peuvent en aucun cas être interprétées comme imposant à un État contractant l'obligation :

a) De prendre des mesures administratives dérogeant à sa législation et à sa pratique administrative ou à celles de l'autre État contractant ;

b) De prendre des mesures qui seraient contraires à l'ordre public ;

c) De prêter assistance si l'autre État contractant n'a pas pris toutes les mesures raisonnables de recouvrement ou de conservation, selon le cas, qui sont disponibles en vertu de sa législation ou de sa pratique administrative ;

d) De prêter assistance dans les cas où la charge administrative pour cet État est nettement disproportionnée par rapport aux avantages que peut en tirer l'autre État contractant. »

Article 3

Le point 6 du Protocole à l'Accord entre la République fédérale d'Allemagne et la République d'Ouzbékistan tendant à éviter les doubles impositions en matière d'impôts sur le revenu et sur la fortune est libellé comme suit :

« 6. S'agissant de l'article 26 :

a) L'autorité réceptrice peut utiliser les données conformément au paragraphe 2 de l'article 26 uniquement aux fins indiquées par l'autorité émettrice, sous réserve des conditions prescrites par l'autorité émettrice et conformément à l'article 26 ;

b) Les renseignements peuvent être utilisés à d'autres fins sans l'autorisation préalable de l'autorité compétente de l'État émetteur visée à la quatrième phrase du paragraphe 2 de l'article 26, uniquement si cette utilisation est nécessaire pour prévenir une menace imminente à la vie, à l'intégrité physique, à la liberté d'une personne ou à des biens immobiliers importants dans un cas particulier et s'il existe un danger imminent. Dans ce cas, une demande est adressée sans délai à l'autorité compétente de l'État émetteur afin qu'elle autorise le changement de finalité subséquent. Si l'autorisation est refusée, l'utilisation ultérieure des renseignements à d'autres fins n'est pas autorisée, et une indemnisation est versée pour tout préjudice causé par l'utilisation des renseignements à d'autres fins que celles prévues ;

c) L'autorité émettrice est responsable de l'exactitude des données à transmettre et, conformément au paragraphe 1 de l'article 26, elle s'assure que les données sont pertinentes et proportionnées aux fins pour lesquelles elles sont communiquées. Ces données sont considérées comme pertinentes lorsque, dans un cas particulier, il est raisonnable de penser que l'impôt est dû à l'autre État contractant et que rien ne prouve que les données sont déjà connues de l'autorité compétente de l'autre État contractant ou que cette dernière pourrait se rendre compte que l'impôt est dû dans ce cas particulier sans ces renseignements. L'autorité réceptrice est informée sans délai de la transmission de données inexactes ou de données qui n'auraient pas dû être transmises. Elle est tenue de rectifier ces données ou de les détruire sans délai ;

d) Sur demande, l'autorité réceptrice informe l'autorité émettrice de l'utilisation des données et des résultats obtenus ;

e) L'autorité réceptrice informe la personne intéressée de la collecte des données par l'autorité émettrice. Cette notification peut être omise lorsqu'il apparaît que l'intérêt public de l'omission l'emporte sur l'intérêt de la personne intéressée à être notifiée ;

f) La personne intéressée, sur demande, est informée des données la concernant qui ont été transmises et de l'usage qui en est fait. L'alinéa e) du paragraphe 2 s'applique le cas échéant ;

g) Si une personne subit un préjudice à la suite de la communication de données dans le cadre de l'échange de renseignements prévu par le présent Accord, l'autorité réceptrice en assume la responsabilité conformément à sa législation nationale. Elle ne peut invoquer à sa décharge vis-à-vis de la personne lésée que le préjudice a été occasionné par l'autorité émettrice ;

h) L'autorité émettrice et l'autorité réceptrice sont tenues de consigner la communication et la réception des données à caractère personnel ;

i) Si le droit interne de l'autorité émettrice relatif aux données à caractère personnel prévoit la destruction des données dans des délais déterminés, cette autorité en informe l'autorité réceptrice. En tout état de cause, les données à caractère personnel sont détruites dès qu'elles ne sont plus requises aux fins pour lesquelles elles avaient été transmises ;

j) Les autorités émettrice et réceptrice sont tenues de protéger effectivement les données à caractère personnel transmises contre les accès, les modifications et les divulgations non autorisés. »

Article 4

Le présent Protocole est soumis à ratification. Il entre en vigueur à la date de l'échange des instruments de ratification et prend effet dans les deux États contractants à compter du 1er janvier de l'année civile suivant la date d'entrée en vigueur du Protocole.

Article 5

Le présent Protocole fait partie intégrante de l'Accord et cesse de produire ses effets à la même date que l'Accord.

EN FOI DE QUOI, les plénipotentiaires soussignés, à ce dûment autorisés, ont signé le présent Protocole.

FAIT à Berlin, le 14 octobre 2014, en double exemplaire, en langues allemande, ouzbèke et russe, tous les textes faisant également foi. En cas de divergence d'interprétation entre les textes allemand et ouzbek, le texte russe prévaut.

Pour la République fédérale d'Allemagne :
[FRANK-WALTER STEINMEIER]

Pour la République d'Ouzbékistan :
[ABDULAZIZ KAMILOV]

No. 53490. Multilateral

AGREEMENT ON ESTABLISHING THE CENTER OF EXCELLENCE IN FINANCE (CEF). BLED, 3 SEPTEMBER 2013 [*United Nations, Treaty Series, vol. 3113, I-53490.*]

RATIFICATION

Montenegro

Deposit of instrument with Government of Slovenia: 11 September 2015

Date of effect: 11 September 2015

Registration with the Secretariat of the United Nations: Slovenia, 4 March 2016

RATIFICATION

Republic of Moldova

Deposit of instrument with Government of Slovenia: 14 August 2015

Date of effect: 14 August 2015

Registration with the Secretariat of the United Nations: Slovenia, 4 March 2016

RATIFICATION

Romania

Deposit of instrument with Government of Slovenia: 2 February 2016

Date of effect: 2 February 2016

Registration with the Secretariat of the United Nations: Slovenia, 4 March 2016

N° 53490. Multilatéral

ACCORD SUR LA CRÉATION DU CENTRE D'EXCELLENCE EN FINANCES (CEF). BLED, 3 SEPTEMBRE 2013 [*Nations Unies, Recueil des Traités, vol. 3113, I-53490.*]

RATIFICATION

Monténégro

Dépôt de l'instrument auprès de Gouvernement slovène : 11 septembre 2015

Date de prise d'effet : 11 septembre 2015

Enregistrement au Secrétariat de l'Organisation des Nations Unies : Slovénie, 4 mars 2016

RATIFICATION

République de Moldova

Dépôt de l'instrument auprès de Gouvernement slovène : 14 août 2015

Date de prise d'effet : 14 août 2015

Enregistrement au Secrétariat de l'Organisation des Nations Unies : Slovénie, 4 mars 2016

RATIFICATION

Roumanie

Dépôt de l'instrument auprès de Gouvernement slovène : 2 février 2016

Date de prise d'effet : 2 février 2016

Enregistrement au Secrétariat de l'Organisation des Nations Unies : Slovénie, 4 mars 2016

No. 53511. Multilateral

AGREEMENT ON THE EURASIAN GROUP ON COMBATING MONEY LAUNDERING AND FINANCING OF TERRORISM. MOSCOW, 16 JUNE 2011 [*United Nations, Treaty Series, vol. 3113, I-53511.*]

RATIFICATION

China

Deposit of instrument with Secretariat of the Eurasian group on combating money laundering and financing of terrorism (EAG): 10 July 2012

Date of effect: 10 July 2012

Registration with the Secretariat of the United Nations: Eurasian Group on combating money laundering and financing of terrorism (EAG), 1 March 2016

RATIFICATION

Kazakhstan

Deposit of instrument with Secretariat of the Eurasian group on combating money laundering and financing of terrorism (EAG): 28 April 2012

Date of effect: 28 April 2012

Registration with the Secretariat of the United Nations: Eurasian Group on combating money laundering and financing of terrorism (EAG), 1 March 2016

N° 53511. Multilatéral

ACCORD RELATIF AU GROUPE EURASIE POUR LA LUTTE CONTRE LE BLANCHIMENT DE CAPITAUX ET LE FINANCEMENT DU TERRORISME. MOSCOU, 16 JUIN 2011 [*Nations Unies, Recueil des Traités, vol. 3113, I-53511.*]

RATIFICATION

Chine

Dépôt de l'instrument auprès de Secrétariat du Groupe Eurasie de lutte contre le blanchiment de capitaux et le financement du terrorisme (GEA) : 10 juillet 2012

Date de prise d'effet : 10 juillet 2012

Enregistrement au Secrétariat de l'Organisation des Nations Unies : Groupe Eurasie de lutte contre le blanchiment de capitaux et le financement du terrorisme (GEA), 1er mars 2016

RATIFICATION

Kazakhstan

Dépôt de l'instrument auprès de Secrétariat du Groupe Eurasie de lutte contre le blanchiment de capitaux et le financement du terrorisme (GEA) : 28 avril 2012

Date de prise d'effet : 28 avril 2012

Enregistrement au Secrétariat de l'Organisation des Nations Unies : Groupe Eurasie de lutte contre le blanchiment de capitaux et le financement du terrorisme (GEA), 1er mars 2016

RATIFICATION

Kyrgyzstan

Deposit of instrument with Secretariat of the Eurasian group on combating money laundering and financing of terrorism (EAG): 16 July 2012

Date of effect: 16 July 2012

Registration with the Secretariat of the United Nations: Eurasian Group on combating money laundering and financing of terrorism (EAG), 1 March 2016

NOTIFICATION

Russian Federation

Receipt by Secretariat of the Eurasian group on combating money laundering and financing of terrorism (EAG): 13 June 2012

Date of effect: 13 June 2012

Registration with the Secretariat of the United Nations: Eurasian Group on combating money laundering and financing of terrorism (EAG), 1 March 2016

RATIFICATION

Kirghizistan

Dépôt de l'instrument auprès de Secrétariat du Groupe Eurasie de lutte contre le blanchiment de capitaux et le financement du terrorisme (GEA) : 16 juillet 2012

Date de prise d'effet : 16 juillet 2012

Enregistrement au Secrétariat de l'Organisation des Nations Unies : Groupe Eurasie de lutte contre le blanchiment de capitaux et le financement du terrorisme (GEA), 1er mars 2016

NOTIFICATION

Fédération de Russie

Réception par Secrétariat du Groupe Eurasie de lutte contre le blanchiment de capitaux et le financement du terrorisme (GEA) : 13 juin 2012

Date de prise d'effet : 13 juin 2012

Enregistrement au Secrétariat de l'Organisation des Nations Unies : Groupe Eurasie de lutte contre le blanchiment de capitaux et le financement du terrorisme (GEA), 1er mars 2016

No. 53515. Austria and China

AGREEMENT BETWEEN THE REPUBLIC OF AUSTRIA AND THE PEOPLE'S REPUBLIC OF CHINA ON THE PROMOTION AND RECIPROCAL PROTECTION OF INVESTMENTS. BEIJING, 12 SEPTEMBER 1985 [*United Nations, Treaty Series, vol. 3113, I-53515.*]

EXCHANGE OF NOTES CONSTITUTING A PROTOCOL AMENDING THE AGREEMENT BETWEEN THE REPUBLIC OF AUSTRIA AND THE PEOPLE'S REPUBLIC OF CHINA ON THE PROMOTION AND RECIPROCAL PROTECTION OF INVESTMENTS. PEKING, 4 SEPTEMBER 2012 AND 17 SEPTEMBER 2012

Entry into force: 18 September 2015, in accordance with the provisions of the said notes

Authentic texts: Chinese and German

Registration with the Secretariat of the United Nations: Austria, 23 March 2016

N° 53515. Autriche et Chine

ACCORD ENTRE LA RÉPUBLIQUE D'AUTRICHE ET LA RÉPUBLIQUE POPULAIRE DE CHINE SUR LA PROMOTION ET LA PROTECTION RÉCIPROQUE DES INVESTISSEMENTS. BEIJING, 12 SEPTEMBRE 1985 [*Nations Unies, Recueil des Traités, vol. 3113, I-53515.*]

ÉCHANGE DE NOTES CONSTITUANT UN PROTOCOLE AMENDANT L'ACCORD ENTRE LA RÉPUBLIQUE D'AUTRICHE ET LA RÉPUBLIQUE POPULAIRE DE CHINE SUR LA PROMOTION ET LA PROTECTION RÉCIPROQUE DES INVESTISSEMENTS. PÉKIN, 4 SEPTEMBRE 2012 ET 17 SEPTEMBRE 2012

Entrée en vigueur : 18 septembre 2015, conformément aux dispositions desdites notes

Textes authentiques : chinois et allemand

Enregistrement au Secrétariat de l'Organisation des Nations Unies : Autriche, 23 mars 2016

[TEXT IN CHINESE – TEXTE EN CHINOIS]

I

第 Peking-ÖB/POL/0225/2012 号

奥地利共和国大使馆

照 会

中华人民共和国外交部：

奥地利共和国大使馆向中华人民共和国外交部致意，并继 2010 年 8 月 4 日第 Peking-ÖB/POL/0298/2010 号照会，就修改 1985 年 9 月 12 日在北京签订的《奥地利共和国和中华人民共和国关于促进和相互保护投资协定》（BGBl. Nr. 537/1986）中第 5 条，谨提出如下补充建议：

(2) Die Bestimmungen des vorstehenden Absatzes sind nicht dahingehend auszulegen, dass sie eine Vertragspartei in gutem Glauben hindern, völkerrechtliche Verpflichtungen oder ihre Rechte und Verpflichtungen als ein Mitglied einer Freihandelszone, einer Zollunion, eines Gemeinsamen Marktes, einer Wirtschafts- und Währungsunion oder jeglicher anderer Form der regionalen Kooperation oder Integration, zu erfüllen.

（2）本条上述内容不影响缔约一方诚信地履行其他国际义务或参与自由贸易区、关税同盟、共同市场、经济或货币同盟或其他任何形式的区域合作或一体化而产生的权利和义务。

如果中方同意以上建议，本照会及中方的复函将作为修改《奥地利共和国和中华人民共和国关于促进和相互保护投资协定》的议定书。该议定书的德、中文文本内容一致，同样具有法律效力，将在协议双方通告本国具备实施条件之日起一个月后生效。

顺致崇高的敬意！

奥地利共和国驻华大使馆

2012 年 9 月 4 日于北京

II

中 华 人 民 共 和 国 外 交 部

(2012)部条字第189号

奥地利共和国驻华大使馆:

中华人民共和国外交部向奥地利共和国驻华大使馆致意，并谨收到大使馆2012年9月4日第Peking－ÖB/POL/0225/2012号照会，内容如下:

[See note I - Voir note I]

中华人民共和国外交部谨代表中华人民共和国政府确认，同意上述内容。

顺致崇高的敬意。

二〇一二年九月十七日于北京

[TEXT IN GERMAN – TEXTE EN ALLEMAND]

I

Zl. Peking-ÖB/POL/0225/2012

Verbalnote

Die Österreichische Botschaft entbietet dem Ministerium für auswärtige Angelegenheiten der Volksrepublik China ihre Empfehlungen und beehrt sich, in Verfolg zur Verbalnote Peking-ÖB/POL/0298/2010 vom 4. August 2010, betreffend die Änderung des Abkommens zwischen der Republik Österreich und der Volksrepublik China über die Förderung und den gegenseitigen Schutz von Investitionen, geschehen in Peking, am 12. September 1985 (BGBl. Nr. 537/1986) nachstehende Ergänzung des Artikels 5 vorzuschlagen:

> „(2) Die Bestimmungen des vorstehenden Absatzes sind nicht dahingehend auszulegen, dass sie eine Vertragspartei in gutem Glauben hindern, völkerrechtliche Verpflichtungen oder ihre Rechte und Verpflichtungen als ein Mitglied einer Freihandelszone, einer Zollunion, eines Gemeinsamen Marktes, einer Wirtschafts- und Währungsunion oder jeglicher anderer Form der regionalen Kooperation oder Integration, zu erfüllen."
>
> （2）本条上述内容不影响缔约一方诚信地履行其他国际义务或参与自由贸易区、关税同盟、共同市场、经济或货币同盟或其他任何形式的区域合作或一体化而产生的权利和义务。

Falls vorstehender Vorschlag die Zustimmung der Volksrepublik China findet, stellen diese Note und die Antwortnote des geschätzten zuständigen chinesischen Ministeriums ein Protokoll zur Abänderung des Abkommens zwischen der Republik Österreich und der Volksrepublik China über die Förderung und den gegenseitigen Schutz von Investitionen dar. Das Protokoll, dessen deutscher und chinesischer Wortlaut in gleicher Weise verbindlich ist, tritt einen Monat nach dem Tag in Kraft, an dem die beiden vertragschließenden Teile einander notifiziert haben, dass die erforderlichen innerstaatlichen Voraussetzungen für das Inkrafttreten dieses Protokolls erfüllt sind.

Die Österreichische Botschaft benutzt auch diesen Anlass, dem Ministerium für auswärtige Angelegenheiten der Volksrepublik China den Ausdruck ihrer vorzüglichen Hochachtung zu erneuern.

Peking, am 4. September 2012

An das
Ministerium für auswärtige Angelegenheiten
der Volksrepublik China

Peking

II

Außenministerium der Volksrepublik China

GZ (2012) bu tiaozi 189

An die Botschaft der Republik Österreich in der Volksrepublik China:

Das Außenministerium der Volksrepublik China entbietet der Botschaft der Republik Österreich in der Volksrepublik China ihre Hochachtung und hat von der Österreichischen Botschaft die Verbalnote Peking–ÖB/POL/0225/2012 vom 4.9.2012 mit folgendem Inhalt erhalten:

[See note I - Voir note I]

Das Außenministerium der Volksrepublik China bestätigt im Namen der Regierung der Volksrepublik China die Zustimmung mit obigen Inhalten.

Das Außenministerium der Volksrepublik China benutzt auch diesen Anlass, der Österreichischen Botschaft den Ausdruck ihrer vorzüglichen Hochachtung zu erneuern.

[Rundsiegel:] Außenministerium der Volksrepublik China
Peking, am 17. September 2012

[TRANSLATION – TRADUCTION]

I

NOTE VERBALE

Beijing, 4 September 2012

Zl. Peking-ÖB/POL/0225/2012

The Austrian Embassy presents its compliments to the Ministry of Foreign Affairs of the People's Republic of China and has the honour to refer to the note verbale Peking-ÖB/POL/0298/2010, dated 4 August 2010, concerning the amendment to the Agreement between the Republic of Austria and the People's Republic of China on the promotion and reciprocal protection of investments, done at Beijing on 12 September 1985 (BGBl. No. 537/1986), through the following proposed addition to article 5:

(2) The provisions of the preceding paragraph shall not be construed as preventing a Contracting Party from complying in good faith with obligations under international law or its rights and obligations as a member of a free trade area, customs union, common market, economic and monetary union or any other form of regional cooperation or integration.

(2)

本条上述内容不影响缔约一方诚信地履行其他国际义务或参与自由贸易区、关税同盟、共同市场、经济或货币同盟或其他任何形式的区域合作或一体化而产生的权利和义务。

If the above proposal is acceptable to the People's Republic of China, this note verbale and the reply thereto from the esteemed competent Chinese Ministry shall constitute a Protocol amending the Agreement between the Republic of Austria and the People's Republic of China on the promotion and reciprocal protection of investments. The Protocol, of which the German and Chinese texts are equally authentic, shall enter into force one month after the date on which both Contracting Parties have notified each other that the required domestic requirements for its entry into force have been fulfilled.

The Austrian Embassy also takes this opportunity to convey to the Ministry of Foreign Affairs of the People's Republic of China the renewed assurances of its highest consideration.

Embassy of the Republic of Austria in Beijing

Ministry of Foreign Affairs of
the People's Republic of China
Beijing

II

MINISTRY OF FOREIGN AFFAIRS OF THE PEOPLE'S REPUBLIC OF CHINA

Beijing, 17 September 2012

GZ (2012) butiaozi 189

The Ministry for Foreign Affairs of the People's Republic of China presents its compliments to the Embassy of the Republic of Austria in the People's Republic of China, and confirms receipt of the note verbale Peking ÖB/POL/0225/2012, dated 4 September 2012, with the following content:

[See note I]

The Ministry of Foreign Affairs of the People's Republic of China, on behalf of the Government of the People's Republic of China, confirms that the above is acceptable.

The Ministry of Foreign Affairs of the People's Republic of China also takes this opportunity to convey to the Austrian Embassy the renewed assurances of its highest consideration.

[Seal] Ministry of Foreign Affairs of the
People's Republic of China

Embassy of the Republic of Austria
in the People's Republic of China

[TRANSLATION – TRADUCTION]

I

NOTE VERBALE

Beijing, le 4 septembre 2012

Zl. Peking-ÖB/POL/0225/2012

L'ambassade d'Autriche présente ses compliments au Ministère des affaires étrangères de la République populaire de Chine et a l'honneur de se référer à la note verbale Peking-ÖB/POL/0298/2010, datée du 4 août 2010, concernant l'amendement de l'Accord entre la République d'Autriche et la République populaire de Chine sur la promotion et la protection réciproque des investissements, fait à Beijing le 12 septembre 1985 (BGBl. n° 537/1986), par la proposition d'ajout suivante à l'article 5 :

2) Les dispositions du paragraphe précédent ne peuvent être interprétées comme empêchant une Partie contractante de se conformer de bonne foi aux obligations découlant du droit international ou à ses droits et obligations en tant que membre d'une zone de libre-échange, d'une union douanière, d'un marché commun, d'une union économique et monétaire, ou de toute autre forme de coopération ou d'intégration régionale.

2)

本条上述内容不影响缔约一方诚信地履行其他国际义务或参与自由贸易区、关税同盟、共同市场、经济或货币同盟或其他任何形式的区域合作或一体化而产生的权利和义务。

Si la proposition ci-dessus est jugée acceptable par la République populaire de Chine, la présente note verbale et la réponse du Ministère chinois compétent à celle-ci constitueront un Protocole amendant l'Accord entre la République d'Autriche et la République populaire de Chine sur la promotion et la protection réciproque des investissements. Le Protocole, dont les textes en langues allemande et chinoise font également foi, entrera en vigueur un mois suivant la date à laquelle les Parties contractantes se seront informées de l'accomplissement des formalités internes requises à cet effet.

L'ambassade d'Autriche saisit également cette occasion pour renouveler au Ministère des affaires étrangères de la République populaire de Chine les assurances de sa très haute considération.

Ambassade de la République d'Autriche à Beijing

Ministère des affaires étrangères de
la République populaire de Chine
Beijing

II

MINISTÈRE DES AFFAIRES ÉTRANGÈRES DE LA RÉPUBLIQUE POPULAIRE DE CHINE

Beijing, le 17 septembre 2012

GZ (2012) bu tiaozi 189

Le Ministère des affaires étrangères de la République populaire de Chine présente ses compliments à l'ambassade de la République d'Autriche en République populaire de Chine, et confirme la réception de la note verbale Peking-ÖB/POL/0225/2012, datée du 4 septembre 2012, dont le contenu est le suivant :

[Voir note I]

Le Ministère des affaires étrangères de la République populaire de Chine, au nom du Gouvernement de la République populaire de Chine, confirme que ce qui précède est acceptable.

Le Ministère des affaires étrangères de la République populaire de Chine saisit également cette occasion pour renouveler à l'ambassade d'Autriche les assurances de sa très haute considération.

[Sceau] Ministère des affaires étrangères de
la République populaire de Chine

Ambassade de la République d'Autriche
en République populaire de Chine

No. 53553. Multilateral

AGREEMENT FOR THE ESTABLISHMENT OF THE AFRICAN LEGAL SUPPORT FACILITY. TUNIS, 19 JUNE 2008 [*United Nations, Treaty Series, vol. 3114, I-53553.*]

ACCESSION

African Development Bank

Deposit of instrument with Director of the African Legal Support Facility: 10 February 2009

Date of effect: 10 February 2009

Registration with the Secretariat of the United Nations: African Legal Support Facility, 1 March 2016

ACCESSION

African Union

Deposit of instrument with Director of the African Legal Support Facility: 23 August 2010

Date of effect: 23 August 2010

Registration with the Secretariat of the United Nations: African Legal Support Facility, 1 March 2016

RATIFICATION

Burkina Faso

Deposit of instrument with Director of the African Legal Support Facility: 1 July 2009

Date of effect: 1 July 2009

Registration with the Secretariat of the United Nations: African Legal Support Facility, 1 March 2016

N° 53553. Multilatéral

ACCORD PORTANT CRÉATION DE LA FACILITÉ AFRICAINE DE SOUTIEN JURIDIQUE. TUNIS, 19 JUIN 2008 [*Nations Unies, Recueil des Traités, vol. 3114, I-53553.*]

ADHÉSION

Banque africaine de développement

Dépôt de l'instrument auprès de Directeur de la facilité africaine de soutien juridique : 10 février 2009

Date de prise d'effet : 10 février 2009

Enregistrement au Secrétariat de l'Organisation des Nations Unies : Facilité africaine de soutien juridique, 1er mars 2016

ADHÉSION

Union africaine

Dépôt de l'instrument auprès de Directeur de la facilité africaine de soutien juridique : 23 août 2010

Date de prise d'effet : 23 août 2010

Enregistrement au Secrétariat de l'Organisation des Nations Unies : Facilité africaine de soutien juridique, 1er mars 2016

RATIFICATION

Burkina Faso

Dépôt de l'instrument auprès de Directeur de la facilité africaine de soutien juridique : 1er juillet 2009

Date de prise d'effet : 1er juillet 2009

Enregistrement au Secrétariat de l'Organisation des Nations Unies : Facilité africaine de soutien juridique, 1er mars 2016

APPROVAL

Chad

Deposit of instrument with Director of the African Legal Support Facility: 14 November 2009

Date of effect: 14 November 2009

Registration with the Secretariat of the United Nations: African Legal Support Facility, 1 March 2016

ACCESSION

Comoros

Deposit of instrument with Director of the African Legal Support Facility: 14 April 2014

Date of effect: 14 April 2014

Registration with the Secretariat of the United Nations: African Legal Support Facility, 1 March 2016

ACCESSION

Congo

Deposit of instrument with Director of the African Legal Support Facility: 18 June 2009

Date of effect: 18 June 2009

Registration with the Secretariat of the United Nations: African Legal Support Facility, 1 March 2016

ACCESSION

Egypt

Deposit of instrument with Director of the African Legal Support Facility: 12 February 2014

Date of effect: 12 February 2014

Registration with the Secretariat of the United Nations: African Legal Support Facility, 1 March 2016

APPROBATION

Tchad

Dépôt de l'instrument auprès de Directeur de la facilité africaine de soutien juridique : 14 novembre 2009

Date de prise d'effet : 14 novembre 2009

Enregistrement au Secrétariat de l'Organisation des Nations Unies : Facilité africaine de soutien juridique, 1er mars 2016

ADHÉSION

Comores

Dépôt de l'instrument auprès de Directeur de la facilité africaine de soutien juridique : 14 avril 2014

Date de prise d'effet : 14 avril 2014

Enregistrement au Secrétariat de l'Organisation des Nations Unies : Facilité africaine de soutien juridique, 1er mars 2016

ADHÉSION

Congo

Dépôt de l'instrument auprès de Directeur de la facilité africaine de soutien juridique : 18 juin 2009

Date de prise d'effet : 18 juin 2009

Enregistrement au Secrétariat de l'Organisation des Nations Unies : Facilité africaine de soutien juridique, 1er mars 2016

ADHÉSION

Égypte

Dépôt de l'instrument auprès de Directeur de la facilité africaine de soutien juridique : 12 février 2014

Date de prise d'effet : 12 février 2014

Enregistrement au Secrétariat de l'Organisation des Nations Unies : Facilité africaine de soutien juridique, 1er mars 2016

ACCESSION

France

Deposit of instrument with Director of the African Legal Support Facility: 4 April 2015

Date of effect: 4 April 2015

Registration with the Secretariat of the United Nations: African Legal Support Facility, 1 March 2016

ADHÉSION

France

Dépôt de l'instrument auprès de Directeur de la facilité africaine de soutien juridique : 4 avril 2015

Date de prise d'effet : 4 avril 2015

Enregistrement au Secrétariat de l'Organisation des Nations Unies : Facilité africaine de soutien juridique, 1er mars 2016

RATIFICATION

Gambia

Deposit of instrument with Director of the African Legal Support Facility: 23 August 2012

Date of effect: 23 August 2012

Registration with the Secretariat of the United Nations: African Legal Support Facility, 1 March 2016

RATIFICATION

Gambie

Dépôt de l'instrument auprès de Directeur de la facilité africaine de soutien juridique : 23 août 2012

Date de prise d'effet : 23 août 2012

Enregistrement au Secrétariat de l'Organisation des Nations Unies : Facilité africaine de soutien juridique, 1er mars 2016

ACCESSION

Islamic Development Bank

Deposit of instrument with Director of the African Legal Support Facility: 11 June 2013

Date of effect: 11 June 2013

Registration with the Secretariat of the United Nations: African Legal Support Facility, 1 March 2016

ADHÉSION

Banque islamique de développement

Dépôt de l'instrument auprès de Directeur de la facilité africaine de soutien juridique : 11 juin 2013

Date de prise d'effet : 11 juin 2013

Enregistrement au Secrétariat de l'Organisation des Nations Unies : Facilité africaine de soutien juridique, 1er mars 2016

ACCESSION

Mali

Deposit of instrument with Director of the African Legal Support Facility: 16 October 2009

Date of effect: 16 October 2009

Registration with the Secretariat of the United Nations: African Legal Support Facility, 1 March 2016

ADHÉSION

Mali

Dépôt de l'instrument auprès de Directeur de la facilité africaine de soutien juridique : 16 octobre 2009

Date de prise d'effet : 16 octobre 2009

Enregistrement au Secrétariat de l'Organisation des Nations Unies : Facilité africaine de soutien juridique, 1er mars 2016

ACCESSION

Mauritius

Deposit of instrument with Director of the African Legal Support Facility: 21 November 2012

Date of effect: 21 November 2012

Registration with the Secretariat of the United Nations: African Legal Support Facility, 1 March 2016

ACCESSION

Morocco

Deposit of instrument with Director of the African Legal Support Facility: 28 June 2013

Date of effect: 28 June 2013

Registration with the Secretariat of the United Nations: African Legal Support Facility, 1 March 2016

ACCESSION (WITH RESERVATION)

Netherlands

Deposit of instrument with Director of the African Legal Support Facility: 18 November 2011

Date of effect: 18 November 2011

Registration with the Secretariat of the United Nations: African Legal Support Facility, 1 March 2016

ADHÉSION

Maurice

Dépôt de l'instrument auprès de Directeur de la facilité africaine de soutien juridique : 21 novembre 2012

Date de prise d'effet : 21 novembre 2012

Enregistrement au Secrétariat de l'Organisation des Nations Unies : Facilité africaine de soutien juridique, 1er mars 2016

ADHÉSION

Maroc

Dépôt de l'instrument auprès de Directeur de la facilité africaine de soutien juridique : 28 juin 2013

Date de prise d'effet : 28 juin 2013

Enregistrement au Secrétariat de l'Organisation des Nations Unies : Facilité africaine de soutien juridique, 1er mars 2016

ADHÉSION (AVEC RÉSERVE)

Pays-Bas

Dépôt de l'instrument auprès de Directeur de la facilité africaine de soutien juridique : 18 novembre 2011

Date de prise d'effet : 18 novembre 2011

Enregistrement au Secrétariat de l'Organisation des Nations Unies : Facilité africaine de soutien juridique, 1er mars 2016

Reservation: *Réserve :*

[TEXT IN ENGLISH – TEXTE EN ANGLAIS]

"With regard to Article XXII, paragraph 2, under (ii), of the Agreement for the establishment of the African Legal Support Facility, the Kingdom of the Netherlands reserves the right, under paragraph 3 of Article XXII, to tax salaries and emoluments paid by the Facility to a member of staff of the Facility, if the member of staff can be qualified as a taxpayer for the Dutch income tax."

[TRANSLATION – TRADUCTION]

En ce qui concerne l'alinéa ii) du paragraphe 2 de l'article XXII de l'Accord portant création de la Facilité africaine de soutien juridique, le Royaume des Pays-Bas se réserve le droit, en vertu du paragraphe 3 de l'article XXII, d'imposer les salaires et émoluments payés par la Facilité à un des membres du personnel de la Facilité, si le membre du personnel peut être considéré comme un contribuable au titre de l'impôt néerlandais sur le revenu.

ACCESSION

Niger

Deposit of instrument with Director of the African Legal Support Facility: 9 December 2014

Date of effect: 9 December 2014

Registration with the Secretariat of the United Nations: African Legal Support Facility, 1 March 2016

ADHÉSION

Niger

Dépôt de l'instrument auprès de Directeur de la facilité africaine de soutien juridique : 9 décembre 2014

Date de prise d'effet : 9 décembre 2014

Enregistrement au Secrétariat de l'Organisation des Nations Unies : Facilité africaine de soutien juridique, 1er mars 2016

ACCESSION

Organization for the Harmonization of Business Laws in Africa

Deposit of instrument with Director of the African Legal Support Facility: 23 June 2009

Date of effect: 23 June 2009

Registration with the Secretariat of the United Nations: African Legal Support Facility, 1 March 2016

RATIFICATION

Rwanda

Deposit of instrument with Director of the African Legal Support Facility: 25 January 2011

Date of effect: 25 January 2011

Registration with the Secretariat of the United Nations: African Legal Support Facility, 1 March 2016

ACCESSION

Sierra Leone

Deposit of instrument with Director of the African Legal Support Facility: 15 May 2012

Date of effect: 15 May 2012

Registration with the Secretariat of the United Nations: African Legal Support Facility, 1 March 2016

ADHÉSION

Organisation pour l'harmonisation en Afrique du droit des affaires

Dépôt de l'instrument auprès de Directeur de la facilité africaine de soutien juridique : 23 juin 2009

Date de prise d'effet : 23 juin 2009

Enregistrement au Secrétariat de l'Organisation des Nations Unies : Facilité africaine de soutien juridique, 1er mars 2016

RATIFICATION

Rwanda

Dépôt de l'instrument auprès de Directeur de la facilité africaine de soutien juridique : 25 janvier 2011

Date de prise d'effet : 25 janvier 2011

Enregistrement au Secrétariat de l'Organisation des Nations Unies : Facilité africaine de soutien juridique, 1er mars 2016

ADHÉSION

Sierra Leone

Dépôt de l'instrument auprès de Directeur de la facilité africaine de soutien juridique : 15 mai 2012

Date de prise d'effet : 15 mai 2012

Enregistrement au Secrétariat de l'Organisation des Nations Unies : Facilité africaine de soutien juridique, 1er mars 2016

RATIFICATION (WITH DECLARATION)

Tunisia

Deposit of instrument with Director of the African Legal Support Facility: 24 December 2010

Date of effect: 24 December 2010

Registration with the Secretariat of the United Nations: African Legal Support Facility, 1 March 2016

RATIFICATION (AVEC DÉCLARATION)

Tunisie

Dépôt de l'instrument auprès de Directeur de la facilité africaine de soutien juridique : 24 décembre 2010

Date de prise d'effet : 24 décembre 2010

Enregistrement au Secrétariat de l'Organisation des Nations Unies : Facilité africaine de soutien juridique, 1er mars 2016

Declaration:

Déclaration :

[TEXT IN FRENCH – TEXTE EN FRANÇAIS]

La République Tunisienne, tout en approuvant l'accord portant création de la facilité africaine de soutien juridique signé la 24 juin 2009 à Tunis, déclare que :

1 – Les experts et consultants effectuant des missions pour le compte de la facilité ne jouissent pas des immunités, privilèges et exemptions prévus dans l'article XXII.

2 – Les étrangers résidant en Tunisie avant leur recrutement par le bureau ou la filiale de la facilité ouvert à Tunis, ne jouissent pas des immunités prévues au paragraphe 1.ii de l'article XXII.

3 – Les ressortissants tunisiens et les étrangers résidant en Tunisie avant leur recrutement par le bureau ou la filiale ouvert à Tûnis, ne jouissent pas des exemptions fiscales prévues au paragraphe 2.ii de l'article XXII.

[TRANSLATION – TRADUCTION]

The Republic of Tunisia, while approving of the Agreement for the establishment of the African Legal Support Facility signed on 24 June 2009 in Tunis, declares that:

1. Experts and consultants carrying out missions on behalf of the facility are not accorded the immunities, privileges and exemptions provided for in article XXII.

2. Foreigners residing in Tunisia prior to their recruitment by the office or subsidiary of the Facility opened in Tunis are not accorded the immunities provided for in paragraph 1 (ii) of article XXII.

3. Tunisian nationals and foreigners residing in Tunisia prior to their recruitment by the office or subsidiary opened in Tunis, are not accorded the tax exemptions provided for in paragraph 2 (ii) of article XXII.

ACCESSION (WITH RESERVATION)

United Kingdom

Deposit of instrument with Director of the African Legal Support Facility: 11 December 2014

Date of effect: 11 December 2014

Registration with the Secretariat of the United Nations: African Legal Support Facility, 1 March 2016

ADHÉSION (AVEC RÉSERVE)

Royaume-Uni

Dépôt de l'instrument auprès de Directeur de la facilité africaine de soutien juridique : 11 décembre 2014

Date de prise d'effet : 11 décembre 2014

Enregistrement au Secrétariat de l'Organisation des Nations Unies : Facilité africaine de soutien juridique, 1er mars 2016

Reservation:

Réserve :

[TEXT IN ENGLISH – TEXTE EN ANGLAIS]

The Government of the United Kingdom of Great Britain and Northern Ireland and the Government of the Isle of Man shall not accord to the African Legal Support Facility or members of the Governing Council, members of the Management Board, the Director and other employees of the Facility, personnel seconded to the Facility, and consultants and experts performing missions for the Facility the immunities, privileges, exemptions, facilities and concessions under Articles XVI, XVII, XVIII, XIX, XX, XXI, XXII, XXIV and XXV.

[TRANSLATION – TRADUCTION]

Le Gouvernement du Royaume-Uni de Grande-Bretagne et d'Irlande du Nord et le Gouvernement de l'île de Man n'accordent pas à la Facilité africaine de soutien juridique, ni aux membres du Conseil d'administration, aux membres du Conseil de gouvernance, au Directeur et aux autres employés de la Facilité, au personnel détaché auprès de la Facilité, aux consultants et experts exerçant des missions pour la Facilité, les immunités, les privilèges, les exemptions, les facilités et les concessions prévus aux articles XVI, XVII, XVIII, XIX, XX, XXI, XXII, XXIV et XXV.

ACCESSION

West African Development Bank

Deposit of instrument with Director of the African Legal Support Facility: 5 April 2011

Date of effect: 5 April 2011

Registration with the Secretariat of the United Nations: African Legal Support Facility, 1 March 2016

ADHÉSION

Banque ouest-africaine de développement

Dépôt de l'instrument auprès de Directeur de la facilité africaine de soutien juridique : 5 avril 2011

Date de prise d'effet : 5 avril 2011

Enregistrement au Secrétariat de l'Organisation des Nations Unies : Facilité africaine de soutien juridique, 1er mars 2016

GOVERNING COUNCIL RESOLUTION ALSF/GC/2012/01 AMENDING ARTICLE VIII AND XXVI OF THE AGREEMENT FOR THE ESTABLISHMENT OF THE AFRICAN LEGAL SUPPORT FACILITY. ARUSHA, 29 MAY 2012

Entry into force: 29 May 2012, in accordance with article VIII of the Agreement

Authentic texts: English and French

Registration with the Secretariat of the United Nations: African Legal Support Facility, 1 March 2016

RÉSOLUTION ALSF/GC/2012/01 DU CONSEIL DE GOUVERNANCE CONCERNANT L'AMENDEMENT DE L'ARTICLE VIII ET DE L'ARTICLE XXVI DE L'ACCORD PORTANT CRÉATION DE LA FACILITÉ AFRICAINE DE SOUTIEN JURIDIQUE. ARUSHA, 29 MAI 2012

Entrée en vigueur : 29 mai 2012, conformément à l'article VIII de l'Accord

Textes authentiques : anglais et français

Enregistrement au Secrétariat de l'Organisation des Nations Unies : Facilité africaine de soutien juridique, 1er mars 2016

[TEXT IN ENGLISH – TEXTE EN ANGLAIS]

AFRICAN LEGAL SUPPORT FACILITY
FACILITE AFRICAINE DE SOUTIEN JURIDIQUE

GOVERNING COUNCIL

Resolution ALSF/GC/2012/01

Adopted at the 7th meeting of the Governing Council, on 29 May 2012

Concerning the amendment of Article VIII and XXVI the Agreement establishing the African Legal Support Facility

THE GOVERNING COUNCIL,

HAVING REGARD to: (i) the relevant provisions of the Agreement establishing the African Legal Support Facility (the "Facility"), in particular Article IV (Membership); Article VII (Governance and Management Structure), Article VIII (Governing Council: Powers), Article IX (Governing Council: Composition and Representation); Article X (Governing Council: Procedure) ("the Agreement"); (ii) the Rules of Procedure of the Governing Council of the Facility (the "Rules");

HAVING CONSIDERED Document ALSF/MEMORANDUM/GC/2012/13, in particular the recommendations contained therein for an amendment to Article VIII paragraph *2 (vi)* and to Article XXVI in view of the amendment of the procedure for modification of the text of the Agreement to allow a wider consultation with all the signatory parties to the Agreement concerning proposed amendments;

HEREBY DECIDES to amend Articles VIII paragraph 2 *(vi)* and Article XXVI of the Agreement as attached hereto; and

DECIDES accordingly that:

INSTEAD OF

"ARTICLE VIII (GOVERNING COUNCIL: POWERS)

1. (...)

2. The Governing Council may delegate to the Management Board all its powers, except the power to:

(i) (...)

(ii) (...)

(iii) (...)

(iv) (...)

(v) (...)

(vi) amend this agreement;

(vii) (...)

(viii) (...).

SHALL READ

"ARTICLE VIII (...)

1. (...)

2. The Governing Council may delegate to the Management Board all its powers, except the power to:

(i) (...)

(ii) (...)

(iii) (…)

(iv) (…)

(v) (…)

(vi) recommend to the parties to the present Agreement, any amendment of this Agreement;

(vii) (…)

(viii) (…)

<u>INSTEAD OF</u>

"ARTICLE XXVI (INTERPRETATION AND SETTLEMENT OF DISPUTES)

1. (…)

2. (…)

3. (…)

<u>SHALL READ</u>

ARTICLE XXVI (INTERPRETATION, SETTLEMENT OF DISPUTES AND AMENDMENT)

1. (…)

2. (…)

3. (...)

4. **This Agreement may be amended by the acceptance of the majority of the parties to this Agreement.**

5. **All amendments shall be proposed by the Governing Council or by at least ten per cent of the parties to this Agreement.**

6. **After the majority of the parties to this Agreement have accepted the proposed amendment, the ALSF shall promptly certify the fact by formal communication addressed to the parties and the amendments shall enter into force three months after the date of the formal communication.**

FURTHER DECIDES that this amendment shall enter into force following the adoption of this Resolution.

[TEXT IN FRENCH – TEXTE EN FRANÇAIS]

AFRICAN LEGAL SUPPORT FACILITY
FACILITÉ AFRICAINE DE SOUTIEN JURIDIQUE

CONSEIL DE GOUVERNANCE

Résolution ALSF/GC/2012/01

Adoptée lors de la 7ème réunion du Conseil de gouvernance le 29 mai 2012

Concernant l'amendement de l'article VIII et de l'article XXVI de l'Accord portant création de la Facilité Africaine de Soutien Juridique

LE CONSEIL DE GOUVERNANCE,

Vu: (i) les dispositions pertinentes de l'Accord portant création de la Facilité africaine de soutien juridique (la "Facilité"), notamment l'Article IV (Membres); l'Article VII (Structure de gestion et de gouvernance); l'Article VIII (Conseil de gouvernance: Pouvoirs); l'Article IX (Conseil de gouvernance: Composition et représentation); l'Article X (Conseil de gouvernance: Procédure) ("l'Accord"); (ii) les Règles de procédure du Conseil de gouvernance de la Facilité (les "Règles");

APRÈS AVOIR EXAMINÉ le Document intitulé: ALSF/MEMORANDUM/GC/2012/13, notamment les recommandations qui y sont consignées relativement à un amendement de l'Article VIII, paragraphe *2 (vi)* et de l'Article XXVI visant la redéfinition de la procédure régissant la révision du texte de l'Accord en vue de permettre une plus vaste consultation des parties signataires au sujet des propositions d'amendement ;

DÉCIDE d'amender l'Article VIII, paragraphe 2 *(vi)* et l'Article XXVI de l'Accord joint aux présentes; et

DÉCIDE en conséquence:

QU'EN LIEU ET PLACE DE :

"ARTICLE VIII (...)

1. (...)

2. Le Conseil de gouvernance peut déléguer tous ses pouvoirs au Conseil de gestion, à l'exception du pouvoir :

(i) (...)

(ii) (...)

(iii) (...)

(iv) (...)

(v) (...)

(vi) de modifier le présent Accord;

(vii) (...)

(viii) (...)

IL FAUDRAIT LIRE:

"ARTICLE VIII (...)

1. (...)

2. Le Conseil de gouvernance peut déléguer tous ses pouvoirs au Conseil de gestion, à l'exception du pouvoir :

(i) (...)

(ii) (...)

(iii) (...)

(iv) (...)

(v) (...)

(vi) de recommander, aux parties au présent Accord, toute proposition d'amendement du présent accord ;

(vii) (...)

(viii) (...)

QU'EN LIEU ET PLACE DE :

« ARTICLE XXVI (INTERPRETATION ET REGLEMENT DES DIFFERENDS)

1. (...)

2. (...)

3. (...) »

IL FAUDRAIT LIRE:

« ARTICLE XXVI (INTERPRETATION, REGLEMENT DES DIFFERENDS ET AMENDEMENT)

1. (...)

2. (...)

3. (...)

4. Le présent Accord ne peut être modifié que par approbation de la majorité des parties au présent Accord.

5. Tout amendement doit être proposé par le Conseil de gouvernance ou par au moins dix pour cent des parties au présent Accord.

6. Dès approbation d'une proposition d'amendement par la majorité des parties au présent Accord, l'ensemble des parties est informé par voie de communication officielle, et l'amendement entre en vigueur trois mois après cette notification. »

DÉCIDE PAR AILLEURS de l'entrée en vigueur dudit amendement dès l'adoption de la présente Résolution.

ANNEX C

Ratifications, accessions, etc.,
concerning League of Nations treaties
and international agreements
registered in March 2016
with the Secretariat of the United Nations

ANNEXE C

Ratifications, adhésions, etc.,
concernant les traités et accords
internationaux de la Société des Nations
enregistrés en mars 2016
au Secrétariat de l'Organisation des Nations Unies

No. 2623. Multilateral

INTERNATIONAL CONVENTION FOR THE SUPPRESSION OF COUNTERFEITING CURRENCY. GENEVA, 20 APRIL 1929 [*United Nations, Treaty Series, vol. 112, LoN-2623.*]

SUCCESSION

Serbia

Deposit of instrument with the Secretary-General of the United Nations: 18 March 2016

Date of effect: 27 April 1992

Registration with the Secretariat of the United Nations: ex officio, 18 March 2016

PROTOCOL TO THE INTERNATIONAL CONVENTION FOR THE SUPPRESSION OF COUNTERFEITING CURRENCY. GENEVA, 20 APRIL 1929 [*United Nations, Treaty Series, vol. 112, C-2623.*]

SUCCESSION

Serbia

Deposit of instrument with the Secretary-General of the United Nations: 18 March 2016

Date of effect: 27 April 1992

Registration with the Secretariat of the United Nations: ex officio, 18 March 2016

N° 2623. Multilatéral

CONVENTION INTERNATIONALE POUR LA RÉPRESSION DU FAUX MONNAYAGE. GENÈVE, 20 AVRIL 1929 [*Nations Unies, Recueil des Traités, vol. 112, LoN-2623.*]

SUCCESSION

Serbie

Dépôt de l'instrument auprès du Secrétaire général de l'Organisation des Nations Unies : 18 mars 2016

Date de prise d'effet : 27 avril 1992

Enregistrement au Secrétariat de l'Organisation des Nations Unies : d'office, 18 mars 2016

PROTOCOLE À LA CONVENTION INTERNATIONALE POUR LA RÉPRESSION DU FAUX MONNAYAGE. GENÈVE, 20 AVRIL 1929 [*Nations Unies, Recueil des Traités, vol. 112, C-2623.*]

SUCCESSION

Serbie

Dépôt de l'instrument auprès du Secrétaire général de l'Organisation des Nations Unies : 18 mars 2016

Date de prise d'effet : 27 avril 1992

Enregistrement au Secrétariat de l'Organisation des Nations Unies : d'office, 18 mars 2016